KAPLAN®

Test Prep and Admissions

MCAT*

Verbal Reasoning
Strategy and Practice

CONTENTS

VERBAL REASONING

WRITING SAMPLE

Verbal Reasoning

CHAPTER ONE

INTRODUCTION

You were introduced to the structure of the Verbal Reasoning section in the first MCAT Strategy and Critical Thinking lesson. In the next four chapters and in the lessons, we'll demystify MCAT Verbal by identifying exactly what makes it such a challenging section. Then we'll introduce you to Verbal Reasoning: **THE KAPLAN WAY** —reading for structure, not detail. On Test Day, you'll be prepared with a powerful arsenal of analytical tactics from our Verbal Reasoning chapters, lessons, and Training Library. You *can* improve your critical reading between now and Test Day; we'll show you how!

THE ANATOMY OF THE PASSAGE

MCAT Verbal Reasoning passages cover a great variety of subjects. Past MCATs have had passages on everything from Native American life in Alaska to Sartre's philosophy. Should you be worried about your possible unfamiliarity with such topics? No way! For one thing, all of the information that you need to answer the questions is in the passage itself. So all you have to do is concentrate on reading and thinking critically. And even better, regardless of whether you're dealing with a humanities text, a social science text, or a science text, every passage can be handled easily if you follow some general principles...the ones we will cover in the next chapter, *Reading the Kaplan Way*. But first, we'll look at how our everyday reading differs from the active reading you'll do on MCAT verbal.

READING ON THE MCAT VS. EVERYDAY READING

Ordinarily, we read for one or both of two simple reasons: to learn something, or to pass the time pleasantly. Needless to say, neither of these reasons has anything to do with the MCAT! Furthermore, on a daily basis we tend to read for content. "What's the deeper meaning here?" we ask ourselves, or "What's this book *about*?" But anyone who tries to read for content during the MCAT is missing the point. There's just no time under strict test conditions to understand everything that's written — and, as we'll see, there's no payoff in it, either.

So what does MCAT reading, as distinct from everyday reading, involve? Broadly stated, it involves two things:

Reading for author **PURPOSE** — the "why" of the text.
Reading for passage **STRUCTURE** — the "how" of the text.

Almost every single MCAT Verbal Reasoning question fundamentally hinges on your ability to step back from the text and analyze *why* the author is writing in the first place, and *how* she puts her text together.

Why so? Why does the MCAT test these particular skills?

Here's the deal: Demanding that we figure out the author's purpose and the passage's structure is the best way to test how each of us thinks about the prose we read. And thinking is always being tested, one way or another, on every MCAT question.

Look at it this way. You have probably written a term paper that begins something like this:

> The purpose of this paper is to examine the Christian imagery employed by John Milton in *Paradise Lost*, and then to compare it to the pagan imagery in *Paradise Regained*. I will show that Milton's views of divinity and predestination, in particular, underwent a metamorphosis, as he....

Most of us would say, *"Sure, I was taught to begin papers with that kind of statement of intent. And yes, I was also told to describe how I planned to achieve that purpose."* In other words, most of us were trained to announce our *why* and *how* right at the beginning of the paper.

Now there are good reasons, of course, to urge students to write in this fashion. If you (the student writer) lay out the *why* and *how* of your paper up front, you're more likely to write with unity and clarity as you go along. Moreover, announcing what you've set out to do helps the grader evaluate whether you've done it. (Remember this when you start to learn the writing sample.)

However, more sophisticated writing — like the prose you'll see on the MCAT — doesn't always reveal its secrets quite so explicitly. Authors always have a purpose, of course, and always have a structural plan for carrying out that purpose. But sophisticated writers may not announce their purposes, which puts an extra burden on the reader to analyze what's stated, read between the lines, and draw inferences.

So, in order to set up the questions — to test how we think about the prose we read — the MCAT editors omit or disguise the statement of purpose, and challenge us to unpack it. Consider this first sentence of a typical passage:

> The great migration of European intellectuals to the United States in the second quarter of the twentieth century prompted a transmutation in the character of Western social thought.

See? We can figure out why the author is writing: His purpose, we might say, is *"to explore how the arrival of European eggheads during the period 1926-1950 changed Western social thought"* (your phrasing might be a bit different, but the gist is probably the same). So there is a definite purpose and structure here; we just have to work a little harder at figuring them out than we're used to. In the next chapter, *Reading the Kaplan Way*, we'll learn to execute a scientific protocol of sorts that will allow us to find the purpose and structure of any passage the MCAT gives us on Test Day.

CHAPTER TWO

READING THE KAPLAN WAY

PRINCIPLES THAT WILL REWARD YOU

MCAT Verbal Reasoning tests your understanding of what the author is thinking and doing. Therefore, your focus as you read must always be on the author. The test writers want you to look beyond content—they want you to draw conclusions about the *why* and the *how* of the text, not the *what* of it—about *why* it has been written and *how* it has been put together, not what it says. As you will see in Kaplan's Verbal 2 lesson, detail questions—those that ask about the *what,* are very rare indeed on the MCAT. By contrast, questions that ask about the *why* and the *how*—global, deduction, evaluation, application and incorporation questions—are the mainstay of the Verbal Reasoning section. That's where critical thinking skills come into play.

The passage exists only because the author has a specific purpose in mind. Therefore, as you read, you need to keep asking yourself "Why?" *"Why are you telling me this, author? Why are you discussing this theory? Why are you citing this opinion? Why are you including this particular detail at this particular place in the text?"* Keep in mind that the author's purpose is usually to convince us to accept his or her specific ideas. Even when the text is more objective—a descriptive "storytelling" text—you have to keep asking *why* and *how,* not *what.*

Details are in the passage only to illustrate what the author is thinking or doing. Therefore, read over details quickly; read them more closely only when questions demand it. There's no payoff in just "getting through the passage" without comprehension; on the other hand, trying to assimilate all of the content is a waste of time. Instead, always boil the passage down to its basics.

Paragraphs are the fundamental building blocks of the passage. Therefore, as you read, take note of paragraph topics rather than specifics. Ask yourself: *"What's the purpose of this paragraph? How does it fit into the overall structure of the passage?"* For example, is the paragraph an author's main idea or a small supporting example? Is the author using an analogy in a paragraph to strengthen her point or to refute someone else's contrary idea?

THE SKILLS BEHIND THE PRINCIPLES

In order to apply these critical reading principles, you have to develop MCAT-specific critical reading skills. The next section of this chapter is designed to help you with this process. We'll explain the concepts and give you drills to help you sharpen the necessary skills.

Pause frequently to summarize.   Don't glaze!

A good summary captures the contents of a block of text in a few words or a sentence without losing any of the text's basic ideas. Consider the following block of text:

> Most of the developed countries are now agreed on the need to take international measures to reduce carbon emissions into the atmosphere. Despite this consensus, a wide disagreement among economists as to how much emission reduction will actually cost continues to impede policy making. Economists who believe that the energy market is efficient predict that countries that reduce carbon emission by as little as twenty percent will experience significant losses to their gross national product. Those who hold that the market is inefficient, however, estimate that costs will be much lower....

A good summary of this text would be something like: *An international policy to reduce carbon emissions has been held up by arguments about how much it would cost.* That's the basic idea here; the rest is just detail.

MCAT answer choices are frequently just paraphrases of what was stated in the passage. Learn to paraphrase and you'll learn to be attuned to correct answer choices.

The key to reading MCAT passages successfully will be to leave behind the habit of reading passively, letting the words glide by, even as your mind wanders to other subjects (like your anxieties about getting into med school, for instance). In our work together, you will learn to read more actively, pausing frequently to quickly summarize and paraphrase what you've just read. **A good reader checks her understanding frequently without getting bogged down on any one section.**

FIND THE TOPIC, SCOPE, AND PURPOSE

Finding the topic, scope, and purpose will force you to check your understanding of each paragraph. Let's define our terms:

The **topic** is the author's basic subject matter—World War I; or volcanoes; or Charles Dickens's *Bleak House.*

The **scope** is the specific aspect of the topic that the author focuses on—the causes of World War I; or competing theories about predicting volcanic eruptions; or Dickens's critique of the English legal system.

The **purpose** is the reason why the author wrote the passage—to dispute a common belief about the causes of World War I; or to describe competing theories about predicting volcanic eruptions; or to support Dickens's critique of the English legal system.

Identifying these parameters of a passage makes it easier to attack. While reading VR passages, most MCAT test takers have two maladaptive tendencies: (1) the tendency to glaze over, so that they realize when their eyes reach the end of a paragraph that they weren't really paying attention, and (2) the tendency to read for detail instead of structure, so that they get bogged down when faced with a patch of dense text or a cluster of thorny details. Because MCAT Verbal passages are challenging, both of these tendencies will always be an issue for most test-takers — you will learn to manage both tendencies by using active tasks, including finding topic, scope, and purpose, to keep you attentive and attuned to structure. And, with practice, you'll find yourself getting "glazed & bogged" less and less.

For most passages, the topic and scope remain the same in the passage. However, within the overall purpose of the passage each paragraph has its own unique purpose, and we will discuss this in greater detail in the next section. In the next section, we'll focus on an irreducible property of every paragraph: its purpose.

Drill #1: Finding Topic, Scope, and Purpose

Instructions: Read each of these paragraphs actively, assigning a topic, scope, and purpose to each.   Then using your understanding of each paragraph, match the numbered statements below with the appropriate paragraph. There may be more than one correct statement for each text. Not every statement necessarily matches up with one of the texts.

A. At the Battle of Gettysburg in July 1863, 75,000 Confederate troops faced 90,000 Union soldiers in one of the largest battles of the American Civil War. For two days, both armies suffered heavy casualties in constant fighting, without either gaining a clear advantage. On the third and final day of the battle, Confederate forces mounted one last effort to penetrate Union lines. But the attempt ended in complete failure, forcing Confederate troops to withdraw far to the south....

B. In January 1863, seven months before the decisive Battle of Gettysburg, President Lincoln issued the Emancipation Proclamation, in which he declared an end to slavery in the United States. Some historians cite Lincoln's edict as proof that he wanted to do away with slavery because he considered it morally repugnant. While Lincoln certainly opposed the institution on ethical grounds, the timing of the proclamation suggests that he was out to weaken the Confederacy rather than to undertake a moral crusade....

C. Gettysburg was a turning point in the Civil War. Before the battle, Confederate forces under General Robert E. Lee had defeated their Union counterparts in a string of major engagements. After the battle, however, Union forces took the initiative, finally defeating the Confederacy less than two years later. By invading Union territory, the Confederate leadership had sought to shatter the Union's will to continue the war and to convince European nations to recognize the Confederacy as an independent nation. Instead, the Union's willingness to fight was strengthened and the Confederacy squandered its last chance for foreign support....

D. The Confederacy had hoped that France and Great Britain would intervene militarily on its side in order to restore the European-American cotton trade. But once President Lincoln issued the Emancipation Proclamation—which changed the focus of the Civil War from a conflict over states' rights to one over slavery—both the French and British concluded that their status in the international community would be jeopardized were they, in effect, to support slavery....

1. argue that the outcome of the Battle of Gettysburg undermined the Confederacy's military and political goals in the Civil War

2. discuss the course of one of the most important battles of the Civil War

3. point out that Lincoln's primary motive for delivering the Emancipation Proclamation was to strengthen the Union in its struggle with the Confederacy

4. describe the effect of the Emancipation Proclamation on the Confederacy's foreign relations

5. convey a sense of the close relations that existed between the Confederacy and European nations before the Battle of Gettysburg

6. settle an ongoing debate among historians about the importance of the Emancipation Proclamation to the Confederacy's defeat at the Battle of Gettysburg

7. propose that the Battle of Gettysburg played a crucial part in changing the course of the Civil War

8. refute the view that the Emancipation Proclamation stemmed from Lincoln's desire to destroy slavery

9. explain the cotton trade's role in turning the international community against the Confederacy

10. show that the Union won the Battle of Gettysburg because it had more troops than the Confederacy

Answers to Drill #1

Statements 1 and 7 match up with Text C: Topic is the Battle of Gettysburg; scope is the battle's role in determining the outcome of the Civil War; and purpose is to assert that Gettysburg was a turning point in the eventual defeat of the South and victory of the North.

Statement 2 matches up with Text A: Topic is the Battle of Gettysburg; scope is the battle itself, and purpose is to describe what happened during the battle.

Statements 3 and 8 match up with Text B: Topic is Emancipation Proclamation; scope is Lincoln's motive for issuing the proclamation; purpose is to argue that Lincoln did so in order to weaken the Confederacy.

Statement 4 matches up with Text D: Topic is Confederate foreign relations; scope is the connection between the Emancipation Proclamation and Confederate foreign relations; purpose is to describe the effect of the proclamation on Confederate foreign relations.

Statement 5 doesn't match up with any text: Texts C and D mention Confederate-European relations, but neither of them speaks of close relations before Gettysburg.

Statement 6 doesn't match up with any text: None of the texts refers to a debate among historians.

Statement 9 doesn't match up with any text: Only Text D refers to the cotton trade, but it doesn't draw any connection between the cotton trade and the international community's rejection of the Confederacy.

Statement 10 doesn't match up with any text: Text A mentions the number of troops each side deployed at Gettysburg, but its purpose isn't to argue that the Union won at Gettysburg because it had more troops.

The Importance of Purpose

When a group of sentences is set apart by indentation (such as a paragraph), this is a significant event. It means that these sentences all have something in common, a distinct unifying idea that justifies setting them apart. Each paragraph, then, must always serve a purpose in the larger context of the passage: an author never writes just to pass the time, but rather to make a point. (And no, it's not just "I want tenure!") In other words, the **purpose** of a paragraph is the major point that the author wants you to take away from a paragraph—e.g., *"World War I was caused by European competition for overseas colonies, not by alliance arrangements in Europe"*; or *"so & so's theory of volcanic eruptions is the most credible because of such & such"*; or *"Dickens's critique of the English legal system was flawed by his inability to understand legal arguments."* **As MCAT test-takers, it is most important that you grasp this purpose in order to ace the questions.** Of course, the author must achieve his purpose with supporting evidence, and this evidence will come in the form of details. What is not important for you as an MCAT test-taker is to memorize these details while you read the passage, because you are free to relocate them if a question requires you to do so. Because you will read for structure, not detail, you will be able to relocate relevant details quickly.

Drill #2: Distinguishing the Purpose of a Paragraph from Supporting Details

Instructions: In your own words, jot down the purpose and the supporting details of each paragraph.

1. In the early 20th century, impoverished southern Black farmers migrated in large numbers to northern cities in search of steady employment. With a rapidly expanding industrial base, Chicago was the destination for much of this wave of emigration. Many of these farmers were eventually able to find jobs in Chicago's factories, but life was not easy for them. They received very low wages for long hours of physically-demanding work. Moreover, they were often torn from their families, with wives and children left behind out of economic necessity. And though discrimination was less intense in the North than in the South, Black migrants were still subject to unfair treatment in matters of pay, promotion, and job security.

   Purpose:

   Supporting Details:

2. Theropods, or three-toed dinosaurs, were traditionally thought of as unsociable, land-bound creatures who preferred to scavenge rather than hunt. But recently uncovered fossil evidence has led to a thorough reassessment of this view. The discovery of numerous sets of three-toed tracks at many fossil sites, for instance, has convinced paleontologists that theropods moved in packs, at least when feeding. Furthermore, some fossil sites were under water when dinosaurs roamed the Earth, indicating that theropods could swim. In fact, paleontologists now think that they were excellent swimmers who experienced little trouble capturing prey in the water. Their ability to swim has also undermined the belief that they were scavengers rather than hunters, because scavengers look for carrion on land, not in the water.

   Purpose:

   Supporting Details:

3. The poetry of the earliest Greeks was completely impersonal. It was folk poetry, whose purpose was to express the thoughts and feelings of the entire community. During the later age of heroes, however, the focus of Greek poetry switched from the community to the individual. This poetry celebrates the lives of important personages such as kings and warriors. In so doing, it reflects the changing nature of ancient Greek life: a society that had initially been free of stark class differences eventually developed a hierarchical structure, with a small ruling elite in control of the masses.

   Purpose:

   Supporting Details:

Answers to Drill #2

1. Purpose: Poor black farmers who migrated to Chicago in search of jobs often found employment, but life remained difficult for them.

    Supporting Details: low wages for hard work; family separation; job discrimination

2. Purpose: Contrary to traditional thinking, recent findings have shown that theropods were sociable hunters capable of swimming, rather than solitary, land-bound scavengers.

    Supporting Details: numerous sets of theropod tracks at fossil sites, including some under water at the time theropods roamed Earth

3. Purpose: The change in Greek poetry from an emphasis on the community to an emphasis on the individual reflected the larger changes in Greek society.

    Supporting Details: folk poetry the norm in early Greek society when no classes existed; heroic poetry the norm later when society ruled by small elite of warriors and kings.

CHAPTER THREE

KEYWORDS

Keywords are the words that authors use to reveal the internal structure of their reasoning. There are different types of Keywords, each of which has a specific function.

The most important Keywords are Evidence, Conclusion, Contrast, and (to a lesser extent) Emphasis — because these are the ideas that will lead you to relevant text to answer the questions.

CONCLUSION KEYWORDS signal that the author is about to sum up or announce his or her thesis. The most common one is *therefore,* to which we can add:

thus	believes	consequently	we can conclude that
in conclusion	so	it can be seen that	Toynbee claims that

Since these Keywords have to do with the author's logic, it's no wonder that they are especially crucial for Verbal Reasoning.

EVIDENCE KEYWORDS tell you that the author is about to provide support for a point. Here are the Big Four Evidence Keywords:

because	for	since	the reason is that

CONTRAST KEYWORDS, of course, signal an opposition or shift. There are lots of these words:

but	however	although	not	nevertheless
despite	alternatively	unless	though	by contrast
yet	still	otherwise	while	notwithstanding

Contrast Keywords are among the most significant in Verbal Reasoning because so many passages are based on contrast or opposition. Almost certainly, something important is happening when a Contrast Keyword shows up.

CONTINUATION KEYWORDS announce that more of the same is about to come up. *And* is probably the most common one in the English language. Others include:

also	furthermore	in addition	as well as
moreover	plus	at the same time	equally

Also (there's a signal for you!), the colon sort of does the same job: It usually tells you that what follows expands upon, or continues, what came before.

ILLUSTRATION KEYWORDS signal that an example is about to arrive. *One example* and *for instance* are the most obvious. But think about these:

As Maya Angelou says,	For historians,
In the words of Hannah Arendt,	According to these experts,
To Proust,	

In each case, what's about to follow is an example of that person's thinking.

SEQUENCE KEYWORDS are the author telling you *"Hey, there's some sort of order at work here."* Some examples are:

Secondly (and thirdly, fourthly, etc.)
Next,
Finally,
On the one hand,
Recently,

When all is said and done, **EMPHASIS KEYWORDS** may be the most welcome. If we're supposed to read for the author's point of view–and we are–what better way than to stumble across words and phrases whose sole purpose is to announce *"I, the author, find this important"*? Note these:

above all	most of all	primarily	in large measure
essentially	especially	particularly	indeed

A KEYWORDS EXERCISE

The best MCAT test takers are attentive to purpose and structure at every moment, and when Keywords come along, they tend automatically to anticipate where the author will probably take the passage next. As a result the reader stays ahead of the author, rather than behind, and is less likely to get confused by dense detail or to lose sight of the structure as a whole.

Each of the following pieces of text—any of which might be found in a Verbal Reasoning passage—ends with a familiar Keyword. After you read it, try to formulate an idea of what ought to follow the Keyword; then look at the three possibilities listed. Choose the one of the three that would be the most logical completion of the sentence: Which one (if any) comes the closest to your expectation?

1. The latest research seems to suggest that people who consume alcohol in moderation may be healthier, on average, than either teetotalers or heavy drinkers. Hence,

    A. people who enjoy a single glass of wine with dinner need not fear that they are endangering their health.

    B. at least one clinical study rates both non-drinkers and heavy drinkers as less psychologically stable compared with moderate drinkers.

    C. without more data, it would be premature to change one's lifestyle on the basis of these findings.

2. The photograph being copied must be in good condition; otherwise,

    A. it should be examined with a magnifying glass under strong white light.

B. its dimensions must be identical to those of the desired duplicate.

C. the duplicate will exhibit the same scratches or smears as the original.

3. The fresco was completed after Giotto's death by an apprentice whose skills were not quite up to the task, and

A. he clearly attempted to imitate the master's strokes.

B. neither the perspective nor the colors are convincing.

C. he had studied with the master for only a short time.

4. The evidence suggesting that the two species of felines may have existed simultaneously on the African veldt is purely circumstantial. For example,

A. with no direct proof to the contrary, many experts still believe that the giant cats died out long before their smaller relatives appeared.

B. fossil traces of both species have been found in separate areas in sediments that are thought to have been laid down by the same floodwaters.

C. since all of the giant fossils found so far have been male, some scientists suspect that the smaller ones represent the females and young of the same sexually dimorphic species.

5. Only one day care facility in this city bases its fees on a sliding scale according to family income, and there are over three hundred children on its waiting list. Consequently,

A. it is nearly impossible for most poor mothers to work outside the home while providing care for their children.

B. the blame for the lack of affordable child care alternatives must be placed on state legislators, who have stymied every attempt to redress the situation.

C. the number of high- and middle-income families who place their pre-school children in day care primarily to give them an educational advantage continues to rise.

6. The purpose of the proposed advertising campaign is, first, to increase public awareness of the company's new logo. For instance,

A. it is hoped that the new commercials will reinforce brand loyalty among consumers.

B. a major portion of the budget has been allocated to create a striking and memorable design.

C. television viewers should be able to identify the design correctly after seeing the commercial only once.

7. Tobacco companies often advertise cigarettes with filter tips or with lower levels of tar and nicotine as "lighter," implying that they are less damaging to health than regular cigarettes. But

A. several studies have shown that people who smoke such cigarettes tend to inhale more deeply, thereby delivering at least as much tar and nicotine to their lungs as if they were smoking regular cigarettes.

B. in manufacturing and marketing these products, the tobacco companies are responding to the widespread awareness and fear, even among habitual smokers, of the harmful effects of smoking.

C. the impression created by these advertisements is that people—particularly young women—who care about their health may smoke these cigarettes without having to worry about developing cancer or emphysema.

8. Many methods of contraception work by preventing sperm from fertilizing the ovum. Alternatively,

   A. latex condoms and diaphragms present physical barriers to sperm; the contraceptive efficacy of these methods can be increased chemically via spermicides.

   B. these methods, however varied their mechanisms, are all prophylactic in nature, in that no embryo is ever created.

   C. pregnancy can be averted after fertilization by causing the fertilized egg to be expelled from the body, rather than implanting in the uterine wall.

9. That Nabokov's novels found a mass audience in the U.S., a country in which relatively few people study foreign languages, is mystifying, especially given

   A. his appeal to academics and literary critics.

   B. his penchant for multilingual puns.

   C. the ribald adult content of his books.

Answer Explanations

1. **A**

   Hence is a Conclusion Keyword, and (A) is the only one of the choices that can reasonably be deduced from the previous sentence. (B) provides additional evidence along the same lines, and would more logically follow a Continuation Keyword like "moreover." (C), which takes a different view, would probably start off with a Contrast Keyword like "however."

2. **C**

   The Contrast Keyword "otherwise" warns of some undesired consequence to follow if the photo is in bad shape; (C) fits the bill. (A) is a precondition to ensure that the original photo is OK; it should take a Conclusion Keyword like "therefore." (B) describes a second requirement that's distinct from the photo's condition; it needs a Continuation Keyword like "also" to set it up.

3. **B**

   "And" expresses continuation, another piece of evidence that points in the same direction. Replacing "and" with a wordier Evidence Keyword, such as "as evidenced by the fact that," would make (B) even more clearly correct. Contrast Keyword "although" would more appropriately introduce (A), which expresses a subtle contrast (the apprentice didn't succeed, though he tried). (C) attempts to explain why the apprentice wasn't up to snuff; an Evidence Keyword like "since" should set up this choice.

4. **B**

   "For example," one of the most common Illustration Keywords, sets the stage for (B), a specific piece of the circumstantial evidence mentioned in the first part of the sentence. (A) suggests an opposing conclusion—that the two species did not coexist—and would probably be introduced by a Conclusion Keyword like "thus." (C) reinforces the main clause's statement that only circumstantial evidence supports the conclusion that the two species coexisted; this choice raises additional evidence pointing to an alternative conclusion, and would be more effectively set up by the Continuation Keyword "in addition."

5. **A**

   The Conclusion Keyword "consequently" leads nicely to (A), a natural result of the first sentence. Placing blame, (B), is not a result but a conclusion, but it can't be introduced by a Conclusion Keyword because it's buttressed by new evidence (the legislators have stymied every attempt to redress the situation). Emphasis Keywords like "in large measure" would serve better. (C) discusses a simultaneous but different trend. At the same time, a Continuation Keyword with subtle overtones of contrast would set it up better.

6. **C**

   Illustration Keywords "for instance" should lead to an example of how the campaign would increase public awareness; (C) would be a reasonable result to hope for. A Sequence Keyword like "secondly" would more effectively indicate that (A) raises a new issue, brand loyalty, that is an additional purpose of the campaign, unrelated to public awareness. (B) requires a Conclusion Keyword like "hence" to show that the previously stated objective mandates a hefty design budget for the new logo.

7. **A**

   "But," one of the bluntest Contrast Keywords in the English language, leads to (A), an outcome diametrically opposed to the claims in the cigarette ads. (B) is an attempt to infer why the tobacco companies would make such claims; Conclusion Keywords like "it can be concluded that" would clarify the logical connection. (C) continues the train of thought begun in the previous sentence, summarizing the subtext of the advertisements; Emphasis Keywords like "above all" would work well here.

8. **C**

   The Contrast Keyword "alternatively" has to introduce contraceptive methods that don't rely on preventing fertilization; (C), preventing implantation after the fact, is a good alternative. (A), which describes specific contraceptive methods that prevent fertilization, would be better introduced by an Illustration Keyword like "for example." An Emphasis Keyword like "essentially" would help (B) point out what all these methods have in common.

9. **B**

   "Especially" is another Emphasis Keyword. (B) is the only choice that would make Nabokov's mass appeal in a linguistically provincial country even more mystifying. His appeal to academic and literary critics might explain his mass readership, or at least render it less mystifying; (A) should thus be introduced by a Contrast Keyword like "despite." (C) would tend to work in favor of Nabokov's mass appeal, rather than against it; a combination of Contrast and Evidence Keywords—something like "though perhaps understandable, given"—would make for a better transition.

CHAPTER FOUR

THE VERBAL REASONING QUESTION TYPES

In your first Verbal Reasoning lesson, you found out how the VR section is put together and how to make the format work for you. You also learned the skills you'll need to read the passages with speed and accuracy, and you practiced applying those skills with MCAT-style passages, using the Kaplan Method.

Along the way, you've been exposed to Verbal Reasoning questions, since your performance on those questions is the best indicator of your proficiency in attacking passages. Now, in Verbal Reasoning 2, our specific focus will shift to the questions. You'll learn about the major VR question types, how to recognize them, the best strategies for finding the right answer, and how to recognize classic wrong answer pathology.

To help you make the most of the lesson, we've identified the major VR question types below. Read the definitions, find out how to recognize them, then practice identifying question types when you tackle the VR passages we've recommended. Keep reinforcing the skills you've built in the last lesson—turn Verbal Reasoning into a real strength on Test Day.

VERBAL REASONING QUESTION TYPES

Every question type requires that you identify one or both of the following:

1) **Main Idea**
   - Questions that ask for the "central thesis," "primary purpose," or "main idea."
   - The correct answer will reflect the overall scope and purpose.

2) **Detail**
   - Questions that ask what was stated in the passage.
   - The correct answer will be very close to the text in the passage.
   - These questions are relatively rare today.
   - When they do appear, they often come in the form of scattered detail: all of the following arguments are made in the passage EXCEPT.

The most common VR questions ask more:

3) **Deduction**
   - Questions that require you to identify assumptions or logical conclusions from your broader understanding of the passage.
   - Creative interpretation isn't rewarded here. The correct answer will be definitely true based on the passage.

4) **Evaluation**
   - Questions that ask how the author put together the argument.
   - Correct answers stick to the scope of the argument and identify how the author moves between evidence and conclusion.

5) **Application**
   - Questions that ask you to apply the ideas in the passage to a different situation or context.
   - These may seem to encourage creative interpretations, but don't be fooled! Correct answers stick closely to the ideas in the passage.

6) **Incorporation**
   - Questions that ask you to incorporate new information into reasoning found in the passage.

THE QUESTION TYPES IN VITRO

Following is an example of each of these question types in their order of frequency on the MCAT. You'll see many more examples in Verbal lesson 2 and, of course, on our Practice Tests and AAMC Practice Materials in the Kaplan Training Library.

DEDUCTION

1. The author of the passage would most likely agree that:
    A. The post-1991 MCAT is superior to the pre-1991 MCAT.
    B. Wilson's theory is over-reaching but represents a desirable ideal.
    C. Because causality is so diffuse, a consilient understanding of science is probably unattainable.
    D. The MCAT is the best predictor of performance in medical school.

EVALUATION

2. The author mentions "third-order discontinuities" primarily in order to:
    A. provide support for the theory of plate tectonics.
    B. account for breaks in magma chambers.
    C. present evidence in support of the magma-supply model.
    D. discredit the notion that ridge morphology depends on magma supply.

APPLICATION

3. Which of the following would be an example of consilience according to Wilson?
    A. A scholar composes a poem about the passing of a vesicle from ER to cis-Golgi.
    B. A neurologist studies neural patterns in the brain of a talented composer.
    C. A historian tests her hypothesis about the causes of revolution by comparing economic data from several nations, some of which later revolted.
    D. An economist studies the writing of William Carlos Williams.

INCORPORATION

4. Based on information in the passage, which of the following new discoveries would best support the author's claim that Winston was a traitor?
    A. A black sword under the sea chest
    B. A red waistband and flannel waistcoat
    C. The absence of gunpowder in the tunnel
    D. Mutinous sailors stranded in the Pacific

DETAIL

5. According to the passage, American migrants in the mid-1840s often:
    I. doubted the economic potential of the Great Plains.
    II. had an overly optimistic image of the Great Plains.
    III. were misinformed by newspaper stories.
    A. I only
    B. II only
    C. I and III only
    D. I, II, and III

GLOBAL

6. The author's central thesis is that:
    A. Consilience is a jumping together of multiple distinct thought processes to arrive at a similar conclusion.
    B. MCAT consilience should supplant the dominant modes of inquiry of those disciplines which it has not yet conquered.
    C. Wilsonian consilience may be impractical, but MCAT consilience is a worthy goal.
    D. Whewell would have contested Wilson's interpretation of consilience.

Verbal Reasoning Test One

Time—85 minutes
Question 1–60

DIRECTIONS: Each of the passages in this test is followed by a set of questions based on the passage's content. After reading each passage, decide on the one best response to each question and mark it on your answer sheet. If you are unsure of an answer, eliminate the choices you know are wrong and choose from the remaining choices. You may refer to the passages while answering the questions.

Passage I (Questions 1–6)

Originally published in 1861, *Incidents in the Life of a Slave Girl Written by Herself* was long regarded as a powerful argument for the abolition of slavery in the United States. Recently, however, its meaning and rele-
5 vance have changed. Thanks to the work of historian Jean Fagan Yellin, it has become clear that the work is not a novel, as was initially believed, but a true account by Harriet Jacobs of her own life—a primary source on the realities of an African-American woman's life under
10 slavery.

Circumstances initially led 19th century readers to receive the book as a work of fiction in the tradition of *Uncle Tom's Cabin*, written as a thinly veiled political tract in the Abolitionist cause. *Incidents* was published
15 anonymously. The title page provided no name other than that of its editor, Lydia Maria Child, a noted aboli-tionist and novelist, whose previous novels had included plotlines and themes similar to those in *Incidents*, fuel-ing speculation that she was the author. Since the first-
20 person narrator of the book, in consideration of others, had "concealed the names of places and given persons fictitious names," there was no way to trace the author-ship of the text beyond Mrs. Child, whose denials served only to deepen the mystery surrounding the book's
25 provenance.

Bur perhaps the most important reason they insisted *Incidents* was a novel was an inability to accept that the woman depicted in the book—who endured the brutali-ty of slavery, hid from her owners in a garret for seven
30 years, and then escaped to the North—could write a work so rooted in the melodramatic literary tradition popular among female readers and authors of the time. In fact, deeply ingrained racial prejudices held by most white Americans (even the abolitionists) made it diffi-
35 cult for them to acknowledge that an African-American was capable of such a powerful and dramatic work under any circumstances.

In the 1980s, Jean Fagan Yellin, struck by the book's attempt to create a sense of sisterhood between white
40 and black women, decided to re-examine the claims of its authenticity made by the narrator and Lydia Maria Child. While others had voiced similar arguments as early as 1947, Yellin went one step farther, meticulously documenting the existence of people and events in the
45 book. Studying the papers of Lydia Maria Child and oth-ers in her circle, Yellin found among them Jacobs' letters and other documents that led to general recognition of Jacobs as the writer.

Answering the charge that a former slave could not pos-
50 sibly have been familiar with the literary tradition the book reflected, Yellin demonstrated that Harriet Jacobs had access to the extensive libraries of abolitionist women. She found that Jacobs' daughter, Louisa, had been educated as a teacher and had transcribed the man-
55 uscript in preparation for its publication. Harriet Jacobs' own letters show considerable literary ability; Louisa standardized her mother's spelling and punctuation. And the author's insistence on anonymity was explained in large part by the fact that the book discussed the unique
60 and difficult situation faced by slave women: the sexual predations of male slave owners and their powerlessness to exert on their own behalf society's standards of chaste womanhood. Such matters would be deemed inappro-priate for a woman to discuss publicly in 1861, but
65 Jacobs saw the necessity of reaching out to her female readership in this manner. *Incidents in the Life of A Slave Girl* is now recognized as a record of harrowing experiences in slavery.

GO TO THE NEXT PAGE.

1. The author probably refers to *Uncle Tom's Cabin* (lines 13–25) primarily in order to:

    A. illustrate the racial stereotyping that is also present in *Incidents*.
    B. argue that it is a poorly written novel in comparison with *Incidents*.
    C. assert that precedent existed for the type of book readers believed *Incidents* to be
    D. provide an example of another novel that was confused with nonfiction.

2. With which of the following statements would the author of the passage most likely agree?

    A. Harriet Jacobs should not have included discussions of sexuality in her book.
    B. American standards of behavior were easy to achieve for most men who were slaves.
    C. *Incidents* was most popular among women readers when it was published.
    D. Novels can provide valuable insights into the history and politics of an era.

3. Each of the following is used by Yellin to support the idea that Harriet Jacobs wrote *Incidents in the Life of a Slave Girl* EXCEPT:

    A. Her daughter was educated as a teacher.
    B. Lydia Maria Child was listed on the title page as its editor.
    C. Discussions of sexuality were deemed inappropriate for a woman in 1861.
    D. The people and events cited in the book did in fact exist.

4. Which of the following ideas is most analogous to the situation described in the passage?

    A. A public figure who is identified with an important political issue writes a novel that dramatizes the issue
    B. Thanks to the use of new technology, an oil well is discovered on land that was formerly the site of a plantation house
    C. The value of work by a scientist who was poorly regarded during his lifetime is increasingly recognized in the years after his death
    D. A painting that was thought to be a forgery turns out after careful analysis to be the work of a well-known artist

5. Suppose that it was a common convention in 19th century literature for former slaves to dictate their memoirs to whites, who then edited the memoirs for publication. What effect would this information have had on the arguments about the authorship of *Incidents*?

    A. It would provide additional support to the idea that Lydia Maria Child wrote the book.
    B. It would lend support to the idea that the book could be a work of nonfiction.
    C. It would weaken Jean Fagan Yellin's contention that Jacobs wrote the book by herself.
    D. It would make the author's choice to remain anonymous less credible to the modern reader.

6. Claims for the authenticity of *Incidents* were made as early as 1947, but its status as nonfiction was not established until the 1980s. Based on evidence in the passage, the best explanation for this delay is:

    A. The identification of characters and locations in the book was not done until the 1980s.
    B. Jacobs' frank discussion of sexuality brought great criticism on the book
    C. The book was forgotten for many years after slavery was abolished.
    D. The libraries of the abolitionists who befriended Jacobs had not yet been discovered

GO TO THE NEXT PAGE.

Passage II (Questions 7–14)

The theory of moral reasoning advanced by Lawrence Kohlberg holds that the thought processes of an individual contemplating a moral dilemma are more revealing than the person's actual behavior in a real situation. On the basis of thousands of interviews attempting to probe such thought processes, Kohlberg concluded that every person passes through three distinct stages of moral reasoning—each divided into two substages. According to Kohlberg, the evidence shows that more persons at "higher" stages of moral reasoning are found in older age groups and that persons observed over a period of years typically advance to a higher level. Having studied subjects in the United States and many other countries, Kohlberg claims cross-cultural validity for his findings.

Within Kohlberg's most basic stage of moral reasoning, the "preconventional" stage, the first substage is that of "punishment-obedience." An individual at this substage will justify a course of action on the basis of tangible consequences such as incurring or avoiding trouble or punishment. A more advanced but still preconventional attitude, the "instrumental relativist orientation," involves reasoning on the basis of satisfying one's own desires and needs. Preconventional reasoning is most commonly observed among young children and preteens.

The next, or "conventional," stage is initially marked by an "interpersonal concordance" orientation, and later by an orientation toward law and order. The former is characterized by a comprehension of "good" or "bad" motives for a particular action; the latter is concerned not with intent but with authority as an absolute—the law must be respected at all times. Adolescents and young adults are usually conventional reasoners.

Kohlberg's final, "postconventional," stage is more independent of prevailing social mores and stresses the individual's personal values. In the "social contract orientation" substage, a person takes social standards into account but not as absolutes: they are valid because agreed on by society, but they apply only within a pertinent sphere and may be disregarded in appropriate circumstances. In the higher substage of, "universal ethical principle orientation," abstract ideals such as human rights, justice, or equality are invoked to justify behavior; deviation from socially accepted standards—even breaking one's own rules—is justifiable if one remains true to one's own underlying ethical ideals. Kohlberg asserts that most adults reason at one of the two postconventional substages.

There appears to be some correlation between the level of moral reasoning attained by an individual and that person's level of cognitive development; Kohlberg's theory is thus regarded as an extension of Piaget's views, which regard cognitive development as occurring in successive stages from the earliest sensorimotor coordination through mastery of "concrete operations" and finally "formal operations." Piaget believed age and external stimuli pushed an individual to higher levels of cognitive development; Kohlberg similarly claims that individuals are capable of such longitudinal movement, although he attributes advances to social development. It is important to realize, however, that Kohlberg's stages are not directly correlative to behavior; what develops is not the degree to which one engages in acts one considers "right" or "wrong," but the kinds of justification offered for doing so.

---

7. Which of the following most accurately describes the passage?

    A. An analysis of the ways in which moral reasoning differs from behavior in real life situations
    B. A critique faulting Kohlberg's theory for not accurately predicting real behaviors
    C. A description of Kohlberg's theory of the stages of moral reasoning
    D. A consideration of that which distinguishes moral thought from immoral behavior

8. The passage suggests that an individual displaying an "interpersonal concordance" orientation would reason on the basis of:

    A. an understanding of law and order.
    B. comprehension of good and bad.
    C. respect for the concept of the social contract.
    D. consideration of the values of justice and equality.

9. Which of the following best describes Kohlberg's conception of the development of moral reasoning, as implied by the passage?

    A. Moral reasoning usually moves from concrete justifications to more abstract and personal ideals.
    B. Human behavior generally becomes increasingly moral in older age groups.
    C. People are increasingly guided by their own personal needs and desires as they mature.
    D. In general, human beings become more conservative in their moral judgments with the passing of time.

GO TO THE NEXT PAGE.

10. According to the passage, a difference between Kohlberg's views and those of Piaget is that:

   A. Kohlberg describes moral behavior while Piaget catalogues cognitive development.
   B. Piaget's stages regard actual behavior while Kohlberg's regard thought processes.
   C. Kohlberg's theory concerns cognitive development through adulthood while Piaget focuses on the development of children.
   D. Kohlberg attributes development of thought processes to social development, whereas Piaget attributes it to age and external stimuli.

11. Which of the following would most seriously *weaken* Kohlberg's theory?

   A. A study that shows "postconventional" reasoners sometimes decide to act against socially accepted norms
   B. A study which concludes that infants and toddlers are not capable of grasping the concept of altruism
   C. An experiment that reveals individuals reason at all three levels of Kohlberg's typology throughout life
   D. A study that strongly suggests that the development of moral reasoning and cognitive development coincide

12. The author most likely uses the phrase "longitudinal movement" (line 58) to mean:

   A. advancement to progressively higher levels of reasoning.
   B. lateral motion between different substages.
   C. exhibition of increasingly moral behavior.
   D. alternation between moral and cognitive development.

13. Which of the following might be indicative of a person in the "conventional" stage of moral reasoning?

   A. A driver who runs a red light in order to reach an appointment in good time
   B. A clerk who witnesses but doesn't report an impoverished woman's shoplifting
   C. A person who believes that police should use whatever means necessary to maintain order
   D. A counterfeiter who flees the country when his scheme is brought to light

14. The last sentence of the passage (lines 59–63) implies that Kohlberg's theory:

   A. helps only in understanding the motives behind moral behavior.
   B. is flawed by its inability to predict specific behavior.
   C. is most concerned with the rationalization of behavior.
   D. is ultimately inferior to the developmental theories of Piaget.

GO TO THE NEXT PAGE.

Passage III (Questions 15–20)

65 million years ago, something triggered mass extinctions so profound that they define the geological boundary between the Cretaceous and Tertiary periods (the K-T Boundary). Approximately 75 percent of all animal
5 species, including every species of dinosaur, was killed off; those species that survived lost the vast majority of their numbers. The Earth exists in a region of space teeming with asteroids and comets, which on collision have frequently caused enormous environmental devas-
10 tation, including extinctions of animal species. Yet few traditional geologists or biologists considered the effect these impacts may have had on the geologic and biologic history of the Earth. Since gradual geologic processes like erosion or repeated volcanic eruptions can
15 explain the topographical development of the Earth, they feel there is no need to resort to extraterrestrial explanations.

An important theory proposed in 1980 by physicists Luis and Walter Alvarez challenges this view. The
20 Alvarezes argue that an asteroid roughly 6 miles in diameter collided with the Earth at the K-T Boundary. Although the damage caused by the meteorite's impact would have been great, the dust cloud that enveloped the planet, completely blotting out the sun for up to a year—
25 the result of soil displacement—would have done most of the harm, according to this theory. Plunged into total darkness—and the resulting drastically reduced temperatures—plant growth would have been interrupted, cutting off the food supply to herbivorous species, the loss
30 of which in turn starved carnivores. Additional species would have perished as a result of prolonged atmospheric poisoning, acid rain, forest fires, and tidal waves, all initiated by the asteroid's impact.

Subsequent research has not only tended to support the
35 Alvarez theory, but has suggested that similar impacts may have caused other sharp breaks in Earth's geologic and biologic history. Research in the composition of the Earth has revealed a 160-fold enrichment of iridium all over the world in a thin layer of sediments corre-
40 sponding to the K-T Boundary. The presence of this element, which is extremely uncommon in the Earth's crust but very common in asteroids and comets, suggest that a meteorite must have struck Earth at that time. Additional physical evidence of such a strike has been
45 found in rock samples, which contain shocked quartz crystals and *microtektites* (small glass spheres)—both byproducts of massive collisions.

Observation of the lunar surface provides further evidence of the likelihood of a massive strike. Since the
50 moon and the Earth lie within the same swarm of asteroids and comets, their impact histories should be parallel. Although some lunar craters are of volcanic origin, over the last 4 billion years at least five impact craters ranging from 31 to 58 miles in diameter have marred the
55 lunar surface. By extrapolation, over the same time span Earth must have experienced some 400 collisions of similar magnitude. Although such an impact crater has not been found, Alvarez supporters don't consider finding it necessary or likely. Geologic processes over
60 65 million years, like erosion and volcanic eruptions, would have obscured the crater, which in any case probably occurred on the ocean floor.

Traditional biologists and geologists continue to deny the validity of the Alvarez theory. They point to the
65 absence of any impact crater; to the fact that iridium, while rare at the Earth's surface, is common at its core and can be transported to the surface by volcanic activity; and to the fact that the Alvarezes, though eminent physicists, are not biologists, geologists, or paleontolo-
70 gists.

---

15. According to the Alvarez theory, the mass extinctions of animal species at the end of the Cretaceous period were caused by:

   A. the catastrophic impact of an enormous asteroid.
   B. processes like erosion and repeated volcanic eruptions.
   C. extreme global warming causing a global firestorm
   D. environmental conditions following a meteorite impact.

GO TO THE NEXT PAGE.

16. The views of those scientists who oppose the Alvarez theory would be strengthened if:

    I. major deposits of iridium were found in the lava flows of active Earth volcanoes.
    II. iridium was absent in sediments corresponding to several episodes of mass extinction.
    III. iridium was absent in fragments of several recently recovered meteorites.

    A. I only
    B. I and II only
    C. III only
    D. I and III only

17. The passage suggests that the author would characterize those who hold the traditional views about the topographical development of the Earth as:

    A. detrimental to scientific progress.
    B. unrivaled at the present time.
    C. correct in challenging alternative views.
    D. unreceptive to new evidence.

18. The author discusses the Alvarezes' description of environmental conditions at the end of the Cretaceous period in order to:

    A. demonstrate that an immense meteorite hit the Earth.
    B. explain why no trace of an impact crater has yet been found.
    C. argue that Earth is vulnerable to meteorite collisions.
    D. clarify how a meteorite may account for mass extinctions.

19. The author's statement that "Earth exists in a region of space teeming with asteroids and comets" is most consistent with the:

    A. the Alvarezes' claim that an asteroid's impact caused atmospheric poisoning, acid rain, forest fires, and tidal waves.
    B. the Alvarezes' view that the resulting dust cloud, rather than the impact of the meteorite, did most of the harm.
    C. Alvarez supporters' argument based on extrapolation from the numbers of craters on the surface of the moon.
    D. traditionalists view that topographical development of the Earth can be explained by gradual geologic processes.

20. Suppose new evidence is found establishing irrefutably that the impact of an asteroid 6 miles in diameter on the moon would result in a crater 500 miles in diameter. What effect would this information have on the arguments made in the passage?

    A. It would strengthen the Alvarez theory, because the moon and Earth lie within the same group of asteroids and comets.
    B. It would weaken the Alvarez theory, because the craters that have been measured on the moon are too small to represent the impact of such a meteorite.
    C. It would contradict the traditional view, because craters that large would certainly have catastrophic effects on Earth's environments.
    D. It would have no effect on any arguments made in the passage, because the size of a crater on the moon isn't relevant to the size of a crater on Earth.

GO TO THE NEXT PAGE.

Passage IV (Questions 21–26)

Gender-based trends in labor are of great interest to historians and sociologists, since these shifts mark a transition in the nation's economic prosperity and are linked to the ever-changing concepts of what constitutes
5 "men's" and "women's" work. Perhaps one of the most significant labor transitions in American history occurred in the evolution from the Colonial era, during which most families farmed or ran small "cottage industries" in their homes, to the Industrial Revolution, when
10 a large segment of the population earned wages in mills and factories. Though both eras were patriarchal, the pre-industrial colonists enjoyed a degree of economic egalitarianism that would all but disappear with industrialization.

15 While the Colonial era is certainly not an example of gender equality, its economic system did allow women some power. The family was a self-sufficient economic unit, and all necessary goods and services were available either within or just beyond the home. Work was con-
20 sidered a civic duty for women, integral to the family's economic survival, and wasn't confined to the home: many women were also shopkeepers, midwives, and even blacksmiths. Instead of being embarrassed by their wives' participation in labor-intensive activities, hus-
25 bands encouraged and relied on it.

With the advent of the Industrial Revolution came stricter definitions of men's and women's roles. The move from a subsistence economy to a market economy all but obliterated the family-based "cottage industries"
30 so prevalent during the Colonial era. The gap between the genders widened, as men and women occupied different social realms and physical workspaces. Thus developed the "doctrine of two spheres"—to men the realm of public visibility and economic opportunity, to
35 women private, domestic responsibility. Women felt themselves further demoted in an already patriarchal society.

While Colonial women had the satisfaction of contributing to the family's economic well-being, the society of
40 the Industrial Revolution, on the whole, appreciated neither their presence in, nor their contributions to, the labor force. Instead of encouraging women to help catalyze industrialization, mainstream society endorsed the disempowering phenomenon known as the "Cult of True
45 Womanhood." Women's roles were both idealized and restricted; women were held to the highest standards of piety, purity, domesticity, and submissiveness. The "moral authority" given to women was nominal in comparison to the *actual* authority that their husbands pos-
50 sessed. While many middle- and upper-class families had the luxury—at least ostensibly—to fulfill these requirements, this was simply not an option for the working class, whose women had to leave the home to put food on the table. This experience could be both
55 personally frustrating and socially limiting.

Men felt the pressure and anxiety created by the Cult of True Womanhood as well, afraid of letting his social status and credibility decrease. The "good-provider role," a position shared by men and women during the Colonial
60 era, was now assigned solely to the man of the household. Many men, for a variety of reasons, could not successfully maintain the position of breadwinner. Some over-performed the good-provider role at the expense of emotional intimacy with their wives and children; others
65 refused the burden and abandoned their families. Caught between these two extremes were the everyday male workers who tried their best to maintain social status and strong familial ties—dual goals that were often unattainable.

---

21. Which of the following general theories is best supported by the passage?

   A. A sharp economic downturn at the end of the Colonial era prompted a move toward the gender-segregated labor system of the Industrial Revolution.
   B. The Colonial era in America was characterized by a social egalitarianism that disappeared with the advent of the Industrial Revolution.
   C. The Industrial Revolution, while known as a time of great progress in American history, caused significant socioeconomic strain for men and women alike.
   D. The beginning of the women's movement in the early 20th century was a backlash against the Cult of True Womanhood created during the Industrial Revolution.

GO TO THE NEXT PAGE.

22. The author most likely mentions the status of the working class during the Industrial Revolution in order to:

    A. compare the economic standing of working class families of the Industrial Revolution and the Colonial era.

    B. examine a section of the population for which socially ideal gender roles were not easily attained.

    C. emphasize the negative attitudes the middle and upper classes had toward the lower class.

    D. discuss a social class that didn't view the Cult of True Womanhood as its ideal.

23. The author provides support for all the following statements EXCEPT:

    A. Women in the Colonial era had greater economic power than did women in the Industrial Revolution.

    B. The development of the "doctrine of two spheres" was closely related to the move from a subsistence economy to a market economy.

    C. The gender segregation prevalent during the Industrial Revolution proved disadvantageous for men as well as for women.

    D. The "doctrine of two spheres" was necessary for economic growth and development during the Industrial Revolution.

24. The author would be most likely to make which of the following claims about the difference between the Colonial period and the Industrial Revolution?

    A. The Industrial Revolution was a time of marked prosperity, while the Colonial era was characterized by economic struggle.

    B. Colonial men were more accepting of women's participation in the labor force than were men during the Industrial Revolution.

    C. Men in the Colonial era found it more difficult to maintain the "good-provider role" than did men in the Industrial Revolution.

    D. Children were less likely to be forced into labor during the Colonial era than during the Industrial Revolution.

25. Which of the following situations would the author be most likely to consider an example of adherence to the Cult of True Womanhood?

    A. A woman works in a garment factory all day and then returns home to clean the house, bathe the children, and cook dinner for the family.

    B. A woman sacrifices the financial advantages of taking a job in a factory so that she can tend to the children and participate in church activities.

    C. A woman opens a clothes-tailoring service in her home so that she can contribute to the family's income without having to work outside the house.

    D. A woman's husband becomes overwhelmed with the pressure of providing for his wife and children and eventually abandons the family.

26. The passage indicates that the author is LEAST likely to agree with which of the following statements?

    A. The Industrial Revolution introduced new social and economic standards to American life that proved to be both helpful and harmful.

    B. The financial contribution of working-class women during the Industrial Revolution was similar to that of Colonial women, but Colonial women received more recognition.

    C. Both the Colonial era and the Industrial Revolution were characterized by gender inequality.

    D. The role a woman played in society was much less important during the Colonial era.

GO TO THE NEXT PAGE.

Passage V (Questions 27–34)

The Augustan Age has been called "The Great Age of Satire," since almost all its major writers produced satirical works. They also wrote *about* satire, and often disagreed with each other. Addison was strongly against
5 the use of satire, claiming that the unkind writers who used it inflicted irreparable harm on their scorned victims. Pope, in contrast, calls satire a "sacred weapon" that permitted oblique criticism in his *Epilogue to Satires*. In his own mock epic, *The Rape of the Lock*,
10 Lady Belinda's tresses are cropped by a suitor while she lingers over her coffee. Samuel Johnson called this a questionable topic for poetic treatment: "below the common incidents of common life." Yet the frivolous story was ideal to lambaste traditional epic machinery and
15 romantic conventions.

Swift had a mixed opinion of satire. On the one hand, he believed it could instruct—that those who were influenced neither by the rebuke of clergy nor by fear of punishment would dread to have their misdeeds and pecca-
20 dilloes published to their neighbors. On the other hand, as P.K. Elkin writes, Swift is the only major Augustan writer who questioned the efficacy of satire on a hardened heart. In the preface to *A Tale of the Tub*, for example, the Tubbian says satirists should give up remon-
25 strating with the notorious, who are insensible to verbal lashes.

In spite of this ambivalence, many of Swift's most famous works—like *An Argument Against the Abolishing of Christianity* and *A Modest Proposal*—are
30 satires. Given his mixed feelings, we might question why he chose to satirize such serious subjects as religion and the politics of famine. Perhaps Swift thought satire effectively conveyed strong opinions. The ironic personae adopted in these works—unreliable narrators—are
35 vital to the force of his message because in questioning the narrator's mind and morals, the reader questions what the narrator says. The juxtaposition of the literal and the veiled meaning of the narrators' words effected complicated, subtle operations on the mind of the read-
40 er. Unless his readers are fools or knaves, they read with increasing discomfort as they sense the seriousness behind the wit and their own complicity in the guilt.

The ironic personae used in these two works are not the same. The narrator of the *Argument* occupies the middle
45 of the road, sharing his society's goals, but disagreeing with the means most people would use to attain them.

The author of the *Proposal*, by contrast, is so extreme that some critics have called him mad—a plausible characterization since the Proposer takes literally the
50 abstract economic principle that people are the riches of a nation: People, the riches of Ireland, can be raised, sold, butchered, and eaten like cattle. There is a difference, too, in the narrators' methods. The Arguer admits the possibility, however slight, that the reader may dis-
55 agree with him. The Proposer, on the other hand, is obsessed with the perfection of his solution. The Arguer argues the right cause for the wrong reasons; the Proposer posits a solution that can't be reasonably entertained.

60 The Arguer and the Proposer share some characteristics, though. Both display Swiftian concern for reason gone awry. Both are outwardly rational, but like the Laputians on the Flying Island, they attempt to see everything one way. The Proposer "can think of no one Objection, that
65 will possibly be raised against this Proposal." The reader, by this time aware of the Proposer's fixation, can and will raise objections. Less obsessive than the Proposer, the Arguer states and refutes objections to his argument, but dismissively, only to forestall demur.

---

27. The information in the passage supports which of the following conclusions concerning Augustan satire?

   I. Satirists could focus both on the foibles of individuals and on larger, societal ills.
   II. Satire could be used to mock literary conventions.
   III. Satire could serve as a formidable weapon for personal revilement.

  A. I only
  B. III only
  C. I and III only
  D. I, II, and III

28. Based on the information provided in the passage, which of the following might be an Augustan satire?

  A. a polemic decrying Lockean ethics
  B. an exposé of patronage at the court of Charles II
  C. a fanciful description of a mythical land
  D. a cleverly disguised attack on a pedantic academic

GO TO THE NEXT PAGE.

29. Based on the passage, we can reasonably assume that the author believes Johnson's criticism of *The Rape of the Lock* represents:

  A. an overly narrow perception of the appropriate content of poetry.
  B. fixation on a minor flaw inhibiting enjoyment of the work as a whole.
  C. a failure to appreciate that the work is intentionally humorous
  D. a conviction that the work mocks the dignity of everyday life

30. The passage implies that, in the opinion of the author, during the period before the Augustan Age:

  A. Satire dealt only with subjects of political and religious importance.
  B. The conventions of heroic poetry were considered above criticism.
  C. Satire was seen as only one among several important literary genres.
  D. Greater political freedom allowed writers to express political ideas directly.

31. The author most probably includes details from the "plot" of *The Rape of the Lock* in order to:

  A. argue that Pope had captured the ideal context for Augustan satire.
  B. contrast Pope's view of satire with Addison's strong objection to its use.
  C. demonstrate a dispute between Augustan writers about the proper subject of satire.
  D. show how frivolous Pope's satire was, as compared to the serious satire of Swift.

32. An assumption apparently made by Addison in his criticism of satire as a genre is that:

  A. satire was potentially beneficial but not generally effective.
  B. any instructional value of satire was outweighed by its harm to individuals.
  C. most readers are unable to comprehend the indirect significance of satire.
  D. the subject matter of satire is the "below the common incidents of common life."

33. The author concludes that Swift chose to write on such serious subjects as religion and politics in the form of satire because:

  A. he concluded that satire was effective even on the hardened hearts of the notorious.
  B. satire was the only genre in which he could use his favorite persona, the unreliable narrator.
  C. the ironic personae used in these satires both display Swift's concern for reason gone awry.
  D. it juxtaposed absurd literal ideas with hidden subtext that was especially effective at involving the reader

34. In citing that both the Arguer and the Proposer are "outwardly rational" (line 62), the author probably intends to draw attention to the fact that:

  A. the Arguer is actually rational, but the Proposer is mad.
  B. both are actually irrational, although in different ways.
  C. both are rational, but in varying degrees and respects.
  D. neither conveys Swift's actual concern for reason gone awry.

GO TO THE NEXT PAGE.

Passage VI (Questions 35–40)

Despite the falling popularity of smoking in the United States, the increase in smoking among young women continues. Whereas older teenage males appear to have reached a plateau in the early 1970s, with approximate-
5 ly 19 percent smoking, over 26 percent of older teenage females are now regular smokers.

A 1989 study examined smoking habits among young women as reported by approximately 600 undergraduate women at four Maryland colleges. Researcher Mary
10 Smith and colleagues examined the respondents' description of parental and peer smoking behavior to determine whether these factors were correlated with their smoking behavior.

The researchers first analyzed the effects of parental
15 smoking on the initiation of smoking. Smith views the initiation of smoking as a function of psychosocial rather than physiological influences since the physical effects of nicotine are not felt until later in life. Smoking behavior of the respondents' mothers was sig-
20 nificantly associated with the college women's own early smoking behavior. Among respondents with mothers who smoked, 56.9 percent of the daughters had smoked or did smoke, while 43.1 percent had never smoked. Forty-six and one-half percent of respondents
25 with nonsmoking mothers had smoked or did smoke, while 53.3 percent of such respondents had never smoked. The smoking behavior of the father during the initiation stage appears to have little or no effect upon the respondents' smoking behavior.

30 The next stage of the smoking career, the maintenance of smoking habits, was less significantly related to the smoking behavior of the primary socialization agents. The smoking behavior of the respondents' fathers seemed to have no effect on their smoking maintenance,
35 while the smoking behavior of the mother was related only to the frequency of smoking, but not the duration of the habit. Of much greater importance to the mainte-nance of smoking habits of respondents was the smok-ing behavior of particular members of her proximal
40 social environment—her closest female friends. Interestingly, smoking habits of even the closest male members of the respondent's social network seemed to have no bearing upon the frequency and duration of the respondents' smoking behavior.

45 According to Smith, cessation constitutes the third stage

of an individual's smoking career; in the Maryland study, cessation was measured by the respondents' categoriza-tions of perceived or actual difficulties associated with giving up cigarettes. Her parents' smoking behavior was
50 not taken into consideration, but the relationship between cessation of smoking and the smoking behavior of members of the respondent's social network was sim-ilar to that cited above: only the smoking behavior of female friends was significantly correlated with the
55 respondent's perceived or actual difficulty in breaking her own habit. Smith and her associates concluded that same-sex relationships are important in every phase of a woman's smoking career.

---

35. According to the passage, a young woman's closest female friends:

   A. have little effect on her smoking habits.
   B. encourage her to smoke heavily.
   C. determine whether she will start smoking.
   D. influence the duration of her smoking habit.

36. The passage suggests that male smoking behavior:

   A. helps to explain female smoking behavior.
   B. influences the smoking habits of other males.
   C. affects women's decisions to stop smoking.
   D. does not account for female smoking habits.

37. Which of the following would most seriously *weak-en* Smith's basic argument?

   A. Mothers have influence over the earliest stages of their daughters' smoking careers.
   B. Close female friends influence the duration, but not the frequency, of young women's smoking.
   C. The maintenance of one's smoking habits is heavily influenced by one's economic status.
   D. The smoking habits of both parents significant-ly influence a daughter's initial decision to smoke.

38. Which of the following most accurately describes the passage?

   A. A refutation of an earlier hypothesis
   B. An explanation of a popular theory
   C. A summary of recent research findings
   D. A description of a controversial study

GO TO THE NEXT PAGE.

39. According to the passage, in the early 1970s the percentage of male smokers:

    A. leveled off at 26 percent.
    B. decreased to 19 percent.
    C. increased to 26 percent.
    D. leveled off at 19 percent.

40. The passage suggests that nicotine:

    A. has no effect on smoking behavior.
    B. has less effect than maternal influence on the initiation of smoking.
    C. affects female smokers more than male smokers.
    D. encourages young women to begin smoking.

GO TO THE NEXT PAGE.

Passage VII (Questions 41–46)

Within the family law setting, a tension has always existed between the state's primary goal of normalizing family relationships and the state's adversarial divorce laws to dissolve those relationships. The divorce
5 process, involving a lawyer bound by adversarial ethics, frustrates the intentions of divorcing spouses to fulfill their state-mandated family obligations. In recognition of this, most states have responded with "no-fault" divorce (which eliminates the need to prove one party
10 "wrong" in order to secure a divorce) in an effort to reduce some of the friction.

Experience has shown that the adversarial nature of the divorce process does not tend to promote fulfillment of post-divorce obligations. Divorce, by its very nature,
15 wreaks havoc in the lives of the individuals involved, and the adversarial process promotes, intensifies, and prolongs that turmoil. The couple whose united love resulted in the birth of children will fight with dogged determination for "possession" of them. Liberalized
20 property distribution schemes provide additional incentives to engage in a battle the spoils of which are obtained at great emotional and psychological cost to all involved. The adversarial lawyer zealously strives to maximize his or her client's rights in the property divi-
25 sion, child custody, and continuing support decisions. It is impermissible for a lawyer to advocate a generous or equitable settlement offer if the "best interests" of the client (by which the law means the economic interests, since that is the only objective standard involved)
30 require seeking a different result. Victory is valued, not peaceful coexistence, and toward that victory, adversarial lawyers will use emotional vulnerability as leverage.

Recent developments suggest that this picture may be changing. For couples facing divorce, professional
35 mediation of the dissolution is an increasingly popular choice that its proponents argue is less expensive, limits the amount of legal bloodshed, and better promotes a comparatively amicable ongoing relationship. Mediation, they claim, allows couples to tailor solutions
40 that define their own responsibilities and encourage mutual compliance. The goal of the attorney is to assist the client in achieving the most amicable divorce possible, to be an instrument of peace trained to influence and facilitate choice in the law office, rather than in court.
45 The chosen course can maximize benefits to all interested parties (including, for example, grandparents and children) and to society, as well as to the individual

client. Counselors, social workers, psychologists, and clergy can also be involved in this cooperative process
50 to help the parties deal with emotional problems. Only if confusion, displacement, fear, anger, and resentment can be dissipated can the parties come to reasonable terms with the drastic changes that will necessarily take place in their lives.

55 Critics, on the other hand, argue that mediation is merely a way for lawyers to involve themselves in the divorces of couples who were already prepared to accept a negotiated, rather than litigated, distribution. Before mediation was generally available, these spous-
60 es would not have fought it out in court, but would have resolved and filed settlement agreements or divorces on their own. The state's version of a "fair" distribution means roughly equal, regardless of the couple's own evaluation of their relative contributions during the mar-
65 riage; regardless even of demonstrably appalling behavior by one spouse, unless it resulted in criminal convictions. Those who believe their spouses don't deserve this state-imposed "fair" distribution will not turn to mediation (and mediators would often refuse their cases
70 if they did). Only when mediation has resolved more significant numbers of divorces will we be able to evaluate the actual impact it has had on the litigiousness of divorce—whether it actually reduces the number of in-court contests, or merely increases the cost of settlement.

---

41. According to the passage, a lawyer involved in the adversarial divorce process cannot advocate an equitable settlement if:

   A. property division, child custody, and support monies are involved.
   B. the result includes any provisions beneficial to the other party.
   C. the result would be economically disadvantageous to the client.
   D. the settlement discourages the fulfillment of the state's primary concerns.

GO TO THE NEXT PAGE.

42. Which of the following statements best describes the organization of the passage?

A. The author calls for a change in methods, outlines the virtues of an alternative approach, and defends it against an anticipated criticism.

B. The author outlines a situation, presents the drawbacks of a procedure, and then discusses an alternative procedure.

C. The author makes a general statement about a situation, discusses two methods of resolving it, and proposes a compromise solution.

D. The author offers a historical account of how different approaches to a problem have developed and supplanted one another.

43. Suppose another writer were to assert that the involvement of the court in the adversarial divorce process is necessary to ensure that divorcing spouses fulfill their legal obligations to their family. The author's response would most likely be:

A. Disagreement: we should seek alternative systems to promote those goals.

B. Outrage: families are being destroyed by the present adversarial system.

C. Acceptance: the author never disputes the importance of the court's role.

D. Neutral: this position would not affect any of the author's own assertions.

44. Which of the following, if true, would most *challenge* proponent's claims about divorce mediation?

A. Most couples who try mediation eventually litigate to resolve their disputes.

B. Even those who use mediation go through some conflict in the divorce process.

C. The adversarial process does not lend itself to settling divorces equitably.

D. Many lawyers choose not to mediate when they divorce their own spouses.

45. By the phrase "merely increases the cost of settlement" in the last line, the author most probably means:

A. mediation will result in a greater number of unfair divorce settlements than adversarial divorce.

B. mediation lawyers, because they receive more training than adversarial lawyers, will require higher fees.

C. the social and emotional costs of settlement are increased by the involvement of another party.

D. couples that would have divorced without using lawyers before, now pay lawyers to "mediate".

46. The author cites the introduction of "no-fault" divorce laws probably in order to:

A. suggest that the states will probably be able to cure the ills of adversarial divorce.

B. emphasize the undeniable damage done by adversarial divorce procedures.

C. demonstrate that it is no longer necessary to consider the mediation alternative.

D. support the view that mediation will definitely improve the outcome in divorces.

GO TO THE NEXT PAGE.

Passage VIII (Questions 47–53)

The harbor seal, *Phoca vitulina,* is a member of the order *Pinnepedia,* and lives amphibiously along the northern Atlantic and Pacific coasts. This extraordinary mammal, which does most of its fishing at night when
5 visibility is low and where noise levels are high, has developed several unique adaptations that have sharpened its visual and acoustic acuity. The need for such adaptations has been compounded by the varying behavior of sound and light in each of the two habitats of the
10 harbor seal—land and water.

While the seal is on land, its ear operates much like that of the human, with sound waves traveling through air and entering the inner ear through the auditory canal. The directions from which sounds originate are distin-
15 guishable because the sound waves arrive at each inner ear at different times. In water, however, where sound waves travel faster than they do in air, the ability of the brain to differentiate arrival times between each ear is severely reduced. Yet it is crucial for the seal to be able
20 to pinpoint the exact origins of sound in order to locate both its offspring and prey. Therefore, through processes of adaptation to the demands of its environment, the seal has developed an extremely sensitive quadrophonic hearing system, composed of a specialized band of tis-
25 sue that extends down from the ear to the inner ear. In water, sound is conducted to the seal's inner ear by this special band of tissue, making it possible for the seal to identify the exact origins of sounds.

The eye of the seal is also uniquely adapted to operate in
30 both air and water. The human eye, adapted to function primarily in air, is equipped with a cornea, which aids in the refraction and focusing of light onto the retina. As a result, when a human eye is submerged in water, light rays are further refracted and the image is blurry. The
35 seal's cornea, however, has a refractive index similar to that of water. Therefore, in water light rays are transmitted by the cornea without distortion, and are clearly focused on the retina. In air, however, the cornea is astigmatic. The result is a distortion of incoming light
40 rays. The seal compensates for this by having a stenopaic pupil, which constricts into a vertical slit. Since the astigmatism is most pronounced in the horizontal plane of the eye, the vertical nature of the pupil serves to minimize its effect on the seal's vision.

45 Since the harbor seal procures its food under conditions of low visibility, some scientists hypothesize that harbor seals have an echolocation system akin to the sensory capabilities of bats, porpoises, and dolphins. This kind of natural and instinctual radar involves the emission of
50 high frequency sound pulses that reflect off obstacles such as predators, prey, or natural barriers. The reflections are received as sensory signals by the brain, which interprets them and processes them into an image. The animal, blinded by unfavorable surroundings or lighting
55 conditions, is thus able to perceive its surroundings. Scientists believe that echolocation in the harbor seal is suggested by the fact that these seals emit "clicks," high frequency sounds produced in short, fast bursts that occur mostly at night, when visual acuity is low.

60 Finally, there is speculation that the seal's vibrissae, or whiskers, act as sensory receptors. Evidence for this is found in the fact that vibrissae are unusually well developed in *Pinnepedia* and are highly sensitive to movement. Scientists hypothesize that the vibrissae may be
65 instrumental in catching prey and, because they are sensitive to vibrations, may sense wave disturbances produced by nearby moving fish, allowing the seal to home in on and capture prey.

Having met the sensory demands of dual habitats, the
70 harbor seal is one of the most interesting animals on earth. Its amphibious existence has demanded a sensory acuity and flexibility matched by few other mammals.

---

47. According to the passage, scientists think vibrissae help harbor seals to catch prey by:

    A. improving underwater vision.
    B. sensing aerial vibrations.
    C. camouflaging predator seals.
    D. detecting underwater movement.

48. The passage implies that a harbor seal's vision is:

    A. inferior to a human's vision in the water, but superior to it on land.
    B. superior to a human's vision in the water, but inferior to it on land.
    C. inferior to a human's vision both in the water and on land.
    D. equivalent to a human's vision both in the water and on land.

GO TO THE NEXT PAGE.

49. The passage supplies information for answering which of the following questions?

   A. Why does the harbor seal do most of its fishing at night?

   B. What proportion of the harbor seal's time is spent on land?

   C. Do all types of seals in the *Pinnepedia* order live amphibiously?

   D. How does the harbor seal's eye compensate for the distortion of light rays on land?

50. Which of the following would most strengthen the claim that harbor seals hunt down prey by echolocation?

   A. The harbor seal's eye has become increasingly efficient underwater over time.

   B. Harbor seals rely on their vibrissae to sense prey at close range and do most of their hunting within very limited areas.

   C. Other members of their order of species are known to possess the facility of echolocation.

   D. Harbor seals are not closely related to bats, porpoises, or dolphins.

51. The author compares harbor seal sensory organs to human sensory organs primarily in order to:

   A. point out similarities among mammals.

   B. explain how the seal's sensory organs function.

   C. show that seals are related to humans.

   D. prove that seals are more adaptively successful than humans.

52. The author of this passage is most likely a:

   A. paleontologist.

   B. zoologist.

   C. taxonomist.

   D. geneticist.

53. According to the passage, harbor seals are found in:

   A. many arctic regions.

   B. most areas with abundant fish populations.

   C. most island and coastal regions.

   D. some North American coastal regions.

GO TO THE NEXT PAGE.

Passage IX (Questions 54–60)

Roman Italy was a world of small communities. Hundreds of small cities, towns, and villages dotted the Italian peninsula, each with a slightly different landscape, history, and social and economic structure, but all
5 sharing certain political, social, and economic institutions, physical structures, and rituals of daily life . . . .

. . . Without this structure of rural communities, the Roman Empire could not have existed. Primitive communications and an underdeveloped bureaucracy made a
10 highly centralized government impossible. The largely autonomous communities maintained civic order on the local level. The local community should therefore be seen as a key element in the success of the Roman system.

15 In spite of the ubiquity and importance of these local communities, they have been rather neglected in recent Roman historical research. The reasons for this are complex and tell us much about the development of Roman historical and archaeological studies. The neglect began
20 with the ancient Romans themselves. Although many Roman writers were born in the small towns of Italy, most migrated at a relatively young age to the capital. They concentrated their attention on the society and events of the city of Rome and on the major political and
25 military events that shaped the Republic and the Empire. Like urbanites the world over, they had little interest in the daily life of the small towns . . . .

Modern students of ancient Rome have not treated this local society much more kindly . . . . The mainstream of
30 ancient historical studies during the eighteenth, nineteenth, and twentieth centuries has been directed to the reconstruction of a national Roman history. This suited the predilections of increasingly professional scholars who viewed Roman history as elite, institutional, and
35 legal history concerned with consuls, generals, and emperors, rather than decuriones and small-town shopkeepers. One important exception to this trend was the great Russian historian Michael Rostovtzeff. He was very much interested in the smaller Roman city with its
40 local bourgeoisie and he tied closely the fate of the larger Empire to the rise and fall of that socioeconomic class. He appreciated the importance of the archaeological remains at a site like Pompeii for understanding aspects of Roman society little reflected written record.
45 Yet Rostovtzeff had few true followers . . . .

Roman agricultural history, and especially the changes in rural social and economic structures that took place during the later Republic has, however, received considerable attention. This was a topic that happened to inter-
50 est the ancient, and modern historians attended to their concerns. Such distinguished social scientists as Max Weber have done research on Roman agrarian history. The debate also included the related issues of Roman slavery and the development of a colonate during the
55 later Empire. Marxist scholars were attracted to these topics, which highlighted class oppression and conflict. Partly as a result of this Marxist concern, we have an especially rich bibliography on such topics as Roman slavery, slave revolts, and the rise of the great estates.
60 Although the Marxist models have sometimes distorted our reconstructions of Roman rural life, there is no question that the approach has stimulated much important research.

Recently, more scholarly attention has been focused on
65 the Roman commercial economy. Research has centered on such questions as the nature of senatorial investment in commerce, the development of sea-borne trade, the rise of major trading center such as Puteoli and Ostia, and even the degree to which the Roman economy can
70 be considered "modern." Less attention has been paid to the development of the regional and local economies and to the combined use of literary, epigraphical, and archaeological information to answer questions related to these local systems.

---

54. The author of this passage would most likely urge support for historical research involving:

   A. Marxist models of social and economic analysis.

   B. a synthesis of archaeological and other nonliterary evidence with literary evidence.

   C. investigations into the genealogies of eminent Roman families.

   D. a reconstruction of the operations of the central bureaucracies that collected taxes and administered justice.

GO TO THE NEXT PAGE.

55. The amount of modern scholarship on Roman agriculture suggests that:

    A. modern scholars often reflect the interests of ancient writers.

    B. modern scholars have actually had long-standing interests in the rural communities of Roman Italy.

    C. modern scholars have had little interest in the rural communities of Roman Italy.

    D. modern scholars have tended to have elitist interests.

56. "The neglect [that] began with the ancient Romans themselves" (lines 19–20) refers to the:

    A. Romans' inability to centralize political power.

    B. incompetence of historians and archaeologists.

    C. urban mind-set of the major Roman writers.

    D. proclivities of recent scholars of Roman history.

57. Suppose that a single, previously unknown artifact from ancient Roman Italy could be unearthed at whim. Which of the following would be most useful to the sort of study that the author seeks to undertake?

    A. A well-preserved plough.

    B. The records of an ancient town council.

    C. A trading ship that had been sunk with a full cargo.

    D. A cache of swords and spears.

58. In the context of the passage, the word *decuriones* (line 36) refers to:

    A. important military officers.

    B. slaves and impoverished peasants.

    C. local political leaders.

    D. powerful noblemen.

59. Which of the following is an observation made by the author but NOT supported in the passage by evidence, explanation, or example?

    A. Political power in the Roman Empire was never highly centralized.

    B. Ancient historians tended to have little interest in life outside of Rome.

    C. Marxist historians have generated a great deal of scholarship on slavery and the great escapes of Roman Italy.

    D. There is little recent scholarship that deals with the local economies of Roman Italy.

60. Which of the following statements is best inferred from the author's observation that Rostovtzeff "appreciated the importance of the archaeological remains at a site like Pompeii for understanding aspects of Roman society little reflected in the written record" (lines 42–44)?

    A. Most of the ancient historians who wrote about Rome had little concern with small cities like Pompeii.

    B. Most modern Roman historians are hesitant to investigate matters not described in the written record.

    C. Rostovtzeff's studies were too arcane to attract the interest of other scholars.

    D. Rostovtzeff's studies provided a good starting point for the work of Weber and of Marxist historians.

STOP. If you finish before time is called, check your work. You may go back to any question in this test booklet.

ANSWER KEY
VERBAL REASONING TEST 1

1. C	18. D	35. D	52. B
2. D	19. C	36. D	53. D
3. B	20. B	37. D	54. B
4. D	21. C	38. C	55. A
5. B	22. B	39. D	56. D
6. A	23. D	40. B	57. B
7. C	24. B	41. C	58. C
8. B	25. B	42. B	59. D
9. A	26. D	43. A	60. B
10. D	27. D	44. A	
11. C	28. D	45. D	
12. A	29. A	46. B	
13. C	30. C	47. D	
14. C	31. C	48. B	
15. D	32. B	49. D	
16. A	33. D	50. C	
17. C	34. B	51. B	

EXPLANATIONS

Questions 1–6: HARRIET JACOBS

PASSAGE I

Topic: *Incidents in the Life of a Slave Girl Written by Herself*, by Harriet Jaocbs

Scope: Change in the texts' relevance

Purpose: To explain why *Incidents* was long regarded as a work of fiction, and how the work of Yellin established that *Incidents* is a true account

Passage Map

¶1: *Incidents* = primary source; not a novel
The key point in this paragraph is that the novel's relevance has changed. The text is no longer merely a piece of fiction arguing for the abolition of slavery; it is now a primary source that provides a true account of slavery from the perspective of an African-American woman.

¶2: why received as fiction
The purpose of this paragraph is to explain the circumstances that led to the perception that the novel was a work of fiction. Two reasons are put forth: one, the title page listed only the editor who was a known abolitionist and novelist; and two, the narration did not list any real names or places thus making the authorship untraceable.

¶3: additional reasons why received as fiction: prejudice against character as well as racial prejudice
19th century readers found it hard to believe that the main character (a brutalized woman who went into hiding for seven years) could have written such a work due to its liter-

ary style. According to the author, this is the "most important" reason that the text was regarded as a novel. Finally, the author adds that racial prejudice also played a role as most white Americans couldn't fathom that an African-American could ever write on such a level.

¶4: why and how Yellin discovered Jacobs
The first sentence explains why Yellin pursued the issue (because she was impressed by the text's attempt to create a sisterhood between white and black women) whereas the second sentence explains how Yellin succeeded.

¶5: how Jacobs learned to write; why Jacobs remained anonymous; why Jacobs wrote the novel
The first half of the paragraph offers evidence as to how a slave like Jacobs developed a literary ability to write with such drama thus answering the "most important reason" specified in the 3rd paragraph.
The passage then explains that Jacobs remained anonymous due to the inappropriateness of the content contained in the book.

Nevertheless, Jacobs felt it was necessary to write the novel to reach out with her fellow females.

Questions:

1. C This question asks you to explain the function of the reference to *Uncle Tom's Cabin*, describing it as a "thinly-veiled political tract in the Abolitionist cause," which occurs in the 2nd paragraph. Readers of Incidents were led by circumstances to see it as the same type of book. Thus, precedent existed for this type of book, which is best expressed by Choice (C). Choice (A) is a distortion of the author's statement that readers held racial stereotypes. Choice (B) sets up a comparison that does not exist in the text—nothing is mentioned about the quality of *Uncle Tom's Cabin*. Finally, Choice (D) distorts several points: *Uncle Tom's Cabin* was not confused with nonfiction, according to the passage, nor is *Incidents* a novel.

2. D This is an Inference (Deduction) question, requiring an answer choice that closely follows logically from language in the passage. The first paragraph discusses the book's value as a powerful argument against slavery, even while people thought it was a novel. Reviewing the other choices, we can eliminate Choice (A), which is a distortion of a detail in the last paragraph: readers in 1861 might have deemed discussion of sexuality inappropriate, but we don't know that the author agrees with that assessment. Choice (B) is incorrect because it's outside the scope of the passage—that it was difficult for women to achieve these standards did not mean that it was easy for men. (C) distorts the idea in the 3rd paragraph that the book was embedded in a literary tradition popular among female readers, but we don't know that this book in particular was popular.

3. B All of these statements are in the passage in one form or another. The question asks which one is not used in support of the idea that Harriet Jacobs wrote the book. Choice (B) is the only one that works here. While Yellin takes Child at her word when she says she is not the author, the appearance of her name on the title page is irrelevant. In fact, that her name appears there is what led some to the opposite conclusion. Choices (A) and (C) are from details in the last paragraph, and (D) is in the 4th paragraph—each is cited by Yellin as part of the evidence that Jacobs wrote the book. (C) is more indirect; it supports the idea that Jacobs would have preferred to remain anonymous and left her name off its cover.

4. D In this question you have to apply the ideas from the passage to another situation. The "situation described in the passage" is that *Incidents* was once thought to be fiction, but was later proven to be nonfiction. Choice (D) fits this scenario best. (A) is on the same general topic as the passage, but this is actually an Opposite answer choice. Choice (B) is incorrect because new technology was not responsible for the resurrection of Jacobs' book, and the mention of the plantation house, while relevant to slavery, does not make the situations parallel. Finally, (C) is incorrect because, even if the situation in question were the recognition of Jacobs as the writer of *Incidents*, she was not poorly regarded during her lifetime as far as we know from the passage, though she may have been unknown.

5. B If former slaves did often dictate their memoirs to whites who then became the editors of the work, it might have provided a precedent for Jacobs' relationship with Child. This would tend to provide support for the idea that Jacobs did write the book, though it proves nothing, since it says nothing about Jacobs and Child specifically. (A) is the opposite of what we're looking for: an editor is not an author. (C) is a distortion of Yellin's notion that the book was nonfiction rather than fiction: she never asserts that Jacobs had to have written the book by herself. Finally, (D) is FUD (Faulty Use of Detail): the author's anonymity is a detail unrelated to the idea posited in the question.

6. A This is an Application question that refers to paragraph 4. There we see that Yellin "document[ed] the existence of people and events in the book," thereby establishing the true nature of the book as nonfiction. Choice (A) is on the mark here. Choice (B) is outside the scope: it might have been true when the book was published, but no such criticism during the period after 1947 is mentioned. (C) is Outside the Scope; the question asks why nothing happened between 1947 and th 1980s, not what happened "after slavery was abolished". (D) might have contributed to the delay if it were true, but the fact that Jacobs had access to the libraries, mentioned in the last paragraph, is only cited as evidence that Jacobs herself is the writer, not that the book

is nonfiction. Moreover, the passage gives us no information about when these libraries were "discovered" (or to suggest that they were ever unavailable).

Questions 7–14: KOHLBERG

PASSAGE II

Topic: Lawrence Kohlberg's theory of moral reasoning

Scope: Basic explanation of the theory's stages

Purpose: To detail Kohlberg's theory of moral reasoning and discuss the relevance of these findings to his findings' correlations to cognitive development

Passage Map
¶1: Kohlberg's theory of moral reasoning: 3 stages

¶2: Pre-conventional reasoning: young children and pre-teens

¶3: Conventional reasoning: young adults

¶4: Postconventional reasoning: most adults

¶5: Similarities and Ddifferences between Piaget and Kohlberg on cognitive development

Questions:
7. C This question asks about the primary purpose of the passage. The author's tone is merely descriptive, and his topic is the stages of Kohlberg's theory of the stages of moral reasoning, so (C) answers this question. The last paragraph of the passage cautions that Kohlberg's theory concerns the justifications behind behaviors but does not describe the behaviors themselves; since the author never compares moral reasoning and behavior in real life situations, neither (A) nor (D) accurately describe the main purpose of the passage. Choice (B) is incorrect because it suggests the author criticizes Kohlberg's theory, whereas he merely describes the theory without judging it.

8. B In paragraph 3, "interpersonal concordance" is characterized by comprehension of "good" and "bad" motives (B); it is the first of the two substages that comprise Kohlberg's "conventional" stage of moral reasoning. An understanding of law and order (A) is the second substage of the conventional orientation, which an individual in the interpersonal concordance orientation would not yet comprehend. Similarly, respect for the concept of the social contract (C) and consideration of the values of justice and equality (D) are the two substages of Kohlberg's most advanced orientation—the postconventional stage; since this follows the conventional stage, the individual displaying an interpersonal concordance orientation would not reason on a post-conventional basis.

9. A To answer this question, which asks about the overall pattern of the development of moral reasoning, you need to make an inference based upon the specific stages Kohlberg creates. Paragraph 2 describes the pre-conventional stage as based on tangible consequences; paragraph 3 sketches the conventional stage as characterized by a comprehension of simple concepts; and paragraph 4 describes the postconventional stage as one based on principles, values and abstract ideals. Therefore, (A) correctly describes a progression from concrete justifications to abstract and personal ideals. (B) concerns human behavior, whereas the last paragraph clearly states that Kohlberg's theory concerns justifications for behavior, not actual behaviors themselves. (C), suggests that people are increasingly guided by their own needs as they mature, but Kohlberg characterizes such an orientation in paragraph 2 as common to young children and preteens, not adults. (D) is wrong because Kohlberg's theory does not discuss conservative or liberal moral judgements; again, his theory concerns patterns of moral reasoning.

10. D The fifth paragraph compares Kohlberg's views to those of Piaget. Since Kohlberg's views regard moral development and thought processes rather than behavior, (A) is wrong in suggesting that Kohlberg's theory has to do with moral behavior. (B) suggests that Piaget's theory regards actual behavior, which the passage neither states nor implies in its discussion of cognitive development. Nor does the author suggest that Piaget focuses on the development of children, while Kohlberg studies adults (C): the passage implies that both theorists are concerned with cognitive development throughout life. Only (D) correctly contrasts the theories of Kohlberg and Piaget—the author clearly states in paragraph 5 that Piaget considers age and external stimuli as factors leading to cognitive development, while Kohlberg claims that social development is responsible for the development of thought processes.

11. C This incorporation question asks you to consider statements that might weaken Kohlberg's theory. Paragraph 4 discusses the postconventional stage of reasoning, which stresses personal values and abstract ideals; (A), then, describes reasoning in accordance with Kohlberg's depiction of this stage. Kohlberg claims in paragraph 2 that young children reason on the basis of their own needs and desires, so a study concluding that infants and toddlers cannot grasp the concept of altruism jibes with the description of this early stage of reasoning (B). The first sentence of the fifth paragraph states that there seems to be a correlation between the development of moral reasoning and cognitive development. Therefore, (D) would merely emphasize the similarities between Kohlberg's and Piaget's views and would not have the effect of weakening Kohlberg's theory. But

since the author states in the first paragraph that we pass through three distinct stages of moral reasoning as we age, (C) would weaken Kohlberg's theory because it suggests that individuals do not progress according to Kohlberg's—or any particular—pattern.

12. A The author mentions longitudinal movement in the last paragraph. The very sentence containing this phrase suggests that longitudinal movement refers to the advancement through progressively higher levels of reasoning. (B) is incorrect because "longitudinal" suggests vertical motion, not lateral, horizontal, motion; furthermore, this paragraph concerns advancement up and through more advanced stages, not movements across and between substages. The first and last sentences of the passage emphasize that Kohlberg's theory concerns not actual behavior, but justifications for behavior, so (C) is wrong. The first sentence of paragraph 5 does suggest a "correlation" between one's level of moral development as related to cognitive development, but the author never suggests any alternating pattern of development, so (D) is wrong. See paragraph 3, which discusses Kohlberg's conventional stage as marked by a basic understanding of "good" and "bad," and later by a concept of law and order.

13. C (C) correctly describes a person in this stage, who would conceivably support any police action because of an unwavering belief in the need for lawful order. A driver who runs a red light (A) is likely considering his or her own needs, which is indicative of preconventional, not conventional reasoning. (D) also describes preconventional reasoning, based on an even more basic desire to avoid punishment. (B) describes postconventional reasoning in that it indicates a deviation from socially acceptable standards, justified by underlying ethical codes.

14. C To answer this question you need to consider the author's tone as well as the information contained in the last sentence of the passage. The author notes that Kohlberg's theory does not concern behavior, but the justifications behind behavior. He does this not to criticize the theory, but to clarify the theory's focus on the rationalization of behavior (C). Both (B) and (D) imply that the author is criticizing Kohlberg's theory, and are therefore incorrect. (A) is wrong because it incorrectly suggests that Kohlberg's theory is only concerned with the motivations leading to moral behavior, while the author is interested in the motivations behind behavior in general.

Questions 15–20:
ASTEROIDAL IMPACT

PASSAGE III

Topic: Cause of KT extinctions

Scope: Alvarez' theory of asteroid impact

Purpose: To discuss Alvarez' theory that an extraterrestrial impact caused the KT extinctions

Passage Map

¶1: KT boundary: cause unknown; few consider extraterrestrial impact for Earth history

¶2: Alvarez theory: extraterrestrial asteroid impact caused KT

¶3: Composition of Earth supports impact theory; mineral composition reveals rocks of extraterrestrial origin

¶4: Observation of lunar surface supports impact theory

¶5: Traditional biologists and geologists critique of Alvarez's theory by traditional biologists and geologists

Questions:

15. D This question emphasizes the importance of reading all the choices before selecting one. Sentences 3-7 of the second paragraph tell us that the Alvarezes believe conditions created by the impact of a meteorite led to mass extinctions at the end of the Cretaceous. While they believe the impact of the asteroid (A) caused great damage, they say it didn't do "most of the harm"—see the third sentence. Choices (B) and (C) are FUDs; such "earthly" processes are the explanation of the "traditional" scientists.

16. A To tackle a "strengthen/weaken" question that cites a particular argument in the passage, have clear in your mind what arguments are given for and against the position before reading the answer choices. The arguments of Alvarez-theory opponents are given in the last paragraph: no crater, iridium comes from the Earth's core, and the Alvarezes are only physicists. There are also several types of evidence supporting the Alvarez theory: iridium, shocked quartz crystals, *microtektites* (all offered as proof of meteorite impact), and the number of craters on the lunar surface: information negating these, or providing alternative explanations, would weaken the Alvarez theory, and strengthen their opponents' view. Look at statement I first, since it occurs three times in the choices. This would clearly bolster the opponents' view—if sufficient iridium deposits come from the earth's core, Alvarez supporters can't rely on them as evidence of impact. Statements II and III, however, would neither strengthen nor weaken either side.

The Alvarezes only addressed a single event of mass extinction at the end of the Cretaceous period; "subsequent research" suggested that other mass extinctions may have been similarly caused, but neither side denies that other mass extinctions could have resulted from different causes. So a lack of iridium (indicating no impact to the Alvarez supporters) at the time of some mass extinctions (statement II) doesn't affect either argument. And iridium is "common" in meteorites, but the Alvarez theory doesn't require that every meteorite contain iridium (statement III).

17. C This isn't easy, but (C) is the only possible correct choice. The author is an objective scientist (or at least science journalist) who wouldn't want "opponents" to give up their view until the new theory has been fully tested against all their criticisms. The traditionalists' arguments are given only briefly, and the author clearly believes the Alvarezes have added something valuable to the study of mass extinctions; but the traditional view isn't dismissed as reactionary or obstructionist, as choices (A) and (D) suggest. (B) is clearly not true; the author believes the new theory not only "rivals", but "challenges" the old one.

18. D This evaluation questions asks why the author includes detailed description of the environmental conditions proposed by the Alvarezes for the end of the Cretaceous period. Look back at the second paragraph; these details clarify the mechanism by which the impact led to extinctions—the crater didn't simply smash all species into extinction. Choice (A) is the wrong verb; this isn't offered as proof of the meteorite's impact, or of anything else. (B) is FUD; the lack of a known crater site is mentioned at the end of paragraph 4, and one explanation for its absence is that such geologic processes wore it away—but that's not relevant to the discussion in paragraph 2. The environmental conditions that result from meteorite collisions (C) isn't evidence that the Earth is vulnerable to such collisions.

19. C The number of asteroids and comets suggested by the author's word "teeming" is an essential part of the argument made by Alvarez supporters about how frequently collisions must have occurred in Earth's history. In fact, the "same swarm of asteroids and comets" is expressly cited in making that argument. (A) and (B) are FUDs; the fact that impact would result in certain effects, or the fact that the dust cloud would do more harm than the impact itself are not affected by the number of impacts that are likely. (D) is contradictory; the number of asteroids and comets, and the consequent implications for the likelihood of a collision with the Earth, if anything, run counter to the arguments of the traditionalists.

20. B The details in the question stem can only relate to the statements in the passage about the impact craters on the moon and the Alvarezes' theory proposing that a 6 mile wide meteorite caused the Cretaceous extinctions. The craters we've measured on the moon are only "31-58 miles in diameter" so (according to the new information) something much smaller than a 6-mile-wide asteroid must have caused them, and the evidence of the number of craters on the moon doesn't support the argument that such an asteroid must have struck the earth. (A) contradicts the correct choice. (C) is FUD; the amount of devastation such a crater would cause isn't relevant if we can't demonstrate that there was such an impact at all.

Questions 21–26: GENDER WORK
PASSAGE IV

Topic: Gender-based trends in US labor

Scope: Evolution of gender roles from Colonial Era to Industrial Revolution

Purpose: To discuss the societal changes in the role of men and women that came along with the change from the Colonial Era to the Industrial Revolution.

Passage Map
¶1: Interest in gender-based trends in labor among sociologists and historians

¶2: Colonial Era: family = self-sufficient; work = civic duty for women

¶3: Industrial Revolution: gender gap widened

¶4: Woman's role in Industrial Revolution

¶5: Man's role in Industrial Revolution

Questions:
21. C During the Industrial Revolution, the "doctrine of two spheres" and the Cult of True Womanhood put unreasonable demands on both men and women. This effect of industrialization is discussed in Paragraphs 4 and 6 and is summarized by choice (C). The reason for the shift from the subsistence economy of the Colonial era to the market economy of the Industrial Revolution is not mentioned, making choice (A) incorrect. While women during the Colonial era enjoyed a greater amount of economic egalitarianism than women during the Industrial Revolution, female colonists were by no means treated as men's social equals, as (B) would imply. Finally, while some early 20th-century feminists may have spoken out against the Cult of True Womanhood, this is never discussed in the passage—therefore, (D) cannot be correct.

22. B The author mentions the status of the working class during the Industrial Revolution (Paragraph 6) in order to examine a section of the population for which, due to financial limitations, socially ideal gender roles were not easily attained (B). The author never mentions the status of the working class during the Colonial era, thus the comparison suggested in choice (A) could not possibly be made. While the author notes that members of the working class had a difficult time attaining the social goals of the middle and upper class, there is no discussion of the middle and upper classes attitude toward the working class, making (C) incorrect. Finally, Paragraph 6 discusses the working class' struggle to conform to the socially ideal Cult of True Womanhood, proving choice (D) incorrect.

23. D All of the answer choices are supported by the passage except for (D). The "doctrine of two spheres" that developed during the Industrial Revolution was a disempowering social phenomenon, not a cause of economic growth and development. The author mentions "economic egalitarianism" in Paragraph 1 and discusses women's integral role in the Colonial economy in Paragraph 2, thus providing support for answer choice (A). In Paragraph 4, the author explains how the gender-based segregation of the physical workspace during the Industrial Revolution led to the creation of the "doctrine of two spheres," lending support to answer choice (B). Lastly, Paragraphs 4 and 6 discuss the challenges that both middle- and working-class men faced due to gender segregation during the Industrial Revolution; these paragraphs provide support for answer choice (C).

24. B The economic contributions of Colonial women were considered integral to their families' survival and thus were encouraged by Colonial husbands, making choice (B) the claim the passage's author would be most likely to make. The author would not agree with choice (A), since economic trials and triumphs were characteristic of both the Colonial era and the Industrial Revolution. Choice (C) is refuted by the passage, which examines the egalitarian economy of the Colonial era in Paragraphs 1, 2, and 3 and discusses men's difficulty in maintaining the "good-provider role" during the Industrial Revolution in Paragraphs 4 and 5. Finally, while choice (D) may be historically true, the treatment of children during the Colonial era and the Industrial Revolution is never mentioned in the passage.

25. B The only choice that the author would describe as an example of the Cult of True Womanhood is (B). During the Industrial Revolution, many women chose (or were forced) to stay out of the workplace in order to spend more time on matters of domesticity and spirituality. Choice (A) is not an accurate description of adherence to the Cult of True Womanhood; rather, it is a description of life in the working class during the Industrial Revolution. A woman with her own tailoring business, as described in choice (C), would not be an adherent to the Cult of True Womanhood, since this sort of financial independence was frowned upon by the strictures of the Cult. (Such a "cottage industry" would have been common during the Colonial era.) Finally, a family facing such familial strife as described in choice (D) would not be an example of the Cult of True Womanhood, since adherence to the Cult required domestic happiness and a stable family unit.

26. D Of the statements provided, the author would be least likely to agree with (D). While women played different roles during the Colonial era and Industrial Revolution, women during both time periods were held to certain social expectations (Colonial women were expected to be active participants in the labor force, while women during the Industrial Revolution were expected to be the moral authorities in their homes). The author of the passage would agree with choice (A), since the Industrial Revolution was a time of great advancement but also of harmful socioeconomic restrictions. The author would also concur with choice (B): the financial contributions of working-class women during the Industrial Revolution were key to economic survival, but these women were not encouraged to join the labor force as Colonial women were. Finally, the author would agree with choice (C); gender inequality during the Colonial era is addressed in Paragraphs 1 and 2, where the author makes it clear that neither the Colonial era nor the Industrial Revolution were periods of total equality between men and women.

Questions 27–34: AUGUSTAN AGE
PASSAGE V

Topic: Augustan Age Satires

Scope: Swift's satires

Purpose: To compare and contrast two of Swift's satires.

Passage Map
¶1: Augustan Age: major writers produced satires and argued about the genre of satire

¶2: Swift: mixed opinion on satire

¶3: Swift wrote satires using unreliable narrators ("ironic personae")

¶4: Difference in the narrators of two of Swift's works

¶5: Similarities in the narrators of two of Swift's works

Questions:
27. D Statement I occurs in three choices, so consider it first. In the second paragraph, Swift refers to satirizing individual foibles, and Swift's two works deal with larger, societal ills. So this statement is true. Statement II is supported by the example of The Rape of the Lock,

in paragraph 1. Statement III can be found in paragraph 1. Addison doesn't like satire because it can be a tool for scorn and ridicule.

28. D The correct answer to this Application question will fit into one of the categories of satire mentioned in the passage. Augustan satire can be "oblique" criticism according to Pope; it can expose personal "misdeeds and peccadilloes" according to both Addison in paragraph 1 and Swift in paragraph 2; and the two works of Swift that are discussed are indirectly and ironically "instructional" on the subjects of religion and politics. Choice (D) matches the second of these types. Choices (A) and (B) emphasize the idea of social reform, without the equally important qualification of making their points indirectly. They are earnest, direct approaches, not satirical. Choice (C) could be a setting for satire, but it's not necessarily satirical in nature.

29. A Johnson criticizes the subject matter of Pope's mock epic. In the next sentence the author claims that Pope used his subject well to "lambaste" conventions. Choice (A) correctly makes the point that Johnson presupposes too narrow a definition. Choice (B) is a Distortion. The author is not accepting that there is a "flaw" which Johnson should overlook. According to the author, the subject matter is "ideal". Choice (C) is Outside the scope of the passage. Nowhere does the author suggest that Johnson misunderstood Pope's intention. Choice (4) also distorts Johnson's meaning. "Everyday life" represents the lowest Johnson thinks a poetic subject can go—it isn't his standard.

30. C If, as the first sentence says, the "Augustan Age has been called 'The Great Age of Satire'" then before that age satire did not have a dominant position; choice (C) comes closest to this idea. Choices (A) and (B) are FUD; satire based on political and religious subjects are mentioned in connection with Swift's works in paragraph 3 and (B) relates to Pope's satire in the first paragraph; but nothing in the passage permits a comparison to the pre-Augustan period on these points. (D) can't be inferred; we have no basis for determining why the Augustans seemed to prefer the "indirect" approach of satire, and no reason to believe the pre-Augustans had "greater political freedom".

31. C After Pope's opinion is contrasted to Addison's, we are given this synopsis of his "plot" in *The Rape of the Lock*. This is followed by Johnson's criticism of its subject matter—the purpose for which the "plot" is included. (A) is a Distortion. The author states in the last sentence of the first paragraph that this story line was ideal for a specific satiric purpose—not that it was ideal for all Augustan satire. (B) is FUD. Pope's position is contrasted to Addison's by refrence to the *Epilogue to Satires*. (D) is a Distortion. Pope's story is "frivolous"—not his satire, which the author believes was "ideal" for its purpose.

32. B Addison thought satire did harm to the persons who were its subject, and concluded that the genre should not be used—he assumed the injury to the individual was more important than any value the work could have for the reader or society as a whole. Those who used satire claimed its value was that it was instructional (according to Swift in paragraph 2), and an effective means of conveying strong opinions (according to Pope in paragraph 1 and Swift in paragraph 3). Choice B comes closest to conveying these points. (A) is Opposite; Addison's view was that satire always hurt its target—so it was effective—but he doubted its benefit. (C) is Outside the Scope and contrary. We don't have any basis to infer Addison's opinion about whether readers understood satire; but if readers didn't get the point, the work would probably not harm its subject. (D) is FUD; this is Johnson's criticism of the subject of one of Pope's satires. And Addison believes that no satire should be written—he doesn't voice any opinion about its proper or improper subject matter.

33. D This issue is discussed in the second half of the third paragraph. Swift felt satire "conveyed strong opinion" well because the "juxtaposition of the literal and the veiled" meanings of the narrator resulted in " complicated, subtle operations" in the mind of the reader. (A) is Opposite; the one thing Swift questioned about satire was whether it could reach those with "hardened hearts" according to the last two sentences of paragraph 2. (B) is a Distortion. We aren't told that this persona was a "favorite" of Swift's and the reason he chose the genre. Rather, the persona is a part of the overall effect Swift sought when he did write satire. (C) is FUD. We are told this is true in the first sentence of the last paragraph; but these are part of the catalog of similarities and differences between the narrators in the two works discussed. Discussion of Swift's reason for choosing satire to begin with is found only in the third paragraph.

34. B In paragraph 3 we see already that both narrators are "unreliable" and that seeing through them is part of the process needed for the reader to see Swift's actual meaning. We are then shown in paragraph 4 the ways that the two narrators are different. The cited text is from paragraph 5, where the author discusses the ways the two are the same. The sentence continues by saying "but ... they attempt to see everything one way". The Keyword "but" tells you this is in contrast to the words "outwardly rational". (A) is FUD. It's true that only the Proposer is called mad (in the middle of paragraph 4); but "mad" doesn't mean "irrational" (and vice versa). (C) is Opposite; the gist of the statement is that they are not rational. The end of that paragraph reiterates that the Arguer is "less obsessive" than the Proposer, but this is not the same as saying he is "rational" in a varying degree or respect. (D) is contradicted by the passage. According to the previous sentence,

both do convey this concern. But this is irrelevant to the author's purpose in the cited text.

Questions 35–41: SMOKERS
PASSAGE VI

Topic: Increasing popularity of smoking among women in the US

Scope: Correlations between smoking behavior of women and their parents' and peers' smoking behavior

Purpose: To analyze the results of a study looking at how parental and peer smoking behavior may or may not correlate with smoking behavior of women.

Passage Map
¶1: Increase in smoking among young women

¶2: Study looked at women's parental and peer smoking behavior

¶3: Smoking behavior of mother (but not father) correlates with daughters who smokeing

¶4: Maintenance of smoking behavior correlates with close female friends (not male)

¶5: Termination of smoking behavior also correlates with smoking behavior of female peers

Questions:
35. D This question concerns the effect of a young woman's closest female friends on her smoking behavior. The third sentence of the fourth paragraph indicates that a young woman's closest female friends play a major role in the maintenance of her smoking habit—that is, the duration of her habit, so choice (D) is our answer. Choice (A) is wrong because it *contradicts* this point. Similarly, choice (C) contradicts information in the passage. The second sentence of the third paragraph says that the smoking habits of a young woman's *mother* influence her decision to start smoking. Although the passage tells us that a young woman's closest female friends heavily influence her smoking habits, we cannot infer that they necessarily encourage her to smoke heavily (B). The effect of a woman's friends on her smoking—whether they encourage her to smoke or not to smoke—depends on their own behavior. They are not necessarily smokers.

36. D This is a detail question about the consequences of male smoking behavior. Information contained in the final sentences of the third and fourth paragraphs and the last two sentences of the fifth paragraph indicates male smoking behavior does not account for female smoking habits (D). Choices (A) and (C) *contradict* this information. As far as we know from the passage, male smoking behavior *does not* significantly affect any aspect of female smoking behavior. Choice (B) is wrong because nowhere in the passage is there anything suggested about the effect of male smoking behavior on other males. The last sentence of the passage discusses the importance of same-sex relationships on smoking behavior, but only in relation to the behavior of women.

37. D This question asks for a *weakener* of Smith's argument. Smith's basic argument is twofold. First, a young woman's smoking habits are heavily influenced by the smoking habits of other females. Second, the smoking habits of males play no role in explaining young women's smoking behavior. If further study confirmed that mothers have influence over their daughters' early smoking careers (A), this would tend to *strengthen* Smith's argument. Choice (B) would also tend to *strengthen* Smith's argument, as it coincides with Smith's conclusions that female friends affect maintenance while mothers affect the frequency of women's smoking. Choice (C) would not really *weaken* Smith's argument. Smith's argument does not exclude the possibility that economic status influences smoking habits. This would not necessarily contradict the theory that her smoking habits were heavily influenced by the habits of other females. If it was discovered that the smoking habits of both parents significantly influence a daughter's initial decision to smoke (D), then this would indicate that the male father's smoking habits are indeed an important factor in influencing female smoking behavior. This would *contradict* Smith's argument and, thereby, would seriously *weaken* it.

38. C This passage is primarily concerned with describing the results of Smith's study, so it is a summary of recent research findings (C). Choice (A) is wrong because no earlier hypothesis about female smoking behavior is ever mentioned in the passage, let alone "refuted." There is no indication anywhere in the passage that this study is either "popular" or "controversial," so choices (B) and (D) are wrong.

39. D The second sentence of the first paragraph indicates that in the early 1970s the percentage of males smoking leveled off at 19 percent (D), logically eliminating any of the other possible answer choices. Choices (A), (B), and (C) *contradict* this information.

40. B This is a detail question about the effect of nicotine on female smoking habits. Nicotine is discussed in the second sentence of the third paragraph, which indicates that nicotine does not become a factor in determining smoking behavior until after the initiation of smoking. The next sentence then tells us that the smoking of mothers is significantly associated with the initiation of smoking in daughters. In other words, nicotine has less effect than maternal influence on the initiation of smoking (B). Choices (A) and (D) *contradict* information in the third paragraph. The first sentence of the

third paragraph tells us that nicotine does have effects on smoking behavior, but these effects come later, after the initiation stage of smoking. Because the passage does not discuss the effect of nicotine on male smoking behavior, we have no basis for concluding that nicotine affects female smokers more than male smokers (C).

Questions 41–46: MEDIATION
PASSAGE VII

Topic: Divorce

Scope: Reducing the adversarial nature of divorce

Purpose: To discuss the recent development of professional mediation as a means to reduce the litigiousness of divorce.

Passage Map
¶1: Tension between state goal of normalizing family relationship and state's divorce laws has led states to create "no-fault" divorce settlements

¶2: Adversarial nature of divorce

¶3: Professional mediation – settling outside of the court room

¶4: Criticism against professional mediation

Questions:
41. C The correct choice paraphrases the author's discussion of the client's "best interests" toward the end of paragraph 2. Choice (A) is FUD; these considerations are mentioned, but not as precluding an attorney from endorsing a settlement. (B) is a distortion; getting the best for your client doesn't mean giving nothing to the other side—what the other side gets is merely irrelevant to such an attorney. (D) is another FUD; the state's interests are only mentioned in the first paragraph, and are never the concern of the adversarial attorney.

42. B As with all Global question types, this one draws on your overall sense of the author's opinion as well as your general sense of the details. The first and second paragraphs give you background—the status quo. The third introduces the benefits of mediation as an alternative, and the fourth discusses the view of its critics, ending with a call for more information. (A) is a distortion on two counts: this author doesn't go so far as to "call for" anything (although it is acknowledged that there are problems in the current adversarial system) and doesn't "defend" the alternative method discussed. (C) is another distortion; the author never proposes a solution, and doesn't attempt to combine aspects of the adversarial and mediation systems. (D) is the wrong tone altogether. This is not a scholarly review of the facts. It opens with two paragraphs of "given" facts, but facts that clearly call for change. And one possible, but never endorsed, alternative is then discussed, with a call for further investigation.

43. A Some attitude questions, like this one, focus on a narrow aspect of the topic, rather than on the passage as a whole. Be careful to answer the specific question asked. While the author doesn't take sides on mediation, the current adversarial system is expressly criticized in the first two paragraphs for frustrating the goal of a return to family normalcy. (B) is a distortion. The author clearly believes the current system isn't working, but doesn't take a crusading tone, and clearly believes that we shouldn't change the current system for one that doesn't really improve matters. So another person arguing that the current system works would be disagreed with, but not violently. (C) is another distortion. It's true the author doesn't "dispute the importance of the court's role"—but only because the court's role is never this author's concern. (D) contradicts the correct answer, even though the author's tone in the passage as a whole can be called "neutral"—a fairly strong opinion is expressed about the failings of the adversarial system.

44. A The object of mediation is to negotiate divorces outside the court, according to its proponents; if most couples who try mediation have to litigate anyway, this goal is defeated and the argument for mediation is weakened. (B) has no effect on the argument; the proponents never claim that there is no conflict in mediation, and the author expressly states in the opening lines of the passage that conflict is inherent in divorce. (C) would strengthen the claims about mediation, rather than weaken them. Even if you accept lawyers as "experts" on the question of divorce (D), what they do when they divorce isn't relevant to the proponent's arguments, either.

45. D The final sentence contrasts the proponent's view that mediation "reduces the number of in-court contests" with the possibility that it "merely increases the cost"—so the latter statement is a reference to the critic's position, as the former is to the "proponent's" statements made in the third paragraph. The paragraph begins by stating that "critics" say mediation just involves lawyers in divorces they wouldn't have been involved in before—choice (D). (A) is a Outside the Scope; this author doesn't discuss whether the results are fair in either adversarial or mediated divorces. The passage focuses on whether we can reduce the social and emotional damage done by the adversarial process of divorce. (Actually, the author suggests that those who aren't seeking the state's version of "fair" distributions will not mediate, so its results will probably be mostly "fair" distributions, at least in that sense—but not because of any virtue in the system.) (B) distorts information provided by the "proponents" in the third paragraph. The comparative fees of the two types of attor-

ney aren't discussed—it's the fact that *any* attorney is involved at all that increases the cost. (C) is another distortion; what is contrasted is adversarial vs. mediated divorce, both of which involve "another party" in the form of a lawyer.

46. B "No-fault" divorce is mentioned in the first paragraph as introduced "in recognition of" the problems, from the state's point of view, that are inherent in divorce. And from the state's point of view, those problems are that the present process makes it less likely that the parties will cooperate after the divorce. So the reference is there to highlight the fact that even the states are concerned with the damage done by the present process. (A) and (C) are FUDs that take this information entirely out of context. The author wouldn't introduce in the first paragraph information that makes the rest of the passage unnecessary. "No-fault" divorce eliminates the need for a party to be proven "wrong", but doesn't affect the need for a distribution of assets and rights, and the author never suggest that other changes in the law will handle this. (D) distorts the author's views; this author doesn't offer any evidence for or against mediation, and no connection is drawn between "no-fault" and mediation..

Questions 47–53: HARBOR SEAL
PASSAGE VIII

Topic: Harbor Seals

Scope: Sensory system adaptations

Purpose: To examine the unique sensory system of harbor seals, and how these adaptations suit its dual habitats of land and water.

Passage Map
¶1: Harbor Seal has developed unique visual and hearing adaptations to cope with varying behavior of sound and light between land and water

¶2: Hearing adaptations under water

¶3: Visual adaptations on land

¶4: Scientists suspect harbor seals have echolocation ability

¶5: Whiskers may act as sensory receptors to help catch prey

¶6: Few mammals approach harbor seal's sensory system

Questions:
47. D This is a detail question about the seal's vibris-

sae. The last two sentences of the fifth paragraph tell us that vibrissae. sense underwater movement, allowing harbor seals to locate and capture prey, so choice (D) is our answer. Vibrissae are whiskers and they have *nothing* to do with improving underwater vision (A). Choice (B) is wrong because vibrissae.detect *underwater* vibrations, not aerial vibrations. The passage doesn't say anything about vibrissae. being used for camouflage purposes (C).

48. B This is a question comparing a harbor seal's vision to a human's vision. The seal's eye is discussed in relation to the human eye in the third paragraph of the passage. There we learn that in the water a harbor seal's vision is clear, while a human's vision is blurry. There we also learn that on land a human's vision is clear, while a harbor seal's vision is slightly astigmatic. In other words, a harbor seal's vision is *superior* to a human's vision in the water, but *inferior* to a human's vision on land (B). Choices (A), (C), and (D) all *contradict* this information.

49. D This is a detail question asking you to determine which one of four questions can be answered on the basis of information in the passage. The last two sentences of the third paragraph tell us *how* the harbor seal's eye compensates for the distortion of light rays on land (D). While the passage tells us that the harbor seal does most of its fishing at night, we are not told *why* the harbor seal fishes at night, so choice (A) is wrong. Information throughout the passage indicates that the harbor seal spends time on land, but nowhere are we told *how much* time the harbor seal spends on land, so (B) is wrong. (C) is wrong because the passage discusses only the harbor seal, not other seals or other members of the *Pinnepedia* order.

50. C This is a question that asks you to decide which statement would most strengthen the claim that harbor seals catch prey through echolocation. If the harbor seal's eye has become more efficient underwater over the course of time (A), it would be reasonable to think that the harbor seal's vision may provide the seal with its means to hunt and the claim that harbor seals hunt down prey by echolocation would be weakened. If harbor seals were known to do most of their hunting in a limited area and rely on their vibrissae to sense prey at close range (B), then vibrissae would provide the seal with its means to hunt and the claim that harbor seals hunt down prey by echolocation would be weakened again. If other members of the *Pinnepedia* order—animals genetically similar to the harbor seal—were known to possess echolocation systems, it would be reasonable to think harbor seals might also possess echolocation to help them hunt at night, so choice (C) is our answer. According to the passage, bats, porpoises, and dolphins all have echolocation systems which they use to catch prey. The fact that harbor seals are not closely related to these species (D), then, would either not affect the claim that harbor seals use echolocation to hunt down prey or, at most, would tend to *weaken* the claim.

51. B This question asks about the author's reason for comparing the sensory organs of harbor seals and humans. These comparisons are made in the second and third paragraphs. In these paragraphs the author illustrates the differences between a harbor seal's ear and eye and a human's ear and eye in order to explain to readers how the seal's sensory organs function (B). He refers to human sensory organs only in order to clarify his points by relating them to something very familiar to readers. Choice (A) is wrong because the author discusses the ways a particular mammal, the harbor seal, has adapted to its environment and only mentions humans by way of comparison. It is true that both humans and seals are mammals, but the author compares the differences between these two mammals. He does not point out similarities. (C) is wrong because nowhere in the passage does the author suggest that seals are related to humans. And the author neither suggests nor argues that seals are more adaptively successful than humans (D).

52. B In order to answer this question it is important to consider the passage as a whole. Of the choices listed, (B), a zoologist, is most likely to have authored the passage because zoologists study individual animal species in depth. A paleontologist (A) is not likely to have written this passage because paleontologists primarily study fossils and this passage is not about fossils. (C) is wrong because taxonomists classify various animals in relation to other species and according to their traits. While this passage briefly touches on the relationship between the harbor seal and other species, these comparisons certainly are not the main thrust of the passage. A geneticist (D) deals with issues at the level of the cell and chromosome. Since the passage doesn't discuss cells or chromosomes, a geneticist is not likely to have written this passage.

53. D This is a detail question about the harbor seal's habitat. According to the first sentence of the first paragraph, the harbor seal lives along the northern Atlantic and Pacific coasts, so choice (D) is our answer. Choice (A) is wrong because the passage says nothing about harbor seals living in arctic regions. Since the passage mentions only two regions where the harbor seal lives and doesn't say whether these regions have abundant fish populations, (B) is wrong. (C) is wrong because the passage tells us that harbor seals live only along coastal regions, but doesn't say anything about island regions.

Questions 54–60: ROMAN ITALY
PASSAGE IX

Topic: Ancient Roman History

Scope: Scholarly Research of Ancient Roman History

Purpose: To discuss the research topics ancient and modern scholars have studied, and critique the scholars' general lack of interest in the critical role of local Roman communities in maintaining the empire.

Passage Map

¶1: Roman Italy was a collection of distinct small communities with similar institutions

¶2: Highly centralized government impossible; local community key to success

¶3: Neglect of role of local communities in Roman historical research

¶4: Modern scholars largely neglected local communities; except for Rostovtzeff

¶5: Agricultural history has received attention

¶6: Commercial economy has begun to receive more attention

Questions:

54. B The author's main purpose in this passage is to point out a deficiency in modern scholarship. The sort of research he would want to see done would remedy this deficiency. The correct choice emphasizes the author's view that a new sort of scholarship is needed. At the end of paragraphs four and six the author expresses his belief that nonliterary evidence should be used in a more sophisticated manner. (A) is wrong because the author describes the work of Marxist historians as useful only in a limited number of specific instances (on matters regarding slavery, slave revolts, great estates) and as having a distorting effect to boot. (C) is wrong because it involves the sort of elitist research that he attributes to the "predilections of increasingly professional scholars." (D) is wrong because the author emphasizes the impossibility of centralized bureaucracy in the second paragraph.

55. A The amount of modern scholarship on Roman agriculture refers to the great amount of scholarship on this particular topic. (A) is correct. Even though the author states the answer explicitly, you may be lead astray. The author, having spent four paragraphs on the lack of scholarly interest in rural communities, devotes a paragraph to the great amount of scholarly interest in agriculture. A subtle difference, a subtle shift that must nevertheless be taken into account! (B) contradicts everything the author says on the matter. (C) is wrong even though taken by itself it is true; it just doesn't jibe with the stem. Though scholars have indeed had little interest in the rural communities, there nevertheless exists a great amount of scholarship on agriculture. (D) is wrong for the same reason as (C): Though scholars have indeed tended to have elitist interests, there never-

theless exists a great amount of scholarship on agriculture.

56. D In paragraph 3, "the neglect [that] began with the ancient Romans themselves" refers to the first sentence of the paragraph: "In spite of the ubiquity and importance of these local communities, they have been rather *neglected in recent Roman historical research.*" The correct choice identifies the group with whom the neglect lies. (A) is wrong because it has nothing to do with recent historical research. (B) is wrong because the word incompetence is, as the student should expect, too negative. A deficiency in the scholarship does not indicate incompetence on the part of the scholars. (C) is wrong because, even though it tells why this neglect began with the ancient Roman writers, it does not refer to the "recent Roman historical research" of modern scholars.

57. B The author's main purpose is to discuss remedying a deficiency in modern scholarship. (B) is correct because "the records of an ancient town council" would seem to be most useful to a scholar who wants to investigate local communities. (A) is wrong because the author notes that there is no lack of scholarship on agricultural matters in the beginning of paragraph five. (C) is wrong because the author specifically refers to an increase in scholarship on Roman commerce—"seaborne trade." (D) is wrong because the author specifically refers to the military interests of both ancient writers and modern scholars in paragraphs three and four.

58. C You do not need to know technical terminology but rather you should be able to figure it out according to its context. To do so here you must note how the author juxtaposes a group consisting of "consul, general, and emperor" with a group consisting of "*decuriones* and small-town shopkeepers." Whatever *decuriones* are, they must be of the same relative social rank as shopkeepers. (C) is correct because the key word in the answer is *local,* for it accords with the author's interest in local communities. (A) is wrong because important military officers would belong in the first group along with generals. (B) is wrong because slaves and impoverished peasants do not fit into this context; they are too humble to be paired with shopkeepers. Moreover, the author notes that scholars have shown great interest in Roman slavery. (D) is wrong for the same reason as (A): Powerful noblemen belong in the group with generals and emperors.

59. D You will most likely have to glance back to check which of these observations do and do not receive substantiation. (D) is correct. The very last sentence in the passage states that "Less attention has been paid to the development of regional and local economies . . . ." Although the author has presented a great deal of information as to why scholars have neglected local matters in general, the student must here note that this observation occurs in a paragraph about the *increase* in scholarly attention to commercial matters. Thus—given a relatively great amount of research into commercial matters—it is something of a surprise that local economies have been neglected, and we read no substantiation for why this is the case. (A) is wrong because the author offers an explanation (lines 8–10). (B) is wrong because the author offers an example (lines 22–30). (C) is wrong because the author offers an explanation (lines 60–62).

60. B   You must recognize first, that Rostovtzeff was an "important exception," that he was interested in local communities, and, second, that Rostovtzeff's research involved using nonliterary evidence to go beyond what was in the written record, that he used an innovative methodology. (B) implies how most modern historians are different from Rostovtzeff (they are "hesitant" to employ the sort of methodology he used). (A) is wrong because it compares apples with oranges: Rostovtzeff is a modern historian. (C) is wrong because the author certainly would not consider Rostovtzeff's studies "arcane"; he thinks that Rostovtzeff was ahead of his time. (D) is wrong because the author makes no connection between Rostovtzeff and Weber nor between Rostovtzeff and Marxist historians; Weber and the Marxists are mentioned in the context of agricultural history.

Materials used in this test section were adapted from the following source(s):

Stephen L. Dyson, *Community and Society in Roman Italy.* ©1992 by the Johns Hopkins University Press.

Verbal Reasoning Test Two

Time—85 minutes
Question 1–60

DIRECTIONS: Each of the passages in this test is followed by a set of questions based on the passage's content. After reading each passage, decide on the one best response to each question and mark it on your answer sheet. If you are unsure of an answer, eliminate the choices you know are wrong and choose from the remaining choices. You may refer to the passages while answering the questions.

Passage I (Questions 1–6)

In 1855, excavations at the site of the ancient city of Larsa, in present-day Iraq, unearthed a large number of tablets traceable to Sumero-Babylonian times, approximately 1900–1500 B.C. The materials appeared to be
[5] receipts, accounts, and tables. Interpretation revealed that the number system of this ancient civilization was sexagesimal (counting was by 10s and 60s). The symbols used were quasi-positional; the symbol for "1" could also signify the powers of 60 and even 10 times
[10] the powers of 60, depending upon the specific nature of the transaction.

It is now known that not only the number system but also the system of linear measure used by the Sumero-Babylonian society was based on 60. A clay tablet
[15] recovered at Larsa some time after the initial findings, believed to be a standard text copied as part of the school curriculum, shows a systematic and progressive sequence of linear measure utilizing units that represented specific quantities of barley, the society's food
[20] staple and currency. Six she (grains) were equal to 1 shu-si (finger), 30 shu-si equaled 1 kush (cubit), 12 kush equaled 1 nindan, 60 nindan equaled 1 USH, and 30 USH added up to 1 beru. The factors used to convert from one unit to another—6, 30, 12, 60, and 30—are
[25] multiples of six, and each is a factor of 60, the base in the sexagesimal number system.

Later excavations revealed that the Sumero-Babylonian mathematical system was a successor of sexagesimal systems that had appeared both in earlier eras and in
[30] other geographical locations. Tablet fragments discovered in the 1920s at Jemdet Nasr in Iraq disclosed that the numerical and linear systems first noted in 1855 probably had been in use as early as 2900–2800 B.C. The pictographic inscriptions appeared to be a precursor of a
[35] Sumerian form of writing known as cuneiform, while the numerical symbols—circles, cuplike shapes, and slashes—were similar to those on the tablets found at Larsa. In both, the notations reflected computation in multiples of 10 and 60 while the basic unit of measure

[40] was the she or grain. The Jemdet Nasr findings are thus considered proto-Sumerian.

Research at Susa, the ancient Elamite city located in present-day Iran, has revealed that even this separate culture probably used the mathematical system noted at
[45] the various Sumerian sites. Initial excavations at Susa uncovered tablets inscribed with both the cuneiform writings and numerals of Sumero-Babylonia. Later excavations there revealed evidence of a society in existence at least a millennium before that of the Elamites.
[50] This proto-Elamite culture, which was roughly contemporary with that of the proto-Sumerians, used numbers and linear measures virtually identical to theirs, despite a completely different style of writing.

---

1. This passage was most likely taken from:

    A. a newspaper feature about ancient market transactions.

    B. a journal article regarding ancient numerical systems.

    C. a lecture on archeological discoveries in the Near East.

    D. an encyclopedia entry on Sumero-Babylonian forms of writing.

2. Based on the information in the passage, which of the following archeological findings is LEAST likely?

    A. A tablet or pictographic writing dating from 2700 B.C. using the units she and shu-si

    B. A tablet containing sexagesimal numbers and cuneiform writing, dating from 3200 B.C.

    C. A tablet inscribed with cups and slashes describing a transaction involving measurement in terms of fingers and cubits

    D. A tablet dating from 1300 B.C. showing a table of measurements with conversion factors of 6, 30, 12, 60, and 30

GO TO THE NEXT PAGE.

3. Which of the following characteristics could be common to both a Sumerian and a proto-Sumerian tablet?

   A. Slashes and circles
   B. Cuneiform inscriptions
   C. Positional notation using the number 0
   D. A system of measure based on the finger as the smallest unit

4. The proto-Elamite society existed approximately:

   A. 2,500–3,000 years ago.
   B. 3,500–4,000 years ago.
   C. 4,500–5,000 years ago.
   D. 5,500–6,000 years ago.

5. Which of the following most probably is the sequence in which the societies mentioned in the passage flourished?

   A. Proto-Elamite, Elamite, Proto-Sumerian, Sumero-Babylonian
   B. Proto-Elamite, Elamite, Sumero-Babylonian, Proto-Sumerian
   C. Elamite, Proto-Sumerian, Sumero-Babylonian, Proto-Elamite
   D. Proto-Sumerian, Proto-Elamite, Elamite, Sumero-Babylonian

6. The author mentions excavations at Susa in order to:

   A. prove that the proto-Sumerian culture was dominant in the ancient Middle East.
   B. explain the ways in which an aspect of proto-Sumerian culture spread to other areas of the ancient Middle East.
   C. support the notion that sexagesimal mathematical systems were used by several ancient Middle Eastern societies.
   D. indicate that the mathematical system used in Sumero-Babylonian times was heavily influenced by proto-Elamite culture.

GO TO THE NEXT PAGE.

Passage II (Questions 7–14)

"Big bang"—the spontaneous explosion that created the universe some 12 billion years ago—initiated processes that led to an uneven distribution of luminous matter throughout the universe. The study of the genesis and
5 evolution of the universe is a relatively young discipline. Before the 20th century, astronomers knew little about space beyond our own galaxy, the Milky Way, and could only speculate about the existence of "external" galaxies. In the 20th century, the development of sophisticat-
10 ed observation technology, including the radio telescope, particle accelerators, and satellites, made it possible for astronomers to study the components and properties of the universe and to formulate theories about its development.

15 One popular theory of the universe's development, introduced in 1972 by Soviet astronomers Zel'dovich and Sunyaev, proposes that gases present in the early universe became quite dense and unevenly distributed in response to gravitational forces. Over time, dense pock-
20 ets of gas formed vast sheets of luminous material, which astronomers refer to as "pancakes." Because these gaseous pancakes were located in regions of the universe where multiple clusters of galaxies now exist, Zel'dovich and Sunyaev reasoned that early in the uni-
25 verse's development the pancakes must have fragmented into galactic clusters and individual galaxies; in other regions of the universe, limited quantities of gas prevented the development of luminous matter, leaving much of space "empty".

30 Zel'dovich and Sunyaev's attempt to explain the development of the universe had its origin in their observations of the distribution of galaxies. Galaxies are grouped in structures called "clusters" that vary in size; small clusters may contain only a few galaxies while the
35 largest clusters may contain many thousands of them. Clusters, in turn, form structures known as "superclusters" that are so large that any individual member galaxy, in motion for billions of years, will have traversed only a fraction of its supercluster's diameter.
40 Astronomers have identified four superclusters thus far, but disagree about their precise boundaries.

Whatever the exact boundaries of superclusters, scientists believe that even these huge structures occupy only a small part of the total area of the universe. Most of
45 space consists of empty regions known as "voids" devoid of luminous matter. Astronomers are still unsure of the exact composition of voids, but speculate that they are made up of non-luminous "dark matter" that cannot be seen and appears, in observation from Earth,
50 as nothing more than vast areas of nothingness.

However, while the Zel'dovich-Sunyaev theory describes and explains the uneven distribution of luminous matter, it only partially accounts for the conditions of the universe today. Zel'dovich and Sunyaev failed to
55 address the continued expansion of the universe. To understand this aspect of the universe's development, astronomers had to refer back to the work of Edwin Hubble, a prominent astronomer of the 1920s and 1930s. Using a technique known as "red shift analysis",
60 Hubble developed the concept of diverging galaxies. In astronomical observation, the more distant a celestial body from the Milky Way, the more its light shifts to the red end of the spectrum, and Hubble observed that the light emitted from galaxies moved further to the red end
65 of the spectrum over time. He concluded that other galaxies must be moving away from our own. The divergence of galaxies was later codified as Hubble's Law, from which astronomers have been able to infer that, in a continuing response to the huge initial release
70 of energy in the "big bang" explosion, celestial bodies— including galactic clusters, superclusters, voids, and the universe itself—are expanding.

---

7. Based in the information in the passage, we can infer that the galaxies are moving:

   A. in a random fashion.
   B. toward the Milky Way.
   C. out of their original clusters.
   D. because of a massive energy discharge.

8. According to the passage, which of the following is true of the composition and properties of the universe?

   A. There are no more than four superclusters in our universe.
   B. Gravitational forces have no effect on concentrations of gas.
   C. Galaxies will eventually assume fixed positions in the universe.
   D. The distribution of galaxies today reflects the effects of gravity on gaseous formations.

GO TO THE NEXT PAGE.

9. We would be justified in concluding that the author considers the Zel'dovich-Sunyaev theory to be:

   A. illuminating, but incomplete.
   B. enlightening and comprehensive.
   C. uninformed, but original.
   D. insightful, but lacking evidence.

10. While observing the movement of galaxies, an astronomer on Earth notices that light emitted from galaxy A is further to the red end of the spectrum than light coming from galaxy B. Based on this astronomer's observations, it can be inferred from the passage that:

    A. galaxy B is further from the Milky Way than galaxy A.
    B. galaxy B is moving away from the Milky Way faster than galaxy A.
    C. galaxy B is diverging at a faster rate than galaxy A.
    D. galaxy B is closer to the Milky Way than galaxy A.

11. According to the passage, astronomers today disagree about the:

    A. utility of "red shift analysis."
    B. existence of "external galaxies."
    C. effects of gravity on "pancakes."
    D. dimensions of superclusters.

12. The author apparently introduces "Hubble's Law" principally in order to:

    A. contradict the theory of diverging galaxies.
    B. explain the technique of "red shift analysis."
    C. prove the existence of "dark matter."
    D. supplement the Zel'dovich-Sunyaev theory.

13. According to the passage, prior to the 20th century astronomers:

    A. used radio telescopes to observe other galaxies.
    B. were only able to study the Milky Way.
    C. knew of the existence of clusters and super-clusters.
    D. formulated the idea of the "big bang."

14. It can be inferred from the passage that at some time in the future:

    I. the huge amount of energy released by the "big bang" explosion will be exhausted.
    II. the Milky Way will be larger than its present size.
    III. the configuration of the universe will remain constant.

    A. I only
    B. II only
    C. I and II only
    D. I, II, and III only

GO TO THE NEXT PAGE.

Passage III (Questions 15–20)

Located on the western borderlands of the Russian Empire and later the Soviet Union, the regions that would one day become Belarus and Moldova had long been part of a buffer zone used to protect Russia from
5   Western influences and military forces. The imperial and Soviet governments attempted to fully integrate the two regions' economies into their own and to Russify their people in order to bind them seamlessly into the their respective empires. For a long time, these efforts
10   seemed to work, but in 1991 Belarus and Moldova declared their independence from the Soviet Union.

In both Belarus and Moldova, many conservatives wish to return to the days of the Soviet Union for a variety of reasons, some economic, some nostalgic, and some fear-
15   ful. Both Belarus and Moldova stated their intention of having democratic political systems, but making the change from a communist government to a real democracy proved difficult, not the least because of officials who viewed democracy as too chaotic and unstable,
20   unlike the predictability that had characterized their previous political lives.

The two countries are a study in contrasts. Belarus is mostly ethnic Belarusian (and overwhelmingly Slavic) in population. The tsars and commissars who sought to
25   meld Belorussia with Russia succeeded to a remarkable extent: independent Belarus still identifies closely with Russia, and Belarusian nationalists are in the minority. But Moldova has a majority population of ethnic Romanians, who are not Slavs. Regardless of Russian
30   and Soviet efforts to Slavicize them, most ethnic Romanians were able to maintain their identity and looked to Romania as the source of their culture. When the Soviet Union began to crumble, Moldova sought to distance itself from Russia, despite the wishes of the
35   Transnistrians, who in 1990 proclaimed the "Dnestr Moldavian Republic," with a pro-Soviet extralegal government, on the east bank of the Nistru River. The Transnistrians want no part of a possible reunification with Romania, where they would be a small minority
40   instead of a powerful political force.

Despite the differences between the two countries, the focal point for those who wish to maintain each country's independence is the same—the national language, the same rallying point as in the revolutions of 1848.
45   Those revolts all failed in their immediate goals, but they eventually led to greater representation of ethnic groups in legislatures and to greater cultural autonomy, including the use of languages that, until then, had been dismissed by the authorities as peasant vernaculars.
50   However, while nationalists in the last century sought to codify (and sometimes even form) a literary language, the task of the nationalists in 1991 was to revive that language and divest it of its Russian and Soviet accretions.

To those who have never undergone forced cultural
55   assimilation, the issue may seem trivial. To those who have had their use of language restricted, however, the matter goes beyond mere defiance. Language is the medium of the culture on which their daily lives and identities are based. To define what language can be
60   spoken is to define the identity not only of the individual but also of the country. Moldovans kept Russian as a language of interethnic communication but subsequently entered a debate as to what their own language was to be called: was it Moldovan or Romanian? President
65   Lukashyenka explained that the term "Moldovan" was used in the constitution for political reasons—to assuage fears of imminent reunification with Romania. Again, politics, language, and emotions were thoroughly entangled. Belarusians, the majority of whom prefer to use
70   Russian in their daily lives, have dealt with the language issue differently. They returned Russian to its status of official language, alongside Belarusian.

---

15. Based on the passage, we can reasonably expect the author to argue that the reason the Transnistrians want to realign with Russia, and not to reunite with Romania, is because:

   I.   they fear the political instability and unpredictability of democratic political systems.
   II. they consider the Nistru River the correct and natural Moldavan boundary
   III. they would be a small and powerless minority if Moldova unifies with Romania.

   A. I
   B. II and III only
   C. I, II and III
   D. III only

GO TO THE NEXT PAGE.

16. Which of the following, if true, would most *weaken* the author's claims about the goals of the Transnistrians?

    A. The Russian government also wishes to establish closer relations with Moldova.

    B. Transnistrian seek to protect economic interests that include illegal sales of arms and drugs.

    C. The majority of Moldovans agree that the Transnistrians should secede from Moldova.

    D. There were no Transnistrians in Moldova during the revolutions of 1848.

17. The author probably mentions the revolutions of 1848 (line 44) in order to:

    A. establish that language has been a point of contention in Soviet states for over a century.

    B. argue that, as those revolutions failed, so too the present nationalist cause is doomed.

    C. point out that language was an artificial issue, since the national language had to be invented.

    D. explain why the Transnistrians have historically felt themselves to be outsiders in Moldova.

18. Based on the passage, the author believes that the major cause of controversy in Moldova today is the issue of:

    A. use of Russian as an official language.

    B. possible reunification with Romania.

    C. the legal status of the Slavic minority.

    D. use of Romanian as an official language.

19. If the president of Belarus were to propose expanding its economic and political union with Russia, we can assume that the majority of the Belarusian population would:

    A. accept any cooperative relations that didn't threaten Belarus independence.

    B. threaten to revolt if Russian influence over Belarus were increased.

    C. support him only if equal unity could be simultaneously established with Europe.

    D. we can't predict any response based on the information in the passage.

20. If we were to learn that much of the leadership in Belarus has traditionally considered their country evenly divided between its pro-Western and pro-Russian provinces, this would be LEAST consistent with:

    A. the author's claim that Belarus was a buffer zone protecting Russia from the West.

    B. the author's assertions about the success of Russification in Belarus.

    C. the explanation for why the Transnistrians wish to unite with Russia rather than with Romania.

    D. the conservatives' wish to return to the days of the Soviet Union.

GO TO THE NEXT PAGE.

Passage IV (Questions 21–26)

The following passage is an abstract of a research report presented at a seminar on the social psychology of children.

We report on the results of a study of the relation between the social behavior of preschool children in the nursery school and home environments. Seventeen male and an equal number of female subjects, aged 35 to 64 months, were selected randomly from three nursery schools, the only prerequisite being a minimum of one sibling in each subject's family.

To assess preschooler behavior, nineteen categories were defined; twelve described fairly specific activities, such as "initiate aggression," "receive aggression," and "fantasy talk," while the remainder constituted the more general classes of behavior, including "solitary play," "parallel play," and "cooperative play," which, according to Parton's social play hierarchy, represent a gradient of increasing maturity levels and correlate with increasing age of the preschooler. Researchers recorded one hour of each child's activity at home in the presence of siblings but no peers, and another hour of each child's activity at nursery school during free play periods. Since a given child might behave atypically during any given session, observations of each subject in each setting were collected in twenty three-minute periods over several sessions.

The collected data suggested different patterns of interactions at nursery school and at home. Among the characteristics used to describe the subjects, the two sibling-independent variables—age and sex of subject—revealed the greatest number of correlations with behavior at school. On the other hand, sibling-related variables such as birth order and sex of siblings were more closely related to the nature of sibling interactions at home. For instance, "solitary play" at school tended to vary inversely with the age of the preschooler. In the home the same behavior most significantly correlated—again inversely—with "having a sister."

Several categories of behavior in nursery school correlated closely with sibling-related variables, indicating that in these instances the home play environment may influence peer interactions outside the home. For instance, "receive aggression" at school correlated most directly with the presence of an opposite-sex sibling at home. "Onlooker behavior" at school correlated direct-ly with "having a sister" and with "having a same-sex sibling." Finally, adult-child interactions at school cor-related significantly with "having a same-sex sibling."

Another analytical approach involved registering correlations between behavior at school and at home. Only one behavioral category—"demonstrate aggression"—revealed consistency across the two settings. Since it is not known whether aggression constitutes learned or innate behavior, the influence of setting in this case is far from clear. To explain the surprising lack of other correlations, it has been hypothesized that individual differences among the various home environments were too great compared to the number of subjects in the study. Another possibility is that, although children's interaction levels increase sharply during the preschool years, it may be too early in the child's socialization process for any correlates to appear. A third possibility—that behavior in the home setting is little influenced by behavior at school, and vice-versa—seems unlikely in light of the correlations between behavior and sibling-related variables discussed earlier.

---

21. The total observation time in the study described in the passage was:

    A. sixty-eight hours.
    B. thirty-four hours.
    C. twenty-three minutes per subject per setting.
    D. spread over the course of several months.

22. Three variables descriptive of preschoolers are listed below. According to the passage, which of them MOST frequently correlate with behavior in the nursery school setting?

    I. Age of subject
    II. Having a same-sex sibling
    III. Sex of subject

    A. I and II only
    B. I and III only
    C. II and III only
    D. I, II, and III

GO TO THE NEXT PAGE.

23. With regard to solitary play in the school, the findings summarized by the passage:

    A. show that this variable constitutes a specific activity.
    B. reveal a close correlation with "having a sister."
    C. tend to confirm Parton's social play hierarchy.
    D. show that this kind of play is rarely demonstrated by preschool children.

24. By inference from the passage, one way to improve this study might be to:

    A. use a larger number of subjects from a larger number of homes.
    B. increase the observation time for each subject.
    C. observe each child in each setting for a single one-hour block of time.
    D. use a smaller number of subjects with more similar home environments.

25. Which child is likely to spend the most time in onlooker behavior at school?

    A. A boy with an older brother
    B. A boy with an older sister
    C. A girl with an older sister
    D. A child who engages in solitary play at home

26. Which of the following hypothetical cases would provide evidence for the influence of the school environment on a toddler's home behavior?

    A. "Receives aggression" at home correlates most closely with a sibling-unrelated variable.
    B. "Receives aggression" at home correlates most closely with birth order.
    C. "Fantasy talk" reveals consistency across the two settings.
    D. "Initiates aggression" at home correlates most closely with "age order in the classroom."

GO TO THE NEXT PAGE.

Passage V (Questions 27–33)

For more than a century, there has been a dispute among scholars over the authorship of the heroic poem *Beowulf*. Was *Beowulf* the work of one author or of several? Can the author or authors be identified as pagan or Christian? Of the theories that have attempted to come to grips with these questions, three have been especially prominent.

The earliest of the three, the "tribal-lay" theory, stresses that *Beowulf* is an amalgam of older Germanic and Nordic tribal myths. Proponents of this theory argue that the poem in its final form is the work of several authors whose earlier works were joined together by a number of later editors. This conclusion is based on the poem's numerous digressions from the main theme. These digressions, including Sigemund's battle with the dragon, are only tenuously linked to the hero Beowulf's struggles with monsters and men. Interestingly, while many critics see the poem as a Christian allegory with Beowulf as the champion of goodness battling the forces of evil, "tribal-lay" theorists seem to ignore the poem's obvious Christian overtones and consider its ethical tone to be a reflection of lay Germanic and Nordic codes of loyalty to tribe and vengeance to enemies.

Like the "tribal-lay" theory, the "growth by accretion" theory supports the notion of multiple authorship. But according to the "accretion" view, *Beowulf* began as a short, simple work of mythology by a single author and was gradually transformed into a long, intricate poem as later authors added to it over a period of several centuries. As evidence in support of this view, scholars point to the mixture of pagan rituals and themes with Christian values. This strange combination of conflicting motifs, some believe, could only have been the result of multiple authorship.

A third theory originates from a paper by J.R.R. Tolkien, entitled "*Beowulf:* The Monsters and the Critics." In his paper, Tolkien argued that *Beowulf* was the work of a single Christian author, probably a member of a royal court, who used pagan material as the basis of his poem. Scholars who believe this "Christian authorship" theory argue that it is not at all surprising that a Christian would have written such a poem. At the time of *Beowulf*'s writing, some time between the years 650 and 850, the bulk of the population of England—including much of the literate strata—was only nominally Christian and still clung to pagan beliefs and practices. Although Christianity had gained a foothold in England, it had yet to displace pagan culture. "Christian authorship" theorists reason that a nominal Christian would have been perfectly comfortable incorporating both pagan and Christian elements into the same work. These scholars further argue that since the Anglo-Saxons were engaged in constant warfare with the Vikings, Scots, and Picts at the time of *Beowulf*'s writing, its author may have deliberately emphasized certain pagan motifs, particularly the cult of the warrior, for the political purpose of bolstering morale among both the aristocracy and the masses at a time when they were under constant military pressure.

Although it is not possible to conclusively prove that one theory is correct and the other two wrong, most scholars favor the Tolkien view. The "tribal-lay" and the "growth by accretion" theories are generally dismissed because of the epic's essential unity despite disparate references and seemingly conflicting motifs. Most scholars find historical analyses of the context of the author's writing provide the best resolutions to the poem's apparent contradictions.

---

27. The author mentions Sigemund's battle with the dragon (lines 15–16) in order to:

    A. show that the Christian theme of good versus evil is central to *Beowulf.*
    B. provide support for the notion that *Beowulf* is an incorporation of more ancient tribal myths.
    C. prove that *Beowulf* is the work of a single pagan author.
    D. provide an allegorical representation of the Anglo-Saxon struggle with Vikings, Scots, and Picts.

28. According to the "Christian authorship" theory, the emphasis on the pagan cult of the warrior in *Beowulf* is a reflection of:

    A. major themes in Germanic and Norse culture.
    B. the author's position as a military official in a royal court.
    C. political upheavals in England at the time of the epic's writing.
    D. an eighth-century decline in Christian faith among Anglo-Saxons.

GO TO THE NEXT PAGE.

29. Which of the following statements are compatible with the ideas of the "growth by accretion" theorists?

   I. *Beowulf* represents the result of contributions made by multiple authors.
   II. Conflicting motifs in *Beowulf* indicate that the poem is not the work of a single author.
   III. The essential unity of *Beowulf* defies the constant turmoil and warfare of the period in which its author wrote.

   A. I and II only
   B. I and III only
   C. II and III only
   D. I, II, and III

30. According to the passage, a major distinction between the "tribal-lay" and "growth by accretion" theorists is:

   A. the degree of emphasis each group places on the epic's historical context.
   B. the different ways in which the theorists interpret the poem's allegorical references.
   C. their varied conceptions of the multiple authorship of *Beowulf*.
   D. the way in which each group accounts for *Beowulf*'s Christian elements.

31. Which of the following would most seriously weaken the "Christian authorship" theory?

   A. During an excavation of an 11th century Norwegian church, archeologists find a partially translated manuscript of *Beowulf*.
   B. Historians now believe that Anglo-Saxon conflicts with the Vikings, Scots, and Picts were much more intense and long lasting than previously thought.
   C. Recently discovered documents indicate that *Beowulf* is an English translation of a Germanic myth of earlier origin.
   D. Some linguists have concluded that *Beowulf* was written by a literate peasant because the poem contains phrases and terms used by peasants but not found in the language of aristocrats.

32. The passage suggests that most scholars favor the "Christian authorship" theory because:

   A. it is able to locate many of the obscure references made in *Beowulf* in Germanic and Norse mythology.
   B. other theories fail to appreciate the significance of Christian elements in *Beowulf*.
   C. it is able to resolve inconsistencies in *Beowulf* by referring to the context in which it was written.
   D. no other theory attempts to explain the epic's disparate references and varied motifs.

33. The author mentions a paper written by J.R.R. Tolkien (lines 35–39) in order to:

   A. lend authoritative support to multiple authorship theories.
   B. discredit the notion that *Beowulf* was written by a Christian.
   C. disprove previous theories regarding *Beowulf*'s authorship.
   D. introduce a contextual analysis of the writing of *Beowulf*.

GO TO THE NEXT PAGE.

Passage VI (Questions 34–39)

The psychological effects of overcrowding have been cited as a cause of urban violence, neurosis, drug addiction, and even war. In 1968, for example, the Kerner Commission identified overcrowded conditions as a major factor in widespread rioting that occurred in many U.S. cities the year before. Such simplistic analyses have frequently been justified by reference to widely publicized animal experiments on overcrowding done in the 1960s.

A classic experiment by Calhoun (1962) demonstrated the existence of a "behavioral sink" among overcrowded rats. In this experiment, caged rats were forced to feed simultaneously in a small central space, thus creating an area of extreme population density. The rats became abnormally aggressive and social organization among them seemed to dissolve; the animals fought violently, mated indiscriminately, and destroyed nests and unprotected young. In other animal studies, enlarged adrenal glands and shrunken reproductive organs were observed in rats, while endocrine disorders and reproductive dysfunctions were detected in a natural population of deer that had reached a high population density. Further, numerous studies of enclosed rats and mice showed a consistent population growth pattern: given an abundant supply of food and water, the populations initially grew rapidly, only to reach a peak from which the growth curve declined, either toward extinction or toward stabilization at a point below the potential capacity of the cage.

While these studies were highly suggestive, more recent research has indicated that factors other than population density may be responsible for the changes in population growth and endocrine functions observed among caged animals. Researchers found that when identical groups of deer mice were placed in cages of equal area and provided with seemingly ideal environments, rates of pregnancy declined and the percentage of young that died before maturity increased until, eventually, population growth ceased. This occurred, however, at widely differing times after the beginning of the experiment, and with a large variation in population size. Hence, while all populations eventually ceased growing, the population density at which this occurred varied. Further, when the area of the cages was doubled there was no significant effect on population growth. The critical factor seemed to be simply that the animals were caged. Other studies indicated that when endocrine changes occurred, they were primarily a function of the number of animals in the enclosed group rather than of density. When group size and density were varied independently, the weight of the adrenal glands was affected by the number of animals in the group, but not by the density of the animal population. Clearly, animal studies justify no simple correlation between overcrowding and pathological behavior.

Analyses of demographic data from urban populations have also shown no consistent relationship between density and psychopathology among humans. While some studies have shown a coexistence of high rates of social pathology with crowded conditions, the causality is obscure, and the effects of density are not readily separated from ethnic and socioeconomic variables.

Several recent theories have distinguished between density, a physical situation, and crowding, an individual psychological perception that too many people are too close. In Haller's social learning theory, for instance, density is equated with "available space," while the amount of space an individual requires to feel free of crowding is termed "acceptable space." Whereas available space can be defined as the number of square feet per person, acceptable space involves numerous variables including sex and individual personality characteristics. Haller proposes that overcrowding is a direct function of the ratio of available space to acceptable space; if the available space is less than acceptable space (the ratio is less than one), by definition the situation is crowded.

---

34. In Haller's theory of social learning, which of the following would necessarily increase crowding?

   A. Increasing acceptable space while keeping available space constant
   B. Increasing available space while keeping acceptable space constant
   C. Decreasing acceptable space while keeping available space constant
   D. Decreasing both available and acceptable space proportionately

GO TO THE NEXT PAGE.

35. According to the passage, animal studies have demonstrated all of the following EXCEPT:

A. changes in adrenal gland size can be found among crowded animals.

B. aggression among crowded rats results from factors other than population density.

C. populations of enclosed rats will not continue to reproduce indefinitely.

D. under high-density conditions, the social organization of rats may disintegrate.

36. It may be inferred that the author thinks the urban riots in 1967:

A. were unrelated to conditions of urban crowding.

B. resulted from psychological effects of crowding.

C. were incorrectly related to Calhoun's classic experiment.

D. show the problems of extrapolating results of animal experiments to the human condition.

37. The passage implies that Haller's social learning theory is valuable in that it:

A. relates incidents of urban rioting to population densities.

B. distinguishes between physical and psychological aspects of overcrowding.

C. proposes that overcrowding has little to do with socioeconomic variables.

D. explains the relationship between social pathology and crowding.

38. According to the passage, the fact that population growth began to cease among deer mice colonies of vastly different population sizes suggests that:

A. caged deer mice populations consistently demonstrate population growth followed by decline.

B. a critical density is not the most important variable in the regulation of population growth.

C. a relationship can be demonstrated between density and the regulation of population.

D. enclosure is a critical factor in producing changes in deer mice adrenal glands.

39. The evidence summarized in the passage best supports the conclusion that:

A. population density is not related to social pathology.

B. the findings of Calhoun and other researchers in the 1960s have been invalidated by more recent studies.

C. Haller's social learning theory provides the best explanation of crowd behavior.

D. numerous variables are relevant in explaining the psychological and behavioral effects of crowding.

GO TO THE NEXT PAGE.

Passage VII (Questions 40–47)

The idea that every human has certain inalienable rights first emerged in the seventeenth and eighteenth centuries. Human rights initially meant simply the right to representative government, as conveyed in the aims of
5 the American and French revolutions of the 1700s, but subsequently was enlarged to encompass freedom of speech, religion, and assembly; an unrestricted press; protection against enslavement and torture or freedom from coercion; and due process or equal protection
10 under the law. A largely twentieth-century concern for economic or "welfare" issues has resulted in the expansion of the definition to include the right to be employed, to own property, and to receive at least minimal levels of food, shelter, health care, and education.

15 Sovereign governments are responsible for the translation of human rights theory into concrete policies, often a difficult and controversial task. There may be occasions when the safeguarding of personal rights impinges upon equally important societal goals. In times of war, for
20 instance, the right to free speech and press has been restrained in the name of "national security." The rationale is that the dissemination of certain information or opinions would endanger all human rights by creating a situation wherein the survival of the government itself is threatened.
25 Another problem is defining the extent of a particular guarantee. For example, the amount of education to which every citizen supposedly is entitled has meant basic literacy to some and university instruction to others.

30 Still another view holds that education is not a right at all but is instead a privilege; it may be bestowed or rescinded at society's will. The protection of human rights also implies the existence of an elaborate network of courts, police, schools, hospitals, and employment
35 opportunities, but providing these is not always practical, especially in developing countries.

Many governments have attempted to guarantee rights not only to their own citizens but also to citizens of foreign nations. However, the issues are even more complex at the
40 international level. First, different governments may have varying interpretations of what constitutes a basic right. Second, even if it is assumed that all political, civil, and economic rights are applicable to all times and places, one nation does not necessarily have the authority to pass judg-
45 ment on another's domestic policies; international legal agreements usually preclude intervention in the internal affairs of other nations. A third, problem is that human

rights and "humanitarian interests" may be used as a facade for selfish geopolitical goals. Fourth, intercession
50 in another nation's internal affairs in the name of human rights may transgress domestic laws specifically prohibiting foreign intervention, thereby violating citizens' rights to a responsive and representative government.

Although occasionally amorphous, mechanisms do exist
55 at the domestic and international levels for ensuring the protection of human rights. Most nations have adopted constitutions or other binding documents that specifically enumerate the rights to which their citizens are entitled. In the international realm, direct intervention is one
60 means of safeguarding human rights, although generally undesirable and illegal. A more palatable option is diplomacy; one or more governments frequently can impel another nation to respect human rights through persuasive tactics, trade agreements, and other "quiet"
65 techniques. A third alternative is the creation of formal international organizations, such as the United Nations, to provide a global forum for discussion of human rights policies. Finally, extra-governmental organizations can draw attention to possible abuses of individual rights by conducting media and public information campaigns.

---

40. The author suggests that a political thinker of the eighteenth century and a twentieth-century counterpart would most likely differ on which of the following?

- **A.** Proper methods of ensuring international human rights
- **B.** The amount of education to which every citizen is entitled
- **C.** The definition of basic human rights
- **D.** The importance of representative government

41. According to the passage, direct intervention by one government in another's domestic affairs is likely to involve which of the following?

- **I.** A violation of citizens' rights
- **II.** Civil unrest in the intervening country
- **III.** A violation of international legal agreements

- **A.** I only
- **B.** II only
- **C.** I and III only
- **D.** II and III only

GO TO THE NEXT PAGE.

42. With which of the following statements concerning the guarantee of human rights would the author be most likely to agree?

    A. Translating human rights theory into policies is impossible because no consensus exists concerning the extent of basic rights.
    B. Many rights can be considered privileges and need not be guaranteed by sovereign governments.
    C. The enforcement of human rights on the international level does not conflict with other geopolitical goals.
    D. Governments lacking sufficient resources may be unable to safeguard their citizens' basic rights.

43. In the second paragraph, the author mentions national security considerations as evidence that:

    A. governments often violate the rights of their citizens for selfish geopolitical goals.
    B. the interests of a government may sometimes conflict with the rights of its citizens.
    C. safeguarding the right to free speech and press is an impossible endeavor.
    D. agreeing on the extent of a particular right is always problematic.

44. The author provides support for which of the following assertions?

    A. The concept of human rights should not be expanded to include the right to an education.
    B. Governments should never attempt to influence the human rights practices of other countries.
    C. Diplomacy is the only rational means of safeguarding human rights on the international level.
    D. Difficulties can arise when putting the concept of human rights into practice.

45. The author mentions all of the following as possible mechanisms for ensuring the protection of human rights EXCEPT:

    A. the creation of constitutions outlining citizens' rights.
    B. the existence of nongovernment groups devoted to publicizing rights violations.
    C. development of a universal definition of human rights.
    D. imposition of diplomatic measures to persuade nations to respect human rights.

46. It can be inferred from the passage that the author considers direct intervention by one country in the internal human rights practices of another to be:

    A. undesirable, and generally in breach of international law.
    B. undesirable, but justifiable if all other methods of intervention have first been applied.
    C. undesirable, but necessary as long as violations of basic human rights continue to occur.
    D. desirable, because everything must be done to ensure human rights for all people.

47. The author organizes the passage by:

    A. making distinctions between two levels of human rights, domestic and international.
    B. explaining what is meant by human rights and then discussing the difficulties and methods involved in safeguarding them.
    C. gradually refining the definition of basic human rights through a series of observations.
    D. presenting an argument in favor of broad human rights and then suggesting techniques to guarantee them.

GO TO THE NEXT PAGE.

Passage VIII (Questions 48–54)

The earliest telescopes were refractors, in that they used lenses to bend incoming light. By using refractive lenses, early astronomers were able to gather light and view images with greater resolution and magnification than possible with the naked eye. But because pioneer telescope makers knew relatively little about optics, their lenses exhibited two serious defects. The first problem, spherical aberration, is a distortion that occurs when a lens with round surfaces fails to focus light from a point object to a point image. The second problem, chromatic aberration, stems from the fact that an ordinary lens refracts different wavelengths of light to slightly different degrees, resulting in a different focal length for each color, and therefore, an out-of-focus image with a colorful halo.

A number of scientists, among them Johannes Kepler, realized that spherical aberration could be corrected simply by using a different shaped lens. A solution to chromatic aberration, however, proved more difficult. When Sir Isaac Newton announced that it seemed impossible to correct chromatic aberration, scientists turned their attention to reflecting telescopes. Like refractors, these telescopes also increased light, resolution, and magnification of an image. But reflectors use curved mirrors in lieu of clear lenses in order to avoid the chromatic distortion of refraction. However, early reflecting telescopes had their problems too: the mirrors they utilized were made of metal alloys, which absorbed light and thus obscured images. One solution to this problem was to build larger telescopes, since bigger mirrors mean greater light reception and brighter images. Unfortunately, the opticians and foundries of the day were not yet up to the challenge. Mirror technology progressed slowly, as did the development of better reflector telescopes.

Chromatic aberration remained a problem in refractors, until Englishman Peter Hall discovered that a compound lens (i.e., one that combined different surfaces) could compensate for the dispersion of different colors by focusing them back together. Unfortunately, his findings were little known. Later, mathematician Leonhard Euler hit upon a similar solution using two lenses with water between them. Soon after, noted optician John Dolland followed Euler's lead and sandwiched a piece of flint glass between two pieces of crown glass, an arrangement that corrected both chromatic and spherical aberration. As a result of this advancement and subsequent modifications, the refractor once again became the telescopic instrument of choice and remained so for about 100 years.

But the refractor continued to have one inescapable limitation—a constraint on the maximum effective lens diameter, which limits the light-gathering property of the telescope. For this reason, as well as because of technical advances in mirror making, the reflector would once again assume prominence. At the Great Exposition of 1851, Varnish and Mellish presented the first chemical technique for layering silver onto glass. The mirrors that ultimately resulted from this breakthrough were silvered on the front and represented a double advantage. First, the silver surface (financially feasible because of the small amount of silver required) increased reflectivity of mirrors some fifty percent. Second, using glass in place of metal eliminated problems of shrinkage and cracking.

The refractor never again surpassed the reflector. With further advances in the development of heat-resistant glass and casting techniques, larger and larger mirrors became possible, and astronomers saw farther and farther into the universe.

---

48. Of the following, the author is most interested in discussing:

    A. how different shapes of lenses influence resolution and magnification in telescopes.
    B. why refractors have become more popular than reflectors.
    C. how two basic telescope designs alternately succeeded each other in importance and popularity.
    D. the ways in which technological constraints have shaped the course of science.

49. The author mentions the views of Sir Isaac Newton (lines 20–22) in order to:

    A. explain why scientists initially turned toward reflecting telescopes.
    B. emphasize the severity of the problem of spherical aberration.
    C. show that early scientists often reached erroneous conclusions.
    D. tacitly challenge the view that Sir Isaac Newton was a brilliant scientist.

GO TO THE NEXT PAGE.

50. According to the passage, chromatic aberration can be corrected by:

   A. a lens with rounded surfaces.
   B. using glass in place of metal alloys.
   C. building larger telescopes for greater light reception.
   D. an arrangement of two lenses separated by water.

51. The author mentions all of the following as problems associated with refractors EXCEPT:

   A. chromatic aberration.
   B. limited lens diameter.
   C. spherical aberration.
   D. overabsorption of light.

52. The passage implies that the development of better telescopes was primarily hindered by:

   A. technological constraints.
   B. imprecise methodologies.
   C. disinterest among scientists.
   D. unavailability of materials.

53. Which of the following would best serve as the concluding sentence of the last paragraph?

   A. However, scientists hope that technological advances will someday bring the refractor into vogue again.
   B. However, it is unlikely that telescope design will progress any further.
   C. But until theorists can solve the problem of spherical aberration, scientists will continue to see only distorted images.
   D. Today, with reflectors integrating ancient knowledge and modern technology, we are able to glimpse the corners of the universe.

54. According to the passage, which of the following characteristics are common to both reflector and refractor telescopes?

   I. Increased resolution
   II. Compound lenses
   III. Light-gathering capacities

   A. I only
   B. I and II only
   C. I and III only
   D. II and III only

GO TO THE NEXT PAGE.

Passage IX (Questions 55–60)

Almost monthly, a college or university fraternity makes the national news because of an escapade of underaged drinking or hazing episode resulting in bodily injury or worse. Such incidents tarnish the image of fraternities as a locus of brotherhood. The response from fraternity leaders to those events is predictable. With diverse memberships, they say, it is impossible for everyone to attain the high goals set by fraternities. Moreover, it's not just fraternity members who behave inappropriately, they note . . . . Besides, proponents of fraternities assert, few other student organizations provide such an impressive array of benefits for their members and the host institution, benefits that far outweigh the occasional problems.

Unfortunately, many of these assertions are at odds with the results of recent research. While the majority of college students drink, fraternity members are much more likely than nonmembers to abuse alcohol . . . . The Harvard University School of Public Health surveyed more than 17,000 students at 140 randomly selected four-year schools and found that 86 percent of those who live in a fraternity house were binge drinkers, compared with 45 percent of nonmembers.

Alcohol abuse is only one area in which the performance of fraternity members falls far short of the espoused values and goals of fraternity life. Even though fraternities declare academic performance as a high priority, during orientation period new members' grades often fall well below campus average. Many professors are convinced that the time-consuming, often inane activities required to pledge a fraternity are the primary cause; candid fraternity members agree . . . .

Fraternity membership has a negative influence on intellectual development. Data from the National Study of Student Learning, conducted at 18 four-year colleges by the National Center on Teaching, Learning and Assessment, show that even after controlling for initial differences in such factors as precollege cognitive development, academic motivation, age and selectivity of the college attended, fraternity men are well behind their nonmember counterparts in cognitive development after the first year of college. The biggest deficit is in the area of critical thinking.

The opportunity to develop leadership skills during fraternity life may also be overstated. Students gain competence in practical and interpersonal skills when they perform tasks requiring sustained effort and commitment, such as planning group and campus-wide events. The majority of fraternity men do not hold positions, in their own group or elsewhere, that demand this kind of performance.

Supporters of fraternities surely will criticize this description of their educational impact. We readily concede that some individuals are unaffected by the anti- intellectual influences common to many chapters. And in some fraternities, alcohol abuse is not the norm, and high levels of intellectual and academic achievement are common. Unfortunately, research suggests that those fraternities are in the minority.

Reforming fraternities clearly is difficult. Drinking and hazing are too deeply embedded in the cultural system of many chapters, where they are part of a complicated system of rewards and sanctions that bond the individual member to the group . . . . What is to be done? Colleges and universities need to assess how fraternities affect their educational missions, and to evaluate the political consequences of trying to change the deeply entrenched fraternity system . . . . Behavioral and educational standards must be set. Fraternities that fail to cooperate should be ineligible for any form of institutional recognition, including the use of campus space for group functions.

Because academic performance, intellectual development, and openness to diversity seem to be negatively related to fraternity membership in the first year of college, policies barring first-year students from joining fraternities is essential. This is especially important on campuses where first-year students now can live in fraternity houses before classes begin; those institutions have little chance to socialize the newcomers to academic values . . . . We need a careful examination of the educational benefits that fraternities provide. Colleges and universities must ensure that fraternity members live up to the standards expected of all students and the standards that fraternities themselves espouse. When groups or individuals fail to meet these goals, administrators and fraternity leaders must act decisively to stem further abuse and reaffirm the institution's overarching educational mission.

GO TO THE NEXT PAGE.

55. According to the passage, the value of fraternities is questionable because of:

A. the abuse of alcohol by fraternity members and its effect on the college campus.

B. the questionable nature of the unimpeded growth of the fraternity system on today's college campus.

C. the National Center on Teaching, Learning, and Assessment's survey of the college fraternal system and its effects on student cognitive development.

D. the intrinsic nature of the fraternal system in relation to the overall educational mission of the college or university.

56. The Harvard University School of Public Health survey, as cited by the authors, demonstrates:

A. the need for university administrators to begin clamping down on underaged drinking.

B. the statistical differences between those who drink and are members of fraternities versus those who are not members.

C. the ability of fraternities to use their influence in promoting alcohol abuse through various pledge functions.

D. all of the above

57. In the passage, the authors fail to take into account:

A. factors such as precollege cognitive development, academic motivation, age, and selectivity of the college attended.

B. that alcohol abuse is not the norm at all fraternities.

C. that there are many fraternities that emphasize intellectual prowess.

D. the cultural and racial differences in fraternity membership.

58. The passage infers that the reason for the lack of critical thinking and leadership skills developed by fraternity members is caused by:

A. excessive alcohol usage by underaged drinkers, thereby creating a series of dependencies.

B. the inherent nature of fraternity culture in which there are few leaders and many followers.

C. residing in a single-sex environment, like a fraternity house, since the gender-specific nature of the organization creates a homogeneous atmosphere, reducing the possibility of cross-gender interaction.

D. the time-consuming, often inane activities required to pledge a fraternity.

59. The following is not recommended by the authors as a possible outcome of questioning the value of the fraternal system:

A. Colleges and universities need to assess how fraternities affect their educational missions.

B. Colleges and universities need to evaluate the political consequences of trying to change the deeply entrenched fraternity system.

C. Colleges and universities need to create policies barring first-year students from joining fraternities.

D. Colleges and universities need to insist that fraternities declare academic performance a high priority.

60. In order to stave off the anti-intellectual experiences of fraternity members, the authors would consider the following progressive steps:

A. involving faculty in the educational supervision of fraternity pledges

B. implementing substance-abuse counseling programs

C. banning all fraternities from campus

D. both choices A and B

STOP. If you finish before time is called, check your work. You may go back to any question in this test booklet.

ANSWER KEY
VERBAL REASONING TEST 2

1. B	18. B	35. B	52. A
2. B	19. A	36. C	53. D
3. A	20. B	37. B	54. G
4. C	21. A	38. B	55. D
5. D	22. B	39. D	56. D
6. C	23. C	40. C	57. D
7. D	24. A	41. C	58. B
8. D	25. C	42. D	59. D
9. A	26. D	43. B	60. D
10. D	27. B	44. D	
11. D	28. C	45. C	
12. D	29. A	46. A	
13. B	30. C	47. B	
14. B	31. C	48. B	
15. D	32. C	49. A	
16. B	33. D	50. D	
17. A	34. A	51. D	

EXPLANATIONS

Questions 1–6:
SUMERO-BABYLONIA
PASSAGE I

Topic: Sexagesimal mathematical system

Scope: Popularity of Sexagesimal mathematical system in ancient Babylonia

Purpose: To report the wide use of the sexagesimal mathematical system in ancient Babylonia, based upon the findings of recent excavations at three sites

Passage Map
¶1: Sumero-Babylonian number system
Strategy Note: underline the word "sexagesimal" but do not lose time thinking about how the system works.

¶2: Linear measure system also based on 60
¶3: Sumero-Babylonian system successor of earlier sexagesimal systems

¶4: Elamites also used same system, as did their predecessors

Questions:
1. B In order to answer a question about the source of a passage, it is vital to consider the passage as a whole. The detached tone, highly specialized subject matter (ancient numerical systems), and detailed historical material used to support the author's points suggest this passage is both academic and, most probably, geared to a rather specialized circle of scholars who study ancient numerical systems. Therefore, this passage most likely comes from a journal article on ancient numerical systems (B). If the passage had come from a newspaper feature on ancient market transactions (A), we would expect a more popular writing style and a greater focus on the details of ancient markets. This passage is not likely to have come from a lecture on archeological discoveries in the Near East (C) because the passage only discusses archeological discoveries to help support and shed light on ancient numerical systems. A lecture on archeological finds in the Near East would probably have been broader, touching on more sites and other kinds of discoveries. And this passage is not likely to have come from an encyclopedia entry on Sumero-Babylonian forms of writing (D) because the passage only briefly mentions Sumero-Babylonian writing (cuneiform) in the course of its discussion of ancient numerical systems.

2. B According to paragraphs three and four, the societies flourishing at approximately 2900-2800 B.C.—the proto-Sumerians and proto-Elamites—utilized sexagesimal number systems but not cuneiform inscriptions. Apparently cuneiform writing did not appear until after 2900–2800 B.C.; such inscriptions would not have appeared in 3200 B.C. The date and style of writing in (A) are appropriate to the types of tablets unearthed at Jemdet Nasr (paragraph three). The mathematical symbols and inscriptions in (C) are appropriate to any of the societies mentioned (except possibly Susa—the passage is not explicit). (D) essentially describes findings like those at Larsa, as discussed in paragraphs one and two; although the date is a little late, you should not assume that the use of the sexagesimal system (or conversion factors characteristic of it) died out immediately following the Sumero-Babylonian period.

3. A These characteristics would have been common to tablets unearthed from both Sumerian and proto-Sumerian sites. Although the societies used different styles of writing—Sumerians employing cuneiform and proto-Sumerians utilizing pictographic inscriptions (B)—each culture used similar mathematical symbols. As stated in sentence three of paragraph three, the numerical symbols of the proto-Sumerians, "circles, cup like shapes, and slashes," were quite similar to those noted on the tablets earlier unearthed at the Sumerian city of Larsa. All number systems mentioned in the passage were *quasi*-positional, and the use of 0 is never mentioned (C). The she (grain), not the shu-si or finger, is the smallest unit mentioned (D).

4. C According to paragraph four, the proto-Elamite culture was "roughly contemporary with that of the proto-Sumerians." The proto-Sumerian culture, as exemplified by the Jemdet Nasr archeological findings discussed in paragraph three, was in existence at approximately 2900–2800 B.C. Therefore, the proto-Elamite society also may be traced to 2900–2800 B.C., approximately 4800–4900 years ago. If you selected (A), you probably failed to add 2,000 years to 2900–2800 B.C. to account for the modern "A.D." Choice (B) is more appropriate to the Sumero-Babylonian and Elamite societies, which can be dated to about 2000-1500 B.C. Finally, you may have chosen (D) if you thought the proto-Sumerians were contemporaries of the Elamites rather than the proto-Elamites. Adding another 1,000 to account for the gap between the Elamites and proto-Elamites would have led to this choice.

5.   D   Of the four societies described in the passage, only two are assigned specific historical dates: the Sumero-Babylonians are said to have flourished in the years 1900–1500 B.C., while the proto-Sumerians existed in the years 2900–2800 B.C. Paragraph four places the proto-Elamites contemporary with the proto-Sumerians; the Elamites were at least 1,000 years later, although there is not enough detail to determine their actual date. Thus, in the final sequence, the proto-Elamites and proto-Sumerians should be placed in immediate proximity to one another, followed by the Elamites and the Sumero-Babylonians (or vice versa). Only (D) fulfills this requirement. Choice (A), while it may sound plausible at first, is inconsistent with the information given. (B) and (C) place "proto" societies later than their successors and are thus easy to reject.

6.   C   Excavations at Susa are discussed in the last paragraph of the passage, where the author tells us that in addition to the proto-Sumerian and Sumero-Babylonian societies the proto-Elamite and Elamite societies also used sexagesimal mathematical systems, supporting the notion that sexagesimal mathematical systems were used by several ancient Middle Eastern societies (C). The author doesn't *prove* that proto-Sumerian culture was dominant in the ancient Middle East (A). In fact, in the last paragraph the author seems to *undermine* the notion of proto-Sumerian cultural dominance by saying that a completely different style of writing was found at Susa in later excavations, revealing a proto-Elamite culture contemporary to proto-Sumerian culture, yet differing from it. The author does not discuss or explain the ways in which aspects of culture spread (B). He merely suggests that they did so, somehow, without detailing the *ways* in which that occurred. And the author never indicates that the mathematical system used in Sumero-Babylonian times was heavily influenced by proto-Elamite culture (D). On the contrary, throughout the passage, the author suggests that it was Sumerian and proto-Sumerian cultures that exerted influence upon neighboring cultures, including those of the Elamites and their predecessors. That is probably why the mathematical system is referred to as "Sumero-Babylonian" and not "Elamite."

Questions 7–14:
ZEL'DOVICH-SUNYAEV
PASSAGE II

Topic: The Development of the Universe

Scope: Zel'dovich and Sunyaev theory on the development of the Universe

Purpose: To explain a popular theory of universe development

Passage Map
¶1: Study of the origins and –evolution of universe is young discipline

¶2: Zel'dovich and Sunyaev theory explaining uneven distribution of luminous matter

¶3: Galaxies are grouped into "clusters"

¶4: Most of space = dark matter

¶5: Failure of theory: does not account for expansion of universe

Questions:
7.   D   The first sentence of paragraph 1 says that the "big bang" resulted in continuing expansion of the universe. The last sentence of the passage adds that galaxies are diverging as part of the continuing expansion of the universe. So, galaxies are moving as a result of a massive energy discharge **D**. Choice (A) is wrong because sentences 5-8 of the final paragraph tell us that galaxies diverge, moving away from each other. Thus, they are not moving in random ways. Sentence 8 of the final paragraph says that other galaxies are moving away from our own galaxy, the Milky Way, so choice (B) is incorrect. There is no suggestion that galaxies are moving out of their original clusters (C). We are told in the final paragraph that celestial bodies, including galactic clusters, are expanding; consequently, galaxies are not leaving their original clusters, but remaining within the boundaries of expanded clusters.

8.   D   The first few sentences of the second paragraph state that gravitational forces in the early universe determined the current distribution of galaxies by concentrating gas in certain regions of the universe, so choice **D** correctly describes an aspect of the universe. Choice (A) is wrong because, according to the sixth sentence of the third paragraph, astronomers have identified four superclusters. This is very different from saying that there are no more than four superclusters in the universe. Choice (B) is incorrect because the first sentence of the second paragraph tells us that gravitational forces have an effect on gaseous "pancakes." Nowhere in the passage is there any indication that galaxies will eventually stop moving, so choice (C) is wrong.

9. A This question asks you about the author's view of the Zel'dovich-Sunyaev theory. At the beginning of the final paragraph, the author notes that the Zel'dovich-Sunyaev theory has contributed greatly to our understanding of the universe. But, he goes on to say that this theory cannot explain the universe's continual expansion. Choice **A** conveys this author's attitude and is our correct answer. Choice (B) is wrong because the author believes the theory is not complete. And the author does not criticize the theory for being "uninformed" (C). Paragraphs 2, 3, and 4 summarize evidence that supports the Zel'dovich-Sunyaev theory, so (D) is incorrect in saying that the author considers it lacking in evidence.

10. D Red shift analysis is discussed in the middle of the last paragraph. According to this technique, the more distant a celestial body from the point of observation, the more its light shifts to the red end of the spectrum. Thus, since the problem tells us that light emitted from galaxy A is further to the red end of the spectrum than light emitted from galaxy B, we can infer that galaxy B is closer to Earth and the Milky Way than galaxy **A**. Choice (A) misinterprets and contradicts the principles behind red shift analysis. And, as far as we know from the information in the passage, red shift analysis tells us something about the relative distance, not the speed, of galaxies A and B; consequently, we cannot infer anything about speed, and choices (B) and (C) are incorrect.

11. D The last sentence of paragraph 3 states explicitly that astronomers disagree about the dimensions of superclusters. Choice (A) is wrong because the final paragraph implies that astronomers agree that this technique is very useful. Paragraphs 2-5 imply that astronomers agree that our galaxy is only one among an enormous number of galaxies distributed throughout the universe (B). The influence of gravity on "pancakes" is a central part of the Zel'dovich-Sunyaev theory, which is popular among astronomers, so it's unlikely that they disagree on the issue of gravity and pancakes (C).

12. D "Hubble's Law" and its relevance are discussed in the final paragraph. The author notes that the Zel'dovich-Sunyaev theory fails to account for the continuing expansion of the universe, but Hubble's Law fills this gap. Thus, the author introduces this law to complement or supplement the Zel'dovich-Sunyaev theory. Choice (A) is wrong because Hubble's Law is the theory of diverging galaxies. (B) is wrong because the author introduces red shift analysis to explain Hubble's Law, not the other way around. Hubble's Law deals with the movement of galaxies and has little to do with dark matter, so the author hardly introduces this law to prove the existence of dark matter (C).

13. B The third sentence of the first paragraph tells us that little about space beyond our own galaxy was known prior to the 20th century, implying that astronomers were restricted to studying the Milky Way. Sentence 4 of paragraph 1 tells us that radio telescopes were not used until the 20th century, so choice (A) can't be right. Since sentence 3 of paragraph 1 informs us that astronomers could only speculate about the existence of "external" galaxies prior to the 20th century, they could not have discovered the existence of galactic clusters and superclusters (C) until the 20th century. Finally, we cannot assume that the "big bang" was formulated prior to the 20th century (D) because the passage tells us nothing about when the big bang idea was formulated.

14. B The passage never mentions or suggests that the huge amount of energy released by the "big bang" explosion will be exhausted (I). However, the last sentence of the passage does indicate that, as a result of the huge energy release at the time of the big bang, today's celestial bodies and bounds of the entire universe continue to expand. On this basis, it makes sense to infer that our galaxy will continue to grow in size over time, so option II is a valid inference. Option III suggests that the configuration of the universe will remain constant in the future. But this is contrary to the notion of the expanding universe that we just referred to from the last paragraph of the passage. Thus, only option II can be inferred from the passage, making choice (B) correct.

Questions 15–20:
BELARUS AND MOLDOVA
PASSAGE III

Topic: Recent independence of Belarus and Moldova from the Soviet Union

Scope: Differences between Belarus' and Moldova's attitudes toward Russia

Purpose: To argue that ethnic and cultural differences explain Belarus' and Moldova's varying attitudes towards Russia

Passage Map

¶1: Russia attempted to "Russify" Belarus and Moldova to buffer itself from West

¶2: Both countries have trouble converting from predictable communism to unpredictable democracy

¶3: Ethnic differences between the two countries predicts the degree to which each country identifies with Russia

¶4: National language = primary issue for those aspiring for independence

¶5: Importance of language

Questions:

15. D Statement III appears in three choices, so we'll consider it first. The Transnistrians are discussed only at the end of the third paragraph; the final words of that paragraph tell us they would lose political power if Moldova reunified with Romania, apparently the explanation of their resistance to such reunification and their pro-Soviet position—Statement III is correct. Statement I is FUD (Faulty Use of Detail); in the second paragraph, we see that "officials" resist democracy for this reason, but we aren't told that the Transnistrians are among them. Statement II is a Distortion; the Transnistrian extralegal government is located on the east bank of the Nistru, but we have no basis for concluding this was considered a natural boundary.

16. B The author presents the Transnistrians as principally concerned with not becoming a small minority in a reunited Romania (instead of the powerful minority they have apparently been in Moldova). If we learn that, in fact, they wish to engage in activities banned in Moldova (and that would be illegal under most governments), then the significance of their status as a political minority would be weakened. The interests of the Russian government (A) or the majority of Moldovans (C) would have no effect, based on the passage—its outside the scope. (D) is FUD; those revolutions are discussed in paragraph 4, and are relevant to the importance of language to a culture, not to the political differences among Moldavans.

17. A (B) is FUD; there is no connection made between the failures of those revolutions and the present situation. (C) is a Distortion; the native languages had been "dismissed" by the Russian authorities—they weren't invented (although we are told a "literary language" needed to be codified or formed). (D) also misuses details; based on the passage, the Transnistrians did not exist in 1848, and their situation doesn't have its roots in the past.

18. B We can see this in the third paragraph, where the Transnistrians are introduced, and in the last two paragraphs, where the "debate" is about the name of their language, which is clearly Romanian-based, but called Moldovan to assuage the fears of the Transnistrians (and perhaps other minorities). The issue of use of Russian (A) is handled lightly by comparison—it's simply kept "as a language of interethnic communication" apparently without debate or strife. (C) is a Distortion; the non-Romanian Transnistrian minority seem to be the most vocal pro-Soviet force in Moldova, but there is no indication that their legal status is at issue. (D) is another Distortion; the debate is not about whether a Romanian language is to be used—the majority of the population are ethnic Romanians, and we can tell the language is "official" because it's referred to as "their own language" and mentioned in the constitution—only the name of the language was in dispute.

19. A We are told in the third paragraph that in Belarus the population is mostly Slavic, that the tsars and commissars "succeeded to a remarkable extent" in "Russifying" the people, that Belarusians identify closely with Russia, and nationalists are in the minority. In the fourth and fifth paragraphs, we find that Belarusians "prefer the use of Russian in their daily lives". Overall, Belarus seems fairly closely allied to Russia; all the resistance to "Russification" appears in discussion of Moldova. However, nothing in the passage permits us to conclude that Belarusians don't wish to maintain their independence.

20. B A new assertion that the country was equally Western and Russian is inconsistent with the statement that in Belarus the "tsars and commissars who sought to meld Belorussia with Russia succeeded to a remarkable extent". (A) wouldn't be true; in fact, we would assume that a country that acted as a "buffer" between two other countries felt the influence of each of those other countries. (C) is FUD; the Transnistrians aren't relevant to statements made about Belarus; they are in Moldova. (D) is also FUD; the position of the conservatives (by definition pro-Russian) wouldn't be affected by the existence of pro-Western influences.

Questions 21–26:

PRESCHOOL CHILDREN

PASSAGE IV

Topic: Social behavior of Children

Scope: Study of preschooler behavior in nursery vs. home

Purpose: To report the findings of a study investigating the behavior of preschoolers in the nursery and the home.

Passage Map

¶1: Study of social behavior of preschoolers in nursery vs. at home

¶2: Study's methods

¶3: Sibling-independent variables had most correlations with school behavior; sibling-related variables had most correlations with home behavior

¶4: Sibling-related variables that correlate with behavior in nursery school

¶5: Only one correlation (aggression) between behavior at school and home

Questions:

21. A Total observation time was sixty-eight hours; thirty-four subjects were observed for two hours each. (B) is only half of the correct amount; you counted either one hour of observation time per subject or seventeen subjects. (C) represents a misreading; in each setting for each subject an hour of observation time was collected in twenty periods of three minutes' duration each. There is no discussion of how long collecting the data took overall (D).

22. B According to paragraph three, the subject's age (I) and sex (III) demonstrate the greatest number of correlations (B). According to paragraph four, "having a same-sex sibling" (II) revealed correlations with both "onlooker behavior" and adult-child interaction in the nursery school, but there is no indication that these correlations extend to other types of behavior, and the question asks which variables correlate "most frequently" with "behavior" in general. Therefore, choice (B), I and III only, is our answer.

23. C According to the study results given in paragraph three, solitary play varies inversely with the age of the preschool child. Paragraph two discussed solitary play in the context of Parton's social play hierarchy, placing this activity early on the scale and implying that Parton would expect to find this type of play more among younger preschoolers and less among older preschoolers. Thus, the study under discussion tends to confirm Parton's hierarchy insofar as the two studies can be compared, and (C) is correct. The study reveals nothing about the specificity or generalness of activities, but the passage defines these categories in paragraph two, where solitary play is said to be a general class of behavior (A). (B) is true of solitary play in the home, not in the nursery school. The study does not suggest that solitary play is rare among preschoolers (D). All we know from the study's findings is that solitary play tended to vary inversely with the age of preschoolers. The findings tell us nothing any more specific about the incidence of solitary play.

24. A The last paragraph suggests one problem with the study might be that differences between the various home environments were too great in relation to the number of subjects in the study; a larger subject pool drawn from more homes (A) would remedy this situation, since you would presumably then get groups of children with similar homes—making it possible to statistically correct for selected home variables and treat home environment as a constant. The author never suggests that observation time per subject is insufficient; nor would increasing such observation time even indirectly remedy the other possible problems discussed in the last paragraph (B). (C) runs contrary to paragraph two, since breaking the observation time into three-minute periods apparently yields more reliable results. The second part of (D) would solve the same problem as choice (A), but reduction of the subject pool would impair the results; in any case, preselecting for similar home environments might distort the study in other ways.

25. C According to paragraph four, "onlooker behavior" most closely related to both "having a sister" and "having a same-sex sibling." Since a girl with an older sister fulfills both these qualifications, (C) is correct. Choices (A) and (B) each involve only one of these characteristics. Solitary play at home (D) appears unrelated to onlooker behavior, but if anything, one would expect these two behaviors to be inversely, not directly, related, since solitary play at home is inversely related to "having a sister" (paragraph three) while onlooker behavior is directly correlated with the same variable.

26. D When sibling-related variables revealed correlations with school behavior (paragraph four), the passage took this as evidence for the influence of the home environment on interactions outside the home; using analogous reasoning, this question requires an example in which some descriptive variable at school correlates with some behavior at home. The only answer choice that does this is (D). In (A), since sibling-unrelated variables (specified in the passage as the age and sex of the subject) are also school-unrelated, the nursery school environment does not influence home behavior. (B) presents an example of the home environment influencing home behavior. (C) offers no indication of causality; school could be influencing home, or vice versa, or some other variable could be influencing both (analogous to "demonstrates aggression" in the last paragraph and creating the same problems of interpretation).

Questions 27–33: BEOWULF

PASSAGE V

Topic: *Beowulf*

Scope: Authorship of *Beowulf*

Purpose: To compare and contrast three prominent theories regarding the authorship of *Beowulf*.

Passage Map

¶1: Authorship of *Beowulf* disputed: one author or several; pagan or Christian

¶2: Tribal-Lay theory: amalgam of Germanic and Nordic myths

¶3: Accretion theory: later authors added on to work of first

¶4: Tolkien theory: single Christian author who used pagan materials

¶5: Critics favor Tolkien theory

Questions:

27. B The author mentions Sigemund's battle with the dragon in his discussion of the "tribal lay" theory in paragraph two. This theory considers *Beowulf* an amalgam of older myths and the work of many authors or editors. Sigemund's battle is mentioned to support this theory (B) because his battle with the dragon is seen as an inconsistency or digression that would characterize such an amalgamation. While the author mentions Sigemund as an example of the digressions suggested by the "tribal lay" theory, he mentions a failure to recognize Christian themes as a source of criticism of the theory. So the author's discussions of Sigemund's battle and Christian themes are for completely different and unrelated purposes, making choice (A) wrong. As discussed above, Sigemund's battle with the dragon is mentioned to support the theory that *Beowulf* is the product of many authors, not a single author (C). Finally, the battles between the Anglo-Saxons and the Vikings, Scots, and Picts are discussed in regard to the "Christian authorship" theory in the fourth paragraph; the author treats these conflicts and Sigemund's battle with the dragon as completely different issues, so (D) is incorrect.

28. C The "Christian authorship" theory, discussed in paragraph four, holds that *Beowulf*'s author might have emphasized pagan motifs—like the cult of the warrior—to boost morale for political purposes during a time of military upheavals. Therefore, the cult of the warrior is a reflection of political upheavals in England at the time of its writing (C). The idea that *Beowulf* illustrates major themes in Germanic and Norse culture is stressed in the "tribal lay" theory, not the "Christian authorship" theory, so (A) is wrong. While the author mentions that Tolkien

argues the Christian author of *Beowulf* was probably a member of a royal court (B), he does not say that the writer was a military official and accounts for the emphasis on the role of the warrior by referring to the historical context rather than the author's background. The "Christian authorship" theory holds that from A.D. 650 to 850, Christian and pagan beliefs coexisted, and implies that Christianity was gradually replacing pagan beliefs, even if some people continued to cling to them. So there is no basis for inferring that *Beowulf*'s emphasis on the pagan cult of the warrior exhibits a decline in Christian faith (D).

29. A The "growth by accretion" theory (see paragraph three) states that *Beowulf* is the product of a number of authors over a period of centuries. Considering that, option I is true, and is part of our answer. Proponents of this theory point to conflicting pagan and Christian themes as evidence of *Beowulf*'s multiple authorship, so option II is also true, and is also part of the answer to this question. However, option III plays upon the "Christian authorship" theory's emphasis upon unity, while also attempting to relate the poem's literary qualities to its historical context. All of this has nothing to do with the "growth by accretion" theory. Therefore, only options I and II are true of "growth by accretion" theorists, making choice (A) correct.

30. C Both the "tribal lay" and "growth by accretion" theories hold that *Beowulf* was written by multiple authors. "Tribal lay" theorists believe that the poem began as works of several authors, later combined by editors (paragraph two). "Growth by accretion" theorists, however, propose that *Beowulf* began as the short work of a single author, later contributed to by numerous authors. Therefore, these two theories agree on multiple-authorship, but differ in their conceptions of what it entailed (C). (A) is incorrect because it wrongly attributes historical analysis to the multiple authorship theories when it is the "Christian authorship" theory that emphasizes the epic's historical context. Paragraph two mentions the poem's allegorical references in relation to criticism of the "tribal lay" theory. But the passage provides no details of the "growth by accretion" theorists' interpretations or perspectives regarding these allegories. Since the passage provides us with no basis for comparing interpretations of the poem's references, (B) is wrong. (D) is wrong in suggesting differences in the ways theorists account for the poem's Christian elements. In fact, the author stresses that "tribal-lay" theorists tend to ignore the poem's "obvious Christian overtones" entirely (see paragraph two). They would hardly "account for" or explain references they do not recognize in the first place. So there is no basis for comparing explanations of Christian elements among theorists.

31. C The "Christian authorship" theory rests on the belief that *Beowulf* had a single Christian author who wrote the poem, based on pagan material, sometime between the years 650 and 850. It is perfectly consistent to think that a partially translated (presumably into Norwegian) manuscript of *Beowulf* may have existed in an eleventh century Norwegian church (A). This would not affect the "Christian authorship" theory, which places *Beowulf*'s birthplace in England around the time of the eighth century. The "Christian authorship" theory argues that the Anglo-Saxons were involved in constant warfare with the Vikings, Scots, and Picts, so the discovery of even more intense or long-lasting conflict among the groups would not weaken this theory (B). The "Christian authorship" theorists speculate that *Beowulf* may have been written by an aristocratic Christian author, but this kind of speculation is not central to the theory. The fact that Tolkien felt *Beowulf* was "probably" written by a member of the royal court suggests that it also might not have been. Therefore, the suggestion that the poem was written by a literate peasant (D) would not weaken the theory significantly. However, if it were discovered that *Beowulf* is an English translation of an earlier Germanic myth (C), the "Christian authorship" theory that *Beowulf* originated in England between 650 and 850 would be severely weakened. Since the theory relies heavily upon and is specific to the epic's historical context, the realization that its origins were other than those suggested by Tolkien would erode the very foundations of the "Christian authorship" theory.

32. C The passage's last paragraph explains why most scholars favor the "Christian authorship" theory: historical analyses of the context in which *Beowulf* was written provide the best resolution to the poem's contradictions or inconsistencies (C). The author does not claim that the "Christian authorship" theory locates references in *Beowulf* in Norse and Germanic mythology (A). It is the "tribal lay" theory that emphasizes Nordic and Germanic sources. And while the "tribal lay" theory does not consider the epic's Christian overtones, the "growth by accretion theory" does, so it would be incorrect to say that scholars favor the "Christian authorship" theory because it it is the only one that appreciates the significance of *Beowulf*'s Christian elements (B). Finally, all three of the theories discussed in the passage attempt to explain the epic's disparate references and varied motifs (D); in fact, all of the theories discussed in the passage attempt such an explanation.

33. D The author mentions a work written by J. R. R. Tolkien, originator of the "Christian authorship" theory, in order to introduce a contextual analysis of the writing of *Beowulf* (D). Although you may recognize Tolkien as the prominent author of *The Hobbit*, the passage's author does not mention Tolkien to lend support to multiple authorship theories (A). In fact, Tolkien's theory contradicts the notion of multiple authorship entirely. According to the second sentence of the fourth paragraph, Tolkien argues that *Beowulf* was

written by a single Christian author, eliminating choice (B). (C) is incorrect because the author of this passage does not attempt to *disprove* previous theories of *Beowulf*'s authorship. While it is true that the author's tone seems to favor the theory of "Christian authorship," he writes in the first sentence of the last paragraph that it would be impossible to conclusively prove or disprove any of the theories.

Questions 34–39: OVERCROWDING
PASSAGE VI

Topic: Overcrowding

Scope: Psychological effects of overcrowding

Purpose: To rebut the perception that overcrowding induces pathological psychological effects.

Passage Map
¶1: Psychological effects of overcrowding believed to cause urban violence

¶2: Calhoun experiment: high population density with caged rats

¶3: Evidence against population density as factor in changes of population growth or endocrine function

¶4: No clear correlation between density and psychopathology

¶5: Haller's definition of "crowded"

Questions:
34. A Haller's theory of social learning is discussed in the last paragraph of this passage. That theory distinguishes available space and acceptable space, and suggests that the perception of being overcrowded results when acceptable space exceeds available space. Therefore, increasing individuals' needs in terms of acceptable space, while keeping available space constant (A), would necessarily increase crowding. Increasing available space while keeping acceptable space constant (B), and decreasing acceptable space—lessening the amount of space individuals need—while keeping available space constant (C) would both *decrease* crowding. Choice (D) would neither increase nor decrease crowding, because this choice suggests varying the factors of available and acceptable space together and in the same manner.

35. B Although this passage suggests that animal studies are of limited value to the study of overcrowding, it cites various findings of pertinent animal studies. Changes in adrenal gland size among crowded animals (A) is mentioned in paragraph two in reference to overcrowded rats. That same paragraph mentions the fact that a population of enclosed rats and mice will not continue to reproduce indefinitely (C), and that in crowded conditions the social order of these creatures will often dissolve (D). Only (B), which claims that aggression among crowded rats results from factors other than population density, is not demonstrated by any of the animal studies cited in the passage. Although the author says that certain animal disorders may result simply from being caged, or from being in a large group, she never mentions studies demonstrating that *aggression* in crowded rats results from something other than overcrowding.

36. C To answer this question about the urban riots in 1967, you need to read the first paragraph carefully to pick up the author's tone and attitude toward various explanations for such events. The fact that the author refers to findings like those of the Kerner Commission as "simplistic analyses" (in the last sentence of the first paragraph) suggests that the author is critical of linking animal studies of crowding to urban violence. Considering this, choice (C), which says that the author feels the riots of 1967 were incorrectly related to Calhoun's classic experiment, best reflects the author's attitude towards these findings. Choices (A) and (B) twist the thrust of the author's criticism in opposite directions. The author never goes so far as to say that the riots were unrelated to conditions of crowding (A). Nor does she claim the riots *resulted* from crowding (B). She merely suggests that crowded conditions may be one factor among many that may have led to those riots. Finally, in discussing animal experiments on crowding in relation to crowding among humans, the author does suggest that applying the results of animal experiments to the human condition may be difficult and tenuous. However, the problem of extrapolating animal findings to humans (D) is a larger problem of research methodology—one that may have been demonstrated by the Kerner Commission's report, but cannot be shown by the urban riots of 1967 themselves.

37. B The author states in paragraph 5 that Haller's social learning theory is valuable in that it distinguishes between density, a physical situation, and crowding, a psychological perception (B). In doing so, its purpose is not to relate rioting simply to density, so (A) is wrong. While Haller's theory implies that the perception of crowding is an individual psychological perception, it does not say that overcrowding has little to do with socioeconomic variables (C), nor does it preclude that possibility. Haller's theory may shed some light on the relationship between social pathology and crowding, or the perception of crowding; however, the theory itself does not explain the relationship between social pathology and crowding (D); that is a relationship which we have yet to clarify.

38. B The third paragraph discusses an experiment with enclosed deer mice populations which suggests that, because population growth declined in colonies of varying sizes and densities, density was not the most important variable affecting population growth (B). (A) exaggerates the experiment's findings in saying that caged deer mice populations *consistently* exhibit a pattern of growth followed by decline. The third paragraph of the passage implies that the deer mice study did not demonstrate a relationship between density and population regulation; since (C) says just the opposite, it is incorrect. While this study does suggest enclosure is a critical factor in population regulation in deer mice, it does not mention enclosure as contributing to changes in adrenal gland size, so (D) is wrong.

39. D This passage suggests that population density, size, and enclosure, as well as ethnic, psychological, and other personal considerations, all contribute to the behavioral effects of crowding; therefore, (D) best reflects the passage's conclusion. While the author implies that one cannot simply say that overcrowding is the main factor leading to social pathology, she does not deny that population density may be one of the many possible factors that may encourage social pathology (A). Nowhere does the author suggest the animal experiments of the 1960s have been invalidated (B). Choice (C) is incorrect since the author treats Haller's social learning theory as just one of the many explanations for crowd behavior, not as the best explanation; be careful not to assume that it was favored simply because it was the last one presented.

Questions 40–47: HUMAN RIGHTS
PASSAGE VII

Topic: Human Rights

Scope: Protecting Human Rights

Purpose: To highlight problems of enacting policies that ensure the protection of human rights at the domestic and international levels.

Passage Map

¶1: Evolution of inalienable human rights

¶2: Problems of translating human rights theory into policy

¶3: Necessary social institutions to protect human rights

¶4: Guaranteeing rights to citizens of foreign nations

¶5: Mechanisms to protect human rights at the domestic and international levels

Questions:

40. C The first paragraph states that the basic meaning of human rights has changed considerably since the eighteenth century: What initially meant simply the right to representative government now encompasses the right to be employed, to own property, and to receive at least minimal levels of food, shelter, health care, and education. This information allows us to infer that an eighteenth-century political thinker's understanding of human rights would differ considerably from that of his twentieth-century counterpart. Choices (A) and (B) involve unrelated details discussed in other parts of the passage—we're given no evidence to infer that our hypothetical political thinkers would disagree on the proper methods of ensuring international human rights or on the amount of education to which every citizen is entitled. No comparison between eighteenth- and twentieth-century conceptions of these issues is mentioned or suggested. There is also no indication that the political thinkers would differ in their opinions of the importance of representative government (D); that the twentieth-century political thinker includes many more things in his concept of human rights does not mean he values representative government less than his eighteenth-century counterpart did.

41. C The author mentions the effects of direct intervention by one government in another's affairs in the third and fourth paragraphs. Option I is supported by the last sentence of the third paragraph, which states that intervention could transgress domestic laws, thereby "violating citizen's rights to a responsive and representative government." Support for Option III comes in the fourth sentence of paragraph three ("international agreements usually preclude intervention") and in the third sentence of paragraph four (direct intervention is "generally undesirable and illegal"). Although the passage states that direct intervention could violate the rights of citizens in the intervening country, no evidence is given that the violation would necessarily lead to "civil unrest" (Option II).

42. D The author discusses the difficulty of guaranteeing human rights in paragraph two. At the end of the paragraph, she mentions that certain economic and social resources are necessary to protect human rights—and indicates that providing them is not always practical. This evidence points to (D). Choice (A) goes too far. True, no consensus concerning the extent of basic rights exists, and the author indicates that putting theory into practice is sometimes difficult, but she never says it is *impossible*. Choice (B) distorts a detail in paragraph two. There the author just states that some people consider education a privilege rather than a right that must be guaranteed. She never goes so far as to say or suggest "many rights need not be guaranteed." The author mentions "geopolitical goals" in the third paragraph, but only to say that some countries interfere in the human rights actions of other countries in order to further their own interests. The author never suggests that such intervention does not conflict with other

geopolitical goals. The very nature of such intervention suggests otherwise. So, there is no support for (C).

43. B The reference to national security considerations comes in the second paragraph, within the author's discussion of how "equally important societal goals" sometimes conflict with the rights of citizens—to ensure its survival during war, for example, a government may have to interfere with certain individual rights, like freedom of speech. Choice (A) involves an unrelated detail—the author does not make reference to "selfish geopolitical goals" until the next paragraph. (C) exaggerates to the point of distortion—the author only says that government interests may sometimes conflict with citizens' rights (like the right to free speech and press), *not* that safeguarding those rights is an "impossible endeavor." Choice (D) refers to an unrelated detail discussed a little later in the second paragraph—where the author uses the example of education. While both do concern the question of the extent and limits of rights, the author's discussion of national security is not specifically aimed at providing evidence that the extent of rights is problematic.

44. D The author uses the entire second paragraph to discuss the difficulties sovereign governments face when they try to, transform, human, rights, theories into, concrete policies; therefore, choice (D) is correct. Choices (A), (B), and (C) distort various details mentioned in the passage. The author mentions halfway through paragraph two that *some people* consider education a privilege rather than a right, but she does not argue that education should not be included among human rights (A). Paragraph three discusses the difficulties involved when a country interferes in the human rights practices of another, but the author never argues that governments should never try to influence one another (B). In fact, in paragraph 4, she details a number of methods countries could use to influence human rights on the international level. Of these, the author feels that diplomacy is more "palatable" than direct intervention, but she never claims that it is the "only rational means" (C).

45. C The author discusses the various "mechanisms" for ensuring the protection of human rights in paragraph four. Choice (A) is mentioned in the second sentence, (B) in the last sentence, and (D) in the fourth sentence. Nowhere does the author mention the development of a "universal definition of human rights," making (C) the correct choice. In fact, the author's discussion of difficulties in translating human rights theory into policies suggests (C) would be highly improbable.

46. A The fourth sentence of the third paragraph states that "international legal agreements usually preclude intervention in the internal affairs of other nations," and the fourth sentence of paragraph four says direct intervention is "generally undesirable and illegal." Choices (B) and (C) are on the right track—the author does consider direct intervention "undesirable"—but she never indicates that it's nonetheless "justifiable" or "necessary" under certain conditions. Choice (D) is out right from the start—this contradicts parts of the passage cited above in the explanation of correct choice (A).

47. B The author outlines the general meaning of human rights and how it has evolved in the first paragraph, then goes on to discuss the difficulties of putting theory into practice on the domestic level (paragraph two), and on the international level (paragraph three). In the last paragraph, she mentions some ways to safeguard human rights on both levels. Choice (B) accurately summarizes this structure. The author does not organize her discussion around any "distinctions" between human rights on the domestic and international levels (A), nor does she refine the definition of human rights through a series of observations (C). Choice (D) is out because the author does not really argue a point. Her tone is merely that of an objective presenter of information.

Questions 48–54: TELESCOPES

PASSAGE VIII

Topic: Telescopes

Scope: Evolution of Telescopes

Purpose: To review the evolution of the telescope from the early days of using a refractive lens to the modern-day large reflectors.

Passage Map
¶1: Early telescopes = refractors but had problems

¶2: Mirrors discovered as solution but technology not yet up to speed

¶3: Compound lens fixed refractor problem

¶4: Mirror technology up to speed

¶5: Reflectors surpass refractors

Questions:
48. C This question addresses the primary purpose of the passage: how the refractor and reflector telescopes alternately developed in response to both scientific discovery and technical innovation. While the author does discuss different shapes of lenses throughout the passage, choice (A) is not the main topic of the passage; the effects of different lenses are considered only in support of the more general discussion of the development of telescope design. (B) contradicts the conclusion that reflectors are currently more popular, so it can't be right. This passage is about ways in which technological constraints have affected the development

of the telescope, but that's just one example of how technological constraints have affected the course of science, so (D) is too broad to be the primary purpose.

49. A See the third sentence of paragraph two. Scientists turned to reflectors because Newton thought chromatic aberration in refractors was unsolvable. (B) is wrong because the passage says that spherical aberration is simply corrected. The thought that chromatic aberration was unsolvable was not mentioned for the purposes of deriding Newton or his ways of thinking. Nothing in the passage or in the author's tone suggests such a purpose, so both (C) and (D) are too judgemental to jibe with the author's intentions.

50. D A straightforward detail question. See paragraph three—Leonhard Euler provided a solution to chromatic aberration using two lenses with water between them. According to the passage, using a lens with rounded surfaces (A) may cause spherical aberration but solves nothing. (B) and (C) refer to improvements made in reflectors, which do not suffer from chromatic aberration.

51. D Problems associated with refractors are discussed in paragraphs 1, 3, and 4. Chromatic aberration (A) and spherical aberration (C) are both mentioned in paragraph 1. Limited lens diameter (B) is discussed in sentence 1 of paragraph four. Only choice (D) is not associated with refractors: over-absorption of light is a problem of reflectors, discussed in paragraph 2.

52. A Various problems with materials and construction of telescopes are discussed throughout the passage, which implies that technological constraints hindered the development of telescopes. The passage never implies (B); it scarcely discusses methodology at all and does not suggest any problem with methods being imprecise. Contrary to choice (C), the author implies that scientists were extremely interested in developing better telescopes. There is no suggestion that materials were scarce or unavailable (D).

53. D Solving this question requires that you make an inference from the tone and focus of the passage as a whole, paying special attention to the last paragraph. Choice (D) reflects the fact that the passage describes a technological history, objectively describes both types of telescopes, is informative in tone, and concludes on a rather optimistic note. (A) suggests that scientists prefer the refractor, which contradicts the passage—particularly its last paragraph, which speaks of the reflector's predominance. (B) does not jibe with the optimistic tone of the concluding paragraph. (C) contradicts information contained in the first sentence of the second paragraph; spherical aberration was easily solved.

54. C The third sentence of the second paragraph states that reflectors, like refractors, increase both light and resolution; therefore, both options I and III are correct. Compound lenses, however, are discussed in paragraph three, but only in reference to refractors; the author never states that compound lenses have been used in reflectors. Since options I and III are common to both types of telescopes, but II is only characteristic of refractors, (C) is the correct answer.

Questions 55–60: Fraternities
PASSAGE IX

Topic: Fraternities

Scope: The negative educational impact of fraternities

Purpose: To describe the negative educational impact of fraternities and to propose policy solutions to the problems they cause

Passage Map
¶1: Fraternity image tarnished due to poor news; frat argues benefits outweigh problems

¶2: Study reveals frat more likely to abuse alcohol

¶3: New members' grades suffer during orientation

¶4: Cognitive development deficit

¶5: Claim of developing leadership overstated

¶6: Exceptions exist; a few frats are ok

¶7: Reforming frats will be difficult; college must weight affect on education vs. political consequences and set standards

¶8: Ban first-year students from joining frats

Questions:
55. D The correct choice is (D) because the entire passage discusses the nature of fraternities in regard to its "overall" relationship with the educational mission of the university. Alcohol use, leadership development, critical thinking skills, etcetera are all part of the greater whole. (A) is wrong because the authors target more than just the alcohol abuse that occurs in some fraternities. This answer is too narrow in scope. (B) is wrong because nowhere in the passage do the authors discuss the growth of the fraternity system on the American college campus today. (C) is wrong because, just like (A), it is too narrow in scope. Alcohol use, leadership development, and cognitive development are *all* part of the larger question of value in relation to the educational mission of the fraternity system on the college campus.

56. D The correct choice is (D) because choices (A),

(B), and (C) are all either cited or implied in order to support statements made throughout the passage.

57. D The correct choice is (D) because although the National Study of Student Learning takes various factors into account in their study, the authors never discuss racial differences in fraternity make-up or how this effects the statistics cited. (A) is wrong because these factors are specifically noted by, and cited by, the authors when discussing the National Study of Student Learning. (B) is wrong because, in paragraph six, the authors do note that alcohol abuse is not the norm at all fraternities. (C) is wrong because, in paragraph six, the authors note that there are some fraternities that stress academics achievement.

58. B The fifth and sixth paragraphs discuss the absence of critical thinking and leadership skills in the fraternity system. The authors specifically note the innate lack of opportunity in the fraternity leadership structure as well as the seeming lack of desire by fraternity members to be involved in outside organizations that may provide these skills. (A) is wrong because, although this statement might be true, it is not mentioned by the authors as a reason for a lack of critical thinking skills. (C) is wrong because this statement was made by the authors in the third paragraph in regard to academic achievement, not leadership or critical thinking skills.

59. D The authors note that fraternities have often paid lip service to the concept of academic achievement within its membership. The authors also mention that there is a large discrepancy between this claim and the reality of the situation. (A) is wrong because paragraph seven specifically states the need for colleges to re-evaluate the relationship between the fraternal system and their educational missions. (B) is wrong because paragraph seven specifically states the need for colleges to examine the political "consequences of trying to change the deeply entrenched fraternity system." (C) is wrong because paragraph eight specifically states "academic performance, intellectual development, and openness to diversity seem to be negatively related to fraternity membership in the first year of college, policies barring first-year students from joining fraternities is essential."

60. D The correct answer is (D) because both faculty supervision and substance abuse counseling would help rectify some of the innate problems noted by the authors. Therefore, the statements (A) and (B) are both steps the authors would consider. (C) is wrong because, although you may assume that this is a logical solution to the problem, the authors never suggest the banning of fraternities from campus as an option.

Materials used in this test section were adapted from the following source(s):

G. Kuh, E. Pascarella, and H. Wechsler, *The Questionable Value of Fraternities.* © 1996 by the Chronicle of Higher Education.

Verbal Reasoning Test Three

Time—85 minutes
Question 1–60

DIRECTIONS: Each of the passages in this test is followed by a set of questions based on the passage's content. After reading each passage, decide on the one best response to each question and mark it on your answer sheet. If you are unsure of an answer, eliminate the choices you know are wrong and choose from the remaining choices. You may refer to the passages while answering the questions.

Passage I (Questions 1–6)

In the famous Harrisburg case of 1971–1972, the defendants—Father Phillip Berrigan and seven other Catholic radicals—were charged with conspiring to raid draft boards, destroy records, and kidnap presidential adviser
5 Henry Kissinger. A team of liberal social scientists, realizing that the highly politicized nature of the case made jury composition an especially crucial factor, volunteered to assist the defense by developing a strategy to effect the selection of a sympathetic jury.

10 The first stage in the project consisted of a telephone survey in which calls were made to 840 randomly selected Harrisburg households to determine the general demographic characteristics of the population. In the project's second stage, the research team interviewed two-fifths of
15 the initial group of 840 in order to pinpoint more exactly their attitudes and prejudices. Respondents were asked about their media contact, faith in the government, prior knowledge of the defendants and their case, and other factors that might bear on their responses as jurors. With the
20 information thus compiled, the sociologists developed a rating system that could be applied to each prospective juror and that, it was hoped, would indicate the attitude he or she would possess going into trial. Certain types—for example, Presbyterians and Episcopalians, the college-
25 educated, and those who had broad contact with the metropolitan news media—were considered potentially hostile to the radical, antiwar defendants; other types, such as African Americans, women, and those with no religious affiliation, were judged more likely to be sympathetic.
30 The defense lawyers were guided by the ratings in their challenges to supposed potentially hostile jurors.

Though the defense was pleased with the initial results, the third and fourth stages of the project—courtroom observation and post-trial follow-up—revealed unfore-
35 seen weaknesses. Most significantly, two jurors rated "likely sympathetic" were the only two who finally held out for the defendants' conviction. In addition, the follow-up study indicated that the jury's deliberations had been influenced as much by the relative weakness of the gov-
40 ernment's case and the unpersuasiveness of its witnesses, as by the predispositions reflected in the initial surveys.

After reviewing the above material, one scholar concluded that it is impossible for researchers to link attributes such as education or religion to social attitudes in a way
45 that yields reliable predictions about actual behavior.

1. The primary purpose of this passage is to:
   A. examine the results of an attempt to apply social science research.
   B. prove the problem-solving relevance of social science methodology.
   C. describe the various methodological procedures of social scientists.
   D. argue that social science research is being exploited for political purposes.

2. The passage suggests that the attempt to profile "sympathetic" jurors failed because of:
   A. the random nature of the telephone survey.
   B. inconsistencies in attitudes and behavior.
   C. the inadequacy of current statistical methods.
   D. haphazard collection of irrelevant demographic information.

3. Which of the following accurately reflects the sequence of steps followed in constructing the profile of a "sympathetic" juror?
   A. Personal interviews, telephone survey, development of a rating system, courtroom observation, post-trial analysis
   B. Development of a rating system, telephone survey, personal interviews, courtroom observation, post-trial analysis
   C. Courtroom observation, development of a rating system, personal interviews, telephone survey, post-trial analysis
   D. Telephone survey, personal interviews, development of a rating system, courtroom observation, post-trial analysis

GO TO THE NEXT PAGE.

4. The passage implies that social scientists made which of the following assumptions prior to the trial?

   A. The news media in Harrisburg supported the radicals.
   B. Individuals are not truthful on surveys of their attitudes.
   C. Religious people are likely to support radical political behavior.
   D. Social science research should be used to achieve political goals.

5. According to the passage, the defendants planned to:

   A. conduct a sit-in.
   B. overthrow the government.
   C. abduct a government official.
   D. vandalize Catholic Church property.

6. According to the profile of "sympathetic" jurors discussed in this passage, which of the following individuals would be least likely to support the radicals?

   A. A poorly educated, irreligious man who ignores the local media
   B. A poorly educated, religious woman who ignores the local media
   C. A highly educated, religious man who avidly consumes local news
   D. A highly educated, irreligious woman who avidly consumes local news

GO TO THE NEXT PAGE.

Passage II (Questions 7–12)

Paleontologists distinguish three major eras in the history of multicellular life: the Paleozoic, Mesozoic, and Cenozoic. The fossil record of this 600-million-year period has traditionally been interpreted as showing continuity and progression; even the unusual extinct organisms are routinely assigned to the phyla occupied by their assumed modern relatives. However, the recent reconsideration of a large group of mainly Paleozoic marine remains, collectively known as the "Problematica," has sparked debate over this practice.

The bizarre banana-shaped *Tullimonstrum* and spiked, spiny *Hallucigenia* are cited by the revisionists as examples of Problematica that cannot be cleanly fit into any modern phylum. These creatures have in fact been deemed morphologically unique enough to warrant phyla of their own. But members of another group of Problematica, the pre-Paleozoic Ediacaran fauna, illustrate the more usual taxonomic practice: they are assigned variously to such phyla as Coelenterata (because of the radial grooves some of them exhibit) or Annelida (because others show bilateral symmetry). Revisionists argue that these classifications reflect superficial morphological similarities while ignoring the fact that Ediacaran fauna utilized a fundamentally different approach to survival from those of their supposed present-day relatives. The Ediacaran fauna carried out gas exchange and absorption of nutrients directly through their external surfaces; this was possible only because of their extremely thin cross-section. Among modern animals, only a few parasites such as tapeworms take this approach, and these creatures are otherwise unlike the Ediacaran fauna. Coelenterates and annelids, on the other hand, have evolved internal organs to provide surface areas for gas exchange and absorption.

The disagreement over the Problematica reflects a more significant breach over the nature of evolutionary selection. Conventional theorists believe that the Cambrian explosion—the yet unexplained appearance of large numbers of multicellular organisms on earth between 570 and 500 million years ago—yielded a few basic phyla: in essence, a large number of organisms that fit into a small number of essentially different "body plans." By the end of the Cambrian, almost all modern animal phyla had evolved. (The plant phyla appeared more slowly.) The remainder of the Paleozoic and the entirety of the Mesozoic and Cenozoic eras were given over to the evolution of a great variety of species using these basic body plans. Extinctions, including those of the Problematica, eliminated species or whole groups of species within these basically viable phyla. The extinction of an entire phylum, such as *Tullimonstrum,* is admitted grudgingly as an exception to the general pattern.

Revisionists interpret the Cambrian explosion as the virtually simultaneous appearance of a much larger number of animal phyla than exists today; each was a separate "experiment" in basic design. Hence, the Problematica are viewed not as unsuccessful variants of viable body plans, but as distinct body plans in their own right. While the Paleozoic seas were filled with large numbers of distinct phyla, the number of species in each phylum was low—often only one or two. In contrast, the Cenozoic seas have a much smaller number of phyla, but many more species—there are at least 20,000 species of fish alone. Hence, the number of marine phyla has fallen, while variation within the surviving phyla has been prodigious.

The revisionists agree with taxonomic traditionalists that modern marine species are products of natural selection, but contend that the selection process eliminated not only particular maladaptive traits, but entire approaches to survival—not only species, but also body plans, and thus entire phyla. The unusual solution to respiration and absorption seen in the Ediacaran fauna, for example, was discarded as a viable alternative for the vast majority of animals at the same time as the Ediacaran fauna themselves were wiped out: given the improbability of duplicating an entire body plan through chance mutation, it was unlikely that this particular approach would ever be tried again. Before the Mesozoic was far advanced, these flawed approaches to survival had been permanently removed from the pool of organisms that would have the opportunity to undergo speciation and evolutionary refinement.

---

7. By inference from the passage, the Problematica:
   A. differed from one another morphologically and in their approach to basic life functions.
   B. had begun to significantly decrease in number by the close of the Mesozoic era.
   C. existed exclusively as marine creatures of the Paleozoic era.
   D. recently have been assigned to their own phylum.

GO TO THE NEXT PAGE.

8. According to the passage, a central difference between the conventional and revisionist interpretations of the fossil record is that:

    A. conventional theorists do not account for the disappearance of Problematica from the late Paleozoic–middle Mesozoic fossil record.
    B. revisionist theorists emphasize the effects of selection for overall design in addition to selection for specific characteristics.
    C. revisionist theorists draw their conclusions from a quantification of the number of species existing in each of the three major eras.
    D. revisionist theorists believe ancient life forms were subject to random and unpredictable evolutionary pressures.

9. Researchers who question conventional paleontologists' conclusions would agree with which of the following statements?

    A. Modern organisms have undergone little change since their initial appearance in the early Paleozoic era.
    B. The depiction of all morphologically unusual life forms as unsuccessful variations upon workable body plans distorts critical patterns of evolution.
    C. Imperfections in the fossil record due to natural phenomena preclude the drawing of any definite conclusions about evolutionary processes.
    D. The Cambrian explosion permanently disrupted the orderly patterns of evolution that had previously existed.

10. According to revisionist paleontologists, no modern species are evolutionary descendents of the *Hallucigenia* because:

    A. the body plan of the *Hallucigenia* was just one of many distinct approaches to survival that arose in the aftermath of the Cambrian explosion.
    B. the organisms arising from the Cambrian explosion became extinct before they could undergo evolution.
    C. the *Hallucigenia* ultimately proved to be unfit in comparison with other species of that phylum and were therefore edged out of their particular niche.
    D. the elimination of the *Hallucigenia* phylum as a result of overall flaws in design implied the extinction of all future variants on that design.

11. It may be inferred that revisionist paleontologists would believe which of the following is true of traditional taxonomic classification?

    A. It reflects the outdated and inaccurate belief that evolution is guided by natural selection.
    B. It imposes constraints upon those who would contest conventional evolutionary theory.
    C. It enables researchers to concentrate on the theoretical rather than the practical aspects of the fossil record.
    D. It is skewed toward phyla containing living representatives.

12. Conventional theorists comparing multicellular life at the beginning of the Cambrian era with that at the beginning of the Cenozoic era would assert that:

    A. the number of phyla increased and the number of species increased.
    B. the number of phyla remained the same and the number of species increased.
    C. the number of phyla decreased and the number of species increased.
    D. the number of phyla decreased and the number of species remained the same.

GO TO THE NEXT PAGE.

Passage III (Questions 13–18)

The use of human subjects in medical experiments has been a troublesome issue for the scientific community, one complicated by the fact that there are really two separate situations in which such research might be appro-
5   priate. Therapeutic experimentation involves the use of new drugs and/or procedures on patients in clinical settings as possible treatments for actual ailments. Nontherapeutic experimentation is conducted upon healthy individuals to determine whether a new treat-
10 ment or substance has undesirable side-effects.

Therapeutic experimentation dates back to the eighteenth century, when the healing effects of bloodletting and castor oil were put to the test against diseases ranging from cholera to pneumonia. The purpose of thera-
15 peutic experimentation is quite clear: to ameliorate an individual's illness. The greatest fear aroused by therapeutic experimentation is that physicians may try new therapies recklessly; many members of the medical community therefore insist that it be undertaken solely
20 with the full consent of the patient, and only after conventional treatments have failed.

Since nontherapeutic experimentation confers no benefit on the subject (at best, participants maintain their current state of health; at worst, their health may seriously
25 deteriorate), it has been more controversial. While the need for nontherapeutic experimentation is now generally accepted, there is still controversy over how best to select or encourage volunteers, given the risk of injury. Money and other enticements have been offered to
30 potential participants, although such inducements generally have been considered unethical. As early as 1721, British critics protested King George's offer of a pardon to condemned prisoners who agreed to submit to variolation (inoculation with infectious smallpox matter) to
35 determine whether subjects would subsequently develop the disease or would instead become immune. It was argued that the prisoners were deprived of a truly free choice, since they faced death sentences if they refused. Commentators have also questioned the propriety of
40 experimenting on medical students, soldiers, and pharmaceutical industry employees, all of whom may be vulnerable to pressure by superiors who may have a vested interest in the project.

The medical community and concerned observers have
45 yet to agree upon the type of individual whose participation in a nontherapeutic experiment could be deemed truly voluntary.

Although those conducting both therapeutic and nontherapeutic experiments have attempted to take precau-
50 tions by pretesting their research on animals and by imposing limits on their field of potential subjects, there remains an inevitable risk for human volunteers. To minimize possible hazards, certain traditional safeguards have been utilized. The so-called "golden rule"
55 of human biomedical research has traditionally mandated that no investigator undertake a project unless he or she would willingly participate in that experiment. In 1929, for example, Dr. Werner Forssman passed a catheter into the right ventricle of his own heart to
60 demonstrate that the procedure was both safe and comfortable. The principle ethical question evoked by the "golden rule" is that a physician's right to experiment on his or her own body does not necessarily entitle the doctor to subject others to the same risk.

65 A second important safeguard has been the securing of an "informed consent" from the volunteer. However, the British Medical Association, among other groups, has questioned whether subjects without a minimal level of scientific or medical knowledge can give a truly
70 informed consent, rather than simply accepting the recommendations of their physicians. The difficult task, faced by all scientists who use human subjects in medical research projects is the dispassionate dissemination of accurate and comprehensible information to potential
75 volunteers.

---

13. According to the passage, reservations have been expressed about all of the following aspects of human biomedical experimentation EXCEPT:

   A. the suitability of the "golden rule" as applied to nonphysicians.
   B. the appropriateness of exposing healthy subjects to risk by testing.
   C. the propriety of recruiting members of the armed forces as volunteers.
   D. the validity of the distinction between therapeutic and nontherapeutic experimentation.

GO TO THE NEXT PAGE.

14. In which of the following ways is therapeutic experimentation different from nontherapeutic experimentation?

    A. It offers volunteers improved health as an incentive.

    B. It cannot be initiated without the consent of the patient's physician.

    C. It is only performed on healthy volunteers.

    D. It has been fully accepted by the medical community, while nontherapeutic experimentation is generally rejected.

15. The variolation of prisoners cited in the passage (lines 31–36) is most similar in principle to which of the following procedures?

    A. Drawing a certain amount of blood from a volunteer with a suspected case of malaria

    B. Inserting a catheter into the heart of a subject experiencing an undetermined cardiac event

    C. Assessing the pain-reducing capacities of a new aspirin

    D. Administering a new sedative and monitoring subjects for allergic reactions

16. On the subject of biomedical experimentation, the scientific community has been:

    A. divided over the necessity of obtaining an informed consent from potential subjects.

    B. more supportive of therapeutic research than of nontherapeutic experiments.

    C. largely opposed to the sentiments expressed by other members of society on this issue.

    D. disillusioned by the government's delayed acceptance of nontherapeutic testing.

17. It may be inferred that the selection of subjects for nontherapeutic research projects is complicated by all of the following EXCEPT that:

    A. potential volunteers usually are unwilling to take part in an experiment which does not offer financial compensation.

    B. potential subjects may be unduly influenced by the opinions of those in relative positions of authority.

    C. researchers and nonscientists who intend to take part in an experiment may have different views as to what constitutes an acceptable level of risk.

    D. potential volunteers often do not have an adequate understanding of a proposed project.

18. The author believes that all scientists who conduct medical experiments involving human volunteers must:

    A. make certain that only people with a background in science or medicine are used as test subjects.

    B. ensure that subjects receive an impartial and intelligible explanation of the project.

    C. refrain from initiating experimental therapy unless conventional treatments have proven ineffectual.

    D. allow research on human subjects only after tests on animals have proved a drug safe.

GO TO THE NEXT PAGE.

Passage IV (Questions 19–24)

The giant panda's isolated existence in a few alpine regions on the periphery of the Tibetan plateau and distinctive black and white markings have made the panda the object of great fascination. While the general public
5 tends to view the panda as a kind of living teddy bear, biologists are not sure how to view this enigmatic species. It defies easy classification. Ever since its discovery in the middle of the 19th century, a controversy has been raging among biologists over the question of
10 the panda's relation to other species.

The discoverer of the giant panda, Armand David, considered the panda a species of bear distinct from any other. Later, biologist Alphonse Milne-Edwards argued that the panda should not be classified as a bear, but
15 should be placed in a distinct family of its own. Over the course of the next 120 years, biologists have alternately placed the giant panda with bears in the *Ursidae* family, with raccoons in the *Procyonidae* family, or in its own *Ailuropodidae* family.

20 Systematists, who classify animal species on the basis of traits, consider the classification of the panda according to whether its traits are "homologous" or merely "analogous" to similar traits in other species. Homologous traits are those which have developed as a result of com-
25 mon ancestry; every species possessing a particular trait is descended from the same ancestor. Every member of the cat family, for instance, has only four toes on its hind feet. The extent to which various species are related is determined by the number of homologous traits they
30 share. The greater the number of homologous traits species share, the closer the relationship among them. Analogous traits, on the other hand, result from convergence, a process whereby species descended from different ancestors develop similar traits due to environmental
35 stimulus. The wings of an eagle and those of a butterfly, for example, perform the same function, but these two species do not share a common ancestry.

Unfortunately, the genetic basis of homologous traits is poorly understood and problems in distinguishing the
40 effects of environment and genes make it difficult to identify analogous relationships. Consequently, such analyses of observed traits have raised more questions regarding the panda's lineage than they have solved. While the giant panda may look like a bear, it also has
45 many traits that bears do not possess. The giant panda, like the red panda (a relation of the raccoon and a mem-

ber of the *Procyonidae* family), is mainly an herbivore, its diet consisting primarily of bamboo. This type of diet has contributed to the development of a more massive
50 head and jaw structure in the giant panda than the typical bear. Giant pandas also have thumbs, which are used to strip leaves from bamboo stalks, while bears do not have a similar digit. Many bears hibernate at certain times of the year, but giant pandas do not. Furthermore,
55 most bears growl or roar, but giant pandas bleat. In terms of chromosome structure, bears have thirty-seven pairs, red pandas have twenty-two pairs, and giant pandas only twenty-one. It is not surprising, then, that emphasis of certain traits to the exclusion of others has made it pos-
60 sible for biologists to argue in support of a variety of different panda classifications.

Tests recently developed to supplement methods of classification based on the observation of traits may help to resolve the issue of the panda's proper classification.
65 These tests are based on the "molecular clock" hypothesis, which contends that the genetic material of populations which are reproductively isolated diverges steadily over time. By examining the genetic material of various species, biologists can determine when they diverged
70 from a common ancestor. Employing a technique known as DNA hybridization, biologists have been able to demonstrate that the giant panda is more closely related to bears than to raccoons. Other methods, including gel electrophoresis, two-dimensional electrophoresis, and
75 immunological surveys, have supported the conclusion that while the giant panda belongs to the *Ursidae* family, its ancestors split from the main *Ursid* line more than fifteen million years ago.

---

19. According to the passage, which of the following is NOT true of homologous traits?

    A. Homologous traits stem from the sharing of a common ancestry.

    B. The degree of relationship among various species can be determined by the number of homologous traits they share.

    C. Homologous traits develop as a result of the process of convergence.

    D. Systematists refer to homologous traits in classifying animals.

GO TO THE NEXT PAGE.

20. By inference from the passage, which of the following most probably represents an analogous trait?

    A. Body hair of humans and body hair of apes
    B. Scales of snakes and skin of humans
    C. Wings of falcons and wings of mosquitos
    D. Thumbs of pandas and digits of raccoons

21. According to the passage, all of the following are methods used in determining relationships among species EXCEPT:

    A. DNA hybridization.
    B. homologous trait analysis.
    C. gel electrophoresis.
    D. NMR spectroscopy.

22. According to the information in the passage, which of the following animals are most closely related?

    A. Four animals that share five homologous traits
    B. Three animals that share five analogous traits
    C. Two animals that share ten homologous traits
    D. Two animals that share ten analogous traits

23. Which of the following best sums up the main idea of the last paragraph?

    A. The giant panda is properly classified as a bear, even though its ancestors split off from the bear family long ago.
    B. Because the giant panda is primarily a plant eater, it deserves to be placed with raccoons and red pandas in the *Procyonidae* family.
    C. Various techniques based on the "molecular clock" hypothesis have not shed any light on the issue of the panda's proper classification.
    D. Biologists are now able to approximate when various species diverged from a common ancestor by examining the genetic material of those species.

24. This passage was most likely written by a:

    A. geologist.
    B. geneticist.
    C. biologist.
    D. chemist.

GO TO THE NEXT PAGE.

Passage V (Questions 25–33)

The term *groupthink* was coined by Irving Janis in 1972 to describe breakdowns in group decision making. Janis claimed that groupthink has led to several disastrous decisions in U.S. foreign policy, such as the Kennedy administration's support for the Bay of Pigs invasion in 1961. According to Janis's hypothesis, groupthink may occur when a highly cohesive group led by a strong leader with a predilection for a specific solution faces a crisis situation. Because individual members fear rejection by the group and desire that the morale of the group remain high, the group excludes outside information, ignores alternative solutions, and may make a decision that, in retrospect, is obviously wrong.

To test groupthink under laboratory conditions, Matie Flowers separated 160 undergraduate students into forty groups of four. Two factors were independently considered in the experiment: style of leadership (open or closed) and group cohesiveness. An open leader was instructed to encourage discussion of all possible solutions and to refrain from offering a solution until each member of the group had expressed his or her opinion. A closed leader was told to state a preferred solution at the beginning of the session and to make clear that the main objective of the group was to arrive at a consensus. In groups defined as having low cohesiveness, the members were strangers, while in groups with high cohesiveness the individuals were acquainted. Each team was presented with the same crisis situation; each member of a team was assigned a role and given a different fact sheet (facts listed depended on the specific role played by the individual).

Individuals led by an open leader offered significantly more solutions than did members of teams with closed leaders. However, cohesiveness had no apparent effect on the number of solutions proposed. Groups with open leaders dealt with significantly more facts in making a decision. Teams with a closed leader mentioned more facts after a decision had been reached than did groups led by an open leader. Cohesiveness had no significant effect on the introduction of facts.

Although some effects of groupthink apparently occurred in the experiment, group cohesiveness was not critical in producing the effects. One likely explanation for this inconsistency suggests that the problem stems from two different conceptions of "high group cohesiveness." Janis had based his concept of group cohesiveness on the behavior of individuals that had worked and socialized together over a long period of time; Flowers, however, grouped individuals who were less intimately acquainted. Thus, the experiment may have failed to simulate the type of high cohesiveness that occurs in real social groups faced by actual crisis situations.

---

25. It can be inferred from the passage that group decision making:

    A. is most successful under a strong leader.
    B. is only successful in highly cohesive groups.
    C. can sometimes lead to disastrous results.
    D. limits the number of possible solutions.

26. According to the passage, the goal of Flowers's experiment was to:

    A. demonstrate that group cohesiveness does not influence groupthink.
    B. contest the theory that groupthink is restricted to crisis situations.
    C. test Janis's hypothesis under laboratory conditions.
    D. prove that groupthink stems from strong leadership styles.

27. The author most likely mentions the 1961 Bay of Pigs invasion (line 5) in order to:

    A. discredit the reputation of the Kennedy administration.
    B. illustrate the long-term effects of policy decisions.
    C. provide an example of the effects of groupthink in a crisis situation.
    D. show that poor decisions are made in crisis situations.

28. Which of the following factors did Flowers attempt to vary in her groupthink experiment?

    I. Style of group leadership
    II. Severity of crises encountered by groups
    III. Degree of cohesion among group members

    A. I only
    B. I and III only
    C. II and III only
    D. I, II, and III

GO TO THE NEXT PAGE.

29. Which of the following would most *weaken* Janis's groupthink hypothesis?

   A. A study that concludes individuals fear being rejected by the group more than making a wrong decision

   B. An experiment that suggests an open leadership style rarely results in faulty decision-making

   C. A theory that implies groupthink is common to government and military organizations

   D. A study that concludes leaders rarely approach a crisis with a solution in mind

30. Which of the following best expresses the author's conclusions regarding the Flowers experiment?

   A. Because group cohesiveness did not influence groupthink, Janis's theory is clearly false.

   B. Because leadership style seems to affect group decision-making processes, Janis's theory is obviously true.

   C. Since group cohesiveness did not seem to affect group decision-making processes, Janis's theory may be true only under certain conditions.

   D. Since group cohesiveness had no significant effect on groupthink, it should not be considered a factor in Janis's schema.

31. According to the passage, the "inconsistency" in research findings, referred to in line 44, probably stems from the fact that:

   A. groups led by closed leaders in Janis's study dealt with facts after, not before, decisions were made.

   B. Flowers believed that strong leadership style was the prime cause of groupthink, while Janis emphasized the role of group cohesiveness.

   C. despite Flowers's expectations, groups with open leaders offered fewer solutions than did those with closed leaders.

   D. Flowers and Janis based their studies on varying concepts of group cohesiveness.

32. This passage was most likely excerpted from:

   A. a lecture to government leaders.

   B. a college-level psychology textbook.

   C. a list of effective management guidelines.

   D. an entry in an encyclopedia.

33. If the passage were to continue, the next topic the author would discuss would probably be:

   A. the likely prospect of groupthink occurring under contemporary conditions.

   B. another possible explanation for Flowers's failure to reproduce all the effects of groupthink.

   C. a second experiment attempting to identify the nature of the relationship between cohesiveness and leadership styles.

   D. other examples of situations in which groupthink led to disastrous foreign policy decisions.

GO TO THE NEXT PAGE.

Passage VI (Questions 34–38)

Kuru, a progressive disorder of the central nervous system, provides an example of how epidemiology, combined with other medical disciplines, can elucidate the cause and means of transmission of a particular disease.
5 Kuru was first discovered by Western medicine in 1956, among Fore-speaking people living in a small mountainous area of Australian New Guinea; outside this region the disease remains unknown. Initial manifestations of kuru include lack of coordination of skilled
10 movements and unprovoked outbursts of giggling. Later the victim develops progressive ataxia (failure of muscular coordination), speech problems, incontinence, and athetosis (involuntary writhing of hands and feet). At no time during the course of the disease is cognitive func-
15 tioning impaired. Degeneration occurs over the course of about nine months and is ultimately fatal. Among those villages identified as foci of kuru, it often accounted for over fifty percent of deaths past infancy; its significance was compounded by the fact that the second
20 most frequent cause of death was reciprocal murders of sorcerers suspected of inflicting kuru on their enemies.

Initial proposals as to the cause of the disease ranged over a gamut of infectious, metabolic, environmental, and sociological variables. To narrow the possibilities,
25 extensive epidemiological studies were undertaken.

First, government censuses and field surveys were used to map the region in which kuru flourished.

Since several tribes in adjacent, environmentally similar regions, with stone-age cultures comparable to that of
30 the Fore people, were kuru free, environmental and sociological factors were discounted as causes of the disease.

The epidemiologists next attempted to learn whether the disease had a hereditary basis by using a linguistic
35 analysis of local dialects to indirectly determine the common or differing ancestries of villages in the region. On the assumption that all dialects in the region sprang from a single original language, tribes with the most similar dialects were presumed to have branched from
40 one another most recently, and so to have more closely related gene pools. Data revealed that hardly anyone but Fore speakers contracted kuru, and that the exceptions all had recent Fore ancestors by intermarriage. Thus, a genetic element is probable in the etiology of kuru.

45 Nevertheless, genetic factors were not necessarily the primary cause of the disease. Assuming a toxic, bacteriologic, or viral involvement, laboratory workers attempted to isolate the unknown agent by inoculating chicks and mice with suspensions of tissue of human kuru
50 patients. The first experiments yielded negative results; however, a later assay using monkeys and chimpanzees as recipients was successful. The isolated causative agent was identified as a virus with an incubation period of several years or longer. (It has since been suggested that
55 the agent may be a prion, a minute particle containing no nucleic acids that is thought to cause other CNS disorders; but this is speculative.)

Apparently kuru is a viral disease in which a genetic predisposition determines susceptibility. The epidemio-
60 logical investigators next turned to the question of how the virus is transmitted from victim to victim. Early researchers had suspected that the Fore custom of ritual ancestor cannibalism might figure in the disease cycle, but the theory had been set aside because neighboring
65 cannibal tribes did not contract kuru. However, a study of the kuru population showed that only women and children contracted the disease, while a separate study of the Fore cannibal practices revealed that if men participated at all, they left the brains to be eaten by the
70 women and children. This suggested that consumption of infected human brains is important in the transmission of kuru, a hypothesis strengthened by the fact that kuru is most successfully transferred experimentally in suspensions of infected brain tissue.

75 The conclusion that kuru is spread through cannibalism is further strengthened by the decline of the disease following the banning of cannibal practices by the Australian government in 1957. In subsequent years, the incidence of kuru dropped dramatically among children. More
80 slowly, incidence in the adult population followed suit. Although no cure for the disease has ever been found, today kuru exists only in a few scattered cases and in laboratories where it has been preserved for scientific study.

---

34. One of the first signs of kuru onset might be:

    A. difficulty in tying a knot.
    B. impairment of social judgment.
    C. general lack of coordination.
    D. difficulty in remembering a story.

GO TO THE NEXT PAGE.

35. Investigators compared kuru-affected and kuru-free areas in an attempt to find all of the following EXCEPT:

    A. sociological differences between tribes.

    B. physiological differences between the inhabitants.

    C. environmental differences between the regions.

    D. linguistic differences among dialects spoken in the regions.

36. One can infer from the passage that the original attempts to isolate an infectious agent in kuru failed because:

    A. early techniques were not sophisticated enough.

    B. researchers were not certain whether to look for a toxic, bacterial, or viral agent.

    C. kuru is a genetically based disease.

    D. original animal models were not sufficiently similar to actual human hosts.

37. By inference from the passage, why did neighboring tribes not contract the disease?

    A. They did not practice cannibalism.

    B. They did not have contact with infected villages.

    C. Both genetic predisposition and infection are needed to contract kuru.

    D. No inference can be drawn from the information presented.

38. After cannibalism was banned, kuru incidence dropped more rapidly in children than in adults. By inference, this might be because:

    A. adults continued to practice cannibalism in secret.

    B. cumulative exposure over many years made adults more susceptible to the virus.

    C. since kuru is a long-term chronic disease, many children who contract it will be adults before the disease is fatal.

    D. because of kuru's long incubation period, many who were infected before 1957 did not show symptoms for years.

GO TO THE NEXT PAGE.

Passage VII (Questions 39–45)

Two important concepts of social philosophy are utilitarianism, which aims to calculate and institute the greatest good for the greatest number, not necessarily excepting the possibility of sacrifice and suffering on the part of a minority; and the notion of the social contract, which states that a society exists by the implicit agreement of all its citizens, and on that basis owes certain obligations to them. These two concepts are contrasting but not necessarily contradictory; nonetheless one or another has often enjoyed ascendancy since their initial formulations by Bentham and Locke, respectively. In this century utilitarianism has long been a *de facto* orthodoxy among political philosophers. The 1971 publication of John Rawls's *A Theory of Justice,* however, gave the contractarian view a needed and welcome restatement.

Since they will determine the "clauses" of the social contract, the nature and needs of the parties must be carefully considered. Rather than adopt an implausible Rousseauean vision of uncorrupted, harmonious "natural man," the new contractarians postulate a group of rational men and women gathered for the purpose of defining a concept of justice that will guide their affairs. They further assume that these people make their decisions behind a veil of ignorance, that is, they are temporarily totally unaware of their position in society—their race, their gender, their place in the social order. Yet the principles at which they arrive will bind them once the veil is lifted.

Starting from this original position it can be logically demonstrated that rational beings would arrive at a decision ensuring the maximum possible justice and liberty for even the least privileged member of society. For who would propose a utilitarian view of justice and risk slavery when the veil was lifted? Would the knowledge that society as a whole derived a greater benefit console him or her in servitude?

Two basic principles would most likely emerge from this hypothetical conclave. First, all would have access to the greatest degree of liberty compatible with a similar liberty for all other members of society. For example, freedom of speech thus would be inviolable, whereas the utilitarian could easily justify its abridgment for a greater social good. Second, social and economic inequality, insofar as they are inevitable, would be arranged such that they inhered in offices and stations available to all and such that whatever benefits accrue from a necessary evil would be distributed to everyone's advantage. Injustice, then, is defined as an unequal distribution of good things, with liberty first among them.

While it can be and has been argued that the blind choosers envisioned by the new contractarians might well decide to gamble on the outcome of the social order, such arguments are ultimately lacking in interest. The point of the contractarian view does not lie in what real people "would" do in an admittedly impossible situation. Rather, it is to provide an abstract model that is intuitively satisfactory and a machinery for making ethical decisions.

---

39. The primary purpose of the passage is to:

A. outline and defend a contractarian view of justice.

B. propose a radical solution to social problems.

C. compare the utilitarian and contractarian theories of justice.

D. explore the political theory of John Rawls.

40. According to the passage, people considering justice behind a "veil of ignorance" (line 25) would:

A. select a principle favoring the group they would belong to when the veil was lifted.

B. select a principle that would be fair to everyone regardless of birth and status.

C. be unable to agree on a single principle.

D. demand an end to social and political inequality.

41. By inference from the passage, utilitarianism and contractarianism necessarily:

A. conflict with each other.

B. agree on major points.

C. start from similar ideas of human nature.

D. involve differing notions of the desirable society.

GO TO THE NEXT PAGE.

42. Assume that an aged parent is being artificially kept alive, causing the family financial and emotional hardships. The passage implies that a utilitarian would most likely respond to this situation by:

    A. balancing the potential burdens on the family against the burdens to society.
    B. arguing that the parent, as a member of the "contracting" unit, had a right to an equal voice in the decision.
    C. keeping the parent alive only if doing so was beneficial to society as a whole.
    D. upholding the parent's right to life against any potential lessening of the family's hardship.

43. Which of the following is an assumption of the contractarian model?

    A. The decision makers act without any knowledge of the consequences.
    B. All members of the contracting group will place a high value on personal liberty.
    C. Justice can only be secured by ensuring that all positions have equal power and status.
    D. The contracting parties will seek to safeguard their liberties at the expense of the rights of others.

44. By inference from the passage, a party to the social contract who decided "to gamble on the outcome of the social order" (lines 53–54) would select a principle of justice:

    A. allowing unequal access to liberty and other social goods.
    B. based on a Rousseauistic vision of humanity.
    C. based on the greatest possible equalization of both personal freedom and material circumstances.
    D. benefiting the gambler in his or her future life.

45. Which of the following would a "new contractarian" regard as an absolute right that must not be abridged?

    A. Personal liberty
    B. Social equality
    C. Economic equality
    D. Racial equality

GO TO THE NEXT PAGE.

Passage VIII (Questions 46–52)

Because the length and amino acid sequences of proteins are infinitely variable, an infinite number of proteins are theoretically possible. Nonetheless, we can describe all proteins by a relatively small number of
5 characteristics, and on that basis separate—both conceptually and physically—any one protein from all the rest.

Of the numerous techniques invented for separating proteins according to size, perhaps the simplest is dialysis.
10 In dialysis a membranous bag with microscopic pores of a defined size is filled with a solution of proteins including the one to be purified. Proteins smaller than the pore diameter will escape; all others will be retained in the bag. Thus, selecting a bag with the right pore size is
15 extremely important. This technique cannot be used to separate the target protein from larger molecules, since all escaping proteins must be discarded.

A technique that can isolate a target protein from both bigger and smaller molecules is gel filtration chro-
20 matography. The protein mixture is passed through a column filled with tiny beads containing microscopic pores. Larger proteins cannot enter the pores, and drop straight to the bottom of the column. Smaller proteins, on the other hand, wind their way in and out of the pores
25 as through a maze, and reach the bottom more slowly. By collecting the effluent in small fractions, one can recover samples containing a single protein of a precise molecular size.

Proteins also may be separated by charge. One of the
30 best techniques for achieving this is ion exchange chromatography. This technique uses a column similar to the one used in gel filtration chromatography, but instead of pores, the beads have either positive or negative charges projecting from their surfaces. If a protein has the oppo-
35 site charge it will stick to the column; otherwise it will flow through without sticking. Proteins that stick can then be washed off by flushing with a salt solution. More than one protein may adhere in a given sample, but even these can be separated, since one protein will
40 adhere more strongly than another and will require a higher concentration of salt in order to wash off.

Gel electrophoresis is a technique to purify protein molecules on the basis of either size or charge. An electric field drives charged proteins through a polymerized
45 matrix, a sort of molecular sieve. Proteins with different overall charges migrate at different rates, and are isolated accordingly. An alternative approach uses detergent to coat each protein with an overwhelming number of charges. Since each protein's native charge is compara-
50 tively negligible, all proteins in the sample will have the same charge density, and will separate strictly by size as they pass through the matrix. Gel electrophoresis is effective only for relatively small amounts of protein, making it an analytical tool more than a preparatory one.

55 Another characteristic of proteins—really a consequence of size and weight—is density. Density gradient centrifugation is the technique of choice for separating proteins according to this characteristic. The protein mixture is layered atop a test tube filled with a density
60 gradient of sucrose solution, ranging from densest at the bottom to least dense at the top. Centrifugation drives each protein to its exact level of neutral buoyancy, whence it can easily be retrieved.

---

46. According to the passage, size is a factor in all of the following separation techniques EXCEPT:

   A. dialysis.
   B. gel filtration chromatography.
   C. ion exchange chromatography.
   D. density gradient centrifugation.

47. A solution contains four different proteins with the following characteristics: Protein W is 440 amino acids long and has an overall charge of (–2); Protein X is 120 amino acids long and has an overall charge of (+2); Proteins Y and Z are both 220 amino acids long and each has an overall charge of (+2). Which of the following series of operations represents the best method of isolating Protein Z?

   A. Dialysis, ion exchange chromatography, density gradient chromatography
   B. Dialysis, ion exchange chromatography, gel filtration chromatography
   C. Gel filtration chromatography, ion exchange chromatography, gel electrophoresis
   D. Ion exchange chromatography, electric field gel electrophoresis, density gradient centrifugation

GO TO THE NEXT PAGE.

48. According to the information in the passage, the best technique for separating large quantities of proteins of equal but opposite charge would be:

    A. to pass the protein solution through a membranous bag with microscopic pores.

    B. to pass the protein solution through a column of beads containing microscopic pores.

    C. to pass the protein solution through a column of beads that have both positive and negative charges on them.

    D. to pass the protein solution through a column of beads that have only positive or negative charges on them.

49. In eluting proteins Q and R from a single ion exchange column, protein Q is found to wash off with a 0.5 M K^+Cl^- solution, while protein R washes off at a K^+Cl^- concentration of 1 M. It is likely that:

    A. Q is more highly charged than R.

    B. R is more highly charged than Q.

    C. both proteins are positively charged.

    D. both proteins are negatively charged.

50. The technique of dialysis is most analogous to which of the following?

    A. Lighter gold nuggets spin to the outer rim of a panning plate as the plate is rotated quickly.

    B. Pebbles fall through the holes in a sifting pan as gold nuggets are caught in it.

    C. Pebbles and gold nuggets both fall through the holes in a sifting pan.

    D. Negatively charged gold nuggets sink to the bottom of a positively charged metal pan.

51. The purpose of this passage is to:

    A. compare techniques of protein separation based on size to techniques based on charge.

    B. explain why gel electrophoresis is more an analytical than a preparatory tool.

    C. establish that dialysis is the simplest technique for separating proteins according to size.

    D. discuss various techniques of protein separation.

52. According to the passage, which of the following is true of gel electrophoresis?

    I. It is useful in separating proteins on a size basis.

    II. It is helpful in preparing large amounts of protein.

    III. It can accomplish results similar to those of ion exchange chromatography.

    A. I only

    B. II only

    C. I and III only

    D. II and III only

GO TO THE NEXT PAGE.

Passage IX (Questions 53–60)

"When we abolished the punishment for treason that you should be hanged and then cut down while still alive, then disemboweled while still alive, then quartered, we did not abolish that punishment because we sympathized with traitors, but because we took the view that this was a punishment no longer consistent with our self respect."

These words, spoken by Lord Chancellor during the 1965 death penalty abolition debates in the British Parliament, illustrate the feeling of most individuals opposed to capital punishment. It's not sympathy towards the murderer that we feel; indeed most of us feel a great deal of anger and revulsion towards murderers and their actions. Our objection is that the death penalty is a complete renunciation of all that is embodied in our concept of humanity. Or more simply put, executions degrade us all.

In today's society, the execution process is far removed from most individual citizens. We may, or may not, be aware of the criminal acts that put an individual on death row—and even then usually only through sensationalized press accounts—but very few of us know of the human being whom society has condemned to death. And even fewer of us have witnessed, or will ever witness, an actual execution. They are carried out in the middle of the night, in the dark, away from us all, to hide what they really are—a barbaric punishment symbolic of our less civilized past. The public is kept as far away as possible from the whole process to keep them from seeing that human beings—real flesh and blood, real people—are being put to death. This deliberate dehumanization of the whole process makes it into "something government does," which in turn allows us to avoid individual responsibility for the consequences of such actions. That is the only way that any state or government can continue with executions without the public's demanding their eradication.

There are acceptable alternatives to capital punishment that are more in line with the values of our supposedly enlightened and humanistic society. The state is supposed to be the pillar of our ideals, and its institutions should emulate the best values of our society. Are not the greatest of these values our compassion, our concern for human rights, and our capacity for mercy? By continuing to conduct executions, aren't we undermining the very foundations of our greatness? As the

Zimbabwean poet Chenjerai Hove wrote: "The death penalty is abominable, as abominable as the crime itself. Our state must be based on love, not hatred and victimization. Our penal code must be based on rehabilitation rather than annihilation: For no legal order can sustain itself unless it reflects an underlying moral order of society."

---

53. According to the author, all of the following statements could be used to support the elimination of the death penalty EXCEPT:

A. Betrayal of one's government does not warrant execution as this brings the government to a level lower than that of the traitor.
B. Rather than be eliminated, murderers need to be assessed and recuperated through government judicial programs.
C. The death penalty violates essential mandates set down in Judeo-Christian law.
D. The modern concept of humanity does not encompass the justification of murder.

54. If another paragraph were to be added to the passage by the author, which of the following would most likely be included in it?

A. Specific details of how executions are carried out.
B. A list of alternatives to capital punishment.
C. A series of quotations from death penalty supporters.
D. Discussions on human rights issues.

GO TO THE NEXT PAGE.

55. Which of the following, if found to be true, would most weaken the author's argument?

    A. Lord Chancellor was a firm supporter of capital punishment.
    B. Most executions are actually conducted in the middle of the day.
    C. Most supporters of capital punishment are also against abortion.
    D. The majority of people feel that a convicted murderer is no longer a part of humanity.

56. The author mentions a speech made by Chenjerai Hove to show that:

    A. more developed countries than the United States have abolished capital punishment.
    B. there are many supporters of executions.
    C. our state must be based on love.
    D. our laws must be changed to provide alternatives to executions.

57. Which of the following arguments would be least likely to be used by an opponent of the author's critics?

    A. Executions are unrealistically capital intensive.
    B. Capital punishment has been proven over time to deter potential criminals from committing acts of violence.
    C. Often, inmates on death row have been wrongly convicted of crimes.
    D. People convicted of treason should be disemboweled while still alive.

58. Which one of the following best describes the tone of the author's argument?

    A. angry and militant
    B. accusatory and pompous
    C. passive and fearful
    D. prescriptive and judgmental

59. Which one of the following is not used by the author to support his point of view?

    A. A speech made during a British Parliament debate
    B. An appeal to the reader's sense of morality
    C. A list of alternatives to capital punishment
    D. The feelings of an African poet

60. It can be inferred from this passage that:

    A. many societies have used the death penalty for punishment in the past.
    B. the U.S. government continues to punish treason with death.
    C. capital punishment is no longer practiced in Zimbabwe.
    D. several media networks broadcast executions live on a pay-per-view basis.

STOP. If you finish before time is called, check your work. You may go back to any question in this test booklet.

ANSWER KEY
VERBAL REASONING TEST 3

1. A	18. B	35. B	52. C
2. B	19. C	36. D	53. C
3. D	20. C	37. C	54. B
4. D	21. D	38. D	55. D
5. C	22. C	39. A	56. D
6. C	23. A	40. B	57. B
7. A	24. C	41. D	58. D
8. B	25. C	42. C	59. C
9. B	26. C	43. B	60. A
10. D	27. C	44. A	
11. D	28. B	45. D	
12. A	29. D	46. C	
13. D	30. C	47. A	
14. A	31. D	48. D	
15. D	32. B	49. B	
16. B	33. B	50. B	
17. A	34. A	51. D	

EXPLANATIONS

Questions 1–6: JURORS

PASSAGE I

Topic: Harrisburg Case

Scope: Jury Selection

Purpose: To discuss the limitations of social science applications with respect to jury selection.

Passage Map

¶1: Harrisburg case: social scientists wish to select sympathetic jury

¶2: Telephone survey to develop rating system

¶3: Jury selection system didn't really work

¶4: One scholar concludes it is impossible to predict jury behavior based on the attributes used

Questions:

1. A The first three paragraphs of this passage describe an application of social science, while the last paragraph assesses its success. So, the primary purpose of this passage is to examine the outcome of an attempt to apply social science research (A) to a "real-life" problem. Choice (B) *contradicts* the thrust of the passage. Contrary to proving that social science methodology is relevant to practical problem solving, this passage suggests its applications may be limited. This passage discusses only *some* of the methodological procedures of social scientists and even those aspects of methodology discussed are *details* supporting the larg-

er discussion regarding the application of *some* procedures, so discussing the various methodological procedures of social scientists (C) is not the main purpose of the passage. Nothing in the content or tone of the passage suggests that the author feels social science research is being "exploited" for political ends (D). Of course, the whole passage implies that social science may be applied toward political ends, but "exploitation" would suggest a stronger point—one that the author himself does not make.

2. B The fourth paragraph suggests that the attempt to profile "sympathetic" jurors failed because social scientists are not able to link personal attributes to social attitudes in a way that could yield accurate predictions about behavior (B). The social scientists did carry out a random telephone survey—standard practice in social science and crucial in deriving a representative sample but nothing in the passage suggests that this had anything to do with the failure to profile "sympathetic" jurors, so (A) is wrong. The passage does not state or suggest anything about the inadequacy of current statistical methods (C). And there is no suggestion that the demographic data collected was irrelevant to the problem or was collected in a haphazard way (D).

3. D This detail question concerns the correct sequence of steps followed in constructing a profile of a "sympathetic" juror. The sequence of steps is discussed in the second and third paragraphs of the passage: telephone survey; personal interviews; construction of a rating system to determine what types of individuals would be sympathetic to the defendants; observation of the application of the rating system to prospective jurors in the courtroom; and finally, post-trial analysis to determine whether or not the rating system for picking out "sympathetic" individuals was useful and accurate. (D) has these steps in the proper order and is the correct answer. Correct choice (D) logically eliminates choices (A), (B), and (C), which have have steps ordered in ways that *contradict* information in the passage.

4. D The fact that the liberal social scientists put their research skills at the disposal of the defendants' attorneys indicates that these social scientists felt social science research should be used to achieve political goals (D)—in this case, exonerating radical political activists. Choices (A) and (C) *contradict* information contained in the second paragraph, which implies that the social scientists believed the local news media were *against* the radicals and clearly states that sociologists believed religious people would be *against* the radicals. The fact that the social scientists used attitude surveys to gather information and based conclusions on that information suggests that they trusted people would be truthful on such surveys, so choice (B) is wrong.

5. C The first sentence of the first paragraph tells us that the defendants planned to abduct Henry Kissinger, a government official (C). The passage does not say anything about a planned sit-in (A). Nowhere in the passage is there any indication that the defendants planned to overthrow the government (B). And choice (D) is wrong because the passage says nothing about plans to vandalize Catholic Church property. The passage merely mentions, in the opening sentence, that the Harrisburg defendants were Catholic radicals.

6. C This question asks you to decide which individual would be *least* likely to support the radicals, in terms of the profile of "sympathetic" jurors developed by the social scientists. According to the second paragraph, the social scientists believed that those who are men, highly educated, religious, and attentive to the local media would be least likely to support the radicals, so choice (C) is our answer. The individual in choice (A) has three qualities that might make him inclined to *support* the radicals—he is poorly educated, irreligious, and inattentive to the local media. The individual in choice (B) also has three qualities that might make her inclined to *support* the radicals—her gender, her poor education, and her inattentiveness to the local media. The individual in choice (D), too, has qualities that approximate the profile of a "sympathetic" juror—her gender and her lack of religious belief. In other words, the individuals described in choices (A), (B), and (D) approximate the profile of jurors who might support the radicals, while the individual described in choice (C) does not.

Questions 7–12: PROBLEMATICA

PASSAGE II

Topic: Problematica

Scope: Taxonomy of Problematica

Purpose: To discuss how the disagreement between conventional theorists and revisionists regarding Problematica reveals a greater disagreement over the nature of evolutionary selection.

Passage Map

¶1: Recent reconsideration of Palezoic marine remains sparked debate of fossil record interpretation

¶2: Revisionists argue that Problematica cannot be fit into any modern phylum

¶3: Conventional theorists' theory of evolutionary selection

¶4: Revisionists theory of evolutionary selection

¶5: Revisionists believe entire phyla (and thus body plans) were eliminated

Questions:

7. A See paragraph two. We know that *Tullimonstrum* (Latin for the Tully Monster, named after its discoverer) and the *Hallucigenia* are assigned their own distinct phyla, while the Ediacaran fauna belong either in a new phylum or phyla (revisionist view) or in one of two modern phyla (conventional view). Thus the three examples of Problematica discussed in the passage all belong in different phyla and are morphologically distinct. In addition, the Ediacaran fauna had an approach to basic life functions distinct from that of nearly all modern animals; by inference it was also distinct from that of *Tullimonstrum* and the *Hallucigenia,* since these animals are described as unusual only in morphology. All this adds up to what is stated in (A). (B) wrongly implies that the Problematica began declining sometime during the Mesozoic; the last sentence of the passage tells us they were gone by the early part of that era. (C), however, goes wrong in the opposite direction: paragraph one describes the Problematica as "mainly" Paleozoic, but the Ediacaran fauna were pre-Paleozoic (paragraph two) and some Problematica survived until the early Mesozoic (last paragraph). (D) implies that all Problematica belong to one phylum; neither revisionists nor conventional theorists think this.

8. B The major difference between the conventional and revisionist theories is that advocates of the former argue that natural selection acted upon each phylum to eliminate some of its "branches"—species—but the phylum itself, with its particular body design, was retained among those species that did survive. (As the last sentence of paragraph three notes, exceptions are admitted grudgingly.) Revisionists, however, take the idea of natural selection further to assert that not only species and particular traits were likely to be eliminated, but also entire approaches to survival (sentence 1 of paragraph five). Therefore, a great many early phyla never made it past the Paleozoic but were instead subject to rapid extinction (B). While there is no direct reference to a disappearance of Problematica from the late Paleozoic–middle Mesozoic fossil record (A), it may be inferred that revisionists base their argument on just such evidence (see last sentence of paragraph five). But this does not mean conventional theorists do not take the post-Paleozoic fossil record into account; they may simply interpret it differently. (C) is incorrect for similar reasons; the revisionists apparently have studied calculations of the number of phyla and species existing in the various eras but the same may be true for conventional theorists. (C) is also a distortion: the comparison of numbers of species is corroborating evidence not the basis of the revisionists' conclusions. It is noted in the passage only that revisionists believe ancient life forms were subject to evolutionary pressures on the basis of overall design and specific characteristics; whether these pressures are viewed as "random and unpredictable" is not specified (D).

9. B Keep in mind that the correct statement not only will be true but should also pinpoint a divergence between conventional and revisionist views. (B) is based on the difference between the conventional view, expressed in paragraph three, and the revisionist view as described especially in sentence two of paragraph four. Conventional theorists try to fit the Problematica into known phyla, adopting any other view only "grudgingly"; they regarded extinctions as involving" species or . . . groups of species within . . . basically viable phyla." Revisionists believe that the Problematica, at least, are *themselves* unsuccessful phyla. On this basis, they argue that natural selection operated upon entire approaches to survival as well as upon particular aspects of each approach. This implies that the conventional theorists distort a major aspect of natural selection. No one holds the view described in (A); despite disagreeing on the significance of the Problematica, everyone agrees that most extant animal phyla had evolved during the Cambrian and that enormous diversification subsequently took place within those phyla (end of paragraph four). The implication in (C) that the fossil record is incomplete seems (and is) valid, but the stated conclusion does not follow logically; indeed, revisionists themselves do draw conclusions from the fossil record. Nothing is suggested in the passage about how revisionists (or anyone else) would view evolution before the Cambrian explosion (D).

10. D Although choice (A) is a true statement, it does not by itself answer the question. That the *Hallucigenia* comprised but one of many post-Cambrian phyla does not explain why they did not undergo evolution and speciation. Revisionist paleontologists would argue that the *Hallucigenia* and other Paleozoic creatures represented an entire approach to survival, one eliminated by processes of natural selection in a relatively brief period of time. The extinction of the entire phylum inherently meant the extinction of all possible variations upon that design, i.e., species (D). (The discussion of this point in the last paragraph specifically concerns the Ediacaran fauna, but clearly applies to the *Hallucigenia* as well.) (B) is too broad. Revisionists believe many organisms arising from the Cambrian explosion did evolve and were the ancestors of modern species, as noted in the first sentence of paragraph five. As with some of the choices to an earlier question, (C) depicts the *Hallucigenia* as one of perhaps a number of species belonging to a particular phylum. But in fact, the revisionists and conventional theorists agree that the Hallucigenia occupy their own phylum (see sentence two of paragraph two).

11. D Revisionist paleontologists believe the traditional system of taxonomic classification reflects the prejudice that all fossils may be grouped within current taxonomic categories. The system therefore is structured around a classification of present-day life forms—into which, the revisionists argue, some extinct forms fit poorly, if at all (D). The revisionists do not dismiss natural selection but instead view it as a mechanism that eliminated entire categories of organisms as well as separate species (A). (B) is never suggested in the passage; besides, the revisionists themselves, by devising their own theory, clearly have overdone any "constraints" imposed by the traditional system of classification. The distinction in (C) is not suggested in the passage, nor is it clear that either approach would be more theoretical than the other.

12. A Paragraph three states: "By the end of the Cambrian, *almost* all modern animal phyla had evolved. (The plant phyla appeared more slowly.)" Since the conventional theory holds that few if any ancient phyla have become extinct, as discussed extensively in earlier explanations, the implication is that more phyla and species were living at the beginning of recent (Cenozoic) times than at the beginning of the Cambrian (A). The same reasoning rules out choice (B). (C) is a revisionist and not a conventional conclusion (see the last sentence of paragraph four). Both revisionists and conventional theorists, regardless of any disagreement over the number of phyla, agree that the number of *species* has increased since the beginning of the Cambrian (D).

Questions 13–18:
HUMAN SUBJECTS

PASSAGE III

Topic: Biomedical Research

Scope: Use of human subjects in research

Purpose: To explain the difficulties of using human subjects in medical experiments.

Passage Map
¶1: Therapeutic experimentation vs. nontherapeutic experimentation

¶2: Therapeutic experimentation history

¶3: Problems with nontherapeutic experimentation

¶4: Definition of truly voluntary needed but not yet agreed to

¶5: Golden Rule of research

¶6: Informed consent

Questions:
13. D The distinction between therapeutic and nontherapeutic experimentation is discussed in paragraph one. There is nothing in the passage to indicate that that distinction has been questioned. The "golden rule" (A) states essentially that physicians advocating human

experimentation should be willing to do unto themselves as they would do unto others; but the last sentence of paragraph four questions whether it is appropriate for a physician to expose test subjects to certain risks even if the doctor is willing to face the same risks. (B) refers to the basic issue of the acceptability of nontherapeutic experimentation, which "has been more controversial" than therapeutic experimentation (paragraph three). (C) is mentioned in the next-to-last sentence of paragraph three.

14. A The purpose of therapeutic experimentation is to "ameliorate an individual's illness" (second sentence of paragraph two); volunteers therefore may be rewarded with their own improved health. But according to sentence one of paragraph three, non-therapeutic experimentation lacks this inherent incentive. (B) is incorrect because the only mention of "permission" concerns the patient's right to approve or reject a research proposal; the physician's role here is not elaborated. (C) is true of non-therapeutic research and not true of therapeutic experimentation (paragraph one). (D) exaggerates a point stated correctly by choice (B) of question 16: the medical community is more supportive of therapeutic research, but such research has *not* been "fully accepted" (paragraph two), nor has nontherapeutic testing been "generally rejected." Both are accepted to some degree but involve unresolved issues.

15. D See paragraph three. The variolation experiment involved inoculating volunteers with infectious smallpox matter to determine whether they acquired immunity. It was thus a *nontherapeutic* experiment; participants would either maintain their health by not developing smallpox, or contract the disease. The only choice that discusses a nontherapeutic experiment, and is thus similar in principle to variolation, is (D). Testing for allergic reactions to a new drug would be a typical nontherapeutic research project; as with variolation, subjects risk their present state of health by taking part in the experiment. Choices (A) and (B) involve subjects with actual health problems, and so are dissimilar to the nontherapeutic principles underlying variolation. (C) is quite vague and may not even involve human experimentation.

16. B According to paragraph two, therapeutic research dates back to the eighteenth century, its "purpose is clear," and the only serious reservation concerns the behavior of the researchers. Nontherapeutic research, however, "has been more controversial" because of limited or unethical incentives, uncertainty over volunteers, and similar questions (paragraph three). There is no mention of a division in the medical community over the *necessity* of informed consent (A); the argument focuses on whether a truly informed consent can be *obtained* from people with no background in science or medicine (sentence two of paragraph five). The sentiments of other sectors of society toward biomedical experimentation are not mentioned, so there is no basis

for (C); nor does the passage describe the scientific community's attitudes towards governments (D).

17. A See paragraph three. Enticements such as money, prison reprieves, and the approval of superiors have all been offered to potential subjects in nontherapeutic experiments. Apparently financial compensation is not the only or most frequent incentive, making (A) an inaccurate statement, and thus the correct choice. According to sentence six of paragraph three, several groups of people may be vulnerable to persuasive tactics on the part of superiors (B). The last sentence of paragraph four implies that the participating doctor's idea of an acceptable risk may be significantly different from the volunteers' ideas (C). (D) paraphrases sentence two of paragraph five.

18. B The author states a personal belief only in the last sentence: "The difficult task faced by all scientists who use human subjects in medical research projects is the dispassionate dissemination of accurate and comprehensible information to potential volunteers." This opinion is paraphrased in correct choice (B). No one recommends that experimentation be limited to volunteers who have a scientific or medical background (A); this choice distorts the discussion of "informed consent" (paragraph five). (C) *is* the view of many doctors (last sentence of paragraph two), but the author expresses no opinion on this point. (D) is never discussed and involves an inherently implausible idea—tests on animals cannot *prove* a drug safe for humans, though they could establish a high probability of safety.

Questions 19–24: PANDA

PASSAGE IV

Topic: Giant Panda

Scope: Classification

Purpose: To document the historical difficulties in classifying the Giant Panda and report the findings of recent tests to resolve the debate.

Passage Map

¶1: Panda's relationship to other species debated

¶2: Panda's classification has varied

¶3: Systematist system of classification

¶4: Differences between panda and other bears

¶5: Molecular biology has helped clarify the panda's proper classification

Questions:

19. C Homologous traits are discussed in the third

and fourth paragraphs, so look there for the answer to this detail question. Choice (A) is mentioned in describing homologous traits in the second sentence of the third paragraph. Choice (B) is mentioned in the fourth and fifth sentences of that paragraph. We know choice (D) is true of homologous traits from the first sentence of the third paragraph. Choice (C), however, is true of analogous traits rather than homologous traits. We learn that from the last two sentences of the third paragraph. Therefore, choice (C) is NOT true of homologous traits and is the correct answer to this question.

20. C This is an application question, asking you to apply your understanding of analogous traits and relationships among animals. Analogous traits develop as a result of environmental stimuli, rather than stemming from common ancestry. The correct answer must present two animals that are not related but possess traits that serve similar functions. Falcons and mosquitos, in choice (C), are not descended from the same ancestor, yet both organisms have developed a similar trait, wings used for flight, so (C) is our answer. Humans and apes are descended from a common ancestor, so their shared trait of having body hair is probably a homologous trait, not analogous, making choice (A) wrong. Choices (B) and (D) are both wrong because while they deal with species descended from different ancestors, the traits in these choices are not analogous. A snake's scales and a human's skin have evolved to meet quite different needs and do indeed perform different functions. Similarly, we can infer that a panda's thumb, which we know from the sixth sentence of the fourth paragraph is quite specialized, and a raccoon's digits probably would not perform the same highly specialized function.

21. D Methods used to determine relationships among species are discussed in the third, fourth, and fifth paragraphs of the passage, with paragraphs three and four detailing the analysis of homologous and analogous traits and the fifth paragraph listing several other methods of verifying lineage. DNA hybridization and gel electrophoresis are mentioned in the last paragraph, so choices (A) and (C) are wrong. Homologous trait analysis is detailed in paragraphs three and four, so choice (B) can't be right. Only choice (D), NMR spectroscopy, is not mentioned in the passage at all, so (D) answers this question.

22. C Solving this application question requires that you apply your understanding of homologous traits, discussed in the third and fourth paragraphs of the passage. We know from the second sentence of the third paragraph that common ancestry, or relatedness, is indicated by homologous traits. So choices (B) and (D) can be eliminated on the grounds that analogous traits do not indicate common ancestry. And we know from the fifth sentence of the third paragraph that the greater the number of homologous traits species share, the closer the relationship among them. So, choice (A) can be

eliminated on the basis that the animals described in this choice share fewer homologous traits than those in choice (C), our correct answer. It is important to note that the number of animals sharing traits has no bearing on the degree of relatedness they share.

23. A The last paragraph of the passage is mainly concerned with resolving the issue of the giant panda's proper classification. The first half of this paragraph tells us about several new techniques of genetic analysis that may help determine proper classification. The last half of this paragraph tells us that, using a variety of new techniques, biologists have come to the conclusion that the giant panda is a bear, even though its ancestors split off from the bear family long ago. So choice (A) best sums up the main idea of the last paragraph. Some of the information in the fourth paragraph does suggest an argument for classifying the plant-eating giant panda as a member of the *Procyonidae* family (B). But this particular question concerns the last (fifth) paragraph, which actually contradicts choice (B); the gist of the last paragraph is that most biologists now consider the giant panda to be a member of the *Ursidae* family. The last paragraph also suggests that various new techniques based on the "molecular clock" hypothesis have provided biologists with information which has allowed them to properly classify the giant panda as a member of the bear family, so choice (C) is wrong. Choice (D) is too vague and general in relation to the specific point made in this passage's concluding paragraph. Although the paragraph does say that biologists are now able to approximate when various species diverged from a common ancestor by examining the genetic material of those species, this is merely supporting information used to help make the main point that the panda is properly classified as part of the bear family.

24. C In order to answer this question it is important to consider the passage as a whole. Of the choices listed, choice (C), a biologist, is most likely to have authored the passage. Biologists study organisms, including the relationships among species, so (C) is a good answer. A geologist, choice (A), is a scientist who studies the earth by examining rock formations. The earth has nothing to do with the contents of this passage, so choice (A) is wrong. A geneticist deals with relatedness at the level of the cell and chromosome and, while parts of the passage touch on chromosome structure, this passage as a whole is less detailed than one would expect of someone as specialized as a geneticist. This passage is more general biology, so (C) is still the better or "more likely" answer to the question than (B). Similarly, a chemist, choice (D), is too specialized to be a likely writer of this passage. This passage does not concern chemistry or even biochemistry, but more general biology.

Questions 25–33: GROUPTHINK

PASSAGE V

Topic: Groupthink

Scope: A lab test of groupthink

Purpose: To report and discuss the lab test of group-think headed by Matie Flowers.

Passage Map

¶1: Irving Janis' theory of groupthink

¶2: Methods and details of lab conditions to test group-think

¶3: Study results

¶4: Failures of the study design

Questions:

25. C In answering this question, it is important to note the difference between groupthink and group decision making in general. The first paragraph of this passage identifies *groupthink* as a breakdown in group decision-making that has led to "several disastrous decisions in U.S. foreign policy." This implies that group decision making can sometimes lead to disastrous results (C). The first paragraph also suggests that groupthink is more likely to occur under a strong leader, which contradicts (A). Similarly, the first and third paragraphs both state that group decision making is more productive and successful in less cohesive groups; highly cohesive groups (B), according to Janis, are more prone to groupthink. The third paragraph of the passage suggests that groups led by open leaders offer more solutions to crises than do groups led by closed leaders. This does not imply that group decision making *in general* limits the number of possible solutions (D). In fact, it suggests that the more people involved in an interactive decision-making process, the more possible solutions result.

26. C The first sentence of the second paragraph states that Flowers's goal was to test the groupthink hypothesis under laboratory conditions (C). It is important to note that Flowers did not set out to necessarily prove or disprove any component of Janis's theory, but merely to test the theory. The last paragraph states that Flowers's experiment suggests that cohesiveness does not necessarily contribute to groupthink (A). This finding was a result of Flowers's experiment, but not something she had set out to prove or disprove, so (A) is wrong. Similarly, Janis's theory discusses groupthink in the context of crisis situations, but nowhere is there any suggestion that the theory is restricted to crisis situations or that Flowers set out to contest such a theory (B). Nor was Flowers's aim to prove that groupthink stems from strong leadership styles (D); though Janis suggests that

groupthink does indeed relate to strong leadership and Flowers's experiment confirms that fact, again, Flowers did not set out to prove, but to test, Janis's theory.

27. C The author mentions the 1961 Bay of Pigs crisis as an example of how groupthink has led to disastrous decisions in foreign policy. (A) is incorrect because the author's tone in the passage is descriptive and informative, and does not seem to condemn or even blame the Kennedy administration for a "disastrous decision." In fact, the author implies that the decision arose as a result of groupthink and not on account of any particular fault on the part of the Kennedy administration. The *long-term effects* of the Bay of Pigs invasion (B) are not discussed in the passage, so (B) is beyond the scope of the passage. While the 1961 Bay of Pigs incident is indeed an example of a poor decision made in a crisis situation, this does not lead to the generalization that poor decisions are made in crisis situations (D).

28. B The second sentence of the second paragraph states that Flowers's experiment tested two factors—style of leadership (I) and group cohesiveness, which is another way of phrasing "the degree of cohesion among group members" (III). Therefore, both options I and III are certainly going to be part of the correct answer. However, the end of the second paragraph states that each team was presented with the same crisis situation. Therefore, option II is incorrect. The correct answer, then, must be choice (B), I and III only.

29. D To answer this application question you need to consider the factors that Janis describes in the first paragraph as contributing to groupthink, and then consider the answer choices according to Janis's theory. (A) would not weaken Janis's groupthink hypothesis because it is in keeping with that theory—the last sentence of the first paragraph says that individual members do indeed fear rejection by the group and suggests that their fear of rejection is greater than their fear of making a wrong decision. Similarly, choice (B) is in accordance with Janis's theory: The passage states that it is a strong leader with a predilection for a specific solution, not an open leader, who is likely to lead a group to a faulty decision. Since the beginning of the passage says that Janis claimed groupthink has led to several disastrous foreign-policy decisions, and nothing in the passage suggests Janis would exclude his theory from either or both government and the military, (C) would not weaken Janis's hypothesis. Since Janis's theory states that an essential contributing factor to groupthink is a strong leader with a predilection toward a specific solution, a study showing that leaders usually *do not* approach crises with such a predilection (D) would weaken Janis's hypothesis; such a study would imply that groupthink stems from different causes than those Janis described.

30. C The answer to this question lies in the fourth paragraph, where the author discusses the reasons

Flowers's experiment did not reproduce Janis's hypothesis regarding group cohesiveness. There you are told that group cohesiveness may be a factor only in groups whose members are very well acquainted. Considering that, the author seems to conclude that Janis's theory is true only under certain conditions (C). To say that the author concludes that Janis's theory is clearly false because group cohesiveness did not influence groupthink (A) is an extreme exaggeration. The author suggests that the validity of the theory, particularly with regard to the cohesiveness of groups, remains a question, but he does not totally disregard the theory. The first sentence of the last paragraph merely suggests that some aspects of the theory have been verified while others have not. The third paragraph does say that Flowers's experiment confirmed Janis's theory regarding leadership styles. But the fourth paragraph mentions that the aspects of the theory regarding group cohesiveness are at question. This does not imply that the author regards Janis's theory as "obviously true" (B). Although Flowers's experiment proved no significant effect of group cohesiveness, the author in no way suggests that, because of this, group cohesiveness should not be considered a factor in Janis's schema (D). Rather, the last paragraph suggests that the role of group cohesiveness in Janis's schema might be clarified and refined.

31. D The "inconsistency" to which this question refers has to do with the fact that while Janis described high group cohesiveness as a factor contributing to groupthink, Flowers concluded that group cohesiveness was not critical in producing the effects of groupthink (see sentence one of paragraph four). The second sentence of paragraph four reveals the probable source of this inconsistency: Janis and Flowers based their studies on different conceptions of "high group cohesiveness" (D). While it is true that groups led by closed leaders dealt with facts after, not before, a decision was made (A), this is not the "inconsistency" to which the author refers at the beginning of the concluding paragraph. Choice (B) attempts to fabricate an "inconsistency" by claiming that Flowers emphasized the role of leadership while Janis emphasized the role of group cohesiveness. In fact, there is no indication that Flowers felt strong leadership style was the "prime cause" of groupthink or Janis believed that both strong leadership and group cohesiveness contributed to groupthink. (C) contradicts information in the third paragraph. In Flowers's experiment, groups with open leaders offered more, not fewer, solutions than did those with closed leaders; therefore, this could not be the source of inconsistency referred to in the fourth paragraph of the passage.

32. B To answer a question about the likely source of a passage, you need to consider the information contained in the passage, its overall tone, and the passage's level of complexity. This passage describes a theory, and then details an experiment designed to test the validity of this theory; the tone of the passage is rather academ-

ic, although it is not couched in specialized language. Considering these factors, the most likely source of this passage is (B)—a college-level psychology book. The passage is not likely an excerpt from a lecture to government leaders (A) because the tone is too academic for a lecture to practitioners like politicians, and because the detailed description of Flowers's experiment is not likely to be of interest to the broad group of "government leaders." The passage is probably not from a list of management guidelines (C) because the format of the passage is not that of a list, and the focus of this discussion of groupthink is not aimed at applications in management. Nor is the likely source of the passage an entry in an encyclopedia (D)—the account of the Flowers's experiment is too detailed for an encyclopedia entry.

33. B Answering this question requires that you consider the focus of the passage as a whole, paying special attention to the last paragraph. This last paragraph considers the fact that Flowers's experiment failed to identify group cohesiveness to be critical to producing groupthink. The author then discusses one possible explanation for this unexpected result. Considering that conclusion, the next topic would probably be another explanation for Flowers's failure to reproduce all the effects of groupthink (B). (A) is incorrect because it would entail an unlikely shift in focus, from the discussion of a laboratory test of a theory, to the possibility of groupthink actually occurring under contemporary conditions. (C) focuses on the relationship between cohesiveness and leadership styles, which is never discussed in the passage, so would be an unlikely topic for the author to turn towards. It is also unlikely that the next topic the author would discuss would be other examples of how groupthink negatively influenced foreign policy (D), since the author provides only one example of such an occurrence, and does so much earlier in the passage, in his introduction.

Questions 34–38: KURU

PASSAGE VI

Topic: Kuru

Scope: Cause and Transmission

Purpose: To provide an example of how epidemiology can elucidate the cause and means of transmission of a particular disease.

Passage Map
¶1: Description of the disease kuru

¶2: Possible causes of disease

¶3: Geographical distribution of kuru mapped: environmental and sociological factors discounted

¶4: Via linguistic analysis, probable genetic element to disease established

¶5: Isolated causative agent

¶6: Transmission of disease

¶7: Ban on cannibalism stemmed disease

Questions:

34. A The symptoms of kuru are stated in the middle of the first paragraph. They are separated into initial and later symptoms. One of the first signs of the disease is "a lack of coordination of skilled movement," which would include such actions as tying a knot (A). A general lack of coordination (C)—progressive ataxia—is a later symptom. Choice (D) is contradicted. Memory is a cognitive function and the passage explicitly states that "at no time during the course of the disease is cognitive functioning impaired." Choice (B) is never mentioned relative to kuru. (B) tempts you with the fact that victims giggle for no reason; but there is no indication that the giggling reflects on the victim's social judgment; it may simply be a nervous system malfunction.

35. B Paragraphs three and four describe the studies of kuru-free and kuru-affected areas. Paragraph three states that kuru-affected regions were mapped. Researchers were able to see that kuru-free and kuru-affected tribes existed side by side in environmentally similar regions (C) and were culturally similar (A). Thus, (A) and (C) were differences that researchers considered, although such differences did not, in fact, exist. In paragraph four, we find that epidemiologists looked at the similarities of dialects in order to determine linguistic differences (D) among kuru-free and kuru-affected tribes. Choice (B), however, was never considered: physiology is not referred to in these two paragraphs.

36. D Researchers attempted to isolate the agent causing kuru by inoculating test animals with infected human tissue. The only difference between the original experiments—which failed—and later, successful attempts is that the original experiments were done on chicks and mice and the later experiments on chimpanzees. The implication is that chicks and mice were not similar enough to humans for the virus to infect the animals. There is no indication that a difference between the original attempts and later successes existed in technique (A) or what the researchers were looking for (B). Although there is a genetic predisposition or susceptibility to kuru, the disease is *caused* by an infectious agent, making (C) incorrect—the experiments failed to find the agent because they were using the wrong subjects, not because the disease is noninfectious.

37. C According to the passage, the difference between kuru-affected and kuru-free tribes was the genetic makeup (pools) of the tribes. Because of this, the investigators concluded that a hypothesized genetic susceptibility is critical for the development of the disease. However, the disease is *caused* by a virus (or perhaps a prion). Both the genetic element and the virus are needed for the disease to develop, as stated in the first sentence of paragraph six and in choice (C). (C) explains logically why neighboring tribes remained kuru-free: no matter who the neighbors met or ate (i.e., whether or not they were exposed to kuru), they could not contract the disease without possessing the hypothesized genetic factor. Choice (A) *would* explain variations in the incidence of kuru, but there is no information in the passage to suggest that there were in fact differences in how cannibalism was practiced. There is no indication that kuru-free and kuru-affected tribes had no contact (B); in fact, there was intermarriage among the tribes. Finally, while the passage may not offer a *definitive* reason why kuru hits some tribes and not others, the presumed genetic factor does provide an explanation, and thus (D) can be eliminated.

38. D From the fifth paragraph you know that kuru has a long incubation period. Thus, even when cannibalism was banned in 1957, individuals who had once practiced cannibalism continued to develop the disease for years afterward. However, soon there was a new generation of children who had never been exposed to the disease and therefore, statistically the disease died out in the youngest age groups first. Although the question asks you to make an inference, you still must be careful to base any answer on only the facts given in the passage. Neither (A) nor (B) has any support in the passage. Each is a potentially important detail that, if true, would probably have been mentioned in the passage. Choice (C) is incorrect for two reasons. First, kuru is not a long-term chronic disease; once an individual develops the disease, degeneration occurs within nine months. (You should distinguish between conditions with a long incubation period, such as kuru, and chronic conditions, which persist for long periods after they become manifest.) Second, *incidence* means the rate at which the disease occurs, and is not a measurement of fatality rates.

Questions 39–45:
SOCIAL PHILOSOPHY

PASSAGE VII

Topic: Social Philosophy

Scope: Contractarian

Purpose: To outline and defend a contractarian view of justice.

Passage Map
¶1: Utilitarianism vs. social contract

¶2: The contractarian philosophy

¶3: Method would lead rational person to ensure maximum possible justice and liberty for all

¶4: Emerging principles of contractarian philosophy

¶5: Criticism and rebuttal regarding the principles that would emerge from the application of the contractarian approach

Questions:

39. A Although the author appears to be outlining a contrast between utilitarianism and contractarianism (C) in the first paragraph, he or she never really follows this up. Rather, the second paragraph explains the setup postulated by Rawls and the new contractarians, and the remainder of the passage explains and justifies the consequences of this setup. Thus, (A) is essentially correct. (See also the editorializing statement at the end of paragraph one.) Two solutions to social problems are described (if indeed that is what these philosophies are), but neither of them appears to be considered radical (B). And while it's true that most of what is discussed is the work of John Rawls, one thing the first paragraph does is set Rawls's ideas into a larger context of contractarianism, so (D) is too narrow.

40. B See paragraphs two through four. The rational beings assumed in Rawls's model would "ensur[e] the maximum possible justice and liberty for even the least privileged member of society" (paragraph three); privileges, where unavoidable, would be potentially available to all and arranged so that their benefits "would be distributed to everyone's advantage" (paragraph three). These points add up to what is stated in (B). The "veil of ignorance" renders the decision makers "temporarily totally unaware" of their membership in various groups [paragraph two—(A)]. Rawls clearly believes that the decision makers *would* be able to agree on a single principle (C), but it would not be one that would end inequality (D) since this is to some degree "inevitable," in Rawls's view (paragraph four).

41. D Although utilitarians call for "the greatest good for the greatest number," it's clear from paragraph one that this may involve sacrificing the interests of a minority. Contractarians, on the other hand, believe society "owes certain obligations" to all its members—which implies that at least some interests of all the members of society must be satisfied, even if this requires reducing the absolute amount of "good" in the world as defined by the utilitarians. Thus, the two ideas start from differing notions of the desirable society, as in (D). Choice (A) is wrong because of the statement in paragraph one that the two systems do not necessarily conflict; on the same basis they do not necessarily agree, either (B). We really don't have enough information to know or even infer the utilitarians' idea of human nature (C), and the same

holds true for contractarians. (We are told that the new contractarians don't believe that people are purely and naturally good, but this is not much to go on, and we know nothing about other contractarians.)

42. C As described in paragraph one, utilitarianism would always prescribe a broad social good over and against a benefit to an individual or minority; in this case the individual is the aging parent, and the family constitutes a sort of secondary minority. Utilitarianism would never balance public and private burdens; only if a social public benefit would accrue or burden be reduced would a utilitarian seek to improve the lot of the family (A); in addition this choice leaves the parent out of the picture. (B) is a contractarian view; utilitarianism is not democratic: it presumes that an absolute knowledge of benefits and burdens can be arrived at which will necessarily lead to one decision, so no one has a "right" to a voice in the decision. (D) presumes that "right to life" is an absolute good, a statement not made in the passage.

43. B Paragraph two makes plain that the members of the contracting group will select what they consider the most beneficial and equitable social structure. Paragraph three goes on to say that one of these rules would be maximum possible liberty, justifying this conclusion by putting the rhetorical question of who would risk slavery when the veil was lifted. But in fact the answer to this question is not at all self-evident. For instance, someone who valued comfort above liberty might consent to a system of well-rewarded servitude. Thus, the contractarians' assertion that their system leads to a free society is only true insofar as choice (B) is assumed to be true. The decision makers actually know the general consequences of their decision (A); they simply remain unaware of the specific personal consequences. The contractarians actually disagree with (C): paragraph four says that justice resides not in equal power and status for all positions, but rather in equal access to positions of varying power or status. Because of the veil of ignorance, it would be impossible for the contracting parties to safeguard their own liberties at the expense of others (D), and, if it were possible, it would not lead to the sort of society the contractarians envisage.

44. A Careful here: Don't try to decide which answer choice is factually true; rather, decide which one would provide a potential reward for a gambler. After spending several paragraphs showing how contractarianism leads to equal access to liberty and other social goods, in the last paragraph the author implies that a gambler might take a chance on altering these results, which would mean unequal access to social goods, as in (A). A Rousseauean vision [(B); paragraph two] assumes everyone is naturally harmonious and implies that there are no social inequities to gamble on; hence a gambler would be unlikely to select a Rousseauean principle. (C), like (B), provides nothing the gambler could gamble for. A gambler behind the veil of ignorance would be unable to create a society definitely favorable to himself or herself (D); the best he or she could do would be to select a principle of justice *more likely* to be of personal benefit.

45. D Let's use elimination. As the second sentence of paragraph four makes clear, personal liberty (A) can be abridged if it interferes with the personal liberty of another (it is freedom of speech that cannot be abridged). Social inequality (B) and economic inequality (C) are inevitable, according to the fourth sentence of the same paragraph. But according to this same sentence, these last two inequalities must inhere in offices and not in accidents of birth; since a person's race is just such an accident, (D) is the correct choice.

Questions 46–52: PROTEINS

PASSAGE VIII

Topic: Proteins

Scope: Separation & Purification of Proteins

Purpose: To review the various procedures that can be used to separate and purify proteins.

Passage Map

¶1: Differentiation of proteins

¶2: Dialysis

¶3: Gel filtration chromatography

¶4: Ion exchange chromatography

¶5: Gel electrophoresis

¶6: Density-gradient centrifugation

Questions:

46. C Size is a factor in all the protein separation techniques except for ion exchange chromatography. The first sentence of paragraph two states that dialysis (A) is the simplest technique for separating proteins according to size. Paragraph three describes how gel filtration chromatography (B) can separate a protein from both bigger and smaller molecules. Again, size is a factor. The last paragraph informs you that density gradient centrifugation (D) separates proteins according to density, "really a consequence of size and weight." Ion exchange chromatography (C) is the only separation technique in the passage which works not on the basis of size, but (as explained in paragraph four) on the basis of charge.

47. A The key to this question is the understanding that the only way to separate proteins Y and Z, identical

in both size and charge, is by density gradient centrifugation, which works on the basis of density. Although the question stem does not tell you that the densities of these two proteins are different, it does not tell you that they are the same. In this case, it is safe to assume that the densities are different and that density gradient centrifugation would work because without this option there is no way of isolating Y from Z. Once this is understood, you can look for the answer choices that contain density gradient centrifugation, (A) and (D), and eliminate those that do not, (B) and (C). Now you must realize that in order to separate both Y and Z from X, you need a separation method based on size since X, Y, and Z all have the same charge, but X is smaller than Y and Z. Then you must realize that in order to separate Y and Z from W, you need a separation method based on either charge or size since W differs from Y and Z in both these aspects. To choose between (A) and (D) then, look for the choice that includes at least one separation technique based on size and one technique based on either size or charge. Choice (D) lists ion exchange, chromatography, and electric field gel electrophoresis, both charge-based techniques. Since no size-based technique is included, (D) is incorrect. Choice (A) lists dialysis, a size-based technique that will serve to separate Y and Z from X, a smaller molecule, but not from W, a larger molecule. Ion exchange chromatography is a charge-based technique that will separate Y and Z from W. Finally, density gradient chromatography will separate Y from Z. So the correct answer is (A).

48. D To separate large quantities of proteins of equal but opposite charge, the best technique would be one based on charge. Choices (A) and (B), dialysis and gel filtration chromatography, respectively, can immediately be eliminated since they are both techniques based on size. Furthermore, the passage states that gel electrophoresis is effective only for small amounts of proteins, not large quantities as the question stem specifies. Choice (C) is charge based, but since the beads have both positive and negative charges on them, this technique will not separate opposite charges, and both proteins will end up sticking to the columns. Choice (D) is the only remaining and correct option. If the protein solution is passed through a column of beads with only positive or negative charges attached, then only the negatively charged proteins or the positively charged proteins will stick to the column while the proteins of the opposite charge flow through and become separated.

49. B An ion exchange column contains beads with a prearranged charge of a single sign, and any proteins with the opposite charge will adhere to the beads; that protein R requires a higher salt concentration to be washed off means that it adheres more strongly than Q (see paragraph four). This further implies that R is more highly charged than Q, so (B) is correct and (A) is incorrect. However, since we don't know the charge on the column, we cannot determine the sign of the charges of proteins Q and R (C, D).

50. B Dialysis is a separation technique based on size. A protein solution is filtered through a membranous bag with pores of a known diameter. Only protein molecules smaller than the diameter of the pores can escape while larger proteins are retained in the bag. Clearly, the only answer choice that parallels this is choice (B), in which smaller pebbles fall through the holes in a sifting pan while nuggets, whose diameters exceed that of the holes in the pan, get caught. Choice (A) is incorrect because it suggests the physical concept of centrifugal force, not integral to dialysis. Choice (C), is incorrect because no separation occurs as both the pebbles and the nuggets fall through holes large enough to accommodate them both. The purpose of dialysis, however, is to allow some component out but to trap others. Choice (D) is incorrect because it suggests separation based on charge, while dialysis is solely based on size.

51. D The passage opens with the statement that although proteins are infinitely variable, they share some characteristics that have become the basis of several separation techniques. The passage continues to describe these separation techniques that are based on either size, charge, or density. Clearly then, the purpose of this passage is to discuss various techniques of protein separation, answer choice (D). Choice (A) is incorrect because, while the passage does discuss both size and charge-based separation techniques, it never compares them on any basis. Choice (B) is incorrect because although the passage does state that gel electrophoresis is more an analytical than a preparatory tool (paragraph five), this is just a detail, certainly not a principal focus of the passage. The passage does state that dialysis is the simplest of the size-based separation techniques (C), but this is not its main point or the purpose of its discussion.

52. C Gel electrophoresis is discussed in the fifth paragraph of the passage. In the very first sentence of that paragraph, the passage states that gel electrophoresis purifies proteins on the basis of either size or charge. Therefore, option I is correct in suggesting that gel electrophoresis is useful in separating proteins on a size basis. Option II, however, is not true. The last sentence of the fifth paragraph informs us that this technique is effective only for relatively small amounts of protein, making it more an analytical than a preparatory tool. Option III is true. We already know that gel electrophoresis is a two-pronged technique that can separate proteins by both size and charge. Ion exchange chromatography separates on the basis of charge, as explained in paragraph four. Since both ion exchange chromatography and gel electrophoresis can separate proteins on the basis of charge, they can achieve similar results. Only I and III are true, so (C) is correct.

Questions 53–60: Capital Punishment
PASSAGE IX

Topic: Death Penalty

Scope: Abolition of Death Penalty

Purpose: To argue for the abolition of the death penalty.

Passage Map

¶1: Lord Chancellor's explanation for change in treatment of traitors

¶2: Rationale of those opposed to capital punishment

¶3: Execution procedure minimizes exposure to public

¶4: Argument against capital punishment

Questions:
53. C Nowhere in the passage does the author rely on the mandates of Judeo-Christian law in justifying why the death penalty should be abolished. In fact, the argument is presented in a noticeably nonsecular manner. (A) paraphrases the last two sentences of paragraph two. (B) mirrors the idea of Hove that the "our penal code must be based on rehabilitation rather than annihilation." (D) is another paraphrase of the second-to-last sentence in paragraph two.

54. B The passage ends with a paragraph about why we should find alternatives to capital punishment, with a quote from Hove accenting the point. The author never gives any details on how executions are actually carried out, nor does he imply at any point that he will do so, making answer choice (A) unlikely. The author is opposed to the death penalty, so he would probably not use any excerpts from the writings of those who favor capital punishment, eliminating (C). The author is more focused on executions than human rights, so he would most likely continue his discussion of the death penalty rather than moving to a new topic of other human rights issues, so (D) is also wrong.

55. D The author uses the argument that capital punishment is a morally wrong because it undermines our views about human rights, so the view that murderers have their human rights suspended after committing their crimes allows executions to continue without any inconsistencies with societal human rights issues. (C) has nothing to do with the argument, as abortion is not mentioned anywhere in the passage. Answer choices (A) and (B) do both undermine certain points made by the author, however they miss the overall scope of the author's view. These two answers are too specific.

56. D No mention is made that Zimbabwe has abol-

KAPLAN

ished executions, or that it is more developed than the United States, so (A) is disqualified. Both the author and Hove are against capital punishment, so the quote is not used to show support for capital punishment, eliminating (B). (C) is included in the quotation, but is not the purpose of the quote, which is to add external support to the author's view that alternatives to capital punishment must be sought.

57. B The question stem asks for an argument least likely to be used by an opponent of the author's critics, which can be simplified to mean that the argument must support capital punishment. Notice the triple negatives, and use the chance to cancel out two of them, leaving the stem asking which is least likely to be used by the author. (A) and (C) are both supportive of the author's overall intentions, the abolition of capital punishment, so they can both be eliminated. (D) has little to do with the overall argument, leaving (B) as the only answer that is opposed to the author's point of view.

58. D The author is not calling for the use of force to enforce his views, so he is not militant, eliminating (A). The author is appealing to human sensibilities, not being accusatory, nor is he being pompously sure of his argument, canceling out (B). The author is fearful, but he is not passively allowing things to happen, as he is asking for change, so (C) is incorrect. The author is being prescriptive of societal views and judgmental towards government practices, so (D) is most likely.

59. C The question asks for which is NOT used by the author. The British Parliament speech is used in paragraph one, the African poet's feelings are expressed in the last paragraph (Hove), and the author appeals to the reader's morality several times during the last paragraph during his "ideals of the state" point. The author never gives a list of alternatives to capital punishment in this passage, so (C) is correct.

60. A The author mentions that the capital punishment is a "barbaric punishment symbolic of our less civilized past," and provides evidence that several other cultures also do or have carried out executions. The author never mentions the U.S. government's punishment for treason, or anything about treason in the United States, so (B) is incorrect. The reader has no evidence that executions have been abolished in Zimbabwe, only that a poet was against them, so (C) is incorrect. The author points out that the media sensationalize some of the criminals' violent acts, but not that the actual executions were broadcast at all, so (D) is wrong.

Materials used in this test section were adapted from the following source(s):

Michael Ross, *Capital Punishment: We Can Live Without It.* © 1995 by the New Thought Journal.

Verbal Reasoning Test Four

Time—85 minutes
Question 1–60

DIRECTIONS: Each of the passages in this test is followed by a set of questions based on the passage's content. After reading each passage, decide on the one best response to each question and mark it on your answer sheet. If you are unsure of an answer, eliminate the choices you know are wrong and choose from the remaining choices. You may refer to the passages while answering the questions.

Passage I (Questions 1–7)

Although many may argue with my stress on the continuity of the essential traits of American character and religion, few would question the thesis that our business institutions have reflected the constant emphasis in the American value system on individual achievement. From the earliest comments of foreign travelers down to the present, individuals have identified a strong materialistic bent as a characteristic American trait.

The worship of the dollar, the desire to make a profit, the effort to get ahead through the accumulation of possessions, all have been credited to the egalitarian character of the society. As Tocqueville noted in his discussion of the consequences of a democracy's destruction of aristocracy: "They have swept away the privileges of some of their fellow creatures which stood in their way, but they have opened the door to universal competition."

A study of the comments on American workers of various nineteenth-century foreign travelers reveals that most of these European writers, among whom were a number of socialists, concluded that social and economic democracy in America has an effect contrary to mitigating compensation for social status. American secular and religious values both have facilitated the "triumph of American capitalism," and fostered status striving.

The focus on equalitarianism and individual opportunity has also prevented the emergence of class consciousness among the lower classes. The absence of a socialist or labor party, and the historic weakness of American trade-unionism, appear to attest to the strength of values which depreciated a concern with class.

Although the American labor movement is similar to others in many respects, it differs from those of other stable democracies in ideology, class solidarity, tactics, organizational structure, and patterns of leadership behavior. American unions are more conservative; they are more narrowly self-interested; their tactics are more militant; they are more decentralized in their collective bargaining; and they have more full-time salaried officials, who are on the whole much more highly paid. American unions have also organized a smaller proportion of the labor force than have unions in these other nations.

The growth of a large trade-union movement during the 1930s, together with the greater political involvement of labor organizations in the Democratic party, suggested to some that the day—long predicted by Marxists—was arriving in which the American working class would finally follow in the footsteps of its European brethren. Such changes in the structure of class relations seemed to these observers to reflect the decline of opportunity and the hardening of class lines. To them, such changes could not occur without modification in the traditional value system.

A close examination of the character of the American labor movement suggests that it, like American religious institutions, may be perceived as reflecting the basic values of the larger society. Although unions, like all other American institutions, have changed in various ways consistent with the growth of an urban industrial civilization, the essential traits of American trade unions, as of business corporations, may still be derived from key elements in the American value system.

GO TO THE NEXT PAGE.

1. If the claims made in the passage about American and foreign labor unions are correct, how would the unions be expected to react during a strike against a corporation?

    A. American labor unions would be less likely than foreign unions to use violence against a corporation.
    B. American labor unions would be more likely than foreign unions to use violence against a corporation.
    C. American labor unions would be less likely than foreign unions to bargain with a corporation.
    D. American labor unions would be more likely than foreign unions to bargain with a corporation.

2. If a critic of the author's viewpoint brought up examples as a rebuttal to the passage, the existence of which of the following phenomena would most strongly *challenge* the information in the passage?

    A. American union leaders who are highly paid to negotiate on behalf of workers
    B. American labor organizations that avoid involvement in non-labor issues
    C. American workers with a weak sense of group solidarity
    D. American corporations that are more interested in helping people than in making a profit

3. Based on the information given in the passage, which of the following is/are NOT true?

    I. American society emphasizes class solidarity over individual achievement.
    II. American unions are less interested in non-labor issues than unions in other democracies.
    III. American labor organizations and American religious institutions share some of the same values.
    A. I only
    B. II only
    C. II and III
    D. I, II and III

4. Suppose that an American union decides that its members should take an active part in national politics. What effect would this information have on the author's view of American unions?

    A. It would support that view.
    B. It would contradict that view.
    C. It would neither support nor contradict that view.
    D. It would support that view only if it could be shown that getting involved in politics was for society's good.

5. In the context of the passage, the phrase *strong materialistic bent*, as used in the sentence, "From the earliest comments of foreign travelers down to the present, individuals have identified a strong materialistic bent as being a characteristic American trait," refers to:

    A. European socialists' view of aristocrats.
    B. European travelers' concern with democracy.
    C. American society's emphasis on acquiring wealth.
    D. American religion's criticism of secular values.

6. According to the passage, all of the following have influenced the outlook of the American labor movement EXCEPT:

    A. secular values.
    B. religious values.
    C. urban industrial civilization.
    D. foreign labor movements.

7. According to the passage, which of the following is a part of the "traditional value system"?

    A. Class solidarity
    B. Individual achievement
    C. Urban industrialization
    D. Marxist ideology

GO TO THE NEXT PAGE.

Passage II (Questions 8-13)

There are a great many symbiotic relationships in the marine environment. A popular one, often noted for the striking beauty of the juxtaposition, is that of the sea anemone and the clown fish. The anemone has poison tentacles which—when they contact passing fish—paralyze the fish and drag the prey in for a meal. The clown fish uses the anemone's tentacle "garden" as a safe haven while attracting prey for the anemone to capture, for it alone is immune to the sting of the anemone.

Another symbiotic relation that remains the subject of scientific puzzlement concerns the relationship between *Scleractinia*, the coral type whose colonization produces reefs, and their symbiotic partners the *zooxanthellae*, the unicellular algae present in the corals' endodermic tissues. It is known that each symbiont plays an integral part in the formation of a reef's protective limestone foundation. The coral polyps secrete calceous exoskeletons which cement themselves into an underlayer of rock, while the algae deposit still more calcium carbonate, which reacts with sea salt to create an even tougher limestone layer.

It is also known that, due to the algal photosynthesis, the reef environment is highly oxygen-saturated, while the similarly high amounts of carbon dioxide are carried off rapidly. All this accounts for the amazing renewability of coral reefs despite the endless erosion caused by wave activity. However, the precise manner in which one symbiont stimulates the secretion of calcium carbonate by the other remains unclear.

Scientists have also proposed various theories to explain the transformation of "fringing reefs," those connected above sea level to land masses, into "barrier reefs" that are separated from shorelines by wide lagoons, and then into free-floating atolls. Though the theory postulated by Charles Darwin is considered at least partially correct, some scientists today argue that the creation of the reef forms has more to do with the rise of sea level that accompanied the end of the Ice Age. However, recent drillings at Enewetak atoll have uncovered a large underlay of volcanic rock, which suggests that Darwin's explanation may have been more valid after all.

Even the name given to the reefs is something of a misnomer. The *Scleractinia* themselves generally comprise no more than 10 percent of the biota of the average reef community: *zooxanthellae* can account for up to 90 percent of the reef mass, along with *foraminifera*, annelid worms, and assorted mollusks. Moreover, reefs can flourish only in shallow, highly saline waters above 70°F., because the algae require such circumstances; yet non-reef-building corals occur worldwide under various environmental conditions, from the Arctic to the Mediterranean, home of the red coral prized for jewelry. The most likely reason that the term "coral reefs" persists is that the brilliant variety of coral shapes and colors makes aesthetic considerations more vivid than biological ones.

---

8. According to the author, some scientists consider the term "coral reef" a misnomer because:

   A. the beautiful shapes and colors of reefs are produced by the *Scleractinia* rather than the *zooxanthellae*.
   B. the coral portion of a reef has little to do with the reef's survival.
   C. "non-reef-building" corals are found throughout the world.
   D. the majority of a reef's substance comprises *zooxanthellae*, *foraminifera*, annelid worms, and assorted molluscs while a small portion comprises the *Scleractinia*.

9. According to the passage, Darwin's theory regarding coral reef transformation is not universally accepted today. Opponents of Darwin's theory would NOT agree with which of the following statements?

   A. Coral reefs change from fringing reefs to barrier reefs, and then to free-floating atolls.
   B. Atolls are farther from land masses than are barrier reefs.
   C. Fringing reefs inevitably developed into barrier reefs because volcanic islands gradually sank into the ocean.
   D. As a result of the end of the Ice Age, increased expanses of water aided in the transformation of fringing reefs into barrier reefs.

GO TO THE NEXT PAGE.

10. Based on the passage, which of the following is probably an assumption of scientists studying coral reefs?

   A. The theories of reef evolution through glacial melting and through volcanic subsidence are mutually exclusive.
   B. The three main types of coral reefs did not develop independently of one another.
   C. *Zooxanthellae* are always found in coral reefs.
   D. Intense calcification single-handedly protects reefs from destruction by waves and other natural causes.

11. The passage mentions the recent drillings at the Enewetak atoll. This reference serves to:

   A. stengthen the claims made by scientists today concerning reef transformation.
   B. weaken the claims made by scientists today concerning reef transformation.
   C. strengthen the claims made by Darwin concerning reef transformation.
   D. weaken the claims made by Darwin concerning reef transformation.

12. Regardless of what Darwin's opponents may think, according to the author, the theory proposed by Charles Darwin:

   A. is less persuasive on the topic of reef formation in light of recent discoveries.
   B. shows that each type of coral reef developed by separate, distinct processes.
   C. accurately described the transformation of fringing reefs into atolls.
   D. focused on the idea of submerging volcanic islands.

13. Suppose that marine biologists discovered that the calceous exoskeletons produced by coral polyps stimulate the *zooxanthellae* to deposit calcium carbonate via a chemical stimulus. How would this finding be relevant to the study of reefs?

   A. It would explain how reefs maintain a high level of oxygen saturation.
   B. It would clarify the symbiotic relationship between *Scleractinia* and *zooxanthellae* during their formation of the protective limestone foundation.
   C. It would identify the chemical components of the reef's protective layer.
   D. It would explain the intense colors and formations often seen in coral reefs.

GO TO THE NEXT PAGE.

Passage III (Questions 14-19)

From time to time history and myth come peculiarly close to one another, casting a new light on old, and often largely dismissed tales. In various Eastern cultures the notion of the winged serpent and the dragon have come down from the ages, only to be cast aside by modern society as fantastic, mythological creations of someone's overactive ancient imagination. Now, it seems, this supernatural beast might have some historical antecedents.

Archaeopteryx lithographica lived during the latter part of the Jurassic period, approximately 150 million years ago, just south of what today is central Germany. This ancient creature combined a reptilian body and tail with bird-like wings and feathers. This strange amalgamation of traits seems like something out of ancient mysticism of the Far East.

This beast has provided a wealth of information about the evolution of flight in birds. However, fossil and skeletal studies indicate that it was not capable of flight. None of the *Archaeopteryx* fossils discovered to date, including the most mature specimens, exhibit an ossified or bony sternum, the wide bone that extends from the chest to the pelvic area in most modern birds. The main purposes of this structure are to protect internal organs during flight and to act as a sturdy anchoring point for the enormous pectoral muscles necessary for flight. There is no indication that *Archaeopteryx* ever developed strong pectoral muscles, and perhaps this is one reason why it never developed a sternum. Instead, it retained reptilian gastral ribs, thin braces in the abdominal region, which were not attached to the skeleton and which served only to support and protect internal organs. Researchers believe that flight would have been highly unlikely in an animal with such skeletal characteristics.

Furthermore, the bones in the manus of *Archaeopteryx* do not seem to have been fused. In modern birds, these bones are fused in order to support the wing. In addition, the ulna of modern birds is marked with small knobs where feathers are anchored firmly to the bone by ligaments. The ulna in *Archaeopteryx*, however, is smooth, indicating that its feathers were not firmly anchored into the skeleton.

Finally, the skeletal characteristics of *Archaeopteryx* seem to indicate that this animal was most adapted to terrestrial movement. Its hind legs and pelvis closely resemble those of bipedal theropods and dinosaurs, suggesting that, like these other bipeds, it was adept at running along the ground. In contrast to the posture of modern birds, whose bodies are suspended at the pelvis like a seesaw with the thighbones horizontal, it stood up on its hind legs with its long reptilian tail serving to balance it as well as enhance its ability to coordinate abrupt changes of direction while running. In modern birds all that remains of the tail is a shrunken, fused structure called a pygostyle. Although the foot of *Archaeopteryx* was bird-like, with fused metatarsals, it was also adapted to running. By way of its peculiar mix of features, it seems to represent a kind of transitionary phase, illustrating an evolutionary leap from reptile to bird and providing insight into the development of flight.

---

14. Suppose that scientists have recently found the skeleton of a bird capable of flight embedded in pre-Jurassic period rock. What effect would this discovery most likely have on their thinking about *Archaeopteryx lithographica*?

    A. It would support the view that *Archaeopteryx lithographica* represented a transitionary species between reptiles and birds.
    B. It would undermine the view that *Archaeopteryx lithographica* represented a transitionary species between reptiles and birds.
    C. It would neither support nor undermine the view that *Archaeopteryx lithographica* represented a transitionary species between reptiles and birds.
    D. It would support the view that *Archaeopteryx lithographica* failed to develop the pectoral muscles necessary for flight.

15. Based on information in the passage, which of the following statements is NOT true?

    A. *Archaeopteryx lithographica's* skeleton is similar to the skeleton of a modern bird.
    B. *Archaeopteryx lithographica's* tail played a larger role in its daily life than the tail of a modern bird plays in its daily life.
    C. Scientists have studied *Archaeopteryx lithographica* in order to learn about the development of flight.
    D. *Archaeopteryx lithographica* shared some characteristics in common with dinosaurs.

GO TO THE NEXT PAGE.

16. In context, the phrase *wealth of information* (line 17) refers to:

    A. knowledge of recent research projects on the evolution of flight.

    B. knowledge about *Archaeopteryx lithographica's* skeletal structure.

    C. knowledge acquired by scientists studying the development of birds.

    D. knowledge of fossil discoveries in what is now central Germany.

17. The author suggests within the confines of the passage which of the following about *Archaeopteryx lithographica*?

    A. It did not have as well-developed a tail as a modern bird.

    B. Its wings had a different function than the wings of a modern bird.

    C. It was less intelligent than a modern bird.

    D. Its skeletal structure made it much larger than a modern bird.

18. Suppose scientists were to find a skeleton of *Archaeopteryx lithographica* that has a sternum similar to the sternum of a modern bird. According to the passage, which of the following beliefs would this finding most strongly *challenge*?

    A. The belief that *Archaeopteryx lithographica* lived in what is today Europe

    B. The belief that *Archaeopteryx lithographica* lived in the Jurassic period

    C. The belief that *Archaeopteryx lithographica* lacked bird-like feathers

    D. The belief that *Archaeopteryx lithographica* lacked the ability to fly

19. Researchers believe that *Archaeopteryx* differs from modern birds for all of the following reasons EXCEPT:

    A. a lack of feathers.

    B. pectoral muscle development.

    C. ossification of the sternum.

    D. knobs found on the ulna.

GO TO THE NEXT PAGE.

Passage IV (Questions 20-27)

Far from being fixed on Earth, scientists now know that Australia has wandered over the face of the planet for billions of years, sometimes lying in the northern hemisphere, sometimes in the south. For 40 million
5 years, after finally cutting the umbilicus with Antarctica, it slowly drifted northwards, in isolation, at about half the rate at which a human hair grows.

Now that the sheep has faltered, Australians ride more and more upon the marsupial's back. To a large
10 extent, but more difficult to quantify, Australia's fauna and flora are being used as a unique resource. In scientific disciplines from reproductive physiology and evolutionary biology to medicine, Australia's native species are hailed as a unique and priceless heritage. They are
15 providing insights into the way the world, and humans themselves, work.

Australia's rainforests—those "unimportant appendages"—are now widely acknowledged as being the most ancient of humanity's land-based ecosystems,
20 which gave rise to most others. Botanical discoveries of worldwide importance are being made in them every year. Australian botanists have recently completed a catalogue of Australian plants, in which they list 18,000 species. Their taxonomic work over recent years has
25 resulted in a 50 percent increase in the number of species in the groups examined. Yet they estimate that about 7,000 undiscovered plant species still exist in Australia. Many surely inhabit Australian rainforests and are members of ancient and bizarre families, like the
30 southern pine (*Podocarpus* species) recently found growing in a steep valley in Arnhem Land, thousands of kilometers distant from its nearest relatives.

Research on newly discovered Australian dinosaur faunas is challenging previous conceptions of what
35 dinosaurs were like. So important are these discoveries that an Australian dinosaur recently made it onto the cover of a major international magazine. It was discovered in one of only two deposits in the world which was laid down near the South Pole during the age of
40 dinosaurs. The chicken-sized species survived three months of darkness each year in a refrigerated world.

Scientists are finally understanding that evolution in Australia, in contrast to evolution on some other continents, is not driven solely by nature "red in tooth and claw." Here,
45 a more gentle force—that of coadaptation—is important. This is because harsh conditions force individuals to cooperate to minimize the loss of nutrients, and to keep them cycling through the ecosystem as rapidly as possible.

20. For which of the following claims does the author of the passage provide some supporting evidence or explanation within the passage itself?

   I. Scientists have yet to catalogue thousands of Australian plant species.
   II. Australia has shifted its position on the Earth's surface over millions of years.
   III. Australia has more plant species than any other continent.

   A. I only
   B. II only
   C. I and II
   D. I and III

21. If asked, the author of this passage would probably give his *greatest* support to which of the following hypothetical actions by the Australian government?

   A. Funding further research on plant species in Australia's rainforests
   B. Cutting down some of Australia's rainforests to make more room for agriculture
   C. Making sure that Australia's flora and fauna get international press coverage
   D. Convincing other governments to fight the greenhouse effect

22. According to the passage, the author suggests which of the following about the process of evolution in Australia?

   A. The plant species that this process has produced in Australia are also found on other continents.
   B. It has not received the attention that it deserves from the international scientific community.
   C. It has been a less violent process in Australia than it has been in other parts of the world.
   D. This process has only taken place over the last 40 million years.

23. Based on the passage, the author would most likely NOT disagree with which of the following statements about dinosaurs?

   A. Australian dinosaurs were generally small in size.
   B. Modern marsupials are descended from dinosaurs.
   C. Dinosaurs became extinct before rainforests appeared.
   D. Not all dinosaur species lived in warm environments.

GO TO THE NEXT PAGE.

24. Based on information in the passage, which of the following is NOT true?

   A. Australia has moved from one hemisphere to the other over time.
   B. Most Australian plant species remain undiscovered.
   C. Important information is being gathered by studying Australian plants.
   D. Australian rainforests are different from other rainforests.

25. In the context of the arguments made by the author, the phrase *unimportant appendages* (lines 17–18) refers to:

   A. the author's view of Australia's rainforests.
   B. a characteristic of Australia's plant species.
   C. the discovery of the southern pine species.
   D. a view of Australia's rainforests that the author dismisses.

26. Suppose that a previously unknown species of plant that is capable of producing medicine is found in an Australian rainforest. How would this information affect the author's opinion of Australian rainforests?

   A. It would support the author's opinion.
   B. It would contradict the author's opinion.
   C. It would neither support nor contradict the author's opinion.
   D. It would contradict the author's opinion only if this species of plant cannot be found anywhere else.

27. According to the passage, all of the following are considered benefits of studying Australian ecosystems EXCEPT:

   A. increasing knowledge of reproductive physiology and medicine.
   B. gaining information concerning evolutionary trends.
   C. furthering the understanding of the uses of hydroelectric power and solar energy.
   D. providing insight into ancient ecosystems.

GO TO THE NEXT PAGE.

Passage V (Questions 28-34)

The latest prominent principle of criminal sentencing is that of "selective incapacitation." Selective incapacitation, like general incapacitation, involves sentencing with the goal of protecting the community from the crimes that an offender would commit if he were on the street. It differs from general incapacitation in its attempt to replace bluntness with selectivity.

Under a strategy of selective incapacitation, probation and short terms of incarceration are given to convicted offenders who are identified as being less likely to commit frequent and serious crimes, and longer terms of incarceration are given to those identified as more crime prone. Selective incapacitation has the potential for bringing about a reduction in crime without an increase in prison populations. This reduction could be substantial.

Reserving prison and jail space for the most criminally active offenders in some instances conflicts not only with other norms of legal justice, but with norms of social justice as well. Repeat offenders fall basically into two categories: those who are prone to violence and those who are not. If we reserve the sanction of incarceration only for the dangerous repeat offender, excluding the white collar offender and certain other criminals who pose no serious threat of physical injury to others, we may end up permitting harmful people from the middle class to evade a sanction that less privileged offenders cannot. Some white collar offenders, after all, impose greater costs on society than many dangerous street offenders.

One of the most pervasive criticisms of selective incapacitation is that it is based on the statistical prediction of dangerousness; because such predictions are often erroneous, according to this point of view, they should not be used by the court. This criticism is related to both the nature of the errors and to the use of certain information for predicting a defendant's dangerousness. Let's first consider the nature of errors in prediction.

Prediction usually results in some successes and in two kinds of errors: "false positives" and "false negatives." The problem of false positives in sentencing is costly primarily to incarcerated defendants who are not really so dangerous, while false negative predictions impose costs primarily on the victims of subsequent crimes committed by released defendants. In predicting whether a defendant will recidivate, the problem of false positives is widely regarded as especially serious, for many of the same reasons that it has been regarded in our society as better to release nine offenders than to convict one innocent person.

A tempting alternative is to reject prediction altogether; obviously, if we do not predict, then no errors of prediction are possible. A flaw in this logic is that, whether we like it or not—indeed, even if we tried to forbid it—criminal justice decisions are now, and surely always will be, based on predictions, and imperfect ones, at that. Attempts to discourage prediction in sentencing may in fact produce the worst of both worlds: the deceit of predictive sentencing disguised as something more tasteful, and inferior prediction as well. If we are to reserve at least some prison and jail space for the most criminally active offenders, then the prediction of criminal activity is an inescapable task. Is selective incapacitation truly an effective and appropriate proposal, an "idea whose time has come," or is it a proposal that carries with it a potential for injustice?

---

28. Suppose the number of dangerous criminals that would be imprisoned under selective incapacitation but otherwise set free is greater than the number of harmless criminals who would be set free under selective incapacitation but otherwise imprisoned. How would this information be relevant to the passage?

    A. It weakens the claim that the goal of selective incapacitation is to protect the community.
    B. It strengthens the claim that there are more violent than non-violent criminals.
    C. It weakens the claim that selective incapacitation would not increase prison populations.
    D. It strengthens the claim that white-collar criminals unfairly receive shorter sentences.

29. Implicit in the author's discussion of the idea of rejecting statistical prediction is the idea that:

    A. statistical prediction will always be imperfect.
    B. a judge may well make more errors than a flawed statistical formula would.
    C. prediction will never attain widespread acceptance in the criminal justice system.
    D. sentencing should not take into account a criminal's future behavior.

GO TO THE NEXT PAGE.

30. Assuming that the author would defend the idea that we should employ statistical prediction in sentencing, which of the following defenses would the author most likely advocate LEAST?

    A. Prediction has always been used in sentencing.
    B. Prediction will reduce the overcrowding in prisons.
    C. Rejecting statistical prediction leaves us with no predictive basis for sentencing.
    D. Making some predictive errors is better than not predicting at all.

31. The author's statement that selective incapacitation may "end up permitting harmful people from the middle class to evade a sanction that less privileged offenders cannot" (lines 26–28) assumes that:

    A. there are more offenders in the lower-class than in the middle-class.
    B. the dangerous repeat offenders are lower-class and not middle-class.
    C. harmful middle-class people can use their money to avoid prison.
    D. lower-class offenders do not deserve to suffer incarceration.

32. Based on the information in the passage, if one's goal is to protect a community, one would employ a predictive formula that:

    A. maximized the number of "false positives" and "false negatives."
    B. minimized the number of "false negatives."
    C. minimized the number of "false positives."
    D. minimized the number of "false positives" and maximized the number of "false negatives."

33. Based on the passage, which of the following would most likely be cited by an opponent of statistical prediction as the reason that prediction should be abandoned?

    A. The possibility of letting a dangerous criminal loose is too great.
    B. The possibility of imprisoning a man who should be allowed to go free is too great.
    C. The court makes more accurate decisions when statistics is employed.
    D. Dangerousness has yet to be adequately defined as a legal concept.

34. Which of the following is a claim made by the author but NOT supported in the passage by evidence, explanation or example?

    A. Selective incapacitation may conflict with norms of social justice.
    B. The criticism of statistical dangerousness is related to the nature of predictive errors.
    C. Under selective incapacitation, first-time offenders would get short terms of incarceration.
    D. Some white collar offenders impose greater costs on society than many dangerous street offenders.

GO TO THE NEXT PAGE.

Passage VI (Questions 35-41)

A cause of fatal mining accidents was once the peculiar configuration of the controls on the trams shuttling along mineshafts. Each tram had a steering wheel that rose straight up from the floor, with a brake pedal on one side and an accelerator pedal on the other. There was no room to turn the tram around, so to reverse direction the driver simply took a seat on the other side of the steering wheel, whereupon what had been the brake became the accelerator, and vice versa. While this may sound ingenious, it proved disastrous.

Many people set an electric burner on high thinking that it will heat up faster that way: they have the mental model of a gas stove, whose knobs actually do increase the heat's intensity. On an electric stove, however, the knob is merely a switch that turns on the burner and then turns it off when a certain temperature is reached.

Consider the humble wristwatch, which has been transformed into a kind of wrist-mounted personal computer, with a digital display and a calculator pad whose buttons are too small to be pressed by a human fingertip. By replacing the watch's conventional stem-winding mechanism with a mystifying arrangement of tiny buttons, the manufacturers created a watch that was hard to reset.

One leading manufacturer was distressed to discover that a line of its particularly advanced digitals was being returned as defective by the thousands, even though the watches actually worked perfectly well. Further investigation revealed that they were coming back soon after purchase and thereafter in two large batches—in the spring and the fall, when the time changed.

Charles Mauro, a consultant in New York City, is a prominent member of a branch of engineering generally known as ergonomics, or human-factors—the only field specifically addressing the question of product usability. Mauro was brought in to provide some help to the watch manufacturer, which was experiencing what Mauro calls the "complexity problem." With complexity defined as a fundamental mismatch between the demands of a technology and the capabilities of its user, the term nicely captures the essence of our current technological predicament.

A growing number of technologists speak of user-centered design as a means of scrupulously maintaining the user's perspective from start to finish, adding technology only where necessary. When confronted by some mystifying piece of high-tech gadgetry, consumers naturally feel that there is something wrong with them if they can't figure it out. In truth it is usually not their fault. Mauro attributes the confusion to the fact that most products are "technology-driven," their nature determined not by consumers and their needs and desires but by engineers who are too often entranced with the myriad capabilities of the microprocessors that lie at the devices' hearts

Much of the work is a matter of finding the "mental models" by which users instinctively interpret a technology. Especially when the workings of a device are invisible, these models may very well be erroneous. The engineers' blindness to consumers' needs may be at the root of a deeper problem—how so much baffling technology enters the market. The problem has been blamed on the "waterfall method": new technological equipment tumbles out of a corporation, never encountering a typical user until it is bought. No single approach will eliminate all the complexity problems posed by current technology. But user-centered design can certainly help solve these problems, if only by encouraging manufacturers to consider the needs and abilities of the average user early on in the product-development process.

35. Based on the passage, an ergonomics expert would be likely to place high value on a product that:

   A. required no instruction at all to use.
   B. did not incorporate modern technology.
   C. could be easily manipulated by hand.
   D. solved complex problems for its user.

36. Suppose a watch manufacturer were to market a watch with a conventional winding mechanism and the watch was returned as defective by the thousands. How would this information affect the argument made in the first paragraph?

   A. It would weaken the argument.
   B. It would support the argument.
   C. It would weaken the argument if the watches were coming back because they didn't run correctly.
   D. It would weaken the argument if the watches were coming back right after the time changed.

GO TO THE NEXT PAGE.

37. The claim in the last paragraph that "no single approach will eliminate all the complexity problems posed by current technology" is:

    A. necessarily true, given the information presented in the passage.
    B. perhaps true, and supported by the information presented in the passage.
    C. perhaps true, but not supported by any information in the passage.
    D. necessarily false, given the information presented in the passage.

38. The author claims that poor design of tram controls was to blame for fatal mining accidents. The designer of the tram controls might best counter this by arguing that:

    A. it should not have been that difficult to adjust to the change in direction.
    B. the driver should not have switched the pedals.
    C. the tram was never intended to move in the reverse direction.
    D. the driver's erroneous "mental model" was to blame for the accidents.

39. When consumers feel that there is something wrong with them if they can't figure a high-tech gadget out, which of the following assumptions are they making?

    A. The gadget was designed for ready use by the average consumer.
    B. Technology can only be understood by engineer-types.
    C. The gadget designers were blind to the consumers' needs.
    D. Everyone is equally capable of understanding new technology.

40. Which of the following would most *weaken* the contention that the nature of technological products is not determined by consumers and their needs and desires?

    A. Many of a product's features are added because they are eye-catching in the showroom.
    B. Consumers are buying more technological products now than ever.
    C. Computers are upgraded so rapidly that new models are obsolete in a year.
    D. The answering machine has come to be regarded as a necessity rather than a luxury.

41. According to one consumer survey, a third of all VCR owners have given up trying to program their machines for time-delayed viewing. How would the author probably explain this fact?

    A. VCR owners have not yet found the correct mental model by which to interpret the VCR.
    B. Those owners have concluded that the VCR was not well designed.
    C. Those trying to program the machine are not as technologically savvy as they should be.
    D. The VCR is the result of technology-driven rather than user-centered design.

GO TO THE NEXT PAGE.

Passage VII (Questions 42-47)

The eminent sixteenth-century philosopher and jurist Jean Bodin denounced those who scoffed at the belief in the existence of witches. Their protestations of disbelief, he declared, showed that they were most like-
5 ly witches themselves. He wrote of the pact that "confessed" witches said they had signed with Satan. It obliged them to ridicule all talk of witchcraft as superstitious invention and contrary to reason. They persuaded many naive persons, Bodin insisted, whose arrogance
10 and self-deception was such that they would dismiss as impossible even the actions of witches that were right before their eyes.

Because self-deception and secrecy from self point to self-inflicted and often harmful ignorance, they invite
15 moral concern: judgments about responsibility, efforts to weigh the degree of harm imposed by such ignorance, and questions of how to help reverse it. If the false belief is judged harmless and even pleasurable, as may be the case with the benevolent light in which most of us
20 see our minor foibles, few would consider interfering. But clearly there are times when people are dangerously wrong about themselves. The anorexic girl close to starving to death who thinks that she looks fat in the mirror, and the alcoholic who denies having a drinking
25 problem, are both in need of help.

Yet the help cannot consist merely in interference, but must somehow bring about a recognition on the individuals' part of their need and the role they play in not perceiving their problem accurately. Judgments about
30 when and how to try to help people one takes to be in self-inflicted danger depend on the nature and the seriousness of the danger, as well as on how rational one thinks they are. To attribute self-deception to people is to regard them as less than rational concerning the dan-
35 ger one takes them to be in, and makes intervention, by contrast, seem more legitimate. But this is itself dangerous because of the difficulties of establishing that there is self-deception in the first place.

Some feel as certain that anyone who does not
40 believe in their deity, their version of the inevitable march of history, or their views of the human psyche deceives himself as they might feel about the self-deception of the anorexic and the alcoholic. Frequently, the more improbable their own views, the stronger is their
45 need to see the world as divided up into those who perceive the self-evident and those who persist in deluding themselves.

Aiding the victims of such imputed self-deception can be hard to resist for true believers and enthusiasts of
50 every persuasion. If they come to believe that all who do not share their own views are not only wrong but actually know they are wrong in one part of their selves that keeps the other in the dark, they can assume that it is an act of altruism to help the victimized, deceived part
55 see through the secrecy and the self-deception. Zealots can draw on their imputing self-deception to nonbelievers to nourish any tendency they might have to a conspiracy theory. If they see the self—their own and that of others—as a battleground for a conspiracy, they may
60 then argue that anyone who disagrees with them thereby offers proof that his mind has been taken over by the forces they are striving to combat.

It is not long before they come to see the most disparate events not only as connected but as *intended* to
65 connect. There are no accidents, they persuade themselves. Calling something trivial or far-fetched counts, for holders of such theories, as further evidence of its significance. And denying what they see as self-evident is still more conclusive proof.

---

42. Focus on the main ideas of the passage. Which of the following general theories would be LEAST in disagreement with the theme of the passage?

    A. One's own beliefs shape one's judgment of the beliefs of others.
    B. One should strive to rid oneself of all self-deception.
    C. One is always aware at least to some degree of one's self-delusions.
    D. One can never conclusively show that another person is deceiving himself.

43. Suppose one knows that a friend is not nearly as physically fit as the friend believes himself to be. According to the passage, one should:

    A. attempt to persuade the friend that he is deceiving himself.
    B. prevent the friend from engaging in strenuous physical activity.
    C. disabuse the friend of his belief if his lack of fitness endangers him.
    D. realize that one may be wrong about the friend's level of physical fitness.

GO TO THE NEXT PAGE.

KAPLAN

44. Given the information in the passage, if someone who believed there was a government conspiracy to cover up visits by extraterrestrials were to watch a TV program that debunks the idea of extraterrestrials, that person would most likely:

A. conclude that the program's producers were part of the conspiracy.
B. begin to suspect that she was suffering from self-delusion.
C. claim that the idea behind the program was trivial or far-fetched.
D. argue that the narrator of the program was himself an extraterrestrial.

45. Based on the information in the passage, the author believes that someone with very unorthodox views of the human psyche is:

A. probably suffering from harmless self-deception.
B. acting as irrationally as an alcoholic or an anorexic.
C. likely to perceive differing views as self-delusional.
D. unable to establish the presence of self-delusion in others.

46. Based on the passage, the author would probably agree that people who believe in a conspiracy theory:

A. believe themselves to be protected from harm.
B. know that in one part of themselves they are wrong.
C. should not be allowed to voice their radical opinions.
D. will not be dissuaded from their belief by even strong evidence.

47. Which of the following, if true, would most *weaken* the author's argument in the first paragraph?

A. The "confessed" witches were burned at the stake by townspeople.
B. A significant percentage of the modern American population believes in witches.
C. The supposed sixteenth-century witches never confessed or signed a pact.
D. Those whom Bodin accused of witchcraft were really witches.

GO TO THE NEXT PAGE.

Passage VIII (Questions 48-54)

Later Maya occupations of the Yucatan Peninsula site called Colha have undergone excavation since 1979. In 1993, researchers made the first systematic effort to document a pre-ceramic presence at the tropical, forest-
5 ed location. Early Colha farmers inhabited the area in two phases. There are stone tools in deeper soil layers dating from 2500 B.C. to 1700 B.C., based on radiocarbon age estimates of accompanying charcoal bits. Comparable dates come from an adjacent swamp, where
10 pollen analysis documents forest clearance by 2500 B.C.

The pollen provides evidence for the existence of several cultivated crops soon thereafter, mainly corn and manioc, a starchy plant. From about 1400 B.C. to 1000
15 B.C., Colha residents made foot-shaped stone tools that were chipped and sharpened on one side. Preliminary scanning electron microscope analysis of polish on these tools suggests that inhabitants used them to cut away vegetation after controlled burning of trees, and,
20 perhaps, also to dig.

An example of the same tool, known as a constrict-ed uniface, also emerged last year at Pulltrouser Swamp, a Maya site 20 miles northwest of Colha with a prelim-inary radiocarbon date of 1300 B.C. to 1000 B.C. for the
25 artifact. Its unusual design led researchers to suspect that Colha might have harbored an extremely early Maya population. Another sharpened stone point retrieved at Pulltrouser Swamp dates to between 2500 B.C. and 2000 B.C. Several other sites in Belize have
30 yielded constricted unifaces, but archaeologists have been unsure of their ages and origins.

Techniques used to manufacture constricted uni-faces show gradual refinement and modification in stone tools of Colha residents living after 1000 B.C.
35 Continuity in stone tool design and manufacture sug-gests that pre-ceramic Maya inhabited Colha, rather than non-Maya peoples who migrated to the area and later left or were incorporated into Maya villages. "None of us had any reason to suppose that Colha would
40 produce a pre-ceramic Maya occcupation," remarks the director of excavations at Cuello, a Maya site that dates to about 1000 B.C. "This is a bit of archaeological serendipity." This is evidence of the earliest known Maya, who cleared and farmed land bordering swamps
45 by 2,500 B.C. The earliest Central American farmers probably settled at the edges of swampland that they had cleared and cultivated. Excavations of pre-ceramic Colha so far have focused on quarry and field areas.

However, some pottery may still show up in early resi-
50 dential structures.

---

48. The recent findings presented by the author in the passage provide new insight into Mayan civiliza-tion because:

    A. Mayans may have settled extensively through-out the Yucatan penninsula.
    B. ceramic pottery may have been used by the Mayans.
    C. Mayans may have settled in regions much ear-lier than previously thought.
    D. stone tools were never used by the Mayans.

49. The passage implies that archaeologists previously believed which of the following theories concern-ing ceramic use and Mayan civilization?

    A. Stone tools were used by the Mayans to create elaborate clay pottery.
    B. The cultivation of crops and the development of pottery occurred simultaneously.
    C. Mayan settlements could be identified by the existence of ceramic pottery remains.
    D. Mayans did not use ceramics unless they inhabited an area near a swamp.

50. Some would argue that the significance of Pulltrouser Swamp and Colha could use some clar-ification. Which of the following statements clari-fies the significance of these sites?

    A. Pottery retrieved at Colha and stone tools dis-covered at Pulltrouser Swamp show that non-Mayans and Mayans co-existed in the Yucatan.
    B. Stone tools retrieved from excavation sites at Pulltrouser Swamp lead scientists to believe that non-Mayan peoples inhabited this area.
    C. The discovery of a uniquely-designed stone tool in a known Maya site indicates that Mayans may have inhabited the sight before 1000 B.C.
    D. The findings at Pulltrouser Swamp and Colha offer scientists no conclusive evidence.

GO TO THE NEXT PAGE.

51. According to the passage, early Colha farmers were probably:

A. Mayans who used stone tools.

B. Mayans who did not use stone tools.

C. non-Mayans who used stone tools.

D. non-Mayans who made ceramics.

52. In the context of the passage, the author quotes the use of the term "archaeological serendipity" (lines 42–43) to refer to:

A. the discovery of stone tools.

B. the unexpected findings that gave researchers a new understanding of ancient settlements.

C. the method used by archaeologists to excavate ancient civilizations.

D. the Mayan's ability to work with their environment.

53. According to the information presented by the author in the passage, analysis of the stone tools retrieved from Colha led researchers to believe all of the following EXCEPT:

A. a population of pre-ceramic Mayans existed who used and designed stone tools.

B. Mayans had settlements prior to 1000 B.C.

C. non-Maya peoples inhabited the area before the Mayans migrated and took over.

D. the tools underwent various stages of development.

54. Which of the following discoveries would lead archaeologists to change their recently-formed opinions on pre-ceramic Mayan populations?

A. Careful study of a "constricted uniface" shows that this tool was used to clear away vegetation.

B. After extensive excavation of the Colha dwellings, researchers discovered ceramic pottery remains dating back to 2500 B.C.

C. Continued excavation at Colha has produced stone tools dating back to 2500 B.C.

D. At a known Maya settlement, archaeologists recently uncovered pottery dating back to 1000 B.C.

GO TO THE NEXT PAGE.

Passage IX (Questions 55-60)

The tsetse fly, belonging to any of approximately twenty species composing the genus *Glossina*, is indigenous to Africa and is found primarily in forests and savannas south of the Tropic of Cancer. Dependent on vertebrate blood for nourishment, the tsetse fly is equipped with a long proboscis which is sharp enough to penetrate most animal skins and powerful enough to enable the tsetse to drink quantities of blood up to three times its own body weight. Measuring less than half an inch in length, this tiny pest has emerged at the center of health and environmental controversies.

At the same time that the tsetse drains blood, it can also transmit a variety of dangerous diseases. A bite from a tsetse fly can induce African sleeping sickness in human beings and nagana, a similar ailment, in domestic livestock. The agent of these diseases is the *trypanosome*, a unicellular, flagellated parasite which feeds primarily on the blood of vertebrates and is generally transmitted by an intermediary leech or insect host, such as the tsetse fly. In humans the *trypanosome* causes damage to the brain and spinal cord, leading to extreme lethargy and, ultimately, death; in livestock, *trypanosomes* destroy red blood cells, causing fatal anemia.

The immune system is ill-equipped to counter *trypanosomes*. As the immune system attempts to counter disease, antibodies are produced to attack microbes whose antigens, surface proteins, are foreign to the body. Various antibodies are specific for particular antigens. However, the *trypanosome* is capable of disguising itself by altering its genetic code, thereby changing its antigen coating in resistance to each new antibody that evolves. This "quick change" has confounded pathologists and made the development of effective vaccines elusive.

A controversy has been sparked between proponents of the elimination of the tsetse fly and African environmentalists. Those in favor of eradication feel that in addition to reducing disease, the removal of the tsetse fly will open immense tracts of land to cattle breeding. This, however, is precisely what the opposition fears. Environmentalists and conservationists dread the day when cattle and livestock, permitted to roam and graze freely, will uncontrollably devour plush African grasslands, converting them into barren desert. They argue that the tsetse fly must remain for the sake of the land.

With efforts to eradicate the tsetse fly largely unsuccessful, a compromise between tsetse control and tsetse elimination need not be forced. Control may offer the only available option for the interests of both health and environment. Since the protozoan cannot be conquered through antibodies or vaccines, scientists have begun efforts to prevent the transmission of the *trypanosome* parasite by eliminating the tsetse. Attempts to eradicate the tsetse fly, however, have met with little success. Rhodesia used to combat tsetse by extensive brush cleaning, game shooting, and chemical attack, yet the fly persisted. Aerial pesticide treatments have produced inconclusive results.

The reproductive cycle of the tsetse fly is such that a larva pupates underground for several weeks before it emerges as an adult fly. This makes repetitive chemical sweeping at intermittent periods an inconvenient necessity. A third method, called the "soft approach," makes use of the tsetse's attraction to the odors of carbon dioxide, acetone, and octenol. Open bottles of these compounds are hung behind black screens and nets permeated with insecticides. Massive numbers of flies, attracted to the chemicals from great distances, are lured into the nets where they are poisoned and die. All of these methods, however, share the weakness of dependence on harmful chemicals, such as DDT, which threaten both the health of the humans who handle them and the environment in which their toxic residues amass.

---

55. All of the following statements correctly describe the relationship between the tsetse fly, the *trypanosome*, and vertebrates EXCEPT:

    A. vertebrate blood provides the nourishment for the transport of *trypanosomes*.
    B. the "bite" of a tsetse fly can kill vertebrates since it often injects a deadly chemical.
    C. both the tsetse fly and the *trypanosome* utilize vertebrate blood for nourishment.
    D. vertebrates may die after *trypanosome* contamination via a tsetse proboscis.

KAPLAN

GO TO THE NEXT PAGE.

56. In the passage, the author does NOT identify which of the following as a characteristic of the tsetse fly?

- **A.** Dependence upon vertebrate blood
- **B.** Ability to transmit a fatal parasite to livestock and humans
- **C.** Ability to alter its genetic code
- **D.** Ability to influence the African cattle population

57. The author of the passage believes that the tsetse fly must be controlled somehow. The passage implies that the tsetse fly must be controlled for all of the following reasons EXCEPT:

- **A.** to prevent the spread of disease throughout the African continent.
- **B.** the fact that many human and animal lives are threatened by *trypanosomes*.
- **C.** the fact that cattle in Africa are reproducing at an alarming rate.
- **D.** the fact that *trypanosomes* cannot be overcome by vaccine.

58. In many warm climates, locusts feed on agricultural crops and lizards feed on locusts. Which of the following is most analogous to the effect that eradicating the tsetse fly would have on African grasslands?

- **A.** Locusts transmit a deadly parasite from the agricultural crops to the lizards.
- **B.** Lizards are dependent upon both the locusts and the grasslands for nourishment.
- **C.** Elimination of the locusts results in bumper wheat crops.
- **D.** Elimination of lizards results in locust infestation and devastation of agricultural crops.

59. According to African environmentalists, which of the following accurately describes the effect the tsetse fly has on the African grasslands?

- **A.** If the tsetse fly population continues to exist, the African grasslands will turn into barren wasteland.
- **B.** If the tsetse fly population continues to exist, the African grasslands will not be able to provide sufficient food supply for African cattle and livestock.
- **C.** Destruction of the tsetse fly population will lead to the conversion of grasslands into desert.
- **D.** Destruction of the tsetse fly population will cause overgrowth of the African grasslands.

60. Suppose that the author was presented with the following options for combating the problems associated with the tsetse fly. Which would the author most likely consider the best solution the tsetse problem?

- **A.** Using repeated insecticide treatment during the fly's pupal period
- **B.** Clearing away large tracts of tsetse infested brush
- **C.** Strictly-regulated use of the "soft approach" in predetermined areas
- **D.** Continued research toward the development of a trypanosome vaccine

STOP. If you finish before time is called, check your work. You may go back to any question in this test booklet.

ANSWER KEY
VERBAL REASONING TEST 4

1.	B	16.	C	31.	B	46.	D
2.	D	17.	B	32.	B	47.	D
3.	A	18.	D	33.	B	48.	C
4.	B	19.	A	34.	D	49.	C
5.	C	20.	C	35.	A	50.	C
6.	D	21.	A	36.	D	51.	A
7.	B	22.	C	37.	C	52.	B
8.	D	23.	D	38.	C	53.	C
9.	C	24.	B	39.	A	54.	B
10.	B	25.	D	40.	A	55.	B
11.	C	26.	A	41.	D	56.	C
12.	D	27.	C	42.	A	57.	C
13.	B	28.	C	43.	C	58.	D
14.	B	29.	B	44.	A	59.	C
15.	A	30.	C	45.	C	60.	C

EXPLANATIONS

PASSAGE I

Topic and Scope:
The author discusses the capitalist nature of American society and argues that American unions derive many of their traits from American values.

Mapping the Passage:
¶s1-4 discusses the capitalist nature of American society and its connection to American notions of equality (European perspective ¶3).
¶5 discusses the difference between American labor unions and those in other democracies.
¶6 outlines the rise of American labor unions and early predictions about the form they would take.
¶7 says that the character of the American Labor movement is derived from the nation's values.

Questions:
1. B Where are the differences between foreign and American labor unions mentioned? ¶5. Scanning down the answer choices shows that you need to focus on the use of violence and bargaining. ¶5 argues that American labor unions are more militant and that bargaining techniques are "more decentralized," though this doesn't indicate whether the American unions are more or less likely to bargain than their foreign counterparts. Scanning the choices armed with these facts turns up (D).

Wrong answers:
(A): Opposite. The author argues that the American unions are more militant than their foreign counterparts.
(C): Out of Scope. We have nothing in the text to indicate the relative likelihood that an American union would bargain.
(D): Out of Scope. As above.
Strategy Point: Scanning answer choices vertically to see if a certain pattern occurs can be helpful in predicting.

2. (D) An incorporation question. We're looking for something that challenges that author's main ideas. Quickly review the main ideas in the passage before scanning the choices. While three of the choices fit characteristics the author mentions, choice (D) indicates that corporations are characterized more by their altruism than by their capitalism, which runs directly counter to the author's point in ¶1.

Wrong answers:
(A): Opposite. The author argues in ¶7 that American labor unions have more full-time salaried officials than their foreign counterparts.
(B): Opposite. The author also makes this point in ¶7 when discussing "narrow self-interest."
(C): Opposite. The author discusses a difference in class solidarity in ¶7.

3. A Look for Roman numerals that counter what the author is arguing. Start with RN II, which appears in three out of four answer choices. Where does the author discuss the difference between American unions and others? Hit the fifth paragraph. The author argues that American unions are more "narrowly self-interested." RN II must therefore be true, and all the answer choices but (A) can be eliminated. RN III is true based on line 56–60. RN I runs counter to the author's main point, most forcefully expressed in ¶s1 and 2, that class solidarity is less important than equality of opportunity.

Wrong answers:
(B): Opposite. As above.
(C): Opposite. As above.
(D): Opposite. As above.

4. B Predict how this new information could be incorporated into the passage. What characteristic of labor unions in general would political action involve? The willingness to engage in non-labor issues. The author argues in ¶7 that American unions are less likely to take part in this sort of activity, and this new information would therefore contradict the author's argument. (B) fits.

Wrong answers:
(A): Opposite. Since political involvement is non-union activity, the author's point about such activity would be weakened.
(C): Opposite. The author makes a clear argument on the point, and so the information must have some impact on the argument.
(D): Out of Scope. The overall good of society isn't a focus of this particular part of the author's argument.

5. C Go back to review the relevant line numbers. Reading the few lines that come afterwards illuminate the meaning of the phrase: the "materialistic bent" seems to be, according to the author, the focus on profit-making and possessions as a mean of advancement. Choice (C) fits.

Wrong answers:

(A): Faulty Use of Detail. The author mentions the opinions of European socialists in the passage, but in reference to Americans.

(B): Distortion. The European travelers are forming an opinion about American characteristics, not necessarily democracy as a whole.

(D): Out of Scope. Though it would seem to fit as a criticism religion might make of secular values, the author never uses it in this way.

6. D   What is the author's main argument about the influences of American labor movements? The author makes the point that American labor unions are most influenced by the American value system and culture. While three of the answer choices are described by the author as being American influences, foreign labor movements are of course not American and so would not have influenced the outlook of their American counterparts. (D) it is.

Wrong answers:

(A): Opposite. The author mentions secular values at the beginning of ¶3.

(B): Opposite. This is mentioned in conjunction with secular values in ¶3 also.

(C): Opposite. This, though not an American value, is mentioned as an influence in ¶7.

7. B   Look for something that fits in with the traditional American system that the author discusses throughout the passage, or eliminate three answer choices that clearly don't fit. (B), individual achievement, is touted in ¶1 as one of the central values of the American system.

Wrong answers:

(A): Opposite. This is a value of foreign democracies, not an American traditional value.

(C): Faulty Use of Detail. While this is mentioned as an influence on American labor unions, it's not a part of the traditional value system.

(D): Faulty Use of Detail. Marxist ideology is described as a quality of foreign labor unions, not American values.

PASSAGE II

Topic and Scope:

The author discusses the formation , transformation, and composition of coral reefs.

Mapping the Passage:

¶1 introduces the notion of symbiotic relationships in a marine environment with the example of the anemone and the clown fish.

¶s2 and 3 discuss the symbiotic organisms responsible for the formation of coral reefs and point out that much of the mechanism for forming reefs remains unknown.

¶4 discusses two theories on the formation of barrier reefs.

¶5 points out that coral reefs contain far more algae than coral, and that the name "coral reef" is therefore a misnomer.

Questions:

8. D   Your map will remind you that a full paragraph discusses the misnomer "coral reef." Summarize the main reason why this is true: Reefs have lots of algae, not much coral. (D) matches the prediction.

Wrong answers:

(A): Faulty Use of Detail. The author argues at the end of ¶5 that this is why the term persists, but it doesn't explain the misnomer.

(B): Distortion. While the reef's conditions for growth depend on the algae, the coral could also play a major role in determining survival.

(C): Faulty Use of Detail. While true as described in ¶5, this doesn't explain why the term "coral reef" would be misleading.

Strategy Point: When a question asks for an answer that is the focus of a whole paragraph, predict by summarizing the paragraph's overall point.

9. C   A question with some tricky wording; be very careful in dissecting it. If an opponent with Darwin's theory wouldn't agree with something, who would agree with it? Darwin! The question is basically asking for something that is part of Darwin's theory. Even armed with this information, the question isn't easy. Darwin's theory is mentioned in ¶4 in a roundabout fashion. Go back to review the details: The author implies that Darwin theorized that volcanic islands caused the transformation. (C) rewards that prediction.

Wrong answers:

(A): Faulty Use of Detail. This is a belief that scientists in general hold (¶5); it's not a component of Darwin's theory specifically.

(B): Faulty Use of Detail. As above, this is just a definition of terms rather than a component of Darwin's theory.

(D): Opposite. This is the alternative to Darwin's theory; opponents of Darwin would probably believe this.

10. B   A difficult question to predict; review the main points of the passage in your map. Remember to eliminate while looking for the correct answer, using the denial test as needed. (B) must be an assumption of the scientists since they study the different types of reefs with the intent of understanding how they transformed from to another. Denying (B) and arguing that the three types developed independently destroys the transformation theories that the author discusses.

Wrong answers:
(A): Opposite. The author argues in ¶4 that Darwin's theory may be "partially true," suggesting that the two theories can coexist to some extent.
(C): Opposite. The author mentions corals without algae in the last part of ¶5.
(D): Opposite. The author shows in ¶s2 and 3 that a variety of factors influence reef renewal.

11. C How does the Enewetak atoll fit into the passage? Mentioned in ¶4, the author argues that it supports Darwin's theories about barrier reef formation. (C) matches the prediction exactly.

Wrong answers:
(A): Out of Scope. While it strengthens the claims of some scientists, it can't strengthen the claims scientists in general since there are competing theories.
(B): Out of Scope. As above.
(D): Opposite. The author states explicitly that the evidence strengthens Darwin's theory.

12. D Review the main elements of Darwin's theory as described by the author in ¶4: Darwin believed that barrier reef formation was caused by submerging volcanic islands, and the author states that this theory is probably partially true. Look for an answer that seizes on one of these points. Choice (D) simply summarizes the theory.

Wrong answers:
(A): Opposite. The author argues in ¶4 that it's more persuasive in light of the evidence gathered at Enewetak atoll.
(B): Opposite. The theory's point is to describe the transformation from one type of reef to another.
(C): Distortion. The author argues that Darwin's theory is probably partially accurate, which also means that it's probably partially inaccurate.

13. B Where is the stimulation of calcium production mentioned? Go back to ¶2, keeping in mind that the author states that this mechanism is not well-known. If it were shown that the coral stimulates the algae to deposit calcium, the mechanism would become clearer. (B) repeats this.

Wrong answers:
(A): Out of Scope. This isn't a point of uncertainty, and has nothing to do with calcium deposits.
(C): Out of Scope. The author says that this is known also; the new evidence would have no bearing on it.
(D): Out of Scope. The author doesn't discuss a connection between calcium deposits and coral colors.

Strategy Point: A good understanding of chains of evidence and points of uncertainty is key— it will be tested often on Natural Science passages.

PASSAGE III

Topic and Scope:
The author describes the skeletal structure of *Archaeopteryx lithographica* and how it illustrates the evolutionary leap from reptile to bird.

Mapping the Passage:
¶1 discusses the coincidental connection between Eastern mythical beasts and real animals.
¶2 gives an overview of *Archaeopteryx*, emphasizing its reptilian and bird-like features.
¶s 3 and 4 discuss skeletal features in *Archaeopteryx* that suggest it probably lacked the ability to fly.
¶5 discusses skeletal features in *Archaeopteryx* that seem adapted for movement on the ground and argues that *Archaeopteryx* is probably a transitional species between reptiles and birds.

Questions:
14. B Where is the Jurassic period mentioned? Go back to the second paragraph. Archaeopteryx lived during the latter part of the Jurassic period. If the fossil of a bird living before this were discovered, what would that do to the theory that Archaeopteryx was a transitional species between reptiles and birds? It would weaken it, as birds would have already existed. (B) repeats this line of reasoning.

Wrong answers:
(A): Opposite. If Archaeopteryx lived after birds, it could not represent a bridge between reptiles and birds.
(C): Opposite. The order of Archaeopteryx and birds in the fossil record is crucial to the author's argument.
(D): Out of Scope. The theory about the development of pectoral muscles wouldn't be affected by the new evidence.

Strategy Point: Always pay attention to dates and time periods when mentioned in questions, particularly in natural science passages.

15. A Quickly consider the main points of the passage and the structure of your map before checking the answer choices. A good map will immediately lead to (A) as untrue: much of the passage deals with the differences between the skeletons of Archaeopteryx and modern birds, so (A) can't possibly be true.

Wrong answers:
(B): Opposite. This is mentioned in ¶5.
(C): Opposite. This is one of the main points of the passage.
(D): Opposite. This is mentioned in ¶5.

16. C Go back to the passage to review the lines in context. For whom is this information valuable? Primarily for the scientists who are studying the evolution of flight. Applying this prediction to the answer choices turns up (C).

Wrong answers:

(A): Out of Scope. No recent research projects are mentioned in the passage.

(B): Out of Scope. While the skeletal structure has been key in supplying the information about flight's evolution, the "information" in the question stem is about the evolution itself, not the skeletal structure.

(D): Out of Scope. As above, though the fossil discoveries provide information on evolution, they are themselves not the information being referred to by the phrase.

17. B Review the main points of the author's argument: Archaeopteryx was a transitional species that had some similarities to birds and quite a few differences. (B) is a specific example of a difference the author implies. If Archaeopteryx couldn't fly, then its wings must have had a function different from that of birds.

Wrong answers:

(A): Opposite. The author argues in ¶5 that its tail was very well-developed, more so than present-day birds.

(C): Out of Scope. Intelligence isn't mentioned in the passage.

(D): Out of Scope. This is tempting if you draw your own conclusions. Remember to stick to the passage: relative size isn't mentioned.

18. D Go back to the passage to review the function of sternum in birds. A sternum is needed to support strong pectoral muscles, which are used to fly (lines 24–27). Therefore, if Archaeopteryx did have a bird-like sternum, it's reasonable to think that it might have flown, directly challenging one of the author's main contentions. (D) matches the prediction.

Wrong answers:

(A): Out of Scope. Sternums or the lack thereof have nothing to do with the geography of the area.

(B): Out of Scope. The author never gives any indication that sternums can be used for dating organisms.

(C): Out of Scope. The passage makes no connection between sternums and feathers.

19. A Review your map to get a grasp of where to find the details in this question. Be aware of the main similarities and differences between Archaeopteryx and birds when tackling the choices. (A) immediately jumps out: since Archaeopteryx did have feathers, it certainly doesn't differ from birds by lacking them.

Wrong answers:

(B): Opposite. This is mentioned in ¶3.

(C): Opposite. This is also mentioned in ¶3.

(D): Opposite. This is mentioned in ¶4.

PASSAGE IV

Topic and Scope:
The author discusses some unique ecological features of Australia.

Mapping the Passage:
¶1 discusses Australia's geographic movement over time.
¶2 argues that Australia's native species provide unique insights into how the world works.
¶3 discusses Australian rainforests and the prospect of undiscovered plant species.
¶4 discusses the importance of Australian dinosaur fossils to the understanding of dinosaurs in general.
¶5 argues that Australia's harsh conditions led to coadaptation and efficient ecosystems.

Note: when there are abrupt transitions between paragraphs, take the whole passage in context in order to determine the topic and scope. Here, each paragraph discusses an individual way in which Australia's ecology is important in scientific research.

Questions:
20. C Take quick stock of where evidence is most likely to appear in the passage before hitting the Roman numerals. Their frequency in the choices and order coincide, so start with RN I. The end of ¶3 states that, by some estimates, 7000 plant species remain undiscovered in Australia. Eliminate (B). ¶1 deals with the substance of RN II. Eliminate (A) and (D), which leaves only (C). RN III can be eliminated as outside the scope; the author never discusses the number of species on other continents.

Wrong answers:

(A): Opposite. As described above.

(B): Opposite. As described above.

(D): Opposite. As described above.

21. A What is the author's point in writing the passage? It seems to be the general promotion of Australian ecosystems. Look for an action that would further this purpose. (A) fits well as an action that would increase knowledge and awareness of a particular Australian ecosystem.

Wrong answers:

(B): Opposite. The author would certainly be horrified by the destruction of part of a unique Australian ecosystem.

(C): Distortion. Though the author thinks that Australian ecosystems should be studied and recognized, there's nothing to indicate that he desires international press coverage.

(D): Out of Scope. While the greenhouse effect is mentioned, fighting it is not.

22. C Where does the author mention evolution, specifically as it applies to Australia? The last paragraph which states that the harsh conditions of Australia forced species to coadapt more (and compete less) than species on other continents. Choice (C) summarizes this point.

Wrong answers:
(A): Out of Scope. There's no basis in the passage for this claim.
(B): Distortion. Though the author thinks that the unique aspects of Australia are worthy of attention, there's nothing to indicate the international scientists have neglected them.
(D): Distortion. Though Australia has been drifting north for this length of time, there's no reason to believe that evolution on the continent wasn't taking place before this. Be careful not to choose an answer choice because you recognize a specific date or name from the passage.

23. D Note the double negative "NOT disagree"— we're looking for an answer choice with which the author would agree. Scan the answer choices. While no answer choice matches a general summary made by the author, (D) coincides with the specific example the author gives of an unusual dinosaur species that hibernated in a cold climate (¶4)

Wrong answers:
(A): Distortion. Though the one specific example of an Australian dinosaur mentioned was small, this doesn't mean that *all* Australian dinosaurs were small.
(B): Out of Scope. There's no basis for this in the passage.
(C): Out of Scope. There's nothing in the passage to suggest this chronology.

24. B Keeping the author's main points and your own map in mind, look for an answer choice which directly conflicts. (B) is false based on the passage. If researchers have listed 18,000 species and believe that 7,000 remain undiscovered, then the majority of the species *have* been discovered.

Wrong answers:
(A): Opposite. This is discussed in ¶1.
(C): Opposite. Species of "worldwide importance" are mentioned in ¶3.
(D): Opposite. This is also mentioned in ¶3.

25. D Go back to review the statement in context, being careful to keep viewpoints straight. While the author uses the phrase in question to refer to Australia's rainforests, he doesn't endorse it: the rest of the sentence refutes it (the "unimportant appendages" are "now widely acknowledged" as leading to discoveries of "worldwide importance"). The author therefore has to be using this phrase ironically. (D) matches the prediction.

Wrong answers:
(A): Opposite. The author takes the opposite view.
(B): Opposite. The phrase refers to Australia's rainforests.
(C): Opposite. As above, the phrase refers to the rainforests in general.

26. A Paraphrase the author's main argument about the Australian rainforests: they're unique and worthy of careful study. How would finding a useful medicine affect this claim? It would validate the idea that the rainforests were worth studying. (A) straightforwardly summarizes this.

Wrong answers:
(B): Opposite. The discovery of useful plants would support the author's claims.
(C): Opposite. As above.
(D): Opposite. It supports the author's claim even more strongly if the plant is unique to the Australian rainforests.

Strategy Point: Straightforward questions like this are easy points if you keep the author's main arguments in mind.

27. C Review the parts of your map that touch on the benefits of studying Australian ecosystems; eliminate answer choices that match up while looking for something that falls outside the scope of the passage. (C) is never mentioned, and it would be difficult to imagine how studying ecosystems could provide insight into hydroelectric or solar power anyway.

Wrong answers:
(A): Opposite. This is mentioned in ¶2.
(B): Opposite. This is mentioned in ¶5.
(D): Opposite. This is mentioned in ¶3.

PASSAGE V

Topic and Scope:
The author discusses the benefits and drawbacks of tying the length of prison terms to a prediction of an offender's likelihood to commit crimes in the future.

Mapping the Passage:
¶s 1 and 2 describe the concept of selective incapacitation and its potential advantages.
¶3 describes a potential injustice of selective incapacitation: more lenient sentences for the better-off.
¶s4 and 5 discuss another potential drawback: errors in statistical prediction that lead to unjust or dangerous sentencing.
¶6 discusses the possibility of rejecting prediction altogether but argues that some form of prediction is necessary.

Questions:
28. C An incorporation question with some difficult initial information to sift through. A quick vertical scan of the answer choices shows that you need to determine whether the information strengthens or weakens various arguments that the author makes. Since the claims in the choices are diverse, try to predict what would happen based on the information alone. If the information in the question is true, then more criminals will be going into

prison than coming out. Looking for an answer choice that touches on this turns up (C). Of course, if the prison population is increasing, the claim that selective incapacitation would not increase the prison population is weakened.

Wrong answers:
(A): Opposite. If more dangerous criminals are being imprisoned, this claim would be strengthened.
(B): Out of Scope. This claim is never made, and the relative numbers of the imprisoned would have no effect on it even if it were.
(D): Opposite. This opinion would be strengthened by the evidence that more dangerous criminals are justly receiving longer sentences.

29. B An assumption question. Where does the author mention the possible rejection of statistical prediction? Focus on the last paragraph. The author argues that some sort of explicit prediction is necessary, because if statistical prediction isn't used, prediction will still creep into sentences anyhow. How will it do so? Presumably through human influence rather than statistics. The author argues that this human prediction will be "inferior." Though the prediction is general, it should lead easily to (B). Use the denial test: If (B) weren't true, then there would be no reason to keep any sort of statistical prediction because judges would be more accurate.

Wrong answers:
(A): Faulty Use of Detail. The author states explicitly in ¶6 that (A) is true. Since this is stated explicitly, it's not implicit in the argument.
(C): Out of Scope. The author never indicates that this is true.
(D): Opposite. The author argues that prediction is necessary, and that sentencing therefore should take future behavior into account.

30. C Another question on statistical prediction: focus on ¶s4-6, reviewing the author's defenses for using statistical prediction. While the author would certainly agree with three of the answer choices, he would disagree with (C) because he believes that all sentencing has an element of prediction to it.

Wrong answers:
(A): Opposite. The author mentions this in ¶6.
(B): Opposite. This is discussed in ¶2.
(D): Opposite. This is discussed in ¶6.

31. B Review the given lines in context. If the less privileged offenders are punished more severely, then they must be predicted to be more dangerous. (B) repeats this. Use the denial test to verify: If the dangerous repeat offenders were middle class instead of lower class, then the harmful people in the middle class would be imprisoned more often, which runs contrary to the author's point.

Wrong answers:
(A): Distortion. While there may be more dangerous offenders, this doesn't mean that there are more offenders overall.
(C): Distortion. Though those in the middle class by definition have more money, there's no indication that they're using it to escape prison terms.
(D): Distortion. Though there may be class inequity in sentencing, this doesn't mean that all lower class offenders are undeserving of prison terms.

32. B A quick visual scan of the answer choices shows that we need to focus on the discussion of false positives and negatives in ¶5. If the sole goal is to protect the community, the best strategy would be to imprison as many potential offenders as possible. This could be accomplished either by maximizing the number of false positives or minimizing the number of false negatives. Scanning the answer choices for a match to this yields only (B).

Wrong answers:
(A): Opposite. Maximizing both would nullify the intended effect.
(C): Opposite. This would achieve the opposite effect.
(D): Opposite. This would also achieve the opposite effect.

Strategy Point: Questions with systematic answer choices generally require a lot of up-front prediction.

33. B Review the arguments that opponents of statistical prediction make. The main argument is that statistical prediction is unfair to the innocent. Only (B) matches this point.

Wrong answers:
(A): Opposite. As mentioned in ¶5, an opponent of prediction would be more in favor of letting a criminal go free than imprisoning an innocent person.
(B): Opposite. An opponent of statistical prediction would argue just the opposite.
(C): Out of Scope. The passage doesn't deal with this at all.

34. D Keep an eye on the map and the text as you look for an answer choice that the author mentions but doesn't back up. The author mentions (D) in ¶3 but provides no supporting evidence or explanation for the claim before moving on.

Wrong answers:
(A): Opposite. This is discussed in detail in ¶5.
(B): Opposite. This is also mentioned in ¶5 and backed up with detailed explanation.
(C): Out of Scope. The author never makes this claim at all.

PASSAGE VI

Topic and Scope:
The author discusses the problems caused by technological complexity and a possible approach to easing them.

Mapping the Passage:
¶s1 and 2 give examples of disconnects between technological design and human thought.
¶s3 and 4 describe the problem of technological complexity and give a supporting example.
¶5 defines complexity and gives an example of a specialist who attempts to combat the problem.
¶6 suggests that many technologists believe products should be designed around the needs of an "ordinary" user.
¶7 describes the origins of complexity: engineers design products without keeping the consumer in mind, and argues that user-centered design may help solve the problem of complexity.

Strategy Point: With passages such as this where the link between paragraphs is not immediately apparent, determine each paragraph's purpose and then look for the overall passage topic. Here, each paragraph discusses problems caused by technological complexity.

Questions:
35. A What do ergonomics experts value? According to ¶5, ease of use. Looking for a product that fits this criterion turns up (A). The example of the watch is helpful in reinforcing this point: the watches weren't defective, and presumably had instructions, but they were too complicated for users to understand.

Wrong answers:
(B): Distortion. Though an ergonomics expert would assert that technology should be easy to use, he wouldn't argue that technology should be eliminated altogether.
(C): Out of Scope. Ease of use doesn't necessarily indicate manipulation by hand. What about an ergonomic bathroom scale?
(D): Distortion. Though complex tasks should be made simpler, this doesn't mean that an ergonomic product has to solve complex tasks on behalf of its user.

36. D An incorporation question with a twist: the new information is very similar to an example in the passage. The only difference is that instead of complicated buttons, the watch has a winding mechanism. The watches could possibly be defective, and so it can't be argued that returning the watches alone strengthens or weakens the argument. If the watches were all being returned when the time changed, though, what would happen to the author's argument? The contention that people returned their watches because the new buttons were too complicated would be weakened; it would

seem more likely that there's a natural correlation between time changes and watch returns, technology or no technology. (D) fits.

Wrong answers:
(A): Distortion. The author's argument can only be weakened under the circumstances described in the passage.
(B): Opposite. Returning presumably ergonomic watches couldn't support the author's argument under any circumstances.
(C): Out of Scope. If the watches are in fact defective, then returning them has no effect on the author's argument since there's no tie to ease of use or technology.

37. C A quick scan of the answer choices' structure shows that you need to gauge the truth or falsity of the statement in context. Go back to the last paragraph to reread the author's points. There's nothing to indicate that the claim is false, but neither is there any support for its truth. It's just a claim the author makes before moving on. (C) restates this.

Wrong answers:
(A): Distortion. There's no information to suggest that the statement must be true.
(B): Distortion. While the statement is perhaps true, there's nothing given in the passage to support it.
(D): Opposite. The author wouldn't provide information in the passage that proved one of the passage's main points false.

38. C How would the designer of the controls potentially respond to the accusation that his design was poor? Review ¶1. The author says that trams were driven in reverse because there was no space to turn the tram around. The designer might point this out and argue that the tram was never designed to be operated in the reverse direction. (C) fits.

Wrong answers:
(A): Out of Scope. Whether or not it should have been difficult to adjust is a different question from whether it was difficult: the evidence shows that it was.
(B): Out of Scope. As described in the passage, there was no alternative but to switch the pedals, which makes this potential response meaningless.
(D): Out of Scope. Though this may be true, it begs the question of why the tram designer didn't take the user's mental model into account when designing the tram.

39. A The situation mentioned is identical to that described in ¶6; use the main ideas from it for reference. If a user can't operate a product and concludes that the fault is with them, what assumption are they making? That the fault doesn't lie with the product. In the context of the passage, products are at fault when they aren't designed with average users in mind. Choice (A) ties these ideas together. Using the denial test confirms the assumption: If the gadget wasn't designed for ready use by the average consumer, then the user would have no reason to believe that the fault lay with him.

Wrong answers:
(B): Distortion. Though the technology may have been designed by engineers, the user isn't necessarily assuming that no one but engineers can figure it out. As far as he knows, the problem lies only with him.
(C): Opposite. If the user assumed this, then there would be no cause to believe that the fault was his own.
(D): Opposite. As above, if this were assumed, there would be no reason for consumers to believe that something was wrong with them.

40. A Look for a fact that will counter the claim that products are created with technology in mind: the right answer choice should indicate that products are somehow user-centered. Armed with this prediction, you can quickly focus on (A). If many features are added because they are eye-catching, then they are being added not because of engineers, but because users are attracted to them.

Wrong answers:
(B): Out of Scope. The rate of buying has nothing to do with the design of the product.
(C): Out of Scope. Obsolescence has no connection with the product's design either.
(D): Out of Scope. Whether consumers feel they need a given product or not has no impact (at least according to the passage) on how a product is designed.

41. D How would the author explain a situation in which consumers give up on trying to master a certain technology? The author's main purpose is arguing that users do this because the technology isn't built around their needs and abilities. Searching for an answer choice that echoes this turns up (D).

Wrong answers:
(A): Opposite. The author argues that technology should be built around mental models, not the other way around.
(B): Out of Scope. The author isn't concerned with what the consumers think about the product as much as with how easily they can use it.
(C): Opposite. The author argues that consumers shouldn't have to be technologically savvy to use a common product.

PASSAGE VII

Topic and Scope:
The author argues that though self-deception does exist, many zealots mistakenly persuade themselves that those who do not share their extreme beliefs are self-deceived.

Mapping the Passage:
¶1 provides an example of someone with extreme beliefs about witches who imagined a conspiracy among those who didn't share those beliefs.
¶s2-4 note that self-deception can be harmless or dangerous and argue that judgments about another's self-deception can be clouded by one's own personal beliefs.
¶5 argues that those with extreme beliefs may consider themselves altruistic by persuading others that they are deceiving themselves by not sharing those beliefs.
¶6 suggests a sort of snowball effect that reassures those with extreme beliefs that they are in fact correct particularly when challenged.

Questions:
42. A A rare global question. Predict by summarizing the main point of the passage: Personal beliefs cloud our opinion of whether others are self-deceived. (A) immediately rewards the careful prediction.

Wrong answers:
(B): Distortion. The author argues in ¶2 that some self-deception is benign, and this isn't the focus of the whole passage anyway.
(C): Faulty Use of Detail. This is the belief of those with strong beliefs of their own, as described in ¶5. It's not the point of the whole passage, however.
(D): Distortion. Another answer choice that doesn't summarize the passage. The author never makes this claim.

43. C What would the author suggest one do in response to someone else's self-deception? Predict based on ¶2: If the deception is harmful, intervene. If not, hands off. Applying this rule to the specific situation yields a course of action identical to (C).

Wrong answers:
(A): Distortion. The author would argue that this should be done only if the friend is in danger, a qualification added in the correct answer choice.
(B): Out of Scope. Deception is the focus of the passage; this answer choice veers off topic.
(D): Distortion. The author argues that people can be wrong about the *beliefs* of others. In this case, the deception is centered on a physical state which the question says can be known.

44. (A) What does the author claim about people who believe in conspiracies? They believe, as the example in the first paragraph demonstrates, that those who deny the conspiracy are in on it. Applying the generalization to the specific situation, the TV watcher would probably think that the television station was part of the conspiracy. (A) fits the bill.

Wrong answers:
(B): Opposite. The viewer, with her extreme views, would be more inclined to believe that *others* are self-deluded.
(C): Out of Scope. There's no evidence in the passage to suggest that the viewer would react this way.
(D): Distortion. The supposed conspiracy is designed to *cover up* aliens; it's not composed of the aliens themselves.

Strategy Point: The MCAT will test you repeatedly on your ability to generalize from a specific situation and to apply that generalization to an analogous situation.

45. C How would the author characterize "very unorthodox views"? Most likely, she'd classify them as extreme views. What is the author's main point about those with extreme views? They perceive others as self-deluded and attempt to rescue them from the supposed deception (¶5). (C) captures the first part of the prediction.

Wrong answers:
(A): Faulty Use of Detail. Though the author argues that self-deception can be harmless, she doesn't suggest that those with extreme views are probably suffering harmlessly from self-deception.
(B): Faulty Use of Detail. Though the author argues that alcoholics and anorexics do behave irrationally, she doesn't suggest that those with extreme views are suffering from the same sort of self-deception.
(D): Opposite. The author suggests that the person with extreme views would at least persuade themselves that others were deluding themselves.

46. D Review the author's points regarding those who believe in conspiracy theories: they tend to hold extreme views and believe that attempts to argue against the conspiracy are in fact a product of the conspiracy itself. Scanning the answer choices armed with this summary turns up (D): if denials are seen as a product of the conspiracy, the conspiracy theorist will only become *more* persuaded of the conspiracy by evidence to the contrary.

Wrong answers:
(A): Out of Scope. This isn't mentioned anywhere in the passage.
(B): Opposite. Rather, they believe that *others* know this, and so can be convinced of the "correct" viewpoint.
(C): Distortion. The author defines their opinions as radical, but never argues that they should be disallowed to voice them.

47. D Summarize the author's purpose of writing the first paragraph: to provide an example of a man who believed in a conspiracy so strongly that any evidence to the contrary was taken as further proof of the conspiracy.

What would weaken the point of this example? If Bodin were actually right! The witch hunt turns up (D).

Wrong answers:
(A): Out of Scope. There's no evidence to suggest that the witches burnt were actually witches. Notice the quotations around "confessed," implying that that the confessions were less than convincing, or were coerced.
(B): Out of Scope. The belief of a population in a different time period doesn't have any impact on the example in question.
(C): Out of Scope. This would seem to be true anyway based on the example, but has no weakening effect in any case.

PASSAGE VIII

Topic and Scope:
The author discusses evidence suggesting that pre-ceramic Mayan culture existed much earlier than originally thought.

Mapping the Passage:
¶s1 and 2 discuss the Colha area and a pre-ceramic settlement that left behind stone tools.
¶3 provides more evidence of stone tools in other areas that give clues to the Mayan culture's age.
¶4 emphasizes that Maya themselves inhabited Colha and explains that Mayan culture may date back to 2500 B.C.

Questions:
48. C A global question testing your grasp of the passages overall point. Predict: Mayans were around long before scientists first thought. (C) fits.

Wrong answers:
(A): Out of Scope. The findings don't discuss the extent to which Mayans settled throughout the Yucatan.
(B): Faulty Use of Detail. Scientists believed this in the first place; it's not the point of the passage.
(D): Opposite. The passage gives evidence that stone tools *were* used (lines 14–16). Another answer choice that focuses on detail instead of the broad picture.

49. C What was the relationship between Mayans and pottery before Colha? Scientists thought that they'd found the oldest Mayan settlements when they found the oldest pottery. In other words, they thought that pottery and Mayan settlements went hand in hand. (C) states this in a slightly different way.

Wrong answers:
(A): Distortion. This answer choice takes different elements in the passage and rearranges them into something completely unfamiliar.

(B): Opposite. The passage suggests that crop cultivation occurred *before* pottery since there are traces of it around Colha.

(D): Distortion. Though some evidence was found near a swamp, that doesn't mean that Mayans didn't use pottery unless they were near a swamp.

50. C Go back to the passage to locate Pulltrouser swamp. Why is it important? It provides evidence that Mayans inhabited the area earlier than anyone thought. Only (C) deals with a conclusion that focuses principally on the Maya, and it matches our prediction.

Wrong answers:

(A): Opposite. The author suggests in ¶3 that the culture was exclusively Maya.

(B): Opposite. As above, the evidence points to a Mayan culture.

(D): Opposite. The author's point in mentioning the findings is to provide evidence for the main point of the passage.

51. A Where are Colha farmers mentioned? Go back to the relevant parts of the map and the passage. A quick scan of the answer choices will show that you're looking for basic traits of the Colha farmers. The passage argues that they were Mayans (the point of the passage) who used stone tools (a primary piece of evidence.) Choice (A) fits.

Wrong answers:

(B): Opposite. The evidence of stone tools in the passage is designed to support the Mayan hypothesis.

(C): Opposite. The point of the passage is that Mayans inhabited these early settlements. Non-Mayans are excluded by the evidence and are outside the scope of the passage anyhow.

(D): Opposite. As above, with the added knock that the evidence shows the Colha culture to be pre-ceramic.

52. B Go back to the last paragraph to review the phrase in context. The director of the excavations states that they didn't expect what they found at the settlement and were lucky to have found it; in other words it was serendipity. (B) encapsulates this.

Wrong answers:

(A): Faulty Use of Detail. This is a piece of evidence that helped to prove the conclusions referred to in the phrase.

(C): Out of Scope. The researcher using the phrase is concerned with unexpected findings, not methods used to reach those findings.

(D): Out of Scope. This is never mentioned in the passage as a concern of the researchers or as a conclusion based on the evidence.

53. C Locate the part of the passage dealing with stone tools to eliminate wrong answer choices quickly, keeping an eye out for an answer choice that doesn't fit

with the overall point of the passage. Even without elimination, (C) jumps out: the point of the evidence in the passage is to show that Mayans were indigenous to the area; (C) contradicts this.

Wrong answers:

(A): Opposite. This is a primary conclusion drawn from the evidence in ¶3.

(B): Opposite. Another conclusion from the stone tools, and the point of the passage.

(D): Opposite. Another conclusion supported by ¶3.

54. B What would change the researchers' opinions? Take stock of the main pieces of evidence that could have an effect: probably something having to do with stone tools, ceramics, or farming that conflicts with the existing interpretation. Scanning down the answer choices with these in mind turns up (B): If pottery remains date back to 2500 B.C., then the Colha settlement wasn't pre-ceramic after all.

Wrong answers:

(A): Out of Scope. This may very well have been a function of the stone tools, but it doesn't go against anything the scientists currently think.

(C): Out of Scope. This would just reinforce the idea that the Mayans were at Colha as far back as 2500 B.C.

(D): Out of Scope. Scientists already knew that Mayans were making pottery in 1000 B.C.; the passage is concerned with a time period before that.

PASSAGE IX

Topic and Scope:
The author discusses the health crisis caused by the tsetse fly and the environmental problems caused by attempts to eradicate it.

Mapping the Passage:
¶1 introduces general information about the tsetse fly.
¶2 discusses diseases caused by the fly.
¶3 discusses the reasons the immune system responds poorly to a parasite transmitted by the fly.
¶4 summarizes the controversy between African environmentalists and those who want to eliminate the tsetse fly.
¶s5 and 6 outline strategies that have been used to destroy the fly itself, and their potential environmental drawbacks.

Questions:
55. B Refer back to your map and the passage to eliminate details that are in the passage, keeping an eye out for one that contradicts a claim made in the passage. (B) suggests a mechanism for illness completely different from the parasitic transmission the passage discusses.

Wrong answers:
(A): Opposite. This is mentioned in ¶2.

(C): Opposite. This can be deduced from information in ¶s 1 and 2 about each of the two organisms.

(D): Opposite. As above, this can be deduced from information about the fly and the parasite in ¶s 1 and 2, respectively.

56. C As in the last question, keep an eye on the passage and the map while looking for a choice that doesn't fit the passage's evidence and explanation. (C) attributes a characteristic of the *trypanosome* parasite (described in ¶3) to the fly itself.

Wrong answers:

(A): Opposite. This is mentioned in ¶1.

(B): Opposite. This is the topic of ¶2.

(D): Opposite. A little removed from the other choices, but this can be inferred from the environmentalists' concerns in ¶4.

57. C Review the passage's arguments for control of the tsetse fly: it spreads a nasty disease that is hard to control once it gets a foothold. This prediction knocks out all choices but (C). In fact, if cattle were reproducing too quickly, it would stand to reason that the tsetse fly should be allowed to flourish in order to keep the cattle population in check (as environmentalists argue in ¶4).

Wrong answers:

(A): Opposite. This can be inferred as a goal of fly control since the disease can't be controlled once it takes hold.

(B): Opposite. This is mentioned in ¶2.

(D): Opposite. This is the topic of ¶3.

58. D Predict carefully. We have an insect and a non-insect in the new situation, but the species are irrelevant: their order in the ecosystem is the relevant piece of information. What are locusts that feed on crops analogous to in the passage? Cattle that feed on grassland. Likewise, lizards feeding on the locusts are analogous to the tsetse fly that feeds on the cattle. Environmentalists argue that eliminating the fly would allow cattle to run wild and destroy the grasslands (¶4). Looking for an answer choice in which eliminating the lizards allow the locusts to run wild and destroy crops turns up (D).

Wrong answers:

(A): Distortion. This answer choice is designed to trap those who draw a parallel between the locust and the tsetse fly without thinking about their roles.

(B): Out of Scope. Drawing the analogy back to Africa would require the tsetse flies to feed on the grasslands, which doesn't happen.

(C): Out of Scope. Again extending the analogy back to Africa, this would be parallel to eliminating cattle, while we're concerned with eliminating the tsetse fly.

Strategy Point: Don't get drawn off-topic in a question by superficial similarities!

59. C Summarize the point made by the environmentalists in ¶4: the fly keeps herd animal populations in check and thereby prevents them from destroying the African grasslands. (C) restates this point.

Wrong answers:

(A): Opposite. The environmentalists argue that the grasslands will disappear if the tsetse fly is *eliminated*.

(B): Opposite. As above, they believe that the tsetse prevents this situation from happening.

(D): Opposite. The environmentalists believe that destruction of the fly will lead to destruction of the grasslands.

Strategy Point: You've now researched this information in ¶4 three times. On test day, make sure to use previous research to answer questions quickly and score easy points.

60. C Review the author's discussion of approaches to controlling the tsetse fly in the last few paragraphs. The author argues that the soft approach is effective, though environmentally touchy, and that active measures should be taken to control the fly population. (C) is the only approach that fits in with this general prescription.

Wrong answers:

(A): Opposite. The author states in ¶6 that flies in the pupal period escape death by being underground, and that insecticide use is therefore potentially ineffective.

(B): Opposite. The author points out in ¶5 that this was tried without success in the past.

(D): Opposite. The author argues in ¶3 that the search for a vaccine isn't likely to be successful anytime soon.

Materials used in this test section were adapted from the following source(s):

Sissela Bok, "Secrets: On the Ethics of Concealment and Revelation." © 1982 by Pantheon Books.

B. Bower, "Maya Beginnings Extend Back at Belize Site." © 1994 by *Science News*.

Timothy Flannery, *The Future Eaters*. © 1994 by Reed Books.

Brian Forst, "Selective Incapacitation: A Sheep in Wolf's Clothing?" © 1984 by *Judicature*.

Seymour Martin Lipset, *The First New Nation*. © 1979 by W.W. Norton and Co., Inc.

John Sedgwick, "The Complexity Problem." © 1993 by *The Atlantic Monthly*.

Verbal Reasoning Test Five

Time—85 minutes
Question 1–60

DIRECTIONS: Each of the passages in this test is followed by a set of questions based on the passage's content. After reading each passage, decide on the one best response to each question and mark it on your answer sheet. If you are unsure of an answer, eliminate the choices you know are wrong and choose from the remaining choices. You may refer to the passages while answering the questions.

Passage I (Questions 1–8)

Physicians have disagreed for years about whether they should be involved in capital punishment of convicted criminals. Some physicians vigorously support participation, often arguing that organs should first be removed
5 for transplantation. One frequent objection to capital punishment is that sometimes techniques don't work the first time, resulting in lingering, painful deaths. If physicians would guarantee that a patient would not die in such a way, they would gain the trust of some patients.

10 For any kind of killing, some physicians favor the creation of "designated killer" technicians. This would free physicians from the taint of killing, keeping their image pure and their hands clean. But is this workable? Insofar as the designated killers are mere technicians, what pre-
15 vents them from abusing their role? Wouldn't it be better for physicians, torn between saving life and honoring patients' wishes, to be reluctant killers? Wouldn't physicians know best what to do if something went wrong?

Many physicians paradoxically endorse mercy
20 killing but refuse to do it themselves. Nor do they think other physicians should kill. Physicians who support mercy killing but who don't want physicians to kill commonly emphasize the importance of maintaining the role of the physician as a healer and preserver of life. One
25 poll of American physicians showed 60 percent favoring euthanasia but less than half would perform it themselves. To such physicians, taking life radically conflicts with the symbolic image of physicians. Such conflict, they say, destroys trust in physicians.

30 Discussing this problem of designated killers in 1988, *New England Journal of Medicine* editor Marcia Angell called the idea "an unsavory prospect." She suggested that mercy killing may one day be the end point of a continuum of good patient care. She asks how any
35 physician can excuse himself from this most basic notion? Dr. Angell concluded, "Perhaps, also, those who favor legalizing euthanasia but would not perform it should rethink their position."

Dr. Angell implies that it is hypocritical to favor
40 mercy killing but would be unwilling to perform it. Is this true? There are at least two schools of thought. Some thinkers believe that if one favors, say, meat-eating, one should be willing to kill and prepare animals for eating oneself. Others conclude differently, seeing no
45 reason why each person who favors a position must be willing to implement it.

Must you be willing to kill a serial murderer to favor capital punishment? Critics say one must. Being face-to-face with one's victims creates basic moral qualms and
50 such moral restraints are important to respect. In Stanley Milgram's studies on obedience, naive subjects under an experimenter's control were dramatically less willing to inflict injury as the victims became closer to subjects under study. In contrast, as the consequences of actions
55 became more remote, such as by pressing a switch which released a bomb on an unseen, unknown populace, it became easier to inflict injury.

---

1. Consider the main points that the author makes throughout the passage. The primary purpose of this passage is to:

    A. speculate on the symbolism of the physician as healer.
    B. portray those doctors who argue against administering euthanasia as hypocritical.
    C. cast and explain the different arguments surrounding euthanasia.
    D. introduce the concept of "designated killers" to a receptive audience.

2. According to the passage, which of the following is most likely to be true of those physicians who favor the creation of so-called "designated killers?"

    A. They believe it is good patient care to provide a continuum of services.
    B. They seek to keep the physician remote from acts of harm.
    C. They understand that it raises a conflict with their opinions on capital punishment.
    D. They fear abuse of the privilege that comes from this unique role.

GO TO THE NEXT PAGE.

3. Suppose the following four scenarios took place in the United States in the next year. Which of these scenarios would strengthen the argument against doctors performing acts of euthanasia?

A. A poll of American physicians shows that more than half are against euthanasia.

B. A string of acts of euthanasia, administered by "designated killers," encounter medical difficulties.

C. Some physicians become more willing to perform euthanasia as they become more informed with the patient's case history.

D. In nations that have legalized physician-assisted suicide, patients with serious health conditions prefer to visit doctors who refuse to perform euthanasia.

4. For which of the following claims does the passage NOT offer supporting evidence?

A. Forty percent of American physicians disagree with or have no opinion concerning the practice of euthanasia.

B. American physicians have debated their role in capital punishment at successive national conferences.

C. The moral difficulties that physicians encounter in capital punishments are not to be dismissed.

D. The *New England Journal of Medicine* has adopted an editorial stance against the suggested use of "designated killers."

5. According not necessarily to the author, but to those in favor of euthanasia specifically, what is a potentially negative aspect of the use of "designated killers?"

A. They would disrupt the continuum of patient care provided by a physician.

B. They might release physicians from an association with death.

C. Their use might prevent lingering, painful deaths.

D. The prescription of euthanasia may become more prevalent as physicians are removed from the act itself.

6. Suppose that the American Medical Association adopted the use of practiced "designated killers" as it is mentioned in the passage. Which of the following might be expected responses, based on information presented in the passage?

A. The *New England Journal of Medicine* issues an editorial condoning the practice.

B. A poll of American physicians shows a great increase in the number of physicians willing to attend to mercy killings.

C. Some physicians note an increase in trust between themselves and patients.

D. The presence of physicians at capital punishment proceedings becomes more widespread.

7. The reader can conclude that a basic assumption of those in favor of using "designated killers" is that:

A. the practice would evolve into a readily available medical option.

B. very few physicians could be convinced to assume the role and duties.

C. physicians would have to be present with the patient in order to conduct euthanasia.

D. many physicians are reluctant to administer euthanasia because they are not in favor of capital punishment.

8. The paradox of physician-endorsed euthanasia is summarized in the passage by which of the following?

A. Many physicians endorse the idea of euthanasia but are unwilling to perform the act or would prefer other physicians to perform it.

B. Many physicians agree with euthanasia and are willing to endorse a cadre of "designated killers" that would perform the act.

C. Many physicians endorse euthanasia because it ends long-term pain and suffering.

D. Many physicians endorse euthanasia and are unwilling to perform it until it is endorsed by a professional association.

GO TO THE NEXT PAGE.

Passage II (Questions 9–13)

In August 1348 the bubonic plague, or Black Death, suddenly appeared in England. Its germs were carried by the fleas on black rats that came into the country on ships from abroad. The first outbreak of the plague was of intense ferocity, for the people had no immunity and persons living close to the margin of subsistence fell victims to the disease.

Returning in 1361, the plague caused high mortality among children born since 1348; there were other visitations in 1368 and 1375. The best estimates place the population of England (exclusive of Wales, Scotland, and Ireland) at about 1.1 million in 1086, about 3.7 million in 1348, about 2.2 million in 1377, and not much more than that in 1450. High farming in the thirteenth century had been based on the scarcity of land, a large population, and a great demand for food—conditions that had forced the peasants to remain on their holdings and to accept the burdens of serfdom. But when the demand for food was less, the profits of agriculture shrank. High farming, which had already been slipping before 1348, came to an end.

The startling fact about those figures is the amazing drop in population between 1348 and 1377. It may be the number of people in overcrowded England already was beginning to decline before the coming of the Black Death. There were floods and famines in the years between 1315 and 1317. Certainly the plague caused a high mortality. In some monasteries the monks all but disappeared (it is thought that half the clergy in England fell victims to the pestilence). The Black Death had its most striking effect on the rural economy. The balance between the number of laborers and the amount of land under cultivation and the relations between lord and peasant were quickly altered. There were deserted villages and many unoccupied peasant holdings. After the first visitation widows and widowers remarried quickly and produced as many children as before; but because of the high mortality among young people this population increase was not maintained later in the century.

The work of the manor could not be performed by the villeins who had survived the plague; the lord had to employ casual labor at wages that doubled within a decade. Moreover, a villein, once tied to his holding by economic necessity, could easily run away to another manor where employment would be offered to him with no questions asked.

Landowners complained bitterly of the labor shortage and of the wages they had to pay. In 1351 they obtained the Statute of Laborers, which fixed wages at the rates before the plague, declared that all landless men must accept work when it was offered to them, and prohibited peasants from moving from one manor to another. For a time the statute had some effect, but in the long run it was useless, for wages continued to rise and employers had to pay them. There was also a scarcity of tenants. Few manors were without vacant holdings; hence the yield was less and income from the land declined. Agricultural products no longer fetched high prices. Yet the cost of luxuries and of manufactured goods was rising.

Thereafter the plague subsided in the rural areas but remained endemic in London and other towns, where it could become active at any time and could spread along lines of communication into the country. It remained in England for more than 300 years.

9. Which of the following was NOT a contributing factor in the dependence of the peasantry on high farming as a means of subsistence?

   A. A large population
   B. A widespread outbreak of plague
   C. A great demand for food
   D. A scarcity of land

10. Look back on the arguments made by the author. Which of the following statements is supported within the passage?

    A. In the long run, the Statute of Laborers was useful in slowing the inflationary pressure on wages.
    B. The plague continued to trouble England sporadically until the end of the seventeenth century.
    C. The demand for food stayed roughly equivalent after the first attack of plague.
    D. It was difficult to break an obligation to one landowner in the wake of the plague.

GO TO THE NEXT PAGE.

11. According to information brought forth by the author in the passage, the economic difficulties brought on by the Black Death were not quickly resolved because:

   A. potential workers were afraid to leave their homes due to the fear of contracting disease.
   B. population gains that might have been made by remarriages were offset by a high infant mortality rate.
   C. many landholdings were left unoccupied, often without recourse.
   D. the Statute of Laborers fixed wages at the pre-plague levels.

12. Of the many economic effects brought about by repeated attacks of plague, the author considers which of the following the most important?

   A. The great demand for food and conversely, the shortage of arable land
   B. The vacancies incurred by landowners due to the plague
   C. The introduction of wage controls in a rapidly fluctuating economy
   D. The alteration of the relationship between landowner and land-worker

13. Which of the following claims would, if true, most substantially *weaken* the author's claim that the plague brought an end to the practice of high farming?

   A. The practice of high farming was reinforced after the floods and famines in the 1310s reduced the amount of arable land.
   B. Immediately following the plague, the profits of agriculture would see a rebound due to the stabilization in wages and food prices.
   C. The numbers of peasants working on English farms decreased throughout much of the years of plague.
   D. The Statute of Laborers began to be strictly enforced when it became apparent that wages were still rising.

GO TO THE NEXT PAGE.

Passage III (Questions 14–19)

In Manhattan, the beauty of the night sky is only a faded metaphor, the shopworn verse of an outdated love song. The stars shine no brighter at midnight in midtown than the ones depicted on the time-dimmed ceiling of the waiting room at Grand Central Terminal. The eternal orange glow of the city lights leaves only the faintest hints of the blackness beyond. And when the sky is truly clear and the clouds do not reflect this amber aura, the brightness of the city environs constrict the pupils so much that only the moon can be seen on most evenings. But over the last few weeks it has been possible, even in Manhattan, to watch the evening star—Venus—descending in the west, presenting her orbit, edgewise, to viewers on Earth.

Venus is the luminous body hanging over New Jersey to the west in the early evening. In spite of the fact that it emanates no light of its own—only reflecting light from its neighbor and provider, the sun—it is brighter than any heavenly object visible from Earth except the sun and the moon. For the moment, Venus becomes apparent at twilight, about a third of the way up the western sky, and it sets around 11. Every night people go to bed wondering what strangely bright star that is. To those who live in New York City, it may be the only star they see when trapped on this tiny little island. Whatever the case, in the morning no one remembers that luminous body any longer.

To say, as one must, that Venus is not a star but a planet seems ungrateful, almost pedantic. Astronomers might have us know that this distinction is not a mere splitting of hairs, but the most basic of divisions, not unlike that of plants and animals. Be that as it may, it is the kind of technicality the English essayist Charles Lamb had in mind when defending the generosity of his personal ignorance almost 200 years ago. "I guess at Venus," he wrote, "only by her brightness." Lamb was no Copernican, and neither are most of us. We are little Ptolemies every one. The sun rises and sets upon us. When one lies upon a meadow late at night, etherized by the fullness of the sky, it is all one can do to imagine the simplest of celestial motions—the pivoting of constellations around the North Star. To impart to each point of light the motions that are proper to it—to do the unimaginable calculus of all those interfering rotations, those intersecting gravities—is simply impossible. It is easier to imagine that one is staring at the ceiling of a celestial waiting room, forever spinning around and around above our heads.

But at the moment, one can almost picture the motion of Venus in its orbit, as if one were looking at a diagram of the solar system. Imagine a line between the sun, at sunset, and Venus, glittering high above the horizon. That, roughly speaking, is the path of the Venusian orbit. When Venus moves toward Earth, as it is doing now, it is the evening star, and when it moves away from Earth, it is the morning star. Even this, to some, might seem like a stretch of the abilities of conceptualization, but it is worth the challenge. For if one can muddle through this mental errand for a moment, it will become clear that a change is about to take place. The moment of transition will occur on June 10, when Venus passes between the sun and Earth. As May wears on, Venus will appear nearer and nearer the sun, until the planet is engulfed by twilight. Venus will come back into view, at dawn, sometime in late July.

For now, the evening star—Hesperus, as it was anciently known—is a steadily waning crescent, no matter how star-like or globular its light appears. It will not return to its present position until sometime in December 1997. And who knows where we will be by then? Surely someone, but not me, not one of the little Ptolemies, that stares up into the night sky and sees a most beautiful display, arranged every night for his personal enjoyment.

---

14. Which of the following would support the author's phrase, "We are little Ptolemies" (lines 37–38)?

A. Most people visualize the night sky from a geocentric point of view and in this way are unable to understand the complex paths of the numerous celestial motions in space.

B. Most people are not as knowledgeable about space as Copernicus or Ptolemy and for them, it is impossible to understand the complexities of numerous celestial motions in space.

C. Those who have studied astronomy are the ones most likely to understand the complexities of numerous celestial motions in space.

D. Those who are aware that Venus is a planet and not a star are still likely to refer to Venus as a star because of its beauty and resemblance to a star in the night sky.

GO TO THE NEXT PAGE.

15. Taking into account all the points made within the context of the passage, the author would most likely support which of the following statements?

    A. Venus can be observed in the sky only once every several years and only between May and late July.
    B. Venus may be observed first in the western sky and then in the eastern sky between May and late July.
    C. Without the astronomical skills of Copernicus, those on Earth are unable to comprehend Venus' orbit even though they may identify it by its brightness.
    D. Environmental and clean-up efforts should be made in Manhattan so that Venus and the other wonders of the night sky are again visible to those that reside there.

16. According to the passage, Hesperus is best observed in the evening when:

    A. Venus is moving toward Earth.
    B. Venus is moving away from Earth.
    C. Venus is passing between the sun and Earth.
    D. the sun's brightness does not make it impossible to see Venus without the aid of a telescope.

17. In the passage, the author describes the beauty of the night sky as all of the following EXCEPT:

    A. pivoting constellations.
    B. a verse in an old love song.
    C. a celestial waiting room.
    D. a stationary display of ethereal lights.

18. The existence of which of the following would most strongly conflict with the author's explanation of the motion of Venus in its orbit?

    A. A scientific article which asserts that Venus moves toward Earth every winter and spring
    B. A scientific article which asserts that Venus may be seen as one of the many points of light surrounding the North Star only at certain times of year
    C. A scientific article which asserts that in late July, Venus will be moving away from Earth
    D. A scientific article which asserts that, standing in the polluted streets of Manhattan, it is impossible to view Venus descending in the west

19. According to information given within the context of the passage, Hesperus is known as the evening star for all of the following reasons EXCEPT:

    A. as Hesperus passes between the sun and Earth, it is globular in form and appears star-like.
    B. until June 10, Hesperus can only be seen at twilight until about eleven o'clock at night.
    C. Hesperus' path toward Earth can be observed only in the evening as it descends in the western sky.
    D. except for the sun and the moon, Hesperus is sometimes the brightest object visible from Earth during the early evening.

GO TO THE NEXT PAGE.

Passage IV (Questions 20–26)

I eschew the notion of racial kinship. I do so in order to be free to claim what the distinguished political theorist Michael Sandel labels "the unencumbered self." The unencumbered self is free and independent, "unen-
5 cumbered by aims and attachments it does not choose for itself," Sandel writes. "Freed from the sanctions of custom and tradition and inherited status, unbound by moral ties antecedent to choice, the self is installed as sovereign, cast as the author of the only obligations that
10 constrain." Sandel believes that the unencumbered self is an illusion and that the yearning for it is a manifesta-tion of a shallow liberalism that "cannot account for cer-tain moral and political obligations that we commonly recognize, even prize"—"obligations of solidarity, reli-
15 gious duties, and other moral ties that may claim us for reasons unrelated to a choice," which are "indispensable aspects of our moral and political experience."

Sandel's objection to those who, like me, seek the unencumbered self is that they fail to appreciate loyal-
20 ties that should be accorded moral force partly because they influence our identity, such that living by these attachments "is inseparable from understanding our-selves as the particular persons we are—as members of this family or city or nation or people, as bearers of that
25 history, as citizens of this republic." There is an impor-tant virtue in this assertion of the value of black life. It combats something still eminently in need of challenge: the assumption that because of their race black people are stupid, ugly, and low, and that because of their race
30 white people are smart, beautiful, and righteous. But within some of the forms that this assertiveness has taken are important vices—including the belief that because of racial kinship blacks ought to value blacks more highly than others.

35 I shun racial pride because of my conception of what should properly be the object of pride for an indi-vidual: something that he or she has accomplished. I cannot feel pride in some state of affairs that is indepen-dent of my contribution to it. The color of my skin, the
40 width of my nose, the texture of my hair, and the vari-ous other signs that prompt people to label me black constitute such a state of affairs. I did not achieve my racial designation. It was something I inherited—like my creed and socio-economic starting place and sex—
45 and therefore something I should not be credited with.

In taking this position I follow Frederick Douglass, the great nineteenth-century reformer, who declared that "the only excuse for pride in individuals is in the fact of

their own achievements." I admire Sandel's work and
50 have learned much from it. But a major weakness in it is a conflation of "is" and "ought." Sandel privileges what exists and has existed so much that his deference to tradition lapses into historical determinism. He faults the model of the unencumbered self because, he says, it
55 cannot account for feelings of solidarity and loyalty that most people have not chosen to impose upon themselves but that they cherish nonetheless. This represents a fault, however, only if we believe that the unchosen attachments Sandel celebrates should be accorded moral
60 weight. I am not prepared to do that simply on the basis that such attachments exist, have long existed, and are passionately felt. Feelings of primordial attachment often represent mere prejudice or superstition, a hang-over of the childhood socialization from which many
65 people never recover.

---

20. With an eye towards the passage as a whole, which of the following represents the author's primary focus?

    A. Identity formation as self-definition according to family, history, and culture, or as self-defi-nition according to independent accomplish-ment
    B. The individual, unencumbered self and the validity of Michael Sandel's position on this type of identity
    C. Racial kinship and how its rejection results in accomplishment
    D. Individual versus group consciousness

21. In the passage the author discusses the political theorist Michael Sandel. In doing so he proposes that Sandel treats individuals' inherited interper-sonal connections with which of the following?

    A. Too little weight
    B. An unjustifiable moral force
    C. An unquestioning reverence
    D. A cursory critical treatment

GO TO THE NEXT PAGE.

22. Through his discussion of the works and beliefs of Michael Sandel, the author suggests all of the following characteristics of the encumbered self EXCEPT:

   A. it maintains many of the interpersonal connections established in childhood.

   B. it is influenced by history.

   C. it is the product of independent accomplishment.

   D. it is manifested in those who embrace racial kinship.

23. The author's indication that Sandel's "deference to tradition lapses into historical determinism" (lines 52–53) suggests that:

   A. Sandel's position undermines the belief that individuals forge their own lives and connections.

   B. historical events can often influence the actions of men in the present.

   C. respecting tradition is ultimately harmful.

   D. individuals should not expend energy paying homage to significant historical events or people.

24. Which of the following might the author find antithetical to his stance on identity, racial kinship, and racial pride?

   A. The right of every student to equal treatment by professors and teachers

   B. The Million Man March, in which 500,000 African-American men gathered for a demonstration of racial solidarity in Washington, DC in 1995

   C. The stance of public municipal hospital emergency rooms to provide all citizens with healthcare regardless of whether or not they are indigent

   D. The recognition of Elijah Lovejoy, a white man murdered in the early nineteenth century for supporting the abolition of slavery

25. The author's attitude toward Sandel's stance on the unencumbered self can best be described as:

   A. impersonal and academic in its consideration of both sides of the issue.

   B. one of strong, yet tempered disagreement.

   C. marginally hostile.

   D. dismissive.

26. The author states his definition of "what should properly be the object of pride for an individual" (lines 36–37) in order to:

   A. exhibit his support of Frederick Douglass's opinion at the end of paragraph one.

   B. undermine what Sandel categorizes as "the unencumbered self."

   C. lay the foundation for his argument against racial solidarity.

   D. ensure that readers do not perceive him as having the yearning that Michael Sandel calls a "manifestation of shallow liberalism".

GO TO THE NEXT PAGE.

Passage V (Questions 27–33)

In a poll conducted for a December 4, 1989 cover story in *Time* magazine entitled "Onward, Women!" the majority of women surveyed (fifty-eight percent) did not consider themselves feminists, though, conversely, a

5 similar majority (sixty-two percent) felt that feminism had been helpful to women. In 1991, the issue of feminism resurfaced in the mainstream media on a broad scale, from the release of the film *Thelma & Louise* to the publication of such books as Naomi Wolf's *The*

10 *Beauty Myth*, Susan Faludi's *Backlash*, and Gloria Steinem's *The Revolution Within: A Book of Self-Esteem*, to the attention given to the issue of sexual harassment in the wake of the Anita Hill/Clarence Thomas hearings. Shortly after the Hill/Thomas hear-

15 ings brought the issue of sexual harassment into the public eye, the music industry was rocked by the announcement of allegations of sexual harassment involving executives at three major record companies and an attorney at a leading L.A. law firm.

20 Even the Rock & Roll Hall of Fame, established in the mid-'80s to recognize the contributions of those involved in the music business, has been criticized for overlooking women's contributions to the industry. Mary Wilson noted this discrepancy in *Supreme Faith*

25 when she wrote about the Supremes' induction into the Hall of Fame in 1988, and her participation in the all-star jam that traditionally occurs after the ceremonies: "It seemed so symbolic of the record industry, and rock and roll in general, that the only two women on stage

30 were Yoko Ono, there to accept her late husband John Lennon's award [the Beatles were inducted into the Hall of Fame in the same year], and me." Out of the nearly one-hundred performers, songwriters, label executives, and promoters now in the Hall of Fame, the only female

35 inductees to date are Aretha Franklin and LaVern Baker, inducted as performers, Carole King (with Gerry Goffin), inducted as a non-performer, and Bessie Smith and Ma Rainey, inducted as "Forefathers."

Though the battle over abortion rights caused

40 women to recognize the underlying fragility of the gains the feminist movement had made, the media focus on other "women's issues" further illuminated the struggles women continued to face in society. A November 3, 1991, story in the *Los Angeles Times* not only discussed

45 the specific allegations mentioned above regarding sexual harassment, it also examined sexual harassment in the record industry as a whole, and revealed the "put up or shut up" bind women who experience harassment are placed in.

50 As a result, instead of going through the legal system, women working in the industry have been driven to create an informal grapevine to pass on information about companies deemed "safe havens" from sexual harassment and to warn each other about the "bimbo

55 hounds" in different record company departments. Fred Goodman and Ira Robbins, after discussing the harassment allegations in a "Rockbeat" column in the *Village Voice,* offered a pungent summary of the lack of respect women receive in the music industry by wryly observ-

60 ing, "We'd be willing to bet a woman will be president of the United States before one runs Sony Music or Warner Bros. Records."

Since then, the increasing threat to women's reproductive freedom in the U.S. has mobilized growing

65 number of women to reawaken from a state of "post-feminist" complacency. Attitudes toward a female presence in the workplace showed little signs of change in other areas of the music industry. An article in *Billboard* in March 2, 1991, noted that though almost half the sales

70 positions in radio were held by women, there were far fewer women working in programming or on-air positions. Phyllis Stark, the article's author, made the observation that "Many women say they simply are not taken seriously"—a perception that has a disturbingly familiar

75 ring. In the same article, Lisa Lyons, a program director at Dayton, Ohio station WAZU, related a story about the necessity of "dressing down" (a tactic similar to the one Gail Colson had adopted when she was managing director at Charisma Records in the '70s) that also sounds

80 depressingly familiar; "I always make it a point to look like a slob. It's a little humiliating and degrading when an artist shakes your MD's [music director's] hand and asks you to sleep with him."

---

27. If given a chance to expand on the points made in the passage in an interview or on a news program, the author might possibly cite all of the following statements as evidence that discrimination towards women exists within the music industry EXCEPT:

    A. the lack of qualified female executives heading major record labels.
    B. the minimal effect the physical appearance of women has on their success in the music industry.
    C. the small percentage of female artists inducted into the Rock & Roll Hall of Fame.
    D. the secure job status of the executives and attorney charged in the sexual-harassment case.

GO TO THE NEXT PAGE.

28. For which of the following statements does the passage provide no support or substantiation?

A. Fewer women than men work as radio personalities or music programmers.

B. Several female executives have been denied promotion to leadership roles within the music industry.

C. Only two female artists were represented at the 1988 Hall of Fame inductions.

D. A majority of women feel that feminism has been helpful to women.

29. Based on the examples provided in the passage, with which of the following assertions is it most likely that the author would disagree?

A. Working women face few pressures to maintain a physically attractive appearance.

B. Women have often tied the success of the feminist movement to the fight over abortion.

C. Women working in the music industry are subject to similar obstacles as working women in other fields.

D. Women working in the music industry have not achieved status commensurate with their contribution to the art.

30. Each of the following is cited by the author in the passage as evidence of the reawakening of feminism EXCEPT:

A. the release of the film *Thelma & Louise*.

B. women's response to the increasing threat of abortion rights.

C. the induction of the first women into the Hall of Fame.

D. the publication of Naomi Wolf's *The Beauty Myth*.

31. Suppose the number of female executives within the music industry has not increased measurably within the past two decades. If this statement is true, what effect would it have on the author's argument?

A. It would support the argument that women already hold too many positions at the executive level.

B. It would contradict the argument that men focus on women's physical appearance.

C. It would support the argument that the number of females inducted into the Hall of Fame will increase rapidly in the coming years.

D. It would support the argument that women are not moving ahead in sectors such as the music industry.

32. Which of the following statements, if true, would most strengthen the author's claims about sexual discrimination in the music industry?

A. Several female candidates were passed over for the top job at Charisma Records in the 1970s.

B. The executives charged with harassment in paragraph one were eventually found not liable for civil damages.

C. Female artists are often included on ballots for induction into the Hall of Fame.

D. The level of training and qualification is the same between men and women in the music industry.

33. The pointed inclusion in the passage of Bessie Smith and Ma Rainey as "Forefathers" indicates that the author believes that:

A. women are slowly beginning to receive their due in the music industry.

B. women have always had a large, if unacknowledged, role in music history.

C. women artists are poorly recognized by even the music industry's highest honors.

D. women had a strong influence on the early development of popular music.

GO TO THE NEXT PAGE.

Passage VI (Questions 34–40)

…Those amused by all the evidence of gullibility should remember the Cardiff Giant. In 1868, in upstate New York, what seemed to be the remnants of a gigantic human being were unearthed. Thousands came to see it at a dollar a view. The director of the New York State Museum called it "the most remarkable object yet brought to light in this country." The first human had been found and was American. The Giant was in fact a badly made gypsum statue, aged with ink, sand, and acid.

Britain has just completed a Research Assessment Exercise in which ten thousand scientists were graded by their supposed peers. A low score means no more money, a high one an extra slice of cake. Its results were predictable. Those who have get more; those who have not get nothing. Expect a wave of fraud inquiries the next time the government inspectors come round. The deceits will be less fun to unravel than was Piltdown since those who commit them are making pathetic efforts to save a career rather than grandiose attempts at fame. There is, certainly, *some* dishonesty. Perhaps there is more than there was. It can be blamed on the intrusion into the laboratory of the moral of the marketplace.

What to accept about the past is, too often, a matter of the spirit of the time. The first human fossil, Neanderthal Man, was, in 1856, dismissed as the remains of a soldier who had crept into a cave and died during Napoleon's retreat from Moscow. A society later entranced by evolution was not yet ready to believe even genuine evidence. As soon as it was, though, the bones brought a political message.

The delighted Germans upon whose territory Neanderthal Man was found ascribed his prominent brow ridges to a habit of frowning while deep in Teutonic thought. Science is the easiest place for a villain to make a living. It is not at all like working in a bank: far from the meticulous process of cross–checking that is its public image, science is a profession that depends uniquely on faith. Nearly all results are accepted and the question of audit scarcely arises. Usually a fraud is safe enough. More than half of all scientific papers are never referred to again, even by their authors.

No doubt there lurk in that academic undergrowth great monsters of deceit. Most, though, have done no harm apart from unmerited tenure for their begetters. Why bother to transplant skin from a black to a white mouse when you can get the same effect with a felt-tip pen? Why not claim that intestinal worms cause cancer (a Nobel Prize was won for that) or that water retains a memory of the substances once dissolved in it even when diluted a billion billion times? Checking the scientific books is a task as joyless as accountancy. Nowadays, though, the clerks have taken over. There is a new demand for double–entry bookkeeping.

Some years ago the U.S. Congress set up the Office of Research Integrity to check a supposed crisis of scientific cheating. Its credentials were dubious, but the inquisitors entangled many scientists in a web of innuendo. More than a hundred fell into its clutches. Nearly all were found innocent but many had their careers damaged. Scientific fraud is quite extraordinarily rare. The reason is simple. Science is a card game against Nature, the ultimate opponent. The hope is to deduce the hand she holds from the few clues she is willing to disclose. It is possible to win every time by faking one's own cards, but that removes the whole point of playing the game.

---

34. Through his repeated references to banking and accountancy, the author of this passage demonstrates his belief that:

A. scientists are becoming more like accountants.

B. scientists are too eager for government grants.

C. science thrives where there is mutual trust.

D. science thrives with constant external scrutiny.

35. In the fifth paragraph. the author mentions the Nobel Prize—"Why not claim that intestinal worms cause cancer (a Nobel Prize was won for that),"—in order to elaborate his point that:

A. some frauds succeed by their very audacity.

B. the scientific élite is easily deceived.

C. the Nobel Prize is awarded for reasons solely based upon scientific merit.

D. the best scientists are often the most unethical.

GO TO THE NEXT PAGE.

36. In the discussion of the Cardiff Giant, why does the author describe the it as an American?

- **A.** To deride the thousands of Americans who paid to see it
- **B.** To show how Americans of 1868, as opposed to Europeans of 1856, were eager to embrace the theory of evolution
- **C.** To imply that the director of the New York State Museum was in on the hoax
- **D.** To illustrate the patriotic pride of nine-teenth–century Americans

37. Several years ago two professors from Utah claimed to have fused atomic nuclei in a test–tube. They received worldwide attention for a few weeks. According to the author, all of the following may have motivated their "cold fusion" lie EXCEPT:

- **A.** their need for grant money
- **B.** their contempt for oversight bureaucracies
- **C.** their desire for international recognition
- **D.** their attempt to protect their job security

38. In the context of the passage as put forth by the author, what effect did the "spirit of the time" (line 24) have on scientists and on people interested in science?

- **A.** It inclined the scientists toward fraud and made the public more susceptible to such fraud.
- **B.** It limited their curiosity about matters of science.
- **C.** It encouraged scientists to seek fame and the public to admire scientists.
- **D.** It inclined them to force scientific evidence into the context of their own national histories.

39. Within the context of the passage, what can be inferred about scientists from the author's card game analogy?

- **A.** That research scientists tend to be very competitive with one other
- **B.** That research scientists face great temptations to cheat when compiling data
- **C.** That research scientists believe that they are probing the secrets of nature
- **D.** That most research scientists "fake their cards," perpetuating their continued recognition

40. Which of the following statements is best inferred from the author's observation that one should "expect a wave of fraud inquiries the next time the government inspectors come round" (lines 15-16)?

- **A.** Government inspectors tend to be like inquisitors and entangle scientists in a web of suspicion.
- **B.** A new oversight policy is likely to reduce the amount of scientific fraud in Britain.
- **C.** Scientists who receive low scores in the Research Assessment Exercise are no less competent than those who receive high scores.
- **D.** Scientists who receive low scores in the Research Assessment Exercise are under pressure to produce interesting research.

GO TO THE NEXT PAGE.

Passage VII (Questions 41–47)

In the 1930s the Payne Foundation funded studies attributing juvenile crime to movie violence, complete with testimonials of youthful offenders that they had gotten larcenous ideas from the silver screen. Legions of censors from the Hays Office monitored Hollywood output to make sure that, at the least, crime didn't pay. In the 1950s, Dr. Frederic Wertham made a name for himself by attributing all manner of delinquencies to the mayhem depicted in comic books. If today's censorious forces smell smoke, it is not in the absence of fire.

In recent years, market forces have driven screen violence to an amazing pitch. As the movies lost much of their audience—especially adults—to television, the studios learned that the way to make their killing, so to speak, was to offer on big screens what the networks would not permit on the small. Thus, decades ago the "action movie"—a euphemism for, among other things, grisly violence—aimed to attract the teenagers who were the demographic category most eager to flee the family room. At the same time, the technologies of special effects steadily advanced to permit more graphic representations. We have witnessed the burgeoning of a genre that budding auteurs throughout the world aspire to imitate.

Aiming to recoup losses and better compete with cable, television programmers struck back; the networks lowered their censorship standards and pruned their "standards and practices" staffs; the deregulatory Federal Communications Commission clammed up; and the local news fell all over itself cramming snippets of gore between commercials.

I have denounced movie violence for more than two decades, all the way back to *The Wild Bunch* and *The Godfather*. I consider Hollywood's slashes, spatters, chainsaws and car crashes a disgrace, a degradation of culture, and a wound to the souls of producers and consumers alike. I also think liberals are making a serious mistake by pursuing their vigorous campaign against violence in the media. However morally and aesthetically reprehensible today's screen violence, the crusades of former Illinois senator Paul Simon and Attorney General Janet Reno against television violence, as well as Catharine MacKinnon's war against pornography are cheap shots.

There are indeed reasons to attribute violence to the media, but the links are weaker than recent headlines would have one believe. The attempt to demonize the media distracts attention from the real causes of—and the serious remedies for—the epidemic of violence.

The sheer volume of alarm can't be explained by the actual violence generated by the media's awful images. Rather, Simon, Reno, and MacKinnon—not to mention former vice president Dan Quayle and the Reverend Donald Wildmon—have signed up for the traditional American pastime. The campaign against the devil's images threads through the history of middle-class reform movements. For a nation that styles itself practical, at least in technical pursuits, we have always been a playground of moral prohibitions and symbolic crusades.

The question the liberal crusaders fail to address is not whether these images are wholesome but just how much real-world violence can be blamed on the media. Assume, for the sake of argument, that every copycat crime reported in the media can plausibly be traced to television and movies. Let us make an exceedingly high estimate that the resulting carnage results in 100 deaths per year that would otherwise not have taken place. These would amount to 0.28 percent of the total of 36,000 murders accidents, and suicides committed by gunshot in the United States in 1992.

That media violence contributes to a climate in which violence is legitimate—and there can be no doubt of this—does not make it an urgent social problem. Violence on the screens, however loathsome, does not make a significant contribution to violence on the streets. Images don't spill blood. Rage, equipped with guns, does. Desperation does. Revenge does. As liberals say, the drug trade does; poverty does; unemployment does. It seems likely that a given percent increase in decently paying jobs will save thousands of times more lives than the same percent decrease in media bang-bang. And once in a while—meaning far too often—some grotesque images inspire emulation.

Both big and small screens have taught impressionable people—or at least reinforced their propensity to practice—thrilling new ways to lacerate flesh. In 1982, after the cable television broadcast of *The Deer Hunter*, several people killed themselves playing Russian roulette, which was featured in the movie. American youths recently were killed and maimed when they lay down on the center strip of a highway, imitating a scene from Disney's movie *The Program*. A few months ago, a 17-year-old French youth blew himself up after learning from an episode of MacGyver how to build a bomb in a bicycle handle, at least according to his mother, who is suing the head of the channel for manslaughter.

GO TO THE NEXT PAGE.

41. The passage suggests that having more stringent controls on media violence would NOT have a great effect on the death rate because:

    A. the numbers of deaths resulting from so-called "copycat" acts of violence composes only a small portion of violent deaths each year.

    B. the number of deaths resulting from so-called "copycat" acts of violence would remain unchanged nonetheless.

    C. networks and film studios lack the personnel to enforce any new regulation.

    D. there exists no definite link between media violence and actual violence.

42. The passage suggests most strongly that the volume of concern regarding media violence is unwarranted because:

    A. America has always been "a playground of moral prohibitions" and ideological quests.

    B. the relationship between the number of annual deaths and deaths attributed to media violence does not merit it.

    C. demonizing the media does little to remedy its ills.

    D. the causes and effects of violence are less certain that critics of media violence believe.

43. Of all of the following, which does the author NOT believe can be linked to violence?

    A. Rage
    B. Poverty
    C. Revenge
    D. Desperation

44. If delivered in a paper that sought to undermine the points of this passage, which of the following statements, if true, would most seriously *weaken* the passage's central argument?

    A. The number of violent acts depicted in the media has remained more or less constant for the past decade.

    B. A Canadian study reported a sixteen-percent increase in violent crimes after exposure to television and film episodes in which violent acts were depicted.

    C. Politicians and celebrities are assisting effectively in diminishing violence.

    D. Films belonging to the "action" genre have found little acceptance at the box office.

45. In the context of the passage, the use of the phrase "traditional American pastime" (lines 53–54) by the author is understood to mean:

    A. making an unpopular stand on a moral issue.
    B. championing a cause with moral overtones.
    C. using popular issues to corrupt political campaigns.
    D. effecting change through sharp criticism.

46. Paying attention to all of the arguments made by the author, which of the following claims does the passage neither directly support nor contradict?

    A. The conclusions of the Payne Foundation studies of the 1930s were scientifically sound.

    B. The marked increase in media violence can be attributed to the continued financial success of those movies and programs that contain scenes of violence.

    C. The movie studios exploited the desire for teenagers to go outside their homes for entertainment by offering films that contained violent scenes.

    D. Television networks responded to the imagery in films by raising their own standards for content.

47. The broadcast networks have recently proposed a system of rating program content, similar to those ratings in the film industry. Which of the following best characterizes the relevance of this statement?

    A. The statement acknowledges that the networks have taken little responsibility in patrolling the content of their programming.

    B. The statement implies that those who speak out against media violence have had significant success in convincing the networks to enforce stricter content standards.

    C. The statement suggests that some convincing evidence supporting a stronger link between media violence and violent acts has been found.

    D. The statement suggests that networks will decrease the amount of shows that contain violent content.

GO TO THE NEXT PAGE.

Passage VIII (Question 48–54)

Boccaccio's donnée is of an upper-class milieu where girls and young men can meet socially at ease and move—thanks to wealth—out of plague-stricken Florence. In fact, it daringly reverses the standard form

[5] of morality, well summed up nearly contemporaneously by Traini's famous *Triumph of Death* fresco in the Campo Santo at Pisa. There, an upper-class, amorous, hedonistic group of young people is depicted as doomed to die. Boccaccio's group consists very much of stylish

[10] survivors. Almost more scandalous than any of the tales they tell among themselves, is their clear-eyed common sense. Since they can do nothing about the plague, they seize the chance of the general disruption of the normal covenances and the absence—or loss—of parents and

[15] guardians, to go off and enjoy themselves, for which they are not punished.

The code of behavior they assume and also promulgate is impressively liberal, civilized and un-prudish. Love is a natural bond between them, neither coarse nor

[20] etherealized. Seven girls who have met by chance at Mass at Santa Maria Novella plan their adventure and then co-opt three young men who happen to enter the church. The three are already known to them, but it is the girls who take the initiative, in a tactful, well-bred

[25] way, making it clear from the start that this is no invitation to rape. One has only to try to imagine Victorian girls—in fiction or in fact—behaving with such a degree of sophistication to see that society by no means advances century by century. Boccaccio is a highly

[30] complex personality who, like many another writer, may have felt that his most famous work was not his best. But the *Decameron* became famous early on, and was avidly read and frequently translated throughout Europe.

[35] Today, only scholars settle down to read his more high-flown romances and classical compilations, or even his "life" of Dante, whom he profoundly admired. The *Decameron* is a thoroughly Florentine book and a thoroughly social one, down to its structure. After the

[40] poetry of the *Divine Comedy*, it is very much prose, in every way. It glories in being undidactic, entertaining and openly—though by no means totally—scabrous. Eventually it shocked and frightened its creator, who thus unwittingly or not recognized the force of its liter-

[45] ary power. He repented and turned moralist and academic, leaving Florence for the small Tuscan town of Certaldo where he had probably been born and where in 1375 he died.

[50] Part of his religious repentance was perhaps expressed by commissioning two altarpieces (sadly, not extant) for a local church. Whatever the medievalism enshrined in the *Divine Comedy*, the *Decameron* speaks for a robustly changed, relaxed vision, one set firmly upon earth. It is the opposite of lonely and ecstatic. It is

[55] a vision closer to that of *Canterbury Tales* than to the spiritual one of *Piers Plowman*.

It has female protagonists who seem mundane if not precisely modern compared with the real women mystics and saints of central Italy of a few generations

[60] before, women whose fierce, intense, sometimes horrifyingly palpable and semi-erotic visions read like real-life cantos from Dante's poem. It is Boccaccio who should more correctly have been painted beside Giotto, for in a certain sense they share standards that are *al nat-*

[65] *urale*. No doubt Boccaccio has idealized a little, but he puts forward a calm, sane case for freedom and humor and good manners between the sexes which, however palely, foreshadows the Shakespearean world of Beatrice and Benedick.

[70] The theme of the stories his group exchange is human behavior—often as it is manifested under the pressure of lust or love. But the group is also shown indulging in chess and music and dancing (even bathing though separated by sex). The ladies frequently laugh

[75] and occasionally blush, while never losing their self-possession and their implicit command of the situation. Never could they be mistaken for allegorical nymphs or bloodless abstractions.

That the diversions of the *Decameron* are set bright-

[80] ly against the gruesome darkness of the Black Death is effective and also realistic. The plague begins the book. It is seen working psychologically as well as physically, horribly corrupting manners and morals, in addition to destroying life. Diversion and escape seem not frivolous

[85] but prudent, especially when provided by a pleasantly sited, well-stocked villa outside Florence, with amenities that extend to agreeable pictures in its rooms. In sharing the group's diversions the reader should be diverted, and Boccaccio says that he is thinking particu-

[90] larly of women, lovelorn women. Their lives are restricted: in love they cannot, unlike men, find relief in sport, travel, and business. It adds another, non-idealistic touch to his portrait of society, just as the retreat to the country is no literary convention but a reminder of the pleas-

[95] ant villas in the hills around the city.

GO TO THE NEXT PAGE.

48. Which of the following statements best summarizes the author's opinion in the passage regarding Boccaccio's view of his own work?

A. Boccaccio held more regard for the *Decameron* than for his later works.

B. Boccaccio was later dismayed but nonetheless convinced by the literary power of the *Decameron*.

C. Boccaccio felt that Dante was a literary figure worthy of high regard.

D. Boccaccio was heartened that the *Decameron* was avidly read and translated.

49. According to the author, the *Decameron* differs markedly from its Italian predecessor *The Divine Comedy*. From the information presented in the passage, which of the following statements can the reader NOT assume about *The Divine Comedy*?

A. It is written in poetic verse.

B. It is set in Florence.

C. It is written in a didactic style.

D. It has a tendency to be tedious.

50. The author chooses to strongly contrast Traini's *Triumph of Death* fresco in Pisa with the *Decameron* because:

A. they represent a correlation between the content of art and literature in medieval Italy.

B. Traini's fresco marks the departure of medieval art from pure religious content.

C. the Decameron's subjects depict chastity rather than the wanton behavior depicted in Triani's fresco.

D. their subjects are so markedly different in representation, despite their roughly contemporary installation.

51. According to the author, the *Decameron* "daringly reverses the standard form of morality" presented in contemporary writing and art. Given that opinion, which of the following conclusions must be true?

A. The *Decameron* was one signal of a new era of humanism.

B. The *Decameron* was a robust, entertaining literary work.

C. The *Decameron* was preceded by didactic, religious themes in medieval literature.

D. The *Decameron* was not followed in suit by other works of secular humanism.

52. The contrast of Boccaccio's heroines to Victorian girls is noted in paragraph 2 to support all of the following conclusions EXCEPT:

A. an age of liberalism of thought and action went into decline with the Victorian era.

B. society advances in a logical progression from century to century.

C. Boccaccio's heroines display a seemingly anachronistic amount of courage and practicality.

D. the *Decameron's* sophisticated interaction between the sexes foreshadowed that of Shakespeare's plays.

53. Suppose that the author claimed that the *Decameron* was more structurally similar to *Canterbury Tales* than to Dante's *Divine Comedy*. If true, this assertion would most likely be used in the passage to:

A. draw a more detailed correlation between both stories as examples of a new humanism.

B. reinforce the notion of the *Decameron* as a sophisticated work atypical of Boccaccio's oeuvre.

C. more fully describe the *Decameron* as a prototype of Italian humanist literature.

D. approach an argument that also links both stories through verse form and rhyming scheme.

54. Some disagree with the author's opinion of the *Decameron*. Which of the following, if true, would most weaken the author's opinion?

A. Boccaccio felt that the *Decameron* was his best work.

B. It was not until the eighteenth century that the *Decameron* became widely read.

C. Boccaccio intended the *Decameron* to be read ironically.

D. Additional chapters that spell the death of several lead characters have recently been discovered.

GO TO THE NEXT PAGE.

Passage IX (Question 55–60)

No one is eager to touch off the kind of hysteria that preceded the government's decision to move against Alar, the growth regulator once used by apple growers. When celebrities like Meryl Streep spoke out against Alar and the press fanned public fears, some schools and parents rushed to pluck apples out of the mouths of children. Yet all this happened before scientists had reached any consensus about Alar's dangers.

Rhetoric about dioxin may push the same kind of emotional buttons. The chemical becomes relatively concentrated in fat-rich foods—including human breast milk. Scientists estimate that a substantial fraction of an individual's lifetime burden of dioxin—as much as 12%— is accumulated during the first year of life. Nonetheless, the benefits of breast-feeding infants, the EPA and most everyone else would agree, far outweigh the hazards. Now environmentalists say dioxin and scores of other chemicals pose a threat to human fertility—as scary an issue as any policymakers have faced.

But in the absence of conclusive evidence, what are policymakers to do? What measure can they take to handle a problem whose magnitude is unknown? Predictably, attempts to whipsaw public opinion have already begun. Corporate lobbyists urge that action be put on hold until science resolves the unanswered questions. Environmentalists argue that evidence for harm is too strong to permit delay. This issue is especially tough because the chemicals under scrutiny are found almost everywhere.

Since many of them contain chlorine or are by-products of processes involving chlorine compounds, the environmental group Greenpeace has demanded a ban on all industrial uses of chlorine. The proposal seems appealingly simple, but it would be economically wrenching for companies and consumers alike. With the escalating rhetoric, many professionals in the risk-assessment business are worried that once again emotion rather than common sense will drive the political process. "There is no free lunch," observes Tammy Tengs, a public-health specialist at Duke University. "When someone spends money in one place, that money is not available to spend on other things." She and her colleagues have calculated that tuberculosis treatment can extend a person's life by a year for less than $10,000—surely a reasonable price tag. By contrast, extending a life by a year through asbestos removal costs nearly $2 million, since relatively few people would die if the asbestos were left in place. That kind of benefit-risk analysis all too rarely informs the decisions made by government regulators.

As the EPA raises anew the dangers of dioxin, the agency needs to communicate its findings to the public in a calm and clear fashion. John Graham, director of the Harvard Center for Risk Analysis, suggests that people should strive to keep the perils posed by dioxin in perspective and remember other threats that are more easily averted. "Phantom risks and real risks compete not only for our resources but also for our attention," Graham observes. "It's a shame when a mother worries about toxic chemicals, and yet her kids are running around unvaccinated and without bicycle helmets."

---

55. If it appeared in an article that the author read, he would most strongly agree with which of the following statements?

A. Asbestos and radon have caused serious health problems in the past that many government officials chose to ignore.

B. Dioxin is the foremost threat to human fertility and needs to be addressed in order to prevent serious health problems in the future.

C. Environmental groups and corporate lobbyists often take polarized stances which eventually are modified by governmental agencies.

D. Thorough research and investigation of environmental problems should be performed by the government before any unnecessary hysteria spreads throughout the public.

56. According to the passage, it is dangerous to react drastically to recently posed health hazards for all of the following reasons EXCEPT:

A. proven precautions are overlooked.
B. public fear leads to irrational action.
C. insurance premiums will increase.
D. economic burdens can occur.

57. In the context of the passage, the author uses the term "whipsaw public opinion" (line 23) to refer to:

A. changing the needs of the community.
B. convincing citizens to accept a polarized viewpoint on health hazards.
C. offering a variety of alternatives for health hazards.
D. acting irrationally in response to government policy.

GO TO THE NEXT PAGE.

58. For which of the following reasons does the author cite the Alar incident in paragraph 1?

A. To show the bureaucracy involved in changing a chemical plant's mode of operation

B. To illustrate the problem in publicly announcing health hazards before conclusive scientific evidence has been formulated

C. To show that drastic reaction is often the best way to solve a crisis

D. To demonstrate that it takes a celebrity to effect public change

59. Which of the following statements, if true, would most weaken the author's argument?

A. The EPA carefully considered the research results of a highly-qualified team of scientists, economists, and public policy makers who researched the asbestos and Alar threats before any governmental action was performed.

B. Large numbers of babies have been born with defects over the last 20 years when levels of Alar have been extremely high.

C. Activist groups, such as Greenpeace, believe that the use of chemicals in our society has reached overwhelming proportions and needs to be regulated immediately.

D. Corporate lobbyists consider economic factors that may make certain precautions economically unfeasible.

60. All of the following are mentioned by the author in the passage in support of the main argument EXCEPT:

A. the idea that people often overlook health threats for which we already possess remedies.

B. biased groups will try to sway citizens into believing that their stance is the only correct way of handling health hazards.

C. public reaction has lead to unnecessary actions that have wasted time and money.

D. chemicals in food and homes have caused too many deaths in modern society.

STOP. If you finish before time is called, check your work. You may go back to any question in this test booklet.

ANSWER KEY
VERBAL REASONING TEST 5

1. C	16. A	31. D	46. A
2. B	17. D	32. D	47. B
3. D	18. D	33. C	48. B
4. B	19. A	34. C	49. B
5. A	20. A	35. A	50. D
6. C	21. B	36. D	51. C
7. B	22. C	37. B	52. B
8. A	23. A	38. D	53. A
9. B	24. B	39. C	54. C
10. B	25. B	40. D	55. D
11. B	26. C	41. A	56. C
12. D	27. B	42. B	57. B
13. B	28. B	43. B	58. B
14. A	29. A	44. B	59. A
15. C	30. C	45. B	60. D

EXPLANATIONS

PASSAGE I

Topic and Scope:
The author discusses the paradox of doctors who support euthanasia but who are reluctant to carry it out.

Mapping the Passage:
¶1 introduces the idea of physicians becoming involved in capital punishment as example of alleviating sometimes painful death.

¶2 states that many doctors favor "designated killer" technicians but that maybe this isn't right decision.

¶3 describes the paradox of physicians who support euthanasia but who would not themselves perform it.

¶4 presents an expert opinion that physicians should have a consistent approach towards mercy killing (Marcia Angell).

¶s5 and 6 describe two positions on ¶4'sparadox: one that physicians who support mercy killing should be responsible for it; the second that they need not.

Questions:
1.   C   A rare global question: review topic, scope, and purpose and then simply find their closest match in the answer choices. While three choices are off topic and/or scope, (C) fits with the overall purpose of describing the conflicting arguments about euthanasia.

Wrong Answers:
(A): **Out of Scope.** The author doesn't deal with this subject in any depth, and certainly not as the overall purpose of the passage.
(B): **Faulty Use of Detail.** While the author implies that some people might believe this about physicians, the author doesn't make it the focus of the passage.
(D): **Faulty Use of Detail.** The author mentions this in ¶3, but it's not the purpose of the passage as a whole.

Strategy Point:
Be sure to keep an eye out for the author's position. When the author takes pains to be objective, as is the case in this passage, questions will almost always test to see whether you've picked up on this.

2.   B   The "According to the passage..." phrasing is a sure cue to refer back to the passage, using your map to direct your focus. Where are designated killers mentioned? Go back to ¶2 to find out what sort of physicians favor this approach: physicians who want to be free from "the taint of killing." Choice (B) rephrases the same.

Wrong Answers:
(A): **Faulty Use of Detail.** Marcia Angell argues in ¶4 that mercy killing will become part of a continuum, but she does this while opposing designated killers.
(C): **Out of Scope.** The author doesn't argue in this part of the passage that a conflict exists, much less that the physicians recognize it.
(D): **Out of Scope.** There's no evidence in the paragraph or elsewhere that doctors fear the designated killer would abuse the privilege.

3.   D   What sort of situation would strengthen the argument that doctors aren't the best people to perform euthanasia? Anything that would conflict with doctors' primary purpose. Scan down the choices for a situation that would fit. (D) would be just such a situation: if patients are avoiding visiting doctors because they fear the euthanasia angle, then the doctor's primary purpose of treating the sick is being overshadowed by the mercy-killing aspect.

Wrong Answers:
(A): **Out of Scope.** The number of physicians favoring euthanasia doesn't necessarily have an impact on whether doctors should perform euthanasia.
(B): **Opposite.** This would tend to strengthen the argument that physicians are the only people qualified enough to perform euthanasia.
(C): **Opposite.** This too would strengthen the argument in favor of physician-administered euthanasia: if physicians favor euthanasia more when they have a close relationship with patients, there would be less moral justification for avoiding the task.

4.   B   Keep an eye out for a statement that either conflicts with the passage or simply has no support. (B) falls into the latter category: the author never mentions formal debate at national conventions.

Wrong Answers:
(A): **Opposite.** This is supported by doing just a little math on the statistics in ¶3: If 60 percent favor, then the remaining physicians either oppose or have no opinion.
(C): **Opposite.** The author supports this throughout the passage: the moral qualms that physicians have are addressed in most parts of the author's arguments.

KAPLAN

(D): Opposite. This statement is supported by all of ¶4: the author notes that the editor has called designated killers an "unsavory prospect."

Strategy Point:
If something in the passage sounds unfamiliar, it probably is! Trust your map and don't get bogged down in looking for details that may not exist.

5. A Where are the downsides of designated killers mentioned? Refer back to ¶s 2 and 4, where the author raises questions about designated killers and the editor of the NEJM raises objections. (A) is the objection raised by the editor: she argues that someday euthanasia will be part of good patient care and that physicians should be in on the action.

Wrong Answers:
(B): Opposite. This is one of the arguments that physicians who favor designated killers make.
(C): Distortion: physicians, not designated killers, would prevent lingering, painful deaths.
(D): Out of Scope. This argument isn't made in favor of physician-sponsored euthanasia.

6. C What would be the effect if practiced designated killers were used? It would presumably reduce the incidence of painful death, since competent euthanasia would be more common. The author argues in ¶1 that if physicians could guarantee that death would not be painful, they'd gain patients' trust. (C) is a reasonable effect in light of this.

Wrong Answers:
(A): Out of Scope. It doesn't follow that a medical journal will condone a practice it had previously condemned just because it's put into practice.
(B): Opposite. If anything, more designated killers would probably mean fewer physicians willing to do the dirty work themselves.
(D): Opposite. As above, if designated killers were common, physicians would feel less burdened to do the killing themselves.

7. B Go back to ¶s 2 and 4 to review the idea of the designated killer. Both those who support and oppose the idea suggest that it provides a degree of removal between the physicians and the act of death. An assumption of this, therefore, must be that physicians won't be the designated killers. If this is denied, the argument falls apart, a sure sign of a sound assumption.

Wrong Answers:
(A): Out of Scope. This would have no effect on the argument: denying it wouldn't necessarily weaken the contention that the use of designated killers is a bad idea.

(C): Opposite. This is essentially the opposite of the correct assumption. The idea of designated killers assumes the absence of the physician.
(D): Out of Scope. This also has no effect on the argument: If it's denied, the argument against designated killers remains just as strong.

8. A This is essentially a global question in disguise. Predict the paradox before hitting the questions: Lots of physicians are in favor of euthanasia, but not as many want to actually do it. (A) fits instantly.

Wrong Answers:
(B): Out of Scope. This doesn't touch on the paradox of physicians who support euthanasia but don't want to get involved. These same physicians may be willing both to endorse designated killers and to perform the act themselves.
(C): Faulty Use of Detail. . This has no element of the paradox either; it's only a piece of the puzzle.
(D): Distortion. While this almost captures the paradox, it introduces the unnecessary element of professional endorsement, which isn't suggested in the passage.

Strategy Point:
Be on the lookout for common question types in uncommon wording; critical thinking on the test often involves untangling the question.

PASSAGE II

Topic and Scope:
The author discusses the causes and effects of the bubonic plague in England.

Mapping the Passage:
¶1 discusses the causes of the bubonic plague.
¶2 describes the dates of its impact and the drops in population caused by the repeated plagues.
¶s3 and 4 describe the effect of the plague on the English economic system.
¶5 describes the responses of landowners to economic pressures caused by plagues and the eventual ineffectiveness of those responses.
¶6 recaps some of the effects of the bubonic plague.

Questions:
9. B Go back to ¶2, where high farming is mentioned. While three of the factors are mentioned as factors, (B) conflicts with the author's argument that the plague *reduced* dependence on high farming.

Wrong Answers:
(A): Opposite. This is mentioned immediately after the introduction of high farming.
(C): Opposite. As above.
(D): Opposite. As above.

10. B An inference question; keep an eye out for an answer choice that fits closely with something mentioned in the passage. (B) simply restates the dates from ¶s1 and 6: If the plagues started in 1348 and lasted for more than 300 years, then they continued until the end of the seventeenth century.

Wrong Answers:
(A): Opposite. This contradicts the author's point in ¶5 that "in the long run the statute was useless."
(C): Opposite. This is the opposite of the author's point in ¶2 that after the plague the demand for food went down drastically.
(D): Opposite. The author argues in ¶4 that it was easy to run away to other landowners with "no questions asked."

Strategy Point:
The MCAT will often base questions on dates; don't take them for granted!

11. B This question asks you to get to the root of the problem caused by the plague. The economic difficulties are attributed in the passage to a labor shortage. According to ¶3, this labor shortage lingered because of high infant mortality.

Wrong Answers:
(A): Out of Scope. The author never discussed people's fears of leaving the home (and in fact ¶4 describes a good deal of movement).
(C): Faulty Use of Detail. This is an effect, not a root cause of the economic difficulty. Landholdings could not be filled without more workers.
(D): Opposite. The Statute's effects are discussed in the passage as being negligible.

12. D What point is the author trying to make in the paragraphs dealing with economics? The overall thrust is that the relationship between landowners and peasants changed when the number of available workers decreased. Since the author spends the most time talking about this change in the relationship, it's safe to assume that this is the most important factor.

Wrong Answers:
(A): Opposite. The author argues that demand for food was decreased because the population was less.
(B): Faulty Use of Detail. While the author does consider this to be a factor in the economic equation, it's not the main effect of the plague, but rather a secondary effect of the low population and changing relationships.
(C): Faulty Use of Detail. As above, this is another secondary effect of the main one: loss of population and changing landowner-peasant relationships.

13. B Go back to ¶2 to review the author's argument that the plague ended high farming. The author argues that the peasantry depended on this sort of farming for subsistence and in ¶5 implies that landowners had

previously taken high profits from the practice. If (B) is true, the second point, made in the last sentences of the passage, is directly contradicted: there would have been fewer reasons for high farming to collapse, and the author's argument would therefore be weakened.

Wrong Answers:
(A): Out of Scope. Even if this were true, it would have no effect on the plague since it occurred several decades before the plague occurred.
(C): Out of Scope. Is incorrect because the population decrease is one of the author's supporting pieces of evidence for the central argument.
(D): Out of Scope. Even if this is true, it has no impact on the fact that the plague brought an end to high farming. This is an *effect* of the plague's impact on high farming, not a fundamental piece of evidence supporting or refuting it.

PASSAGE III

Topic and Scope:
The author discusses the orbit of Venus and its appearance from earth.

Mapping the Passage:
¶1 states that at the time of the passage's writing, Venus was visible as the "evening star."
¶2 describes the appearance of Venus and the times at which the planet is visible.
¶3 describes the difficulties in understanding the motion of the stars simply by looking.
¶4 argues that it's possible to nearly imagine the motion of Venus in orbit and describes this motion.
¶5 discusses Venus's orbit and when it will return to its current position.

Questions:
14. A Go back to review the author's point in context. The author follows the "little Ptolemies" statement with the elaboration that "the sun rises and sets upon us." Looking for an answer choice that fits this earth-centered point of view immediately turns up (A).

Wrong Answers:
(B): Distortion. While the author discusses the astronomers, he's not using them to compare their *knowledge* to regular people, but to contrast their different astronomical views.
(C): Out of Scope. The author is arguing that "most of us" have little knowledge of astronomy and so don't understand the complexities of space. The case of those who do have this knowledge is outside the scope of the comment.
(D): Out of Scope. While this might be true, it doesn't tie into the author's point about Ptolemies: most don't understand the complexities of the universe.

15. C   Go back to ¶3 to review what the author says about Copernicus. The author mentions Lamb who says that he sees Venus by its brightness. The author follows this with the statement, "Lamb was no Copernican, and neither are most of us." Paraphrase this: Copernicus had a good enough grasp of astronomy to understand what Venus was doing, but we can't. (C) captures all of this.

Wrong Answers:
(A): Opposite. While the author implies that the appearance of Venus changes over a long period of time, this doesn't mean that Venus is only visible during a certain range of years. The author also argues in ¶4 that Venus *isn't* visible between May and July.
(B): Opposite. The author argues in ¶4 that between May and July, Venus isn't visible.
(D): Out of Scope. While the author mentions in ¶1 that it's difficult to see much in the Manhattan sky, there's no indication from the author that environmental efforts should be made.

Strategy Point:
Paraphrase difficult or confusing text, especially when it's essential to an answer. Paraphrasing is one method of prediction.

16. A   Take a moment to predict where the answer will be in the passage. While ¶2 might be tempting, as it discusses time, we already know we're looking for Venus in the evening. We need another criterion. A quick scan of the answers shows that they have to do with orbit. Go to ¶4. The author says that when "Venus moves toward earth....it is the evening star." (A) rewards the careful and targeted research.

Wrong Answers:
(B): Opposite. When it's moving away, Venus is the morning star.
(C): Opposite. The author suggests that when this happens, Venus isn't visible at all.
(D): Opposite. Rephrase the double negative. If this were true, Venus would best be visible in the evening when the sun's brightness made it possible to see Venus. This doesn't make sense; the author doesn't argue that the sun's brightness is responsible for Venus' exceptional visibility.

17. D   In All...EXCEPT questions keep an eye out for answer choices that contradict what the passage says. (D) immediately jumps out: The author argues in ¶3 that we see the stars rotating. Therefore, the night sky wouldn't be a stationary display.

Wrong Answers:
(A): Opposite. The author mentions this in ¶3.
(B): Opposite. The author mentions this in ¶1.
(C): Opposite. The author mentions this in ¶3.

18. D   The right answer will conflict with the author's explanation of Venus' motion. A scan of the answer choices shows that they're pretty dense. Don't take time to evaluate each one fully; look for something that will immediately contradict the author. (D) does just this. The author says in ¶1 that it's possible to watch Venus "descending in the West" from Manhattan, and (D) is simply the opposite.

Wrong Answers:
(A): Opposite. The author makes points in ¶4 suggesting that this is exactly what happens, and, therefore, that Venus is the evening star in the winter and spring months.
(B): Opposite. Paraphrase: this choice basically says that Venus can only be seen in the sky at certain times of the year. The author backs this up in ¶4.
(C): Opposite. The author says in ¶4 that this happens.

Strategy Point:
When faced with a series of difficult answer choices, evaluate only as much as you need to. Very often, the right answer will be easy to spot, and getting bogged down in the choices that come before will waste time.

19. A   Review the location of the author's main points about the evening star, primarily in ¶s 1 and 4. As usual with this question type, keep an eye out for something that contradicts the author's argument. (A) not only does this, but also makes no sense. The author argues in ¶4 that Venus is invisible when passing between the earth and the sun, which makes sense if one has to look in the direction of the sun to see Venus.

Wrong Answers:
(B): Opposite. This is a combination of the author's points in ¶s 2 and 4 about Venus' visibility during time of day and month.
(C): Opposite. The author makes this point in ¶1.
(D): Opposite. The author states this explicitly in ¶2.

PASSAGE IV

Topic and Scope:
The author discusses the idea of self-determination and contrasts it with idea of racial pride.

Mapping the Passage:
¶1 describes Michael Sandel's idea of "the unencumbered self." Sandel disagrees with the idea, while the author supports it.
¶2 acknowledges that elements of racial pride can serve a valuable purpose but go too far in valuing the qualities of one race over another.
¶3 describes the author's view that pride should rest in personal accomplishments rather than race.
¶4 describes weaknesses in Sandel's view.

Strategy Point:
Be sure that you understand the conflicting viewpoints in the passage. Many questions will have answer choices that trap the careless test-taker who confuses distinct points of view.

Questions:

20. A The question is essentially asking the scope of the author's argument. Take a moment to predict this before scanning the choices. (A) takes some paraphrasing to untangle, but fits the author's main focus: self-identity in relation to race and history.

Wrong Answers:
(B): Faulty Use of Detail. This is the scope of ¶s1 and 2, but not that of the entire passage.
(C): Distortion. The author doesn't argue that rejecting racial kinship *causes* individual accomplishment, only that the two can go hand-in-hand.
(D): Out of Scope. The author discusses racial pride, but this doesn't necessarily mean the same thing as group consciousness, which is never discussed in the passage.

21. B Carefully review the scope of the question and both Sandel's and the author's opinions on it. What do they both think about inherited connections? The author thinks that they're overrated, Sandel that they're important. Only (B) and (C) roughly fit this breakdown. Of those, (B) fits the author's argument more closely; the author argues in ¶ 4 that Sandel accords the connections mentioned in the question with moral weight.

Wrong Answers:
(A): Opposite. The author believes that inherited connections should be valued *less*, and so wouldn't think this.
(C): Distortion. While Sandel does think that inherited connections are important, there's nothing in the passage to suggest that he has reverence for them, let alone that it's unquestioning. The author discusses Sandel's reasoning at length, suggesting that his views on the matter are carefully-reasoned.
(D): Opposite. The author takes pains to show that Sandel goes into the topic in depth, well beyond a cursory critical treatment.

22. C Carefully examine the wording of the question, which asks about the *encumbered* self. Since the author is a big fan of the unencumbered self, he'll presumably feel negatively towards the encumbered self. (C) conflicts with the author's point in ¶1 that the unencumbered self is "free and independent." If this is true, the encumbered self must be the opposite.

Wrong Answers:
(A): Opposite. The author discusses the encumbered self as the product of childhood attachments in ¶4.
(B): Opposite. The author discusses history as a foundation and even to some extent definition of the encumbered self in ¶s1 and 4.

(D): Opposite. This fits with the author's contention that racial pride and the encumbered self go hand-in-hand.

Strategy Point:
Read carefully! Missing a negative or a lack of one can easily lead to the wrong answer even with otherwise perfect reasoning.

23. A Go back to review the lines in context. Why does the author think that Sandel's deference to tradition is negative? It gets in the way of the unencumbered self and the ability to make one's own decisions. (A) says the same.

Wrong Answers:
(B): Distortion. While Sandel might believe this, the author would argue that history doesn't necessarily shape individual destinies.
(C): Distortion. Though the author thinks that one shouldn't be bound to tradition, he wouldn't go so far as to argue that it's harmful to respect it.
(D): Distortion. As above, though the author would argue that we shouldn't be bound to past people and events, we shouldn't necessarily ignore them altogether either.

24. B The author's view is that one should make one's own decisions without being tied to ideas of race and history. Look for an answer choice that contradicts this: Since (B) is an event consisting of a single race gathering to advance racial identify, the author would take issue. He thinks that racial identity should take a back seat to individual decisions.

Wrong Answers:
(A): Opposite. The author would be in favor of treatment that isn't based on race or history.
(C): Opposite. Since the author is in favor of an individual identity that isn't based on history, which poverty tends to be, he'd be all for hospitals that didn't discriminate based on economic conditions.
(D): Opposite. The author would have no problem with recognizing an individual achievement. In this case, the achievement would be all the better in the author's eyes since it was an attempt to eliminate a system based on race.

25. B Untangle the question carefully. What does the author think about Sandel's stance on the unencumbered self? Sandel doesn't support the unencumbered self; the author does. Therefore, the author must disagree with Sandel. Three answer choices express disagreement, but only (B) reflects the sort of evenhanded discussion in which the author engages.

Wrong Answers:
(A): Opposite. The author definitely takes a side, and does so in a personal fashion, referring to himself in the first person throughout the essay.

(C): Distortion. There's no evidence of hostility in the argument against Sandel's position.

(D): Distortion. Though the author disagrees with Sandel, there's no dismissiveness: he "admire[s] Sandel's work and [has] learned much from it." (lines 49–50).

Strategy Point:
Pay attention to the author's tone in addition to the overall stance. Many answer choices will distort the author's position with extreme wording.

26. C An evaluation question: read the lines, paying careful attention to your map in the process. The author mentions the quoted phrase immediately after saying that he rejects racial pride. It's reasonable to think that the purpose of the phrase, then, is to set up the argument that racial pride is unjustified. (C) says the same.

Wrong Answers:
(A): Faulty Use of Detail. The author does support Frederick Douglass, but to support the idea that racial pride is unjustified, not as an end in itself.

(B): Opposite. The author supports the unencumbered self.

(D): Opposite. The author describes his view as the same one that Sandel considers to be "shallow liberalism." In any case, the author doesn't use this phrase to convince his readers to feel any particular way about him.

Strategy Point:
Always map with an eye to purpose rather than simple summary. Ask why the author writes something.

PASSAGE V

Topic and Scope:
The author discusses the harassment and hurdles facing women in the music industry.

Mapping the Passage:
¶1 describes a recent reawakening of feminism in response to threats to its objectives.
¶2 describes discrimination against women at the Rock & Roll Hall of Fame.
¶s3 and 4 describe discrimination against women in the recording industry.
¶5 describes harassment of women at radio stations.

Questions:
27. B Look especially for an answer choice that runs counter to the overall theme of the passage: (B) does this. The author suggests throughout the passage that the physical appearance of women is a major factor in industry success (the WAZU description in the last paragraph is a prime example).

Wrong Answers:
(A): Opposite. The author discusses this in ¶5.
(C): Opposite. The author discusses this in ¶2.
(D): Opposite. If this is true, it would further reinforce the idea that women in the industry are subject to discrimination.

28. B Read carefully; you're looking for a statement that provides *no* support. This is an identical task to An "All...EXCEPT" question. Three of the choices are supported in the passage, while one statement, (B), isn't made at all. Though it seems a plausible situation, the author doesn't specifically say that this has happened.

Wrong Answers:
(A): Opposite. The author discusses this in ¶5.
(C): Opposite. The author backs this claim in ¶2.
(D): Opposite. This claim is made and supported in ¶1.

Strategy Point: Don't draw your own conclusions! While (B) may seem like a plausible situation, the passage never mentions it.

29. A Look for a choice that runs counter to the author's main arguments about the barriers that women face. (A) immediately recommends itself: the author argues directly that women are pressured to maintain a certain physical appearance, which (A) denies.

Wrong Answers:
(B): Opposite. The author alludes to abortion in ¶2 when discussing the "fragility of gains" in advancement. Women therefore have at times tied the battle over abortion to the idea of overall gains in the feminist movement.
(C): Opposite. This can be inferred from the author's discussion of broad barriers to advancement and the segue to a specific example, the record industry, in ¶s1 and 3.
(D): Opposite. This follows from the author's argument in ¶2 that women are underrepresented in the Hall of Fame.

30. C Look for a choice that isn't used in the passage as an example of the "reawakening of feminism," as cited in ¶1, keeping in mind the author's main points about women's advancement. While the three wrong answer choices are all predictably in the first paragraph, (C) is not only in the wrong paragraph but is also used as an example of barriers to feminist progress rather than as an example of its reawakening.

Wrong Answers:
(A): Opposite. The author supports the reawakening of feminism with this example in ¶1.
(B): Opposite. This is mentioned in ¶3 as a wake-up call to women over the "increasing fragility" of gains in women's rights.
(D): Opposite. This is also mentioned in ¶1 in conjunction with feminism's reawakening.

31. D An incorporation question; evaluate the statement in the context of the passage. If the number of female record executives has remained the same, this would support the author's contention that the music industry is stifling women's progress. (D) fits perfectly.

Wrong Answers:
(A): Opposite. The author would argue that women hold too *few* positions.
(B): Out of Scope. The argument wouldn't touch directly on the issue of appearance, though it could also be argued that if women are held back, it might be because men do focus too much on appearance. This would also run counter to the choice.
(C): Opposite. The author seems pessimistic about chances for improvement in women's prospects in the record industry.

Strategy Point: don't over-think easy questions. Take the quick points and move on.

32. D The author's argument is that women are unfairly kept from advancing in the industry and are therefore discriminated against. Look for an answer choice that would strengthen this position. (D), if true, reinforces the idea that the lack of advancement is unfair and that discrimination therefore occurs.

Wrong Answers:
(A): Out of Scope. Though this would be an example of women who aren't promoted, there's no evidence that it's *unfair* behavior, and therefore discrimination.
(B): Out of Scope. If the executives were found to be not liable for damages, that would weaken the idea that harassment took place. It would have no effect on the argument about *discrimination* however.
(C): Opposite. If female artists are often on the ballot, this would suggest that their lack of inclusion is not necessarily due to discrimination.

33. C Why would the author take particular note of the inclusion of women as "forefathers?" The name itself suggests that women are improperly recognized in the industry and are made to fit into a category that is technically worded in such a way as to exclude them. (C) summarizes this point.

Wrong Answers:
(A): Opposite. The author is making the opposite point: that when they are recognized, it's in an improper fashion.
(B): Faulty Use of Detail. Though the author believes this, it doesn't address why the author is miffed about the induction of these women as "forefathers."
(D): Faulty Use of Detail. Though the author would certainly believe this also, it doesn't address the issue discussed in the question.

PASSAGE VI

Topic and Scope:
The author discusses the motivations for scientific fraud and its implications.

Mapping the Passage:
¶1 discusses the example of a large fraud: the Cardiff Giant.
¶2 provides an example of a British scientific award structure that encourages fraud, and states that fraud is a result of pressures similar to those in economic situations.
¶3 describes initial reactions to the Neanderthal Man, arguing that society more readily believed the discovery when cultural beliefs changed.
¶4 argues that fraud is relatively easy to get away with in science.
¶5 points out that the biggest frauds are often the most successful.
¶6 provides an example of newly increased scrutiny in scientific research, and states that fraud is self-defeating.

Questions:
34. C Why does the author bring up accounting and banking? To give examples of situations in which, due to constant oversight, fraud is rare. By contrast, the author says in ¶4, science depends on "faith." ¶2 provides an example of how an attempt to systematize science like accounting can backfire. Choice (C) most closely summarizes the overall range of references.

Wrong Answers:
(A): Distortion. Though the author mentions accounting and states in ¶4 that there have been attempts made to evaluate science in an accountant-like fashion, there's no evidence that scientists are becoming more like accountants.
(B): Out of Scope. There's no evidence from the passage that this is the case, and it has nothing to do with the accounting references.
(D): Opposite. The author uses ¶s3 and 6 to provide examples of science *not* thriving under scrutiny.

35. A Go back to the line reference, paying attention to your map summary also. The author is making the point that some frauds are successful precisely because of their size and audacity. (A) most closely matches this.

Wrong Answers:
(B): Distortion. Though the author argues that some deceptions have been too easily accepted, this doesn't mean that the scientific elite as a whole is easily deceived.
(C): Opposite. The author is making the point that at least in this case, the Nobel Prize was awarded even when there *wasn't* scientific merit.

(D): Distortion. Though the biggest frauds may be the most unethical, they're certainly not perpetrated by the best scientists.

36. D Why did the American provenance of the Cardiff giant have any relevance? The author suggests that people were proud that the first man happened to be an American. (D) states the same.

Wrong Answers:
(A): Distortion. The word "deride" is extreme—the author at most lightly criticizes the "gullibility" of those who paid to see the Cardiff Giant.
(B): Out of Scope. Though the author makes a point about evolution in ¶3, it's not made specifically in relation to Americans or to the Cardiff Giant.
(C): Out of Scope. The author never suggests this.

37. B The question provides an example of scientific fraud and asks what could have motivated it. This is essentially a scattered-detail question in disguise: eliminate answer choices that the author cites as causes for scientific fraud. Only (B) is excluded: the author never cites contempt for oversight committees in the passage.

Wrong Answers:
(A): Opposite. The author raises this possibility in the last paragraph.
(C): Opposite. This would be consistent with the Nobel Prize-winning motives of ¶2.
(D): Opposite. The author argues in ¶2 that scientists may engage in fraud to protect their career.

38. D Review the lines with an eye to your map. The author makes the point that people were more willing to believe the Neanderthal discovery when it fit in with social trends (¶3). (D) comes close to this, and fits well with the example of Germans who considered one feature of the Neanderthal to be evidence of their own perceived national history (¶4).

Wrong Answers:
(A): Out of Scope. There's no evidence from the passage that this was the case.
(B): Out of Scope. Another choice not supported by the paragraph or the passage.
(C): Out of Scope. Though scientists may seek fame, the author doesn't suggest that they specifically seek it out because of the national consciousness of any given time.

39. C Review the analogy in the last paragraph in context and paraphrase its meaning: science is an attempt to discover the laws of nature, and faking science defeats the purpose of discovery. A prediction along these lines should lead you immediately to (C).

Wrong Answers:
(A): Distortion. The analogy of the game isn't intended to suggest that competition exists. The "game" is between scientists and nature, not between scientists themselves.
(B): Out of Scope. While scientists may be tempted to cheat, the author isn't pointing this out through the card game analogy.
(D): Opposite. The author argues explicitly that fraud is "quite extraordinarily rare," contradicting this choice.

40. D Why does the author think that one should expect a wave of fraud inquiries? Look at the context and the purpose of the paragraph. The author argues that the pressure to produce research in order to get grant money will foster an atmosphere that encourages cheating. (D) summarizes this.

Wrong Answers:
(A): Distortion. This is a distortion of the point made in ¶6 that a specific organization did this at a specific time.
(B): Opposite. The author is arguing that fraud will *increase* under the British system.
(C): Out of Scope. Though the author might not like the British method, there's no evidence that he thinks scientists are of equal caliber regardless of their score.

PASSAGE VII

Topic and Scope:
The author argues that crusades against violence in media, and especially film and television, are misguided because media violence causes very little actual violence.

Mapping the Passage:
¶1 provides examples of previous crusades against media violence.
¶s2 and 3 acknowledge that film and television violence has increased drastically in recent years.
¶4 says that a prominent backlash against television violence exists. The author agrees that filmed violence is a "disgrace" and argues that liberals go too far in fighting violence in media.
¶5 argues that the link between media violence and actual violence is weak.
¶6 argues that the campaign against media violence is part of a long American tradition of moral crusades.
¶7 argues that by any measure, the amount of violence caused by media violence is very small.
¶8 accepts that media violence contributes to a climate of violence but argues that it is not a significant factor in triggering violence.
¶9 acknowledges that occasionally actual violence comes as the result of emulating filmed violence.

Questions:
41. A Why does the author argue that the campaign against media violence is misguided? He essentially

argues that media violence is not a big deal, a drop in the bucket. (A) states the same.

Wrong Answers:
(B): Out of Scope. Though this might be true, it's not the basis of the author's objection to the campaigns against media violence. He's more concerned with the argument that the problem isn't big to begin with.
(C): Out of Scope. This argument isn't made anywhere in the passage.
(D): Distortion. The author acknowledges that there is an occasional definite link, but makes the argument that the frequency is very low.

42. B Predict by again reviewing the author's main point: the level of concern is unwarranted because the amount of actual violence caused by media violence is too low to merit such attention (¶7). (B) quickly rewards the efficient prediction.

Wrong Answers:
(A): Faulty Use of Detail. The author makes this point in ¶s1 and 6, but only to suggest that there's a tradition of such campaigns against violence and vice. The main point is that media violence simply doesn't do that much damage.
(C): Faulty Use of Detail. Though this can be inferred from the author's point in ¶5, it doesn't provide the author's reason *why* demonizing the media doesn't do much good.
(D): Out of Scope. Though this also might be able to be inferred from the passage, it's not the author's main point about why crusades against media violence do little good.

43. B While the author lists three of these factors as causes of violence, he says only that liberals attribute violence to (B), not that he himself considers that to be a cause.

Wrong Answers:
(A): Opposite. This is mentioned in the eighth paragraph.
(C): Opposite. As above, and in the same place.
(D): Opposite. Also in the same place.

44. B What is the author's central argument? That media violence doesn't cause much actual violence, and so there should be little worry about it. Look for a choice that establishes the link that the author denies: (B) does just this, suggesting that media violence *does* cause actual violence.

Wrong Answers:
(A): Out of Scope. Though this would contradict the author's point in ¶2, it wouldn't weaken the overall argument that there's little link between violence and its representation.

(C): Out of Scope. Even if this were true, the author would respond that the violence reduced probably isn't caused by the media in the first place.
(D): Out of Scope. Though this would also contradict a point made in ¶2, it doesn't weaken the author's argument that an overall link is weak.

45. B Go back to the referenced line numbers. What does the author argue that the American pastime is? The author says that it's the "campaign against the devil's images" and expands this by arguing that America loves "moral prohibitions and symbolic crusades." (B) fits.

Wrong Answers:
(A): Distortion. The author never argues that the stands being made are unpopular. If anything, they're *too* popular.
(C): Out of Scope. The author never mentions the corruption of political campaigns.
(D): Distortion. Though most of this choice is right, there's no indication that the change that's being effected comes about as a result of criticism that's particular sharp.

46. A Look for an answer choice that reflects a claim the author simply leaves alone without evaluating. (A) is such a claim: the author mentions the Payne Foundation study in ¶1 but doesn't refute it or provide evidence in support of it.

Wrong Answers:
(B): Opposite. The author makes this point in ¶2.
(C): Opposite. This point is also made in ¶2.
(D): Opposite. The author *contradicts* this point in ¶3.

47. B If the broadcast industry is just now proposing a rating system, what could have been the cause of this? Quite possibly the backlash to the increased violence that the author discusses. (B) says the same: those who have spoken out against media violence *have* made an impact on the networks.

Wrong Answers:
(A): Opposite. This choice would suggest that the networks *have* taken action to at least patrol the content of their programming, though they might not necessarily change that content.
(C): Out of Scope. The stations might simply be reacting to pressure. There's no suggestion that the action is being taken because they've acknowledged a link between violence in the media and the real world.
(D): Out of Scope. Though the networks will *rate* content, this doesn't mean that they'll change it.

PASSAGE VIII

Topic and Scope:
The author discusses Boccaccio's *Decameron* and its relevance to changes in the literature and society of the time.

Mapping the Passage:
¶1 describes the characters in the book as embodying a liberal code of behavior.

¶2 introduces the Boccaccio and his "most famous" work, the *Decameron* argues that different ages can either progress or regress from earlier ones and provides examples of other ages that compare to and contrast with Boccaccio's.

¶3 describes the book as principally being a Florentine and social book and describes Boccaccio's reaction to his own book.

¶s4 and 5 describe the book as a more natural and less spiritual book than the *Divine Comedy*.

¶6 argues that the focus of the book is human behavior rather than abstraction.

¶7 uses the plagues of the time to show that the book is realistic rather than idealistic.

Questions:
48. B Review ¶3 to get a prediction to this question. The author says that Boccaccio recognized the power of his own book and was horrified by it. (B) says the same.

Wrong Answers:
(A): Out of Scope. Though this isn't mentioned in the passage, if Boccaccio repented writing the *Decameron*, it would be safe to assume he preferred whatever he wrote later.
(C): Faulty Use of Detail. The author mentions in several points that Boccaccio did believe this, but this doesn't answer the question of what he thought of his own work.
(D): Out of Scope. This isn't mentioned in the passage, though it can be inferred that Boccaccio would have been unhappy about this also, since he didn't like the *Decameron*.

49. B The question gives hints as to how to figure out the answer to this question: If the *Divine Comedy* differs greatly from the *Decameron*, look for an answer choice that describes a quality the *Decameron* possesses. (B) fits, and there's no evidence in the passage that the *Divine Comedy* is set in Florence anyhow.

Wrong Answers:
(A): Opposite. The author says in ¶3 that the *Divine Comedy* has this quality.
(C): Opposite. This can be inferred from the contrast to Dante's work in ¶s 3 and 4.
(D): Opposite. As above, the author describes the *Decameron* in contrast to Dante's work as being "entertaining," and so it's safe to infer that the *Divine Comedy* wasn't.

50. D Go back to ¶1 to review the use of the fresco. The author argues that the *Decameron* "daringly reverses" the morality shown in the fresco, also noting that both works of art were created at about the same time. (D) summarizes this.

Wrong Answers:
(A): Opposite. Both the question and passage suggest that the two works of art contrast, while this answer choice suggests that they correlate.
(B): Opposite. The author suggests that the fresco is in keeping with the tradition of medieval religious art.
(C): Opposite. The author argues the opposite about both of these works of art.

51. C If the *Decameron* daringly reverses morality in art, and if the morality described in the book is described as relatively unrestrictive, what can be inferred? That morality was portrayed *more* restrictively in art before. (C) rewards the careful reasoning.

Wrong Answers:
(A): Out of Scope. While this might be true, it doesn't tie into the reversal of morality mentioned.
(B): Out of Scope. As above.
(D): Out of Scope. As above.

52. B Go back to the passage to review the author's point in using the Victorian example. The overall idea is that the Victorian era marked a regression to morals more restrictive than the ones that Boccaccio describes. All the choices support this except for (B), which directly contradicts the author's point in ¶2 that society *doesn't* necessarily progress.

Wrong Answers:
(A): Opposite. This is suggested by the author's description of more restrictive morality in ¶2.
(C): Opposite. This reinforces the idea that Boccaccio's characters were unusual for their time, a point reinforced by the reference to the morals of the Victorian era.
(D): Opposite. The author mentions this in ¶2 as a contrast to Victorian habits and morals.

53. A An incorporation question. How would the author use the idea that Boccaccio's book is more similar to the *Canterbury Tales* than Dante's book? Go back to ¶4, where the books are mentioned. The author already considers the *Decameron* and the *Canterbury Tales* similar, and would use further similarity to reinforce the point that they were reflective of a new style of writing and society. (A) matches up with this prediction.

Wrong Answers:
(B): Opposite. The author argues in ¶s 2 and 3 that the *Decameron* is *less* sophisticated than Boccaccio's other works.
(C): Out of Scope. This might be true, but there would be no reason that the author would use a similarity to *The Canterbury Tales* to advance this point.

(D): Out of Scope. The author isn't as concerned with the style as with its implications, which this answer choice doesn't discuss.

54. C Predict the author's main point about the book before searching for a weakener. The author argues that Boccaccio's book was an unusually realistic representation of society. If (C) is true, the argument that the *Decameron* is realistic would be turned on its ear: a book meant to be read ironically would *not* be realistic. Further, if the book were meant to be ironic, it would have a didactic purpose, which the author specifically argues against.

Wrong Answers:
(A): Out of Scope. Even if this is true, which would weaken the author's point about Boccaccio's opinions, it doesn't undercut the author's *main* point.
(B): Out of Scope. The reading of the book is less important than what the book actually says, and thus this would have no effect on the author's argument.
(D): Opposite. This would strengthen the author's argument that the book realistically deals with death.

PASSAGE IX

Topic and Scope:
The author discusses the threat posed by dioxin and suggests that fears about the toxin may be overblown.

Mapping the Passage:
¶1 provides an example of another case of hysteria over a toxin that outran scientific knowledge.
¶2 states that some claim that dioxin is a threat and that the reaction to dioxin may also be overly emotional.
¶3 rhetorically asks if there can be any meaningful response.
¶4 describes responses to the dioxin threat, expresses skepticism at some environmentalists' proposals, and suggests that common sense and risk analysis should guide decisions about threats.
¶5 quotes an authority to argue that levels of risk should be kept in perspective.

Questions:
55. D Predict by recalling the author's main points: fears about certain toxins are often overblown and should be tempered by common sense and science. (D) simply repeats this.

Wrong Answers:
(A): Out of Scope. There's no evidence from the passage that the government has ignored these problems. The author might also dispute the seriousness of these health problems, as it's argued in ¶4 that asbestos fears are exaggerated.
(B): Opposite. The author argues roughly the opposite: dioxin isn't the threat many make it out to be.

(C): Out of Scope. While this might be true, there's no evidence from the passage that the government modifies extreme environmental stances.

56. C Look for an answer choice that either contradicts something that the author says about reactions or simply isn't included in the passage. (C) fits the latter: the author never mentions the effect of drastic reactions on insurance premiums.

Wrong Answers:
(A): Opposite. This is the point made in the last paragraph: it's more effective to worry about safety methods that have been proven to improve safety.
(B): Opposite. This can be inferred from various statements in the passage: the author believes that drastic reactions generally represent irrational thought that can itself be dangerous if it leads to the neglect of proven safety measures.
(D): Opposite. The author makes this point in ¶4.

57. B Refer back to the passage. Who wants to "whipsaw public opinion?" Both corporate lobbyists and environmental groups, each of represent extreme viewpoints. Each of these groups want to convince the public of their own view. (B) matches this.

Wrong Answers:
(A): Out of Scope. There's no discussion about changing the *needs* of the public, only the opinion.
(C): Opposite. Groups with an extreme viewpoint won't present a range of alternatives, as evidenced by the examples in ¶s1 and 4.
(D): Distortion. Though the author might believe that extreme groups are acting irrationally, this isn't related to the attempt to change public opinion.

58. B An evaluation question. Why does the author mention Alar? It's another example of a situation in which mass hysteria took hold before science was able to give a clear view of the risks of the toxin. (B) repeats this.

Wrong Answers:
(A): Out of Scope. The author doesn't discuss this.
(C): Opposite. The author believes that drastic reactions are a bad way to respond to public health crises, and that measured response is better.
(D): Opposite. The author is suggesting that the publicity that Alar generated wasn't necessarily warranted, and so the celebrity appearance would also be unwarranted.

59. A Look for something that counters the author's main point, which you should review briefly again before hitting the answers: health fears are often exaggerated and should be tempered by careful study. (A) is an example of a situation in which the sort of careful study that the author suggests took place, and its subject was a health crisis the author believes was overblown. If government action on asbestos and Alar took place only after careful study, the author's main examples in favor of her point would be worthless and the argument therefore would be weakened.

Wrong Answers:
(B): Out of Scope. The author argues that public fears about Alar outpaced science, but doesn't suggest that Alar was completely harmless. This choice would only weaken the author's argument if that contention had been made.
(C): Out of Scope. The author considers at least one view of Greenpeace extreme, and her argument thus wouldn't be affected by further opinions of the group absent any additional evidence.
(D): Out of Scope. As above, this is another example of an extreme viewpoint. Even if this is true, the author has acknowledged extreme viewpoints in the argument already.

60. D A scattered detail question. Look for a choice that isn't stated or conflicts with the author's main ideas. (D) conflicts with the author's suggestion that fears about chemical toxins have been overblown, a point made most clearly in the last paragraph.

Wrong Answers:
(A): Opposite. The author quotes Graham, who makes this point in the last paragraph.
(B): Opposite. This point is made regarding lobbyists and environmental groups in ¶4.
(C): Opposite. The author mentions this most clearly when discussing asbestos in ¶4.

Material used in this test section has been adapted from the following sources:

Gillian G. Gaar, *She's A Rebel*. © by Seal Press.
Todd Gitlin, "Media Violence Does Not Cause Societal Violence." © 1994 by The American Prospect.
Steve Jones, "Crooked Bones." Reprinted with permission from *The New York Review of Books*. © 1997 by Nyrev, Inc.
Randal Kennedy, "My Race Problem—And Ours." *The Atlantic Monthly* Vol. 279 No. 5 May 1997 p. 56.Michael Levey, *Florence: A Portrait*. © by Harvard University Press.
J. Madeleine Nash, "Keeping Cool about Risk." © 1994 by *Time, Inc.*
"Hesperus Descending" (Editorial) *The New York Times*. © 1996 by *The New York Times*.
Gregory E. Pence, *Classic Cases in Medical Ethics*, pp. 54 - 55. © by McGraw-Hill, Inc.
David Harris Wilson and Stuart E. Prall, *A History of England, Third Edition*. © 1984 by Holt, Rinehart and Winston, Inc., reprinted by permission by permission of the publisher.

Verbal Reasoning Test Six

Time—85 minutes
Question 1–60

DIRECTIONS: Each of the passages in this test is followed by a set of questions based on the passage's content. After reading each passage, decide on the one best response to each question and mark it on your answer sheet. If you are unsure of an answer, eliminate the choices you know are wrong and choose from the remaining choices. You may refer to the passages while answering the questions.

Passage I (Questions 1–9)

Since 1789, the Constitution has granted the President the authority to veto legislation passed by Congress. The threat of a veto in many cases precipitates compromise on the content of a bill that would be
5 otherwise mired in debate before it reached the President. The "regular" veto is a qualified negative veto, which necessitates a two-thirds vote by Congress to be overridden. The "pocket" veto, on the other hand, is exercised when a bill sits on the President's desk with-
10 out being signed before Congress has adjourned (and is therefore unable to override the veto). Opponents of the pocket veto allege that its absolute nature grants the President excessive power. They liken it to a prerogative of the English Kings that the Framers vehemently
15 despised. The argument also embraces a vast body of commentary on the "Imperial Presidency," that is, the growing accumulation of power in the executive relative to the legislative branch.

These arguments, in claiming an imbalance of fed-
20 eral powers, misrepresent the pocket veto. Unlike the royal prerogative, the pocket veto is exercised by a democratically-elected leader pursuant to a clearly defined constitutional procedure in which presentation of a bill by Congress may be arranged so as to thwart the
25 possible execution of the pocket veto. Moreover, an absolute veto forecloses further action on a proposal whereas Congress may overcome a pocket veto by insti-tuting a reintroduction and passage of the rejected bill in a subsequent term.

30 The "Imperial Presidency" developed from the encroachment of executive action into areas where it has been assumed that the legislative branch retains supremacy. The legislative process, however, clearly orders shared responsibility between the President and
35 Congress. One should not mistake Presidential powers granted to block legislation for those that would, in effect, supplant congressional authorization. The latter threatens to override the constitutional system of checks and balances; the former situation, typified by the pock-
40 et veto, is a part of that system of checks and balances.

The arguments raised in *Kennedy* and *Barnes* implicitly claim that a regular veto would be overridden, or not exercised at all. Consequently, the pocket veto grants the President a special political tool against "pop-
45 ular will" as exercised by Congress. Herein lies the fun-damental disagreement over the pocket veto. Opponents press for the President to defer to a seemingly inevitable congressional victory while proponents of this second type of veto stand behind its historical use by the
50 President to stall or delay legislation he thinks unwise. If circumspection and deliberation are the more valued aspects of the lawmaking process, even the most bla-tantly political use of the pocket veto passes muster. Historical practice favors the President's role as an inter-
55 loper.

---

1. As used in the last sentence, the word "interloper" most nearly means:

    A. one who unjustly assumes power through the use of force.
    B. one who acts as a liaison between different parties.
    C. one who prevents certain actions from occur-ring.
    D. one who thinks carefully before acting.

2. The author's conclusion that opponents of the use of the pocket veto misrepresent its power depends on which of the following assumptions?

    A. A democratic leader elected through constitu-tional procedure cannot accumulate too much legislative power.
    B. In a democracy, the legislative and executive branches are balanced by the authority of the judicial branch.
    C. Royal prerogatives no longer exist in modern governments.
    D. The pocket veto limits the President's power to counteract a Congressional motion.

GO TO THE NEXT PAGE.

3. The author refers to *Kennedy* and *Barnes* in the passage in order to:

    A. prove that Congress opposes the pocket veto as a limit to its legislative power.
    B. suggest that the validity of the pocket veto has been a matter of judicial concern.
    C. show how the pocket veto's weaknesses override its strengths.
    D. praise how the pocket veto can delay the legislative process.

4. The passage suggests that which of the following would be the likely consequence if overwhelmingly popular legislation is deferred by the President's use of the pocket veto?

    A. The vetoed legislation would be reintroduced by Congress.
    B. Congress would be powerless to pass similar legislation.
    C. The President would override the system of checks and balances.
    D. The pocket veto would be detrimental to future legislative efforts.

5. The author suggests that opponents of the pocket veto would most likely agree that:

    A. the President should not be allowed to exercise legislative authority.
    B. use of the pocket veto unfairly removes power from the legislative branch.
    C. Congress should have the right to override the pocket veto.
    D. the absolute veto should be reinstated by Congress.

6. The author would consider a "blatantly political use of the pocket veto" (lines 52–53) to be:

    A. unjustified, since the will of the congressional majority should be respected.
    B. unwise, since the President should be perceived to stand above partisan politics.
    C. appropriate if the President has pledged in advance to block the legislation in question.
    D. legitimate because it can force further consideration of a bill the President opposes.

7. It can be inferred that the author considers which of the following to be the strongest argument *against* the positions opposing the pocket veto taken in *Barnes* and *Kennedy*?

    A. A return veto of the legislation in question would not have been overridden.
    B. A return veto of the legislation in question would probably have been overridden.
    C. The President would have been unlikely to use a return veto, because of fear of public opinion.
    D. In certain cases, the Constitution allows the President to delay legislation which has majority support.

8. The author would be most likely to agree with which of the following statements about the "Imperial Presidency"?

    A. It represents an unprecedented threat to the continuity of American institutions.
    B. It is more in keeping with the present English system of government than with the American.
    C. The pocket veto is not really an example of tendencies toward an "Imperial Presidency."
    D. It has been the cause of increasingly frequent use of the pocket veto.

GO TO THE NEXT PAGE.

Passage II (Questions 9-15)

The term "editor" covers a number of functions ranging from one who makes acceptance decisions or is responsible for commissioning and organizing a publishing program; to someone internal who deals with the production process (production editor) or is responsible for copy-editing typescript and/or electronic manuscripts. Further complicating the attempt at classification, an additional and important role of the copy-editor may involve substantive changes to the text—either by "polishing" the language or by "developing" the prose—to make it clearer or more appropriate for its purpose. As Renni Browne has said, "Editors don't make up for lack of talent...What editors make up for more than anything else is a lack of objectivity."

Most copy-editors of literature consider it their main duty to present the text as the writer intended. As Thomas McCormack says, "the primary rule of editing is, first do no harm." This sounds simple, but aside from the question of whether the author's intentions can ever be known, it is not necessarily clear what is actually intended. The actual cases are so diverse that any singular maxim probably does more harm than good.

Circumstances abound in which pressure has been applied to authors by their editors to alter their work. The publisher of the first edition of *The Red Badge of Courage* moderated Stephen Crane's uncompromising depiction of the horrors of war. The publisher of the first edition of *Women in Love* toned down much of the explicit nature of D.H. Lawrence's sexual passages. In both cases, the changes were "authorized" insofar as the authors accepted them. But then, on the other hand, what other option did they face except not seeing their work published at all. Can this situation be construed as the authors' "free" acceptance of the editorial alterations, and do the author's intentions endure?

More recently, there has arisen a trend in editing that is well illustrated by the declaration adopted in 1992 by the Board of Directors of the Association of American University Presses: "Books...should also be at the forefront in recognizing how language encodes prejudice. They should also be agents for change and the redress of past mistakes." This "politically correct" movement seeks to eliminate un-intended perpetuation of prejudices in literature, but with obvious, inherent dangers and difficulties.

Not all difficult problems for editors are caused by moral, political, ethical or even marketing issues. Punctuation, mainly thought of as part of an author's individual style, is not usually considered controversial. In spite—and partly because—of this, punctuation is what publishers traditionally feel most free to alter as mere, neutral "correction" (a gross example is the unskilled and unnecessary editing of Emily Dickinson's eccentric, but eloquent, punctuation in early editions of her works). First editions in particular tend to present the publisher's "house style" rather than the author's own punctuation. The obvious course for an editor might be to return to the author's manuscript wherever possible. But publishing-house re-punctuation is so routine that many authors have actually counted on it for the correct punctuation of their work; in such cases, the manuscript would contain punctuation (or a lack thereof) that the author never expected to see reproduced in print. *Jane Eyre* provides an interesting quandary for an editor. We have Charlotte Brontë's original manuscript. We also have a letter from Brontë to her publisher, thanking him for correcting her punctuation. Which punctuation is more authentically "Brontëan": Brontë's own, or that which Brontë explicitly preferred to her own?

The thorniest situation of all, perhaps, involves *authorial* revisions made long after publication. W.H. Auden, in subsequent editions of his work, altered his own earlier poems to accord with his later political and religious opinions. One fancies that the young Auden would have been furious at the old Auden's liberties. Yet both are Auden—which has the greater authority?

---

9. It is most reasonable to conclude that the author of the passage would agree with which of the following general statements about the proper role of the editor?

  A. An editor should restore passages censored in earlier editions.

  B. When the author's manuscript is available, an editor should be faithful to its punctuation.

  C. Editorial decisions are too complex to be made on any other basis than case-by-case.

  D. An editor should respect the author's present (or, in the case of a deceased author, final) intentions.

GO TO THE NEXT PAGE.

10. Which of the following can be inferred about the text of *Jane Eyre* from the passage?

   A. Following the punctuation of the manuscript would make the book more difficult to read.

   B. The punctuation of the first edition misrepresents the intentions of the author.

   C. Bronte made a mistake by allowing her publisher to correct her punctuation.

   D. Bronte requested that the publisher make corrections to her punctuation.

11. Based on information in the passage, which of the following new discoveries would potentially be a legitimate basis for a new edition of a literary work?

   I. An author's original manuscript

   II. A first edition incorporating the publisher's revisions

   III. A second edition thoroughly emended by the author

   A. I only

   B. III only

   C. I and II only

   D. I and III only

12. According to the applicable points outlined by the author in the passage, which of the following aspects of an author's original work is most likely to be altered or deleted by a publisher?

   A. Sexually explicit passages

   B. Explicit descriptions of violence

   C. Unconventional punctuation

   D. Expressions of currently unpopular political opinions

13. Based on the information given in the passage, which of the following situations would the author probably consider the most difficult decision for an editor?

   A. Pope rewrote *The Dunciad*, directing the satire against a completely different person.

   B. Dickens changed the ending of *Great Expectations* at a friend's suggestion before its publication in book form.

   C. Whitman printed *Leaves of Grass* himself and continued to produce new, expanded editions for almost 40 years.

   D. James Joyce's poor eyesight made it difficult for him to proofread his manuscripts.

14. If the following options were presented in a series of papers in response to this passage, which of the following would the author probably consider an acceptable resolution of the problem presented by the revisions made by Auden to his earlier works?

   A. Publishing a text with the young Auden's words in one typeface, showing the old Auden's changes in another typeface

   B. Refusing to reprint any version until the literary community had resolved which version represented the author's true intent

   C. Publishing the old Auden's words, but including the young Auden's words in footnotes

   D. Treating the young Auden and the old Auden as separate authors, and publishing both with appropriate acknowledgements

15. The author cites the edits made to Emily Dickinson's punctuation in early editions of her works most probably in order to:

   A. provide an example demonstrating how difficult it can be to decide how to edit an author's work.

   B. provide an example of the wrong decision made in a situation where the right decision should have been easy.

   C. argue against ever making any changes to an author's punctuation, which the author considers to be done excessively.

   D. argue that the decisions to be made, even in changing something as neutral as punctuation, are never easy.

GO TO THE NEXT PAGE.

Passage III (Questions 16-21)

Over the past two decades, courts have gone far in their interpretations of civil rights legislation to ensure African-American participation throughout the work force. Much ground has been gained in this fight against
5 an institutionalized inequality that has become ingrained in our collective psyche. There are some, though, who remain concerned that the situation of African-American managers has made only limited progress in certain industries.

10 It is particularly disturbing (contributing to what Martha Kim has called "a deceptive and manipulative sense of false hope") to find relatively few African-American executives in an industry whose work force consists primarily of African-Americans, namely pro-
15 fessional team sports. In the 2001 Racial and Gender Report Card published by the Center for Sport in Society of Northeastern University, which analyzed the composition of players and administrators in professional leagues, only the Women's National Basketball
20 Association and the National Basketball Association scored well. According to the report, generally "who's running the league doesn't look like who's playing in the league." Questions are being posed as to whether general employment principles are properly applicable
25 to the sports business, or whether the sports industry in fact enjoys a special status similar to baseball's antitrust exemption. With a growing number of African-Americans achieving the educational standards as well as the practical experience required for executive posi-
30 tions, it is foreseeable that the professional team-sport industry will soon face challenges to its executive employment decisions.

The organizational structures of clubs and leagues are similar to other large businesses. It is within these
35 two organizations that the absence of African-American executives is most noticeable. Some professional club owners justify the absence of African-American executives at these levels by alluding to clubs' and leagues' organizational structure as being familial in nature.
40 Whether this characterization justifies the exclusion of African-American executives is questionable at best. It is worth noting that the Supreme Court, clarifying the burden of proof in discrimination cases in a decision issued June 12, 2000 (Reeves v. Sanderson), confirmed
45 that a plaintiff's evidence of discrimination, combined with sufficient evidence for a reasonable judge to reject the employer's "nondiscriminatory" explanation, is adequate to sustain a finding of intentional discrimination.

The sports industry is within the purview of Title
50 VII of the Civil Rights Act of 1964, which exists to prohibit intentional discrimination in employment on the basis of race, color, religion, sex or national origin. However, recent legal developments call into question whether the principles applied to assure lower level jobs
55 will be applied to protect African-American executives from discrimination while seeking upper level positions. The courts have traditionally been willing to assess an applicant's qualifications in resolving claims of discrimination. Yet courts in upper level cases often profess a
60 lack of expertise and refuse to assess an applicant's qualifications. This, in effect, works to make it virtually impossible for a successful suit brought by an executive to occur, since it involves prohibitively difficult proof that the employer has subjected comparably qualified
65 individuals of different races to different treatment.

The Supreme Court has not yet confronted the issue of which Title VII standards and rules should apply to discrimination cases involving African-American executives. Lower federal courts have seemingly begun to
70 distort these standards in cases involving executive and professional employees. Given that executive positions have unique characteristics, resolution of these actions becomes all the more difficult. Rules developed to deal with lower level Title VII cases may not always be
75 applicable to executive employment cases.

---

16. In paragraph 4, the author claims that courts have hesitated to deal with Title VII cases involving executive employment decisions due to their lack of expertise in that area. This conclusion of the courts is based on which of the following assumptions?

    A. Proper assessment of a candidate's qualifications for a position requires substantive knowledge of a particular field.

    B. Courts should not be expected to evaluate candidates based on their educational and professional experience.

    C. Executive candidates possess skills and training that are more difficult to quantitatively assess than the skills and training of lower-level employees.

    D. Discrimination cases involving executive employment are more time-consuming and costly to courts than cases of lower-level employment discrimination.

GO TO THE NEXT PAGE.

17. Which of the following would be analogous to the situation described in paragraph 2 regarding the absence of African-American executives in a field with many African-American athletes?

A. The Board of a non-profit Protestant Church youth organization consists solely of middle-aged men and women.

B. A social service agency, which serves minority and disadvantaged youths, is run by a management team of suburban professionals.

C. Fewer than half of the managers of a national feminist bookstore company, which employs mostly female cashiers and clerks, are women.

D. A state anti-smoking campaign is organized and implemented by a group of smokers and non-smokers.

18. The author of the passage mentions the Supreme Court in the final paragraph in order to:

A. prove that courts have been slow to respond to Title VII cases initiated by African-American executives who have been denied upper-level positions in professional team sports.

B. suggest that upper courts need to provide standards for the proper application of Title VII posits in upper-level employment discrimination cases.

C. explain that the lower courts have been more willing to handle executive employment decision cases under the auspices of Title VII.

D. argue that the Judicial Branch of the federal government should set precedents for treating executive employment cases that are protected by Title VII.

19. The author suggests which of the following about the relatively low number of African-American executives currently employed in the sports industry?

A. It is attributable to flaws in the American educational system.

B. It is caused by baseball's antitrust exemption.

C. It is the result of African-American executives' lack of managerial experience.

D. It does not compare favorably with the industry's labor force as a whole.

20. The author responds to the argument that clubs' and leagues' organizational structure is familial by:

A. contending that the argument is fallacious.

B. challenging the motivations of those making the argument.

C. implying that the argument, even if true, should be overridden by more important considerations.

D. stating that the argument cannot be accepted without further proof, and is probably libelous.

21. The author's assertion that the sports industry will "soon face challenges to its executive employment decisions" (lines 31–32) assumes that African-American executive candidates:

A. are now the most qualified applicants for executive positions.

B. have joined forces in a collective bargaining position.

C. are likely to sue non-minority executive candidates who are hired in their place.

D. are no longer willing to be victimized by hiring practices they perceive as unfair.

GO TO THE NEXT PAGE.

Passage IV (Questions 22-27)

Thunderstorms generally develop in the late afternoon or evening hours, when moist, daytime air rises into the upper atmosphere as temperatures cool and denser, nighttime air slides in underneath. Clouds of
[5] water droplets, generally supercooled (droplets whose temperature has fallen below 0 degrees Celsius but have not yet frozen), condense around dust particles in the air until a critical density is reached, at which point it begins to rain. Cloud-to-ground lightning occurs when a
[10] discrepancy in electric charge develops between a cloud and the earth. For reasons that are not widely agreed upon, a charge begins to build up in this mixed water and ice region. When this discrepancy reaches a certain "breakdown potential," the surge of electric charge
[15] known as lightning moves downward between the negative and positive charge centers in 50-yard sections called step leaders. Eventually, it encounters something on the ground that is a good connection, and, with the circuit complete, the charge is lowered from cloud to
[20] ground. This entire event usually takes less than half a second. It is by preventing the requisite charge polarization that scientists hope someday to discourage the creation of cloud-to-ground lightning, thereby making storms safer and easier to "weather."

[25] Many authorities adhere to a hypothesis for cloud electrification theory which emphasizes that the charging process occurs when a supercooled droplet of water collides with an ice particle of precipitation size (a hailstone)—the precipitation model. At this moment a large
[30] portion of the droplet freezes—resulting in a negative charge on the forming hailstone—while a smaller portion, still lingering in its supercooled state, dissociates itself—taking on a positive charge. The relatively heavy hailstone, responding to gravity, then begins to fall,
[35] while the extremely light supercooled droplet is carried by updrafts to higher regions of the cloud. Assuming the veracity of this account of charge separation, scientists guess that they would be able to discourage polarization by reducing the quantity of supercooled water in a
[40] cloud. To this purpose they have conducted preliminary seeding experiments, in which they have attempted to initiate the freezing of excess water by dropping large quantities of dry ice and silver iodide into potential thunderclouds, the results of which are, however, as yet
[45] inconclusive.

A more recent convection model of the polarization process is offered by Bernard Vonnegut and Charles B. Moore, who contend that the primary cause of electrical charge formation in clouds is the capture of ionized
[50] (electrically charged) gas molecules by water droplets. The ions, so the theory goes, are absorbed by the droplets and transported by updrafts and downdrafts to various portions of the cloud. Vonnegut and Moore suggest that, in order to combat the effects of this transport
[55] of ions, it would be necessary to modify the properties of ions beneath accumulating clouds. In support of this explanation of cloud polarization they conducted a series of "space charge" experiments. Suspending a high-voltage wire above nine miles of Illinois country-
[60] side, Vonnegut and Moore released large quantities of ions into the atmosphere below, forming clouds. By means of airplanes specially equipped for electrical measurements, they determined that the ions were being distributed to differing regions of the clouds.

---

22. Which of the following options best summarizes the author's main point in the passage?

   A. Several recent breakthroughs have increased our understanding of the causes of lightning.
   B. Charge polarization in clouds can result both from the freezing of supercooled droplets and from the modification of ion properties.
   C. The standard explanation of the causes of lightning is inaccurate and should be modified.
   D. Scientists are not yet agreed on either the causes of cloud-to-ground lightning or the methods of controlling it.

23. It can be inferred from the information in the passage that the term "breakdown potential" as used in line 14 of the passage refers to:

   A. a charge polarity sufficient to cause lightning.
   B. the intensity of the lightning bolt.
   C. the distance between the negatively charged earth and the positively charged cloud.
   D. the duration of the lightning event.

GO TO THE NEXT PAGE.

24. According to points made in the passage by the author, scientists agree that lightning can occur when:

    A. ions are transported by updrafts to higher regions of a thundercloud.
    B. supercooled droplets collide with hailstones in clouds.
    C. a difference in charge exists between a cloud and the ground.
    D. dry ice is released into a potential thundercloud.

25. According to the author, the "precipitation" and "convection" accounts of cloud polarization differ with respect to:

    I. the role of gas ions in causing polarization.
    II. the ability of water droplets to carry an electric charge.
    III. whether air currents play a part in the process of polarization.

    A. I only
    B. III only
    C. I and II only
    D. II and III only

26. Which of the following statements would be LEAST consistent with the account of cloud polarization offered by Vonnegut and Moore?

    A. Charge is transported within clouds via updrafts and downdrafts.
    B. Lightning is caused by a discrepancy in electric charge between a cloud and the ground.
    C. Water droplets are capable of carrying an electrical charge.
    D. Lightning occurs when positively and negatively charged droplets are absorbed by hailstones.

27. It can be inferred that in relation to their theory of charge polarization in clouds, Vonnegut and Moore's "space charge" experiments:

    A. provided supporting but not conclusive evidence for the theory.
    B. definitively proved the theory.
    C. greatly weakened the theory.
    D. disproved a competing theory and thus indirectly strengthened Vonnegut and Moore's theory.

GO TO THE NEXT PAGE.

Passage V (Questions 28-34)

Virginia Woolf made an original contribution to the form of the novel, but was also a distinguished essayist, a critic for *The Times Literary Supplement*, and a central figure of the Bloomsbury group. Dialogic in style and
5 continually questioning what may be the reader's opinion (her rejection of an authoritative voice links her to the tradition of Montaigne), her critical essays, when examined carefully, reveal a thematic and technical complexity that rivals her novels.

10 Some of her most rigorous essays suggest that the personality of the author can be fixed if sufficient evidence can be amassed and if its logical implications are followed. In "The Novels of Turgenev," Woolf pursues the problem of interpretation on the part of the reader by
15 providing a detailed report of her own response to Turgenev. She does this in order to make possible the question that leaps the gap between reader and text. That question—"what principles guided Turgenev?"—focuses on the fictional strategies that must have been in oper-
20 ation in order to have produced Woolf's experience. Thus Woolf accounts for this by reconstructing Turgenev's method. But she pushes farther insofar as she asserts that the method must be a sign of a deeper informing power, the mind of Turgenev itself. This dis-
25 tance can be traversed by interpretation, Woolf argues, because writers like Turgenev achieve a level of personality beneath the surface distinctions among individuals. Her greatest examples of this impersonal power in the English language are Jane Austen and Shakespeare.
30 According to Woolf, these authors write with a "clarity of heart and spirit" that allows their potential for genius to express itself "whole an entire." Unencumbered by impediments that would be erected by such feelings on their part as fear, hatred, or dependency, we are allowed
35 by their art to make contact with what is most deeply personal, and therefore most widely human, in them.

But one of the riches of Woolf's essays is that they critique this very same possibility of closing the gap that exists between author and audience. This is evinced in
40 Woolf's awareness of the contemporary artist's self-consciousness: the enemy of human contact and knowing. There seem to be so many barriers on the road to the deepest level of self that the journey there is impossible, but it is this level of self through which the gap must be
45 closed. In fact, Woolf asserts that the journey *is* impossible for the modern writer. In "How It Strikes a Contemporary," Woolf contrasts writers of the past— Chaucer is her most powerful example—who believed

wholeheartedly in an atemporal order verified by the
50 entire culture, with modern writers who have lost this advantage. Woolf suggests that, if, for writer and reader, no way to a shared, universal level of experience is available, the very ground of the interpretive enterprise is removed.

28. Which of the following would most weaken Woolf's assertion that the distance between reader and writer can be traversed by interpretation?

   A. Contemporary writers are unable to construct a deep meaning for each reader because they focus primarily on personal distinctions rather than similarities.
   B. Every reader reacts differently to the same text and yet each constructs for himself/herself a similar idea of the author's personality and presence.
   C. Past writers were governed by a strong sense of individualism, which made it impossible for them to appeal to human commonalities.
   D. Authorial intent or perspective remains an abstract idea unless the writer is able to confirm or deny the reader's interpretation.

29. According to the points elucidated by the author within the passage, all of the following are characteristic of Woolf's essays EXCEPT that:

   A. they focus primarily on examining whether or not a reader's experience of a text can reveal the original authorial presence.
   B. they are written in a more technically and thematically complex manner than are her fictional works.
   C. they betray Woolf's skepticism about the very idea she is attempting to demonstrate and justify.
   D. they frequently utilize examples from other writers in order to illustrate and support her conclusions.

GO TO THE NEXT PAGE.

30. Based on points made by the author of the passage, Woolf mentions Chaucer in her essay "How It Strikes a Contemporary" in order to:

    A. prove that writers of the past were more adept at bridging the gap between reader and author.

    B. indicate how a cultural mindset allowed previous authors to universalize the human experience.

    C. argue that contemporary writers share a similar culture and yet are unable to achieve the same interpretive results as writers of the past.

    D. suggest that modern writers are so concerned with class and gender distinctions that they are unable to be objectively critical of their own work.

31. The author of the passage would be most likely to agree with which of the following statements?

    A. Woolf's attempts to reconstruct the narrative techniques of other authors are admirable but flawed.

    B. Although Woolf remains objective in her analysis of other fictional works, she allows her own personal preferences to interfere with her conclusions.

    C. Woolf's essays often embody a contradictory and self-critical nature.

    D. Woolf proffers examples from past writers in order to disguise her ignorance of contemporary narrative methods.

32. According to the passage, Woolf views a belief in an atemporal world order as:

    A. defining the literary customs of modern writers.

    B. being inadequate to the task of eliminating divisions in human society.

    C. having evolved from a belief in a temporal world order.

    D. contributing to the distinctiveness of past literature.

33. The passage implies that, in her essay "The Novels of Turgenev," Woolf assumes that:

    A. stable and defining qualities of an author's personality are discernible in his or her fiction.

    B. interpretation involves a compromise between the reader's perspective and the perspective of the author.

    C. a reader's experience of a novel's text is determined by a standard set of fictional principles.

    D. making contact with an author's mind requires the use of critical reasoning more than intuition.

34. In the passage the author refers to common perspectives of contemporary writers. He does this in order to:

    A. exemplify a contemporary preoccupation with separateness.

    B. identify manifestations of contemporary cultural patterns in literature.

    C. suggest parallels between past and present literature.

    D. refute the idea that self-consciousness is an affliction.

GO TO THE NEXT PAGE.

Passage VI (Questions 35-40)

The cathedral of Notre-Dame de Paris, the construction of which began between 1150 and 1155, was planned to be the tallest space in Gothic architecture. The construction and design were crafted by the most
5 skilled artisans and directed by Jean de Chelles and Pierre de Montreuil, and being built on a site sacred since Roman times (a temple of Jupiter was once built on the Ile de la Cite, the small Parisian island which houses the great cathedral), Notre Dame's vaulted ceil-
10 ings rise some 33 meters above the floor, more than eight meters higher than any of its early Gothic predecessors. In fact, the height increase of more than one-third over previous buildings, was the apex of the entire era. Nevertheless the structural configuration of the
15 Paris choir (the eastern part of the cathedral where services are sung), which was built first, is essentially similar to that of earlier, smaller churches. The outward thrust of the interior vaults against the high window wall (the clerestory) is resisted only by stone quadrant arch-
20 es hidden under the sloping roof of the adjacent gallery.

In designing the somewhat wider nave, however, with its lighter and more open structure, the Paris builders evidently decided that the concealed quadrant arches were insufficient to support the high clerestory.
25 The increased width translated into greater outward thrust of the vaults than of the choir. More importantly, in building the choir the craftsmen must have become aware of a new problem for which experience with lower churches could not have prepared them: wind
30 speeds are significantly greater at higher elevations. Wind pressure, it is now known, is proportional to the square of wind speed. It is presumed that a concern for this led the builders of the Paris nave to introduce the flying buttress (an exposed support, higher up on the
35 wall than a concealed quadrant arch) just before 1180.

In less than two decades the flying buttress became the stylistic hallmark of Gothic building, and its origin and dissemination in the Middle Ages have long interested historians. As has been revealed by modern struc-
40 tural analyses of a number of medieval buildings, early designers learned from experience, making use of any various flaws and imperfections that developed in actual buildings , in contrast to today's engineers, who rely on instrumented prototypes to ascertain the structural
45 behavior and soundness of a design. The master masons of later cathedrals, such as those at Chartres and Bourges, seem to have been aware of flaws in the original buttressing scheme at Paris and to have modified their own designs accordingly.

35. The author suggests that the flying buttress:

   A. was often flawed by a cracked mortar.
   B. shared structural similarities with the quadrant arch.
   C. presented a solution to an ancient construction problem.
   D. was considered more a stylistic than a structural feature.

36. Which of the following would most *weaken* the author's conclusion that medieval designers learned from experience?

   A. Historians have discovered that a later cathedral was constructed with the same flying buttresses as at Notre-Dame.
   B. Ruins of a fortress prove that the foundation was inadequately prepared for the weight of the corner towers.
   C. Cracks in the mortar of an abbey indicate that workers used poor-quality materials which led to collapse of some exterior walls.
   D. Analysis of several prisons indicate that structural problems were resolved by subsequent engineering innovations.

37. If the author attended a hypothetical conference on medieval building techniques, with which of the following statements would he most likely agree?

   A. Historical analysis of extant medieval architecture is of little practical use to modern designers.
   B. Medieval engineers and architects were talented technological innovators.
   C. Flying buttresses and stone arches have erroneously come to be associated exclusively with Gothic cathedrals.
   D. Notre Dame provides historical scholars with evidence of construction foibles common during the Middle Ages.

GO TO THE NEXT PAGE.

38. Based on the passage, which of the following helps to resolve the paradox that the first part of Notre Dame was built according to models from existing smaller churches although the cathedral itself was planned to be the tallest space in Gothic architecture?

    A. Initial attempts to heighten and widen the nave were unsuccessful, so builders had to abandon this goal of the project.
    B. The first architect was a devout Catholic who resisted any proposed changes to traditional church structures.
    C. Builders were unprepared for the increased wind pressure on the taller structure.
    D. The acoustical needs of the choir were best accommodated by lower ceilings and a narrower span.

39. The author mentions the cathedrals of Chartres and Bourges in order to:

    A. provide examples of superior architectural design in Gothic cathedrals.
    B. point out flaws in the buttressing system of the cathedral of Notre-Dame.
    C. indicate that medieval cathedral builders learned through observing each other's designs.
    D. support the contention that these cathedrals were derivative in design.

40. The author gives a detailed description of the mathematical formula for wind pressure in the second paragraph in order to:

    A. further explain the necessity of strong buttressing.
    B. suggest that flying buttresses provided insufficient support.
    C. underscore the inadvisability of concealing the quadrant arches.
    D. provide evidence that craftsmen understood wind loading well before 1180.

GO TO THE NEXT PAGE.

Passage VII (Questions 41-46)

The Dutch cartographer, Abraham Ortelius, first suggested in 1596 that the Americas were "torn away from Europe and Africa"; but there was little evidence to support his hypothesis. In England in 1620, Francis
5　Bacon also noted that the similarity of many of the edges of various continents suggested that they once might have fit together like puzzle pieces. Evidence mounted gradually over the course of the next few centuries that continents were once joined: fossils of simi-
10　lar plant and animal species found on widely separated continents, long and linear zones of deformed rocks occurring at the edges of continents, and certain geologic and glacial features shared across different continents.

German meteorologist Alfred Wegener proposed in
15　1912 that the continents were all joined in a common landmass he named "Pangaea"—whose etymology was derived from the Greek meaning "all land"—which began breaking up approximately 200 million years ago. In fact, precursors of this theory existed in maps depict-
20　ing the joined continents, which had, it may be noted, been drawn almost a century earlier, but it was Wegener who was the first to combine the accumulating evidence for continental drift into a common framework—to weave seemingly dissimilar, unrelated facts into a theo-
25　ry. His proposal was not well received, however; it remained unclear how the continents actually moved, and science had not developed accurate radiometry to date the fossils or the linear belts of rock at the edges of continents. Geologist Arthur Holmes proposed in 1929
30　that the hot and melted rocks that made up the mantle of the Earth, the layer just beneath the Earth's thin crust, flowed upward, downward, and laterally, pushing apart regions of ocean floor or allowing nearby regions to collide and overrun each other; but again little evidence
35　existed to support the idea. In the following decades, magnetic studies of the ocean floor, showing that the orientation of rocks had changed over the course of recent geologic time, helped confirm Holmes' ideas that ocean plates were the cause of the rifts and valleys on
40　the ocean floor, as well as of the larger movement of landmasses. As the rock cooled, iron atoms contained within it oriented themselves to the magnetic poles of the earth. Not only has magnetic north deviated over the northern polar region over time, but in a fairly regular,
45　periodic cycle, the magnetic poles of the earth have actually flipped, changing the orientation of the earth's magnetic field, in effect making compasses point south.

By the early-1960s, a wealth of new evidence (much of it from studies of the ocean floor) formed a
50　picture of what caused continents to drift. The sedimentary rocks of an oceanic origin were different from predial samples previously found, and geologists reasoned from this that continents were not simply upwellings of ocean floor. Continents are built of blocks of crust vary-
55　ing in age, size, rock composition, structure, and fossil assemblage (fauna and flora), with relatively stable, older interiors (the oldest rocks of which are more than 3 billion years old); the sea floors are significantly younger. The theory of mantle convection currents and
60　sea-floor spreading became the prevailing explanation of how large plates of the Earth's crust continually move upward, downward, and to the side, allowing the separation of and collision of landmasses well above the moving ocean plates. In 1994, however, Seiya Uyeda
65　concluded that subduction (the gravity-controlled sinking of a cold, denser oceanic slab into the subduction zone) "plays a more fundamental role than seafloor spreading in shaping the earth's surface features" and "running the plate tectonic machinery." Current analy-
70　sis of seismic waves and other geophysical studies continue to vastly expand our understanding of the Earth's interior and the components of plate tectonics theory.

---

41. Current studies show that the oldest ocean floors are merely 200 million years old, considered fairly young geologically. This finding would most likely:

    A. strengthen the idea that the Earth's molten mantle gradually replaced older continents, which were swept back into the ocean depths.
    B. strengthen the idea that plates moved because of a high degree of ocean floor movement and turnover.
    C. weaken the idea that ocean floors did not become continental landmasses by vertical motion.
    D. weaken the idea that it is the ocean floors that cause land movements above them rather than land movements occurring on their own.

GO TO THE NEXT PAGE.

42. Over the past 20 million years, Arabia is thought to have split off from Northern Africa, and the Sea of Japan has formed as Japan has moved East. What relevance does this information have to the passage?

    A. It suggests that Arabia and Japan should be considered their own separate continents.
    B. It decreases the likelihood that Wegener was correct about the formation of Pangea.
    C. It suggests that plate tectonics is a current phenomenon that did not stop with the break-up of Pangea.
    D. It strengthens the assumption that magnetic fields can be used to study the movement of ocean plates.

43. The author most likely mentions the work of the Dutch cartographer Abraham Ortelius in order to:

    A. show that the idea of plate tectonics is not new, although most evidence supporting it dates to the 20th century.
    B. compare the state of Dutch and English cartography in the 16th century.
    C. draw a strong contrast between Ortelius' pioneering views and those of Wegener and Holmes.
    D. show that cartography was sufficiently advanced in the 16th century that predictions could be made about continental drift.

44. According to the author, the primary significance of the discovery that molten uprisings continually reshape the ocean floor is that:

    A. these uprisings provide a mechanism for the continental drift that has clearly occurred.
    B. it shows how sensitive the Earth's crust is to geologic activity taking place beneath it.
    C. ocean floor movement lends strong support to the idea that the super-continent Pangea once existed.
    D. the movement of deep ocean plates offers an explanation for magnetic and seismic measurements that have perplexed scientists for decades.

45. According to the passage, all of the following statements are true EXCEPT:

    A. long, linear zones of rock on continental edges were recognized long before fossils on continental edges were accurately dated.
    B. mantle convection currents help to explain seismic phenomena long measured by oceanographers and other studying continental drift.
    C. fossils of similar plant and animal species can be found on widely-separated continents only in the long, linear, coastal rock zones of those continents.
    D. the Earth's crust is a thin, hard layer of solid rock, while the mantle is a molten, flowing sublayer of the crust.

46. Based on information in the passage, one can reasonably conclude that the author believes, with respect to the theory of plate tectonics, that:

    A. evidence from the earth's surface has been more important than evidence from the ocean floors in substantiating the theory.
    B. it is now well established that subduction is the primary mechanism by which the continents are caused to move over the earth's surface.
    C. wide acceptance of Wegener's theory was the cause of the increased interest in studies of the ocean's floor in the mid-20th century.
    D. the theory succeeded by drawing on information developed in such diverse geophysical studies as paleontology (the study of fossils) and seismology (the study of earthquakes).

GO TO THE NEXT PAGE.

Passage VIII (Questions 47-52)

What would be required for successful direct protection of human rights? The authority to command violating parties to do otherwise? The ability to enforce such a command? Overwhelming political pressure
5 directed against human rights violations to the exclusion of other interests? No United Nations human rights body has such authority and power.

The United Nations' primary raison d'etre in the human rights field as acted upon by the Human Rights
10 Committee is long-term. It may be that the sum total of UN activity in this field is supposed to socialize or educate actors into changing their views and policies on human rights over time toward a cosmopolitan human rights standard as defined by United Nations instru-
15 ments. Conversely one can say that the entirety of UN human rights activity is to dispense or withhold a stamp of legitimacy on member states according to their human rights record. It can be persuasively argued that in some cases a ruling regime lost ground in its struggle
20 for legitimacy in the eyes of important actors because of violations of aforementioned rights. The United Nations' definition of human rights probably contributed to the process.

At some point, socialization and manipulation of
25 legitimacy must directly change specific behavior and must lead to direct protection by some actor. In a few situations this linkage can already be demonstrated. In the case of *Filartiga v. Peña Irala* in the United States, a federal court held torture to be prohibited by customary
30 international law, using United Nations instruments and actions as part of its reasoning. "Once a tort can be considered to be in violation of the law of nations, Sec. 1350 allows immediate access to a federal court.... It is now generally accepted by the United States and the
35 vast majority of other member nations of the United Nations that gross violations of human rights are, as a matter of international law, a legitimate concern of the world community." This case opened the possibility of express prosecution of torturers of any nationality who
40 appear in the jurisdiction of the United States. Other courts in the U.S. have also used United Nations instruments and activities as part of their decisions, and other states beyond the U.S. show some influence from UN instruments in their legal and administrative decisions.
45 The 1998 Pinochet extradition case in London, described by Human Rights Watch as a "wake-up call" to tyrants everywhere, was decided on the basis that both Britain and Chile had ratified the United Nations Convention against Torture.

47. According to various points made by the author of the passage, all of the following are ways in which the UN can exert influence over human rights EXCEPT:

   A. by persuading member states to change certain laws to avoid human rights violations.
   B. by enforcing a UN command to cease any behavior that does not adhere to UN standards.
   C. by recognizing certain countries based on their human rights record.
   D. by affecting the legal and political policies of member states.

48. The passage suggests that the author would most likely agree with which of the following statements?

   A. The UN has done little to affect the protection and establishment of human rights.
   B. Human rights violations should be the primary concern of the UN.
   C. International policies can be influenced by UN activities and proclamations.
   D. Future human rights court cases may turn to UN policies for assistance.

49. Paragraph 2 shows that the UN's primary actions on human rights can be divided into two distinct approaches. This division is based on which of the following assumptions?

   A. Refusing to approve a governmental regime cannot result in a change in policies on human rights issues.
   B. Socializing member states with poor human rights records produces effective legal and political changes.
   C. Human rights violations cannot be justified by ignorance of the UN cosmopolitan human rights standard.
   D. Ruling regimes that violate human rights have occasionally lost legitimacy due to UN efforts.

GO TO THE NEXT PAGE.

50. According to the passage, which of the following is a potential problem with the UN's activity on human rights?

    A. Member states often ignore UN recommendations regarding human rights violations.

    B. The Human Rights Committee is unable to effect any short-term political changes.

    C. Significant influence by the UN on human rights is difficult to achieve through long-term means.

    D. Non-member states demonstrate a high amount of human rights violations that continue unabated.

51. The author mentions the case of *Filartiga v. Peña Irala* primarily in order to:

    A. describe United Nations human rights activity that led to direct protection by an actor.

    B. demonstrate the dangers of the UN's concentration on long-term effects.

    C. provide evidence that torture is prohibited by international law.

    D. cite a case in which the UN withheld legitimacy from a target state.

52. Regardless of what the rest of the passage might be arguing, the author's principal concern in the first paragraph is most likely to:

    A. propose changes that would increase UN effectiveness in enforcing human rights.

    B. indicate indirectly the shortfalls of UN human rights activity concerned with short-term change.

    C. explain the UN's function in the field of human rights by giving examples.

    D. describe the major activity of the UN in the field of human rights.

GO TO THE NEXT PAGE.

Passage IX (Questions 53-60)

The combination of consonant-vowel syllabic glyphs and logographs in ancient Mayan gave the scribes a variety of choices with which to write the words of their texts in detail. For example, one very common honorific title in Maya texts is *ahaw*, meaning "lord" or "noble." *Ahaw* may be written in logographic form as a head in profile, with the distinctive headband or scarf that marked the highest nobility in Maya society. But it is also possible to write the word as a combination of three phonetic, syllabic signs: *a-ha-wa*. Likewise, the word *pakal* ("shield") can be indicated by a depiction of a shield or by the combination of syllabic elements *pa-ka-la*.

Mayan signs are by nature highly pictorial, often representing in considerable detail animals, people, body parts and objects of daily life. The pictorial principle is taken to the extreme in inscriptions composed of "full-figure" glyphs, in which individual signs and numbers become animated and are shown interacting with one another. None of this should be taken to mean that the Maya only wrote in simple pictures. The Maya wrote both logographically and phonetically, and within their phonetic system alone, the Maya had multiple options. All English words are formed from various combinations of only 26 phonetic signs. By contrast, all Maya words can be formed from various combinations of nearly 800 consonant-vowel glyphs, each representing a full syllable. Sounds are formed by combining a particular consonant with one of the five vowels (hence a *syllabary*, rather than an alphabet).

Because many Maya signs remain undeciphered, it's not possible to state precisely the relative proportions of logographic and syllabic signs. But a significant number of the logograms have been deciphered and the number of deciphered syllabic signs keeps growing. Epigraphers have filled more than half of the syllabic grid, meant to plot the consonants of the spoken Maya language against its vowels and thus represents the totality of signs needed to write the language. It must be remembered that the discovery of the structure of the syllabic elements—Knorozov's main contribution—was made a little more than 30 years ago. Furthermore, the consonant-vowel syllables that are already understood are the common ones.

Nonetheless, the pace of phonetic decipherment is bound to increase in the coming years as more resources are trained on it. One aspect of Maya writing that may complicate this progress is the fact that different signs can be allographs. Such equivalences are common in Maya texts (there are at least five different signs that could be chosen to represent the Maya syllable *ba*). Each scribe chose from several different signs to convey the sounds. In evaluating a particular phonetic interpretation of a syllable, it's helpful to identify as many as possible of the variant forms; so the process of recognizing allographs depends on the slow work of comparing many texts in order to find variant spellings of the same word.

---

53. The author mentions Knorozov in the third paragraph in order to:

   A. prove that the recent discovery of Maya signs has led to its lack of decipherment.
   B. offer an explanation for what may appear to be a relative paucity in the completion of the Maya sign syllabic grid.
   C. argue that expert linguists have been stymied in their attempts to decipher and understand many allographic Maya signs.
   D. show how the understanding of other linguistic structures may improve the comprehension of Maya syllabic signs.

54. As used in the passage by the author, the term "logographic" most closely refers to:

   A. a written phonetic representation of a word.
   B. a syllabic division of an individual word.
   C. an imagistic representation of an idea.
   D. a visual picture of an idiomatic phrase.

55. The author of the passage would be LEAST likely to agree with which of the following statements?

   A. Languages whose writing is composed of pictorial signs can demonstrate a remarkable degree of complexity and detail.
   B. Linguistic signs based on syllabic or phonetic coding may be easier to decipher than those based on visual images.
   C. Logographic languages are restricted to the expression of simple ideas because of their emphasis on image.
   D. The existence of allographs in Maya signs indicates the complexity of this linguistic system.

GO TO THE NEXT PAGE.

56. The author's conclusion that Maya scribes were able to write the words of their texts in detail depends on which of the following assumptions?

   A. Individual signs could be combined to illustrate interaction or animation.
   B. The availability of two distinct types of signs enabled the Mayas to represent words in a variety of ways.
   C. Certain ideas or concepts could only be represented logographically and not syllabically.
   D. The only way to record words in detail is through a combination of sign types.

57. According to information put forth in the passage by the author, which of the following might best address some of the decipherment problems associated with Maya signs?

   A. Additional financial and scholarly resources should be directed towards this linguistic effort.
   B. More attention should be focused on identifying logographic signs than on categorizing syllabic signs.
   C. Scholars should prioritize the completion of Knorozov's syllabic grid.
   D. Careful study of comparative texts should continue in order to evaluate phonetic interpretation of each syllable.

58. In the course of the argument of the passage, the author implies which of the following about the ratio of logographic to syllabic signs in Maya writing?

   A. Researchers disagree about the correct way to determine it.
   B. Its practical value has failed to attract serious attention.
   C. A meaningful ratio may never be established.
   D. More work must be done before the ratio can be determined.

59. The author discusses the words *ahaw* and *pakal* in order to:

   A. estimate the number of meanings that some common Maya words may possess.
   B. compare the flexibility of Maya logographs to that of consonant-vowel syllables.
   C. illustrate the difficulty of understanding detailed Maya texts.
   D. demonstrate that Maya words may appear in both logographic and syllabic form.

60. The author mentions that the structure of syllabic elements was discovered "only a little more than 30 years ago" in order to suggest that:

   A. the translation of difficult syllables has been unwisely neglected.
   B. scholarly standards are more exacting today than they were 30 years go.
   C. filling in the syllabic grid is more time-consuming than phonetic decipherment.
   D. the half-completed grid should not be considered an unimpressive accomplishment.

STOP. If you finish before time is called, check your work. You may go back to any question in this test booklet.

ANSWER KEY

VERBAL REASONING TEST 6

1. D	16. A	31. C	46. D
2. A	17. C	32. D	47. B
3. B	18. B	33. A	48. D
4. A	19. D	34. A	49. A
5. B	20. C	35. B	50. C
6. D	21. D	36. A	51. A
7. D	22. D	37. B	52. B
8. C	23. A	38. D	53. B
9. C	24. C	39. C	54. C
10. A	25. A	40. A	55. C
11. D	26. D	41. B	56. D
12. C	27. A	42. C	57. D
13. A	28. A	43. A	58. D
14. D	29. B	44. A	59. D
15. B	30. B	45. C	60. D

EXPLANATIONS

PASSAGE I

Topic and Scope:
The author discusses the pocket veto and arguments on whether it allows the President too much power.

Mapping the Passage:
¶1 gives background on the Presidential veto and introduces both the pocket veto and an argument against it.
¶2 argues that the pocket veto isn't absolute because Congress has ways of getting around it.
¶3 argues that the pocket veto is part of the system of checks and balances.
¶4 points out a flaw in the pocket veto: it can delay legislation, summarizes final arguments for and against the pocket veto, and argues that history favors continued use of the veto.

Questions:
1. D Read the lines in context to get an idea of the author's opinion of the President's role as "interloper." The author says immediately above this comment that "if circumspection and deliberation" are valued, the pocket veto is acceptable. Therefore, when the President exercises it, he's acting as an agent for thoughtfulness. (D) fits.

Wrong Answers:
(A): Opposite. The author argues that the President is justified in use of the veto, and rather than seizing power, is preserving a system of checks and balances.
(B): Out of Scope. The author doesn't suggest that the President is serving as a bridge between parties, only that he acts to preserve a system of checks and balances.
(C): Faulty Use of Detail. Though the President *is* preventing certain actions from occurring when he exercises the veto, the author is more concerned in this part of the passage with emphasizing the aspect of careful thought associated with it.

2. A Where does the author reject the view that the pocket veto holds too much power? This is primarily found in ¶2, where the author argues that the pocket veto plays by the rules by following constitutional procedure. He contrasts this to the royal system, a situation which he argues *does* have too much power. Look for an assumption that ties into this argument. While both (A) and (C) might initially seem tempting, (C) can be denied without harming the author's argument. However, the author *must* believe (A): if he didn't, the argument that constitutional actions aren't an abuse of power wouldn't make sense.

Wrong Answers:
(B): Out of Scope. The author isn't discussing the judicial branch, only the balances between the executive and legislative branches.
(C): Out of Scope. Even if they do still exist, it doesn't affect the author's argument about a democratically elected government.
(D): Opposite. The author doesn't believe that it limits the President's power at all; the argument is over whether it gives him *too much* power.

Strategy Point:
Don't spend too much time predicting an assumption if one doesn't come easily. Review the relevant part of the argument, find an answer choice that touches on the same points, and use the Denial Test to verify that it is a critical assumption.

3. B Go back to ¶4 to review the mention of Kennedy and Barnes. It's not necessary to completely understand what it is, only why it's used. Since these are court cases that seem to be dealing with the pocket veto, (B) seems to make sense: if there have been at least two court cases on the matter, then the judicial branch has clearly concerned itself with the matter.

Wrong Answers:
(A): Out of Scope. Even if this is true, these two court cases wouldn't be mentioned in order to prove a point about Congress.
(C): Opposite. The author is mentioning a flaw in this paragraph, but he's in favor of the pocket veto: he wouldn't believe that the weaknesses override the strengths.
(D): Distortion. Though the author agrees that the veto can delay legislation, he says that this is the only potential flaw of the veto, and so he wouldn't be inclined to praise this aspect in particular.

4. A What does the author present as a response to a veto of popular legislation? The author says that the pocket veto isn't absolute because legislation can just be reintroduced. Thus, (A) is a likely course of action.

Wrong Answers:
(B): Opposite. The author argues that the pocket veto is acceptable precisely because Congress can pass similar legislation.
(C): Opposite. The author argues that the pocket veto is a valuable part of the system of checks and balances.
(D): Opposite. The author argues that there are ways around the pocket veto, and so it doesn't get in the way of future attempts to pass legislation.

5. B What do opponents of the pocket veto argue? Go back to ¶1 to review if necessary. Those who oppose the pocket veto says that it gives the President too much power at the expense of Congress. (B) most closely fits this.

Wrong Answers:
(A): Out of Scope. Neither the author nor opponents of the veto suggest that the President does exercise legislative authority, only that the veto serves as a check on this authority.
(C): Distortion. While opponents of the veto think that it grants the President too much power, there's no evidence that their solution would be to allow an override of the pocket veto.
(D): Opposite. If opponents of the pocket veto dislike that type of veto, they'd hate an absolute veto. The author says in ¶1 that opponents of the veto already describe it as absolute.

6. D What would the author think about using the pocket veto just for political ends? Since the author seems to think that any constitutionally awarded power is justified, he'd probably support it in this case too. Going back to the line references reinforces this: the author says that even this case would be justified because it allows for greater "circumspection and deliberation." (D) summarizes both the author's potential response and the reasons.

Wrong Answers:
(A): Opposite. The author argues in the last paragraph that it's justified even when blatantly political.
(B): Opposite. The author says that the veto would be justified and argues that it would allow more time for thought, which would contradict the assertion that it is unwise.
(C): Out of Scope. Though the author would consider it appropriate, he doesn't mention this as a reason.

7. D A trickily-worded question. You need to find arguments against the opposition to the pocket veto. Paraphrase it: you're looking for arguments in support of the pocket veto in ¶4, where the cases are mentioned. Line 49 says that the pocket veto is supported because it's been historically justified. (D) comes closest to this, and is supported by the author's overall argument that the pocket veto is Constitutionally justified.

Wrong Answers:
(A): Opposite. The author says that a return veto probably would have been overridden in the cases in question.
(B): Faulty Use of Detail. The author says in ¶4 that this is the case, but it's too specific: it doesn't address the question of why the veto is justified in general.
(C): Opposite. The author argues that the President sometimes does use the veto to override popular legislation; there's no reason to believe he wouldn't in this case also.

8. C Where does the author discuss the "Imperial Presidency"? Target ¶s 1 and 3. Predict the author's opinion on it: the author thinks that while an imperialistic presidency with absolute powers is bad, the current presidency isn't like that because it operates under Constitutional procedures. (C) reinforces this in the context of the pocket veto specifically.

Wrong Answers:
(A): Out of Scope. The author only refers to the phenomenon of the "Imperial Presidency" to show that the current system isn't that bad; he doesn't think that it exists in America, and so it can't be a threat.
(B): Distortion. The author suggests that this type of presidency is similar to the "prerogative of the English Kings," but there's no suggestion that the present English system is like this.
(D): Opposite. The author doesn't think that the current presidency is imperial, and therefore the "Imperial Presidency" can't be the cause of pocket vetoes.

PASSAGE II

Topic and Scope:
The author discusses literary editors, their function, and challenges they face.

Mapping the Passage:
¶1 discusses the general role of editors.
¶2 discusses a central tenet, and the difficulties editors encounter in following it.
¶3 gives examples of editing that has taken the form of censorship possibly harmful to the author's intent.
¶4 argues that the new trend of editing in a politically correct fashion is difficult and dangerous.
¶5 says that punctuation is the most common type of edit, and discusses the difficulties associated with this.
¶6 states that the most difficult editing situation is when authors have edited themselves after long periods of time.

Questions:
9. C The author says a lot about authors, but predict the overall thrust of the passage: editing is difficult and should be done with caution. Choice (C) fits with the author's contention in ¶2 that any universal rule is a bad

idea and "probably does more harm than good." It's better, then, to make decisions on a case-by-case basis.

Wrong Answers:
(A): Distortion. Though the author argues in ¶3 that censorship of certain works occurred and doesn't seem to be a fan of the process, there's nothing in the passage to indicate that the author thinks the censored sections should be restored.
(B): Opposite. The author argues that this particular type of correction is common and suggests that in some cases authors rely on this editing.
(D): Distortion. Though in the last paragraph the author raises the question of whether authorial revisions should be respected, he doesn't come to a set conclusion.

10. A Why does the author mention *Jane Eyre*? It's an example of a book where editing was useful because the author preferred the editor's punctuation to her own. If this is true, (A) makes sense. Inferior original punctuation would make the original manuscript more difficult to read.

Wrong Answers:
(B): Opposite. The author argues that Bronte preferred the corrected punctuation, and so it's safe to assume that it more closely reflects her intentions.
(C): Out of Scope. The author doesn't suggest anywhere that Bronte was unwise to allow corrections.
(D): Distortion. Though Bronte approved of the changes to the punctuation, the passage doesn't suggest that she actively requested that the changes be made.

11. D When would a new edition be justified? Presumably when the new edition was closer to the original intent of the author than the previous editions. Look at each Roman Numeral with your prediction in mind. Start with RN I, which appears in three choices. Since the author believes that the editor should present what the author intended, an original manuscript would be reasonable cause for a new edition. For the same reason, the author probably wouldn't agree that RN II would present justification since the publisher might be straying from the original intent, as is the case in the examples in ¶3. RN III is similar to what Auden does as described in the last paragraph. Since the author's intent has changed, it's reasonable to assume that a new edition is justified. (D) catches both of the correct points.

Wrong Answers:
(A): Opposite. As above.
(B): Opposite. As above.
(C): Opposite. As above.

12. C What does the author say the most common type of editorial revision is? The author explicitly states in ¶5 that it's punctuation, arguing that it's what "publishers traditionally feel most free to alter." Bank the easy points from (C) that come from careful prediction.

Wrong Answers:
(A): Faulty Use of Detail. Though the author mentions this type of edit in the context of *Women in Love* in ¶3, there's definitely no suggestion that it's the most common type of edit.
(B): Faulty Use of Detail. As above, this is mentioned only in conjunction with *The Red Badge of Courage*.
(D): Faulty Use of Detail. This goes along with the discussion of political correctness in ¶4, but there's no evidence that it's the most common type of edit.

13. A Predict what the author would consider the most difficult editorial situation. It's stated explicitly in the last paragraph: the "thorniest situation...involves *authorial* revisions made long after publication." Looking for an answer choice in which the author fundamentally changes his own work after publication immediately turns up (A).

Wrong Answers:
(B): Out of Scope. Though Dickens changes his work in this case, it's *before* publication, and so falls outside the author's concern.
(C): Distortion. Though this is an example of an author revising his work, he's not changing the substance, but rather adding to it. The author would presumably think that this was less of a problem for an editor than if Whitman had fundamentally changed the text itself.
(D): Out of Scope. This doesn't touch at all on an author revising his manuscripts after publication.

14. D What is the fundamental problem with Auden? The author argues in the last paragraph that the two phases of Auden are so different that the young Auden would have been upset at the old Auden's revisions. Though it's difficult to predict an answer, look for a solution that fits with this general view. (D) most closely does this, keeping both of the author's sides in existence without tainting one with the other.

Wrong Answers:
(A): Distortion. Though this would keep the two somewhat separate, it would still mingle them, and make the meaning more difficult to understand to boot.
(B): Opposite. The author suggests that *both* versions represent the author's true intent, just at different stages in the author's life.
(C): Distortion. This would subordinate the younger Auden to the elder Auden: the author seems to suggest that one can't easily make a judgment call on which one "has the greater authority."

15. B Go back to review the Emily Dickinson reference in ¶5. The author cites her "eccentric but eloquent" punctuation and implies that editors should have kept their hands off of it. (B) fits this: it would have been simple to leave the punctuation as it was, and changing it made the text worse.

Wrong Answers:

(A): Out of Scope. Though the author believes this, Dickinson isn't being used as an example to prove this. If anything, this editing situation would have been easier than usual if done correctly because it could have been left alone.

(C): **Distortion.** The author believes that changes are sometimes warranted (as in the case of *Jane Eyre*) even if they weren't in the case of Dickinson.

(D): Out of Scope. A very similar answer to (A): Though the author certainly believes this too, Dickinson isn't being used as an example of the difficulty of editing.

PASSAGE III

Topic and Scope:
The author discusses Title VII and its relevance to the lack of African-Americans in upper-level administrative positions in sports.

Mapping the Passage:
¶1 introduces the topic of how civil rights legislation has not affected African Americans equally in terms of managerial positions.

¶2 notes that African-Americans have made only limited progress in obtaining executive positions in sports.

¶3 gives the sports industry's justifications for not hiring many African-American executives.

¶s 4 and 5 discuss Title VII and the difficulties in applying it to cases of high-level racial discrimination in sports.

Questions:

16. A   Go back to ¶4, where the court stances on Title VII cases are mentioned. The author says that "courts in upper level cases often profess a lack of expertise and refuse to assess an applicant's qualifications." If courts aren't taking the cases for this reason, they must be assuming that it's necessary to possess expertise in order to rule on such cases. (A) says the same.

Wrong Answers:

(B): Distortion. Though the courts claim not to have enough information in these particular cases, that doesn't mean that they shouldn't ever be expected to evaluate candidates based on qualifications. The fact that the courts stated that they didn't have enough information in these cases implies that in some cases they *do*. The author says as much in lines 59–62.

(C): Distortion. The court isn't bowing out because the evaluation is more difficult, but rather because it simply doesn't have enough information.

(D): Out of Scope. Even if this is the case, it has not been given as the reason the courts are unwilling to evaluate.

17. C   Review the basics of the situation described in the second paragraph, summarized by the statement that "who's running the league doesn't look like who's playing in the league." Look for a similar situation. (C)

fits most closely. The company is targeted towards women and run on the lower levels by women, but women aren't in the upper-level executive positions: the same discrepancy found with African-Americans in sports.

Wrong Answers:

(A): Out of Scope. Though there's a gap between the membership of the organization and the board of the organization, there's no evidence that the Board runs the organization. The difference in this case is also one of age, which might be a justifiable difference, as opposed to race: review the Title VII criteria in line 52.

(B): Out of Scope. There's no evidence that the people running the organization aren't themselves minorities or from disadvantaged populations.

(D): Out of Scope. There's no necessary gap between membership and group oversight here, and so it can be safely eliminated.

18. B   Go back to the last paragraph to figure out why the author mentions the Supreme Court. The author says that the Supreme Court hasn't determined which Title VII standards should apply in the cases the author is concerned about and says that the lower courts have started distorting the standards. The implication is that the Supreme Court should resolve the discrepancy. Choice (B) fits with this.

Wrong Answers:

(A): Distortion. The author isn't suggesting that courts have been slow to respond, but only that their response hasn't been adequate.

(C): Distortion. Though the author says that lower courts have taken the issues up, he argues that they've distorted the standards. The Supreme Court isn't mentioned to show that the lower courts have been more willing to resolve the disputes, but rather to show that they've done so badly.

(D): Distortion. The author wants the Supreme Court to set guidelines, but doesn't necessarily argue that this should be broadened out to all executive cases under Title VII: he's concerned with a very narrow range of cases.

19. D   Review the main points made in ¶1 and 2 about African-American executive positions in sports. The author argues in the first few lines that more progress has been made in the general workforce than in sports specifically. (D) rephrases this point: hiring of executives in the sports industry needs to catch up.

Wrong Answers:

(A): Opposite. The author argues that the gap is because of discrimination, not education.

(B): Distortion. The author argues in ¶2 that "questions are being posed" whether the sports industry is immune from general labor laws like baseball is through its antitrust exemption. This is an analogy, though, not a cause-and-effect relationship.

(C): Opposite. The author argues that that a "growing number" are achieving "the practical experience required for executive positions," which directly contradicts this choice.

20. C Review the argument in ¶3 that the question refers to. The author responds that "Whether this characterization justifies the exclusion of African-American executives is questionable at best." The author's focus is therefore not on the validity of the argument, but whether it's enough, even if true, to justify discrimination. (C) says roughly the same thing.

Wrong Answers:
(A): Out of Scope. The author might believe this, but attacks the argument on whether it justifies discrimination.
(B): Out of Scope. The author isn't concerned with why the argument is being made, only whether it justifies the effects.
(D): Out of Scope. The author never claims that the argument is libelous and, again, doesn't attack it as being an unproven argument.

21. D Review the lines in context. If the industry will soon face challenges to its executive discrimination, the clear implication is that those who are discriminated against will be the ones making the challenges. (D) reflects the most likely assumption based on this: those who are discriminated against understandably feel that the hiring practices are unfair.

Wrong Answers:
(A): Distortion. The author believes that these candidates are qualified, but there's no evidence in the passage that they're the *most* qualified.
(B): Out of Scope. There's no evidence for this in the passage.
(C): Out of Scope. Though candidates who are discriminated against might be reasonably expected to sue the companies doing the discriminating, there's no reason to believe that they'd sure the people hired in their place.

PASSAGE IV

Topic and Scope:
The author describes two theories of cloud electrification and their possible impact on controlling lightning formation.

Mapping the Passage:
¶1 describes the mechanism of lightning formation and notes that scientists hope to someday control it.
¶2 introduces two competing theories of cloud electrification, convection and precipitation, and describes the older theory of precipitation.

¶3 describes the convection model of cloud electrification.

Questions:
22. D A rare global question. What is the author's main purpose? To describe the competing theories on cloud charge and to describe how they might help to control lightning. (D) fits well.

Wrong Answers:
(A): Out of Scope. The author doesn't discuss recent breakthroughs, and only one of the theories presented has evidence described.
(B): Faulty Use of Detail. Though this is mentioned in the passage, it's not the main idea of the passage.
(C): Distortion. The author presents two competing theories, but doesn't endorse one or the other or argue that they're inaccurate.

23. A Go back to the referenced line numbers to read about breakdown potential. The passage says that lightning occurs after the "breakdown potential" is reached. Only (A) catches this cause-and-effect relationship.

Wrong Answers:
(B): Opposite. The breakdown potential is required for lightning to occur, but it's not a characteristic of the lightning itself.
(C): Out of Scope. The author doesn't mention the distance between the earth and cloud.
(D): Opposite. As with (B), this is a quality of the lightning rather than a precondition for it.

24. C Though scientists differ on the causes of cloud electrification, you can deduce from this fact alone that they believe that cloud electrification exists. By definition, then, even the scientists who differ on the causes must both agree with (C), that there's a charge difference between cloud and ground.

Wrong Answers:
(A): Faulty Use of Detail. While scientists who argue for the convection model in ¶3 believe this, not all scientists do.
(B): Faulty Use of Detail. This is a part of the precipitation argument in ¶2.
(D): Opposite. This is a potential way to *stop* lightning from forming and also a test of the precipitation hypothesis as described in ¶2.

Strategy Point:
When a Natural Science passage presents competing theories, be on the lookout for areas of agreement as well as points of difference.

25. A The statements are evenly distributed in the answer choices, so begin anywhere. The convection model is based on the idea of gas ions in lines 49–50; the precipitation model doesn't include this. Therefore RN I is a point of difference. Both theories mention charged water droplets and air currents in their respective paragraphs, though, though they differ on why these are important. (A) alone thus catches all the differences.

Wrong Answers:
(B): Opposite. As above.
(C): Opposite. As above.
(D): Opposite. As above.

26. D Review ¶3 to review the convection theory. The main tenet of the convection model is that water droplets capture ionized gas molecules which are transported in updrafts and downdrafts. With an eye to the paragraph, look for a choice that conflicts with or is not part of the theory. (D) is part of the precipitation theory described in ¶2 and doesn't factor into the convection theory.

Wrong Answers:
(A): Opposite. This is mentioned in line 52.
(B): Opposite. This is mentioned in ¶1 and is the basis for both theories.
(C): Opposite. As described in ¶3, this must be true in order for the ionized gas particles to be transported.

Strategy Point:
In Natural Sciences with two theories, something that weakens one theory will often be a main point of the other.

Strategy Point:
Proper names, italicized text, and titles can all be a useful way to quickly zero in on relevant concepts and text.

27. A Predict how the evidence cited in ¶3 affected the convection theory. The author doesn't endorse one theory or the other, so it certainly couldn't have proven it. The author says that the experiment "determined that the ions were being distributed to differing regions of the clouds," which reinforces the fundamental point of the theory. (A) fits with the predicted effect on the argument.

Wrong Answers:
(B): Distortion. If it had proven the theory, the author wouldn't have described the two theories as both viable.
(C): Opposite. As expected, the convection theorists' own experiments supported their theory.
(D): Opposite. The evidence supports the convection theory, but doesn't do anything to disprove a competing theory.

PASSAGE V

Topic and Scope:
The author discusses Woolf's essays and in particular their focus on problems of interpretation between the author and reader.

Mapping the Passage:
¶1 introduces Woolf and compares her fiction and criticism.
¶2 discusses a particular essay, "The Novels of Turgenev," and describes how Woolf uses her own experiences as a reader to understand the author's method.
¶3 says that Woolf's essays argue that the gap between the reader and author may not be able to be closed, and that the author's self-consciousness has much to do with this.

Strategy Point:
Don't spend excessive time trying to understand every point of a difficult passage. Rely on topic sentences and keywords to help illuminate the structure of the paragraphs.

Questions:
28. A Take a moment to review the point referred to in the question. Woolf argues that readers can understand the writer's intent and personality through interpretation (as described in lines 24–27). Look for an answer choice that would challenge this idea. (A) is a detail mentioned in ¶3, therefore one may be inclined to say that this argument of Woolf's cannot weaken her earlier point. But the third paragraph specifically states that Woolf critiques her own theories and (A) is given as a prime example that weakens her earlier point.

Wrong Answers:
(B): Opposite. This would strengthen Woolf's idea that individual readers can use their own experience to discover the author's original intent and personality.
(C): Out of Scope. Even if this is true, it would still presumably be possible for individual writers to use their own experiences to figure out what the author was getting at.
(D): Out of Scope. While it is true that Woolf thinks that interpretation can close the gap between reader and writer, while (D) says that the writer has to directly confirm interpretations for them to be valid. (D) is merely a claim that contradicts Woolf and does not give any meaningful support; it is therefore not as damning as (A).

29. B Look for an answer choice that isn't mentioned in the passage or that directly contradicts what the author says about Woolf's essays. (B) is a distortion of what the author says: go back to ¶1 to review what the author does say when comparing the essays to the fiction. The essays "reveal a thematic and technical complexity that rivals her novels." If it rivals that of the novels, it's not necessarily exceeding, as the answer choice suggests.

Wrong Answers:
(A): Opposite. This is the main focus of the author's argument.
(C): Opposite. This is an implication of ¶s 3 and 4. The author says that Woolf believes "the gap between reader and author may be eliminated" in ¶3 but in ¶4 says that Woolf's essays "critique the very possibility of closing the gap between reader and writer."
(D): Opposite. This is supported by the discussions of Turgenev, Austen, and Shakespeare in ¶3.

30. B Review the discussion of Chaucer in ¶4. Reviewing the lines above and below the mention will, as usual, help to figure out what's going on. The author says that "There seem to be so many barriers on the road to the deepest level of self that the journey...is impossible for the modern writer." Chaucer is used as an example of how this wasn't true in the past, and how writers wrote works "verified by the entire culture." (B) summarizes these points.

Wrong Answers:
(A): Distortion. Woolf wanted to suggest that this was true, but didn't want to prove it. This choice is too strong.
(C): Distortion. Though Woolf believes the second part of this choice, she doesn't believe that contemporary writers share a similar culture.
(D): Distortion. Woolf believes that these factors lead to self-consciousness, but there's no indication that it prevents them from being objectively critical of their own work.

31. C Look for an answer choice that fit with the author's opinion of Woolf's essays, looking for something that captures the general scope of the passage. The author spends time discussing (C) between the second and third paragraphs. Since Woolf argues for the importance of bridging the gap between reader and writer and then argues that this might be impossible in modern times, her essays are critical and self-contradictory. The author is clearly a fan of the effect.

Wrong Answers:
(A): Out of Scope. The author doesn't suggest that anything about Woolf's essays is flawed.
(B): Distortion. Though Woolf believes that personal experiences are necessary to determining the original writer's opinion, there's no indication that those personal preferences are interfering with anything she determines.
(D): Out of Scope. The author never suggests this. This is another answer that can be eliminated as being far too negative to match with the author's tone.

32. D Scan the passage to find where and in what context Woolf mentions the "atemporal world order." This is mentioned favorably when describing Chaucer in lines 46–47. The author argues that the modern writers who have lost this have "lost their advantage." (D) is the only choice that reflects this positive outlook.

Wrong Answers:
(A): Opposite. The author argues that the "atemporal world order" is true of past writers, not modern.
(B): Out of Scope. This goal isn't mentioned, but the author believes that there were fewer divisions in human society when this world order existed.
(C): Out of Scope. What came before the "atemporal world order" is never discussed in the passage.

Strategy Point:
Use distinctive phrases as cues to review the relevant text in the passage. Don't guess! Common phrases will often be attached to distorted answer choices.

33. A Paraphrase the main point that Woolf is trying to make in the second paragraph: readers can use their own personal experiences to understand the personality and motivations of the writer. Looking for an assumption necessary to this argument turns up (A), which simply restates the point that readers can figure out part of the author's personality. If (A) isn't true, the argument falls apart: this is a sure sign of a critical assumption.

Wrong Answers:
(B): Opposite. Woolf is arguing that the reader's perspective can be used to discover the perspective of the author; there's no discussion of compromise.
(C): Opposite. Woolf is arguing that the reader uses personal experiences, not standards, to interpret the text.
(D): Opposite. If personal experiences are most necessary to understanding the author, then it would seem that intuition is more important than critical reasoning.

34. A Review the relevant lines. What are the common themes referred to? The author mentions self-consciousness and anger as themes that get in the way of writers presenting their true personalities. (A) summarizes this: contemporary writers are preoccupied with ideas of separateness.

Wrong Answers:
(B): Distortion. These themes aren't sources of cultural patterns, but rather the result of the cultural patterns. Woolf believes that this writing is a product of the culture, not the cause of it.
(C): Opposite. Woolf believes that the present themes contrast, not parallel, past themes.
(D): Opposite. Woolf does believe that self-consciousness is an affliction.

PASSAGE VI

Topic and Scope:
The author describes the innovations developed during the construction of the Notre Dame cathedral and their influence on other medieval building projects.

Mapping the Passage:
¶1describes the cathedral as the tallest example of Gothic architecture, and notes that the choir was similar to earlier churches.
¶2 describes how the flying buttress was probably developed during the construction of Notre Dame to provide stability against wind pressure at higher elevations.
¶3 notes that architectural innovations were developed during actual building.
¶4 notes that innovations were quickly transmitted between medieval building sites.

Questions:
35. B   A lot of information on the flying buttress in the passage; review your map for an idea on what parts of the passage to target. (B) repeats the author's statement at the end of ¶2 that the flying buttress was "similar in structure to the concealed quadrant arch."

Wrong Answers:
(A): Distortion. This is a distortion of the author's point in ¶3 that cracked mortar often led to innovation.
(C): Opposite. The author argues that the flying buttress came about in response to unexpected wind pressures at great heights. Notre Dame was the first to reach those heights, and so the problem wasn't ancient.
(D): Opposite. The author argues that the innovation came about in response to the very practical concern of wind pressure.

36. A   Keep an eye out for an answer choice that would run counter to the idea that medieval builders learned from the mistakes and innovations of earlier buildings. (A) jumps out: ¶3 points out that designers of subsequent cathedrals noted and corrects flaws in the buttress system of Notre-Dame. If builders repeated the same design that led to these flaws, it's likely that they weren't aware of them to begin with.

Wrong Answers:
(B): Out of Scope. This doesn't include any mention of earlier innovations, and so is outside the scope of the question.
(C): Out of Scope. As above, there's no indication that builders were unaware of earlier innovations here.
(D): Opposite. This would strengthen the author's argument that innovations were effectively transmitted to other building sites.

37. B   Predict the question by quickly reviewing the author's main points: Notre Dame was an example of

the fact that innovation spread quickly through the medieval system of building. (B) is a valid inference based on this idea: if medieval engineers *weren't* talented innovators, there would have been no system of innovation for the author to write about.

Wrong Answers:
(A): Out of Scope. The author argues that historians *are* interested in medieval architecture, but doesn't deal with its usefulness to modern design.
(C): Distortion.   The author says in ¶3 that flying buttresses are a "stylistic hallmark of Gothic building," but doesn't argue that people wrongly associate them only with Gothic cathedrals.
(D): Distortion. The author argues that Notre Dame provides evidence of innovation in response to building difficulties. The focus isn't on the mistakes, but on their solutions.

38. D   Review the paradox that the author discusses in ¶1. Most of the building was tall, but the choir space was small. Looking for an answer that would reasonably explain this turns up (D). If the choir needed lower ceilings, then it would make sense that Notre Dame's designers accommodated that need.

Wrong Answers:
(A): Opposite. The author argues at the beginning of ¶2 that the nave *was* wider.
(B): Out of Scope. The author never mentions anything associated with this.
(C): Faulty Use of Detail. This explains why flying buttresses were used to help reinforce the tall structures, but it has nothing to do with the low choir.

39. C   Review the author's inclusion of the other cathedrals in the last paragraph, referring to your map. The other cathedrals are used to illustrate the idea that innovation was shared among building sites in medieval times. (C) paraphrases this.

Wrong Answers:
(A): Distortion. The author is concerned with innovation, but not in order to show that the design in Gothic cathedrals was somehow superior.
(B): Distortion. The author argues that innovation came in response to flaws, but doesn't mention the cathedrals in order to point out flaws in buttressing.
(D): Distortion. The author isn't arguing that the cathedrals were derivative in design, only quick to adapt innovations from other cathedrals.

40. A   Review the point made about wind pressure. The author isn't concerned with wind pressure for its own sake, but rather to demonstrate that flying buttresses were a useful innovation in helping the cathedral hold up against the higher wind pressure at higher altitudes. (A) says the same.

Wrong Answers:
(B): Opposite. The author argues that the buttresses *did* provide enough support.
(C): Out of Scope. The author doesn't discuss whether this concealing was good or bad.
(D): Opposite. The author implies that builders *didn't* understand wind loading. This is reinforced by the mention in line 28 that wind loading is *now* well known.

PASSAGE VII

Topic and Scope:
The author discusses the gradual development and acceptance of the theory of plate tectonics.

Mapping the Passage:
¶1 states that the theory of plate tectonics evolved gradually and gives the earliest version of the theory of continental drift.
¶2 discusses Wegener's theory of "Pangea" and Holmes' idea that magma is responsible for continental flow. Ocean floor evidence supports this.
¶3 discusses new ocean floor evidence suggesting that the sea floor is younger than the continents.

Questions:
41. B Where does the author discuss the age of ocean floors? Go back to ¶3 to review what the evidence about sea floor age is used for. Young ocean floors support plate tectonics because they indicate that the sea floor is constantly moving, which in turn pushes the continents. (B) matches this.

Wrong Answers:
(A): Opposite. The evidence suggests that continents are very old compared to the sea floor, which means that while the sea floor changes the continents stay relatively intact.
(C): Opposite. This view is found in lines 53–54. The newness of the ocean floor would support the idea that continents and seabeds were made of different stuff.
(D): Opposite. This is essentially the same idea of (B), which is strengthened by the evidence given.

42. C How can you use the dates in the question? The passage states in ¶2 that Pangea began breaking apart 200 million years ago. If landmasses are still breaking apart long after, (C) must be true as a consequence.

Wrong Answers:
(A): Out of Scope. The author doesn't discuss the criteria that make up a continent, and so there's no basis to judge whether this would support (A).
(B): Opposite. If landmasses are breaking apart from larger ones, this would lend some support (though not proof) to the idea that the continents were once all part of the same landmass.

(D): Out of Scope. Since the movement of these landmasses has nothing to do with magnetic fields, this choice can safely be eliminated.

43. A An evaluation question. Use your map to assist in predicting. Ortelius is mentioned in ¶1, which discusses early versions of continental drift theories. (A) is immediately attractive.

Wrong Answers:
(B): Out of Scope. The author isn't concerned with cartography; this choice is off the passage's scope.
(C): Opposite. The author wants to show a *continuum* between the older theories and the newer theories; saying that there's a contrast does just the opposite.
(D): Out of Scope. As with (B), the author isn't concerned with cartography.

Strategy Point:
Evaluation questions reward mapping for structure rather than for detail.

44. A As with the last question, find the general area in the passage this is mentioned. Molten uprisings are mentioned in ¶4 in order to suggest a way that continents could move, which even scientists who already believed continental drift was occurring had been at a loss to do. (A) summarizes this.

Wrong Answers:
(B): Faulty Use of Detail. Though this is true, it's not the primary significance of the finding.
(C): Faulty Use of Detail. As above, while this is true, the author's more concerned with describing a mechanism for continental drift.
(D): Out of Scope. The author doesn't suggest that this has perplexed scientists for decades or that the new evidence would clear up the confusion.

45. C Keep an eye out for an answer choice that contradicts the author's main points about continental drift. (C) distorts the point made in lines 9-13. The author mentions that this is *one* place that similar fossils can be found, but also lists other locations as well.

Wrong Answers:
(A): Opposite. This is true because the linear zones in ¶1 were recognized very early on, long before fossil dating was possible.
(B): Opposite. This is the point of ¶4.
(D): Opposite. This can be found in lines 29-31.

Strategy Point:
Watch out for extreme wording; words like "only," "always," and "never" will always be backed up by the passage if they're true.

46. D The question may be hard to predict, but as always keep the author's major point in mind: plate

KAPLAN

tectonics has gradually been accepted over time as diverse evidence has built to support it. (D) echoes this, as fossils and earthquakes are both cited as evidence in the passage.

Wrong Answers:
(A): **Opposite.** This contradicts the author's emphasis on sea floor data in ¶s 3 and 4.
(B): **Distortion.** The author argues in ¶3 that this is just one of two opinions of what played a more "fundamental role" in continent movement.
(C): **Distortion.** ¶2 says that Wegener's proposal was "not well received," and there's no suggestion that later studies came about as the result of excitement for his theory.

PASSAGE VIII

Topic and Scope:
The author discusses the United Nations' current role in improving human rights and suggests a future course of action.

Mapping the Passage:
¶1 questions how human rights might be best protected and states that the United Nations has no such power currently.
¶2 states that the form this work takes is twofold: attempts to change views and policies, and to award or withhold approval based on nations' policies.
¶3 argues that the UN must work for short-term change and points out that UN policies influence national politics.

Questions:
47. B Predict by recalling what the author says the UN can *not* do: ¶1 argues that the UN can't back up its commands with force. (B) says the same.

Wrong Answers:
(A): Opposite. The author argues in ¶s 2 and3 that the UN has done just this in its policies against torture, for example.
(C): Opposite. This is one of the methods of effecting change mentioned in ¶2.
(D): Opposite. The author mentions this in ¶3, with torture again as an example.

48. D Predict by summarizing the author's general point: the UN needs to have a short-term impact in order to effect long-term change. (D) follows from this and from the author's discussion of court cases that already do rely on the UN for human rights standards. If *Filartiga* did this in the past, it's reasonable to believe that future cases will do the same.

Wrong Answers:
(A): Distortion. The author argues that the UN needs to do *more*, but argues throughout the passage that the UN *has* had an impact on human rights.
(B): Out of Scope. While the author thinks that human rights should be one concern of the UN, there's no comparison to other tasks that the UN undertakes, and so it can't be said that human rights should be the *primary* concern.
(C): Out of Scope. The author is only concerned with how the UN affects national politics, and especially national human rights issues. International politics is outside the scope of the court cases and situations mentioned.

49. A What would be a possible assumption underlying the argument that the UN needs *two* approaches instead of just one? Predict: The UN needs two approaches because one or the other by itself isn't going to cut it. (A) matches the prediction. If refusing approval *could* change behavior by itself, there would be no reason for the other method, education. Since there obviously is a need, the author must assume that each individual approach is insufficient by itself.

Wrong Answers:
(B): Opposite. This is the flip side of the assumption in (A). The author would believe that *both* approaches are necessary, and this answer choice suggests that one alone is sufficient.
(C): Out of Scope. The author mentions this standard in lines 13–14. While this information might tie into one of the two approaches, it doesn't provide an assumption necessary to explain why there are two approaches in the first place.
(D): Out of Scope. As above, this is an assumption that likely underlies the description of the second approach. However, it doesn't answer the question of why the UN requires two approaches.

Strategy Point:
Be sure to answer the question rather than just simply selecting an answer that looks true. Compare difficult answer choices back to the question to make sure that they address what is being asked.

50. C Predict by paraphrasing the author's overall point again: Long term change is nice, but it has to be backed up somewhere along the line with short-term change. (C) captures this point, made most implicitly in the first lines of ¶3: "directly" changing "specific behavior" is an immediate, short-term goal and is more effective than long-term options.

Wrong Answers:
(A): **Out of Scope.** The author doesn't spend time discussing whether the UN is usually obeyed or not, and is more concerned with what the UN does rather than with how others respond.

(B): Opposite. The author is arguing that they should do this.
(D): Out of Scope. The author never makes this claim in the passage.

51. A Start your prediction broadly: what is the purpose of the paragraph in which the court case is mentioned? To argue that the UN should effect short-term change. Double-check by scanning the relevant text to see if the case backs this up: it's an example of a short-term effect brought about directly by UN policies. (A) summarizes the point.

Wrong Answers:
(B): Opposite. This is a case in which the UN had a short-term effect.
(C): Faulty Use of Detail. While this is probably true based on the information in the passage, the author isn't trying to prove this point, but rather that the UN can effect change in the short term.
(D): Out of Scope. The UN isn't making a decision in the court case; a US court is. There's no mention of the UN withholding legitimacy.

Strategy Point:
Use your map to form a broad prediction and then narrow it down, if needed, with information from the passage.

52. B Review your map for a quick prediction. The author presents rhetorical questions to show that the UN doesn't have many tools to enforce short-term change. (B) says the same.

Wrong Answers:
(A): Out of Scope. Though the author touches on this later on in the passage, he's not yet concerned with discussing it in ¶1.
(C): Out of Scope. This is the focus of ¶2 rather than ¶1.
(D): Distortion. Though the author does briefly describe the UN's function, most of the paragraph is concerned with describing what it doesn't do.

PASSAGE IX

Topic and Scope:
The author discusses the nature and in particular the complexity of Maya writing.

Mapping the Passage:
¶1 explains that pictoral and phonetic representations in Maya writing can often be used interchangeably for the same word.
¶2 points out that in the system of Maya writing signs can be either pictoral or phonetic.
¶3 describes progress in deciphering the "syllabic grid."
¶4 suggests that the speed of decipherment will increase, but may be slowed down by allographs, different signs that represent the same sound.

Questions:
53. B As usual, use your map to get a rough prediction. Knorozov is mentioned in ¶3, which deals with progress in detangling the syllabic grid. A check of the passage shows that his purpose is to illustrate just this. (B) fits.

Wrong Answers:
(A): Distortion. The author isn't trying to prove that Mayan signs have done anything, only to detail progress. This choice is too extreme.
(C): Distortion. The author argues in ¶4 that allographic signs might make decipherment a longer process, but doesn't argue that it's stymied the experts.
(D): Out of Scope. The author doesn't discuss other linguistic structures, and so this can be safely eliminated as being outside the passage's scope.

54. C Go back to ¶2, where the author says in line 22 that the Maya wrote both "logographically and phonetically." Since the phonetic symbols are described as syllabic sounds made of consonants and vowels, logographs must be the other type of representation: pictoral symbols. The author backs this up with examples throughout the passage. (C) simply paraphrases the idea of pictoral representation.

Wrong Answers:
(A): Opposite. This is phonetics, the other way Mayans wrote.
(B): Opposite. As above, this is an example of phonetic communication.
(D): Distortion. Though logographs are visual representations, the author never suggests that they can represent an entire phrase, but rather only a single word.

55. C Paraphrase the author's main idea: Mayan writing is complex for several reasons but is steadily being deciphered. Based on this, the author would disagree with (C): Mayan writing *doesn't* convey simple writing, the author would argue, because it's more than just "simple picture writing."

Wrong Answers:
(A): Opposite. This is the opposite of the correct answer: the author would argue that Mayan is just such a language, and that it can indeed represent complexity.
(B): Out of Scope. The author never makes this comparison, and so it's impossible to say whether the author would agree with this statement or not.
(D): Opposite. This summarizes the point of ¶4: allographs add a layer of complexity to the language that make deciphering it more difficult.

Strategy Point:
Remember that questions asking for a statement that the author would be least likely to agree with may contain wrong answers that are Out of Scope, even though most wrong answer choices will be things that the author does agree with.

56. D Where does the author draw this conclusion? Go back to ¶1: scribes were able to write in detail by using phonetic representation; instead of a single sign they could string multiple signs for syllables together. (D) is therefore a necessary assumption: the only reason that Mayans were able to write in detail was because they had multiple syllabic signs to put together.

Wrong Answers:
(A): Faulty Use of Detail. The author makes this claim in lines 18–20, but it has nothing to do with writing in detail.
(B): Faulty Use of Detail. This is also true, and comes from the right part of the passage, but it doesn't address an assumption behind the argument that Mayas could write "in detail," i.e., write using phonetics. Try denying it: even if this wasn't true, the Mayans could still presumably write in detail, even if it were just in one way.
(C): Out of Scope. The author never suggests that this is the case. Denying the assumption results in an intact argument, a sure sign that it's irrelevant to the argument being made.

57. D What does the author consider the main problems in deciphering Mayan signs? The pesky issue of allographs. The author says in the last lines of the passage that deciphering allographs depends on comparing many texts. (D) says the same.

Wrong Answers:
(A): Distortion. A tempting answer choice. The author argues at the beginning of ¶4 that the pace of decipherment will increase as more resources are trained on it, but stops short of saying that more resources *should* be trained on it, or suggesting what form those resources might take. (A) changes a statement of fact to a recommendation as well as interpreting "resources" far more specifically than can be justified by the passage.
(B): Opposite. Since allographs are phonetic representations, the author would argue that if anything there should be more attention given to syllabic signs.
(C): Opposite. The author argues in ¶3 that finishing the grid isn't a huge deal; since many of the grid's symbols are very rare, there's no pressing need to get it done. Allographs are a bigger issue.

58. D Where does the author talk about ratios between the two types of signs? Review the beginning of ¶3. The author says that it's impossible to "state precisely the relative proportions" because many of the signs are undeciphered. The clear implication is that as these signs *are* deciphered, the ratio will become clearer. (D) fits.

Wrong Answers:
(A): Out of Scope. The author suggests that the lack of a ratio is due to a lack of information, not because of disagreement.

(B): Out of Scope. The author never suggests a practical value that is being ignored.
(C): Opposite. The author seems confident that the signs *will* be deciphered, which indicates that someday a ratio will also be able to be established.

59. D What is the purpose of ¶1, where these words are mentioned? Review your map: Maya words can appear in both pictoral or phonetic form. (D) rewards the careful mapper with quick points.

Wrong Answers:
(A): Distortion. The author suggests that the same *meaning* can have different *words*, not that the same word has different meanings.
(B): Opposite. The author suggests that the phonetic representations are more flexible because they allow for writing "in detail."
(C): Faulty Use of Detail. The author agrees that it is difficult to understand some difficult texts, but this is a point from ¶4 rather than from ¶1.

60. D Why is it important that the syllabic structure was only discovered a relatively short time ago? It explains the fact that there hasn't been a complete decipherment of the structure. (D) paraphrases this: half-done in thirty years isn't bad.

Wrong Answers:
(A): Opposite. The author implies that though these syllables will eventually be deciphered, it's not that critical because they are in rare texts anyhow.
(B): Out of Scope. The author never makes this claim in the passage.
(C): Faulty Use of Detail. While this might be true based on the fact that most of what remains undeciphered is from the syllabic grid, the author's more concerned with showing that a lot of progress has been made rather than comparing it unfavorably to the progress made in the other system of writing.

Verbal Reasoning Test Seven

Time—85 minutes
Question 1–60

DIRECTIONS: Each of the passages in this test is followed by a set of questions based on the passage's content. After reading each passage, decide on the one best response to each question and mark it on your answer sheet. If you are unsure of an answer, eliminate the choices you know are wrong and choose from the remaining choices. You may refer to the passages while answering the questions.

Passage I (Questions 1–6)

Almost all James Baldwin's protagonists—from John in *Go Tell It on the Mountain* to Arthur in *Just Above My Head*—are involved in an agonizing quest for self. According to Baldwin, suffering, if endured coura-
5 geously and creatively, leads to self-knowledge and self-acceptance. With no internal conflicts, one can finally open up to another person. Suffering, thus, has humanizing power and redemptive potential.

If many of the black characters in Baldwin's fiction
10 are presented as morally superior to most of the white characters—an aspect of his works that has annoyed many critics—it is not because those characters are black, but because blackness inflicts additional suffering on them—because "the American Negro identity origi-
15 nates from an extreme situation" created by "estrangement from his past." But for Baldwin this is never an entirely private battle; it can be achieved only in spiritual communion with others.

Tradition, or heritage, is what one carries from a
20 cultural past involuntarily; accepting it is indispensable to achieving self-discovery. This idea of finding selfhood and strength through community is elaborately developed in Baldwin's poignant novel *If Beale Street Could Talk*. Here the family—symbolic of communi-
25 ty—emerges as a source of enduring strength to the individual. The Rivers family is nurturing and protective. Because it is united in love and commitment, it is able to offer stiff resistance to external oppression. The various members of the family as well as Fonny Hunt
30 emerge as individuals who can unite communally to battle for justice. Baldwin's implication is clear: one ought to establish one's individual identity and find one's center within oneself, not in opposition to but in harmony with one's reality and communal identity. And the indi-
35 vidual, while strengthening the community, draws strength from it in return. Baldwin's recipe calls for a self-identity, confrontation and acceptance of reality, and finally, open, committed relationships.

Again, the bridge of suffering can enable one to
40 define oneself through a compassionate understanding of the other. This idea of conquering the void of otherness through recognition and acceptance of another's humanity is examined in the novel *Just Above My Head*, in which the narrator, Hall, attempts to understand him-
45 self by gaining an understanding of his brother's anguished life. He succeeds largely because he examines his brother's life with compassion and loving commitment. David in *Giovanni's Room*, on the other hand, fails, first because he fails to forge his human identity
50 through an acceptance of his own sexuality and the suffering it entails; and second, because he lacks the capacity for communion with and commitment to another individual. David asks himself "Can I love a man" rather than "Can I love Giovanni." By doing this, he
55 misses the point.

---

1. The author implies that, to James Baldwin, all of the following elements contribute to a character's self-understanding EXCEPT:

    A. a capacity to form close relationships.
    B. sympathy for the difficulties of others.
    C. endurance of personal hardship.
    D. a commitment to personal independence.

2. As it is used in the end of the second paragraph in the line, "But for Baldwin this is never an entirely private battle; it can be achieved only in spiritual communion with others," the phrase "spiritual communion" most nearly means:

    A. involvement in religious worship.
    B. commitment to racial equality.
    C. an ability to endure suffering.
    D. sympathetic relationship with others.

GO TO THE NEXT PAGE.

3. The author calls *If Beale Street Could Talk* "poignant" because it:

   A. portrays the tension between the individual and the community.
   B. details the hardships that plague the Black community.
   C. illustrates the need for a traditional family structure.
   D. presents a situation in which a united community overcomes hardship.

4. Implicit in the author's discussion of the relationship between self-discovery and group experience in the third paragraph, is the idea that Baldwin:

   A. is an advocate of social reform in the Black community.
   B. presents the interrelation between individual and community as a theme common to all humankind.
   C. never abandons the belief that suffering is a necessary component of the search for self-discovery.
   D. believes self-discovery is attained by sacrificing part of the communal identity.

5. If given the task of analyzing the passage on the surface level, the overall structure of the passage could best be described as:

   A. defending a controversial thesis.
   B. tracing the development of a literary theme.
   C. reconciling two contradictory literary interpretations.
   D. suggesting an agenda for social change.

6. The author mentions various texts throughout the passage. He brings up *Giovanni's Room* principally in order to:

   A. provide an example of a character for whom suffering leads to self-discovery.
   B. lend support to the notion that self-discovery is tied to compassion for others.
   C. suggest that self-awareness rests in one's communal identity.
   D. illustrate the idea that suffering and moral superiority are linked.

GO TO THE NEXT PAGE.

Passage II (Questions 7–14)

Lee Bollinger, rejecting traditional models of the defense of free speech as inadequate, defends it with a model designed to take into account changes in the function of speech attributable to the emergence of a society
5 marked by stability and widespread consensus on essential values. This new, "self-restraint model" justifies free speech from a different perspective. Although staunchly supporting free speech, the self-restraint model inverts the relationship between speech and tolerance. Under
10 traditional models, the value of tolerance is subordinated to the value of speech. The self-restraint model, however, often subordinates the value of speech to that of tolerance. Traditional justifications of the free speech principle originated in the belief that speech is entitled
15 to greater tolerance than other kinds of activity.

A review of the traditional justifications reveals two distinct models of explanation. Although both these models link the need to protect speech to its inherent value, they agree on little else. According to the classi-
20 cal model, freedom of speech serves an indispensable function in democratic self-government. Meiklejohn uses the traditional New England town meeting as a paradigm for a self-governing society.

From this perspective, the free speech principle
25 need only protect political speech—the facts, theories, and opinions relating to any issue on which the citizens must vote. Meiklejohn insists that even extremist views cannot be withheld from voting citizens, if these views bear on any public issue. Protection of free speech,
30 including extremist political speech, serves the collective interests of a self-governing society, made up of all rational, equal, and fully participating citizens. Predicated on the belief that speech itself is valuable, this theory ascribes positive value to a very broad range
35 of speech, including any that may be offensive to many people.

In contrast to the serene and optimistic, the fortress model is built on a foundation of pessimism, individualism, relativism, and self-doubt. According to Holmes,
40 speech represents not so much a free marketplace of ideas as a kind of "counsel of despair." Freedom of speech is necessary to the discovery of truth; but, although any belief held by an individual is ultimately likely to prove false, individuals tend to feel certain
45 about their beliefs and consequently justified in requiring others to conform. From Holmes' perspective, the government and any majority of the people pose a great danger of intolerance. In order to protect speech from the natural tendency to censor nonconforming views,
50 the fortress model prescribes overprotection of speech. This strategy establishes a broad "buffer zone" that encompasses extremist speech because its protection substantially diminishes the probability that inherently valuable speech will be suppressed. Even if speech is so
55 extreme that it cannot seriously be considered to contribute to the discovery of truth—like the most extreme views propounded by the Nazis—it still ought not to be censored, for once unleashed censorship cannot be reasonably expected to remain confined to worthless views.

---

7. It can be inferred from the passage that Meiklejohn's model of free speech would NOT necessarily extend protection to:

   A. speech expressing extremist political viewpoints.
   B. extremist speech that is not political.
   C. views that reject the legitimacy of democratic government.
   D. political opinions that the majority of citizens find offensive.

8. According to conclusions that can logically be drawn from the passage, it can be inferred that Holmes would agree with all of the following statements EXCEPT:

   A. in order to protect useful speech, it is necessary to protect extremist speech.
   B. views that have the most value to society deserve the most protection.
   C. it is less harmful to tolerate extremist speech then to censor potentially valuable speech.
   D. censorship of extremist views makes it more likely that nonextremist views will also be censored.

9. Based on points brought up and argued by the author, it can be inferred from the passage that all of the following are true of Bollinger's model EXCEPT that it:

   A. affirms that the justification for protecting free speech may change as society evolves.
   B. conceives the relationship between speech and tolerance differently than do the classical and fortress models.
   C. does not protect speech as fully as the classical and fortress models.
   D. applies to a society which shares agreement on fundamental values.

GO TO THE NEXT PAGE.

10. It can be inferred from the passage that speech is viewed as a fundamental value in the:

    I. classical model.
    II. fortress model.
    III. self-restraint model.

    A. I only
    B. I and II only
    C. II and III only
    D. I, II and III

11. A law prohibiting any speech that stigmatizes or victimizes an individual or group on the basis of race, religion, or sex could be effectively criticized using the:

    I. classical model.
    II. fortress model.
    III. self-restraint model.

    A. I, II and III
    B. II and III only
    C. II only
    D. III only

12. As described in the passage, Meiklejohn's conclusion that all political speech is valuable to a democratic society assumes which of the following?

    A. In order to make the best possible decisions, members of a democratic society need to consider all views.
    B. Many views that are unpopular when first expressed are eventually accepted by a majority of citizens.
    C. Some useful social reforms were considered extreme when they were first proposed.
    D. Protection of free speech is most essential in a small self-governing community, where all can join in the decision-making.

13. Turning an eye to the greater structure of the passage, which of the following best describes the function of the last three paragraphs of the passage?

    A. The author describes two theories and links each to the historical situation in which it was proposed.
    B. The author refers to a traditional way of viewing a question and examines two contrasting approaches that spring from that view.
    C. The author establishes contrasts between two approaches to a question and then explores their points of agreement.
    D. The author discusses two theories and the opposed conclusions that follow from them.

14. The author indicates that Meiklejohn's and Holmes' understanding of free speech is similar in that both:

    A. believe that free speech ultimately leads to the discovery of truth.
    B. favor extending the right of speech to those who express extremist doctrines.
    C. consider that censorship involves the suppression of valuable speech.
    D. justify free speech by referring to the citizen's right to be informed of all views relevant to public issues.

GO TO THE NEXT PAGE.

Passage III (Questions 15–20)

Although he rejected the prevailing Neo-Romanticism of the late forties and early fifties, Philip Larkin was no admirer of modernism. Like many in the English middle-class, for example, he thought Picasso a
5 fake, and believed that an artist should "make a horse look like a horse."

When some disparaged his work as "limited" and "commonplace," Larkin replied, "I'd like to know what dragon-infested world these lads live in to make them so
10 free with the word 'commonplace'." His irritation stemmed from his view that poetry "was an act of sanity, of seeing things as they are." He thought that the connection between poetry and the reading public, forged in the 19th century by such poets as Kipling,
15 Housman and Brooke, had by the mid-20th century been destroyed by the growing unintelligiblity of English poetry to the general reader. He attributed this in part to the emergence of English literature (along with the other arts) as an academic subject, demanding poetry that
20 required elucidation.

He saw no such need to explain his own work. When asked to expand on *The Whitsun Weddings*, he remarked that the intent of each poem was clear enough in itself, and he would only add that "the poems had
25 been written in or near Hull, Yorkshire, with a succession of 2B pencils during the years 1955 to 1963." Influenced by the poetry of Thomas Hardy, he made the mundane details of his life the basis for tough, unsparing, memorable poems that rejected the Victorian belief
30 in a benevolent God, exploring life with a post-religious stoicism. The poems themselves are deceptively simple. Through the details of advertisements, train-stations, and provincial towns, they transform into something elevated and strangely beautiful the central issues of ordi-
35 nary life in the language of ordinary speech. His underlying themes of love, solitude, and mortality express intense personal emotion while they strictly avoid sentimentality or self-pity, using rough-hewn rhythms and colloquial diction with an extraordinary variety of
40 meters and stanzaic forms. These qualities were quickly identified, if not always appreciated, by reviewers. As the critic Donald Hall put it (only half-admiringly)," [Larkin's poem] 'At Grass' is the best horse picture ever painted."

45 Some critics went so far as to call him anti-social. In an interview, Larkin questioned why he was described a melancholy man, protesting—self-deprecatingly—that he was actually "rather funny." Neither of these adjectives reflect the beauty of his poetry that is
50 the source of a deep, abiding pleasure.

Philip Larkin earned a living as a librarian until his death of cancer in 1985. His first poem was published in 1940, but he earned his reputation as one of England's finest poets with the publication of *The Less
55 Deceived* in 1955, which was subscribed to by almost all recognized young English poets: Amis, Bergonzi, Boyars, Brownjohn, Conquest, Davie, Enright, Hamburger, Hill, Jennings, MacBeth, Murphy, Thwaite, Tomlinson, and Wain. His status was con-
60 firmed with the release in 1963 of *The Whitsun Weddings* (the title poem of which may be the finest in all his work), and again with *High Windows* in 1974. The mood of each of these thin volumes changed considerably from poem to poem; but, for all their range,
65 they were clearly the products of a singular and accomplished poetic sensibility.

---

15. It can be justifiably concluded based on the author's points throughout the passage that Larkin would have thought that the poetry of Brooke:

    A. required elucidation due to its academic orientation.
    B. addressed issues important to everyday life.
    C. could be easily understood by the general reader.
    D. was not a suitable subject for academic discussion.

16. The author quotes Larkin as saying "I'd like to know what dragon-infested world these lads live in to make them so free with the word 'commonplace'" in lines 8–10 in order to:

    A. show how Larkin dismissed critics of his work by pointing out their personal failings.
    B. show how Larkin mocked his critics for implying that everyday experience must be trivial.
    C. suggest that Larkin's critics attacked his work to make their own lives seem more glamorous.
    D. show that Larkin did not believe that the events he wrote about were actually common.

GO TO THE NEXT PAGE.

17. The author's primary concern in this passage is to:

 A. show that Larkin's verse was informed by his views on poetry.
 B. describe how Larkin created verse of lasting value based on ordinary events.
 C. compare schools of poetry from the 19th and 20th centuries.
 D. explain how the general reader became alienated from English poetry by the mid-20th century.

18. The author cites the description of one of Larkin's poems by one of his critics as "the best horse picture ever painted." This quotation serves several purposes, including to demonstrate:

 I. that critics considered Larkin's poetry poor and funny.
 II. the commonplace subject matter of Larkin's work.
 III. that critics often blurred Larkin's poetry with Larkin's views.

 A. I only
 B. I and II only
 C. II and III only
 D. II only

19. In the third paragraph, the author cites Larkin, in response to the request that he expand on the meaning of his poetry, as saying "the poems had been written in or near Hull, Yorkshire." Larkin's purpose in making this comment was most likely to:

 A. support Larkin's argument that poetry should be self-explanatory.
 B. strengthen Larkin's argument that poetry should deal with the commonplace.
 C. weaken the critics' argument that poetry should not deal with the commonplace.
 D. refute the argument that English poetry had become less intelligible to the reader.

20. Based on the information provided in the passage, we can assume that Larkin would be LEAST likely to write a poem taking as its subject:

 A. a devout song of praise to God.
 B. the working day of a London businessman.
 C. the death in war of an upper-class academic.
 D. a current, happy love affair.

GO TO THE NEXT PAGE.

Passage IV (Questions 21–27)

Because it impinges upon so much—from bilingual education, political correctness, and Afro-centered curricula, to affirmative action and feminism—the current discussion on multiculturalism is essential to under-
5 standing Western academic culture today. Charles Taylor's account of the development of multiculturalism out of classical liberalism traces it through changing conceptions of what he terms "the politics of recognition."

10 Deft as his historical account may be, any analysis of the motivations for multiculturalism solely in terms of "recognition" must remain fundamentally incomplete. In his analysis are two central demands for recognition underlying classical liberal thought: the demand
15 for the equal recognition of human dignity, and for recognition and respect of all human beings as independent, self-defining individuals. Multiculturalism, according to Taylor, rejects both of these ideals and their political application in an official "difference-blind" law
20 (which focuses on what is the same in us all). Instead, it embraces laws and public institutions that recognize and even foster particularity—that cater to the well-being of specific groups. These two modes of politics, then, both having come to be based on the notion of equal respect,
25 come into conflict.

Taylor acknowledges that it can be viewed as a betrayal of the liberal ideal of equality when the multiculturalist calls for a recognition of difference rather than similarity, and seeks special treatment for certain
30 groups—such as aboriginal hunting privileges or the "distinct society" of Quebec. However, he plausibly argues that to recognize only sameness is to fail to recognize much that is necessary for real "recognition", since we are all cultured individuals with personal his-
35 tories and community ties. Still, Taylor does not stray far from classical liberalism, insisting that multiculturalism be able to "offer adequate safeguards for fundamental rights."

The more extreme forms of multiculturalism, which
40 Taylor disavows, commit the crucial error of reducing all ethical and normative standards to mere instruments of power, because in doing so any distinctly moral arguments for these positions become absurd. Though Taylor seems correct to reject this diminution, he's
45 wrong to think that the "recognition" model alone can sufficiently account for the demands made by various minority groups for both the promotion of discrete cultural identities and the transformation of the dominant

culture. For what many in these groups desire is much
50 more than mere recognition or approval: it is the power to more effectively and independently control their own destinies.

It's even become common to disdain the respect or solidarity professed by those in the dominant group in
55 an attempt to consolidate separate cultural identities. How Taylor misses this fact is not clear, since even his favorite example of Quebec's distinct society presents a case in which the primary function of the demand for recognition is to acquire the power necessary for those
60 within to maintain, promote and even enforce their way of life. Taylor understands that the Quebeçois want more than to merely preserve their culture, or to have others appreciate it. They also want to create a dynamic, autonomous society in which future generations will
65 participate as part of a common project. Unfortunately, he does not consider how this fact undercuts the notion of "recognition" as an adequate lens through which to view their project.

---

21. The author's primary purpose in the passage is to:

    A. criticize Taylor's definition of liberalism.
    B. define the concept of multiculturalism.
    C. defend an account of the historical development of multiculturalism.
    D. assess the adequacy of a thesis about the nature of multiculturalism.

22. According to the passage, extreme multiculturalists make which of the following mistakes:

    A. they wrongly disdain the solidarity professed by those in the dominant group.
    B. they undercut their position by eliminating any moral arguments that they could make for their view.
    C. they overestimate the distinctness of their position from classical liberalism.
    D. they argue for their position on moral grounds, rather than pointing to the practical benefits of their views.

GO TO THE NEXT PAGE.

23. According to the argument posed by the author in the passage, multiculturalism may be seen as a betrayal of liberal ideals because:

    A. classical liberalism is not concerned with the well-being of minority groups.
    B. it abandons the demands for equality that characterize classical liberalism.
    C. a failure to recognize what is different about individuals can be a failure to fully recognize individuals.
    D. it is not capable of respecting diversity or offering adequate safeguards for basic rights.

24. The author's two references to the "distinct society" of Quebec are primarily intended to:

    I. give an example of a multiculturalist demand.
    II. give an example for which Taylor's analysis is inadequate.
    III. give an example of a group for which special treatment is sought.
    A. I only
    B. III only
    C. I and II only
    D. I, II, and III

25. Which of the following can most reasonably be inferred from the passage about the author's attitude toward the two classical liberal ideals of equality mentioned in the passage?

    A. They are adequate for most contexts in which recognition is demanded.
    B. They do not safeguard fundamental rights for individuals in aboriginal groups.
    C. They reflect a disguised attempt by a privileged group to maintain its power over other groups.
    D. They reflect an impoverished conception of the individual person.

26. Based on the information provided in the passage, it would be most reasonable to expect the author to agree that Charles Taylor's "politics of recognition" model is:

    A. admirable, but flawed.
    B. of limited use.
    C. historically deft.
    D. an unmitigated failure.

27. In the context of the passage as whole, the statements made in paragraph 3 can best be characterized as which of the following?

    A. A criticism of an argument is raised, and then shown to be superficial.
    B. A weakness in an argument is revealed, and then developed.
    C. An opinion is related, and then a subsequent position is stated.
    D. A cultural trend is outlined, and then a defense of that trend is given.

GO TO THE NEXT PAGE.

Passage V (Questions 28–33)

The rate at which pollen settles is dictated principally by the size and density of the grain. The slower the settlement rate, the greater the dispersal range. Numerous species reduce the density of their pollen
5 grains through air cavities in their walls. The grains of many species quickly dehydrate after release.

There is a limit, however, to the lower range of pollen size. The smaller a particle becomes, the more difficult its capture, because as airflow carrying particles
10 sweeps past surfaces, inertia represents a principal component of the mechanism for capture. Usually considered a "primitive" feature in textbooks, wind-pollination has, in fact, reappeared independently in many plant groups relatively recently in geological time: whole
15 plant families have adapted to wind-pollination—like the oaks (Fagaceae) and grasses (poaceae) that dominate valleys in Central California—and some flowering plants have simplified their flowers, becoming more like the pines.

20 General textbooks still often give the impression that the anemophilous syndrome is rather uninteresting, often defining it mainly as a combination of negatives: a lack of nectar, scent, petals, etc. With the evolution of terrestrial life about 400 million years ago, wind
25 replaced water as the primary vector by which plants moved male sex cells. Wind pollination has traditionally been viewed as a reproductive process dominated by random events—the vagaries of the wind and weather. This view seems justified by the potential hazards a
30 pollen grain is subject to when transported over long distances.

Pollen loss through happenstance is compensated for in wind-pollinated plants to a large degree by pollen-to-ovule ratios that greatly exceed those of insect-polli-
35 nated species. And unlike the sticky pollen grains of plants pollinated by insects, the pollen grains of wind-pollinated plants are smooth and dry, to avoid clumping and precipitating, and the stigma of the female is huge, sticky, and feathery, the better to catch any floating
40 pollen grains. Similarly, wind-pollinated plants typically evolved to grow in stands, such as pine forests, corn fields and grasslands. Indeed the wind vector is only useful in large, near-monoculture populations.

However, recent research has shown that several
45 remarkably sophisticated mechanisms for dispersal and capture are characteristic of wind-pollinated plants. Pollen release is often tied to the recognition of unambiguous environmental clues. The devices that operate to prevent self-pollination are also sometimes extremely
50 intricate. Recent findings, consistent with the primary biological principle that structure relates to function, have revealed another dimension in the adaptations that compensate for wind pollination's inefficiency. Many species take advantage of the physics of pollen motion
55 by generating aerodynamic environments within the immediate vicinity of their reproductive organs. Two biological features appear to be critical in this process: the density and size of the pollen grain and the morphology of the ovulate organ.

60 The shape of the female organ creates patterns of airflow disturbances through which pollen grains travel. The obstructing organ causes airflow to separate around windward surfaces and creates turbulence along leeward surfaces as ambient wind speeds increase. Because the
65 geometry of female organs is often species-specific, airflow disturbance patterns that are also species-specific can be generated. The speed and direction of this pattern combines with the physical properties of a species' pollen to produce a highly synergistic pattern of pollen
70 collision on windward surfaces and sedimentation on leeward surfaces of reproductive organs. The aerodynamic consequences of this synergism can significantly increase the pollen-capture efficiency of an ovulate organ.

---

28. In general, according to the author of the passage, pollen grains that would have the greatest dispersal range would have which of the following characteristics?

   I. Small size
   II. Dryness
   III. Low-density

   A. I only
   B. I and II only
   C. I and III only
   D. I, II and III

29. According to the passage, processes that take place on leeward surfaces of reproductive organs include, but are not necessarily limited to:

   A. the separation of airflow and sedimentation of pollen.
   B. turbulence and pollen collision.
   C. turbulence and the separation of airflow.
   D. turbulence and sedimentation of pollen.

GO TO THE NEXT PAGE.

30. Based on the information set forth in the passage, all the following mechanisms serve to reduce pollen loss in wind-pollinated plants EXCEPT:

    A. retention of pollen within the male organ when weather conditions are not conducive to dispersal.

    B. growth of plants in large populations with few species.

    C. creation of species-specific air-flow disturbance patterns by the morphology of the ovulate organ.

    D. development of intricate mechanisms to prevent self-pollination.

31. If, due to an El Niño condition off the Pacific coast, rainfall levels in a particular growing season were abnormally high, it is most reasonable to conclude, based on the passage, that the:

    A. amount of pollen released by wind-pollinated species would be less than normal because of sophisticated mechanisms tied to environmental clues.

    B. amount of pollen released by wind-pollinated species would be greater than normal to compensate for the greater resulting pollen loss.

    C. pollen-to-ovule ratios of wind pollinated species would be unaffected by the change in weather.

    D. amount of seed produced and released by wind-pollinated species would be greater than normal.

32. Based on the information in the passage, it must be inferred that the author believes the study of pollination:

    A. is considered uninteresting by the majority of scientists.

    B. requires knowledge of aerodynamics.

    C. is an interdisciplinary field.

    D. has only recently begun to be taken seriously.

33. Based on passage information, it is reasonable to conclude that wind-pollinated plants are LEAST likely to be found:

    A. in tropical rain forests of South America.

    B. in the taiga and other northern European coniferous forests.

    C. in the valleys of California.

    D. along river banks in temperate climates.

GO TO THE NEXT PAGE.

Passage VI (Questions 34–40)

The media's particular understanding of the ways of influence and decision-making in government colors the way they describe political reality. It also defines their responsibility in reporting that reality; contemporary reporters are in many ways the grandchildren of the Progressive muckrakers.

Few aspects of American politics reinforce this Progressive world-view as effectively as the American way of campaign finance. Its cash is an easy measure of influence, and its PACs are perfect embodiments of vested, selfish interests. In assuming that public officials defer to contributors more easily than they do to their party, their own values, or their voting constituency, one has the perfect dramatic scenario for the triumph of wealthy special interests over the will of majorities and the public interest.

Much has been made recently about campaign finance reform. Various politicians and voters' rights groups have petitioned for a reworking of the campaign finance laws that govern how political candidates can solicit and spent money on their races for office.

As Liebling showed us, there is no end to the supply of anecdotes about the failings of American journalism with which to trigger outrage or amusement. But diversions aside, the problem is really one of approaching media coverage of public life more systematically. "Bias" is a word with many meanings. It suggests a single explanation—one of conscious, even willful preference—for a range of instances in which the message misinterprets or misconveys the reality. The media have been attacked as biased in a partisan direction by both Democrats and Republicans, and from both the left and the right. To be sure, media partisanship was apparent in earlier times, when the partisan press was little more than a propagandist for the party it favored.

But that overtly biased style seems to have given way in the 20th century to a media more concerned with gaining audience than political proselytes, and an electronic media fearful of government regulation if it strays into political controversy. Few objective observers of, for instance, the reporting of campaign finance would argue that conventional biases are operating here. There is no singling out of Democrats or Republicans, liberals or conservatives. All political action committees (PACs) and all campaign contributions and expenditures tend to be treated alike. Rather one has to look to more intrinsic and ingrained forms, to the structural biases of American newspapers and the political assumptions of their reporters, editors, and headline-writers. Structural biases are rooted in the very nature of journalism—in its professional norms, in marketplace imperatives, in the demands of communicating information to an unsophisticated audience.

Stories need identifiable actors, understandable activity, and elements of conflict, threat or menace. They cannot be long, and must avoid complexity—must focus on the horserace rather than on the substance of a campaign; on controversy, personalities and negative statistics rather than on concepts. These define the "good" story. As for political assumptions, all observers bring a "cognitive map" to American politics—a critical posture toward politics, parties, and politicians. For some it may be as simple as "all politicians are crooks"; for others it involves an understanding of the distribution of power and influence in America.

Systematic bias and political assumption, finally, meet in an analytical conundrum. A systematic bias dictates that newspapers print stories that will be read. But does the press publish the story because readers have been conditioned by newspapers to accept and believe such accounts, or does it publish the story because of its conviction that it represents political truth? Is there really any difference? Ultimately, the Progressive view of reality becomes a part of the imperatives of publishing a newspaper.

---

34. In the course of presenting his arguments, the author suggests that structural biases in American journalism result primarily—but not necessarily exclusively—from:

- **A.** problems intrinsic to the publishing and marketing of newspapers.
- **B.** suppositions of journalists about the integrity of public officials.
- **C.** reporters' cynicism about the public's level of intelligence.
- **D.** growing competition among newspapers for a shrinking audience.

GO TO THE NEXT PAGE.

35. The author contends that conventional political prejudices are not reflected in journalists' accounts of the finance activities of political parties. He supports this contention with the observation that:

    A. the press maintains an attitude of caution toward political misconduct.
    B. the public dislikes journalism that is colored by overt prejudice.
    C. political action committees are hotly opposed by most American journalists.
    D. journalists do not cite specific parties as exclusively blameworthy.

36. According to the passage, which of the following would indicate structural biases inherent in journalists' work?

    A. An article that adheres loyally to Progressivist dictates
    B. An article that successfully masks its biased opinions
    C. An article that is informed by political sophistication
    D. An article that is entertaining and easy to comprehend

37. The author suggests in the passage that the American system of campaign finance:

    A. is unjust and should be reformed.
    B. has exclusively served the interests of the wealthy.
    C. is an easy target for journalists.
    D. has been unfairly singled out for criticism by politicians.

38. Which of the following best describes the "analytical conundrum" referred to in the sentence, "Systematic bias and political assumption, finally, meet in an analytical conundrum," in the last paragraph?

    A. Newspapers promote Progressive ideas in which they do not believe.
    B. Since systematic biases and political assumptions have similar effects, it is difficult to differentiate their roles in journalistic publishing decisions.
    C. Systematic biases and political assumptions exert contradictory and conflicting pressures on newspaper publishers.
    D. Readers' preferences for dramatic news accounts reflecting Progressive ideas, rather than journalists' objective understanding of the political system, determine what is published.

39. The author most probably puts the word "good" in quotes in line 57 in order to:

    A. suggest approval of journalists' concern with marketplace imperatives.
    B. indicate that journalists have their own distinct criteria for measuring the value of a news account.
    C. emphasize the high standards adhered to by journalists in writing newsworthy articles.
    D. call attention to the difficulties of writing a professional piece of journalism.

40. The author would most probably determine that the media's evaluation of the effects of PACs on public officials is:

    A. fair minded.
    B. sophisticated.
    C. uninformed.
    D. simplistic.

GO TO THE NEXT PAGE.

Passage VII (Questions 41–46)

The recognition of exclusive chattels and estate has really harmed and obscured Individualism. It has led Individualism entirely astray. It has made gain, not growth, its aim, so that man has thought that the important thing is to have, and has not come to know that the important thing is to be. The true perfection of man lies, not in what man has, but in what man is.

This state has crushed true Individualism, and set up an Individualism that is false. It has debarred one part of the community from being individual by starving them. It has debarred the other part of the community from being individual by putting them on the wrong road and encumbering them. Indeed, so completely has man's personality been absorbed by his trinkets and entanglements that the law has always treated offenses against a man's property with far more severity than offenses against his person.

It is clear that no authoritarian socialism will do. For while under the present system a very large number of people can lead lives of a certain amount of freedom and expression and happiness, under an industrial barrack system, or a system of economic tyranny, nobody would be able to have any such freedom at all. It is to be regretted that a portion of our community should be practically in slavery, but to propose to solve the problem by enslaving the entire community is childish. Every man must be left quite free to choose his own work.

No form of compulsion must be exercised over him. If there is, his work will not be good for him, will not be good in itself, and will not be good for others. I hardly think that any socialist, nowadays, would seriously propose that an inspector should call every morning at each house to see that each citizen rose up and did manual labor for eight hours. Humanity has got beyond that stage, and reserves such a form of life for the people whom, in a very arbitrary manner, it chooses to call criminals.

Many of the socialistic views that I have come across seem to me to be tainted with ideas of authority, if not of actual compulsion. Of course, authority and compulsion are out of the question. All association must be quite voluntary. It is only in voluntary associations that man is fine. It may be asked how Individualism, which is now more or less dependent on the existence of private property for its development, will benefit by the abolition of such private property. The answer is very simple. It is true that, under existing conditions, a few men who have had private means of their own, such as Byron, Shelley, Browning, Victor Hugo, Baudelaire, and others, have been able to realize their personality, more or less completely.

Not one of these men ever did a single day's work for hire. They were relieved from poverty. They had an immense advantage. The question is whether it would be for the good of Individualism that such an advantage be taken away. Let us suppose that it is taken away. What happens then to Individualism? How will it benefit? Under the new conditions Individualism will be far freer, far finer, and far more intensified than it is now. I am not talking of the great imaginatively realized Individualism of such poets as I have mentioned, but of the great actual Individualism latent and potential in mankind generally.

---

41. In paragraphs three through five, the author is primarily concerned with:

    A. rejecting the enforcement of Socialist policy by governmental coercion.
    B. advocating membership in voluntary organizations.
    C. refuting arguments in favor of the eight-hour workday.
    D. proposing reforms in the treatment of criminals.

42. The author of the passage most likely mentions Byron, Shelly, Browning, Hugo, and Baudelaire in an effort to:

    A. give examples of the harmful effect of money on Individualism and art.
    B. call attention to the rarity of artistic genius.
    C. define what is meant by the phrase "realize their personality".
    D. stress the importance of financial independence.

GO TO THE NEXT PAGE.

43. Which of the following would the author be most likely to consider an example of "enslaving the entire community"?

    I. South Africa under apartheid, where rights of citizenship were denied to the Black majority, and granted in full only to the White minority

    II. Cambodia under the Khmer Rouge, where the urban population was forcibly deported to the countryside to perform agricultural labor

    III. Sweden under the Social Democrats, where all citizens pay high taxes to support extensive social programs

    A. I only
    B. II only
    C. I and II
    D. II and III

44. As used in the fourth paragraph of the passage, the phrase "the people whom, in a very arbitrary manner, it chooses to call criminals" implies which of the following?

    A. All actions should be permitted.
    B. Notions of justice are open to question.
    C. No one would commit crimes in a Socialist society.
    D. Criminals are better suited for mandatory labor than other people.

45. Suppose for a moment that Baudelaire was actually not wealthy, and often had to work to earn money. What relevance would this information have to the arguments posed by the author within the passage?

    A. It would refute the author's claim that artists require independent wealth to create.
    B. It would refute the author's claim that poets are people who can realize their own personality.
    C. It would strengthen the author's claim that the acquisition of wealth leads Individualism astray.
    D. The central thesis of the passage would remain equally valid.

46. Based on the information in the passage, we can assume that the author is most likely to agree that:

    A. most people who have sufficient private property are fully realized individuals.
    B. even with sufficient private property, most people never realize their individuality.
    C. artists are less likely than others to be dependent on private means to realize themselves.
    D. no artists can realize themselves except with substantial private means.

GO TO THE NEXT PAGE.

Passage VIII (Questions 47–54)

Since the time of Darwin, morphological structures have been used to identify phylogenetic relations. For example, the similarity between a man's arm and a bat's wing is taken as evidence of their common origin.

5 There are innumerable examples of this in nature. From the whiskers of lions and domestic cats to the bone structure in the fins of a whale and that of a human hand, it seems one would be hard pressed to fine an attribute in a particular species that did not illustrate some kind of 10 relationship to another species.

Similarities in behavior patterns can also serve in reconstructing evolutionary history. It is not always clear, however, how certain types of innate behavior evolved through natural selection. In its modern form 15 the Darwinian interpretation of evolution asserts that evolution consists of changes in the frequency of appearance of different genes in populations, and that the frequency of the appearance of a particular gene can only increase if the gene increases the "Darwinian fit-20 ness" (the expected number of surviving offspring) of its possessors.

The discovery of a genetic predisposition to be especially responsive to certain stimuli was an important contribution to the study of evolution. Genetically deter-25 mined responses must be subject to the pressures of natural selection. Hence innate behavior must evolve. Ethologists were able to show how a motor pattern employed in a noncommunicatory context such as feeding could evolve into a ritualized form employed as a 30 signal in, say, courtship.

Differentiation in innate behavior patterns could be traced to selection pressures arising from the environment. There are many instances of animal behavior patterns that seem not to contribute to the survival of the 35 individual displaying that behavior. The classic example is the behavior of the worker bee: this insect will sting an intruder and thereby kill itself in defense of the hive. The problem is evident: How can a gene that makes suicide more likely become established? The concern over 40 this type and other types of apparently anomalous behavior led to the development of a new phase in the study of the evolution of behavior: a marriage of ethology and population genetics.

Animal behavior was formerly thought to consist of 45 simple responses, some of them innate and some of them learned, to incoming stimuli. Complex behavior, if it was considered at all, was assumed to be the result of complex stimuli. Over the past 60 years, however, a group of ethologists, notably Konrad Lorenz, Nikolaas 50 Tinbergen and Karl von Frisch, have established a new view of animal behavior. Studying whole patterns of innate animal behavior in natural environments (rather than focusing primarily on learned behavior, as animal behaviorists do), they have shown that the animal brain 55 possesses certain specific competences, that animals have an innate capacity for performing complex acts in response to simple stimuli. As Gould put it in 1982, "Rather than encompassing merely the rigid and impoverished behavioral repertoire of primitive organisms, 60 instinct has been shown to possess a stunning flexibility and overwhelming richness. As a result, we no longer need to invoke the barren behavioristic tenet of learning as an 'explanation' of complexity."

---

47. In the context of the arguments being made by the author in this passage, the term "phylogenetic" (line 2) most closely means:

    A. structural.
    B. inter-species.
    C. innate.
    D. functional.

48. Disregarding, for a moment, later studies of animal behavior, the passage suggests which of the following about early studies of animal behavior?

    A. Innate responses to stimuli were regarded as evidence of animal brain function and mass.
    B. Scientists believed that animals were capable of complex behavior only if such responses were learned.
    C. Most researchers did not investigate whether or not simple responses to stimuli modified over time.
    D. Complex responses to stimuli were used to prove that animal behavior was largely innate rather than acquired.

GO TO THE NEXT PAGE.

KAPLAN

49. Which of the following scenarios would be most analogous to the example given by the author of the worker bee?

- **A.** A male spider reacts to intruding predators by releasing venom that kills both the predator and itself.
- **B.** A female marsupial abandons her weakest offspring as prey for her natural enemies in order to protect the rest of her brood.
- **C.** The youngest member of a canine pack sacrifices himself by fatally wounding an attacking predator so that the pack itself can escape.
- **D.** A drone ant kills an insect preying on his collective by stinging the insect's eyes.

50. The author of the passage would be most likely to agree with which of the following statements?

- **A.** Unusual animal behaviors can be understood in terms of natural selection when they are studied in the context of procreation patterns and needs for survival of that particular species.
- **B.** Overpopulated animal colonies often weed out their excess or weak members by abandoning them to their natural predators.
- **C.** Darwin's evolutionary theories of natural selection have been unnecessarily modified by modern scientists in order to make them accord with observations of animal behavior patterns.
- **D.** The evolution of certain types of innate animal behavior demonstrate the inadequacy of the notion of "Darwinian fitness" as an approach to studying evolution.

51. Of the following choices, which are used to construct the author's argument in this passage?

- **I.** Evidence and refutation of faulty logic
- **II.** Rhetorical questioning
- **III.** Explanation of research findings

- **A.** I and II.
- **B.** II and III.
- **C.** III only.
- **D.** I and III.

52. The author's attitude toward the concept of the evolution of behavior can best be described as:

- **A.** critical of its unconventional interpretations of Darwinian theory.
- **B.** enthusiastic about its applicability to all types of innate behavior.
- **C.** skeptical of its validity when applied to cases of morphological similarities.
- **D.** cautiously approving of its ability to address a variety of behaviors.

53. Which of the following is most closely analogous to the specific accomplishment of ethologists described in lines 27–30?

- **A.** A lawyer building a controversial legal argument around a variety of previous judicial decisions
- **B.** A doctor diagnosing a patient's illness after consulting with a number of medical specialists
- **C.** A student making a formal commitment to a course of study after many years of indecision
- **D.** A historian establishing an underlying link between two seemingly unrelated phenomena

54. Which of the following statements best describes the organization of lines 1-13 of the passage?

- **A.** A scientific paradox is pointed out, then a possible interpretation is set forth.
- **B.** A scientific trend is outlined and an example of that trend is given.
- **C.** A theoretical position is summarized, then a conclusion is drawn.
- **D.** A scientific viewpoint is related, then a subsequent position is stated.

GO TO THE NEXT PAGE.

Passage IX (Questions 55–60)

Let us consider whether women as a group have unique, politically relevant characteristics, whether they have special interests to which a representative could or should respond. Can we argue that women as a group
5 share particular social, economic, or political problems that do not closely match those of other groups, or that they share a particular viewpoint on the solution to political problems? Framing the working definition of "representable interests" in this fashion does not mean that
10 the problems or issues are exclusively those of the specified interest group, any more than we can make the same argument about other types of groups more widely accepted as interest groups.

The fact that there is a labor interest group, for
15 example, reflects the existence of other groups such as the business establishment, consumers, and government, which in a larger sense share labor's concerns, but often have viewpoints on the nature of, or solutions to, the problems which conflict with those of labor.

20 Nor does our working definition of an interest group mean that all of the potential members of that group are consciously allied, or that there is a clear and obvious answer to any given problem articulated by the entire group that differs substantially from answers
25 articulated by others. Research in various fields of social science provides evidence that women do have a distinct position and a shared set of problems that characterize a special interest.

Many of these distinctions are located in the insti-
30 tution in which women and men are probably most often assumed to have common interests, the family. Much has been made of the "sharing" or "democratic" model of the modern family, but whatever democratization has taken place, it has not come close to erasing the division
35 of labor and, indeed, stratification, by sex. Time-use studies show that women spend about the same amount of time on and do the same proportion of housework and child care now as women did at the turn of the century. To say that women are in a different social position from
40 that of men and therefore have unique interests to be represented is not, however, the same as saying that women are conscious of these differences, that they define themselves as having special interests requiring representation, or that men and women as groups now
45 disagree on policy issues in which women might have a special interest.

Studies of public opinion on the status and roles of women show relatively few significant differences
50 between the sexes, and do not reveal women to be consistently more feminist than men. On the other hand, law and public policy continue to create and reinforce differences between women and men in property and contract matters, economic opportunity, protection from violence, control over fertility and child care, education-
55 al opportunities, and civic rights and obligations. The indicators generally used to describe differences in socioeconomic position also show that the politically relevant situations of women and men are different. Women in almost all countries have less education than
60 men, and where they achieve equivalent levels of education, segregation by field and therefore skills and market value remains.

---

55. Based on the information put forth in the passage, with which of the following statements about the status of women would the author be LEAST likely to agree?

   A. In the modern family, housework and child care are more equitably divided than in the past.
   B. As groups, men and women do not necessarily disagree on issues of interest to women.
   C. Women have special interests to which representatives could respond.
   D. Women do not have full control over issues relating to their own fertility.

56. Which of the following would the author be most likely to consider a necessary characteristic of a group having "representable interests" (lines 8–9)?

   A. The problems of the group are unique to its members.
   B. The group's proposed solutions to their problems differ radically from those proposed by other groups.
   C. Members of the group are not already represented as individuals.
   D. Members of the group tend to have similar opinions about the handling of particular political problems.

GO TO THE NEXT PAGE.

57. It can be inferred from the passage that which of the following statements is true of men and women as groups?

    A. In public opinion polls on women's issues, men's responses do not differ in a consistent way from those of women.
    B. Developments in recent years have given men more control over child care issues.
    C. Women are becoming more aware of their differences from men than in the past.
    D. Men do not wish to recognize the special interests of women.

58. According to the passage, which of the following experiences do modern women have most nearly in common with women who lived in 1900?

    A. They are represented only as individuals and not as a group.
    B. They spend about the same amount of time on housework.
    C. They experience significant discrimination in employment.
    D. The proportion of women among those designated as representatives is lower than among the represented.

59. Based on the passage, of the following issues the author is most concerned about the problem of:

    A. the history of women's demands for representation as a group.
    B. recent changes in the status of women in society.
    C. opposing views concerning women's awareness of their own special interests.
    D. the criteria that would justify group representation for women.

60. The passage offers the most support for concluding that which of the following is an important problem confronting women today?

    A. Women are in a different socioeconomic position from that of men.
    B. Men differ greatly from women in the answers they propose for women's problems.
    C. Women do not qualify as an interest group, because they have not all banded together to pursue common goals.
    D. A lack of educational opportunities has inhibited women from voicing their concerns.

STOP. If you finish before time is called, check your work. You may go back to any question in this test booklet.

ANSWER KEY
VERBAL REASONING TEST 7

1.	D	16.	B	31.	A	46.	B
2.	D	17.	B	32.	C	47.	B
3.	D	18.	D	33.	A	48.	C
4.	B	19.	A	34.	A	49.	C
5.	B	20.	A	35.	D	50.	A
6.	B	21.	D	36.	D	51.	B
7.	B	22.	B	37.	C	52.	D
8.	B	23.	B	38.	B	53.	D
9.	C	24.	D	39.	B	54.	D
10.	B	25.	D	40.	D	55.	A
11.	D	26.	B	41.	A	56.	D
12.	A	27.	D	42.	D	57.	A
13.	B	28.	D	43.	B	58.	B
14.	B	29.	D	44.	B	59.	D
15.	C	30.	D	45.	D	60.	A

EXPLANATIONS

PASSAGE I

Topic and Scope:
analyzes the elements of self-discovery in James Baldwin's novels.

Mapping the Passage:
¶1 and 2 discuss the role of suffering in Baldwin's idea of self-identity.
¶3 argues that Baldwin's self-identity also relies on an identification with community and tradition.
¶4 argues that Baldwin's idea of self-discovery also relies on the understanding of others.

Questions:
1. D Be careful with the "all...EXCEPT" wording. Predict what the wrong answer choices will look like: they'll be things that do contribute to self-identity. Eliminate choices based on your map: While the first three match up with points made in the passage, (D) contradicts ¶4, which argues that personal independence can get in the way of understanding others.

Wrong Answers:
(A): Opposite. This is the subject of ¶4
(B): Opposite. This also a point that follows from ¶4.
(C): Opposite. This is the subject of ¶1.

2. D Review the line in the context of the map. The term comes up in the end of paragraph 2 and then is explained in paragraph 4. The point of the paragraph is that self-discovery relies on the understanding of others. (D) alone matches with this.

Wrong Answers:
(A): Out of Scope. A common meaning for the phrase, but nothing like what the author refers to in this passage.
(B): Out of Scope. Racial equality is never specifically mentioned in the passage and is far outside the scope of understanding others.
(C): Faulty Use of Detail. This is the scope of ¶1 rather than ¶4.

3. D Focus on the structure of the passage rather than the particular details. The book in the question is mentioned in ¶3. Review your map: ¶3 discusses the role community unity plays in forming self-identity. Chances are that the answer choice will therefore deal with that aspect of the book. (D) fits both with the map and with a close, though in this case unnecessary, reading of the text.

Wrong Answers:
(A): Opposite. The book is used to show that the individual must identify with the community, rather than stand in tension with it.
(B): Out of Scope. Though it may do this, the author isn't concerned specifically with the Black community.
(C): Out of Scope. As above, though this may be true, the author is concerned primarily with discussing the role of community, not of family specifically.

4. B Predict using your map: Baldwin believes that group experience is necessary for self-identity. Only (B) is on scope. Baldwin must believe that this is true; were it not, it wouldn't be generally applicable, as Baldwin clearly intends it to be.

Wrong Answers:
(A): Out of Scope. While this might be true, it's not mentioned in the passage and has nothing to do with the relationship between individual and community.
(C): Faulty Use of Detail. This is perhaps implicit in the discussion of suffering in ¶4, but doesn't tie into group experience.
(D): Opposite. Baldwin believes that self discovery can be attained only through communal identity; this argues the opposite.

5. B A rare type of evaluation question that asks you to evaluate the whole structure of the passage. Predict: the author is concerned only with Baldwin's idea of self-identity, and spends the passage discussing the elements Baldwin believes are necessary to achieve it. (B) fits.

Wrong Answers:
(A): Out of Scope. There's no thesis prevented that the author is defending, and certainly no hint of controversy.
(C): Out of Scope. The author only discusses one interpretation: Baldwin's own.

(D): Out of Scope. While Baldwin likely believed that social change was necessary, the author is only concerned with Baldwin's idea of self-identity.

Strategy Point: When faced with abstract answer choices, compare them back to the passage to find concrete parallels.

6. B Where is Giovanni's Room mentioned? Go back to ¶4 to review. The paragraph deals with personal interactions with others. Only (B) relates to this idea. Specifically, the book describes someone who fails to achieve self-identity because he lacks compassion for others.

Wrong Answers:
(A): Faulty Use of Detail. ¶1 deals with this point, but Giovanni's Room supports the points of ¶4.
(C): Faulty Use of Detail. This is the topic of ¶3.
(D): Faulty Use of Detail. This point is also mentioned in ¶1.

PASSAGE II

Topic and Scope: discusses three models for justifying free speech.

Mapping the Passage:
¶1 describes a third model, the self-restraint model.
¶2 introduces two models justifying free speech.
¶3 describes Meiklejohn's classical model.
¶4 describes Holmes' fortress model.

Questions:
7. B Predict by summarizing the classical model as described in ¶3: free speech is necessary in order to protect free political activity. Meiklejohn wouldn't necessary argue that non-political speech has to be protected: "the free speech principle need only protect political speech." (B) falls under this category of non-protected speech.

Wrong Answers:
(A): Opposite. The main idea of the classical model is that *all* political speech has to be protected.
(C): Opposite. Since this would be a form of political speech, the classical model would protect this also, extreme as it is.
(D): Opposite. These opinions could also be considered political, and the classical model would therefore protect them, offensive or not.

8. B What does Holmes advocate? The fortress model as described in ¶4, which argues that all speech should be protected in order to keep the majority from censoring the opinions of the minority. Look for an answer choice that somehow runs against this. (B) fits the bill: if Holmes believes that speech should be protected in order to prevent the dominance of one

viewpoint over another, he certainly wouldn't believe that some views deserve more protection than others.

Wrong Answers:
(A): Opposite. The fortress model argues that even extreme speech has to be protected in order to make sure that useful speech isn't eventually censored as well.
(C): Opposite. This also follows from the idea that no speech should be censored so that useful speech can be protected.
(D): Opposite. Holmes believes that protecting extremist speech increases the odds that useful speech will be protected. Therefore, if extremist speech *is* censored, useful speech is more likely to be censored as well.

9. C Review Bollinger's model in the last paragraph. Bollinger argues that free speech is less important than is tolerance, and that those who speak should exercise self-control. While three choices fit with what is described in ¶1, (C) contradicts the author's description of the self-restraint model as "staunchly supporting free speech."

Wrong Answers:
(A): Opposite. This follows from the point in paragraph 1 that the self-restraint model believes that the function of speech changes along with society.
(B): Opposite. This summarizes the author's argument in paragraph 1 that Bollinger's model "inverts" the traditional relationship between speech and tolerance.
(D): Opposite. This reiterates the point in line 5.

10. B While this is a Roman Numeral question, it may be easier to simply predict than to go through choice by choice since the Roman Numerals are in this case simply the three different models. Scan the relevant parts of the passage to predict whether each model considers speech a fundamental value or not. The last lines of paragraph 1 state that traditional models consider free speech to be entitled to more tolerance than other activities, while the first paragraph argues that the self-restraint model considers tolerance more important than free speech. Therefore, it's safe to assume that the two traditional models consider free speech a fundamental value, while Bollinger's model doesn't.

Wrong Answers:
(A): Opposite. As described above.
(C): Opposite. As above.
(D): Opposite. As above.

11. D Another Roman Numeral question with the same set-up. The question is trickily worded; take time to decipher it. What model would criticize laws prohibiting intolerant speech? In other words, what model would *tolerate* intolerant speech? While the classical model only requires tolerance for political speech and the self-restraint model actually subordinates free speech to tolerance, the fortress model protects *all* speech, and (D) is therefore the correct answer.

Wrong Answers:
(A): Opposite. As described above.
(B): Opposite. As above.
(C): Opposite. As above.

12. A Review the classical model: why does it want to protect political speech in particular? Meiklejohn implies that free speech is useful because it allows a variety of viewpoints to be heard when considering political decisions. (A) is thus an underlying assumption. Try denying it: if members *don't* need to consider all views, then the justification for protecting free speech under the classical model disappears.

Wrong Answers:
(B): Out of Scope. Even if this is true, it's not necessary to the argument that political speech depends on free speech to be of maximum effectiveness.
(C): Out of Scope. As above, even if this assumption were denied, Meiklejohn's argument would remain intact.
(D): Distortion. This is a distortion of Meiklejohn's community model. Even though he uses the model of a small community, he doesn't necessarily believe that free speech is *more* important in such a community.

13. B Review your map to predict a quick answer to the question: The two traditional models are introduced and explained. (B) fits perfectly.

Wrong Answers:
(A): Out of Scope. Though two theories are described, there's no historical backdrop for them in the passage.
(C): Out of Scope. Though there are contrasts between the two models, the author is principally concerned with discussing the contrasts rather than discussing the points of similarity.
(D): Distortion. While two theories are discussed, the conclusions of both models are essentially the same: free speech should be protected. While they differ on the details of the conclusion, the author focuses far more on the different arguments that lead to that similar conclusion.

14. B What do the two traditional models have in common? Predict: They both value free speech above tolerance, and therefore tolerate extremist speech. (B) rewards the careful prediction.

Wrong Answers:
(A): Faulty Use of Detail. This is mentioned as a hallmark of the fortress model, but not mentioned when discussing the classical model.
(C): Faulty Use of Detail. (C) is another of Holmes' views: censoring speech eventually leads to the censorship of both useful and worthless views.
(D): Faulty Use of Detail. This is a tenet of the classical model, but not the fortress model.

PASSAGE III

Topic and Scope: discusses Philip Larkin's style of poetry and critics' reaction.

Mapping the Passage:
¶1 introduces Philip Larkin by explaining his artistic tastes.
¶2 describes Larkin's response to critics and gives Larkin's artistic view: art should be simple and easily accessible.
¶3 analyzes Larkin's poetry and mentions some critical reaction.
¶4 mentions a perception of Larkin as antisocial and provides the author's own positive view of Larkin's poetry.
¶5 gives some background on the career of Larkin.

Questions:
15. C Where is Brooke mentioned? He's an example in ¶2 of an English poet who had forged a "connection between poetry and the reading public." (C) summarizes the fundamental point about Brooke: he had connected easily with the reading public.

Wrong Answers:
(A): Opposite. This was a trait of the poetry that was replacing Brooke's style of poetry.
(B): Distortion. Though the passage suggests that Brooke was easy to understand, there's nothing about his subject matter; he could have written about issues easy to understand but unimportant to everyday life.
(D): Distortion. Larkin believed that the new poetry came about as a result of academic study of English literature, but this doesn't mean that the poetry that came before *wasn't* suitable.

16. B Go back to ¶2 to review the lines in context. Larkin said this when responding to critics who said that his work was too "commonplace." What must Larkin have believed? Not necessarily that his work *wasn't* commonplace, but that being so wasn't such a bad thing. (B) paraphrases this response.

Wrong Answers:
(A): Out of Scope. Larkin never mentions any personal failings in the response. He's concerned with showing that the ordinary isn't such a bad thing.
(C): Distortion. Though Larkin's critics might have considered his poems commonplace, that doesn't mean that they thought their own lives were glamorous, or that they were attacking his poetry to make themselves look better.
(D): Opposite. Larkin took pride in writing about common things; he disputed critics' assessment of their importance, not of their commonness.

17. B A main idea question. Predict the right answer based on purpose, scope, and topic. A vertical scan is helpful in this case too: "describe" most closely matches

KAPLAN

what the author does. A check of the answer choice shows that it holds up. The author is concerned with describing Larkin's verse particularly in the context of the subjects he uses.

Wrong Answers:
(A): Faulty Use of Detail. Though the author does mention Larkin's views on poetry, and shows how they tied in with what he wrote about, the purpose of the topic is broader than just to show this relation.
(C): Out of Scope. This doesn't include Larkin specifically, a necessary element.
(D): Out of Scope. As above, this summary skims over Larkin, with whom the passage is mainly concerned.

18. D   Review the quote at the end of ¶3. The critic is referring to a specific poem of Larkin's. The lines above suggest that the critic is responding to the commonplace elements in the poem. Since the response is only half-admiring, the critic is complimenting the poem while at the same time noting its subject matter. The only RN that fits with these various purposes is RN II. RN I distorts the critics' view, and neglects the good half of the "half-admiringly." RN III is off the scope: While Larkin's own views and his poetry were intertwined, there's no evidence that the critics were focusing on some element of Larkin's views that wasn't in his poetry.

Wrong Answers:
(A): Opposite. As described above.
(B): Opposite. As above.
(C): Opposite. As above.

19. A   Review the quote in context. Right above the anecdote, the author says, "He saw no such need to explain his own work." Larkin likely made the arguably pointless comment about where the poem was written, then, in order to back this idea up. (A) says the same.

Wrong Answers:
(B): Faulty Use of Detail. Though Larkin believed this, the comment is made to support an entirely different point.
(C): Faulty Use of Detail. As above, though critics did suggest this, Larkin's tackling a different issue in this quote.
(D): Opposite. Larkin *did* believe that poetry had done this, and isn't interested in proving that in this quote anyhow.

Strategy Point: Explanations of an example's relevance can very often be found above or below the quoted lines. Read in context!

20. A   What would Larkin be least likely to write a poem about? Predict: something not commonplace. Only one of the choices fits this: (A) represents something that is intangible and lofty, definitely not commonplace.

Wrong Answers:
(B): Opposite. Very commonplace.
(C): Opposite. While the choice tries to trick you with the academic angle, death in war would still seem "real" enough for Larkin's tastes.
(D): Opposite. Another commonplace subject.

PASSAGE IV

Topic and Scope: critiques Charles Taylor's analysis of multiculturalism and its focus on recognizing diversity.

Mapping the Passage:
¶1 introduces Taylor's analysis of multiculturalism and argues that it is incomplete.
¶2 describes the two liberal demands for recognition that multiculturalism rejects: recognition of human dignity and individualism.
¶s3 and 4 describes Taylor's idea that multiculturalism betrays the liberal idea of equality. Taylor argues that recognition of diversity is essential but that extreme multiculturalism goes too far.
¶5 argues that the recognition model is insufficient and provides an example.

Strategy Point: Pay close attention to authorial points of view. Whenever the author's viewpoint is different from other viewpoints in the passage, the contrasts will be tested.

Questions:
21. D   A main idea question. Predict: the author is discussing Taylor's analysis of multiculturalism, with emphasis on demonstrating that it's incomplete. Only (D) includes both a theory of multiculturalism and a critique of it.

Wrong Answers:
(A): Distortion. The author criticizes Taylor, but not his definition of liberalism.
(B): Out of Scope. The author is concerned with critiquing Taylor's view, not merely defining multiculturalism.
(C): Opposite. The author is *critiquing* Taylor's view, not defending it.

22. B   Review the beginning of ¶4, where the author discusses extreme multiculturalism. He states that these "commit the crucial error of reducing all...standards to mere instruments of power..." and in doing so make moral justifications "absurd." (B) paraphrases the second part of the point.

Wrong Answers:
(A): Faulty Use of Detail. This is true of some minority groups, as described in the beginning of the fifth paragraph, but doesn't refer to extreme multiculturalism.

(C): Distortion. Taylor is the one making comparisons between multiculturalism and liberalism, not the extreme multiculturalists themselves.

(D): Opposite. The author argues that the extreme multiculturalists have *lost* the moral arguments.

23. B Go back to ¶3, where the author describes Taylor's view on multiculturalism as betrayal of liberal ideals. The liberal idea that is being specifically betrayed is that of equality. (B) summarizes this.

Wrong Answers:

(A): Distortion. Though liberalism doesn't concentrate on minority groups to the extent that multiculturalism does, there's no evidence that it's not concerned at all.

(C): Opposite. This is Taylor's response to multiculturalism's betrayal rather than the betrayal itself.

(D): Opposite. Taylor specifically argues in the same paragraph that multiculturalism should be able to accomplish this.

24. D Review the answer choices in with focus on the paragraphs dealing with Quebec: ¶s 3-5. Start with RN I: The Quebecois are used as an example of one society's "demand for recognition." RN II is backed up by the author's point in the end of the passage: Taylor doesn't fully consider the implications of his example of Quebec. Finally, RN III is supported in lines 29–31. The Quebecois demand for a distinct society is described as "special treatment." (D) is therefore the correct answer.

Wrong Answers:

(A): Opposite. As described above.

(B): Opposite. As above.

(C): Opposite. As above.

25. D Review ¶s 2 and 3, where the liberal ideals are discussed. The correct idea may be difficult to predict exactly, so paraphrase Taylor's main argument about liberal ideals: multiculturalism betrays them for legitimate reasons. While three answers can be quickly eliminated, (D) alone is left. (D) reflects the idea that recognizing only sameness is an incomplete conception. Since the author says that this is "plausible," it's reasonable to assume that the author would agree with Taylor's view.

Wrong Answers:

(A): Opposite. This is roughly the opposite of the correct answer choice: Taylor argues that liberal ideals are inadequate, and the author seems to agree.

(B): Distortion. Taylor and the author are concerned with how multiculturalism safeguards rights, not the liberal ideals.

(C): Out of Scope. This is never discussed.

26. B What is the author's main contention about Taylor's ideas? They're incomplete. (B) most closely matches this.

Wrong Answers:

(A): Distortion. While (A) is tempting, the author never says that Taylor's model is admirable.

(C): Faulty Use of Detail. While the author does describe Taylor's historical account as "deft," he has a different opinion about the model itself.

(D): Distortion. The author argues that the model is incomplete, but not that it is a complete failure.

27. D An evaluation question. Review the lines discussed: the author says that Taylor acknowledges that multiculturalism betrays liberalism, and then "plausibly argues" that it's good for it to do so. (D) summarizes this.

Wrong Answers:

(A): Out of Scope. Taylor is defending multiculturalism's betrayal of liberal principles; this choice includes no defense.

(B): Distortion. Though Taylor does present a potential weakness in multiculturalism, he doesn't develop it, but rather argues that it isn't in fact a weakness.

(C): Distortion. This suggests that two ideas are presented, rather than the single idea of multiculturalism's betrayal of liberal ideals.

PASSAGE V

Topic and Scope: discusses the evolution and unique adaptations of wind pollination.

Mapping the Passage:

¶s1 and 2 describe adaptations specific to pollen grain size.

¶s2 and 3 elaborate on the traditional view of wind pollination as primitive and suggest that wind pollination has independently evolved several times.

¶4 describes wind pollination and the traditional view of it.

¶5 describes recent evidence and introduces two sophisticated features of wind pollination: pollen grain size and ovulate organ morphology.

¶6 describes adaptations specific to ovulate organ morphology.

Questions:

28. D Where does the author discuss pollen grains? Go back to ¶s1 and 2. Since the Roman Numeral choices are fairly short, it's probably fastest in this case not to worry about searching for the one that appears most frequently; start in order. The author discusses in ¶s1 and 2 that small, low-density grains are preferable, which validates RNs I and III. Dryness can be inferred from the author's point that many pollen grains "quickly dehydrate after release." Therefore, all RNs are valid and the answer choice must be (D).

Wrong Answers:
(A): Opposite. As described above.
(B): Opposite. As above.
(C): Opposite. As above.

29. D A detail question. Go to ¶6 to find the mention of leeward surfaces. They're mentioned in two places: when discussing turbulence and sedimentation. (D) is therefore correct.

Wrong Answers:
(A): Opposite. Separation takes place on the *windward* surface.
(B): Opposite. Collision takes place on the windward surface also.
(C): Opposite. As above, separation is a windward-surface phenomenon.

30. D A scattered detail question. You're looking for an answer choice that *doesn't* function to prevent pollen loss. While three of the choices can be eliminated based on the text of the passage, (D) is an adaptation with an entirely different function. Preventing self-pollination is never discussed in the context of pollen loss; it's useful only to prevent inbreeding.

Wrong Answers:
(A): Opposite. This is mentioned in ¶4.
(B): Opposite. This paraphrases the author's point in ¶3 that "the wind vector is only useful in large, near-monoculture populations."
(C): Opposite. This is the topic of ¶6, which is focused with adaptations necessary for pollen capture.

31. A Where does the author discuss something that might have to do with rainfall? ¶5 states that pollen grains aren't released when "humid or wet conditions might cause pollen grains to clump or fall." Therefore, it's reasonable to guess that the plants would avoid releasing pollen. (A) says the same.

Wrong Answers:
(B): Opposite. For the reasons the author describes in ¶5, the amount would be *less*.
(C): Opposite. Since there's less pollen being released, the pollen-to-ovule ratio will necessarily be less also.
(D): Opposite. If pollen release is less, it's reasonable to infer that seed production will be less also.

32. C A difficult question to predict, but try to review the author's main points: Wind pollination hasn't been considered that interesting as compared to other types of pollination, but all sorts of new evidence shows that it's very sophisticated. (C) alone can coexist with this prediction, and is backed up by the fact that the author discusses both botany and various "vectors" that affect pollination, suggesting that a knowledge of the different vectors (wind, water, insects, etc.) is useful for understanding pollination.

Wrong Answers:
(A): Distortion. Though *wind* pollination might be considered uninteresting by *textbooks*, there's no indication that pollination in general is considered uninteresting by scientists in general.
(B): Distortion. Though the author suggests that a knowledge of aerodynamics is needed for *wind* pollination, that's not necessarily true of pollination in general.
(D): Distortion. As with choice (A), though *wind* pollination hasn't been taken seriously by textbooks, there's nothing to suggest that pollination in general hasn't been taken seriously by the scientific community at large.

33. A Predict: where would wind pollinated plants not do well? Probably in a place without much wind and with lots of moisture. (A) looks good: tropical rain forests certainly match both these criteria.

Wrong Answers:
(B): Opposite. This is a dry, windy biome. Perfect for wind pollination. Conifers are specifically mentioned in the passage as wind pollinators.
(C): Opposite. The author mentions certain plants in central California valleys in ¶2 as having recently adapted to wind pollination.
(D): Opposite. Since the plants are right by a riverbank, they might be less likely to wind pollinate, but they would still be far more likely to use wind pollination by a river (which doesn't guarantee humidity) than in a tropical rain forest (which does).

PASSAGE VI

Topic and Scope: discusses biases inherent in American journalism.

Mapping the Passage:
¶1 describes how media's understanding and view of politics shades their reporting on it.
¶s2 and 3 give an example of this in a specific situation: campaign financing.
¶s4 and 5 argue that outright political bias is less prevalent in modern America than are structural biases and political assumptions.
¶6 describes both structural bias and political assumption.
¶7 describes the circular relationship between the media and public: the media writes what the public will buy, but the public buys what the media has conditioned it to want.

Questions:
34. A Where does the author discuss the reasons for structural bias? Review the beginning of ¶6: the author says that the structural biases are "rooted in the very nature of journalism." (A), which suggests that bias

comes from intrinsic issues with the industry, reflects this view.

Wrong Answers:
(B): Faulty Use of Detail. This describes political assumptions, not structural biases.
(C): Distortion. Though the passage mentions that structural bias arises partly from "the demands of communicating information to an unsophisticated audience," the passage doesn't say that reporters are cynical about readers' intelligence, only that the intelligence may in fact *be* unsophisticated.
(D): Distortion. Though the passage mentions "marketplace imperatives" it doesn't go so far as to say that the audience is shrinking.

35. D A difficult question, especially in its wording; be sure to take the time to paraphrase it. Why aren't conventional political prejudices found in reporting much anymore? The author argues in ¶s4 and 5 that they've been supplanted by structural bias and political assumptions, and says, "There is no singling out of Democrats or Republicans..." and then specifically mentions that all campaign contributions are treated in the same way. (D) fits with all this, arguing that individual parties aren't exclusively singled out.

Wrong Answers:
(A): Distortion. Though the press doesn't bash one party over the other in its treatment of misconduct, there's nothing in the passage to suggest that it's *cautious* about all this.
(B): Opposite. If anything, the last paragraph suggests that the public is more willing to buy prejudiced accounts.
(C): Distortion. Though the author argues in ¶2 that they're an eager target, there's no evidence that the journalists oppose them. They just write negatively about them.

Strategy Point: If a question looks difficult, skip it and come back to it after doing all the others; work from the other questions may help you answer it!

36. D Go back to the beginning of ¶6 to review what structural biases consist of. Most of structural bias has to do with selling newspapers to an unsophisticated audience, so look for a situation that exemplifies this. (D) fits perfectly.

Wrong Answers:
(A): Opposite. This would go against the author's idea that most journalism isn't overly partisan anymore. Even though newspapers *are* progressive according to the author, they wouldn't adhere loyally to the dictates of one position.
(B): Opposite. As above, the author doesn't think that the media is overly biased in its opinions.

(C): Opposite. The author says that the media has to play to an unsophisticated audience, and so this would suggest something that went *against* structural bias.

37. C What is the author's main point about campaign financing? The author argues in ¶2 that it's targeted by journalists because it's easy to write about and fits all the right stereotypes. (C) paraphrases this.

Wrong Answers:
(A): Distortion. Though journalists might write this in their stories, the author doesn't indicate that he himself believes it.
(B): Distortion. As above, there's no evidence that the author believes this.
(D): Distortion. Though it's singled out by journalists, there's no evidence of *politicians* singling it out, which wouldn't make sense as it's the system that keeps them elected.

38. B Summarize the main idea of ¶7: it's hard to tell systematic bias from political assumption because the newspapers write (with their political assumptions) what the public wants to read (thus driving systematic bias).(B) paraphrases this.

Wrong Answers:
(A): Faulty Use of Detail. Though the author argues in ¶s 2 and 7 that newspapers support a "Progressivist world view," it does nothing to describe the "conundrum" described in ¶7.
(C): Opposite. The author is arguing that they have more or less the *same* effect, which is why they're so hard to tell apart.
(D): Faulty Use of Detail. While this might be true, it's only part of the puzzle. This choice includes the element of systematic bias (the desires of the audience) but nothing about the political assumptions of those writing the newspapers.

39. B Why would the author put "good" in quotation marks when discussing what makes a good story? Read the lines above: the author is describing how structural biases affect the composition of the story. It's logical to infer that the author doesn't think that these are necessarily good trends, but rather that the story is judged good or bad by whether it sells papers. (B) fits this: journalists know what sells, and judge "goodness" based on that.

Wrong Answers:
(A): Distortion. Though journalists are concerned with marketplace imperatives, the author doesn't necessarily approve.
(C): Opposite. If anything, the author is arguing that the standards are lower because of structural bias.
(D): Out of Scope. The author is discussing how stories suffer from structural bias; there's no attempt to defend journalists by talking about how hard it is to write.

40. D Review the main points of the author's argument about campaign financing? What is it an example of? A media system that plays to the interests of an unsophisticated public by oversimplifying easy targets. (D) captures this, while each of the other three answer choices go too far one way or the other.

Wrong Answers:
(A): Opposite. The author would argue that in these stories, fairness is secondary to structural biases and political assumptions.
(B): Opposite. The author argues that the media plays to an unsophisticated audience by writing unsophisticated pieces. This is the direct opposite of the correct answer.
(C): Distortion. Though the media might be simplistic in its treatment of campaign finances, the author never suggests that it doesn't have the information needed to write the story. If anything, it's highly informed and simply uses the information poorly.

PASSAGE VII

Topic and Scope: argues for the abolishing private property in order to foster individualism.

Mapping the Passage:
¶s1 and 2 explain how private property has harmed individualism.
¶s3 and 4 argues that socialism cannot be compulsory.
¶5 argues that while most socialists don't advocate compulsory socialism, authority is still overemphasized.
¶s5 and 6 tie individualism and private property together, and gives examples of people who were able to achieve individualism through wealth and ¶6 argues that individualism will benefit from the elimination of personal property.

Questions:
41. A What do the first two paragraphs deal with? Predict: The author believes that socialism cannot be compulsory. (A) immediately recommends itself.

Wrong Answers:
(B): Distortion. Though the author believes that socialism should be voluntary, there are no specific organizations that the author is recommending membership in.
(C): Out of Scope. The author mentions an eight-hour workday, but isn't concerned with discussing its merits.
(D): Out of Scope. The author also mentions criminals, but isn't particularly worried about their treatment in these paragraphs.

Strategy Point: When all the answer choices in a question are the same type of word (such as a verb or an adjective) try a "vertical scan" to get an idea of which word fits best with the author's tone. This is particularly useful on global and evaluation questions.

42. D Where are these individuals mentioned? Look over your map of ¶5. These were all individuals who were able to maximize their individuality because they were so rich that they didn't have to work. Only (A) and (D) involve money, and (D) alone fits with the author's overall point in the paragraph.

Wrong Answers:
(A): Opposite. While this choice does talk about money, and while the author's overall point is that property should be abolished, in this paragraph the author is giving examples of artists who had an "immense advantage" by being rich. Money therefore must be helpful to individualism.
(B): Out of Scope. While the author might believe that genius is rare, the scope of the paragraph is on money and its advantages to individualism.
(C): Distortion. The author does define this; it's simply individualism. The focus of the paragraph is on money, however.

43. B Where does the author use the phrase mentioned in the question? It's mentioned in ¶4, where the author is arguing against compulsory socialism. Look for choices that exemplify compulsory socialism. Start with RN II, which appears in three choices: In this example, part of the population is forced to perform a certain type of labor, which certainly would qualify as compulsory socialism. Look at RN I: No socialism is suggested in this example, only segregation. RN III represents socialism, but there's no suggestion that it's compulsory socialism. (B) must be correct.

Wrong Answers:
(A): Opposite. As described above.
(C): Opposite. As above.
(D): Opposite. As above.

44. B Find the phrase mentioned in the question: it's in ¶4. Review the context: The author argues that "humanity has got beyond" enforced manual labor, and that it saves that for the criminals. He also mentions that criminals are labeled such "in a very arbitrary manner." What does this imply about the author's opinions towards society and criminals? He seems to think that the notion of criminality that society has isn't necessarily just. (B) paraphrases this.

Wrong Answers:
(A): Distortion. Though the author thinks that the label of "criminal" might be arbitrary and that people shouldn't be forced to work, this doesn't mean that all actions should be permitted.
(C): Out of Scope. The author never suggests this.
(D): Distortion. Though society seems to think that this is true, the author doesn't necessarily agree, especially since he considers ideas of criminality to be very arbitrary.

45. D Use your predictions from Question 42 to help here. What is Baudelaire used as an example of? Someone who was able to cultivate his genius because he didn't have to hold down a day job. If Baudelaire did have to work, this would weaken the author's idea of wealth as an advantage to attaining individuality. However, since he's one of six examples, it wouldn't weaken it all that much; the author would have plenty to fall back on. The only "weakeners" in the choices are outright refutations, which is far too strong an effect on the argument. It's clear that this information contradicting the author wouldn't strengthen the argument, though, so only (D) is left: The author's main points might not have as much evidence as they did, but there's still plenty for them to remain valid.

Wrong Answers:
(A): Distortion. As described above, it would only ever-so-slightly weaken it.
(B): Out of Scope. Even if Baudelaire did have to work, he could still be a poet who recognized his own personality.
(C): Opposite. Baudelaire doesn't tie into this part of the argument, but if he was individualist and did have to work for private property, the author's argument would be weakened.

46. B An inference question without any hint as to specifics, which means that the answer will probably tie into the author's main idea. Predict it: Compulsory socialism is bad, but private property should be eliminated because it gets in the way of individuality. (B) fits most closely. The author believes that only a few people are able to achieve individuality with the help of wealth, but that "mankind generally" is a different matter.

Wrong Answers:
(A): Distortion. While the author mentions a few artists who were, he argues just that: that only a few have been able to achieve individuality with wealth.
(C): Opposite. The author only mentions artists who were dependent on private means to achieve their individuality.
(D): Distortion. Though the author believes that some artists had an advantage because of their private means, there's no indication that this is the only way that self-realization can occur.

PASSAGE VIII

Topic and Scope: discusses the relationship between evolution and instinctive animal behavior.

Mapping the Passage:
¶s1 and 2 introduce Darwin and the notion of morphological structures.

¶3 states that relating behavior to evolution has both solved and raised problems.
¶4 argues that innate behavior must evolve.
¶5 suggests that some behaviors don't contribute to individual survival in a classic Darwinian sense, and states that these behaviors are best explained in relation to population genetics.
¶6 describes a traditional view of complex animal behavior (complex behavior comes from complex stimuli) and a new view: complex behavior can be innate and arise from simple stimuli.

Questions:
47. B Review the word in context. The author states that "morphological structures have been used to identify phylogenetic relations." While this might not immediately help, compare it to the example below. The arms of both man and bat presumably are morphological structures, and "phylogenetic relations" must therefore refer to the "common origin" of both structures. (B) most closely fits this idea, and is the only answer choice that makes sense when read back into the sentence.

Wrong Answers:
(A): Out of Scope. Structures are being compared, but the word deals with something *describing* the structures.
(C): Out of Scope. The author is concerned with the relationship between structures, not how they were obtained.
(D): Out of Scope. As above, the relationship between two different structures is being considered, not the function of one single structure.

Strategy Point: Don't be intimidated by complex or confusing wording in a passage. If a word or phrase is important to understanding the passage, there will always *be sufficient context to infer its meaning.*

48. C Where are early studies of animal behavior mentioned? Go to ¶6 for the "traditional" view. Summarize the view: early studies suggested that simple responses were due to simple stimuli, complex responses a result of complex stimuli. The new view, by contrast, is that complex behaviors can evolve over time. Therefore (C) is a valid inference: early studies didn't see a need to investigate whether complex behavior evolved since the scientists believed that complex behavior only existed as a result of complex stimuli.

Wrong Answers:
(A): Out of Scope. There's nothing in the passage to suggest this.
(B): Distortion. This distorts the point in ¶6 that animal behaviorists focus primarily on learned behavior. No link between complex behavior and learned behavior is mentioned.
(D): Opposite. This is a hallmark of the new theory rather than the old one.

49. C Go back to ¶5 to review and paraphrase the example of the worker bee. Why is it relevant? It represents an example of behavior that doesn't help the survival of the individual organism, which sacrifices itself, but protects the overall community. Find an answer choice that matches up with these criteria: (C) does so.

Wrong Answers:
(A): Distortion. Though the individual dies, it's not to protect a community.
(B): Distortion. An individual is sacrificed for the good of the community in this scenario, but it's not an instance of self-sacrifice.
(D): Out of Scope. There's no element of sacrifice in this choice.

Strategy Point: When a question asks you for a situation similar to one in the passage, all major elements of the two points must match. Eliminate answer choices that depart significantly from these main points.

50. A Predict by reviewing the author's main ideas: complex behavior can evolve and has to be related to community as well as individual survival. Choice (A) paraphrases this, essentially summarizing the passage.

Wrong Answers:
(B): Out of Scope. The author never suggests any sort of animal behavior that would lead to this situation.
(C): Opposite. The author argues that Darwin's theories are appropriate for studies of animal behavior, and are modified appropriately (to explain self-sacrificial behavior, for example
(D): Opposite. The author argues that Darwin's ideas are important to understanding complex behavior.

Strategy Point: Questions that ask you about the author's opinion without providing context are fairly rare and will usually deal with the author's main ideas.

51. B Since you're looking for things used to build the author's argument, this is an evaluation question, though an unusual one in that it includes Roman numerals. Evaluate each RN using your map and the passage to find support or refutation. RN III appears in three choices, so start there. The author describes research in ¶4 as well as its significance. The choice is now between (B) and (D). If one RN can be eliminated, the other must be true, and vice versa. The author relies on rhetorical questioning in ¶5 but never mentions faulty logic. (B) must therefore be the correct answer.

Wrong Answers:
(A): Opposite. As above.
(C): Opposite. As above.
(D): Opposite. As above.

52. D What does the author think about evolution? Predict: Evolution explains a lot of innate behavior, but

has to be taken in conjunction with population genetics to explain strange cases like the self-sacrificing bee. (D) describes an attitude that most closely fits this view.

Wrong Answers:
(A): Opposite. If anything, the author is supportive of the idea that classic Darwinism has to be modified in order to be broadly applicable.
(B): Distortion. Though the author thinks that evolution is a valuable tool to explain behavior, there's no unqualified enthusiasm for it: the author believes it has to be modified to more fully explain some behaviors.
(C): Opposite. The author discusses morphological similarities as an example of evolution's applicability, and therefore wouldn't be cautious about applying it to these examples.

53. D Paraphrase the "specific accomplishment." The ethologists showed that simple instincts used one way could evolve into more complex behaviors used another way. Looking for an answer choice that roughly meets these criteria eliminates everything but (D): just as ethologists demonstrated a link between the different behaviors, so the historian shows a link between seemingly unrelated phenomena.

Wrong Answers:
(A): Out of Scope. Nothing in this choice involves a link such as the one made between animal behaviors.
(B): Out of Scope. As above, there's no link between two different situations or behaviors.
(C): Out of Scope. Just as the last two choices, there's no link between previously unlinked behaviors.

54. D An evaluation question: use your map to help answer. How does the author open the passage? The "traditional view" is described, and a new theory that is supplanting it is introduced. (D) restates this.

Wrong Answers:
(A): Out of Scope. The author doesn't describe a paradox in need of resolving.
(B): Distortion. A *theory* is being discussed rather than a trend.
(C): Distortion. Though a theoretical position is summarized, there's no conclusion immediately drawn from it. Rather, the conflicting viewpoint is introduced.

Strategy Point: Be on the lookout for a classic MCAT passage structure introducing a traditional view and a new view that contrasts with the former. Identifying this pattern can make mapping much easier.

PASSAGE IX

Topic and Scope: discusses the question of whether women should be represented as their own political group.

Mapping the Passage:
¶s 1-3 provide the author's definition of a legitimate political interest group.

¶4 cites research supporting the idea that women as a group fit this definition. The author provides evidence on the amount of housework and childcare.

¶5 argues that despite these differences, women may not be generally conscious of them and then goes on to cites further evidence in support the idea fit the definition of a political interest group.

Questions:
55. A Look for an answer choice that runs counter to the author's general argument or to a specific point made. (A) directly contradicts the author's point in ¶4 that the amount of housework and child care performed by women is about the same as it was at the turn of the century.

Wrong Answers:
(B): Opposite. This follows from the author's argument at the end of the passage that women are not significantly more feminist than men.
(C): Opposite. The author makes this point in ¶s 4 and 5 when describing issues particularly relevant to women.
(D): Opposite. This is implicit in the author's reference to fertility in ¶5.

56. D Go back to ¶s 1 and 2, where the author discusses the criteria for representable interests. The author implies in ¶1 that groups with representable interests "share a particular viewpoint on the solution to political problems." (D) paraphrases this.

Wrong Answers:
(A): Opposite. The author states in ¶1 that the problems *don't* need to be "exclusively those of the specified interest group."
(B): Opposite. The end of ¶3 states that a legitimate political group doesn't need to have a view "that differs substantially from answers articulated by others."
(C): Distortion. The author distinguishes between individual and group representation in the first sentence, but doesn't suggest that members of a group can't be represented individually.

57. A The author discusses differences between men and women in ¶s 3-5, so focus your search there. The author suggests that notwithstanding all the differences between men and women, there's no evidence that "men and women as groups now disagree on policy issues in which women might have a special interest." (A) follows logically from this.

Wrong Answers:
(B): Distortion. While the author argues in ¶5 that differences in child care are being reinforced, there's no indication that they're doing so in such a way that gives more control to men.

(C): Opposite. The author argues in ¶5 that women aren't particularly aware of their differences with men.
(D): Distortion. The author suggests that men and women aren't that aware of the differences, but this doesn't imply that men are unwilling to do so.

58. B Where does the author mention the year 1900? Though it's not specifically stated, author mentions the turn of the century in ¶4. Review the context: evidence shows that women spend about the same amount of time working around the house as they did around 1900. (B) matches up.

Wrong Answers:
(A): Distortion. This distorts the point made in the first sentence. There's no point of comparison on this point with the turn of the century.
(C): Out of Scope. This is never mentioned in the context of the turn of the century.
(D): Out of Scope. Another choice that has no relation to the turn of the century.

59. D Predict by reviewing the author's purpose in writing the passage. The author wants to discuss whether women constitute a politically representative group; (D) summarizes this.

Wrong Answers:
(A): Out of Scope. The author only discusses history in passing, and only to support arguments in favor of the main focus: political representation for women.
(B): Distortion. Though the author alludes to the changing status of women in ¶5, it's again less a concern than the appropriateness of political representation.
(C): Out of Scope. The author never mentions opposing views.

60. A Most of the support that the author provides is in the form of evidence listed in ¶s 3-5; keep this in mind when evaluating the answer choices. Socioeconomic position is discussed in ¶5. The author suggests that the socioeconomic status of women and men is different, and provides a list of evidence supporting this at the beginning of the paragraph.

Wrong Answers:
(B): Opposite. This contradicts the author's suggestion in ¶5 that women and men have few differences in their degree of feminism.
(C): Opposite. The author argues in ¶3 that it's not necessary that the members of an interest group be "consciously allied."
(D): Out of Scope. The author never suggests that a lack of education is getting in the way of voicing concerns.

Verbal Reasoning Test Eight

Time—85 minutes
Question 1–60

DIRECTIONS: Each of the passages in this test is followed by a set of questions based on the passage's content. After reading each passage, decide on the one best response to each question and mark it on your answer sheet. If you are unsure of an answer, eliminate the choices you know are wrong and choose from the remaining choices. You may refer to the passages while answering the questions.

Passage I (Questions 1–7)

Before there were books, before, even, there was the written word in civilization, there must surely have been stories told. Relating stories to one another is a unique way that we, as humans, communicate thoughts,
5 needs, desires, and instruction. Whether it be the true story of what happened on the way to the well yesterday—a story meant to instruct about the latest water situations—or a dramatic retelling of a long-ago battle—a cautionary tale meant to warn against unnecessary war-
10 fare—stories have the unique ability to bring home information and instruct in a way a mere recitation of the facts cannot.

The Tale, the Parable, and the Fable are all common and popular modes of conveying instruction—each
15 being distinguished by its own special characteristics. The true Fable, if it rises to its high requirements, ever aims at one great end and purpose: the representation of human motive, and the improvement of human conduct, and yet it so conceals its design under the disguise of
20 fictitious characters, by clothing with speech the animals of the field, the birds of the air, the trees of the wood, or the beasts of the forest, that the reader receives the advice without perceiving the presence of the adviser. Thus the superiority of the counselor, which
25 often renders counsel unpalatable, is kept out of view, and the lesson comes with the greater acceptance when the reader is led, unconsciously to himself, to have his sympathies enlisted on behalf of what is pure, honorable, and praiseworthy, and to have his
30 indignation excited against what is low, ignoble, and unworthy.

The true fabulist, therefore, is charged with a most important function. He is neither a narrator, nor an allegorist, he is a great teacher, a corrector of morals, a cen-
35 sor of vice, and a commender of virtue. In this consists the superiority of the Fable over the Tale or the Parable. The fabulist is to create a laugh, but yet, under a merry guise, to convey instruction. Phaedrus, the great imitator of Aesop, plainly indicates this double purpose to be
40 the true office of the writer of fables.

The Fable partly agrees with, and partly differs from the Tale and the Parable. It will contain, like the Tale, a short but real narrative; it will seek, like the Parable, to convey a hidden meaning, not so much by
45 the use of language, as by the skillful introduction of fictitious characters; and yet unlike to either Tale or Parable, it will ever keep in view, as its high prerogative, and inseparable attribute, the great purpose of instruction, and will necessarily seek to inculcate some
50 moral maxim, social duty, or political truth.

The Tale consists simply of the narration of a story either founded on facts, or created solely by the imagination, and not necessarily associated with the teaching of any moral lesson. The Parable is the designed use
55 of language purposely intended to convey a hidden and secret meaning other than that contained in the words themselves; and which may or may not bear a special reference to the hearer, or reader.

---

1. According to various points made within the passage, the author would agree with all of the following EXCEPT:

   A. instruction can be communicated successfully through more than one type of narrative construct.
   B. the use of rhetorical devices is incompatible with the didactic purpose of narrative writing.
   C. education is more effective when a reader arrives independently at an understanding of the intended lesson.
   D. humor in fables can be a useful educational device.

GO TO THE NEXT PAGE.

KAPLAN

2. The passage suggests that the fable is superior to the parable and the tale for none of the following reasons EXCEPT:

   I. the fable contains a moral lesson within its narrative.
   II. the parable's message may be too enigmatic for a reader to comprehend.
   III. the tale is a chronicle of recent historical events.

   A. I only
   B. I and II
   C. II and III
   D. I, II, and III

3. The author's conclusion that the parable and tale are inferior narrative forms for conveying instruction depends on the assumption that:

   A. readers learn most successfully when an educational lesson is integrated within an entertaining narrative framework.
   B. a long and purely descriptive narrative relies too heavily on the author's creative powers of imagination.
   C. faulty historical accuracy subverts the instructional goal of the tale.
   D. most authors are not sufficiently trained in the art of persuasion to successfully communicate a moral lesson to their readers.

4. According to the passage, which of the following is NOT a requirement for a narrative text to be classified as a fable?

   A. Use of fictional characters, such as personified animals and natural objects
   B. Inclusion of social, moral, or political references relevant to contemporary readers
   C. Constant awareness of and attention to a particular instructional goal
   D. Figurative or poetic language to demonstrate the author's creative talent

5. Another fabulist, Phaedrus, is referenced by the author in paragraph three. The author brings this fabulist to the reader's attention in order to:

   A. prove the hypothesis that learned philosophers can be effective fabulists.
   B. counteract potential criticism of the author's analysis of different narrative forms.
   C. support the idea that fables provide readers with education and entertainment.
   D. illustrate Aesop's influence on his fellow writers.

6. Which of the following, if true and presented in the context of an argument, would most *weaken* the author's conclusion as to the efficacy of moral instruction through fables?

   A. Readers never perceive fictional ideas or lessons as relevant to their own lives.
   B. Most readers can identify with non-human characters.
   C. Excessive use of rhetorical language makes fabulist texts incomprehensible.
   D. Studies have shown that readers learn most successfully when they are diverted.

7. Which of the following best characterizes the claim that the fabulist is a "great teacher, a corrector of morals, a censor of vice, and a commender of virtue?"

   A. It is an analysis of the importance of the fabulist's role in society.
   B. It is a conclusion that fabulists should be honored above writers of parables or tales.
   C. It is appreciation for the fabulist's ability to multi-task.
   D. It advocates increased honor and respect for the fabulist.

GO TO THE NEXT PAGE.

Passage II (Questions 8–13)

Until the 1970s it was assumed that, despite the very large number of species that appeared during the Cambrian explosion, nearly all fit into the same rather small number of phyla that exist today. Each phylum—
5 a group of organisms with the same basic pattern of organization, such as the radial symmetry of jellyfish and other coelenterates or the segmented structure of worms and other annelids—was seen as evolutionarily stable.

10 Innumerable individual species have arisen and died out, but development and extinction were assumed to take place within existing phyla; the elimination of entire phyla was thought to be extremely rare. A diverse group of marine fossils, known collectively as the
15 Problematica, present difficulties for this interpretation. They show patterns of organization so bizarre that it is hard to fit any of them into present-day phyla. They include the banana-shaped Tullimonstrum and the spiked, spiny Hallucigenia, creatures whose very names
20 reflect the classifier's discomfort.

The "Ediacaran fauna," which respired, absorbed nutrients, and eliminated wastes directly through their external surfaces, are also included among the Problematica. Theirs was an approach taken by only a
25 few modern multicelled creatures (such as tapeworms) that are otherwise totally unlike them. Several theorists have argued that the Problematica are not just hard to classify—they are evidence that the conventional view of the Cambrian explosion is wrong. They contend that
30 the Cambrian explosion represented the simultaneous appearance of a much larger number of animal phyla than exists today. Each was a separate "experiment" in basic body design, and the Cambrian seas teemed with many different phyla, or basic body plans, each repre-
35 sented by only a few species.

Today, the number of phyla has fallen drastically, but each surviving phylum contains a much larger number of species. The Problematica, then, were not unsuccessful variants within present-day phyla; each repre-
40 sented a distinct phylum in its own right. Revisionists contend that the selection process eliminated not only particular unfavorable traits, but entire body plans and approaches to survival. The Ediacaran fauna, for example, represented a particular structural solution to the
45 basic problems of gas and fluid exchange with the environment.

This approach to body engineering was discarded at the same time as the Ediacaran fauna themselves were wiped out; given the improbability of duplicating an
50 entire body plan through chance mutation, it was unlikely that this particular approach would ever be tried again.

Revisionists and conventional theorists agree that modern marine species are products of natural selection.
55 Up until 30 years ago, the pattern of early marine animal evolution seemed to be well established. Most present-day marine animal phyla had appeared during the "Cambrian explosion," an extraordinary burgeoning of multicellular life in the warm seas of the Cambrian peri-
60 od, between 570 and 500 million years ago.

---

8. The author implies that revisionists would view efforts to classify the Problematica in present-day phyla:

   A. enthusiastically.
   B. optimistically.
   C. skeptically.
   D. with indifference.

9. The description by the author in the third paragraph of how the Ediacaran fauna carried out respiration, absorption, and excretion tends to support the view that the Ediacaran fauna:

   A. were probably not members of any present-day phylum.
   B. had physiological processes different from those of any other known organisms.
   C. could not absorb or excrete fluids.
   D. were members of the same phylum as Tullimonstrum.

10. The passage implies that in spite of what may have been the case at other points in the Earth's history, present-day phyla contain:

   A. only a few species each.
   B. species more dissimilar than many phyla in the Cambrian period.
   C. many species showing basic structural similarities.
   D. species that undergo no evolutionary change.

GO TO THE NEXT PAGE.

11. Based on the information presented in the passage, it is clear that the author mentions coelenterates and annelids in order to give examples of:

  A. phyla that died out because their body plans were not viable.
  B. the structural patterns characteristic of some modern phyla.
  C. phyla that are closely related to the Problematica.
  D. phyla that have evolved since the Cambrian period.

12. The passage implies that conventional and revisionist theorists disagree about all of the following EXCEPT:

  A. the accuracy of the conventional view of early marine evolution.
  B. the probable number of marine animal phyla during the Cambrian period.
  C. the likelihood of entire phyla becoming extinct.
  D. the applicability of the theory of natural selection to the Cambrian period.

13. According to the passage, the Problematica are difficult to classify because:

  I. some had unusual shapes.
  II. some of them functioned physiologically differently from modern organisms.
  III. they became extinct at the end of the Cambrian period.

  A. I only
  B. II only
  C. I and II only
  D. I and III only

GO TO THE NEXT PAGE.

Passage III (Questions 14-20)

Though he left us with numerous great works and, to be sure, is widely regarded as America's first internationally renown author, Washington Irving's sometimes enigmatic tendencies and techniques have left literary critiques and academics to ponder his motives more than 140 years after his death.

One such trait that raises the proverbial eyebrow of the community of readers and critiques is Irving's repeated, and varied, use of pseudonyms throughout his career. Whether it be the name Diedrich Knickerbocker that Irving took for his humorous *A History of New York from the Beginning of the World to the End of the Dutch Dynasty* or that of Geoffrey Crayon, Gentleman for his internationally acclaimed collection of short stories, *The Sketch Book*, Irving used various pseudonyms to achieve myriad effects from masking his young age to establishing a tone for his works.

One of the most well-known female writers to adopt a pen name was George Sand, born Aurore Dupin in 1804, who became one of the most prolific and admired French authors—female or male—during the nineteenth century. The true identity of George Sand did not remain a secret for long, for after 1830 the author used this name in her everyday life, and close friends commonly referred to her as "George."

Most portraits of the author as an adult are entitled simply *George Sand* and make no reference to her given name. Her son, too, adopted this new last name even though association with his famous author-mother did not bring him any obvious benefits, other than to indicate that his relationship with his mother was closer than that of his sister. Given that the name "George Sand" is radically different from Aurore Dupin's birth name, many readers have wondered how the author formulated her masculine pen name.

At least two possible answers spring to mind. The first, as indicated in Curtis Cate's biography *George Sand*, is that the idea for this pseudonym arose from a collaboration with her first lover, Jules Sandeau, with whom she co-authored several articles as well as a full-length novel entitled *Rose et Blanche*. On the advice of their publisher, the lovers signed this latter work under the name "J. Sand." Once Aurore's writing began to overshadow that of Jules, she decided to sign her solo works as "Georges Sand," which eventually became simply "George Sand." Since her own literary output was a great success in the 1830s-1850s, she quickly became known by this name, and began to use her pen-name on a daily basis.

By continuing to use the name initially assigned to collaborative writings with her lover, perhaps Aurore hoped to maintain her connection to Sandeau. Perhaps she fondly remembered their time together and wished to have a permanent reminder of their relationship. Or perhaps she simply realized that it would be much more expedient to continue to write under a name which was already familiar to her audience thanks to the joint works she and Sandeau had published.

Given that George Sand began writing under this masculine name at around the same time as she began to roam around Paris in pants and a jacket—typically male clothing—it is not hard to understand why she chose a masculine pseudonym, since, like her choice of clothes, this male identity gave her more freedom of expression, both literally and figuratively. And once she became known as a successful author under this name, there was no reason to change it. Writing under a false name allowed her to distance parts of her character—her roles as wife, mother, and lover—from the creative and literary parts that formed the basis for her role as an author. Using a male name set her apart and added to her persona as an unusual and fascinating woman. And in the end, the reason why she chose this particular pen-name is not nearly as important as the vast quantity of writing—articles, letters, novels, plays—that forms her legacy to the field of French literature.

The name could have a more symbolic meaning as well which would give more credit to the author herself. Taking each letter of "Sand" as an allusion to names, places, or people from Aurore's life, this name can be seen as a representation of Aurore's childhood and early married life. The "A" stands for "Aurore," her given first name; likewise, the "D" stands for "Dupin," her given last name, or perhaps for "Dudevant," her married name; the "N" is for "Nohant," her childhood home, which she loved, and which became a refuge for her from Paris throughout her life; and finally, the "S" maintains her link with her first lover by indicating "Sandeau." Even if George did create the name, however, she was well aware of the similarity to her lover's name, and was equally aware that many of her readers would make this connection. As an intelligent and perceptive woman, she recognized that such an association with a male author would help to validate her early writing career before she had succeeded in establishing her own reputation as a talented and publishable author.

GO TO THE NEXT PAGE.

14. The author's attitude towards the use of male pseudonyms by female authors as noted in the passage can best be described as:

    A. skeptical of the usefulness of pseudonyms.
    B. critical of the women's adoption of a male name.
    C. appreciative of female authors' efforts to be published at any cost.
    D. intrigued by the creation of a pseudonym.

15. According to the passage, the following were all possible reasons for George Sand to create a pseudonym EXCEPT:

    A. she began publishing collaborative works with Jules Sandeau.
    B. her new name reflected important parts of her life.
    C. she was not able to publish any works under her own given name.
    D. the works published under her pen name sold well.

16. With which of the following statements would the author most likely agree?

    A. Aurore Dupin should have written works under her own name once the secret of her pseudonym was revealed.
    B. By writing under a pseudonym, George Sand created for herself a new identity which allowed her to transcend the limitations of society.
    C. George Sand owed her early success to her partner, Jules Sandeau.
    D. The choice of a masculine pseudonym was restrictive for George Sand and forced her to live as a man throughout her life.

17. The author mentions Curtis Cate in order to:

    A. refute his claims about the reason for Aurore Dupin's choice of a male pseudonym.
    B. provide support for a plausible explanation of the creation of Aurore Dupin's pseudonym.
    C. advocate the reason for Aurore Dupin's pseudonym as presented in this particular biography.
    D. show that biographers do not always write accurately about their subjects.

18. According to the passage, there was widespread use of the pseudonym George Sand. Based on the points the author brings up, which of the following is NOT proof of this widespread use?

    A. Members of her family used part of her pseudonym for themselves.
    B. Aurore Dupin's lovers and close friends called her "George."
    C. Portraitists and the general public knew her predominantly by her pen name.
    D. Early book reviews of her works never referred to her given name.

19. Regardless of the facts set forth in the passage, the author implies that the second possible reason for George Sand's pen name is:

    A. more appealing since it demonstrates the author's creativity and independence.
    B. equally plausible as the first reason even though it has no relevance to the writer's family.
    C. too sentimental for such a rational and innovative writer.
    D. based on reading she did during her childhood and early married life.

20. According to information put forth by the author within the confines of the passage, George Sand's male pen name and her choice of clothing are related because:

    A. both acknowledge her strong masculine side.
    B. both provide evidence of her androgyny.
    C. both freed her from stereotypical female constraints.
    D. both permitted her to succeed in a patriarchal society.

GO TO THE NEXT PAGE.

Passage IV (Questions 21-26)

Five times as many workers may be needed to construct a power plant as to operate it. The numbers may be even more disproportionate for a major pipeline or dam. When the construction ends, a substantial reduction in population is virtually guaranteed. Hence, there may be no justification for providing an infrastructure necessary to maintain adequate levels of service during the construction period.

Money necessary to build water systems, schools and roads and to fund salaries and maintenance costs is mismatched by traditional taxing programs. The construction project is usually not subject to local property tax until it nears completion, which may be five years after the impact has occurred. Alternative sources of tax revenue cannot begin to cover the cost of providing the necessary services. Even if some governments have money, they may not be the right governments. Some entities may suffer the impact of development without being able to tax it. For example, a development may be located in the county just outside the limits of an incorporated city. The county will be entitled to tax the property while the city may receive most of the project population and demand for services.

The 1960s and 1970s witnessed a new boomtown era in the West. The typical contemporary boomtown is fueled by a quest for energy in the form of a fossil-fueled electric generating plant, a hydroelectric dam or a new mine. The energy project is typically located near a small community or is forced to start a community from scratch. Often, the boomtown is poorly planned and under-financed. Longtime residents find their community changed for the worse and newcomers find the town an undesirable place to live.

The boomtown is characterized by inadequate public services, undesirable labor conditions, confusion in community structure, and deterioration of the quality of life arising from rapid population growth due to a major economic stimulus. Accelerated growth is the most distinguishing characteristic of a boomtown.

Studies have shown that large-scale development in sparsely populated areas causes major social problems. Housing, street and water systems construction, school development and police and fire protection lag far behind population growth. Rent and property tax increases join with a rise in the general cost of living to harm persons on fixed incomes. Education in the community may suffer. One result of boomtown living is higher incidence of divorce, depression, alcoholism and attempted suicide. Until recently, planners have ignored or understated such problems. While the boomtown promotes an "us against them" mentality — the old timers versus persons brought to the community by the boom — the fact remains that all parties suffer. Newcomers may blame old-timers for a lack of support just as old-timers may blame them for a deterioration of community life. Consequences of the boomtown also harm the project developer. The undesirable community results in poor worker productivity and frequent worker turnover, factors that delay construction and push projects over budget. Problems of rapid growth in some boomtowns are compounded by the fact that most of the population disappears with the completion of project construction.

---

21. It can be inferred from the passage that which of the following are possible ways in which a boomtown is affected by poor planning and under-financing?

    I.   Unsatisfactory labor conditions
    II. Inadequate police protection
    III. Poor community relations

    A. II only
    B. I and III only
    C. II and III only
    D. I, II, and III

22. The passage suggests that there is often a lack of services associated with boomtowns. The author claims that all of the following are possible causal factors for the lack of services associated with a boomtown EXCEPT:

    A. the expected loss of a substantial number of residents after the completion of a project.
    B. lack of support from long-time residents.
    C. the location of an energy project just outside the limits of an incorporated city.
    D. the time lag between the beginning of project construction and the onset of tax payments for it.

GO TO THE NEXT PAGE.

23. Based on information provided in the passage, improved public services in boomtowns could result from which of the following?

    A. Establishment of an adequate infrastructure during project construction

    B. Increased support by long-time residents

    C. Better enforcement of tax programs

    D. Limiting services to the anticipated levels necessary for towns' long-term needs

24. The tone of the author's discussion of traditional taxing programs in regard to boomtowns can best be described as:

    A. outraged.

    B. concerned.

    C. disbelieving.

    D. complacent.

25. The author would be most likely to agree with which of the following statements concerning community life in a boomtown?

    A. Old-timers suffer the most from the new developments that occur because of energy project construction.

    B. A smaller number of boomtown residents would suffer from depression or alcoholism if planners did not understate such problems.

    C. Project developers would experience less worker turnover if they acknowledged the complaints of long-time residents.

    D. An "us against them" mentality is unproductive because all residents suffer from a boomtown's failings.

26. Consider the fifth paragraph independent from the passage. Which of the following best describes the organization of that paragraph?

    A. A finding is cited and then discussed.

    B. A prediction is made but then qualified.

    C. A point of view is set forth and then justified.

    D. A proposal is presented and then dismissed.

GO TO THE NEXT PAGE.

Passage V (Questions 27-32)

In general, the impossible must be justified by reference to artistic requirements, or to the higher reality, or to received opinion. With respect to the requirements of art, a probable impossibility is to be preferred to a thing improbable and yet possible. And by extrapolation, it goes without saying that the improbable impossibility makes for a not too enticing option while the probable possibility will not even be discussed here as it, by its very nature, tends towards the mundane.

The poet being an imitator, like a painter or any other artist, must of necessity imitate one of three objects—things as they were or are, in the past—be it ancient or near—and in the present—as he observes those things around him or those things that are observed by others contemporary to him; things as they are said or thought to be, be they products of philosophical discourse, a study in divinity, or the mythos of a people; or things as they ought to be as often expressed in laments for the state of affairs in a society. The vehicle of expression is language—either current terms or, it may be, rare words or metaphors. There are also many modifications of language which we concede to the poets. Add to this that the standard of correctness is not the same in poetry and politics, any more than in poetry and any other art.

Within the art of poetry itself there are two kinds of faults—those which touch its essence, and those which are of the cause of a lack of advertence. If a poet has chosen to imitate something, but has fallen short through want of capacity, the error is inherent in the poetry. But if the failure is due to a wrong choice—if he has represented a horse as throwing out both his off legs at once, or introduces technical inaccuracies in medicine, for example, or in any other art—the error is not essential to the poetry. These are the points of view from which we should consider and answer the objections raised by the critics.

As to matters which concern the poet's own art. If he describes the impossible, he is guilty of an error; but the error may be justified, if the end of the art be thereby attained—if, that is, the effect of this or any other part of the poem is thus rendered more striking. If, however, the end might have been as well, or better, attained without violating the special rules of the poetic art, the error is not justified, for every kind of error should, if possible, be avoided. Again, does the error touch the essentials of the poetic art, or some accident of it? For example, not to know that a hind has no horns is a less serious matter than to paint it inartistically.

Further, if it be objected that the description is not true to fact, the poet may perhaps reply—"But the objects are as they ought to be": just as Sophocles said that he drew men as they ought to be; Euripides, as they are. In this way the objection may be met. If, however, the representation is of neither kind, the poet may answer—"This is how men say the thing is." This applies to tales about the gods. It may well be that these stories are not higher than fact nor yet true to fact. But anyhow, "this is what is said." Again, a description may be no better than the fact.

---

27. Assuming that the poet's artistic goals are achieved, the passage implies that which of the following would NOT be an example of a justifiable error?

   A. Describing a lioness as a hunter in a metaphor for the behavior of predatory government officials
   B. Using awkward language to create an analogy between a ruler's hand as a symbol of authority and a city's capitol as a symbol of power
   C. Creating anachronistic errors by mentioning inappropriate historical or contemporary events
   D. Representing human characters as improbably courageous or strong

28. The author brings up the ancient Greek poets Sophocles and Euripides to make a point within the passage. According to the information cited in the passage, they differ from each other because:

   A. Euripides' characters provide ideal models of human behavior.
   B. Sophocles portrays people as common public opinion supposed them to be.
   C. the characters in Sophocles' work are meant to inspire improved human behavior and actions.
   D. humans are unfavorably described by Euripides in order to show detrimental behavior to avoid.

GO TO THE NEXT PAGE.

29. The author's argument that the poet is "an imitator, like a painter or any other artist" suggests that the author would be most likely to agree with which of the following statements?

    A. Different types of creative or aesthetic talent have different means of representation.
    B. Creating text and chiseling marble are similar forms of representation.
    C. The visual arts are superior to the rhetorical arts.
    D. The forms of imitation found in poetry are inefficient.

30. Which of the following is NOT discussed in the passage?

    A. Examples of appropriate linguistic and rhetorical devices that can be effectively used by a poet
    B. The difference between possibility and probability as represented in art
    C. Reasons a poet can give to justify the description of what might be considered an impossible situation
    D. The manner in which a poet expresses ideas or communicates an aesthetic

31. Without the author present, the greater purpose for writing this passage can only be speculated upon. The author's reason for writing this passage would most likely be to:

    A. persuade readers that poets can be useful chroniclers of historical events.
    B. describe potential errors in poetry and conditions under which they are justified.
    C. analyze the three important forms of artistic imitation utilized by poets.
    D. justify the most common types of errors committed by poets.

32. According to the passage, the impossible can be an acceptable element of poetry because:

    A. all other artistic imitations are representations of reality that are impossible to believe.
    B. readers believe improbable events when they are described in poetic language.
    C. an improbable possibility is preferable to an event that is impossible yet probable.
    D. the poet's use of language satisfies the necessary artistic requirements.

GO TO THE NEXT PAGE.

Passage VI (Questions 33–40)

For better or for worse, race places a very large part in people's perception of others in the world and in their own society. The notion of one's own race often influ-
5 ences the actions and interests of an individual (either towards or away from activities typically associated with a group) and, in many cases, the perception of another individual's race influences the perceiver's actions toward that individual. Races are inaccurate as biological categories. The existence of racism, and the
10 genesis of our racial taxonomies themselves in the history of colonialism and slavery, argue for abandoning racial categories altogether.

Few would deny the importance of racial categories in our everyday lives, nor the social problems and con-
15 flict race has caused. Less well known are the scientific problems with race: racial categories cannot be reconciled with what scientists know about human biological diversity. Biological races are branches of a species that have been unable to reproduce with each other for a
20 significant period of time. Their separation may be due to geographic or other barriers, but anatomically, members of different races can interbreed, since they are of the same species.

Breeds of domesticated dogs are an example of
25 races cultivated by humans. In contrast, human groups have interbred for our entire history as a species, and none have been isolated long enough to be considered true races. The American racial classification system is no more scientifically valid than are other racial tax-
30 onomies, local conceptions of race affirmed in other societies or countries. Racial taxonomies in different countries are not biological races, but rather what anthropologist Charles Wagley calls "social races."

Racial classification presupposes that people with
35 certain phenotypes share a common recent ancestry that others do not share. However, physical traits are not a reliable indicator of recent shared descent. There are no sharp borders between human groups, as there are between so-called races, because physical traits change
40 gradually. Anatomical features in human populations represent adaptations to evolutionary forces: skin color is an adaptation to latitude, facial shape to climate or altitude, and blood type to endemic diseases. Any particular trait is shared by groups of people of varied her-
45 itages, people who adapted to similar conditions in different parts of the world. Since different features do not vary together, no assortment of traits can accurately delineate any group as a true race.

If race were biological, different societies would
50 understand race in similar ways. In fact, societies use widely varying criteria to determine race. Nor are these criteria all internally consistent. Although most Americans believe that appearance or genetics form the basis of race, in the United States, a person's race, legal-
55 ly, is determined by his ancestry, the race of his parents. Further, some state laws, legacies of slavery, place biracial individuals into the race of the minority parent, without regard to chromosomes or physical appearance. In Brazil, on the other hand, people do not consider
60 ancestry when identifying a person's race, and there exist many more racial categories than in the US. Race in Brazil derives solely from appearance. One's race can change from day to day, and may differ from the race of one's family, including that of full siblings. The
65 racial taxonomies in Brazil and the United States differ, but neither one is based on scientific principles.

---

33. According to the passage, there are various problems with a biological notion of race. As articulated by the author, they include all of the following EXCEPT:

   A. different cultures have different systems for classifying races.
   B. phenotypic differences among human groups do not exist.
   C. shared anatomical features do not accurately reflect shared ancestry.
   D. no human group has ever been secluded for long enough to form a biological race.

34. The passage cites Brazil as a country in which racial definitions have a meaning that might not otherwise be readily apparent. The author suggests that a person who is Brazilian might change his race by:

   A. altering his birth certificate.
   B. marrying a person of a different race.
   C. having his DNA tested.
   D. getting a sun tan.

GO TO THE NEXT PAGE.

35. The overall purpose of this passage is to:

    A. present a hypothesis that may explain a recent discovery.

    B. compare and contrast two methods of classification.

    C. criticize the basis of a popular belief.

    D. describe worldwide variations in a cultural phenomenon.

36. The author of this passage would be most likely to agree with which of the following statements about abandoning racial classification?

    A. We can improve our society through conscious and concerted effort.

    B. The United States' racial classification system should be replaced with that of Brazil.

    C. It would be disastrous for scientists to strip people of their valued beliefs.

    D. All beliefs that are not scientifically sound should be abandoned.

37. The passage discusses several problems with the biological notion of race. Which of the following illustrates one of these problems?

    A. A person of European ancestry is called "white," even though her skin is really not white, but a shade of pinkish-beige.

    B. A person from New Guinea might be mistaken for African American due to physical features, although New Guinea is in Asia and not in Africa.

    C. A person of African origin is descended from the original line of humanity, since human beings first evolved in Africa.

    D. A person of mixed racial ancestry in the USA would be classified based solely on his appearance, although it does not reflect his genetic make-up.

38. If the information presented by the author in the passage is correct, then which of the following conclusions can be correctly drawn from that information?

    A. Racial classifications in different parts of the world are gradually becoming more and more similar.

    B. Racial classifications in different parts of the world are gradually becoming more and more distinct.

    C. Racial classifications in different parts of the world may be related to historical events in those regions.

    D. Racial classifications once represented human diversity accurately, but due to migrations in the past 500 years, they are no longer valid.

39. If it were true that humans had formed biological races, which of the following would also be true?

    A. Members of two races would not be able to produce viable offspring.

    B. There would be more racial groups than are currently recognized.

    C. An individual's chromosomal makeup, ancestry and appearance would all coincide in identifying that person's race.

    D. Members of each race would have had no contact with members of other races for a very long period in their past.

40. The author presents the example of racial classification in the United States in the passage most probably in order to show that:

    A. racial taxonomies may be logically inconsistent and widely misunderstood.

    B. the system of racial classification in North America is grounded in scientific research.

    C. individuals should be allowed to choose and to change their own racial identification.

    D. racial classifications are most accurate when they take all factors (appearance, ancestry, and DNA) into account.

GO TO THE NEXT PAGE.

Passage VII (Questions 41–46)

Gautier was indeed a poet and a strongly representative one—a French poet in his limitations even more than in his gifts; and he remains an interesting example of the manner in which, even when the former are surprisingly
5 great, a happy application of the latter may produce the most delightful works. Completeness on his own scale is to our mind the idea he most instantly suggests. Such as his finished task now presents him, he is almost sole of his kind. He has had imitators who have imitated every-
10 thing but his spontaneity and his temper; and as they have therefore failed to equal him we doubt whether the literature of our day presents a genius so naturally perfect. We say this with no desire to transfer Gautier to a higher pedestal than he has fairly earned—a poor ser-
15 vice, for the pedestal sometimes sadly dwarfs the figure. His great merit was that he understood himself so perfectly and handled himself so skillfully. Even more than Alfred de Musset (with whom the speech had a shade of mock-modesty) he might have said that, if his glass was
20 not large, as least it was all his own glass.

There are a host of reasons why we should not compare Gautier with such a poet as Browning; and yet there are several why we should. If we do so, with all proper reservations, we may wonder whether we are the richer,
25 or, at all events, the better entertained, as a poet's readers should before all things be, by the clear, undiluted strain of Gautier's minor key, or by the vast, grossly commingled volume of utterance. It is idle at all times to point a moral. But if there are sermons in stones, there are profitable
30 reflections to be made even on Théophile Gautier; notably this one—that a man's supreme use in the world is to master his intellectual instrument and play it in perfection.

He brought to his task a sort of pagan bonhomie which makes most of the descriptive and pictorial poets
35 seem, by contrast, a group of shivering ascetics or muddled metaphysicians. He excels them by his magnificent good temper and the unquestioning serenity of his enjoyment of the great spectacle of nature and art. His world was all material, and its outlying darkness hardly
40 more suggestive, morally, than a velvet canopy studded with silver nails. To close his eyes and turn his back on it must have seemed to him the end of all things; death, for him, must have been as the sullen dropping of a stone into a well. His observation was so penetrating
45 and his descriptive instinct so unerring, that one might have fancied grave nature, in a fit of coquetry, or tired of receiving but half-justice, had determined to construct a genius with senses of a finer strain than the mass of human family.

41. In the passage, the author suggests that the French poet Théophile Gautier's talents included all of the following EXCEPT:

   A. an innovative and unique artistic view of nature.
   B. the ability to quickly and immediately compose poetry.
   C. extensive training in rhetorical and literary techniques.
   D. a strong understanding of his world and himself.

42. For what purpose can it reasonably be concluded does the author reference other writers in this passage, including Musset and Browning?

   A. To prove that Gautier, as a poet, was unique among his contemporaries
   B. To show that Gautier's poetry was representative of French lyricism at the time
   C. To criticize Gautier's limited talent and creativity
   D. To refute the idea that Gautier's colleagues could easily imitate his style

43. Which of the following, if true, would most *weaken* the author's conclusion that Gautier's artistic gifts more than compensated for his creative limitations?

   A. Gautier's poems are still studied more frequently than any of his prose writing.
   B. Close study of Gautier's life has revealed that he frequently collaborated with other writers.
   C. During the early 1800s, Gautier's primary success came from his critical reviews of art.
   D. Numerous later writers acknowledged Gautier's work as an influence on their writing.

44. As used in the passage, the words "pagan bonhomie" (in the first sentence of the last paragraph) refer to:

   A. Gautier's extravagant and debauched lifestyle as revealed through his poetry.
   B. the unique descriptions of nature that are essential to Gautier's work.
   C. Gautier's lack of modesty and his desire for lasting notoriety.
   D. a particular attitude towards the world that set Gautier apart from his contemporaries.

GO TO THE NEXT PAGE.

45. Without regard for what other critics of the genre might purport, according to the passage, what is the primary reaction a reader should have to poetry?

    A. Poetry should produce a strong emotional response within the reader.

    B. A reader should enjoy and be entertained by poetry.

    C. Readers should learn a moral, social, or political lesson from poetry.

    D. Poetry should provide readers with ideas that are relevant to their own lives.

46. The author makes a few noteworthy remarks about Gautier's attitude towards death. This attitude would most support which of the following conclusions?

    A. None of Gautier's literary works focused on human frailty.

    B. Gautier believed that people are inherently linked to the divine.

    C. The fleeting passage of time was a common poetic theme that Gautier neglected.

    D. In his poetry, Gautier often focused on the vibrancy of human and natural life.

GO TO THE NEXT PAGE.

Passage VIII (Questions 47-53)

The study of the analog position of mental representation has many fascinating branches which help illuminate the inner workings of our minds and how we perceive images in our mind's eye. This theory points to the link between the time is takes to solve mental problems and their complexity.

In a now-famous study, Stephen Kosslyn asked subjects to imagine an animal, such as a rabbit, next to either an elephant or a fly. When the image was formed, Kosslyn would ask whether or not the target animal had a particular attribute. For example, Kosslyn might say, "elephant, rabbit," and then "leg." He found that it took subjects longer to answer when the target animal was next to the large animal than when it was next to the small animal. Kosslyn interpreted this to mean that subjects had to zoom in on the image to detect the particular feature. Just as one has difficulty seeing details on small objects, so the subjects could not simply mentally "see" details on the smaller object in their mental image.

Second, Kosslyn and colleagues demonstrated that the time it takes to scan between two points depends on the distance between the two points [in a memorized image]. In one experiment, subjects memorized an array of letters separated by different distances. Kosslyn found that the farther apart the letters were from each other, the longer it took to answer questions about one of the letters. One of the principal hypotheses of the analog position of mental representation, which is the idea that mental processing requires one to move sequentially through all intervening steps to solve a problem, is that mental images have regular properties. In a similar experiment, Kosslyn had subjects memorize pictures of objects like a plane or a motorboat. Then he had them focus on one part of the object (e.g., the motor) and move to another (e.g., the anchor).

He found that the time it took to determine whether the second part was present depended on the distance between the two parts in the memorized picture. In one of his more famous experiments of this type, Kosslyn and colleagues had subjects memorize the location of various objects (such as a hut or a tree) on a fictional map. Subjects were then told to focus on one object and then scan the image to determine whether another object was or was not on the map. The amount of time it took to locate objects that were present on the memorized map was linearly related to the distance between the objects.

Using a completely different paradigm, Shepard and Feng tested the amount of time that it would take for subjects to specify whether two arrows on unfolded blocks matched up. They found a linear relationship between the number of folds between the arrows and the time it took to make this judgment, suggesting that subjects went through a discrete series of organized steps in order to solve this problem.

The final type of experiment showing that mental images have regular properties is perhaps the most famous: mental rotation experiments. In 1971, Shepard and Metzler tested subjects' abilities to make complex figure comparisons. They presented subjects with a three dimensional "standard" figure and a comparison figure which was either identical to the standard figure, or its mirror image; the comparison stimulus was rotated, either clockwise or into the third dimension. Shepard and Metzler found that the time needed to judge whether the comparison stimulus was identical or a mirror image depended directly on the size of the angle between the target orientation and the orientation of the standard.

---

47. According to the way it is presented by the author in the passage, the analog position of mental representation argues that:

   A. mental processing requires one to go sequentially through all intervening steps to solve a problem.
   B. one typically uses short cuts to solve mental problems.
   C. it should take longer to solve more complex problems.
   D. most problems are not able to be solved by people without help.

48. According to the scanning experiments mentioned in the passage, it should take longer to scan longer distances because the subjects:

   A. believe that there is no relationship between distance and time.
   B. have to keep time with a metronome set up by the experimenter.
   C. form a mental picture of the scene and go through all the intervening positions in the picture.
   D. are tricked by the experimenter into taking a longer time.

GO TO THE NEXT PAGE.

49. Which of the following conclusions not presented in the passage might be an alternate explanation for the map experiments described by the author?

    A. Subjects forget where the objects are.
    B. Subjects know that it should take longer to move longer distances and so answer accordingly.
    C. Subjects consult actual maps for the distances and this takes them more time the greater the distance.
    D. It takes subjects longer to start scanning longer distances and so it ultimately takes them longer to finish.

50. According to the passage, why does Kosslyn say it takes longer to identify attributes of objects when they are next to a bigger object than when they are next to a smaller object?

    A. Because one scans objects in order of size from larger to smaller
    B. Because the larger object covers the smaller object and one must move it out of the way
    C. Because large and small objects have all the same features and so interfere with each other
    D. Because one must zoom into see parts of the smaller object when it is next to a larger object

51. If it were the case that subjects simply respond as the experimenters encourage them to do, based on information in the passage one would expect:

    A. that the pattern of results would be just as they are.
    B. that there would be a non-linear relationship between distance and reaction time.
    C. that the relationship between distance and reaction time is constant.
    D. that one could create any relationship between distance and reaction time.

52. Based on the passage, which of the following patterns of results would contradict the analog position?

    I. It takes longer to scan longer distances.
    II. There is no relationship between scanning time and distance.
    III. It takes less time to scan longer distances.

    A. I only
    B. II and III
    C. I and III
    D. I, II, and III

53. Other researchers have found that subjects can alter the amount of time it takes to scan images based on the instructions they are given. What implications does this have for the analog view?

    A. It implies that the analog view is more likely to be correct since subjects are scanning as they believe they should.
    B. It implies that the analog view is more likely to be correct since subjects do not have control over the rate at which they scan.
    C. It implies that the analog view is less likely to be correct because subjects might be scanning as they believe they should.
    D. It implies that the analog view is more likely to be correct since subjects can control the rate at which they scan.

GO TO THE NEXT PAGE.

Passage IX (Questions 54-60)

Never accept anything as true that you do not clearly know to be so; that is, carefully avoid jumping to conclusions, and include nothing in judgments, other than what presents itself so clearly and distinctly to the
5 spirit that you would never have any occasion to doubt it. Then, divide each of the difficulties being examined into as many parts as can be created and would be required to better resolve them. Order your thoughts, by starting with the simplest ideas, which are the easiest to
10 comprehend, to advance little by little, by degrees, up to the most complex ideas, even believing that an order exists among those which do not naturally follow one another. And last, always make deductions so complete, and reviews so general, so as to be assured of omitting
15 nothing.

When I was younger, I had studied a bit—in the field of philosophy, logic, and in the field of math, geometric analysis and algebra—the three arts or sciences that seemed as though they should contribute something
20 to my methodological approach.

But while examining these fields, I noticed that, in logic, syllogisms and the bulk of other logical theorems serve only to explain to others the things that one already knows, or even to speak without judgment of
25 things that one doesn't know, rather than to teach others anything; and, although logic contains, in effect, many true and just precepts, there are yet among these so many others mixed in, which are superfluous or refutable, that it is almost sickening to separate one from
30 the other.

As for geometric analysis and modern algebra, in addition to the fact that they don't treat anything except abstract ideas, which seem to be of no use whatsoever, geometry is always so restricted to the consideration of
35 figures that it can't stretch the intellect without exhausting the imagination; and algebra subjects one to certain rules and numbers, so that it has become a confused and obscure art that troubles the spirit rather than a science that cultivates it.

40 All of this made me think that it was necessary to look for some other methodological approach which, comprising the advantages of these three, was at the same time exempt from their defaults. And, just as the multitude of laws often provides rationalization for vice,
45 such that any State is better ruled if, having but a few vices, it closely monitors them, thus likewise, instead of following the great number of precepts which compose logic, I thought that I would have enough with the four

preceding, as long as I made a firm and constant resolu-
50 tion never—not even once—to neglect my adherence to them.

---

54. According to the passage, the author gave up the study of logic. He did so for all of the following reasons EXCEPT:

  A. he did not gain sufficient knowledge to impart his learning to others.

  B. he was unable to separate valid logical theories from those which seemed invalid.

  C. he could not understand the rational methodology upon which logic is based.

  D. he did not learn anything new from his philosophical and analytical studies.

55. As presented within the context of the passage, the first precept of the author's methodological approach is based on the assumption that:

  A. true comprehension depends primarily on rational comprehension and analysis.

  B. theories can be accepted as true if they are perceived intellectually and instinctively.

  C. relying solely on intellectual prowess is a valid way of determining the validity of a theory.

  D. scholars must study philosophy and mathematics in order to understand abstract ideas.

GO TO THE NEXT PAGE.

56. Which of the following best expresses the author's attitude towards the existence of vice in a State?

   A. National vices should be considered equivalent to deductive flaws in logic.

   B. Vices can be justified or excused through legal channels.

   C. An effective government must eradicate all vices in its rulers and citizens.

   D. Certain vices may be unavoidable, but can be kept under control through careful observation.

57. According to the passage, which of the following statements are true about geometry?

   I. Geometric analysis is not useful for a logical methodology.

   II. Geometry focuses too narrowly on shapes and lines.

   III. Geometry is largely visual, so comprehension requires both intellect and imagination.

   A. II only

   B. I and II

   C. I, II, and III

   D. III only

58. The author takes time in the passage to describe his study of philosophy and mathematics in an effort to:

   A. justify his precepts as being validly based on personal knowledge and experience.

   B. demonstrate the relationship between logic, geometry, and algebra.

   C. provide a scholarly model for his readers so that they can expand their study of logic.

   D. refute prior logicians' theories and indicate their flaws.

59. The author would be LEAST likely to agree with which of the following statements?

   A. Logic is an inappropriate field of research for young scholars.

   B. A scholar should always treat the subject of his or her study in its entirety.

   C. Orderly study is based on the principle that a whole is the sum of its parts.

   D. Teaching is one of the motivations for studying abstract ideas and theories.

60. Based on the point of view taken by the author in the passage, the author's primary concern in developing his method is:

   A. objective examination of prior methodologies.

   B. thorough grounding in a variety of academic disciplines.

   C. consistent adherence to his principles.

   D. extensive research in the natural sciences.

STOP. If you finish before time is called, check your work. You may go back to any question in this test booklet.

ANSWER KEY
VERBAL REASONING TEST 8

1. B	16. B	31. B	46. D
2. B	17. B	32. D	47. A
3. A	18. D	33. B	48. C
4. D	19. A	34. D	49. B
5. C	20. C	35. C	50. D
6. A	21. D	36. A	51. D
7. C	22. B	37. B	52. B
8. C	23. A	38. C	53. C
9. A	24. B	39. D	54. C
10. C	25. D	40. A	55. B
11. B	26. A	41. C	56. D
12. D	27. B	42. A	57. B
13. C	28. C	43. B	58. A
14. D	29. B	44. D	59. B
15. C	30. A	45. B	60. C

EXPLANATIONS

PASSAGE I

Topic and Scope:
The instructional purpose and narrative techniques of the fable.

Mapping the Passage:
¶1 introduces the importance of stories in conveying information.
¶2 argues that the fable communicates a moral in "disguise," hiding the instructor.
¶3 argues that those who tell fables ("fabulists") have an important function and must both instruct and entertain.
¶s4 and 5 compares the fable to the tale and the parable. .

Questions:
1. B Since there's no information in the question to narrow your options, predict the author's overall view. The structure of the fable allows a moral to be communicated effectively. Eliminating the answer choices that the author *does* agree with leaves you with (B). The author must disagree with (B); he argues in ¶2 that it's precisely the use of rhetorical devices that makes the fable able to effectively convey instruction.

Wrong Answers:
(A): Opposite. The first sentence of ¶2 lists three narrative types that can convey instruction.
(C): Opposite. This point is made in the second paragraph: the author believes that the fable is effective because the "superiority of the counselor...is kept out of view."
(D): Opposite. The author discusses humor in ¶3, saying that the "fabulist is to create a laugh, but yet, under a merry guise, to convey instruction." Humor is therefore part of the process of teaching.

2. B First translate the language: look for "none of the...reasons EXCEPT" means look for a reason. Where does the author talk about the superiority of the fable? ¶s 4 and 5. Evaluate RN I: The author argues that *unlike* the other two forms of narrative, the fable always keeps its moral in mind. RN I fits, eliminate (C). RN II is a bit tougher to evaluate. Can we infer that the parable's message might be too enigmatic? Yes. The Parable is "intended to convey a hidden...meaning" which "may or may not bear a special reference to the hearer" (¶5), while the fable conveys a hidden meaning for "the great purpose of instruction." The parable therefore can be too enigmatic in comparison. RN II is also correct, eliminate (C). Finally, check RN III. Even though the statement might be true, it does nothing to explain why the fable is superior, and so can be eliminated.

Wrong Answers:
(A): Opposite. As described above.
(C): Opposite. As above.
(D): Opposite. As above.

3. A An assumption question: evaluate the evidence and the conclusion carefully. The conclusion, of course, is that the other two narrative forms are inferior to the fable when it comes to teaching. What is the evidence? Essentially the whole passage. Why does the author believe that the fable is superior? Predict: its structure, and especially its humor, make the lesson easy to digest. The author must therefore assume that readers do in fact get the lesson better when it's in this framework. (A) fits.

Wrong Answers:
(B): Distortion. While a tale may rely on the author's imagination, as described in ¶5, there's no reason to believe that a tale relies *too* much on this, or that it makes the tale inferior.
(C): Distortion. As above, though a tale may or may not rely on historical accuracy, there's no relation between this and any instructional goal.
(D): Out of Scope. The author never says anything about training.

4. D What are the criteria of a fable? Either eliminate answer choices that can be found in the text or find an answer choice that is clearly *not* a quality of a fable. While three of the answer choices are details from the passage, (D) suggests that a fable's author uses figurative language to display his own talent, while the passage argues in ¶2 that the author in a fable should be invisible.

Wrong Answers:
(A): Opposite. This is mentioned at the beginning of ¶2.
(B): Opposite. This is mentioned at the end of ¶4.
(C): Opposite. This is also mentioned at the end of ¶4.

5. C A handy evaluation question that gives you not only the example, but its place in the passage. Go back to ¶3 to review. The author argues that Phaedrus

KAPLAN

"plainly indicates this double purpose to be the true office of the writer of fables." What is the double purpose? Read above: fabulists should be humorous and instructional at the same time. (C) says the same.

Wrong Answers:
(A): Out of Scope. It is irrelevant whether Phaedrus was a learned philosopher; the author's purpose is to describe the role of fabulists, not their individual characteristics.
(B): Out of Scope. The author doesn't suggest any possible criticism, and so wouldn't be responding to it.
(D): Distortion. Though Phaedrus is described as an imitator of Aesop, the author isn't concerned with comparing the two, but rather indicating why they were effective fabulists.

6. A Paraphrase the author's conclusion mentioned in the question: fables are particularly good at conveying instruction. Look for an answer choice that would attack this conclusion. (A) does this: If readers don't perceive fictional ideas as relevant to their lives, then the fable, which is fictional, would *not* be good at conveying instruction.

Wrong Answers:
(B): Opposite. This would strengthen the author's argument that the fable, which often uses non-human characters, is a useful instructional tool.
(C): Faulty Use of Detail. This is one of the properties of a parable, not a fable.
(D): Opposite. This would support the author's argument that the fable helps readers learn through humor, which is a form of diversion.

Strategy Point:
An argument can be weakened by countering the evidence, assumption, or conclusion. When a question asks you to weaken a certain part of the argument, be sure to paraphrase it before finding the weakener.

7. C A question asking you to characterize a claim will usually be an evaluation question. Why does the author make this point about fabulists in the third paragraph? Predict: the fabulist has several functions in society. Look for an answer choice that fits this. While (A) may be tempting, (C) is the only answer choice that captures the fact that the fabulist has many roles.

Wrong Answers:
(A): Distortion. Though the author believes that the fabulist has an important role, the comment isn't analyzing the role, and is more concerned with making the point that the fabulist has several roles.
(B): Distortion. Though the author believes that fables are a better means of communicating instruction, there's no indication in the passage that those who tell fables are more worthy of honor than are those who tell other sorts of tales.

(D): Distortion. As above, though the author has a high opinion of fabulists, there's no argument in the passage that they should get more respect than they are now.

PASSAGE II

Topic and Scope:
Traditional and revisionist theories on phyla in early marine evolution

Mapping the Passage:
¶s1 and 2 discuss a traditional theory of phyla evolution.
¶s2 and 3 present fossil evidence, the Problematica, that challenges the traditional view of phyla and ¶3 presents theorists who argue that the Problematica disprove the traditional view.
¶s4 and 5 present the new view's main tenet: natural selection involved not only experiments with individual traits within a phyla, but also with whole phyla.
¶6 reviews the traditional theory of phyla evolution.

Questions:
8. C If the author is implying something, you know that you'll have to deduce something not stated explicitly in the passage. Review the main point of the revisionist argument: The Problematica disprove the traditional view. What is the traditional view? That most everything can be classified according to existing phyla. What can be inferred, then, about classifying the Problematica according to existing phyla? The revisionists would think that it was fundamentally misguided. (C) is the only choice that reflects this negative view.

Wrong Answers:
(A): Opposite. Revisionists consider the Problematica phyla in their own right, so they wouldn't agree that they should be shoehorned into modern-day phyla.
(B): Opposite. As above, there's nothing in the revisionist view to support this optimistic tone.
(D): Opposite. Revisionists would actively oppose the classification mentioned in the question, and so they wouldn't express indifference.

9. A Before reading the text closely, predict based on your map. What does ¶3 present? Evidence that challenges the traditional view that everything can be classified according to presently-existing phyla. (A) rewards the strong map instantly.

Wrong Answers:
(B): Opposite. The author says that the Edicarian physiological processes took an approach "taken by only a few modern multicelled creatures," which means that these processes were not unique.
(C): Opposite. The author states explicitly in lines 21 and 22 that they *could* absorb and excrete.

(D): Distortion. Though the Tullimonstrum phylum is part of Problematica too, the author doesn't suggest that it and the Edicarian fauna are part of the same phylum.

10. C What does the author say about modern phyla? The author says in ¶1 that there is a small number of modern phyla, and in ¶4 that "the number of phyla has fallen drastically, but each surviving phylum contains a much larger number of species." This information along with the definition of a phylum in lines 5 and 6 as a group of organisms with the same basic body pattern leads to (C), which simply combines the two facts.

Wrong Answers:
(A): Opposite. There are *many* species in each phylum, as the author explicitly states.
(B): Out of Scope. The author doesn't discuss the relative similarities *within* phyla.
(D): Opposite. The first line of ¶6 contradicts this claim; both sides of the issue agree on the presence of natural selection.

11. B Where are these organisms mentioned? They're in ¶1 and so probably are used to illustrate the traditional view. A quick look at lines 7 and 8 backs this up: they're used as examples of traditional phylum stability. (B) fits the prediction that they illustrate the traditional view of modern phyla.

Wrong Answers:
(A): Opposite. Since they're examples of presently existing phyla, they can't have died out.
(C): Opposite. These are modern-day organisms, while the whole point of the Problematica species is that they were in completely different phyla that died out.
(D): Distortion. Though many species evolved in the Cambrian period, there's no suggestion that these organisms specifically evolved after the Cambrian, nor is there any reason why the author would want to provide examples in this paragraph of species that did.

12. D Evaluate the wording carefully. The two sides disagree on all the answer choices except the correct one, which means that they *agree* on the correct choice. Predict a point of agreement between the two sides. ¶6's opening line gives a big hint: The two sides agree that "modern marine species are products of natural selection." (D) jumps out quickly when the prediction is made beforehand.

Wrong Answers:
(A): Opposite. The basis of the revisionist view is that the conventional view of static phyla is wrong.
(B): Opposite. Traditionalists think that there were only a few phyla with lots of species; revisionists believe that there were many phyla, as discussed in ¶3.
(C): Opposite. Since revisionists believe that many ancient species fit into existing phyla and revisionists believe that they belonged to now-extinct phyla, the

two sides would disagree on whether phyla are likely to become extinct.

13. C Where are the Problematica discussed? Evaluate the Roman Numerals with an eye to ¶s2 and 3. Start with RN I, which appears in three choices: The author says in lines 16–17 that their patterns of organization were bizarre, and that this makes it hard to fit them into modern phyla. RN I therefore fits, eliminate (B). Evaluate RN II: The Edicarian fauna are an example of different physiological functioning, so this statement is valid also. At this point, only (C) is a viable answer choice, and there's no need to evaluate RN III. A quick look at RN III shows a statement with no support in the passage: the author doesn't discuss when the Problematica went extinct, only that they did.

Wrong Answers:
(A): Opposite. As described above.
(B): Opposite. As above.
(D): Opposite. As above.

PASSAGE III

Topic and Scope:
The origin of Aurore Dupin's pen name, George Sand

Mapping the Passage:
¶1 introduces the topic of pseudonyms and brings up the example of Washington Irving.
¶2 expands on the Irving example.
¶s3 and 4 introduce Aurore Dupin's pen name, George Sand.
¶s5 and 6 discuss one possible origin of the name: a take-off on the name of her first lover.
¶7 discusses possible reasons for Dupin's choice of a specifically male pen name.
¶8 discusses a second possible origin: each letter refers to part of Aurore Dupin's life.

Questions:
14. D In questions that ask you for the author's tone, a vertical scan can be helpful. The choices start out with "skeptical, critical, appreciative, intrigued." Which of these would best fit the author's purpose of discussing the origin of Dupin's pen name? Intrigued fits most closely with the author's descriptive function and doesn't carry the charges of the other three. Looking at the whole answer choice validates the hunch: the author spends most of the passage theorizing about how the male pen name might have come about.

Wrong Answers:
(A): Opposite. The author never suggests in the passage that the pen name wasn't useful. In fact, it's suggested in the last paragraph that it gave Dupin *more* freedom.
(B): Out of Scope. The author doesn't express any sort of negative opinion regarding Dupin's choice of names, but is rather interested in why she chose it.

(C): Distortion. Though the author suggests that the male pen name gave Dupin more freedom, there's no suggestion that female authors in *general* should do whatever it takes to be published, including taking a male name.

Strategy Point: Keeping the author's tone, positive, negative, or neutral, in mind can help you easily eliminate answer choices with positive or negative charges.

15. C A scattered detail question; look for a choice that isn't mentioned specifically in the passage or eliminate the three that are. While three of the answer choices reflect the topics of paragraphs in the passage, (C) is outside the author's scope: no attempts to publish under her given name are discussed.

Wrong Answers:
(A): Opposite. This is the theory discussed in ¶5.
(B): Opposite. This is the second theory, described in ¶8.
(D): Opposite. ¶7 mentions this advantage of a male pen name.

16. B A broad deduction question that will probably touch on the author's main points. Predict: The pen name George Sand has a variety of possible origins, and was useful for writing without the limitations of her actual place in society (a "wife, mother and lover," ¶7). (B) fits in with this latter point, most extensively described in ¶7.

Wrong Answers:
(A): Opposite. The author argues in ¶7 that "there was no reason to change" her pen name.
(C): Distortion. While the author mentions in ¶5 that Dupin's early work was in collaboration with Sandeau, there's no evidence that she owed her early success to him.
(D): Distortion. The author argues that George Sand took on certain masculine elements, which gave her *more* freedom.

17. B Where is Curtis Cate mentioned? You can find him as the author of a George Sand biography in ¶5. Since this paragraph introduces the Jules Sandeau theory, Cate is probably mentioned to introduce or to bolster this view. (B) fits with the prediction that Cate is brought up to explain a possible origin of "George Sand."

Wrong Answers:
(A): Opposite. Rather than refute his claims, the author takes them seriously as a one potentially valid explanation.
(C): Distortion. Even though the author presents the theory as possibly true, the author doesn't go so far as to advocate this theory as the correct answer.

(D): Out of Scope. The author is concerned with presenting a theory about Dupin's pen name, not with criticizing Cate in any way.

Strategy Point:
When two or more theories or explanations are presented in a passage, be aware of which (if any) theory the author favors or opposes.

18. D Be sure to understand what the question is asking. You're asked to find an answer choice which *isn't* "proof" of the fact that the pen name was widely used. Proof is simply another way of describing evidence, so either eliminate details that support the conclusion that there was widespread use of the pseudonym or find a choice that isn't mentioned. While three of the answer choices come from ¶s3 and 4, (D) is never suggested. Even though most *portraits* of Dupin only refer to her as "George Sand," there's nothing said about what the book reviews did.

Wrong Answers:
(A): Opposite. Her son did this, as described in lines 28-29.
(B): Opposite. This is nearly an exact quote from lines 24-25.
(C): Opposite. This is mentioned in lines 26-27.

19. A Predict the second possible reason from your map of ¶8: "George Sand" is an acronym that represented parts of Dupin's life. Since the question asks what the author *implies,* you know that the answer won't be as simple as a straight rehashing of the paragraph's topic. What does the author say about this theory? It gives more credit to Dupin herself. Since the author is clearly a fan of George Sand, it would seem that all else being equal, this explanation would be preferable because it reflects Dupin's own creativity. (A) says the same.

Wrong Answers:
(B): Opposite. A big part of this theory is that it contains *many* references to the author's family.
(C): Distortion. The author argues that this theory is more sentimental, but doesn't suggest that Sand is particularly rational or innovative, or that sentimentality would detract from Sand's personality.
(D): Out of Scope. Among the various things that may have contributed to the name, the author doesn't mention any reading that she did. This choice tries to trap you with the phrase "childhood and early married life," which is mentioned in ¶8 in a different context.

20. C Where is George Sand's preference for male clothing mentioned? Review the mention in ¶7. The author mentions both the pseudonym and the male clothing to argue that "this male identity gave her more freedom of expression..." (C) paraphrases this.

Wrong Answers:
(A): Distortion. Though she had more freedom from taking on certain masculine character traits, the author doesn't suggest that she was personally masculine.
(B): Distortion. As above, though certain external qualities reflected masculinity, there's nothing to suggest that Dupin herself was androgynous (neither masculine nor feminine)..
(D): Distortion. A tempting answer choice. The author wants to show that she had more freedom of expression, but doesn't suggest that she wouldn't have succeeded otherwise.

PASSAGE IV

Topic and Scope:
Rapid growth and infrastructure problems in '60s and '70s western boomtowns

Mapping the Passage:
¶1 notes that the population drop after a project is completed makes problems worse.
¶2 describes the reasons that money is scarce for infrastructure.
¶s3 and 4 describe the causes of modern boomtowns and introduce problems caused by the growth.
¶5 describes social problems and their negative impact on the project that caused the problems in the first place.

Questions:
21. D Where are consequences of poor planning mentioned? While the author discusses them throughout the passage, there's a particular focus in ¶s3–5. RN I is mentioned explicitly in line 35 and expanded on in ¶5. RN II is mentioned in line 43. Note that at this point, all the answer choices except for (D) are eliminated, so you can save time by not evaluating the last statement! RN III is discussed in the context of the "us against them" mentality described in the second half of ¶5.

Wrong Answers:
(A): Opposite. As described above.
(B): Opposite. As above.
(C): Opposite. As above.

22. B An "All...EXCEPT" question, so either eliminate or look for an off-scope answer choice. (B) is the only statement not suggested in the passage as a cause for lack of services. Although resentment among "old timers versus persons brought to the community by the boom" (¶5) can occur, there's no reason why the lack of support from long-time residents would lead to a shortage of schools, housing, etc..

Wrong Answers:
(A): Opposite. This is the topic of ¶1.

(C): Opposite. An energy project is one of the types of projects the author mentions at the beginning of the passage as causing all the problems listed in the passage.
(D): Opposite. This is discussed throughout ¶2.

23. A What is the main problem in a boomtown? Predict: There's not enough infrastructure to field the services needed to support spike in population. It can be inferred that if there *were* enough infrastructure, things would be better. (A) says the same.

Wrong Answers:
(B): Distortion. A lack of support by long-time residents is one of the problems, not a cause of the public services shortage.
(C): Distortion. The author doesn't suggest that tax programs aren't well-enforced, only that their structure prevents much tax revenue from being collected when it's needed.
(D): Opposite. The author argues that problems arise when services don't rise to the short-term level needed by the town. When services stay at the level needed in the long term, the short-term residents are underserved.

24. B What does the author think about the traditional systems of taxation as described in ¶2? Predict: The author thinks that it leads to a "critical problem." (B) is the only choice that reflects that worry about the effects of too few taxes.

Wrong Answers:
(A): Distortion. Though the author thinks that the inefficient taxation is a problem, there's no hint of outrage, which is far too extreme.
(C): Out of Scope. There's nothing to suggest that the author is at all astonished by the taxation programs.
(D): Opposite. The author thinks that the problem is "critical," which suggests that the tone is anything but complacent.

25. D What is the author's main point about community life? Review the last paragraph: Boomtowns often suffer from divisions between the long-time and the short-term residents that end up hurting everyone. (D) paraphrases this.

Wrong Answers:
(A): Distortion. Though the long-time residents do suffer, there's no suggestion in the passage that they suffer *more*.
(B): Distortion. The author suggests in line 47 that these problems are a "result of boomtown living" but doesn't suggest that these problems specifically would be lessened with greater planning. Remember that valid inferences *must* be true based on the passage.
(C): Distortion. As above, though the author mentions worker turnover in lines 58–59 and says that it's due to an undesirable community, it's not necessarily true that simply acknowledging long-time resident complaints

would by itself improve the community enough to prevent turnover.

26. A An evaluation question. Since it's asking you for the organization of a single paragraph, go back to take a closer look at the structure of ¶5. The author cites a conclusion from studies, and then elaborates both on the conclusion and on its implications. (A) is the only answer choice that parallels this structure: fact and follow-up discussion.

Wrong Answers:
(B): Out of Scope. There's no prediction made to be qualified.
(C): Out of Scope. The author specifically begins with findings from studies, not a point of view.
(D): Out of Scope. As above, the author is presenting objective findings, not a debatable proposal.

PASSAGE V

Topic and Scope:
The subjects of poetry, and in particular how factual errors when writing about those subjects can be justified for artistic reasons.

Mapping the Passage:
¶1 discusses when writing about impossible things is and isn't justified.
¶2 introduces three subjects of poetry and suggests that poetry doesn't need to strive for absolute correctness.
¶3 describes two faults in poetry: errors in the poetry itself and factual errors.
¶4 discusses when errors in poetry itself are and are not justified.
¶5 mentions ways poets can respond to alleged factual errors.

Questions:
27. B When is an error in poetry not justified? Easier to predict by remembering when an error *is* justified. In ¶2 the author divides errors into faults in the poetry itself and errors in the subject matter, arguing in ¶3 that errors in the poetry itself are justified if the effect is "rendered more striking." Justifications for factual errors are described in ¶4. Look for an answer choice that doesn't meet these criteria. (B) does this: it's an example of an error inherent to the poetry which, since it's awkward, doesn't create a more striking effect. As an essential error without a higher purpose, it's therefore not justified.

Wrong Answers:
(A): Out of Scope. There's nothing in this metaphor to suggest any obvious errors, justifiable or otherwise.
(C): Opposite. This is a factual error, but since the poet's artistic goals have been achieved, it's forgivable for any of the reasons in ¶4.
(D): Opposite. This also might be a factual error, but could be justified again by the responses in ¶4: the poet

would argue that humans are being portrayed as they *should* be.

28. C Review the comparison of Sophocles to Euripides in ¶5. The passage says that "...Sophocles said that he drew men as they ought to be; Euripides, as they are." Paraphrase: Euripides portrayed people realistically; Sophocles' subjects weren't factually correct, but reflected what he thought people ought to act like. (C) closely follows from this.

Wrong Answers:
(A): Opposite. Euripides portrayed people realistically; this answer choice states the opposite.
(B): Opposite. Sophocles portrayed his subjects idealistically, which suggests that his portrayals were not at all like people's view of reality.
(D): Distortion. Though Euripides portrays people realistically, there's no evidence that he portrays them especially unfavorably in order to get a moral across.

29. B If the author believes that the poet's role is to imitate like any other artist, what must he also believe? That the basic task of all art is the same: imitation. The author would therefore agree with (B); since both poetry and sculpture are art, they are both similar in their task of imitation.

Wrong Answers:
(A): Opposite. The author in fact believes that different types of artistic talent are *similar* in that they all imitate the same basic subjects.
(C): Out of Scope. No superiority is suggested, nor would it make sense for the author to argue this if the basic task of all art is the same.
(D): Out of Scope. Though the author believes that poetry can have errors, there's no suggestion that poetry's way of representing things is inefficient.

30. A A simply-worded question that asks for a detail not found in the passage. Either eliminate answer choices that are in the passage or look for something that's not discussed. (A) is never mentioned in the passage. Though the author argues that rhetorical devices can be justified in poetry, no specific examples are provided.

Wrong Answers:
(B): Opposite. The author discusses this difference in various parts of the passage, and in the last paragraph especially.
(C): Opposite. This is the topic of ¶5.
(D): Opposite. The author discusses the way that the poet represents things in the second half of ¶2.

31. B did the author write the passage? Consider his main topic: describing poetical errors and conditions under which they are and are not justified. Look for an answer choice that takes this topic into account. A vertical scan might be helpful since all the choices start with verbs. While "persuade" and "justify" sound at odds with the author's descriptive purpose, "describe" and "analyze" sound promising. Check these choices first. (B) recaps what the author discusses in the passage, and it's reasonable to assume that the author's purpose is simply to describe these points.

Wrong Answers:
(A): Out of Scope. The author believes that poets are mainly imitators, not chroniclers, and so wouldn't be concerned with accomplishing this.
(C): Faulty Use of Detail. Though the author mentions these types in ¶s2 and 4, the overall purpose of the passage is broader.
(D): Faulty Use of Detail. As above, though the author does this in the passage at various points, the purpose of the passage isn't to categorically justify errors, but to describe when they are and are not justified.

32. D When is writing about the impossible justified? The author addresses this directly in ¶4, saying "If he describes the impossible...the error may be justified, if the end of the art be thereby attained..." (D) repeats this: if the artistic goal is reached, it's okay to describe the impossible.

Wrong Answers:
(A): Out of Scope. The author never argues that the impossible is justified when everything else is equally impossible.
(B): Out of Scope. This is never suggested either, and the author doesn't suggest that poets describe the impossible with the hope of fooling readers into believing it.
(C): Opposite. The author argues the opposite in the last sentence of the first paragraph. Be careful not to confuse the wording!

PASSAGE VI

Topic and Scope:
Problems with traditional ideas of race and racial classification.

Mapping the Passage:
¶1 introduces the topic of race and outlines some of the problems it has caused.
¶2 discusses scientific problems inherent in defining race, including biological diversity.
¶3 argues that human races are social, rather than biological races.
¶4 argues that physical traits are not necessarily indicative of ancestry.
¶5 contrasts the flexible Brazilian concept of race to the restrictive American one, but says neither is scientific.

Questions:
33. B An "all...EXCEPT" detail question, which means that you should be looking for an out of scope or contradictory answer choice. (B) fits the latter category. The author discusses a variety of phenotypical differences that *do* exist in human populations (skin color, facial shape, blood type, etc., ¶4). The author argues that these differences aren't tied to discrete races, not that these differences don't exist at all.

Wrong Answers:
(A): Opposite. This is the purpose of contrasting America and Brazil in ¶5.
(C): Opposite. This closely paraphrases the point made in ¶4.
(D): Opposite. The author makes this point almost word-for-word in ¶3.

34. D What does the Brazilian system of racial classification consist of? Review ¶5: Race consists of physical features and not ancestry. Though it would be hard to predict an exact answer in this application question, you *can* predict that you're looking for an answer choice that involves some change in physical features. (D) jumps out immediately when the prediction is made beforehand.

Wrong Answers:
(A): Opposite. This might have an effect on ancestral classifications, which aren't part of the Brazilian model.
(B): Opposite. Marrying someone of a different race doesn't change one's own physical features.
(C): Opposite. This is closer to the American "ancestry" model than the Brazilian model.

35. C A global question with verbs starting out each of the answer choices: do a vertical scan! What is the author trying to do in the passage? Discredit the traditional notion of race. Scanning the choices only yields one tempting verb in "criticize." In fact, (C) supports the prediction. The popular belief is that distinct racial categories exist, and the author attacks the foundations of this belief.

Wrong Answers:
(A): Out of Scope. Though the author alludes to scientific evidence that humans don't have distinct racial categories, there's no recent discovery that the author specifically wants to explain.
(B): Faulty Use of Detail. Though the author does this with America and Brazil in ¶5, it's meant to support a larger point, not to be the point itself.
(D): Faulty Use of Detail. Though, as above, the author does this with Brazil and America, it's not the main point of the passage.

36. A Predict what the author would say about abandoning racial classification: It's a good idea, and will have significant benefits. (A) fits this general argument.

Wrong Answers:
(B): Distortion. The author mentions Brazil as an example of a system differing from that of America's, but notes at the end of ¶5 that it's not scientifically valid either. The author would be in favor of eliminating all systems of racial classification.
(C): Opposite. The author argues that these "valued beliefs" are causing problems that would disappear if they were stripped.
(D): Distortion. Though the author mentions one particular set of beliefs that should be abandoned as unscientific, this doesn't mean that all unscientific beliefs should be abandoned. A classic MCAT over-generalized wrong answer.

37. B An application question, and your prediction will necessarily be general as a result. Still, make sure you have a prediction. The general problems with race come from classification that's arbitrary and not based on "real" definitions of race. (B) is such a situation, specifically tying into the author's argument that race doesn't effectively represent ancestry. This situation would be likely in the Brazilian model, which the author considers unscientific and therefore problematic.

Wrong Answers:
(A): Out of Scope. This is more an example of semantics than anything, and doesn't touch on the fundamental problem outlined by the author: people create racial categories that have no valid basis in ancestry.
(C): Out of Scope. Human ancestry in general is outside the scope of the passage; this answer choice focuses on ancestry to the exclusion of race.
(D): Opposite. This contradicts the author's point in ¶5 that America does classify people based on ancestry.

38. C A question which asks you for an inference in a roundabout fashion. Remember that the correct answer won't be explicitly stated in the passage, but must follow from what the author says. While three choices don't, (C) logically follows from the author's point in the last paragraph that some racial classifications are "legacies of slavery," which suggests historical influence on racial categories.

Wrong Answers:
(A): Out of Scope. Though the author discusses current differences in classification, she doesn't discuss any trends over time.

(B): Out of Scope. As above, the author discusses no trends over time.
(D): Out of Scope. The author never suggests that racial classifications were accurate to begin with.

39. D What does the author say is true of biological races? As described in ¶2, biological races are able to interbreed anatomically but haven't been able to practically do so for a long time. (D) reflects this point, backed up by the author's point that humans don't have races because populations haven't been isolated for a long enough period of time.

Wrong Answers:
(A): Opposite. The author states in ¶2 that "members of different races can interbreed, since they are of the same species."
(B): Out of Scope. Since the author doesn't acknowledge true human races, there's no way to compare numbers of racial groups.
(C): Faulty Use of Detail. Though these things are variously used to define race now, the author's scientific definition of race listed in ¶2 doesn't include any of these criteria.

40. A Why does the author discuss American racial classification in ¶5? Predict: The idea of race is arbitrary and doesn't make much sense. (A) fits this, and is supported by the author's argument that legal definitions of race in America are different from what Americans believe makes up race.

Wrong Answers:
(B): Opposite. The author argues in ¶5 that it's not "based on scientific principles."
(C): Opposite. The author is arguing that racial classification should be abolished altogether, not that individuals should classify themselves.
(D): Opposite. The author argues that racial classifications are always inaccurate because races don't exist.

PASSAGE VII

Topic and Scope:
The poet Gautier and his unique qualities.

Mapping the Passage:
¶1 argues that Gautier was a flawed poet, but was nevertheless unique and talented.
¶2 argues that Gautier was able to be uniquely himself in his poetry.
¶3 argues that Gautier was uniquely interested in life and nature.

Questions:
41. C The presence of "suggests" in the question indicates that you'll probably be looking for inferences

or paraphrases from the text. Since the question is an "All...EXCEPT" structure, use your map and the text to eliminate choices that fit with the passage or look for a choice that contradicts or doesn't touch on what the author argues. (C) fits the latter: the passage doesn't discuss Gautier's educational background, and therefore nothing can be inferred about it.

Wrong Answers:
(A): Opposite. This is discussed in ¶3; Gautier's treatment of nature is, according to the author, "of a finer strain than the mass of human family."
(B): Opposite. This follows from the author's discussion of Gautier's "spontaneity" in line 10.
(D): Opposite. This can be inferred from ¶s 2 and 3, in which the author discusses Gautier's self-understanding and keen observation of Nature.

Strategy Point:
Remember that when a question is set up in such a way that three answer choices are statements with which the author would agree, the correct answer will either contradict the author or be off-scope. Though answer choices that contradict are much more common, be aware of the other type as well.

42. A Why does the author mention other poets? Evaluate the examples in the passage individually. At the end of ¶1 the author compares Gautier to Musset to say that Gautier was even more unique than Musset was: for Gautier, "Even more than Alfred de Musset....if his glass was not large, at least it was all his own glass." When comparing Gautier to Browning in ¶2, the author argues that it's possible to be more entertained by Gautier than Browning, and then goes on to say that "a man's supreme use in the world is to master his intellectual instrument..." which again suggests Gautier's uniqueness. The author suggests in lines 9 and 10 that Gautier was unique when he says he was never fully imitated. Finally, in the last paragraph, the author argues that Gautier "excels" other descriptive poets by his personal qualities, which yet again emphasizes uniqueness. Therefore there is overwhelming evidence for (A)!

Wrong Answers:
(B): Faulty Use of Detail. Though the author suggests this in the first sentence, it has nothing to do with Gautier's comparison to other poets, since French lyricism isn't mentioned again in the passage.
(C): Opposite. The author is very positive about Gautier. Though limitations are mentioned, the author focuses more on his exceptional creativity.
(D): Faulty Use of Detail. Though the author argues in the first paragraph that others have tried and failed to imitate Gautier completely, there's no claim that Gautier's colleagues could easily imitate his style to refute in the first place.

43. B Break the question down a bit before predicting. What are Gautier's artistic gifts? Mainly his uniqueness, ability to entertain, and powers of observation. If these were the things that overcame his limitations as a poet, you can predict that the right answer will somehow diminish these qualities. (B) does just this. If Gautier collaborated with other writers, then he wasn't particularly unique, and at least one quality that the author uses to justify Gautier's limitations doesn't exist.

Wrong Answers:
(A): Out of Scope. The study of Gautier's poems has no impact on Gautier's value as a poet by itself since it doesn't impact the author's evidence or conclusion.
(C): Out of Scope. As above, even if this were true, Gautier's reviews wouldn't have any effect on the value of his poems.
(D): Out of Scope. Though this would indicate that the writers who were influenced by Gautier were less unique, it does nothing to harm Gautier's own uniqueness.

Strategy Point:
An argument can be weakened by attacking its evidences, assumptions, or conclusions.

44. D Review the phrase in context. "Pagan bonhomie" apparently makes the other descriptive poets seem not-so-descriptive. Keep reading. Why does he dwarf these poets? Among other things, because of "his magnificent good temper and the unquestioning serenity of his enjoyment of the great spectacle of nature and art." Pagan bonhomie must therefore be some sort of view of life in general that the other poets don't share. While (B) is tempting, (D) comes closer to capturing the author's overall point that Gautier's attitude set him apart, not just his descriptions of nature alone.

Wrong Answers:
(A): Out of Scope. The author never claims that Gautier had this sort of lifestyle. Eliminate this choice immediately for its negativity.
(B): Faulty Use of Detail. Though Gautier did have unique descriptions of nature, the author's more concerned with pointing out the difference in his overall personality.
(C): Out of Scope. Another answer choice far too negative for the author's tone. The author never suggests that Gautier lacked modesty, and in fact argues the opposite at the end of the last paragraph.

45. B Where does the author discuss the reader's reaction to poetry? It's buried in ¶2; the author says, "...we may wonder whether we are...the better entertained, as a poet's readers should before all things be...." Therefore, the author believes that the first role of poetry is to bring enjoyment. (B) says the same.

Wrong Answers:

(A): Out of Scope. Though this might be true, the author never discusses this.

(C): Out of Scope. As above, the author never discusses poetry and moral lessons. Though the author discusses a "moral" in line 28, it's not a moral in poetry, but rather a lesson to be learned from Gautier in general.

(D): Out of Scope. Again, though it may be true, the author never argues that this is the case.

46. D What does the author say about Gautier and death? The last paragraph says, "...death, for him, must have been as the sullen dropping of a stone into a well." In other words, Gautier wouldn't have been a fan of death. If Gautier wasn't focused on death, what must he have been focused on by default? Life. (D) matches this, and is supported by the author's overall discussion in the paragraph of Gautier's natural subject matter.

Wrong Answers:

(A): Distortion. Though the author believes that Gautier wasn't fascinated by death, this doesn't mean that he avoided everything negative. Frailty would be considered a part of life, which is within the scope of Gautier's subject matter.

(B): Out of Scope. The author says only that Gautier focused on natural subjects; there's no information from which to draw an opinion on his ideas of the divine.

(C): Out of Scope. This too has no support. As part of life rather than death, it would be well within Gautier's scope, and there's no reason to believe he neglected this.

PASSAGE VIII

Topic and Scope:
Experiments supporting the theory of analog mental imaging

Mapping the Passage:
¶1 introduces the analog hypothesis of mental imaging and states that four types of experiments support the idea that mental images have regular properties.

¶2 describes the 1st experiment highlighting the mind's reaction to relative sizes of mental images.

¶3 describes the 2nd experiment demonstrating perceptions of distance in mental images.

¶4 describes the 3rd experiment suggesting that problems can be solved mentally by manipulating mental images.

¶5 describes the 4th experiment suggesting that the time needed to mentally compare figures depends on how similar those figures initially appear.

Questions:

47. A This question simply asks you to summarize the hypothesis described in ¶3. The fastest way to predict here it to read the text. The analog position is "the idea that mental processing requires one to go sequentially through all intervening steps to solve a problem." (A) repeats this almost word-for-word.

Wrong Answers:

(B): Opposite. This contradicts the argument that mental processing has to proceed step-by-step.

(C): Faulty Use of Detail. Don't get sidetracked by the information in ¶1. This follows from the analog position, as supported by the experiments in the passage, but it's not the analog position itself.

(D): Out of Scope. There's no support for this statement in the passage.

48. C What reason would the analog position give for the fact that it takes longer to scan long distances in a mental image? Review the relevant parts of the passage, ¶2 in particular. The experiment suggests that people are building a mental map since the map is "fictional". Because the analog position suggests that one has to go through steps to solve a problem, it would be reasonable to infer that it takes longer to scan long distances because those doing the scanning are "looking" at all the intervening space in between the two given objects. (C) summarizes this.

Wrong Answers:

(A): Out of Scope. There's nothing to suggest that those in the experiment don't believe that this relationship exists. The experiment is concerned with their mental images rather than their opinions.

(B): Out of Scope. There's no evidence for this in the passage.

(D): Out of Scope. As above, there's simply no support for this in the passage.

49. B An unusual question. What would an alternate explanation do to the conclusions drawn from the experiment? It would weaken it, and this question can therefore be treated as a classic "weaken" question. Look for evidence that would weaken the passage's conclusions. (B) does this: if subjects change their answer based on what they think the answer should be, the argument that they take longer because they're referring to a mental map is weakened.

Wrong Answers:

(A): Distortion. This choice contradicts the basis of the experiment. Since subjects in the experiments had to memorize the positions of the objects, subjects who forgot the positions wouldn't be part of the experiment's focus.

(C): Out of Scope. The experiment is designed to deal only with "fictional" maps, and so any explanation that involves real maps would be implausible.

(D): Out of Scope. The passage states that response times depend on distance, but there's no reason to believe that it would take longer to begin scanning longer distances as opposed to shorter ones.

50. D Where is Kosslyn mentioned? In ¶s2 and 3. Since the question mentions big and small objects, focus on the experiment described in ¶2. Review the text to determine why Kossyln believes it takes longer to identify small objects next to large ones: Kosslyn believes "subjects had to zoom in on the image to detect the particular feature." (D) says the same.

Wrong Answers:
(A): Out of Scope. This isn't suggested in the passage.
(B): Out of Scope. Kosslyn's experiment says nothing about this either.
(C): Out of Scope. This is also unsupported by the passage.

51. D Though it's not immediately obvious, this is an incorporation question because you're given new information and asked how it will affect the passage. What would be the case if subjects simply responded in the way they thought the experimenters wanted them to? Predict: the experiment wouldn't prove anything except the experimenters' own biases. (D) restates this: whatever relationship the experimenters want, they'll get.

Wrong Answers:
(A): Out of Scope. Though this might be true, it misses the point that the results would be invalid because the experimenters could engineer any result they wanted.
(B): Opposite. It would make more sense that the subjects would show a *linear* relationship, since the experimenters, in keeping with the analog model, were expecting that.
(C): Out of Scope. As with (A), even though this constant relationship might be reflected, it misses the point that *any* relationship is possible if the subjects are simply following the experimenters' lead.

52. B Paraphrase the analog position before answering this to make evaluation easier: solving a problem requires step-by-step thought, and mental images have properties that can be tested. Start with RN I, which restates the conclusion of an experiment *supporting* the analog hypothesis. Since you're looking for statements that *contradict* it, eliminate (A), (C), and (D). Only (B) is left, and there's no need to evaluate the other remaining choices. RNs II and III contradict RN I and the conclusions of the map experiments, and are therefore valid elements of the correct answer.

Wrong Answers:
(A): Opposite. As described above.
(C): Opposite. As above.
(D): Opposite. As above.

53. C Another incorporation question which asks you to take new evidence and determine how it would affect the passage. The new information sounds suspiciously like that given in question 51 and the correct answer to question 49. Predict the result again: If subjects change

their responses based on what they think "should" happen, then the results of the experiment should be called into question, as the subjects are simply reflecting experimental bias. (C) captures this.

Wrong Answers:
(A): Opposite. For the reasons described above, if subjects are scanning in the way they think they should, the experiment is more likely revealing experimental bias than the actual mental images it sets out to describe.
(B): Opposite. Another "more likely to be correct" choice that can be eliminated immediately. A lack of subject control over scanning contradicts the information in the question anyhow, since it's stated explicitly that subjects *can* alter the time they spend scanning.
(D): Opposite. As with the other answer choices, this can be immediately eliminated because it suggests that the analog model would be strengthened. Even if subjects can control the rate at which they scan, as the question suggests, the analog model would still be weakened by this conscious response.

Strategy Point:
The same point will often be tested repeatedly throughout a passage's questions. Don't reinvent the wheel! Use your previous work to save time and to maximize your points.

Strategy Point:
Don't spend excess time evaluating an answer choice once you are sure that it's incorrect. If you know that the correct answer choice weakens an argument, there's no use spending time evaluating an answer choice that claims the argument is strengthened.

PASSAGE IX

Topic and Scope:
The development of a particular method of thought.

Mapping the Passage:
¶1 discusses the four principles of thought: don't accept anything as true unless it's known to be so, divide difficulties into individual parts that can be resolved, build ideas from simplest to most complex and make deductions complete so that nothing is left out.
¶s2 and 3 discuss the author's background and problems with logic.
¶4 discusses the author's problems with geometric analysis and algebra.
¶5 discusses the author's desire to find a new way of thinking and mentions four principles of thought.

Strategy Point:
Passages written in the first person are rare. When they appear, keep an eye out for a potentially strong authorial opinion.

Questions:

54. C Remember that "According to the passage..." will almost always signal a detail question. Use your map to predict where the details will likely be. Go back to ¶s2 and 3 to review the author's reasons for abandoning logic. Three answer choices are details in this first paragraph, but (C) isn't supported: There's no evidence that the author didn't understand logic.

Wrong Answers:
(A): Opposite. This follows from the author's argument that logic serves "only to explain to others the things that one already knows."
(B): Opposite. This is a paraphrase of the last lines in paragraph three.
(D): Opposite. This also follows from the author's argument that logic only explains what one already knows.

55. B Review the author's first precept in ¶1: Don't accept anything as true unless it's known to be true. Be sure to look through the rest of the (short) paragraph for evidence and support. The author's first precept depends on the assumption that the author's perception of truth is valid. (B) restates this. If in doubt, try the denial test: if theories can't be accepted as true by being perceived intellectually, then the author's attempt to know what is true in this way is unworkable.

Wrong Answers:
(A): Opposite. The author argues that he'll only believe what he perceives to be true, which means that knowing the truth is ultimately a subjective process. (A) argues that comprehension is ultimately based on rational analysis rather than personal knowledge, which the author rejects.
(C): Opposite. As above, the author believes that it's necessary to rely on personal opinion in addition to pure intellect.
(D): Distortion. Though the author argues that these disciplines are used for understanding abstract ideas, there's no argument that these things must be studied to understand abstract ideas. Even if this were true, it wouldn't have an impact on the author's argument in ¶1.

56. D Where does the author mention vice in a State? Go back to review the example in ¶5. The author says that a "State is better ruled if, having but a few vices, it closely monitors them..." Paraphrase: it's best to keep a close eye on the few flaws present. (D) restates this point.

Wrong Answers:
(A): Out of Scope. The author never makes a comparison between vices and logic.
(B): Faulty Use of Detail. The author argues that many laws can rationalize vices, which is exactly why it's better to stick to just a few rules. This answer captures only the

author's introduction to the main point: it's better to have a few rules that are always followed.
(C): Distortion. The author argues that it's best to have a few vices, but never suggests that it's advisable or even possible to get rid of all vice.

Strategy Point:
Questions and answers that follow complicated paragraphs will often make you earn the points by paraphrasing points in the passage. Get in the habit of restating difficult points in simpler words when predicting answers.

57. B Another detail question. Focus your work in this question on ¶4, where geometry is discussed. First tackle RN II, which appears in three choices. The author argues that geometry is "so restricted to the consideration of figures" that it ends up being limited. RN II paraphrases this, eliminate (D). RN I states that geometric analysis isn't useful for logical analysis. The author argues that geometry not only deals too much with figures, but also doesn't "treat anything except abstract ideas, which seem to be of no use whatsoever," suggesting that it's not useful for logic. RN III, however, contradicts the author's point that geometry stretches the intellect at the expense of the imagination. (B) catches the legitimate statements.

Wrong Answers:
(A): Opposite. As described above.
(C): Opposite. As above.
(D): Opposite. As above.

58. A An evaluation question. Why does the author describe his former study of philosophy and mathematics? Predict: He wants to show that they weren't useful by themselves, and that he needed new precepts that combined all their advantages (¶5). Look for an answer choice that ties into this. (A) is reasonable. If the author wanted to create a new system based on the old ones, he'd mention his studies in the other fields in order to show that he had the necessary background to form these new ideas.

Wrong Answers:
(B): Distortion. Though the author wants to combine parts of these fields, he's not concerned with discussing their relationship to each other so much as with describing how they fit into his new way of thinking.
(C): Opposite. The author argues in ¶3 that the study of logic by itself is pointless, so he wouldn't want to help readers expand their study of logic.
(D): Distortion. Though the author does argue in ¶3 that much logic is flawed, his purpose in mentioning his own study isn't to refute specific theories, but to describe his new method of thinking.

59. B Since you have no information in the question to narrow your focus, you can be reasonably sure that the right answer will be something with which the author generally disagrees. The shortcomings of the old systems and the four precepts make up the meat of the passage, so look for something that conflicts with the author's negative view of traditional methods of thought and his positive view of his own precepts. (B) does the latter. The second precept argues that difficulties should be broken up into many small pieces that can be individually evaluated; (B) argues that subjects should never be broken up. The author would clearly disagree.

Wrong Answers:
(A): Opposite. This follows from the author's argument in ¶3 that logic isn't particularly useful.
(C): Opposite. This is simply the opposite of the correct answer choice. The author would agree that it's possible to understand a big problem by breaking it down in to smaller problems.
(D): Opposite. The author argues in ¶3 that logical theorems "serve only to explain to others the things that one already knows..." which suggests that the author is concerned with teaching abstract ideas in addition to simply learning them.

Strategy Point:
In questions that ask you to find a statement with which author disagrees, it is often much faster to find a choice that conflicts with the main points than to eliminate the three choices with which he would agree.

60. C Where does the author discuss the reasoning behind his method? ¶5 is concerned almost entirely with this. The author argues that it was enough for him to have four principles as long as he was sure "never—not even once—to neglect my adherence to them." (C) is a close paraphrase of this particular concern about consistency.

Wrong Answers:
(A): Distortion. Though the other methodologies played a role in the author's new system, he doesn't suggest that his primary concern is the examination of these old systems. He's more concerned with having a few simple principles.
(B): Distortion. As above, though the author suggests that he has this thorough grounding, he believes that it's better to have simple principles that are always followed.
(D): Out of Scope. The natural sciences aren't mentioned at all in the passage.

Materials used in this test section were adapted from the following source(s):

Henry James. *French Poets and Novelists.* London: Macmillan and Co., 1884

Verbal Reasoning Test Nine

Time—85 minutes
Question 1–60

DIRECTIONS: Each of the passages in this test is followed by a set of questions based on the passage's content. After reading each passage, decide on the one best response to each question and mark it on your answer sheet. If you are unsure of an answer, eliminate the choices you know are wrong and choose from the remaining choices. You may refer to the passages while answering the questions.

Passage I (Questions 1–6)

Some writers have so confounded society with government, as to leave little or no distinction between them, whereas they are not only entirely different, but have different origins. Society is a blessing brought
5 forth naturally by our wants, uniting our affections and promoting our happiness. Government is a necessary evil originating from the need to restrain our vices.

Suppose a small number of persons represent the first peopling of any country, or of the world. In this
10 state of natural liberty, a thousand motives will excite them to society: the strength of one is so unequal to his wants, and his mind so unfitted for perpetual solitude, that he is soon obliged to seek assistance and relief from another, who in turn requires the same. Considering the
15 slavish times in which it developed, the form of government known as "constitutional monarchy" is granted to have been a noble creation. When the world was overrun with tyranny, the least remove therefrom was a glorious rescue. However, government, if unchecked, evolves
20 over time to a form so complex that a nation may suffer for years without being able to discover in which part the fault lies; and every political physician will advise a different medicine.

Four or five united in a society would be able to
25 raise a dwelling, but one might labor out the period of life without accomplishing anything. Disease or misfortune could soon reduce an individual to a state in which he could easily perish. As time passes, however, in proportion as they surmount their early difficulties, the peo-
30 ple will inevitably relax in their duty and attachment to each other; and this laxity will point out the necessity for each to surrender a part of his property in order to establish some form of government to protect the rest. Here then is the origin of government: the inability of moral
35 virtue to govern the world; here, too, is the design and end of government: freedom and security.

And it unanswerably follows that whatever form of government which appears most likely to ensure the protection which constitutes government's essential pur-
40 pose, with the least expense, is preferable to all others.

As the community expands, public concerns will increase and the distance at which the members are separated may render it inconvenient for all to meet on every occasion. Thus the members may consent to leave
45 the legislative part to be managed by a number of chosen representatives, who are supposed to have the same concerns as those who appointed them, and who will act in the same manner as the whole would, if present.

That the interest of every part of the colony may be
50 attended to, the whole may be divided into convenient parts, each part sending its proper number. And so that there be assured a common interest with every part of the community, on which the strength of government depends, prudence will point to the need for frequent
55 elections, thereby assuring that the elected return and mix often with the community.

---

1. As evidenced by the arguments posed by the author in each paragraph, the primary purpose of the passage is to:

    A. chronicle the development of a particular form of government.
    B. advocate a simple form of representative government.
    C. contrast society and government.
    D. distinguish representative government from constitutional monarchy.

2. Which of the following best reflects the author's intended meaning of the word "society" as used throughout the passage?

    A. Social relationships, customs, and practices
    B. The socially dominant members of a community
    C. Established organizations or foundations
    D. Political practices and institutions.

GO TO THE NEXT PAGE.

3. The author concluded in the passage that the essential purpose of government is protection of property. In doing so the author assumes that:

   I. there actually existed a time in which the disparity between an individual's needs and wants motivated cooperation, and not transgressions against property.

   II. the part of property surrendered to establish some form of government is less than that which would be lost if it were left unprotected.

   III. the moral laxity resulting from reduction in hardship results in acts against property, rather than failure to assist those experiencing disease or misfortune.

   A. I, II, and III
   B. II and III only
   C. I and II only
   D. I and III only

4. The second paragraph discusses the theoretical beginnings of society and the impetus for government to be formed. In this paragraph the author implies that constitutional monarchy is a form of government that:

   I. is better than the form that immediately preceded it.

   II. could be improved by more disciplined examination of the problems which it has evolved.

   III. has outlived its usefulness.

   A. I, II, and III
   B. I and II only
   C. I and III only
   D. II and III only

5. It can be inferred from the passage that its author would most probably respond to the view that the resources of government should be employed to relieve the effects of poverty by stating that:

   A. since the strength of an individual must be recognized to, at times, be unequal to his needs, it is natural for government, once it has evolved, to perform such functions.

   B. these activities should be performed by individuals or associations outside of government.

   C. since poverty is correlated with crime against property, government must perform these functions if non-governmental efforts are not fully effective.

   D. this should be decided by the representatives elected by the people as a whole.

6. A contemporary of the author wrote: "Government is a contrivance of human wisdom to provide for human wants. Men have a right that these wants should be provided for by this wisdom." Based on this quotation and the passage, it can be inferred that the two authors would probably agree with respect to:

   A. what constitutes the essential purpose of the government.

   B. whether government is justified because it is necessary or because it is beneficial.

   C. whether the best form of government is the simplest.

   D. whether certain rights of an individual should be recognized in relation to the state.

GO TO THE NEXT PAGE.

Passage II (Questions 7–12)

In 1979, a team of scientists from Berkeley working near Gubbio, Italy, discovered a layer of clay that revolutionized theories concerning the disappearance of the dinosaur, which had centered on the assumed gradual climatic change. Beneath the two-centimeter-thick layer lay limestone containing fossil organisms from the late Cretaceous, while above it was limestone with early Cenozoic fossils.

Positionally, then, the Berkeley group could place the clay in a period roughly contemporaneous with the disappearance of the dinosaur approximately 63 million years ago. They found that the clay stratum contained an iridium level thirty times greater than that of clays in adjacent strata. As iridium is distributed fairly evenly over time through micrometeoritic impact, the researchers knew that the anomalous matter in the clay must have originated extra-terrestrially; the high iridium level, moreover, indicated a sudden deposition in an exceptional, catastrophic event.

The subsequent finding of similarly enriched marine rocks from the end of the Cretaceous in Spain, Denmark, and New Zealand has led the Berkeley group to the conclusion that 500 billion tons of material was suddenly deposited on the earth in the period of less than 150 years represented by the two-centimeter-thick stratum. To fully grasp the magnitude of this event one must remember that all of this material would have initially been suspended in the atmosphere. For the better part of that 150 years there would have been so much foreign matter in the atmosphere as to blot out nearly all of the available sunlight. Scientists are sharply divided on the possible causes of so cataclysmic an event. The possibility that the deposition occurred as an aftereffect of a supernova has been discounted: radioactive isotope Pu-244 was absent from the clay, and neither Ir-191 nor Ir-193 were present in significant proportions.

Those who maintain that the material came from within the solar system contend that the earth must have collided during the late Cretaceous with an astral body large enough to have distributed the iridium-rich material over the globe. An asteroid of the required mass would have been approximately ten kilometers in diameter; a comet would have to have been twice as large, since comets are largely composed of ice water.

Trying to fathom the scale of such an event as this is mind boggling. It is true that from space, an object 10-20 miles across colliding with earth would be akin to something smaller than a grain of sand landing on a basketball, it is also the case that an object twenty miles across that landed on earth would be nearly twice as tall as Mt. Everest (the tallest mountain on Earth) and further across than the length of Manhattan. Furthermore, when the body came crashing to Earth it would have been ablaze in an inferno caused by the friction of entry into our atmosphere. To the argument that there is no geological evidence of the impact of such massive objects, Richard Grieve has replied that the clay layer could have resettled after the impact in the form of fallout. Frank Kyte of UCLA asserts that a comet, if disrupted by the earth's gravitational field, would have exposed the surface to a deluge of debris that would not have created major craters. Alternatively, the Berkeley group suggests that an asteroid may have landed in the sea; such a collision would have produced tidal waves eight kilometers high, swamping large areas of the earth.

Whatever the type of body and mode of impact, Walter Alvarez of the Berkeley team argues that the primary effect of the catastrophe was to disrupt the planetary ecology through the suspension of vast clouds of matter in the stratosphere. The effects of the initial impact would have been greatly multiplied, Alvarez argues, as photosynthesis was impeded by the blockage of sunlight; there would then have been a massive disruption at the base of the dinosaur's food chain.

---

7. The passage discusses a new discovery that may change the way scientists think about one aspect of dinosaurs. It can be inferred that the discovery described in the passage may "revolutionize" (lines 2–3) which aspect of current theories about dinosaurs?

   A. The geographical extent of the presumed habitation of the dinosaur
   B. The approximate date at which dinosaurs are thought to have become extinct
   C. The assumption that dinosaurs became extinct because of a change in their natural environment
   D. The rate at which the extinction of the dinosaur is thought to have occurred

GO TO THE NEXT PAGE.

8. According to the passage, the Berkeley group used which of the following to support their hypothesis on the disappearance of the dinosaur?

    I. A comparison of the fossil records of various marine strata

   II. A comparison of different clay strata near Gubbio, Italy

  III. A comparison of marine strata in several locations

  A. I only
  B. III only
  C. I and II
  D. II and III

9. According to the information presented by the author throughout the passage, scientists used the analysis of the isotopes present in the clay to:

  A. estimate the age of the stratum more exactly.
  B. determine the extent of meteoritic impact upon the earth.
  C. derive a hypothesis concerning the effect of the impact of an extraplanetary body on the earth's ecology.
  D. eliminate a possible theory concerning the enriched clay's formation.

10. It can be inferred from the passage that scientists assessing the possible causes of the deposition of iridium-rich material are most divided over:

  A. the manner in which deposition of the clay would have caused the extinction of the dinosaurs.
  B. whether the iridium originated from within or without the solar system.
  C. whether the debris was deposited as a result of the impact of a comet or an asteroid.
  D. how a collision of the required magnitude could have occurred without leaving primary evidence of impact.

11. Judging from the information in the passage, Walter Alvarez' theory concerning the extinction of the dinosaur would be most strengthened by:

  A. discovery of plentiful dinosaur fossils in strata older than the clay layer.
  B. the absence of plant fossils in Cenozoic deposits that were plentiful in Cretaceous strata.
  C. discovery of elevated levels of iridium in rocks above and below the Spanish and Danish clay strata.
  D. the development of a consensus among scientists on the probability of cometary impact.

12. Based on the way in which the author argues in the passage, which of the following correctly states the relationship between the hypotheses of cometary impact, asteroid impact, and stratospheric suspension?

  A. The hypothesis of stratospheric suspension is consistent with both of the others and helps explain how either might have led to the extinction of the dinosaur.
  B. The three hypotheses are mutually exclusive and each adequately explains the extinction of the dinosaur.
  C. The theory of stratospheric suspension is consistent with asteroid, not cometary, impact, and necessary to explain how it could have led to the extinction of the dinosaur.
  D. The three hypotheses taken together provide a possible explanation for the extinction of the dinosaur.

GO TO THE NEXT PAGE.

Passage III (Questions 13–18)

The notion of the Great Plains as a vast roaming ground for cowboys and their herds of cattle became popular more recently than some might think. Let us first put aside that now cliché notion of a lawless Wild
5 West with gunslingers and bandits running rampant and shootouts in front of salons every day at high noon. To be sure the west was a dangerous place, but the vast majority of the mystique surrounding the times and places comes more from East Coast writers and later
10 imaginations than anything else. The image of a Great Plains populated by cattle herds and homesteaders was slow to emerge. Much of the settling of the West happened in land grabs after the Civil War.

In spite of the conventional interpretation, a survey
15 of source material reveals that the image of the plains as Desert was restricted in 1825 to certain portions of the country and to certain segments of the population. Analysis of newspapers and periodical literature indicates that the Desert image was strongest in the rural
20 areas of the Northeast and weakest in the rural areas of the South and trans-Appalachian West. Acceptance of the Desert concept was more likely among the well-educated elite, particularly in the Northeast, and acceptance of a "Garden" notion was greater among the rural popu-
25 lations, particularly in the South and West.

American historians have argued that the myth of the Great American Desert dominated the pre-Civil War view of the Great Plains. It was this conception of the plains as Desert, according to the traditional interpreta-
30 tion, that caused the American folk migration westward to leap over the region during the 1840's and the 1850's. Who, it was thought, would want to settle in a land devoid of rain, fertile ground in which to cultivate crops, and lacking in the rich abundance of fauna that populat-
35 ed the forests of the east coast and supported the need for meat and furs. This conventional understanding is neither completely invalid nor necessarily incorrect; but it is too simplistic to be fully satisfying. To claim the universal acceptance of stereotyped images of the Great
40 Plains is to ignore the presence of a considerable array of data to the contrary.

By the middle of the 1840's, the concept of the plains as Desert had become prevalent, but even then the Desert image was not the exclusive one. The year 1845
45 is critical, for it marked the beginning of the migration of Americans across the Plains to Oregon and California. An examination of the sources of American images of the plains in that year does not support the contention that the folk migration failed to halt on the
50 Great Plains because that region was viewed unfavorably by the migrants. By 1845 the American frontier was bursting with what one Missouri newspaper editor called "perfect Oregon fever." But those who encouraged migration to Oregon did not deny the agricultural
55 potential of the Plains. They simply made Oregon the logical and desirable culmination of the American drive to the Pacific.

This notion of Manifest Destiny was so pervasive during that time. It was considered by most Americans
60 to be not merely a right, but a duty to settle the continent from shore to shore, plowing through the middle of the country to reach the inevitable destination. To substantiate the point that the folk elements of American society did not see the plains as Desert, one need only look at
65 the records of those who crossed the Plains on their way to Oregon or California. A survey of the diaries from the years preceding the Civil War uncovers only 17 references to Desert conditions in the Great Plains.

---

13. According to the information presented by the author in the passage, American migrants traveling throughout the United States in the mid-1840's often:

    A. doubted the economic potential of the Great Plains.
    B. had an overly optimistic image of the Great Plains.
    C. had geographical destinations other than the Great Plains.
    D. were misinformed by newspaper stories.

14. Which of the following can be inferred from the passage about the diaries left by American migrants in the mid-nineteenth century?

    I. They described the transformation of the Great Plains into productive farmland.
    II. Their contents have been ignored or overlooked by some historians.
    III. They contain little useful information about the Great Plains.
    A. I only
    B. II only
    C. III only
    D. I and II only

GO TO THE NEXT PAGE.

15. All of the following can be found in the author's argument about the Great Plains EXCEPT:

    A. a contrast between the views of Americans who lived in different regions.
    B. a comparison of written and oral accounts of the migration experience.
    C. a general description of people who believed the Great Plains to be a Desert.
    D. an indication as to when westward migration activities increased in scope.

16. Which of the following best summarizes the author's attitude toward the traditional view as posed in the passage that most Americans regarded the Great Plains as Desert?

    A. It ignores conflicting evidence.
    B. It is irrelevant to historical understanding.
    C. It is substantially correct.
    D. Its importance has been unappreciated.

17. The passage suggests that in spite of what might be commonly believed by the public and taught in schools today, the image of the Great Plains as Desert:

    A. led to mass migration to the shores of the Pacific.
    B. developed in the aftermath of the Civil War.
    C. was more common in the 1840s than in the 1820s.
    D. contributed to population growth in the South.

18. According to the passage, at certain points in the history of the United States, various individuals most likely thought of the Great Plains as Desert. Which of the following individuals was most likely to think of the Great Plains as Desert?

    A. A banker in the Northeast in 1825
    B. A farmer in the South in the 1820s
    C. A Mormon migrant in the late 1840s
    D. A gold miner in California in the 1850s

GO TO THE NEXT PAGE.

Passage IV (Questions 19–25)

From the beginning, Johannes Kepler (1571-1630) was convinced that the basic astronomical verities must have a geometrical interpretation. This conviction has been shared by all the great natural philosophers, from Pythagoras to Einstein—the conviction that the cosmos was laid out according to a mathematical design and that this design is "simple" and accessible to human intelligence. For Kepler, mathematics meant the pure geometry of the Greeks.

His early scientific career is especially interesting because the ideas that seemed to him to be the most significant, and which he tried to exploit for the rest of his life, appear to a modern reader to be almost completely mad. It was the fact that he could never get them to work that drove him to make the series of astronomical discoveries that appear to us to be so significant.

God was for Kepler a master Greek geometer, and the "book of the world" must therefore be contained among the theorems of Euclid. One theory was that there are only five "perfect solids." A perfect solid (the most familiar example is the cube) is a solid all of whose faces are "perfect" plane figures (in the cube, these figures are squares). The other perfect solids are the tetrahedron, octahedron, dodecahedron, and icosahedron. There were known to be six planets - Mercury, Venus, Earth, Mars, Jupiter, and Saturn, in order of increasing distance from the sun, around which, Kepler believed, the planets moved in circular orbits.

Carrying on with his geometry, he considered a universe in which a cube, a tetrahedron, a dodecahedron, an icosahedron, and an octahedron would be arranged concentrically, one inside another; the orbit of Mercury would be fitted within the first of these perfect solids, the orbit of Venus outside it, and outside each of the other solids the orbit of another planet. This, he thought, might make it possible to calculate the interplanetary distances and also explain why there were no more than six planets.

With the superior vision of hindsight, it is all too easy for us to pass judgment on the weakness of Kepler's youthful notion. (Apart from anything else, we know that there are *nine* planets.) In fact, however, had Kepler's mysticism not also been coupled with a fanatic obsession to make his theory fit the observed facts quantitatively, he might as well have gone down in scientific history as just another visionary crank, along with the more unenlightened alchemists who abounded at that time.

It is interesting to note that Newton also devoted his "spare" time to alchemy. What would have driven this man of science, this father of our modern physics, to spend his free time trying to turn base metals into gold? Undoubtedly, this fact shows us that the desire for wealth often trumps the pursuit of pure science, even in the most noteworthy of individuals. This combination of mysticism and devotion to the "facts" as he knew them was Kepler's great strength. Einstein characterized the interrelation between mystic intuition and the need to deal with hard facts as a formula that "Science without religion is lame. Religion without science is blind."

---

19. Which of the following statements most nearly captures the author's central argument as articulated in the passage?

    A. The originality of Kepler's early scientific work can be fully appreciated by studying its influence on the mature work of Newton and Einstein.
    B. Kepler's early beliefs were often erroneous, but his mysticism coupled with an attachment to scientific fact led to many of his later, key discoveries.
    C. Kepler laid the groundwork for our current understanding of the universe in his early studies of the pure geometry of the Greeks.
    D. An investigation of Kepler's youthful work yields relatively few clues about the method he employed in his most remarkable work.

20. The passage suggests that which of the following scientific beliefs held by Kepler in his youth was, in fact, correct?

    A. The planets are arranged concentrically, within perfect solids.
    B. The orbit of the planets are circular.
    C. The number of perfect solids is equal to the number of planets
    D. There is an underlying order to the cosmos which is accessible to the human intelligence.

GO TO THE NEXT PAGE.

21. It can be inferred from the passage that Kepler and most alchemists shared which of the following?

    A. Opposition to a union of science and religion
    B. Skepticism about the value of quantitative data
    C. Disbelief in the idea that the cosmos corresponds to a mathematical design
    D. Reliance on the intuitive powers of the mind

22. According to the passage, which of the following is true about the "five perfect solids"?

    A. They have inspired the work of all great natural philosophers.
    B. They are each formed by plane figures with four equal sides.
    C. They were originally posited in a Euclidean theorem.
    D. They yielded important measurements of distances among six planets.

23. As it is used by the author in the passage, the phrase "the book of the world," probably refers to:

    A. a mathematical account of the plan of the universe.
    B. a treatise written by Kepler explaining the pure geometry of the Greeks.
    C. a comprehensive history of human knowledge.
    D. a text presumed to have been of divine origin.

24. The author quotes Einstein in the sixth paragraph. His primary purpose in doing this is to:

    A. suggest that Kepler's thought was misconstrued by Einstein.
    B. clarify a difference between scientific and religious thought.
    C. indicate the extent of Einstein's personal admiration of Kepler.
    D. emphasize a particular attribute of Kepler's own method and outlook.

25. Which of the following statements is implied by the author in paragraphs five and six?

    A. The history of science is full of scientists who have failed to esteem what was of greatest significance in their own work.
    B. It is during periods of youthful enthusiasm that the fundamental guidelines to the most important scientific discoveries nearly always emerge.
    C. Such is the paradox of the human personality that, despite such problems, Kepler became one of the most determined seekers of cosmic harmony in history.
    D. Kepler, too, was aware of the dangers of pure speculation conducted without taking into consideration observed phenomena.

GO TO THE NEXT PAGE.

Passage V (Questions 26-32)

Frailty of understanding is in itself no proper target for scorn and mockery. But the unintelligent forfeit their claim to compassion when they begin to indulge in self-complacent airs, and to call themselves sane critics, meaning that they are mechanics. And when, relying upon their numbers, they pass from self-complacency to insolence, and reprove their betters for using the brains which God has not denied them, they dry up the fount of pity.

If a hale man walks along the street upon two sound legs, he is not liable to be chased by crowds of cripples vociferating 'Go home and fetch your crutch.' If a reasoning man edits a classic rationally, he is. What a critic is, and what advantage he has over those who are not critics, can easily be shown by one example. Cicero's oration *pro rege Deiotaro* was edited between 1830 and 1840 by Klotz, Soldan, and Benecke. The best MS then known was the Erfurtensis, and all three editors pounced on this authority and clung to it, believing themselves safe. In 1841, Madvig, maintaining reason against superstition in Cicero's text as I now maintain it in Juvenal's, impugned 17 readings adopted from the Erfurtensis by these editors, and upheld the readings of inferior MSS. We now possess MSS still better than the Erfurtensis, and in 12 of the 17 places they contradict it; they confirm the inferior MSS and the superior critic.

But there are editors destitute of this discriminating faculty, so destitute that they cannot even conceive it to exist; and these are entangled in a task for which nature has neglected to equip them. What are they now to do? Set to and try to learn their trade? That is forbidden by sloth. Stand back and leave room for their superiors? That is forbidden by vanity. They must have a rule, a machine to do their thinking for them. If the rule is true, so much the better; if false, that cannot be helped: but one thing is necessary, a rule. A hundred years ago it was their rule to count the MSS and trust the majority. But this pillow was snatched from under them by the great critics of the 19th century, and the truth that MSS must be weighed, not counted, is now too widely known to be ignored.

The sluggard has lost his pillow, but he has kept his nature, and must needs find something else to loll on; so he fabricates, to suit the change of season, his precious precept of following one MS wherever possible. Engendered by infirmity and designed for comfort, no wonder if it misses the truth at which it was never aimed. Its aim was purely humanitarian: to rescue incompetent editors alike from the toil of editing and from the shame of acknowledging that they cannot edit.

---

26. The author's discussion takes the reader to the topic of the Erfurtensis MS in paragraph two. The example of this manuscript is relevant to the claim that:

    A. the Erfurtensis MS is not very reliable.
    B. no single MS can be assumed to be always right.
    C. Madvig was a lazy editor.
    D. MSS must be weighed, not counted.

27. According to the various arguments put forth by the author of the passage, which of the following are true about the editing of classics?

    I. It has not been undertaken in the case of Cicero.
    II. It is sometimes undertaken by people who are unable to do it correctly.
    III. There were important advances in the field during the 19th century.

    A. I and II only
    B. II and III only
    C. I and III only
    D. I, II and III

28. Suppose that the author is present at a panel discussion on the topic of this passage where all of the following statements are made by other panelists. According to the arguments he has put forth in the text, the author is LEAST likely to agree with which of the following statements?

    A. It should not be assumed that the majority of the MSS of a classical text are correct.
    B. Madvig was a better editor than Klotz, Soldan, or Benecke.
    C. It is a mistake to think that one MS of a particular text is better than another.
    D. There is no simple rule for editing that eliminates the need for critical discrimination.

GO TO THE NEXT PAGE.

29. In spite of what may or may not appear in the first paragraphs of the passage, the bulk of the passage is devoted to showing:

    A. that incompetent editors have developed methods for avoiding the difficulties of responsible editing.
    B. that the Erfurtensis MS is no longer considered the best MS of Cicero's *pro rege Deiotaro.*
    C. that it was discovered in the nineteenth century that MSS must be weighed, not merely counted.
    D. that Cicero was editing more often during the 1830s than during any other decade.

30. As used in the passage, the word "mechanics" (line 5) refers to:

    A. people who do not study classical literature.
    B. the great critics of the 19th century.
    C. editors who follow fixed rules instead of using their own judgment.
    D. able-bodied people who can walk without crutches.

31. Which of the following general theories would be most consistent with the passage?

    A. The editor of a classical text should select one MS of that text at random, and follow that MS as closely as possible.
    B. The editor of a classical text should compare all available MSS of that text, determine which is the best, and follow that MS as closely as possible.
    C. The editor of a classical text should compare all available MSS of that text, and wherever the MSS give different readings, follow the reading given by the majority of the MSS.
    D. The editor of a classical text should compare all available MSS of that text, and wherever the MSS give different readings, follow the reading that seems most likely on its own merits to be correct.

32. Suppose that a new MS of Cicero's *pro rege Deiotaro* were discovered, that agreed with the Erfurtensis MS in all 17 places that Madvig departed from it. What relevance would this information have to the passage?

    A. It would weaken the author's claim that Madvig was right to depart from the readings of the Erfurtensis MS.
    B. It would strengthen the author's claim that automatically following either a single MS or the majority of MSS is a form of superstition.
    C. It would have no relevance, because the author argues that the editor's judgment should outweigh the authority of any MS.
    D. It would have no relevance, because this hypothetical new MS would not necessarily be the best MS.

33. Based on the passage, which of the following could be a reasonable defense of the practice of following one MS of a classical text as closely as possible?

    I. An editor's task is to report the contents of an MS, not to evaluate them.
    II. A modern editor's judgment is unlikely to be more reliable than that of an ancient or medieval scribe.
    III. Use of a single MS makes it possible to edit a text more quickly.

    A. I and II only
    B. II and III only
    C. I and III only
    D. I, II, and III

GO TO THE NEXT PAGE.

Passage VI (Questions 34–40)

Pesticides (including insecticides, fungicides, nematicides, and herbicides) are chemicals used in agriculture to increase production by combating organisms that damage or destroy plants. However, pesticides by
5 their very nature can result in serious harm to wildlife both by directly killing animals and through more subtle effects on reproduction, development and behavior. Organophosphates are pesticides that interfere with the enzyme cholinesterase, which is essential for the proper
10 functioning of the nervous systems of insects, as well as of humans and other vertebrates. Toxic exposure to organophosphates results in fatal respiratory failure. The first indicator of toxic absorption is a reduction in the enzyme cholinesterase in red blood cells, and contact
15 with insecticides is the only known cause of a marked depression of this enzyme.

In a recent study, researchers collected specimens of both adult and tadpole Pacific treefrogs from sites located both within the Sierra Nevada (representing
20 northern and southern areas) and also to its west (representing the foothills and the Pacific coast of California). When cholinesterase levels were then examined they were significantly lower in tadpoles taken from the mountains east of the San Joaquin Valley, such as
25 Yosemite and Sequoia National Parks, than in those taken from similar sites farther north in the Sierra Nevada, which lie east of the Sacramento Valley where agricultural activity is less intense.

Moreover, lower cholinesterase activity levels were
30 correlated with distance away from the coast and toward the higher elevations of the Sierra Nevada. Similar, although less significant, trends were seen in adult frogs. Concentrations of particular organophosphate pesticides in the collected tadpoles and adult frogs were also mea-
35 sured. More than fifty percent of the adult frogs and tadpoles at Yosemite National Park had measurable levels of diazinon and chlorpyrifos, compared to only nine percent at coastal sites. Since both diazinon and chlorpyrifos degrade very rapidly in organisms, the detection of
40 either compound indicates recent exposure to the chemicals. The red-legged frog is now listed as threatened under the U.S. Endangered Species Act, and the mountain yellow-legged frog and Yosemite toad have been proposed for listing. Many amphibian population
45 declines have occurred in some of the state's most seemingly pristine areas, such as the Sierra Nevada mountain range of eastern California which includes Sequoia,
Yosemite, Kings Canyon, and Lassen Volcanic National Parks as well as Lake Tahoe and Mt. Whitney.

50 Because the southern parts of the Sierra Nevada lie east of the intensely agricultural San Joaquin Valley, environmentalists have suspected that pesticide use may be responsible. Pesticides could be transported from the San Joaquin Valley to the Sierra Nevada on the prevail-
55 ing eastward summer winds, and then affect populations of amphibians that breed in mountain ponds and streams.

---

34. All of the following are important to supporting the claim that insecticides are responsible for declines in amphibian populations in the Sierra Nevada EXCEPT:

A. incidence of measurable levels of organophosphates was higher in amphibians from sites east of the San Joaquin Valley than in sites east of the Sacramento Valley.

B. the red legged frog is now listed in as threatened under the U.S. Endangered Species Act.

C. incidence of measurable levels of organophosphates was higher in Yosemite National Park than along the coast of California.

D. cholinesterase activity levels were highest in coastal areas.

35. In the passage, the author most likely mentions that population declines have occurred in seemingly pristine areas (line 46) in order to emphasize that:

A. while there has been some damage to the environment of the Sierra Nevada, it is not irreparable.

B. appropriate action should be taken to restore the Sierra Nevada to its former purity.

C. environmental damage and its causes may not be apparent to casual observers.

D. because some amphibian species are still abundant in the Sierra Nevada, casual observers do not realize how many are seriously threatened.

GO TO THE NEXT PAGE.

KAPLAN

36. There are many assumptions in the scientific community about the misunderstood Pacific treefrog. Which of the following conclusions about Pacific treefrogs can be most reasonably inferred from the passage?

    A. Pacific treefrogs are likely to be proposed for listing as threatened under the U.S. Endangered Species Act.
    B. Phasing out use of organophosphates in the San Joaquin Valley is warranted as it will prevent loss of Pacific Treefrog populations.
    C. Pacific treefrogs are less abundant in the Sierra Nevada than in coastal areas.
    D. Pacific treefrogs are currently more abundant than red-legged frogs.

37. If the author of the passage met a biologist who argued that the decline in California amphibians should not be attributed to pesticides as amphibian species are declining world wide for unknown reasons, he would probably respond that:

    A. while California amphibians may be subject to factors that are causing world wide declines, their decline may also be exacerbated by environmental factors particular to this area.
    B. declines in California amphibians have been more dramatic than those which have occurred in most other areas.
    C. pesticide use may be responsible for much of the world wide decline in amphibian populations.
    D. intensity of agricultural cultivation has been increasing world-wide.

38. With respect to pesticides, the author takes time in the passage to assert that they:

    A. are transported for long distances by wind currents.
    B. are detrimental to both insects and vertebrates.
    C. are not used in the Sierra Nevada.
    D. have benefits in agricultural applications.

39. The function of the first paragraph in relation to the passage as a whole is to:

    A. critique the scientific study alluded to in the first paragraph.
    B. present evidence to support a hypothesis intro-duced in the first paragraph.
    C. provide more details with respect to the geographical information introduced in the first paragraph.
    D. provide more specific examples of the harmful effects of pesticides mentioned in the second paragraph.

40. An article about lawn care indicated that about 40% of the nation's private lawns are treated with pesticides and that homeowners use three to six times as much pesticide per acre as farmers do. If true, this would weaken the author's argument by casting doubt on the premise that:

    A. organophosphates are dangerous to the nervous system.
    B. organophosphate levels were measurable in only nine percent of the coastal frogs.
    C. there is an inverse correlation between the amount of pesticides released into the environment and the populations of certain amphibian species
    D. the levels of cholinesterase activity were lower in amphibians from the coast and from areas east of the Sacramento Valley.

GO TO THE NEXT PAGE.

Passage VII (Questions 41–46)

With the collapse of the "dotcom" bubble in 2001 and the new trend towards outsourcing information technology labor demands, it becomes imperative to analyze the state of the economy which has brought us
5 to this place. With the explosion of the technology industry in the late 1990s, the US ushered in the so-called "new economy." Based largely on speculation and a "cash in" mentality, the new economy bustled along until the bottom fell out and it came crashing back
10 to earth. But what set the stage for this collapse to happen was put into motion years earlier.

The growth of productivity is defined as the rate of growth in product less the rate of growth in the labor used in production. Productivity can be affected by fac-
15 tors such as: amount of capital invested in production, methods used in production, educational or demographic composition of the labor force, business climate, global competition, and cost of environmental and safety regulations. Capital investment was booming in the
20 U.S. in the post-1995 period, nearing a historic peak as a percentage of the U.S. gross domestic product. Furthermore, that part of capital invested in information technology, including computers, software, and communications equipment, rose to more than fifty times what
25 it had been in 1975. Because of its high gross rate of return in improving methods of production, capital investment in information technology should have a particularly large impact on overall productivity.

For the past five years the big news for the U.S.
30 economy has been a noticeable productivity growth spurt, which many have attributed to new information and communication technologies. The rate of growth in U.S. productivity had not been so high since the period extending from the end of World War II through the
35 1960s. In the early 1970s, productivity growth dropped suddenly. Apart from normal cyclical movements low productivity growth continued until the mid-1990s. Then, performance of the U.S. economy accelerated to a truly extraordinary level. From 1995 to 1999 real gross
40 domestic product grew at an average rate of about 4 percent per year, and the rate of growth in labor productivity returned to the pre-1970 rate of increase.

The revolution in technology is, at least in some sense, a worldwide phenomenon. Therefore, one would
45 expect the recent trend in the rate of growth in productivity in the U.S. to be shared by other developed countries. However, marked differences exist. Although the U.S. had the lowest rate of overall productivity growth

in the 1981-95 period, in the post-1995 period the U.S.
50 rate of productivity rose to third among the countries, behind only Ireland and Australia. In several other developed countries, including France, Italy, Japan, the United Kingdom, the Netherlands, and Spain, overall productivity growth slowed quite sharply. The questions
55 then arise: Why are these trends in productivity growth so different; and does this difference illuminate anything about the role of the new technologies? Regression analysis of the rate of growth in productivity in each of these countries in the late 1990s, both as a function of
60 the country's share of spending devoted to information technology and as a function of its number of internet servers, reveals a positive correlation that passes the test for statistical significance. Therefore, with due deference to the problems of international comparison, the
65 data appears to reinforce the view that utilization of the new technologies has been important in raising productivity in the U.S. in recent years.

---

41. According to the passage, a resurgence in productivity occurred in:

   I. the U.S. in the late 1990s.
  II. Ireland in the late 1990s.
 III. developed countries other than the U.S. in the 1981-95 period.

  A. I only
  B. II only
  C. III only
  D. I, II, and III

42. In concluding that utilization of new technologies has been important in raising productivity in the U.S. in recent years the author assumes all of the following EXCEPT:

  A. other factors affecting productivity did not become significantly more favorable in this period.
  B. the revolution in technology is a world-wide phenomenon.
  C. amount of spending on information technology and number of internet servers are valid measures of utilization of new technologies in production.
  D. the share of spending devoted to information technology and the number of internet servers are a cause of productivity growth.

GO TO THE NEXT PAGE.

43. If the passage were to continue, the next topic the author would discuss would most probably be:

   A. what factors caused the drop in the growth of U.S. productivity in the early 1970s.

   B. what factors prevented the productivity growth spurt in the U.S. form continuing.

   C. the relative importance of other factors in fostering productivity growth in the U.S.

   D. why different developed countries invested different shares of total spending on capital investment in new technologies.

44. If given the opportunity to rebut all of the following comments, with respect to the change in productivity growth in the U.S. in the late 1990s, the author would most probably agree with which of the following statements?

   A. This change is typical of the type of change that is a natural part of the tendency of economies to cycle through periods of higher and lower growth.

   B. This particular change is more remarkable than other changes that have occurred in the last half-century and, therefore, warrants a particular explanation.

   C. The factors that caused this change should be identified so that they may be fostered in countries that are not experiencing strong productivity growth.

   D. Investment in information and communication technologies has played a significant role in fostering the productivity gains in the U.S.

45. In paragraph 2, the author is primarily concerned with:

   A. defining productivity and identifying the types of factors that can affect its growth.

   B. noting a correlation between a peak in capital investment and a peak in the growth of productivity.

   C. emphasizing the impact of the amount of capital invested on the degree of improvement in methods used for production.

   D. introducing a explanation that will then be tested by further investigation.

46. The author provides evidence in the passage that could help to identify:

   A. the reason productivity growth in the late 1990s was greater in the U.S. than in some other developed countries.

   B. the reason productivity growth in the U.S. was greater in the late 1990s than in the U.S. in the period extending from the 1970s through the early 1990s.

   C. the reason U.S. productivity growth surged in both the late 1990s and in the period from the end of World War II through the 1960s.

   D. the reason productivity growth in France, Italy, Japan, United Kingdom, Netherlands, and Spain slowed in the post-1995 period.

GO TO THE NEXT PAGE.

Passage VIII (Questions 47-54)

Should the soft spring breath of kindly appreciation warm the current chilly atmosphere, flowers of greater luxuriance and beauty would soon blossom forth, to beautify and enrich our literature. If these
[5] anticipations are not realized, it will not be because there is anything in our country that is uncongenial to poetry. If we are deprived of many of the advantages of older countries, our youthful country provides ample compensation not only in the ways in which
[10] nature unveils her most majestic forms to exalt and inspire, but also in our unshackled freedom of thought and broad spheres of action. Despite the unpropitious circumstances that exist, some true poetry has been written in our country, and represents an earnest of
[15] better things for the future and basis to hope that it will not always be winter with our native poetry.

Whenever things are discovered that are new, in the records of creation, in the relations of phenomenon, in the mind's operations, or in forms of thought
[20] and imagery, some record in the finer forms of literature will always be demanded. There is probably no country in the world, making equal pretensions to natural intelligence and progress in education, where the claims of native literature are so little felt, and where
[25] every effort in poetry has been met with so much coldness and indifference, as in ours.

The common method of accounting for this, by the fact almost everyone is engaged in the pursuit of the necessities of life, and that few possess the wealth
[30] and leisure necessary to enable devotion of time or thought to the study of poetry and kindred subjects, is by no means satisfactory. This state of things is doubtless unfavorable to the growth of poetry; but there are other causes less palpable, which exert a more subtle
[35] but still powerful antagonism. Nothing so seriously militates against the growth of our native poetry as the false conceptions that prevail respecting the nature of poetry.

Stemming either from a natural incapacity for
[40] appreciating the truths which find their highest embodiment in poetry or from familiarity only with more widely available, but lower forms, such notions conceive of poetry as fanciful, contrived, contrary to reason, or lacking the justification of any claim to
[45] practical utility. These attitudes, which admittedly may have some origin in the imperfection that even the most partial must confess to finding in our native poetry, nevertheless also can have the effect of dis-

[50] couraging native writers of undoubted genius from the sustained application to their craft that is essential to artistic excellence.

Poetry, like Truth, will unveil her beauty and dispense her honors only to those who love her with a deep and reverential affection. There are many who
[55] are not gifted with the power of giving expression to the deeper sensibilities who nevertheless experience them throbbing in their hearts. To them poetry appeals. But where this tongue-less poetry of the heart has no existence, or exists in a very feeble degree, the
[60] conditions for appreciating poetic excellence are wanting. Let no one, therefore, speak of disregard for poetry as if it indicated superiority.

Rather, it is an imperfection to be endured as a misfortune. Despite prevailing misconceptions, there
[65] always remain at least a few who appreciate fine literature. Why do these not provide sufficient nourishment for our native artists? Here, we must acknowledge the difficulty that so many of us, as emigrants from the Old Country, cling to memories of the lands
[70] we have left, and that this throws a charm around literary efforts originating in our former home, and it is indisputable that the productions of our young country suffer by comparison.

---

47. In the passage, the author makes various inferences regarding the country being written of. Which of the following inferences about the country is LEAST supported by evidence from the passage?

   A. It was recently settled by immigrants.
   B. It possesses unspoiled beauty.
   C. It lacks a system of higher education.
   D. It is characterized by a relatively low standard of living.

GO TO THE NEXT PAGE.

48. The passage asserts that which of the following are reasons for the indifference toward native poetry that the author finds in his country?

   I. There has been insufficient edification of most of the population.

  II. The highest achievements of native poets do not rise to the level achieved by poets of the immigrants' homeland.

 III. Nostalgic feelings orient readers toward the literature of their former home.

  A. I and II only
  B. II and III only
  C. I and III only
  D. I, II, and III

49. An important contrast is made throughout the passage. The author developed this contrast between:

  A. the subtle and the palpable.
  B. false claims and real facts.
  C. the appreciable and the insignificant.
  D. the practical and the impractical.

50. Suppose that the passage does not stand on its own, but is excerpted from an introduction to a book. This book would most likely be:

  A. a textbook on the techniques for writing good poetry.
  B. a volume comparing the poetry of two countries.
  C. a volume of recent native poetry.
  D. a volume of essays on poetry and criticism.

51. In the sentence, "But where this tongue-less poetry of the heart has no existence, or exists in a very feeble degree, the conditions for appreciating poetic excellence are wanting" (lines 58–61), the author most probably uses the phrase "tongue-less poetry of the heart" in order to:

  A. emphasize that poetry is more commonly experienced through reading, rather by being heard.
  B. emphasize a defect that exists in those who devalue poetry.
  C. emphasize that appreciation of poetry is not limited to those who can write it.
  D. express compassion for those who lack the gift of writing poetry.

52. The author probably considers which of the following "unpropitious circumstances" (lines 12–13) most essential to explaining the state of native poetry?

  A. Lack of available resources for the study of poetry
  B. Failure of native poets to devote themselves to learning their craft
  C. Prevalent misconceptions about poetry
  D. Nostalgia of emigrants for their home country

53. Which of the following statements, made by poets about the creative process, is closest to the opinions expressed in the passage about what constitutes "true" poetry?

  A. "Like a piece of ice on a hot stove the poem must ride on its own melting. A poem may be worked over once it is in being, but may not be worried into being."
  B. "My method is simple: not to bother about poetry. It must come of its own accord. Merely whispering its name drives it away."
  C. "If there's room for poets in this world . . . their sole work is to represent the age, their own age, not Charlemagne's."
  D. "The only way of expressing emotion in the form of art is by finding an "objective correlative"; in other words, a set of objects, a situation, a chain of events which shall be the formula of that particular emotion; such that when the external facts, which must terminate in sensory experience, are given, the emotion is immediately evoked."

54. By "native literature" the author most probably means:

  A. literature authored by the aboriginal people of his home country.
  B. literature authored by people who make his country their home.
  C. literature authored by people born in his country.
  D. literature produced in and reflecting the circumstances and environment of his country.

GO TO THE NEXT PAGE.

Passage IX (Questions 55-60)

Without entering now into the *why*, let me observe that the printer may always ascertain when the dash of the MS. is properly and when improperly employed, by bearing in mind that this point represents *a second* [5] *thought—an emendation*. In using it just above I have exemplified its use. The words "an emendation" are, speaking with reference to grammatical construction, put in *ap*position with the words "a second thought." Having written these latter words, I reflected whether it [10] would not be possible to render their meaning more distinct by certain other words.

Now, instead of erasing the phrase "a second thought," which is of *some* use—which *partially* conveys the idea intended—which advances me *a step* [15] *toward* my full purpose—I suffer it to remain, and merely put a dash between it and the phrase "an emendation." The dash gives the reader a choice between two, or among three or more expressions, one of which may be more forcible than another, but all of which help out the [20] idea.

It stands, in general, for the words—*"or, to make my meaning more distinct."* This force *it has*—and this force no other point can have; since all other points have well-understood uses quite different from this. [25] Therefore, the dash *cannot* be dispensed with. It has its phases—its variation of the force described; but the one principle—that of second thought or emendation—will be found at the bottom of all. That punctuation is important all agree; but how few comprehend the extent of its [30] importance!

The writer who neglects punctuation, or mis-punctuates, is liable to be misunderstood—this, according to the popular idea, is the sum of the evils arising from heedlessness or ignorance. It does not seem to be known [35] that, even where the sense is perfectly clear, a sentence may be deprived of half its force—its spirit—its point—by improper punctuation. For the want of merely a comma, it often occurs that an axiom appears a paradox, or that a sarcasm is converted into a ser- [40] monoid. There is *no* treatise on the topic—and there is no topic on which a treatise is more needed.

There seems to exist a vulgar notion that the subject is one of pure conventionality, and cannot be brought within the limits of intelligible and consistent *rule*. And [45] yet, if fairly looked in the face, the whole matter is so plain that its *rationale* may be read as we run. If not anticipated, I shall, hereafter, make an attempt at a mag-

azine paper on "The Philosophy of Point." In the meantime let me say a word more of *the dash*.

[50] Every writer for the press, who has any sense of the accurate, must have been frequently mortified and vexed at the distortion of his sentences by the printer's now general substitution of a semicolon, or comma, for the dash in the MS. The total or nearly total disuse of the lat- [55] ter point, has been brought about by the revulsion consequent upon its excessive employment about twenty years ago. The Byronic poets were *all* dash.

---

55. According to the arguments presented in the passage by the author, which of the following are true about the dash?

   I. It is often replaced by printers.
  II. It is overused by some writers.
 III. It serves a unique, necessary function.

  A. I and II only
  B. II and III only
  C. I and III only
  D. I, II and III

GO TO THE NEXT PAGE.

56. According to the passage, the newspapers' printers' practice of replacing dashes in authors' manuscripts with other punctuation marks is due to:

   A. the overuse of the dash by authors during the period closely preceding writing of the passage.

   B. the widespread ignorance of the importance of punctuation.

   C. the fact that the dash serves no function that is not better served by other punctuation marks.

   D. the fact that authors seldom have second thoughts about their work.

57. The passage indicates that if given the chance to respond to the following claims, the author is LEAST likely to agree with which of the following statements?

   A. There is a single ideal way in which any thought can be expressed.

   B. The rules of punctuation are simple and rational.

   C. Punctuation helps to convey the writer's intended meaning and tone.

   D. Most people do not understand the correct use of punctuation.

58. The author most likely mentions his intention to write an article entitled "The Philosophy of Point" in order to:

   A. remind the reader that grammar is a branch of philosophy.

   B. indicate the possibility of explaining correct punctuation concisely.

   C. furnish his own credentials as an expert on punctuation.

   D. emend his statement about punctuation.

59. According to the passage, which of the following is true of the relationship between words or phrases separated by a dash?

   A. Each word or phrase partially conveys the author's meaning.

   B. The second word or phrase renders the first one superfluous.

   C. The first word or phrase states the main topic, and the second states the sub-topic.

   D. The two words or phrases pertain to separate topics.

60. As used in the fourth paragraph of the passage in the sentence, "For the want of merely a comma, it often occurs that an axiom appears a paradox, or that a sarcasm is converted into a sermonoid," the words "axiom" and "paradox" refer to:

   A. two kinds of statement that require the use of the dash.

   B. two kinds of Byronic poem.

   C. two kinds of article that may be rejected by a printer.

   D. two kinds of statement that are different in tone.

STOP. If you finish before time is called, check your work. You may go back to any question in this test booklet.

ANSWER KEY
VERBAL REASONING TEST 9

1. B	16. A	31. D	46. A
2. A	17. C	32. C	47. C
3. D	18. A	33. A	48. C
4. C	19. B	34. B	49. A
5. B	20. D	35. C	50. C
6. D	21. D	36. D	51. C
7. D	22. C	37. A	52. C
8. D	23. A	38. D	53. A
9. D	24. D	39. B	54. D
10. D	25. D	40. C	55. D
11. B	26. B	41. A	56. A
12. A	27. B	42. B	57. A
13. C	28. C	43. B	58. B
14. B	29. A	44. D	59. A
15. B	30. C	45. D	60. D

EXPLANATIONS

PASSAGE I

Topic and Scope:
Government's origin and purpose

Mapping the Passage:
¶1 contrasts society and government.
¶2 describes formation of societies and governments and argues that governments eventually become too complex.
¶3 describes a prototypical society's beginning and its eventual need for government.
¶4 argues that simple government is best and describes the formation of a government from this society.
¶5 describes the final form the government might take.

Questions:
1. B A rare Global question right off the bat in the section. Remember that a good Global answer will generally include the author's purpose, scope, and topic. What does the author want to accomplish in the passage? The main intent of the passage is to advocate as simple a government as possible. (B) says the same.

Wrong Answers:
(A): Distortion. Though the author does describe a hypothetical government's formation (¶s 4 and 5), he or she does so as an illustration that a simple government is the best.
(C): Faulty Use of Detail. This is a detail used to introduce the topic in ¶1.
(D): Faulty Use of Detail. The author discusses both of these in order to advocate simple government, not to contrast the two.

2. A Where is the prototypical society mentioned? Go back to ¶s 2 and 3. The author discusses a small number of people who attach to one another in order

"to seek assistance and relief from another." The author also argues in ¶1 that "society is a blessing brought forth naturally by our wants, uniting our affections and promoting our happiness." The author is thus envisioning society as a group of people united by personal relationships and actions. (A) says the same.

Wrong Answers:
(B): Out of Scope. The author doesn't mention any sort of social dominance in the passage.
(C): Out of Scope. The author is concerned with discussing how society forms, and so focuses on its early form consisting of informal relationships. The author would probably argue that anything established has more to do with government than society.
(D): Opposite. The author argues that society *isn't* interchangeable with government, and therefore wouldn't agree with defining society in a political context.

3. D An assumption question; look for the author's conclusion and evidence. The conclusion is given in the question: the purpose of government is to protect property. What is the author's evidence? Review the passage: The author argues for this conclusion based on the hypothetical history given in ¶s 2 and 3, with the conclusion made in ¶3 when the author discusses "the necessity for each to surrender a part of his property in order to establish some form of government to protect the rest." What assumptions are necessary to connect this evidence to the conclusion? The author must first believe that the hypothetical history is valid and that things actually happened in a similar way, which RN I echoes. The author must also assume that when people relax their duties as described in ¶3, that their property is in fact in danger, which RN III states. RN II isn't necessary to the argument: even if the part of property surrendered was greater, the author could still argue that as long as this was the least amount of property necessary to surrender, the government was still legitimate. (D) includes both necessary assumptions.

Wrong Answers:
(A): Opposite. As described above.
(B): Opposite. As above.
(C): Opposite. As above.

4. C Review the author's discussion of constitutional monarchy in ¶2. The author believes that constitutional monarchy was good because it was better than everything else at the time ("the least remove" from the previous form "was a glorious rescue"), but that "if unchecked" it becomes "so complex that a nation may suffer for years." Compare this prediction to the choices: RN I restates the point that constitutional monarchy was better than the alternative at the time, and RN III paraphrases the author's idea that it's too complex. RN II is out of scope: the author isn't concerned with improving constitutional monarchy, but rather abolishing it altogether in favor of a simpler form of government. (C) includes RNs I and III only and is therefore correct.

Wrong Answers:
(A): Opposite. As described above.
(B): Opposite. As above.
(D): Opposite. As above.

5. B Predict what the author would think about this argument: Since the author believes that government should be kept as simple as possible, and that its only legitimate function is to protect property, he or she wouldn't take kindly to adding another function to government. Looking for an answer choice that reflects this turns up (B), which restates the point: government should stick only to protecting property.

Wrong Answers:
(A): Opposite. Though the idea is dressed up in complicated wording lifted from the passage, it's misapplied here: the author would think that it's *not* natural for government to take on this duty.
(C): Out of Scope. There's nothing in the passage to suggest that the author believes this correlation exists, and so it can't be inferred that the author would believe that this is a valid principle.
(D): Opposite. The author does argue that representatives should decide issues, but also believes that this should happen within a limited government that serves only to protect property.

6. D First characterize the answer choices: If the right answer is something that the two will agree on, each of the wrong answers represents a point of *disagreement*. Either find the point of agreement or eliminate statements on which they must disagree. What is the relevance of the quote to the author's argument? While the quote says that government is designed to "provide for human wants," the author argues in ¶1 that *society* comes from these wants. Any agreement must lie elsewhere. The second part of the quote mentions individual rights, and the author argues in ¶3 that the purpose of government is "freedom and security." Therefore, both the author and his contemporary would likely agree that government should respect individual rights; (D) says the same.

Wrong Answers:
(A): Opposite. The author believes that government should protect property and *society* should serve human wants, while his contemporary believes that *government* should serve human wants; they disagree on this issue.
(B): Opposite. The author believes that government is a necessary evil, and therefore justified out of necessity. His contemporary, though, believes that it provides for human wants, and is therefore justified because of its benefits.
(C): Opposite. Since the author's contemporary believes that government should provide for human wants, his

ideal government is not necessary the smallest. The author, however, believes that size should in fact be kept to a minimum.

PASSAGE II

Topic and Scope:
The iridium layer's impact on theories of dinosaur extinction

Mapping the Passage:
¶s 1 and 2 describe the Berkeley group's discovery of the iridium layer and its significance to dinosaur extinction.
¶3 discusses conflicting theories for the cause of iridium deposition.
¶s4 and 5 elaborate on various theories that an asteroid or comet was responsible for the iridium layer.
¶6 presents Alvarez's mechanism for extinction: debris from impact blocked sunlight, impeded photosynthesis, and harmed the dinosaurs' food chain.

Questions:
7. D Read the phrase in context. The author argues that the discovery of the iridium layer revolutionized theories about dinosaur extinction. What is true about these theories? Immediately afterwards the author says that they "had centered on the assumed gradual climatic change." The implication is that the iridium layer suggests a fast climatic change. (D) is therefore correct: it's likely that the discovery will change the time frame that scientists had used.

Wrong Answers:
(A): Out of Scope. The author doesn't discuss any geographic angles of the theories.
(B): Distortion. Though theories about the length of time over which the extinction occurred may have changed, the author notes that the iridium layer was found in "a period roughly contemporaneous with the disappearance of the dinosaur," which suggests that the date of extinction was already well-established.
(C): Out of Scope. The author doesn't suggest that this is an assumption of traditional theories, and if it was, it wouldn't change: the impact theory, at least as described by Alvarez, says the same thing.

8. D A detail question. Review the Berkeley groups hypothesis: lots of material was deposited in a very short span of time, suggesting a quick extinction. Any support that they have must be in the form of the iridium evidence listed in the first two paragraphs. RN I doesn't pass the test: fossils are mentioned in ¶1, but not in the context of marine strata. RN II, however, repeats the fact that the group compared the iridium strata with the nearby strata from the late Cretaceous and early Cenozoic. Only (D) remains as an answer choice, and there's no need to look at RN III. RN III has to be true from the information in lines 21-23: the Berkeley group compared their findings with marine rocks from various other locations.

Wrong Answers:
(A): Opposite. As described above.
(B): Opposite. As above.
(C): Opposite. As above.

9. D Review ¶3: Why are isotopes important? Predict: They rule out the possibility that the iridium deposits were caused by a supernova. (D) says the same in slightly vaguer terms.

Wrong Answers:
(A): Out of Scope. The passage doesn't discuss any such attempt to estimate the age of the iridium layer.
(B): Out of Scope. The isotopic information is useful only to determine that the iridium wasn't extrasolar, not to determine what type of object from within the solar system hit or how extensive the damage was.
(C): Faulty Use of Detail. Alvarez has a hypothesis that does this, but it doesn't rely at all on the isotopic data.

10. D Review ¶s 4 and 5, which discuss the divisions between scientists. While the scientists seem to be in agreement about the fact that the impact came from within the solar system, ¶5 describes three different hypotheses in response to the claim that there's no geological evidence of impact. The division therefore seems to be over why there's no obvious point of impact. (D) paraphrases this.

Wrong Answers:
(A): Out of Scope. Alvarez provides a hypothesis for this, but there's no evidence that it's challenged.
(B): Opposite. The author says in ¶3 that the supernova possibility "has been discounted," and therefore there's presumably no disagreement over it.
(C): Opposite. It seems there is less disagreement about this than why there is no impact site, since ¶4 describes attempts to explain why there's no impact site.

11. B What would strengthen Alvarez's theory? Predict: Something to do with plants, since Alvarez's theory deals with planetary ecology and photosynthesis. Only (B) mentions plants at all, and cites evidence that would potentially support Alvarez. The author states in ¶1 that the iridium layer falls between the late Cretaceous and early Cenozoic; if plants are missing in the Cenozoic, then something catastrophic happened in between the two time periods, which would support Alvarez's theory.

Wrong Answers:
(A): Out of Scope. What happened to dinosaurs *before* the iridium was deposited has no relevance to the extinction theories.
(C): Opposite. This would weaken Alvarez's theory: if iridium from other places is deposited over many layers, then it's less likely that a catastrophic event was

responsible for its deposition, and therefore less likely that an impact occurred, as Alvarez assumes.
(D): Out of Scope. What scientists think has no impact on Alvarez's evidence or theory; only actual evidence does.

12. A A complicated question; take time to understand and predict before hitting the answer choices. How does Alvarez's theory of "stratospheric suspension" tie into asteroid and cometary impact theories? The author says that Alvarez posits his theory "whatever the type of body and mode of impact," which suggests that it doesn't matter whether the cause was comet or asteroid. (A) paraphrases this; Alvarez's theory works with either and explains a possible mechanism for extinction.

Wrong Answers:
(B): Opposite. Only Alvarez's theory provides a mechanism of extinction, and it's compatible with either of the other two theories, as described above.
(C): Opposite. As described above, Alvarez's theory is compatible with either, and in any case, there's no indication that it's *necessary* to explain extinction.
(D): Opposite. The asteroid and comet theories are presumably mutually exclusive, since either an asteroid or a comet hit.

PASSAGE III

Topic and Scope:
Popular perception of the myth of the Great American Desert in the mid-1800s

Mapping the Passage:
¶1 puts into context the notion of the "Wild West."
¶2 lists the geographical differences in acceptance of the myth of the Great American Desert.
¶3 describes the myth and the traditional view that it was widely-held in the mid-1800s. The author argues that it oversimplifies the case, though.
¶s4 and 5 argue that the Plains were overlooked partially out of a desire to get to Oregon, not out of a belief that the Plains were a desert, and cite more evidence supporting the contention that many Americans did not regard the Plains as desert.

Strategy Point:
Very often, when a traditional view is presented, a new view will be offered that argues that the traditional view is too simplistic or too black-and-white.

Questions:
13. C The mid-1840s are mentioned in ¶s3 and 4. Review the author's basic points: Not everyone thought the plains were the desert, and many settlers simply passed the Plains up because they were on their way to Oregon. (C) reflects the latter point.

Wrong Answers:

(A): Opposite. The author states in the same lines that "those who encouraged migration to Oregon did not deny the agricultural potential of the Plains." For the purpose of settling, agricultural potential in the Plains was presumably equivalent to economic potential.

(B): Distortion. Though the author argues that settlers generally didn't have an overly *pessimistic* view of the Plains as a desert, there's no indication that their view skewed too far in the opposite direction.

(D): Opposite. Newspapers are cited in ¶2 as a data source for investigating the myth of the Great American Desert; the author argues that those who did accept the desert images were mainly the elite, who presumably weren't the main migratory population.

14. B Review the author's discussion of diaries, which occurs at the end of the passage. Paraphrase the main conclusion from the diaries: not many settlers thought of the Plains as desert. RN I doesn't necessarily follow from this since there's no discussion of any sort of transformation. RN II, however, must necessarily follow: the author argues that American historians have argued that the desert myth dominated American thought in the mid-1800s, which they wouldn't do if they hadn't overlooked the information in the diaries. (B) is the only answer choice left, and there's no need to evaluate RN III. RN III must be false, however, for the same reason RN II is true: if the diaries provide information challenging a major historical argument, then they *are* providing useful information.

Wrong Answers:

(A): Opposite. As described above.

(C): Opposite. As above.

(D): Opposite. As above.

15. B An unusual question in an "All...EXCEPT" format that asks you to evaluate the author's argument. A quick scan of the answer choices show that they focus on structure rather than particular details. Look for something that the author doesn't do: (B) fits the bill. The author never mentions oral accounts, and so there can be no comparison of them with something else.

Wrong Answers:

(A): Opposite. This is the subject of ¶2.

(C): Opposite. The author describes the type of person most likely to believe the desert myth at the end of ¶2.

(D): Opposite. The author mentions in ¶4 that the year 1845 marked the beginning of broad migration.

16. A What is the author's opinion of the traditional view? Review ¶3: the author doesn't say that the traditional view is completely wrong, and in fact takes pains to say that it's *not* "completely invalid nor necessarily incorrect." The author believes that it's "too simplistic" and ignores "a considerable array of data to the contrary." (A) summarizes this neatly.

Wrong Answers:

(B): Opposite. This choice is far too negative in tone, and since the author says that the traditional view is not completely invalid, it must have some historical relevance.

(C): Opposite. The author argues that it's too simplistic, which means that it can't be "substantially correct."

(D): Opposite. The author argues that the traditional view has been overhyped if anything and that a more nuanced historical analysis should take its place.

17. C An inference question. The author argues in ¶4 that by the mid-1840s the "concept of the plains as Desert had become prevalent," but says in ¶2 that in spite of the traditional claim that most Americans viewed the Plains as desert by 1825, evidence suggests otherwise. Therefore, (C) is a valid inference: the view was prevalent in the 1840s but not in 1825, and was therefore more common in the 1840s.

Wrong Answers:

(A): Out of Scope. The author never suggests that the misconception of the Plains as desert led to the migration to Oregon, and in fact argues that settlers migrated to the Pacific even though they were aware that the Plains *weren't* desert.

(B): Opposite. The author only discusses *pre*-Civil War views, as specifically stated at the beginning of the passage, and says that the image of Plains as desert was prevalent in the 1840s, well before the Civil War.

(D): Out of Scope. There's no discussion of population growth in the South.

18. A Predict: What type of person thought that the Plains were desert? The author says in ¶2 that the view was "more likely among the well-educated elite, particularly in the Northeast." (A) alone is a specific example of a northeasterner and an elite.

Wrong Answers:

(B): Opposite. A southern farmer wouldn't be a well-educated northeastern elite, and so would be less likely to believe the myth of the desert than the banker mentioned in the correct choice.

(C): Opposite. As above.

(D): Opposite. As above.

PASSAGE IV

Topic and Scope:
Kepler's combination of mysticism and devotion to facts, and they influenced his theories.

Mapping the Passage:
¶1 describes Kepler's view of the link between astronomy and geometry.
¶2 introduces the topic of Kepler's strange ideas from his early career.

¶s3 and 4 describe Kepler's early beliefs about the solar system: Kepler believed that the planetary orbits corresponded to Euclidean perfect solids.

¶s5 and 6 argue that though his ideas may seem wrong in hindsight, Kepler's mysticism and obsession with factual verification made him a great scientist (on par with Newton and Einstein).

Questions:

19. B A Global question: Paraphrase by reviewing the author's topic, scope, and purpose. The author argues that Kepler's mystical beliefs were factually incorrect, but, when coupled with his devotion to factual verification, led to his later valid, and important, astronomical discoveries. (B) paraphrases this.

Wrong Answers:

(A): Out of Scope. The author brings up Newton and Einstein in ¶6 as examples of other scientists who had a mystical bent, but does so only to show that Kepler's mystical inclinations weren't unusual among great scientists.

(C): Opposite. The author suggests that those ideas of Kepler that were based on the early Greek geometry were erroneous (¶s 4-5).

(D): Out of Scope. The author never discusses Kepler's "most remarkable work," and so it can safely be eliminated as the main point of the passage.

20. D An inference question. Kepler's specific early beliefs are mentioned in ¶1, so target your search there. Look for a belief that the author suggests has some connection to our modern knowledge. (D) is a likely candidate. The author mentions this belief in lines 6–9, and immediately above says that it is a "conviction shared by all the great natural philosophers," including Einstein. If all natural philosophers share the belief, a prominent modern scientist among them, it's reasonable to infer that it's a valid belief.

Wrong Answers:

(A): Faulty Use of Detail. This belief was based on the faulty idea that there were six planets (the author points out that this must be false as "we know that there are nine planets" (¶5)).

(B): Faulty Use of Detail. Though Kepler believed this also, there's no indication from the passage that this is in fact correct, and so we cannot infer that it is (and, of course, common knowledge now is that planetary orbits are elliptical).

(C): Opposite. Kepler believed that there were *six* planets and *five* perfect solids, so there couldn't be an exact correspondence between the two groups. Even if there were, one of the author's main points is that the idea of a geometrical correspondence between solids and planetary orbits is faulty.

21. D Another inference question. Since alchemists are mentioned in the question, find the specific mention of them in the passage: they first appear in line 47.

Review the surrounding lines. The author says that if Kepler hadn't been concerned with the facts, he would have been just like the alchemists. Therefore, concern with the facts separates Kepler from the alchemists, but what is similar between them? Mysticism is mentioned, elaborated on in line 58 as "mystic intuition." (D) captures the idea that both Kepler and the alchemists shared this reliance on mystic intuition.

Wrong Answers:

(A): Out of Scope. Religion is mentioned only in Einstein's quote and in the beginning of ¶3 ("God was for Kepler a master Greek geometer"), far from the mention of alchemists.

(B): Opposite. While the alchemists might have been skeptical, the author is adamant that Kepler's embrace of quantitative data separated him from run-of-the-mill mystics.

(C): Opposite. The author says in ¶1 that Kepler fervently believed this.

22. C A detail question. The author states that the five perfect solids came from a theory of Euclid; (C) rewards your research with quick points.

Wrong Answers:

(A): Distortion. The author says in lines 3–6 that the conviction of a mathematical design was inspiring, not the solids in particular.

(B): Faulty Use of Detail. The author states that this is how the cube is formed, but it's not necessarily true of the other solids.

(D): Opposite. The author cites Kepler's belief in the applicability of the perfect solids to planetary orbits as something that seems crazy now, and so there's no reason to believe that they provided the measures of distances that Kepler thought they would.

23. A Review the phrase in context: it's mentioned in line 18. Kepler believed, according to the author, that the "God was for him a master Greek geometer, and the 'book of the world' must therefore be contained among the theorems of Euclid." Paraphrase the sentence: Kepler believed that God created the world according to mathematical principles. The "book of the world" is therefore likely a metaphor for the mathematical blueprint of the universe. (A) paraphrases this.

Wrong Answers:

(B): Distortion. The "book of the world" is a metaphor for God's plan for the world, not an actual text.

(C): Out of Scope. Kepler was concerned with the mechanism of the universe, not with human knowledge.

(D): Distortion. Though the author suggests that Kepler believed that the universe had a divine origin, the text is again metaphorical.

24. D An evaluation question. Review Einstein's quote at the end of the passage. The author prefaces the quote by saying that "Einstein characterized the interrelation between mystic intuition and the need to deal with hard facts..." This is the combination of qualities that the author attributes to Kepler in the lines above, and the quote is therefore likely used to support the author's characterization of Kepler. (D) paraphrases this.

Wrong Answers:
(A): Out of Scope. There's no evidence that Einstein was referring to Kepler when making the quote; rather, Einstein was making a general comment that the author uses to support his own opinion of Kepler.
(B): Distortion. The author doesn't want to clarify a difference in scientific and religious thought, but rather to show how to the two can work together productively as they did in the case of Kepler.
(C): Out of Scope. As with (A), there's no indication that Einstein's quote referred specifically to Kepler.

25. D An inference question (if the author is implying, you're inferring!). A quick scan of the answer choices shows that the statements are fairly broad and complex; you'll have to do as much evaluating of the choices themselves as the text. Predict by summing the author's point in ¶s 5 and 6: Kepler's strength was that he combined mystical intuition with a devotion to the facts. Evaluating the choices with this summary in mind quickly isolates (D), which is the only choice dealing with facts. It's reasonable to infer that Kepler was so concerned with facts because he knew that his speculation required verification, which is exactly what (D) argues.

Wrong Answers:
(A): Out of Scope. The author doesn't mention scientists who made a discovery that was paid little heed.
(B): Out of Scope. The author mentions Kepler's youthful ideas, but doesn't focus at all on what part youth had to play in them.
(C): Out of Scope. The author is concerned foremost with Kepler's eventual "real" discoveries rather than with his search for cosmic harmony, and also believes that his focus on mysticism *enhanced* the search rather than hindering it.

PASSAGE V

Topic and Scope:
Editing as critical interpretation vs. blind adherence to manuscripts

Mapping the Passage:
¶1 argues that rational editing is looked down on by poor editors.
¶2 supports the point above with an analogy and introduces an example of a scholar editing based on an out-of-favor manuscript and ultimately being proven correct.

¶3 argues that editors who are lazy and untalented prefer to edit based on catch-all rules and the older rule: to trust the majority of manuscripts.
¶4 describes the new rule: to trust one manuscript whenever possible, which the author dislikes.

Questions:
26. B What is the author's point in discussing the Erfurtensis MS? Use your map to predict: The Erfurtensis MS was the preferred manuscript of most editors, but was ultimately proven to be flawed. Since the author writes the passage to show that it's better to rationally analyze manuscripts than to blindly stick to a single one, it's reasonable to predict that the Erfurtensis MS is an example supporting this point. (B) states the same thing.

Wrong Answers:
(A): Distortion. Though the Erfurtensis MS has errors, the author doesn't suggest that it was generally unreliable. It *did* have flaws, but the author wants to show that relying on a single manuscript can cause problems, not to prove any particular point about the Erfurtensis MS.
(C): Opposite. The author argues in ¶4 that lazy editors stick to single manuscripts; Madvig is an example of an editor who didn't do this, but compared multiple manuscripts in order to edit rationally.
(D): Faulty Use of Detail. The author mentions this in line 39, but doesn't bring up the Erfurtensis MS to support this point, rather the point made in ¶2 that good editing requires reason rather than "superstition."

27. B Since the whole passage deals with the editing of classics (since classics would be the main type of work requiring comparison of manuscripts), there aren't many clear predictions that can be made. Review the author's main points: many editors are too lazy to do the job properly and reason is required to edit well. Start with RN I, which appears in three choices. RN I is directly contradicted by the example in ¶2: Madvig's method of editing is cited by the author as an example of proper editing. Only (B) is left, and you can move on without evaluating the remaining two statements! RN II paraphrases a broad point of the whole passage: many editors don't edit well. RN III paraphrases the end of ¶3, which suggests that things were changed by "the great critics of the 19th century."

Wrong Answers:
(A): Opposite. As described above.
(C): Opposite. As above.
(D): Opposite. As above.

28. C An inference question in a "LEAST" format. Characterize the choices: The author would agree with the three wrong choices, and would not agree with the correct choice. Since there's no clue in the question, the right answer will likely touch somehow on the author's main points. Review these before checking the answers. The author would disagree with (C) because much of the argument in the passage is that editors should *not* blindly stick to a single manuscript. If all manuscripts were of equal value, though, sticking to one manuscript wouldn't be a problem. The author also mentions in ¶2 that at one time the Efurtensis manuscript was the best known, and that better ones were subsequently found, again reinforcing the idea that the author believes manuscripts have different levels of quality.

Wrong Answers:
(A): Opposite. This is the rule that the author says lazy editors once followed: "...it was their rule to count the MSS and trust the majority." Since this is cited as a crutch for editors, the author would agree that this is not a good way to edit.
(B): Opposite. The author makes this point in ¶1: the three inferior editors stuck blindly to the single text, while Madvig applied reason to his editing, which the author considers a superior method.
(D): Opposite. The author argues in ¶3 that poor editors look for simple rules and compares the rules to crutches in ¶1. The main point of the passage is that reasoning must be valued above simple editing rules.

29. A An unusual question phrasing that sounds suspiciously like a global question. What does the author do through most of the passage? Predict: The author points out how bad editors edit and argues that good editing requires the application of reasoning. Only (A) ties in broadly to this, paraphrasing the first half of the prediction.

Wrong Answers:
(B): Faulty Use of Detail. The author says in ¶2 that "we now possess MSS still better than the Erfurtensis," but the *bulk* of the passage isn't devoted to this incidental point.
(C): Faulty Use of Detail. The author implies this in lines 38-40, but it is again only an incidental point that's not mentioned again in the passage.
(D): Out of Scope. Though the author discusses bad editors who edited Cicero during this time period in ¶2, there's no evidence that this was the high-water mark for the editing of Cicero.

30. C Review the word in context: the author says that "the unintelligent forfeit their claim when they....call themselves sane critics, meaning that they are mechanics." Therefore, "mechanics" must refer to unintelligent critics. What is true about the unintelligent critics? Predict: They follow rules blindly without basing their editing on reasoning. (C) states the same, simply defining the unintelligent critics.

Wrong Answers:
(A): Opposite. The author believes that there *are* unintelligent critics who study classical literature, as the example in ¶2 shows.

(B): Opposite. Presumably the author considers the great critics of the 19th century great (line 39); "mechanics" refers to *bad* critics.
(D): Out of Scope. This confuses the metaphor that the author uses, and would be wrong anyhow: the able-bodied people in the metaphor are the *good* critics, while the author is referring to the "unintelligent" when speaking of "mechanics."

31. D An unusually worded question. Scanning the answer choices shows that you're dealing with an application question. Each of the answer choices describes a possible method of editing. What does the author think that intelligent editing consists of? Predict: Editors shouldn't stick to one text or simply follow the majority, but should compare texts and use reason when the manuscripts are different. Searching the choices for a match turns up (D).

Wrong Answers:
(A): Opposite. This would be an example of the "precious precept of following one MS wherever possible," which the author says is a rule used by bad editors.
(B): Opposite. This would be better than picking a manuscript at random, but would be another example of following the one manuscript rule that the author attacks in ¶4.
(C): Opposite. The author cites this as a rule of bad editors: "A hundred years ago it was their rule to count the MSS and trust the majority."

Strategy Point:
When the wording of a question looks unfamiliar, scan the structure of the answer choices to get a feel for what the question is asking.

32. C An incorporation question. Since the new information deals with the example in ¶2, focus there, but be sure to keep the author's overall point in the passage in focus. What would the author think of a manuscript that agreed with Erfurtensis where Madvig departed? It might be tempting to think that it would weaken the author's point, but the author's point in ¶2 is that the *editor* is the important factor: "Authority itself has crossed over to the side of reason..." Therefore, a new manuscript that supported Erfurtensis rather than Madvig would be interesting, but it would take nothing away from Madvig's *reasoning* and so should have no effect on the argument.

Wrong Answers:
(A): Opposite. As described above, there would be no effect since the author thinks that authority rests with the editor rather than any particular manuscript.
(B): Distortion. The author mentions "superstition" in order to contrast bad editing with editing based on reason, but isn't actually trying to make a point about superstition. Additionally, there's no reason why a

manuscript that *supported* the manuscript used by the bad editors would support the author's point.

(D): Distortion. While the new manuscript would have no relevance, it's not because of the relative quality of manuscripts. The author believes that the *editor* is the ultimate authority.

33. A Analyze the question. Following one manuscript would be a trait of what the author considers a bad editor. How might an editor who does this respond to the author's criticism? Since the author argues that the editor is more important than the manuscript, an editor might respond that the manuscript is more important than the editor. Now evaluate the choices. RN I follows from the prediction: If the manuscript is the most important part of the process, then the editor should simply report it rather than to try to judge its veracity. Eliminate (B). RN II follows a similar line of reasoning. Even if the editor *is* more important, it's better to stick to the manuscript since the ancient editors were presumably closer to the original version. Eliminate (C). RN III, however, would only support the author's contention that using a single manuscript is a sign of bad editing. The author argues that use of a single manuscript keeps editors from having to deal with the "toil of editing," and this says the same. (A) is therefore correct.

Wrong Answers:
(B): Opposite. As described above.
(C): Opposite. As above.
(D): Opposite. As above.

PASSAGE VI

Topic and Scope:
Pesticides and the decline of California amphibian populations

Mapping the Passage:
¶1 describes the mechanism of pesticide toxicity for the enzyme cholinesterase.

¶s2 and 3 describe experimental evidence suggesting that pesticides negatively affect amphibian species and describe the decline in amphibian populations in various areas of California.

¶4 suggests a mechanism by which pesticides would be transported through wind to contaminate the Sierra Nevada.

Strategy Point:
Be sure to understand cause-and-effect relationships in Natural Science passages. A simple flowchart that diagrams what the passage says can be an effective form of mapping.

Questions:
34. B An "All...EXCEPT" question. The correct answer will *not* be important to supporting the claim that

pesticides are responsible for amphibian declines. Either eliminate choices based on evidence in the passage or look for a statement that would not support the argument. (B) recommends itself; while being listened as threatened would indicate that the red-legged frog's population is low, it says nothing about *why* the population is low. There must be more of a connection for this to affect the argument either way.

Wrong Answers:
(A): Opposite. Since the author states in ¶1 that organophosphates are pesticides, higher levels of the organophosphates in the amphibians east of an agricultural zone would support the theory that pesticides are making their way into the amphibians' ecosystem and thus reducing populations.
(C): Opposite. As above, the fact that levels are higher east of agricultural areas than they are on the coast supports the idea that pesticides from farms are lowering populations.
(D): Opposite. Be sure you're clear on the relationship between pesticides and cholinesterase. Pesticides *reduce* cholinesterase. Therefore, a higher level near the coast would indicate that there's a lower level east of the farms, which means that there is more pesticide contamination east of the farms.

35. C Review the lines in context. Why would the author want to make a point about population declines in "seemingly pristine" areas especially? Predict: Even though the areas *seem* pristine, they might not in fact be so if amphibian populations are declining; they might be contaminated by pesticides that simply aren't obvious. (C) says the same.

Wrong Answers:
(A): Out of Scope. The author only discusses contamination; anything about repair is outside the author's topic, and wouldn't have anything to do with the specific mention of "seemingly pristine" areas anyway.
(B): Out of Scope. As above, the author never discusses whether or how to fix the damage caused by pesticides.
(D): Distortion. Casual observers might not realize that there's *pollution*, but the author never argues that amphibians are abundant.

36. D Where are treefrogs mentioned in the passage? The author discusses Pacific treefrogs at the beginning of ¶2 when describing a study showing reduced cholinesterase levels. Why were Pacific treefrogs studied rather than one of the threatened species that the author mentions in ¶3? Predict: The threatened frogs are probably harder to find by definition since there aren't many left. Therefore, (D) is a valid inference: Pacific treefrogs must be more abundant than the threatened red-legged frog.

Wrong Answers:

(A): Out of Scope. There's no information in the passage that suggests the Pacific treefrog is threatened with extinction, only that it has been affected by pesticides also.

(B): Out of Scope. The author only discusses contamination; there's no information to make an inference about what should be done about that contamination.

(C): Out of Scope. The author only discusses the levels of toxins and cholinesterase in Pacific treefrogs, and never discusses their relative population sizes in specific areas.

37. A An application question. How would the author respond to a scientist who thought that pesticides *weren't* responsible for the Californian amphibian decline since the same thing was happening all over the world? The author could reasonably respond that the California populations were perhaps being reduced for the same unknown reasons, but that pesticides were making the situation worse. It's quite possible, in other words, that there could be *multiple* reasons for the declines, of which pesticides are one. (A) says the same.

Wrong Answers:

(B): Out of Scope. Though this would perhaps support the idea that there's something else acting on the California populations, it doesn't specifically implicate pesticides and so wouldn't support the author's point that pesticides are responsible.

(C): Opposite. While this answer choice might be tempting, the premise of the question is that amphibian levels are declining worldwide for *unknown* reasons. Presumably the author's summary of pesticide action on organisms is well-known, and so if pesticides were responsible for the worldwide decline the causes wouldn't have been unknown.

(D): Opposite. As above, this would suggest that pesticides were responsible for the worldwide declines. But if the amphibian populations are declining for unknown reasons, it's probably not because of pesticides.

38. D A detail question. Where are pesticides primarily mentioned? Focus your search on ¶s 1 and 4. (D) follows directly from the author's point in the first sentence of ¶1: Pesticides are useful in attacking organisms that harm plants.

Wrong Answers:

(A): Distortion. Though the author says that pesticides might be transported "on the prevailing eastward summer winds," there's no way to tell whether they're in fact transported a long distance.

(B): Distortion. The author states in ¶1 that organophosphates are harmful to both insects and vertebrates, but doesn't assert this about pesticides in general, as the question requires.

(C): Out of Scope. While this sounds plausible, the author never discusses potential pesticide *use* in the Sierra Nevada, only contamination from pesticides used elsewhere.

39. B An evaluation question; refer to your map. What is the author's purpose in writing the third paragraph? Predict: The author wants to describe a mechanism by which some pesticides can harm animal populations. The answer choices are abstract, so compare them to your prediction piece-by-piece. (B) holds up: The mechanism of action is evidence, and it supports the hypothesis in ¶3 that pesticides are in fact hurting the frog population.

Wrong Answers:

(A): Out of Scope. While the author *does* allude to a scientific study in ¶3 by mentioning that amphibian populations are declining (someone had to study that), the author never critiques the study.

(C): Out of Scope. The author doesn't discuss any geographic information in ¶1.

(D): Distortion. Though the author does provide examples of harmful effects in ¶1, there are no harmful pesticide effects mentioned in ¶2; there's only the suggestion of a link between pesticide use and amphibian population decline.

Strategy Point:
Read abstract answer choices back into your prediction and the passage; match abstract points to their parallel in the passage.

40. C An incorporation question. Read carefully: the question already says that the information given weakens the argument; you have to determine what *part* of the argument is weakened. Why would the author's argument be weakened if homeowners use a lot more pesticide than do farmers? The author's evidence suggests that amphibian populations are lower downwind of agricultural areas, while they're relatively higher in the coastal regions. However, the coastal regions may very well have many lawns requiring a lot of pesticide. If amphibian levels are relatively high in this high-pesticide area and lower in an area that may in fact have *less* pesticide in the environment, the correlation that the author tries to establish is severely weakened. (C) is therefore correct. Note that the three wrong answer choices are all specific pieces of evidence, while (C) draws a conclusion from that evidence. You could have also gotten the right answer by realizing that new evidence is more likely to weaken a conclusion rather than old evidence.

Wrong Answers:

(A): Out of Scope. As explained above, the use of pesticides on lawns has no effect on the mechanism that the author describes, and therefore wouldn't weaken this part of the argument.

KAPLAN

(B): Out of Scope. The new evidence doesn't replace any of the author's evidence; the specific measurement of organophosphate levels wouldn't be affected by evidence on lawn care.

(D): Out of Scope. As above, since the new evidence is unrelated to the author's own evidence, there's no weakening effect.

PASSAGE VII

Topic and Scope:
The role of information technology in a recent spike in American productivity

Mapping the Passage:
¶1 gives background about the dotcom boom and asks what the precursors to the condition were.
¶2 describes a productivity spike and the possible explanation some have given for the spike: information technology.
¶3 defines productivity growth and suggests that heavy investment in information technology should have led to an increase in productivity.
¶4 discusses productivity and technology investment in other countries, and concludes that the data supports the argument that information technology was important to American productivity gains.

Questions:
41. A A detail question; evaluate it carefully. What is a resurgence? It's a rise to previous levels; if it were just a rise, it would be a surge, but not a *re*-surgence. Only the United States has enough data in the passage to infer a resurgence from: the author says at the end of ¶2 that "the rate of growth in labor productivity returned to the pre-1970 rate of increase." While other nations are mentioned, their previous levels aren't mentioned. Therefore, RN I must fit, while the other ones don't. (A) fits.

Wrong Answers:
(B): Opposite. As described above.
(C): Opposite. As above.
(D): Opposite. As above.

42. B An assumption question, but in an "All...EXCEPT" format that's rare for this type. Remember that an assumption is an unstated belief bridging evidence and conclusion. The conclusion is given: the author believes that information technology has raised American productivity. What is the evidence? Review the map: The author uses data on technology investment in the U.S. and other developed nations. Look for a choice that is *not* necessary to connect these. (B) fits for a few reasons. Perhaps most obviously, it's explicitly stated: the author says at the beginning of ¶4, "The revolution in technology is...a worldwide phenomenon." Since an assumption is unstated, (B) must not be an assumption essential to the argument.

Furthermore, using the denial test (which here you want to fail!), if this weren't true and the revolution *weren't* a world-wide phenomenon, it would do nothing to diminish the impact of information technology *within* the United States.

Wrong Answers:
(A): Opposite. The author must assume that other factors aren't significant; if they were, then the author couldn't make the argument that information technology is the major factor responsible for the surge in productivity.
(C): Opposite. The author uses these measures when discussing levels of technology investment in ¶4. If these weren't valid measures, the author's point in mentioning them would be moot.
(D): Opposite. If the author believes that these are valid measures of information technology and concludes that information technology was responsible for the productivity gains, an assumption must be that those measures were themselves responsible for the gain, as this choice suggests.

Strategy Point:
The Denial Test can be used to test whether an assumption is necessary to an argument. If it is, denying the assumption will cause the argument to fall apart. If the argument holds up even when the assumption is denied, the assumption isn't critical to the argument.

43. B Review the topic and scope of the passage: the author is concerned with information technology's role in boosting American productivity in the recent past. Look for an answer choice that sticks as closely as possible to topic and scope. (B) does this: It's reasonable to guess that the author would continue the paragraph by talking about the next stage of these trends in the same topic and scope: information technology and its effect on productivity.

Wrong Answers:
(A): Out of Scope. The author discusses the 1970s in ¶3, but only as background to discuss the current productivity spurt. It's more reasonable to think that the author will continue by talking about the future trajectory of the productivity gains.
(C): Out of Scope. The author doesn't mention any other possible causes for the increase in productivity and believes that information technology is the primary cause, and so it's unlikely that there would be a drastic shift that discussed other causes.
(D): Out of Scope. The author only discusses other countries to shed light on *American* productivity gains. Going into greater depth regarding other countries would veer out of scope.

44. D This odd wording means that you can ignore the entire "rebut" portion of the question stem. You're just looking for the statement with which the author would agree. An inference question: Predict by reviewing the author's main point about U.S. productivity growth in the late '90s. The author believes that it was the result of heavy investment in information technology. (D) says the same, simply summarizing the author's main point.

Wrong Answers:
(A): Opposite. The author believes, as argued in ¶3, that this particular surge in productivity was "extraordinary," and therefore by definition *not* typical.
(B): Out of Scope. The author doesn't discuss other changes, which could encompass any number of subjects, and so there's no way to compare how the author feels about this particular change relative to others, or whether it merits a particular explanation.
(C): Out of Scope. A classic case of confusing description with prescription: while the author explains a possible cause for the productivity gain, there's no discussion of what should be done with this information.

45. D An evaluation question: Predict by reviewing your map of ¶2. The author's main intent is to define productivity growth, and to suggest that the investment in informationtechnology should have led to a growth in productivity. (D) most closely describes the author's purpose of providing a possible explanation, and suggests that the explanation is given with the intent of following it up with further evidence, which the author does in fact provide in ¶4.

Wrong Answers:
(A): Faulty Use of Detail. Though (A) might be tempting because the author does define productivity and identify the factors that can affect its growth, this choice neglects the second half of the paragraph, which provides an explanation for a growth in productivity.
(B): Distortion. The author describes a correlation between investment and productivity, but doesn't describe peaks in either.
(C): Distortion. As above, while the author proposes a broad correlation between investment and productivity, there's no specific discussion of how much investment is required for a certain amount of productivity.

46. A An unusual question type; review by looking at your map for concentrations of evidence. Most evidence is presented in ¶3 and ¶4, so it's likely that the right answer will either have to do with American productivity growth or with other countries. (A) combines the two: in lines 58-65 the author discusses data that help explain why U.S. productivity growth beat out that of other countries.

Wrong Answers:
(B): Out of Scope. Though the author argues that the difference in productivity between these time periods

was due to technology investment, there's no specific evidence from both time periods to support this.
(C): Out of Scope. As above, though the author says that this happened, there's no data to back up the claim for productivity growth in the earlier time period.
(D): Out of Scope. The evidence in ¶4 doesn't discuss why these countries in particular experienced a slowing in productivity, only why the U.S. outpaced them.

PASSAGE VIII

Topic and Scope:
The state of poetry in the author's country.

Mapping the Passage:
¶1 says that some native "true poetry" has been written and that greater attention to poetry will produce benefits.
¶s2 and 3 describe the country's indifference to poetry, an explanation, and the author's rebuttal to the explanation.
¶4 describes the false conceptions that discourage native poets from writing quality poetry.
¶5 argues that poetry should be more appreciated.
¶6 argues that the country's immigrant population causes "old word" poetry to be valued over native poetry.

Strategy Point:
Save clearly difficult passages until the end of the test, and don't get bogged down. Even the most difficult of passages will have manageable questions.

Questions:
47. C An inference question in a disguised "All...EXCEPT" format. Either eliminate three choices that *must* follow from the passage or look for something that doesn't necessarily or cannot follow. (C) contradicts the author's suggestion that the country being written about is highly educated, "making equal pretensions to natural intelligence and progress in education."

Wrong Answers:
(A): Opposite. This is a valid inference based on the author's point in ¶6 that very many in the country have emigrated from other countries.
(B): Opposite. The author describes in ¶1 a "youthful country...in which nature unveils her most majestic forms to exalt and inspire."
(D): Opposite. The author argues in ¶3 that "few possess the wealth and leisure necessary to enable devotion of time or thought to the study of poetry..." which implies a relatively low standard of living.

Strategy Point: Note how much the passage tells you, and how much it doesn't. Although the author could be describing the U.S., he or she never states such. Therefore don't fill in the blanks with your own perceptions of the U.S.

48. C

A detail question: Review your map to get a feel for the reasons the author gives for the country's indifference to poetry. RN I is difficult to decipher in that it requires knowledge of what "edification" means. If you don't know, guess or move on to the next Roman Numeral! "Edification" means instruction or enlightenment, and the author does in fact argue that the country's population is unenlightened, as described at the end of ¶2 and the beginning of ¶3. RN II may be tempting from a quick review of ¶6, but distorts the author's argument. The author argues that *in spite* of the new country's quality poetry, immigrants read old world poetry because of nostalgia. The issue isn't quality, but homesickness. There's no need to evaluate RN III at this point unless you skipped RN I. RN III is correct for the same reasons that RN II is wrong: immigrants are reading their homeland's poetry because of nostalgia.

Wrong Answers:
(A): Opposite. See above.
(B): Opposite. See above.
(D): Opposite. See above.

Strategy Point:
Notice that if you didn't know what "edification" meant, you could have skipped the choice and still gotten the right answer with certainty after evaluating the other two! Use the setup of Roman Numeral questions to your advantage.

49. A A difficult question. If you're having trouble finding the right answer, it may be easier to eliminate. Start off by predicting a basic contrast in the passage: The author believes that poetry is all sorts of good, but that people don't appreciate it as much as they should. Why is poetry not appreciated in the country the author discusses? The author argues that people don't understand poetry as well as they should. Something palpable is easily accessible, and something subtle isn't. Even if you didn't know the definition of palpable, you could guess that since the choices are presented as contrasts it means the opposite of subtle. This contrast fits in with the author's general argument made throughout the passage that people simply lack a grasp of poetry's finer points. This claim is made in ¶3, when the author says that poetry isn't accepted for "other causes less palpable." In ¶4 the author argues that those who don't appreciate poetry are either incapable of doing so or are more familiar with "widely available, but lower forms," which again suggests a contrast between the subtle and the less so. In ¶5 the author argues that only those who pay careful attention to poetry appreciate it, and in ¶1 the author contrasts a "chilly atmosphere" with a more subtle spring breath. (A) is therefore correct as a contrast made throughout the passage, while the other choices are made only in certain parts of the author's argument.

Wrong Answers:
(B): Faulty Use of Detail. The author makes this distinction at the end of ¶3, but doesn't mention it throughout the rest of the passage.
(C): Faulty Use of Detail. The author implies in ¶6 that some who do not appreciate poetry consider it insignificant, but doesn't make the claim again.
(D): Faulty Use of Detail. As above and as argued in ¶s2-4, the author suggests that those who don't appreciate poetry fail to do so because they consider poetry impractical.

50. C What scope of poetry is the author concerned with? Predict: The author wants to discuss the state of poetry in one particular country. (C) therefore makes the most sense; it's the only answer choice that would justify this focus on the poetry of a single country.

Wrong Answers:
(A): Out of Scope. The author isn't so much concerned with instructing people how to *write* poetry as why they should *appreciate* poetry.
(B): Out of Scope. Though the author does compare old world and new world poetry in ¶6, it's not itself the focus of the passage.
(D): Out of Scope. Another answer choice that doesn't include the author's focus on a particular country, which is an integral part of the passage.

51. C Review the line in context. The author defines the phrase in the lines above when saying that there are "men who are not gifted with the power of giving expression...who nevertheless experience the throbbing in their hearts." Paraphrase: Some people can't write it, but they can still appreciate it. (C) says the same.

Wrong Answers:
(A): Out of Scope. The author is distinguishing between those who can and cannot create, not between ways of communicating poetry.
(B): Out of Scope. The author is describing those who *do* value poetry.
(D): Distortion. The author is talking about people who lack the gift of writing poetry, but doesn't express sympathy toward them. Rather, the point is to show that appreciation can exist even when the person can't write poetry.

52. C Review the phrase in the context of the structure around it. The author has just finished listing all the reasons why poetry isn't properly appreciated, and then says that some true poetry has been written "despite the unpropitious circumstances that exist." It's reasonable to guess that these circumstances are those things that keep true poetry from being written. The author argues in the paragraphs above that this is primarily due to misconceptions about poetry or a lack of understanding. (C) fits.

Wrong Answers:
(A): Faulty Use of Detail. This is an argument made in ¶3, but it's one that the author considers "by no means satisfactory."
(B): Faulty Use of Detail. The author argues that this does happen, both immediately after this phrase and at the end of ¶4, but as the result rather than the cause. Native poets don't devote themselves to their craft *because* of misunderstandings about poetry.
(D): Faulty Use of Detail. Though the author mentions this as one reason for the lack of poetry, it's not the main reason, and the author seems to treat this reason with some forgiveness. It therefore likely wouldn't fall under the negative "unpropitious circumstances" that the author discusses.

53. A An application question. Predict by reviewing what the author considers true poetry to be. The author argues in ¶4 that it's *not* "fanciful or contrived," but that it requires "sustained application to...craft that is essential for artistic excellence." Look for an answer choice that fits with this idea of poetry. (A) most closely fits, describing poetry that can be edited and made better, but that can't be artificially contrived from the start.

Wrong Answers:
(B): Opposite. Though the author believes that poetry must be uncontrived, it's also made clear that good poetry requires a lot of work to perfect. This answer choice suggests the opposite.
(C): Out of Scope. The author discusses poetry that is tied to a particular country, but says nothing about poetry tied to a particular time.
(D): Opposite. This description of poetry would likely be something the author would label as contrived, and therefore more in keeping with misconceptions of poetry than with what "true" poetry is.

54. D What is the author describing when discussing "native literature"? The author argues that poets within the country should produce more literature for the people in the country. The author clearly believes that immigrants can be part of this native literature since the country is described as "young" and the author describes himself as part of a group of "emigrants from the Old Country." Furthermore, the author focuses in ¶1 on what true poetry should be by discussing the nature of the country itself rather than the nature of the poets. (D) therefore most closely fits with what the author is trying to convey.

Wrong Answers:
(A): Out of Scope. The author is concerned with poetry that comes from and concerns a specific country, but there's no indication that only aboriginal poetry can be considered native.
(B): Distortion. Though this might be an important part of native poetry, the author is more interested in poetry

that takes on the characteristics of the country rather than poetry written by any particular group of people.
(C): Distortion. As above, the author is concerned with a national poetry rather than the specific origin of the poets themselves.

PASSAGE IX

Topic and Scope:
The use of punctuation, and in particular the dash

Mapping the Passage:
¶s1-3 explain the main use of the dash: to present multiple expressions describing the same idea.
¶4 argues that punctuation is extremely important to the meaning of language.
¶5 suggests that the topic of punctuation has not been sufficiently explored.
¶6 introduces the dash and notes that it has gone out of style in the press.

Questions:
55. D A detail question in Roman Numeral format: target the last three paragraphs, all of which deal exclusively with the dash. RN I is stated directly in ¶6: the author describes "the printer's now general substitution...for the dash." RN II follows closely afterwards; the author argues that this backlash against the dash came as a result of "its excessive employment about twenty years ago." RN III can be inferred from the author's general argument, and also the point in ¶3 that the dash is necessary and "*cannot* be dispensed with." (D) includes all three statements.

Wrong Answers:
(A): Opposite. As described above.
(B): Opposite. As above.
(C): Opposite. As above.

56. A Use your work from the previous question to help yourself on this question. Statements II and III above together deal with the reason why printers have gotten in the habit of removing dashes. Review ¶5: The dash-censoring "has been brought about by the revulsion consequent upon its excessive employment about twenty years ago." In other words, writers used it too much, so now it's kibosh. (A) says the same.

Wrong Answers:
(B): Faulty Use of Detail. Though the author mentions this in ¶4, a totally different reason is given for why printers dislike the dash.
(C): Opposite. The author argues vehemently in the next paragraph that the dash *does* serve a purpose that other punctuation can't replace.
(D): Out of Scope. Authorial second-guessing is never mentioned in the passage.

57. A You're looking for a right answer that *isn't* a valid inference. Since there's not much information to go on in the question, the answer will probably have something to do with the author's main points. Predict: Punctuation is important, and the dash is unique—it allows multiple expressions of the same thought, something that other punctuation can't accomplish. (A) immediately recommends itself.

Wrong Answers:
(B): Opposite. The author argues in ¶5 that it's a "vulgar notion" to think that punctuation doesn't follow simple rules. Therefore, the author certainly believes that it does.
(C): Opposite. This sums up the author's argument in ¶4.
(D): Opposite. This also follows from the author's suggestion that "few comprehend the extent" of punctuation's importance.

58. B Where is "The Philosophy of Point" mentioned? Go back to ¶5 and review your map: The author wants to argue that writing can follow clear and consistent rules. It's a good bet, then, that the author mentions the article in order to reinforce this point. (B) says the same, suggesting that the article would be the author's attempt to explain exactly what the rules of punctuation are.

Wrong Answers:
(A): Distortion. Though the author puts the word "philosophy" in the title, there's no suggestion that there's anything philosophical about grammar.
(C): Out of Scope. The author never suggests that the purpose of the proposed magazine article would be to reinforce his credentials.
(D): Distortion. Though the author wants to expand on his statement that punctuation follows simple rules, he's not interested in emending—that is, modifying—his argument about punctuation.

59. A A detail question. What does the author argue about different expressions separated by a dash? Predict: The main point of the dash is to separate multiple thoughts that together get at the meaning—"which *partially* convey the idea intended." (A) says the same.

Wrong Answers:
(B): Opposite. The author argues that each phrase partially conveys the author's idea—each expression is useful.
(C): Opposite. Each expression approaches the main thought partially, and so there's no subdivision of purpose as this answer choice suggests.
(D): Opposite. The author states that each expression conveys the *same* idea.

60. D Review the lines in context. The author states that "it often occurs that an axiom appears a paradox, or that a sarcasm is converted into a sermonoid." Why does this happen? Look above: "...a sentence may be deprived of...its point...by improper punctuation." The words are therefore examples of how one point becomes another with bad punctuation. (D) most closely fits: by defining the statements as different in tone, the choice reinforces the idea that incorrect punctuation can change the tone of a statement.

Wrong Answers:
(A): Out of Scope. The author is discussing the improper use of punctuation in general in ¶4.
(B): Out of Scope. The only time that the author mentions Byron is to say in ¶6 that the Byronic poets used the dash, a point irrelevant to ¶4.
(C): Out of Scope. The author doesn't mention printers until ¶6, and then only in reference to the dash, which is out of the scope of ¶4.

Verbal Reasoning Test Ten

Time—85 minutes
Question 1–60

DIRECTIONS: Each of the passages in this test is followed by a set of questions based on the passage's content. After reading each passage, decide on the one best response to each question and mark it on your answer sheet. If you are unsure of an answer, eliminate the choices you know are wrong and choose from the remaining choices. You may refer to the passages while answering the questions.

Passage I (Questions 1–7)

Polychlorinated biphenyls are heavy, syrupy hydrocarbons that were first synthesized in the 1880s. Because they conduct heat but not electricity and are water-insoluble, fire-resistant, and extremely stable
5 (withstanding temperatures of up to 1600° F), they were found, in the 1930s, to be extremely useful as components in cooling systems and electrical equipment (transformers and capacitors). They were widely used for these purposes and also in the composition of
10 sealants, rubber, paints, plastics, inks, and insecticides.

PCBs were banned in 1979, after researchers linked them to cancer and developmental problems in humans. However, PCBs persist in the environment for extremely long periods. Because of an affinity for fat, they have a
15 marked tendency to accumulate in living organisms; increasing in concentration as they move up the food chain.

In the course of the twentieth century, increasing awareness of how chemical wastes can affect public
20 health and the environment resulted in restriction of dumping. However, where dumping had already occurred, uncontrolled or abandoned hazardous wastes remained at sites such as warehouses, landfills, and even rivers. To locate, investigate, and clean up the worst of
25 these sites nationwide, Congress in 1980 established the Superfund Program, administered by the Environmental Protection Agency (EPA). Under Superfund, companies found responsible for pollution can be financially liable for the cost of cleanup. Due to dumping over a period of
30 35 years by two capacitor manufacturing plants located along the northern part of the Hudson River in New York State, EPA has estimated that 1.1 million pounds of PCBs have accumulated.

Field surveys of the river have found substantial
35 contamination in 40 submerged sediment "hot spots," 5 exposed shoreline remnant deposits, dredge spoils on riverbanks, and estuary sediments. Today, because of PCB contamination, human consumption of fish caught in the most affected areas of the Hudson River is pro-
40 hibited. But, while fish consumption remains the most potent route of PCB exposure, exposure can also occur through other routes. Eight municipalities currently draw drinking water from the Hudson and another, New York City, draws it during emergencies.

45 Although many take positions on whether dredging will have positive or negative consequences to the Hudson River Valley, there is only perfunctory attention to the ultimate fate of the dredged PCBs. EPA's report recommending dredging indicates that, due to opposi-
50 tion of local residents, neither a landfill nor a thermal treatment facility (for high temperature incineration) can be locally-sighted and the PCBs should therefore be transported to a solid waste landfill outside of the area. The report does not, however, identify a specific loca-
55 tion.

Furthermore, air along the river contains elevated concentrations of PCBs, and individuals living along the River show PCB residue in their bodies, paralleling the river's contamination. The EPA has recommended that
60 PCBs be removed from the river bottom by dredging, thus reducing contamination and possibly eventually permitting revitalization of commercial fishing, which once generated $40 million income annually. However, the corporation blamed for the dumping argues that
65 dredging may "stir up" the PCBs (which they describe as now "lying undisturbed" in the riverbed), causing the water, air, and riverbanks to become even more contaminated. Some area residents echo these concerns and also argue that dredging will subject them to years of
70 unacceptable noise, disruption, and curtailed recreational activities.

GO TO THE NEXT PAGE.

1. Based on information provided by the author of the passage, it can be inferred from the passage that PCBs are:

   I.   heavier than water.
   II. toxic to fish.
   III. readily biodegradable.

   A. I only
   B. I and II only
   C. I and III only
   D. II and III only

2. An "estuary" is defined as the part of a wide, lower course of a river where its current is met by the tides. Information contained in the passage indicates that PCBs in estuary sediments most probably:

   A. originate from an additional source of pollution not yet discovered.
   B. indicate that PCBs in the river do not necessarily remain where they were originally deposited.
   C. are present at a background level typical of the earth's environment as a whole.
   D. indicate that all the PCBs currently in the river can be expected to eventually end up in the ocean.

3. Based on information contained in the passage as a whole, it can be inferred that the opinion of the company responsible for PCB pollution of the Hudson River, with respect to the appropriateness of clean-up, is most probably:

   A. at least as objective as the opinion of area residents.
   B. reflective of its overriding concern with its public image.
   C. financially motivated.
   D. indicative of its lack of connection to commercial fishing interests.

4. According to the passage, the EPA differs from local residents and the company responsible for PCB contamination in that it affirms that it bases its recommended action on benefit to:

   A. commercial fishing interests.
   B. residential interests.
   C. the environment as a whole.
   D. recreational activities.

5. Suppose a local newspaper in a Hudson River community was preparing an editorial. Which of the following pieces of additional information would be most helpful to it in determining whether it should support the EPA recommendation to remove PCBs from the Hudson River by dredging?

   A. How present PCB levels in the river compare to levels that existed prior to industrialization
   B. To what extent equipment to be used for dredging can remove the PCBs without causing their release into the air and into upper river currents
   C. How the PCBs will be disposed of after removal from the river
   D. The expected cost of the dredging operation

6. It can be inferred from the passage that the justification used for prohibiting individuals from consuming fish caught in contaminated sections of the Hudson River is that the individuals may thereby:

   A. reduce the level of PCBs in their bodies.
   B. avoid any further increase in the level of PCBs in their bodies.
   C. mitigate the accumulation of PCBs in their bodies.
   D. prevent cancer and developmental problems.

7. Which of the following is stated by the author but is not explained by facts or data contained in the passage?

   A. Individuals who live along the Hudson have a concentration of PCBs in their bodies that parallels the concentration of the substances in the river.
   B. PCBs were useful as components of electrical equipment and cooling systems.
   C. PCBs accumulate in living organisms.
   D. What should be done about PCBs which contaminate the environment is controversial.

GO TO THE NEXT PAGE.

Passage II (Questions 8–14)

With equal justice, the council of Pisa deposed the popes of Rome and Avignon; the conclave was unanimous in the choice of Alexander V, and his vacant seat was soon filled by a similar election of John XXIII, the
5 most profligate of mankind. But instead of extinguishing the schism, the rashness of the French and Italians had given a third pretender to the chair of St. Peter.

Such new claims of the synod and conclave were disputed: three kings, of Germany, Hungary, and
10 Naples, adhered to the cause of Gregory XII, and Benedict XIII, himself a Spaniard, was acknowledged by the devotion and patriotism of that powerful nation. The rash proceedings of Pisa were corrected by the council of Constance; the emperor Sigismond acted a
15 conspicuous part as the advocate or protector of the Catholic church; and the number and weight of civil and ecclesiastical members might seem to constitute the states-general of Europe. Of the three popes, John XXIII was the first victim: he fled and was brought back a pris-
20 oner: the most scandalous charges were suppressed; the vicar of Christ was only accused of piracy, murder, rape, sodomy, and incest; and after subscribing his own condemnation, he expiated in prison the imprudence of trusting his person to a free city beyond the Alps.

25 Gregory XII, whose obedience was reduced to the narrow precincts of Rimini, descended with more honour from the throne; and his ambassador convened the session, in which he renounced the title and authority of lawful pope. To vanquish the obstinacy of Benedict XIII
30 and his adherents, the emperor in person undertook a journey from Constance to Perpignan. The kings of Castile, Arragon, Navarre, and Scotland, obtained an equal and honourable treaty; with the concurrence of the Spaniards, Benedict was deposed by the council.

35 The harmless old man was left in a solitary castle to excommunicate twice each day the rebel kingdoms which had deserted his cause and the synod of Constance proceeded with slow and cautious steps to elect the sovereign of Rome and the head of the church.
40 On this momentous occasion, the college of twenty-three cardinals was fortified with thirty deputies, six of whom were chosen in each of the five great nations of Christendom, – the Italian, the German, the French, the Spanish, and the English: the interference of strangers
45 was softened by their generous preference of an Italian and a Roman, and the hereditary, as well as personal, merit of Otho Colonna recommended him to the conclave. Rome accepted with joy and obedience the no-

50 blest of her sons; the ecclesiastical state was defended by his powerful family; and the elevation of Martin V is the era of the restoration and establishment of the popes in the Vatican.

---

8. According to points made by the author about both of the following, it can be inferred that a goal shared by the Council of Pisa and the Council of Constance was to:

   A. reunite the Catholic Church under a single pope.
   B. forge an alliance between the most powerful nations in Europe.
   C. obtain for the Catholic Church the protection of the Emperor Sigismond.
   D. appoint a native Roman to the papacy.

9. According to what the author states in the passage, why was the Council of Constance more successful than the Council of Pisa?

   I. The Council of Constance made sure that it had the support of the most important European powers.
   II. The Council of Constance elected a pope who was more virtuous than any of his rivals.
   III. The Council of Constance elected a pope who was already respected by the Roman people.

   A. I and II
   B. I and III
   C. II and III
   D. I, II, and III

10. For what purpose does the author distinguish between "the most scandalous charges" against John XXIII, and the charges of which he was actually accused?

    A. To demonstrate the leniency of the Council of Constance
    B. To suggest how serious the suppressed charges must have been
    C. To give an example of John XXIII's political influence
    D. To show the importance of electing an Italian to the papacy

GO TO THE NEXT PAGE.

11. Reflecting on the various points brought up by the author in the passage, how did the Spanish contribute to the resolution of the division within the Catholic Church?

   A. They encouraged the cardinals to revolt, and they deposed the two reigning popes.
   B. They opposed the French and Italians, and they supported Benedict XIII.
   C. They protected the Catholic Church, and they prosecuted John XXIII.
   D. They agreed to the deposal of Benedict XIII, and they helped to elect Martin V.

12. It can be inferred that the author would agree with which of the following statements about Benedict XIII, Gregory XII, and John XXIII?

   A. Benedict XIII was the best of the three.
   B. Gregory XII was the best of the three.
   C. None of the three deserved to be pope.
   D. John XXIII had the best claim to having been legitimately elected.

13. By the explanation of circumstances, the passage points out that John XXIII was not generally acceptable to Catholics throughout Europe. The author suggests that if John XXIII had been generally acceptable, which of the following would have resulted?

   A. Benedict XIII and Gregory XII would not have been deposed.
   B. The Council of Constance would not have taken place.
   C. The Catholic Church would not have been reunited.
   D. The papal seat would not have been moved back to Rome.

14. As opposed to the makeup of the Council of Pisa, at the Council of Constance, why were the 23 cardinals joined by 30 deputies?

   A. To make sure that their choice for pope was acceptable to the most important European states
   B. To prevent them escaping
   C. To protect them from governmental interference
   D. To make sure that they maintained a proper level of decorum

GO TO THE NEXT PAGE.

Passage III (Questions 15–21)

Previous investigations into the workings of memory usually tested episodic memory, which describes the recall of specific events, as well as the ability to remember names and the whereabouts of items like car keys.
5   This ability usually remains intact until the mid-sixties, when people often become forgetful of things like recent events and minor details. While some researchers suggest that this well-known decline in episodic memory in the elderly stems from degeneration of the frontal lobes
10 of the brain, many scientists believe that such memory loss is largely due to retirement: after the demands of work stop, most people no longer exercise their mental faculties as strenuously. Thus, regular mental "exercise" might curtail memory loss.

15 But episodic memory comprises only part of this intricate brain function. Memory researchers have identified two other types of memory, neither of which seems to deteriorate with age. Contemporary research into how the mind stores and retrieves information refutes the no-
20 tion of the inevitable decline in memory. New studies suggest that we have more than one kind of memory, and imply that elderly people who suffer from forgetfulness can utilize other types of memory to compensate for the decline.

25 This new conception of memory stems from a shift in methodology of memory research. While older studies of memory and aging involved comparisons between different age groups, recent investigations tested the same group of people over a number of years. Such lon-
30 gitudinal data more clearly establishes the relationship between memory and aging. Through these studies of older adults, researchers concluded that there exist three major kinds of memory, only one of which declines in old age.

35 Semantic memory, which describes our ability to recall knowledge and facts as well as events in the distant past, does not seem to lessen over the course of a lifetime. In fact, such memory may be even sharper in elderly people than in the young or middle-aged. When
40 a group of men and women in their sixties were tested on a specific vocabulary list and retested on the same list a decade later, the group had improved their scores by an average of six words—an increase researchers consider substantial. Such studies suggest that by taking
45 notes or mulling over events, elderly people who suffer from forgetfulness can store more information in the semantic memory, thus compensating for episodic memory loss.

50 Implicit memory deals with the tremendous variety of mental activities we perform without making any intentional effort. Examples of these include actions like driving a car, touch-typing, or riding a bicycle. Scientists have learned through observations of amnesi-
55 acs that this type of memory is distinct from both episodic and semantic memory. In one such study, an amnesiac patient who had been an avid golfer before developing a memory problem remembered which club to use for each stroke; however, he forgot that he had played a hole within minutes of having done so.

60 In addition, further studies of amnesiacs have shown that people with these disorders can learn new facts but cannot remember when and where they had learned them. Studies of people in their sixties and seventies showed similar results: like amnesiacs, older peo-
65 ple are able to learn from new experience as well as younger people, but often have difficulty remembering the source of their knowledge or skill. While the findings are encouraging, it must be noted that such studies do not deal with memory problems associated with ill-
70 ness, disease, or injury to the brain.

15. Based on the information in the passage, the author implies that advanced age might adversely affect which of the following?

   I.   Memory of details of a recent conversation
   II. Recollection of childhood memories
   III. Ability to perform routine tasks

   A. I only
   B. II only
   C. III only
   D. I and II only

16. With regard to new research into memory and the various points brought up in the passage, the author's attitude might be described as one of:

   A. unbridled enthusiasm.
   B. wary skepticism.
   C. reserved optimism.
   D. unbiased objectivity.

GO TO THE NEXT PAGE.

17. The primary purpose of the passage is to:

   A. discuss the ways in which a new theory of memory challenges common assumptions regarding memory and aging.
   B. explain why past investigations into memory tested only episodic memory.
   C. describe recent research into the functioning of the brain.
   D. consider the reasons why episodic memory diminished in later years.

18. It can be inferred from the passage that the author understands that recent developments in memory research can be attributed largely to:

   A. scientists' efforts to dismantle stereotypes regarding the abilities of elderly persons.
   B. recent discoveries that distinguish age-related forgetfulness from disease and injury-related memory loss.
   C. the realization that mental exercise frequently diminishes memory loss.
   D. new methodologies that clarify the relationship between memory and aging.

19. According to studies and evidence put forth by the author of the passage, older people often forget recent events but remember the distant past because:

   A. childhood events exist as part of implicit memory.
   B. episodic memory declines while implicit memory does not.
   C. episodic memory declines but semantic memory improves with age.
   D. retired elderly people make few demands on their semantic memory.

20. The passage suggests that an elderly person who cannot remember how to tie her shoes is most probably suffering from:

   A. amnesia.
   B. semantic memory loss.
   C. episodic memory loss.
   D. implicit memory loss.

21. Based on the information in the passage, the author would probably agree with which of the following statements regarding memory problems associated with illness, disease, or injury?

   A. Since many elderly suffer from such organic dysfunctions, memory research remains more theoretical than practical.
   B. Scientists do not anticipate that these studies will contribute to our understanding of these disorders as well.
   C. It is likely that researchers will turn toward these more critical problems in the near future.
   D. Since such disorders do not conform to the tripartate model of memory, most researchers are not interested in them.

GO TO THE NEXT PAGE.

Passage IV (Questions 22–28)

Carolus Linnaeus, who developed a framework for modern systems of taxonomy and classification in the 1700s, actually undertook his research with the hope of discovering patterns of God's creation. Georges LeClerc (1707-1788) proposed a mechanism for calculating the age of the Earth using molten spheres of iron and measuring cooling times, after which he proposed that the Earth was at least 75,000 years old and perhaps as old as three million years.

Some students may feel that we should not focus on the past, and that our thoughts should be trained on new knowledge and invention, rather than antiquated ideas. What these students do not understand is the importance of the old ideas in shaping our current understanding of the world around us, and that an outright dismissal of past theories simply because they have been rejected by new evidence may limit our understanding of current theories.

There is value of learning about hypotheses that were once espoused to explain an observed phenomenon, but that have now been long disproved and invalidated. Darwin's theory of natural selection as the mechanism for evolution is all too often taught in a vacuum in high school biology classrooms, as if this brilliant naturalist developed a groundbreaking theory on natural order which had never before been contemplated in any form. It is only by learning about the gradual development of evolutionary theory, and the role of some religious individuals in shaping this theory, that students may come to see the logic and power behind Darwin's relatively simple ideas. Many of the contributions upon which Darwin built his ideas came from scientists who were staunch creationists themselves.

These scientists believed that all organisms on Earth had been placed here through "special creation," by God, because there was little evidence at the time to support evolution. LeClerc also perceived that species were not fixed and could change over time; he even proposed that closely related species, such as the horse and donkey, had developed from a common ancestor and had been modified by different climactic conditions. Yet, LeClerc was a devout Christian creationist and devoted much of his writing to the debunking of evolutionary ideas. Despite their commitments to religion, LeClerc and Linnaeus both gave Darwin crucial raw material to work with—their ideas concerning the similarities between related species and possible connections with common ancestors cried out for a reasonable explanation.

For centuries before Darwin, data that challenged the biblical account of creation was surfacing in many fields of research. As explorers began to study the forces that shape the Earth, such as mountain building and volcanic eruptions, accounts from scripture and assertions that the Earth was very young began to be called into question. Uniformitarian geologists such as Charles Lyell felt that the only reason mountains and other features of the Earth's terrain had been built the way they had was because of long, gradual processes that shaped these structures. There was no way, he felt, that the Earth could be several thousand years old as asserted in the Bible. In addition, the discovery of new plants, animals, and fossils as explorers traveled to uncharted regions of the world aroused suspicion about the paucity of animal and plant "kinds" in the Bible. Improvements in scientists' abilities to estimate the age of the Earth and the relative ages of fossils also pushed people to question old assumptions.

---

22. Taking into account all that was argued by the author, the main idea of this passage is that:

    A. religious scientists before Darwin greatly influenced his formation of the theory of natural selection.
    B. similarities between species of plants and animals were too great to ignore as people attempted to explain relationships in nature.
    C. Darwin relied on a great deal of information from those who lived before him as he formed his well-known conclusions about the mechanisms of evolution.
    D. old ideas should not be dismissed simply because they are old and disproved.

23. The passage points out that in the past, various scientific findings stood in contrast to the Bible's creation story. Findings that challenged Biblical accounts of creation included all of the following EXCEPT:

    A. similarities between related species, such as donkeys and horses.
    B. indications that mountain building processes took tens of thousands of years.
    C. findings of a great diversity of new plants and animals across a variety of habitats.
    D. fossil findings indicating that the Earth was, in fact, tens of thousands of years old or more.

GO TO THE NEXT PAGE.

24. If the author were teaching a class on evolution in a university in the Unites States, the passage suggests that the class would spend a significant amount of time discussing:

    A. the origins of Darwin's theory of natural selection.
    B. details of Darwin's theory of natural selection.
    C. the Biblical account of creation.
    D. taxonomy and classification and their importance in Darwin's ideas.

25. According to the information from the passage, Georges Le Clerc's ideas on evolution may have been closest to those of:

    A. Darwin, because LeClerc focused much of his research on understanding similarities between related plants and animals.
    B. Linnaeus, because they were both devout Christians who attempted to explain natural phenomena in a supernatural light.
    C. Lyell, because both scientists concluded that the supposed age of the Earth could not account for certain measured features.
    D. Linnaeus, because both scientists gave Darwin important raw material to work with as Darwin formulated his ideas on natural selection.

26. The author's discussion of Darwin's theory in paragraph 3 of the passage suggests that:

    A. Darwin does not deserve the credit he is given for his ideas on evolutionary theory.
    B. Darwin's theories should be presented in the context within which they were originally conceived.
    C. Darwin's ideas would be properly devalued if people knew the religious background from which his ideas stemmed.
    D. Darwin's ideas are simple enough that he didn't need much help in formulating them.

27. With respect to his claim that students need to understand and appreciate old theories, the author asserts that:

    I. Darwin's theory of natural selection cannot be understood or applied without the knowledge of evolutionary hypotheses that came before him.
    II. even now-debunked concepts, such as LeClerc's melting iron spheres to calculate Earth's age, are important in building a complete picture of how Darwin came to his revolutionary theory.
    III. learning about Linnaeus' classification schemes would help students see how Linnaeus' work gave Darwin a body of knowledge that needed proper explaining.

    A. I and II
    B. II only
    C. II and III
    D. I, II, and III

28. According to the passage, the idea that mountains and other structures take a great deal of time to form was an idea championed by:

    A. catastrophists.
    B. Darwinists.
    C. creationists.
    D. uniformitarians.

GO TO THE NEXT PAGE.

Passage V (Questions 29–33)

In the fast new choreography of American compassion, explanation is twirled into excuse, and the spotlight's shine endows feelings with a prominence that facts could only hope for. Perception has become more important than reality. In homes, classrooms, and workplaces, we prefer to understand viewpoints rather than discern truths.

After recounting the prevalent view of Nicholas II, which faults the last czar for failure to recognize dire conditions of the day, neglect of astute advisors, and reliance instead on sources incompetent to influence state behavior, Y. S. Bark, in *Nicholas the Unlucky*, concedes that Nicholas was a poor leader. She then adds, "What few acknowledge is that none of this mattered. By Nicholas's time, and surely unbeknownst to Nicholas, czarism had become an anachronism. Its collapse was inevitable." Bark's main contention is that Nicholas II was a doomed figure who had the misfortune of presiding over, but not responsibility for significantly contributing to, the calamitous demise of Czarist Russia in 1917.

The product of an accomplished historian known for nice scholarship on inter-war diplomatic history, Bark's first foray into popular political biography proceeds with a deft review of the social, economic, and political conditions of Nicholas's day. In every respect but governance, Nicholas's Russia was, or was rapidly becoming, modern. Political alliances with Europe proper had existed for centuries, as had kinship with European art and literature. Developments in technology, communication, and transportation only increased the magnitude of Russia's Europeanness.

After 1860, even Russian economic life began, however embryonically, to resemble Western forms. Only governance remained unchanged, yet it was governance that most needed transformation. Then begins a confused attempt to vindicate Nicholas: "At the time, calls came for a compromise of czarism, yet it was in their tradition that the czars saw the *sine qua non* of Russian life. This was the impossible situation confronting Nicholas. Given these circumstances, it is implausible to suppose that Nicholas should have viewed the abandonment or even compromise of autocracy as Russia's salvific hope. To the contrary, turbulent times are perfect for redoubling the faith of ages; the first reaction to discomforting ideas is hatred. (The rest is detail—witness history's smile on stalwart Woodrow Wilson.)"

Nicholas the Unlucky is ultimately unsatisfying because Nicholas is a poor choice for arguing historical inevitability and historical compassion. Like monarchism at the same time, czarist absolutism may have been doomed. Perhaps no czar after 1895 could have saved it. But citing the size and force of a tidal wave does nothing to exonerate a leader who all but tore down the dyke and let it in. Worthwhile sources claim, not that Nicholas originated the causes of the revolution, but that at best he did nothing to alleviate them, and at worst he intensified them. Monarchists' astute, if reluctant, embrace of modernity in Prussia and Japan attests to how the demise of monarchy can be delayed. And while, like Nicholas, the Hohenzollerns of Austria-Hungary did not outlast World War I, they had faced the assault of modernity beginning much earlier, and probably would have fallen earlier, in 1848, had they behaved as Nicholas did. These facts deserve some room in the spotlight. For all of us, from schoolchildren to leaders and even historians, perception may seem to be more important than reality. Sooner or later, reality avenges itself.

To demonstrate Nicholas's unshakable faith in the czarist tradition, Bark devotes an entire section to Count Pobedonostsev, by whom Alexander III, Nicholas's father, was tutored in childhood and closely advised as Czar. A singular influence on Nicholas's own development, Pobedonostsev in his memoirs wrote of "…Parliamentarism, which…has deluded much of the so-called 'intelligence'…although daily its falsehood is exposed more clearly to the world." Grounded in the inalienable Russian truth that the czar was "the Little Father, God's chief earthly agent and protector," Nicholas's commitment to autocracy, in Bark's view, rendered major reform unthinkable.

GO TO THE NEXT PAGE.

29. As used in the end of the fourth paragraph in the statement: "The rest is detail—witness history's smile on stalwart Woodrow Wilson," the words "The rest is detail" refer to:

   A. Bark's belief that popular commitment to core values, even though the values are subjective, is essential to persevering through periods of national turmoil.

   B. Bark's implication that policies advanced by Woodrow Wilson, though more successful than those of Nicholas, similarly reflected a strong commitment to traditional beliefs.

   C. the author's contention that weighing the merits of alternative reform policies is less important than a ruler's overall commitment to reform.

   D. the author's assumption that Woodrow Wilson's activist policies do not constitute a reasonable basis for comparison to Nicholas's conservative policies.

30. The author's discussion in the passage of the Hohenzollerns assumes which of the following?

   A. In at least some significant ways, the political challenges faced by the rulers of Austria-Hungary around 1848 resemble those faced by Nicholas around 1917.

   B. Like Nicholas, Hohenzollern rulers perceived themselves as having not only a historical, but also a divine, mandate.

   C. For the purposes of historical analysis, modernity and Europeanness can be treated as interchangeable terms.

   D. Nicholas should have implemented the same policy reforms as those affected by rulers in Japan, Prussia, and Austria-Hungary.

31. The author claims in lines 56–59 that Nicholas at least failed to alleviate, and at most exacerbated, the causes of the collapse of czarism in 1917. The support offered for this conclusion is:

   A. weak; the author neglects to name a czar in the period after 1895 who could have saved czarism from collapse.

   B. weak; the author fails to acknowledge the depth of the reluctance with which monarchists in other nations confronted modernity.

   C. strong; by asserting that reality avenges itself, the author directly undermines the primary hypothesis of *Nicholas the Unlucky*.

   D. strong; the author provides several comparative illustrations of cases in which collapse was averted or forestalled.

32. Suppose that a chapter in *Nicholas the Unlucky* recounted the following episode. In 1915, a group of advisors urged Nicholas to address the concerns of urban workers, who had been participating in increasingly widespread and violent strikes. In response to the advisors' urgings, the Empress Alexandra, Nicholas's wife, advised, "You are the *Autocrat* and they dare not forget it." The advisors were soon dismissed, replaced with "more biddable, less able men." The strikes eventually contributed to the onset of the Russian Revolution. What relevance would this episode have to the passage?

   A. It would provide counter-evidence to Bark's contention that Nicholas was a misunderstood but able leader.

   B. It would be consistent with reasons for which Nicholas has traditionally been regarded as a poor ruler.

   C. It would contradict Bark's claim that, after 1860, the Russian economy slowly began to modernize.

   D. It would confirm Bark's view that, by the time of Nicholas's reign, czarism was doomed.

33. Which of the following, if true, would most *challenge* the author's assertion that "the compassion craze has swept up biography?"

   A. Most readers regard as unflattering Bark's portrayal of Count Pobedonostsev in *Nicholas the Unlucky*.

   B. For their subjects, many biographers choose figures who the biographers believe ought to be viewed in a forgiving and sympathetic light.

   C. Nicholas genuinely believed that his attempt to preserve czarism was in the best interest of the Russian people.

   D. Several decades ago, when Bark wrote *Nicholas the Unlucky*, she had very little exposure to American cultural values.

GO TO THE NEXT PAGE.

Passage VI (Questions 34–39)

The extent to which analysis of social phenomena is compatible with the scientific method is a hotly contested question. Among international relations scholars, historico-deductivist opponents of positivism claim that
5 in the pursuit of objective depictions of the causes, course, and consequences of international phenomena the character and operation of which are purported to exist independently of the observer, positivists miss or dismiss the implicit attitudes, values, and ideologies em-
10 bedded in their work, which personalize and subjectivize their conclusions. Positivism, these critics contend, attempts to impose on world politics a coherent facticity akin to that of the natural sciences, but to which the basic nature of world politics is indisposed. As
15 Dougherty put it, "Aristotle warns in the *Nichomachaean Ethics* that the precision of an answer cannot exceed that of its question, but the positivists want clocks and necessity where there are really clouds and contingency."

20 For historico-deductivists, the problem of *a posteriori* overdetermination is a case in point. In the natural sciences, replicability and verifiability afford the findings of laboratory experimentation potentially nomothetic status. In international relations, however, such
25 lawlike generalizations about cause and effect are rarely if ever possible, not only because events are unique, but also because of the multiplicity of potential causes. Whether World War I resulted from a disequilibrium in the international distribution of power, the ascendancy
30 of government factions committed to aggression, or the accuracy of an assassin's bullet, is, ultimately, unknown. For opponents of positivism, it is better to recognize darkness than to pretend to see light.

While some leading positivists, most notably
35 Pastore, admit as "knowledge" only the sum of all tested propositions, for most it is the very cloudlike nature of political phenomena that requires a clocklike approach. Conceding that their subject does not permit nomothetic propositions, the majority of positivists appear commit-
40 ted to Williams' more moderate rule: "The propensity to error should make us cautious, but not so desperate that we fear to come as close as possible to apodictic findings. We needn't grasp at the torch with eyes closed, fearing to be blinded."

45 Positivists point to the potential of scientific analysis to yield counterintuitive truths. A frequently cited example is Grotsky's study of the role of non-state actors in international trade. Published at a time when many
50 scholars were convinced that multinational organizations had effectively "elbowed the traditional sovereign nation-state…out of analytical existence in our field," Grotsky's research of the structure, timing, and variance of state expenditures on foreign direct investment effec-
55 tively restored the state to its position as the dominant unit in international relations scholarship. Despite several efforts, historico-deductivists who had championed the new relevance of non-state actors have not, as yet, successfully refuted Grotsky's findings—a considera-
60 tion that bodes well for those of us who believe that an end to this longstanding debate, which has produced much timely and relevant research, is not necessarily to be desired.

In addition to claiming that critics have mischarac-
65 terized their methodological commitments, positivists also contend that the historico-deductivist approach is subject to many of the same criticisms leveled against positivism. For example, on the twentieth anniversary of her seminal article depicting the Peloponnesian War as
70 the archetypal case of power politics in action, Nash, perhaps the exemplar of the historico-deductivist school, revisited her earlier findings, only to conclude that the interaction between the Athenians and Spartans included significant instances of cooperation and reci-
75 procity. Even as Nash's confederates praised the "illuminating evolution" in her thinking, many positivists questioned whether Nash's antipodal findings corresponded to a shift in her initial assumptions over time. The implication, of course, is that if positivists' commit-
80 ments at the level of proto-theory color their eventual conclusions, then they are not alone in this regard.

GO TO THE NEXT PAGE.

34. According to information given by the author in the passage, which of the following is true of *a posteriori* overdetermination?

    I. It presents a challenge to scholars' ability to produce nomothetic statements about world politics.

    II. It exemplifies the analytical confusion created by unique events that often have multiple effects.

    III. It suggests that the historico-deductivism is better suited than is positivism to the study of international relations.

    A. I only

    B. III only

    C. I and II only

    D. II and III only

35. As used in the passage by Williams at the end of the third paragraph in the statement, "We needn't grasp at the torch with eyes closed, fearing to be blinded," the word "torch" refers to:

    A. propensity to error.

    B. nomothetic propositions.

    C. political phenomena.

    D. methodological commitments.

36. As described in the passage, historico-deductivist claims about the problem of *a posteriori* overdetermination in the study of political phenomena depend on the unstated assumption that:

    A. positivists' methodological commitments preclude positivists from providing a fully scientific account of the onset of World War I.

    B. complex social occurrences such as wars are ultimately insusceptible to scholarly analysis.

    C. replicability is a more severe obstacle than is verifiability to the scientific study of world politics.

    D. a causal claim that stipulates multiple indistinguishable causes for a certain effect is not likely to be a nomothetic proposition.

37. Which of the following would Dougherty be most likely to describe as "clocks and necessity where there are really clouds and contingency?"

    A. A historico-deductivist study of World War I

    B. A historico-deductivist study of the Peloponnesian War

    C. A positivist study of the nature of reciprocity in the relations among sovereign states

    D. A chemist's study of the behavior of a certain gas under conditions of standard temperature and pressure

38. The principle underlying which of the following is most analogous to "Williams's more moderate rule" (line 40)?

    A. A student's estimation of her work is more important than either the grade awarded the work by the student's instructor or the opinion of the work expressed by the student's peers.

    B. The proficiency of an expert musician may reflect intelligence different in form from, but nonetheless equal in degree to, that of an accomplished painter or a pioneering physicist.

    C. If a worker were certain that he could never earn more than $50,000 per year, this in itself would not be a reason for him to refrain from trying to improve his lot at $20,000 per year.

    D. Hazardous road conditions constitute sufficient reason for a motorist to cancel her travel plans, even if the motorist is extremely reluctant to do so.

39. It can reasonably be inferred that the author of the passage is a:

    A. professor of history.

    B. professor of international relations.

    C. diplomat.

    D. journalist.

GO TO THE NEXT PAGE.

Passage VII (Questions 40–47)

Between 1965 and 1970, welfare caseloads more than doubled and costs tripled. The Nixon administration was unable to secure a legislative majority for comprehensive welfare reform. Legislative welfare reform
5 raised contentious issues of who is entitled to support, how much, and on what terms—precisely the types of issues that have defied political resolution throughout welfare's history.

As a mechanism of policy change, the Nixon ad-
10 ministration turned to a common managerial tool—performance monitoring. Middle-level officials at the Office of Management and Budget (OMB) and the Department of Health, Education and Welfare (HEW) crafted quality control—a system for monitoring the ac-
15 curacy of state welfare payments—into an instrument for indirectly influencing states to become more restrictive in the provision of welfare. Quality control's manifest purpose was to achieve fiscal accountability.

Through this instrument HEW could monitor state
20 welfare payments and withhold federal reimbursement from those that it deemed to be improper. However, quality control also served a latent, political function, partly reflected in its design. It penalized states only for overpayments and payments made to ineligible individ-
25 uals. Part of the administrative strategy employed by Nixon in his second term involved efforts to circumvent legislative obstacles and to begin to curb the provision of welfare administratively. It was not used to hold states accountable for underpayments, erroneous de-
30 nials, unreasonable delays, or administrative practices that discouraged applications.

Quality control's effectiveness depended on the uncoordinated responses of street-level bureaucrats in hundreds of local welfare offices to new demands that
35 administrative reform imposed at the workplace. For example, welfare workers translated administrative concern for procedural uniformity into demands that welfare applicants routinely produce scores of documents of dubious relevance to their eligibility.
40 Applicants who could not meet these procedural demands, whether reasonable or not, were denied welfare.

Administrative reform traded errors of liberality for errors of stringency. Behaviors directed toward the helping aspects of welfare policy were virtually displaced as
45 workers responded to incentives to maximize measured attributes of performance, namely procedural uniformity and productivity. At the same time, worker discretion to make unreasonable procedural demands was virtually unchecked.

50 Quality control did not overtly breach the integrity of theoretical entitlement to welfare promised by statute and supported by legal precedent. Rather, it seemed designed to protect this promise. But in practice, quality control appears to have initiated a process of effective
55 disentitlement. Its adverse effects were unmeasured and unobserved, leaving quality control's manifest legitimacy unimpaired. Government institutions and officials were thus insulated from the effects of their actions. In this sense, quality control ironically eroded the govern-
60 ment accountability that it was ostensibly intended to guarantee. Furthermore, through quality control, federal authorities could indirectly influence state administrative practices without directly encroaching on areas of nominal state authority. Performance measurement
65 backed by fiscal sanctions proved to be a relatively potent, if imperfectly cast, instrument for penetrating a decentralized bureaucracy.

---

40. According to the passage, which of the following led directly to the implementation of quality control in the welfare system?

  A. Difficulty in passing legislation to address the growing problems with the welfare system

  B. Additional costs and less federal support for welfare programs

  C. Complaints of corruption and fraud amongst welfare administrators

  D. Ineffective efforts on the part of the executive branch to stem the increase in welfare caseloads

41. All of the following are mentioned in the passage by the author as adverse effects of quality control EXCEPT:

  A. undue emphasis on administrative paperwork and procedures.

  B. arbitrary and inconsistent penalties for state welfare agencies.

  C. a decrease in the number of people who were eligible for welfare benefits.

  D. lack of accountability for certain systematic infringements of the welfare system.

GO TO THE NEXT PAGE.

42. Suppose the author of the passage was invited to comment on the statements outlined below made in the course of a political debate. The author would most likely agree with which of the following statements?

    A. Federal attempts to make the welfare system more fiscally responsible helped to make the system more effective in its dealings with welfare recipients.
    B. State authorities should continue to maintain a certain amount of control over the welfare offices within their jurisdiction.
    C. Welfare reform can best be achieved through a combination of legislation and revised administrative policies and procedures.
    D. Quality control measures instituted during the Nixon administration have been unjustly accused of causing disentitlement of deserving welfare recipients.

43. In paragraph 4, the phrase "uncoordinated responses of street-level bureaucrats" is used in order to:

    A. support the author's claim that unreasonable administrative procedures caused many applicants to be denied welfare benefits.
    B. refute the theory that quality control was used to hold states to a higher standard of accountability in their fiscal administration.
    C. prove that quality control policies were implemented to serve a political rather than a social agenda.
    D. provide a potential reason for the ineffectiveness of performance monitoring on general welfare reform.

44. What does the author of the passage suggest about the use of common managerial tools to effect policy changes in the welfare system?

    A. Procedural changes in welfare agencies should be established in ways that assure adherence to regulations for both workers and applicants.
    B. Administrative reform methods like performance monitoring may cause welfare organizations to become overly restrictive in their policies.
    C. State payments and federal reimbursement funding can be effectively monitored through changes in welfare administration at the national level.
    D. Implementation of quality control methods helped to hold the federal government accountable for its actions.

45. It can be inferred that quality control was interpreted to include which of the following activities?

    A. Holding states responsible for unreasonable delays in the welfare process
    B. Making states accountable for overpayments
    C. Easing the rules for federal reimbursement
    D. Changing the statutory rules for welfare eligibility

46. It can be inferred that the author would support which of the following steps to counteract the negative effects of the quality control system on welfare entitlement?

    A. Passage of a law limiting the number of welfare applications
    B. More careful screening of welfare caseworkers
    C. Increases in welfare spending by the government
    D. Enforcement of state accountability for underpayments and other actions which affect welfare recipients adversely

GO TO THE NEXT PAGE.

Passage VIII (Questions 47–53)

After being formed deep within the earth, hydrocarbons migrate upwards, following a complex path of minute cracks and pore spaces, and will eventually reach the surface and be lost unless they encounter impermeable rocks (such as dense shale) through which they cannot travel. If the rock within which they are trapped is highly permeable (such as sandstone) the hydrocarbons can be extracted by drilling through the impermeable seal, and tapping into this permeable reservoir.

Our dependence, as a nation—and as a world, on fossil fuels is only increasing as the global population increases and our reliance on technology expands. There are few things that people in first-world countries do anymore that do not require an external power source of some kind. And in spite of the popularization of renewable sources of energy and nuclear energy, the chief source of power in the world is still derived from fossil fuels.

There are a number of different types of traps, but they can be divided into two broad categories. Structural traps are formed by deformation after the rocks have been formed, for example by folding or faulting. Stratigraphic traps are formed when the loose sediments that will eventually be turned into rocks were laid down. For example if the sea level rises and the permeable sands of a beach are covered with estuarine mud, the buried sediments will, under compression, become sandstone capped by impermeable siltstones, forming an ideal reservoir and trap.

By now the locations of all obvious reserves of oil and gas have been discovered. The need to expand oil and gas reserves therefore, brings with it a need to find hydrocarbon reservoirs that are difficult to locate using current geological and geophysical means. To do so, geologists look for rock formations that constitute the seals and reservoirs within which hydrocarbons could be trapped.

Structural traps tend to be easier to locate and are the source of most of the known hydrocarbon reserves. Expanding our reserves therefore means locating more stratigraphically trapped hydrocarbons. The primary means of exploring for oil where there is no surface expression of the underlying geology is by seismology. When a seismic pulse transmitted into the earth encounters an interface where the density changes, typically the surface between two beds or an unconformity with velocity-density contrasts, some of the energy is reflected back upwards. A string of seismophones record these reflections and after extensive computation seismologists can build up a visual record of the intensity of each reflection and the time taken for it to reach the surface.

The primary limitation of the seismic method for locating stratigraphic traps is resolution: It is not possible to resolve features that are thinner than a seismic wavelet. The most common stratigraphic traps (with the possible exception of carbonate reservoirs) are in sandstone layers that are much thinner than a seismic wavelet. Seismic wavelets can be narrowed by increasing the frequency of the seismic pulse. However, high frequencies are selectively attenuated as the pulse travels through the earth, so there are limits to how much resolution can be improved by simply generating higher frequency pulses, or by filtering out the lower frequency components of the seismic source. Moreover, the density contrasts between oil-bearing sandstones and the shales that provide stratigraphic seals for the oil are often very small, so that the reflectivities, and hence the strength of the reflection, will be so low that the events may not be observable above background noise.

Recent developments such as zero phase wavelet processing and multivariate analysis of reflection waveforms have decreased noise and increased resolution. In the future it is hoped that these techniques, and greater understanding of stratigraphy itself, will prove fruitful in expanding hydrocarbon reserves.

---

47. As opposed to other essays written on the same topic, it is likely that the primary purpose of this passage is to:

   A. explain how hydrocarbons are formed and trapped within the earth.
   B. detail how seismologists can locate hidden deposits of hydrocarbons.
   C. contrast the relative difficulty of locating structural traps and stratigraphic traps.
   D. discuss the formation of hydrocarbon reserves and how they can be located.

GO TO THE NEXT PAGE.

48. According to the passage it is often difficult to distinguish reflections from the interface between oil bearing sandstones and the shales that provide stratigraphic seals from background noise because:

   A. high frequencies are attenuated as they travel through the earth.
   B. there is little density contrast between the oil bearing sandstone and the shales which provide stratigraphic seals.
   C. the frequency of the seismic pulse is not high enough.
   D. they are thinner than the seismic wavelet.

49. The example of a stratigraphic trap formed by a rise in sea level (lines 25–29) is brought up to make a certain point. It used by the author of the passage principally to:

   A. contrast a typical stratigraphic trap with a typical structural trap.
   B. explain why sandstones covered by siltstones make ideal reservoir and trap.
   C. illustrate the point that stratigraphic traps are formed when sediments were laid down.
   D. show why stratigraphic traps can be difficult to locate seismically.

50. According to the passage, all of the following are needed if oil is to be extracted from a reservoir EXCEPT:

   A. an impermeable seal above the reservoir.
   B. an original source of hydrocarbons below the reservoir.
   C. high density contrast between the reservoir rocks and the stratigraphic seal.
   D. high permeability within the reservoir.

51. It can be inferred from the passage that, regardless of what angle the author may be trying to present, carbonate reservoirs are:

   A. less dense than sandstone reservoirs.
   B. easily located by seismology.
   C. an important type of stratigraphic trap.
   D. at least as thick as a seismic wavelet.

52. Based on the points made throughout the passage, which of the following best describes how the author views seismology as a tool in locating hydrocarbons?

   A. Of limited effectiveness but showing promise
   B. Intrinsically flawed
   C. Effective and profitable
   D. Theoretically useful but ineffectual in practice

53. Which of the following developments in seismic technique would the author view as the greatest aid in the detection of stratigraphic traps?

   A. The discovery of a means of increasing the attenuation of high frequency seismic wavelets within the earth
   B. The development of a seismic source with an extremely high frequency that does not attenuate over distance
   C. The development of a means of filtering all noise out of seismic sections
   D. Further research into the origin of stratigraphic traps

GO TO THE NEXT PAGE.

Passage IX (Questions 54–60)

American culture changed forever in the latter part of the twentieth century with the advent of pop music. Before the 1950s music defined its own circles, but, at best, only shaded the frame of popular American cul-
5　ture. The birth of Rock and Roll forever changed that as larger and larger numbers of youth came, not only to identify with the music they were listening to, but to identify themselves by that music.

We use pop songs to create for ourselves a particu-
10　lar sort of self-definition, a particular place in society. The pleasure that a pop song produces is a pleasure of identification: in responding to a song, we are drawn into affective and emotional alliances with the performers and with the performers' other fans. Thus music, like
15　sport, is clearly a setting in which people directly experience community, feel an immediate bond with other people, and articulate a collective pride.

At the same time, because of its qualities of abstractness, pop music is an individualizing form. Songs
20　have a looseness of reference that makes them immediately accessible. They are open to appropriation for personal use in a way that other popular cultural forms (television soap operas, for example) are not—the latter are tied into meanings which we may reject.

25　This interplay between personal absorption into music and the sense that it is, nevertheless, something public, is what makes music so important in the cultural placing of the individual. Music also gives us a way of managing the relationship between our public and pri-
30　vate emotional lives. Popular love songs are important because they give shape and voice to emotions that otherwise cannot be expressed without embarrassment or incoherence. Our most revealing declarations of feeling are often expressed in banal or boring language and so
35　our culture has a supply of pop songs that say these things for us in interesting and involving ways.

Popular music also shapes popular memory, and organizes our sense of time. Clearly one of the effects of all music, not just pop, is to focus our attention on the
40　feeling of time, and intensify our experience of the present. One measure of good music is its "presence," its ability to "stop" time, to make us feel we are living within a moment, with no memory or anxiety about what has come before us, what will come after. It is this
45　use of time that makes popular music so important in the social organization of youth. We invest most in popular music when we are teenagers and young adults—music ties into a particular kind of emotional turbulence, when

issues of individual identity and social place, the control
50　of public and private feelings, are at a premium. What this suggests, though, is not that young people need music, but that "youth" itself is defined by music. Youth is experienced, that is, as an intense presence, through an impatience for time to pass and a regret that it is
55　doing so, in a series of speeding, physically insistent moments that have nostalgia coded into them.

---

54. The author's primary purpose in this passage in discussing popular music is to:

   A. account for the importance of popular music in youth culture.
   B. contrast several sociological theories about popular music.
   C. compare popular music with other forms of popular culture.
   D. outline the social functions of popular music.

55. While there are obviously many differences between the two, the author of the passage suggests that one similarity between popular and classical music is that both:

   A. articulate a sense of community and collective pride.
   B. give shape to inexpressible emotions.
   C. emphasize the feeling of time.
   D. define particular age groups.

56. It can be inferred from the passage that the author's attitude towards love songs in popular music is that of being:

   A. bored by the banality of their language.
   B. embarrassed by their emotional incoherence.
   C. interested by their expressions of feeling.
   D. unimpressed by their social function.

57. The author probably refers to sport in paragraph 2 primarily in order to:

   A. draw a parallel.
   B. establish a contrast.
   C. challenge an assumption.
   D. introduce a new idea.

GO TO THE NEXT PAGE.

58. Regardless of what the purpose of the passage is as a whole, in the last paragraph, the author is predominantly concerned with:

   A. defining the experience of youth.
   B. describing how popular music defines youth.
   C. speculating about the organization of youth movements.
   D. analyzing the relationship between music and time.

59. The author cites which one of the following in support of the argument that popular music creates our identity?

   A. Pop songs are unpopular with older age groups.
   B. Love songs shape our everyday language.
   C. Pop songs become personalized like other cultural forms.
   D. Popular music combines public and private experience.

60. In a debate on the importance of popular music in the social organization of youth, which of the following, if true, would most *weaken* the author's argument?

   A. Popular songs often incorporate nostalgic lyrics.
   B. Young people are ambivalent about the passage of time.
   C. Older people are less interested in popular music than young people.
   D. Pop songs focus our expectations on the future.

STOP. If you finish before time is called, check your work. You may go back to any question in this test booklet.

ANSWER KEY
VERBAL REASONING TEST 10

1. A	16. C	31. D	46. D
2. B	17. A	32. B	47. D
3. C	18. D	33. D	48. B
4. A	19. C	34. A	49. C
5. B	20. D	35. B	50. C
6. C	21. B	36. D	51. D
7. A	22. C	37. C	52. A
8. A	23. A	38. C	53. B
9. D	24. A	39. B	54. D
10. B	25. C	40. A	55. C
11. D	26. B	41. C	56. C
12. C	27. C	42. B	57. A
13. B	28. D	43. D	58. B
14. A	29. B	44. B	59. D
15. A	30. A	45. B	60. D

EXPLANATIONS

PASSAGE I

Topic and Scope:
PCB contamination of the Hudson River and possible cleanup

Mapping the Passage:
¶1 describes PCBs and what industries and products made use of them.
¶2 describes PCB toxicity, the ban on PCBs, and the problem that PCBs remain in the environment.
¶3 describes the historical context of chemical dumping and cleanup.
¶4 describes PCB pollution in the Hudson River.
¶5 notes that the fate of PCBs *after* dredging has received little attention.
¶6 describes competing views over cleanup: the EPA wants to dredge PCBs, while corporations and some citizens argue that this will do more harm than good.

Questions:
1.   A   A Roman Numeral inference question with little information to go on in the question. RN I appears in three out of the four answer choices, so evaluate it first. What in the passage would provide information about the relative weights of PCBs and water? If the solution to removing PCBs from the river is to dredge, then PCBs must be at the bottom of the river, which means that they must be heavier than water. Eliminate (D). There's no suggestion that PCBs are toxic to fish; just the opposite! If "fish consumption remains the most potent route of PCB exposure," that must mean that the fish are relatively healthy (at least until eaten). RN III goes against the main thrust of the passage: if PCBs *were* biodegradable, there would be no need to dredge at all. (A) must be correct.

Wrong Answers:
(B): Opposite. As described above.
(C): Opposite. As above.
(D): Opposite. As above.

2.   B   Another inference question, but this time with quite detailed information in the question stem. Where are estuaries mentioned? Go back to ¶4: estuaries are mentioned in the discussion of sites where PCB contamination was found. If estuaries are downriver near the sea and the contamination came from manufacturing plants located on the banks of the river, what has to be true? Predict: The PCBs must have traveled from the plants to the estuary sediment. (B) rewards the careful reading and reasoning.

Wrong Answers:
(A): Out of Scope. While there's no reason this couldn't be true, nor is there a reason that it *must* be true; the passage doesn't mention any additional sources. Furthermore, since an estuary is the wide part of a river, even the PCBs from a new pollution source would have to travel to get to where they were found.
(C): Opposite. ¶4 mentions the presence of "substantial contamination" in estuary sediments.
(D): Distortion. Though the PCBs have clearly moved from the source of pollution to the estuaries, there's nothing to say that they must *keep* flowing. The tides flowing back into the river could keep them in the estuary, for example.

3.   C   A third inference question. What is true about the company responsible for the PCB pollution? Go back to the passage: the company argues in ¶6 that cleanup is unnecessary, and the author notes in ¶3 that companies responsible for pollution can be liable for the cost of cleanup. Look for an answer choice that ties into this information. (C) is a necessary inference: if the company argues against cleanup and may also be held financially liable for the cleanup, it's likely that its opposition to the cleanup is financially motivated.

Wrong Answers:
(A): Opposite. The author would presumably argue that the company's view is less objective than the residents since the latter group doesn't have a financial responsibility for the cleanup, while the former does.
(B): Out of Scope. Public image isn't mentioned anywhere in the passage.
(D): Distortion. What solution would the fishing industry presumably be pushing for? Cleanup, which the author says could eventually revitalize that industry. However, the fact that the company opposes cleanup doesn't necessarily mean that it does so because it doesn't care about commercial fishing. There are less roundabout ways of explaining the company's motivation.

4.   A   A nastily-worded question. Be sure to take the time to figure out exactly what it's asking. Differences between the EPA and the other two groups are mentioned in ¶6. The question asks how the EPA differs on the basis of its recommendation for cleanup. The EPA bases its recommendation on the belief that dredging will reduce contamination and may revitalize commercial fishing. Predict where the difference *isn't*: it's not on environmental concerns, because the company and the residents also base their argument on environmental benefit. Neither the company nor residents are associated with commercial fishing; this is therefore a valid difference. (A) fits.

Wrong Answers:
(B): Opposite. Presumably reduced contamination will further residential interests, which the residents clearly also believe since some oppose dredging on the belief that it will *increase* contamination.
(C): Opposite. Even if the EPA *is* concerned with the environment as a whole, for which there's no basis in the passage, it's arguable that the residents have a similar environmental concern.
(D): Opposite. This is a reason that residents who oppose dredging, not the EPA, cite.

5. B An application question. How would a local newspaper apply to information in the passage? It would presumably reflect the interests of local residents. What information would help a paper that reflects the views of local residents come to a conclusion about dredging? Predict: Information that answered the concerns in ¶6. (B) would do just this, since a concern mentioned in ¶6 is that dredging might stir up pollution.

Wrong Answers:
(A): Out of Scope. Since ¶1 mentions that PCBs were first synthesized in the 1880s, pre-industrial levels must have been nil. Anyway, understanding this historical context wouldn't be valuable for deciding whether cleanup is a good idea.
(C): Out of Scope. Since the EPA has already decided that the PCBs would be transported outside of the area, as mentioned in ¶5, the exact area wouldn't be a concern of local residents.
(D): Out of Scope. Since the cost of the dredging operation would probably be borne by the company not the community, as mentioned in ¶3, this information should also be irrelevant.

6. C Why are individuals prohibited from eating fish from contaminated areas of the Hudson? Review the mechanism described in ¶2: PCBs increase in concentration as they move up the food chain, and so eating fish from contaminated areas would increase the PCB concentration in the person eating the fish. It can be inferred that the fish ban is in place to prevent this from happening; (C) fits.

Wrong Answers:
(A): Distortion. Though not eating the fish may reduce the rate of *increase* in PCB concentration, there's no indication that simply avoiding contaminated fish will reduce PCB concentration overall.
(B): Distortion. As above, though not eating the fish will reduce the rate of increase, this doesn't mean that it will eliminate the increase altogether; there are still other possible sources of contamination.
(D): Distortion. Simply reducing the rate of increase won't necessarily eliminate all risk factors for cancer and developmental problems, which could come from any number of sources, non-fish-borne PCBs included.

Strategy Point:
Watch out for answer choices like (A) that try to confuse a reduced rate of increase with an overall decrease, or vice versa.

7. A Look for an answer choice that is both stated and that has no clear support in the passage. (A) is stated at the beginning of ¶6. Though individuals along the river show PCB residue paralleling that in the river, they can't have accumulated the PCBs from fish, the "most potent route of PCB exposure," because fish consumption is banned. Air pollution by PCBs isn't listed as a major source of contamination in humans, and so there must be another reason for the contamination that isn't stated.

Wrong Answers:
(B): Faulty Use of Detail. ¶1 mentions this fact, but provides explanation for why PCBs were so useful. Note the "Because..." at the beginning of the sentence introducing the fact, a sure tip-off that the statement has justification.
(C): Faulty Use of Detail. This is mentioned in ¶2 and is also prefixed by a "Because..." and a reason: PCB affinity for fat causes accumulation.
(D): Faulty Use of Detail. ¶6 describes the controversy over what should be done about PCBs, and explains the various reasons that each group gives for its position.

PASSAGE II

Topic and Scope:
The resolution of a schism in the Catholic Church through the office of the pope.

Mapping the Passage:
¶1 describes the Church's schism and actions taken by the Council of Pisa to name a pope.
¶2 describes the disorganized group of popes and pretenders that followed (first John XXIII).
¶3 continues to describe the popes, and how Gregory XII and Benedict XIII were deposed from the throne.

¶4 describes step the Council of Constance (rather than Pisa) took to elect a new Pope that would be universally acknowledged.

Strategy Point:
Remembering that structure is more important than detail will help you to get through tough passages efficiently!

Questions:

8. A   What is the main problem implied in the passage? A schism in the Church is mentioned, as well as the presence of multiple Popes. Therefore, it's inferable that the councils met in order to whittle down to a single Pope and so to eliminate the schism. (A) says the same.

Wrong Answers:

(B): Distortion. Though the schism clearly fell along national lines, as evidenced by the fact that different countries supported different Popes, there's no evidence that the councils tried to create national alliances, but rather only to eliminate the national schisms.

(C): Distortion. The Emperor's protection of the Catholic Church is mentioned in lines 14–16, but there's no indication that the two councils were convened to obtain this protection; it seems to have already been there by the time of the second Council.

(D): Faulty Use of Detail. The Council of Constance did this when it made the decision of a Pope "softened by their generous preference of an Italian and a Roman," but the Council of Pisa had no role in this.

9. D   The passage as a whole compares the two councils, so there's no quick place to look in the passage for the correct statements. Predict what the answers will look like: they'll involve steps the Council of Constance took to undo the damage caused by the Council of Pisa. RN I is supported by the middle of ¶2, and especially by the comment that "the number and weight of civil and ecclesiastical members might seem to constitute the states-general of Europe." RN II can be inferred from the point in ¶4 that the new Pope was widely perceived as noble: "Rome accepted with joy and obedience the noblest of her sons." RN III is supported by the same, and (D) is therefore correct.

Wrong Answers:

(A): Opposite. As described above.
(B): Opposite. As above.
(C): Opposite. As above.

10. B   An evaluation question. Where are the "most scandalous charges" mentioned? Go back to line 20. Immediately after this mention of "most scandalous charges" comes a list of pretty nasty crimes. What is the author trying to say? Predict: if the crimes mentioned were relatively harmless, then the others must be awfully bad. (B) says the same.

Wrong Answers:

(A): Distortion. The author isn't suggesting that the serious crimes were suppressed out of leniency; the Council obviously brought some pretty nasty charges against John XXIII.

(C): Opposite. John XXIII's political influence wasn't that strong if he was brought to the Council as a prisoner, and the author reinforces this point by saying that he had been unwise to trust "his person to a free city beyond the Alps."

(D): Out of Scope. The role of the Council in electing an Italian has nothing to do with the charges brought against John.

Strategy Point:
Evaluation questions particularly reward careful reasoning and reference back to the text. Make sure you do both!

11. D   Review the passage for mention of the Spanish. The first sentence of ¶2 states that one of the three Popes, Benedict XIII, was recognized as legitimate by the Spanish because he himself was a Spaniard. The Spanish are next mentioned at the end of ¶3: "with the concurrence of the Spanish, Benedict was deposed by the council." Finally, the Spanish are mentioned in ¶4 as taking part in the election of a new pope. Predict how the Spanish helped: they gave up their own pope, and helped to elect a new one. (D) repeats this nearly word-for-word.

Wrong Answers:

(A): Out of Scope. The author never says that the Spanish did this.

(B): Faulty Use of Detail. Though the Spanish *did* do both of these things, there's no way that this would contribute to resolving the schism. They resolved the schism by later doing the opposite: collaborating with the other nations and giving up Benedict.

(C): Out of Scope. There's no indication that the Spanish did this either.

12. C   What do these three Popes have in common? They were all Pope at the same time, and the author describes how they were each eliminated in favor of a Pope that everyone could agree on. What is the author's attitude towards the three Popes? Predict: He believes that they contributed to the schism and that everyone was better off under Martin. The author says that Benedict and Gregory were deposed "with equal justice" and that John was "the most profligate of mankind," suggesting an overall low opinion of the three. (C) fits.

Wrong Answers:

(A): Out of Scope. The author doesn't mention who he believes the best of the three to be.

(B): Out of Scope. As above.

(D): Out of Scope. The author doesn't say that one election was more legitimate than the others, and in any case speaks very poorly of John in general.

13. B What would have happened (or not have happened) if John XXIII was acceptable to all Catholics? Review ¶1, where John's election is first discussed: The author says that "instead of extinguishing the schism, the rashness....had given a third pretender to the chair of St. Peter." In other words, electing John had made the schism worse. If it *hadn't*, as the question supposes, there would have been no need for a second Council to fix all the damage. (B) says the same.

Wrong Answers:
(A): Distortion. More likely that Benedict and Gregory wouldn't have been recognized in the first place, since everyone would have united behind John.
(C): Opposite. There's no reason to believe that the schism would had remained if everyone had been united behind John as the legitimate Pope.
(D): Out of Scope. There's no evidence one way or the other to say what John would have done about the location of the Papacy.

14. A Review the mention of deputies in ¶4: the author says that the "cardinals [were] fortified with thirty deputies; six of whom were chosen in each of the five great nations of Christendom." Why were they chosen from each of the great nations? Predict: To encourage unity in the decision. (A) paraphrases this.

Wrong Answers:
(B): Out of Scope. There's no mention of escape in the passage, nor would there be a motive for anyone to escape.
(C): Opposite. If anything, the deputies were there to *encourage* government interference, so that the nations would all have a say in who the next Pope was.
(D): Out of Scope. The author says nothing about decorum, and there's no reason why deputies chosen from the great nations would help with that.

PASSAGE III

Topic and Scope:
Specific types of memory loss in old age

Mapping the Passage:
¶1 describes episodic memory, which declines in old age, as well as some possible explanations for the decline.
¶2 gives a traditional view that memory loss and old age are directly correlated, and a new view which suggests that more than one kind of memory exists and that not all of them necessarily deteriorate in old age.
¶3 describes new methodology in studies which has led to the new view.
¶4 describes semantic memory, which the author argues may *improve* with age.
¶s5 and 6 describe implicit memory, which isn't affected by age.

Questions:
15. A What type of memory will advanced age affect? Predict: Only episodic memory will be affected. Review what episodic memory is: the "recall of specific events," as well as names and locations. Only RN I is an example of this type of memory, while RN II is an example of semantic memory and RN III is an example of implicit memory. (A) is therefore correct.

Wrong Answers:
(B): Opposite. As described above.
(C): Opposite. As above.
(D): Opposite. As above.

16. C What is the author's tone in the passage? First ask yourself why the author thinks the research is relevant. The last paragraph states: "While the findings are encouraging, it must be noted that such studies do not deal with memory problems associated with illness, disease, or injury to the brain." Note the keyword "while": the author is optimistic, but not wildly so. (C) rewards the careful attention to structure with a very close paraphrase of this prediction.

Wrong Answers:
(A): Distortion. The author's optimism is tempered by the keyword "while" and the idea that the new research only has limited applicability.
(B): Opposite. The author doesn't seems skeptical of the new research at all, but rather optimistic that it's better than the old approach.
(D): Distortion. While the author is arguably objective, there's a clear bias in favor of the research (hence the optimism).

17. A A main idea question, tucked unusually in the middle of the question set. Predict, using topic, scope, and purpose to guide your prediction: the author wants to describe new research in the field of memory and aging. (A) paraphrases this closely.

Wrong Answers:
(B): Faulty Use of Detail. This is the purpose of ¶3, but not of the whole passage.
(C): Distortion. While the passage does this, its focus is far more specific. This choice is far too broad.
(D): Faulty Use of Detail. The author suggests some explanations for this in ¶1, but it's only one small part of the passage.

Strategy Point:
When predicting the answer to a main idea question, construct your paraphrase as Topic, Scope, and Purpose. Many correct Main Idea answers will follow this order.

18. D What explanation does the author give for the recent developments in memory? The author says in ¶3 that the "new conception of memory stems from a shift in methodology of memory research." (D) says almost exactly the same, adding just enough (a mention of aging) to allow it to qualify as an inference rather than a detail.

Wrong Answers:
(A): Out of Scope. The author is very clear that the advances have come from new methodologies, not from any attempt to dismantle stereotypes.
(B): Distortion. The author states in the last paragraph that the new research can't be applied to disease and injury-related memory loss, but this distinction follows the new research; the new research didn't come about because of this distinction.
(C): Faulty Use of Detail. This is one theory, taken from ¶1, for how memory loss can be avoided, but it's not the source of the new research.

19. C What are the two types of memory discussed in the question? Remembering recent events is episodic memory, while remembering distant events is semantic memory. What does the author say about the two types of memory? Review: Episodic memory declines with age, while semantic memory improves. (C) says the same thing.

Wrong Answers:
(A): Opposite. The author states explicitly that remembering distant events (i.e. childhood memories) falls under semantic memory.
(B): Out of Scope. Episodic and semantic memory, not episodic and implicit memory, are being compared.
(D): Out of Scope. One possible explanation for the decline in *episodic* memory is that it's not often exercised, but the author never says the same about semantic memory.

20. D What type of memory deals with routine events? Predict: implicit memory. (D) rewards an organized understanding of the passage with quick points.

Wrong Answers:
(A): Opposite. The author argues in ¶s5 and 6 that amnesiacs can *retain* implicit memory.
(B): Opposite. Semantic memory involves distant events and facts, not basic skills.
(C): Opposite. Episodic memory involves recent events rather than basic skills.

Strategy Point:
When a passage lists different types of one thing with clear distinctions between the types, make sure that you have a good handle on the distinctions; they will be tested in the questions.

21. B What does the author say about illness, disease, and injury? Review the last paragraph: the author argues that the new research has nothing to say about memory loss caused by these factors. (B) fits with this; the author is summarizing scientific research, and so in this

paragraph is likely summarizing the researcher's views that the new research has nothing to say about unnatural memory loss.

Wrong Answers:
(A): Opposite. The author seems hopeful that the results *are* practical, since only practical results would be encouraging.
(C): Distortion. Though the author suggests that new research would be needed to shed light on these studies, there's no suggestion that there *will* be new research in these areas.
(D): Out of Scope. The author doesn't discuss scientific interest in these disorders at all.

PASSAGE IV

Topic and Scope:
The importance of the historical precursors to Darwin's theory of natural selection

Mapping the Passage:
¶1 Discusses Linnaeus and LeClerc (Creationists), who helped pave the wave for evolutionary theory with some of their insights.
¶2 argues that understanding old ideas is important to understanding modern theories.
¶3 states that Darwin's theory of natural selection was developed in the context of older ideas.
¶4 notes that many of these older ideas came from scientists who were creationists and discusses LeClerc further.
¶5 describes pre-Darwinian data that challenged the Biblical account of creation.

Questions:
22. C A main idea question. Predict using topic, scope, and purpose. The author argues that Darwin's theory of natural selection didn't exist "in a vacuum," (as unfortunately it is taught in many schools, ¶3) but that the theory experienced "gradual development" that had started before Darwin was born. (C) paraphrases this.

Wrong Answers:
(A): Faulty Use of Detail. Though religious scientists did influence Darwin's theory, the author's main focus is on the fact that there were earlier (and perhaps false) ideas in general that influenced Darwin's theory.
(B): Faulty Use of Detail. This paraphrases the claim in lines 46–49, but it's not the main idea of the passage, which again focuses on the idea that evolution wasn't a completely new idea when Darwin proposed it.
(D): Faulty Use of Detail. The author makes this claim in ¶2, but it's used as a way of introducing a discussion of the ideas that preceded Darwin's theory. Since the bulk of the passage is devoted to explaining these theories rather than the argument that new ideas shouldn't be dismissed, it's safe to assume that the author is more concerned with the specifics of natural

selection's precursors than with the general idea that old ideas shouldn't be dismissed.

23. A   A scattered detail question. All the choices challenge Biblical accounts of creation except (A): there's no reason why similarities between closely-related species would challenge evolution. The passage makes explicit note of LeClerc's suggestion that horses and donkeys could have arisen from a common ancestor, but that it could have happened in the context of Biblical creation.

Wrong Answers:
(B): Faulty Use of Detail. Charles Lyell uses this detail as evidence that the earth must be much older than suggested in the Bible (¶5).
(C): Faulty Use of Detail. This detail, mentioned in ¶5, "aroused suspicion about the paucity of animal and plant 'kinds' in the Bible," thereby challenging the creationist view.
(D): Faulty Use of Detail. The ability to estimate the "relative ages of fossils," mentioned at the end of ¶5, "pushed people to question old assumptions," the implication being that the assumptions involved the correctness of Biblical creation.

24. A   What does the author focus on specifically in regard to evolution? Predict: the theory's scientific precursors. Further, the author specifically complains in ¶3 about high school biology classes that teach Darwin's theory in a vacuum. It's reasonable to infer, then, that the author would spend a lot of time teaching the background to Darwin's theory. (A) paraphrases this.

Wrong Answers:
(B): Out of Scope. The author is mainly concerned with the background of the theory. Details are presumably important, but there's no evidence from the passage that the author would focus on the details especially.
(C): Distortion. While the author might focus on this as a way of discussing precursor theories, the focus would be on the theories themselves, and not on Biblical creation.
(D): Distortion. Taxonomy is associated regarding Linnaeus (¶1), and so the author would presumably discuss it, but only in the context of how it led up to Darwin's theory. (A) states this more comprehensively.

25. C   What are the main tenets of LeClerc's theories? Review ¶s1 and 4: LeClerc believed that some species may have been modified from a common ancestor, and also argued that the earth "was at least 75,000 years old and perhaps as old as three million years." Summarize: LeClerc believed in very limited evolution and in an earth much older than that suggested by the Bible. Scanning the answer choices for a scientist with similar views turns up only (C): Lyell also believed that the age of the earth had to be much older than originally assumed.

Wrong Answers:
(A): Out of Scope. There's no evidence that LeClerc did this; the only mention of animals in the context of LeClerc is his suggestion that species could change over time.
(B): Distortion. Though both LeClerc and Linnaeus are described as creationists, the author never suggests that they tried to explain natural phenomena through supernatural means.
(D): Faulty Use of Detail. Though both scientists did give Darwin raw material to work with, as explicitly stated in lines 45–46, their ideas on evolution weren't necessarily similar.

26. B   What is the main idea of ¶3? Predict: The author believes that those studying Darwin's theories should study the ideas preceding those theories. (B) paraphrases this and is essentially a summary of ¶3.

Wrong Answers:
(A): Distortion. Though the author believes that Darwin's ideas have to be understood in context, there's no suggestion that Darwin doesn't deserve credit for his theory.
(C): Out of Scope. The author speaks very positively of Darwin and never suggests that his ideas should be devalued at all. The author discusses religion in order to show that ideas essential to evolution coexisted with creationism, not to show that the theory of evolution is false.
(D): Distortion. Though the author does described Darwin's ideas as "relatively simple," there's no suggestion that Darwin required no help in formulating them. If anything, he was helped by the theories that had come before.

Strategy Point:
Correct answers to inference questions are sometimes nothing more than summaries of the given paragraph or lines. A strong map will help you to get these points quickly.

27. C   Where does the author talk about the need for students to understand old theories? Focus on ¶s2 and 3, keeping the author's main point in mind: old theories help shed light on more modern ones. Note that RN II doesn't need to be checked; it's in *all* of the answer choices! Evaluate RN I: Arguing that Darwin's theory can't be understood at all without knowing its context distorts the author's main point. The author argues that understanding can be limited by not knowing context, not that it's impossible. Only (C) is left. RN III doesn't need to be evaluated either at this point, but it must be true: It's an example of a precursor theory that puts Darwin's discoveries in context. Though there's no need to evaluate RN II while timing the passage, note now why it's correct: the author uses LeClerc in the passage to give examples of theories which aren't necessarily correct, but which are useful in understanding how the idea of evolution evolved.

Wrong Answers:
(A): Opposite. As described above.
(B): Opposite. As above.
(D): Opposite. As above.

28. D A detail question. Who specifically argued that mountains take a long time to develop? The author states explicitly in lines 56–60 that Lyell did, as well as "uniformitarian geologists" like him. (D) fits the bill.

Wrong Answers:
(A): Out of Scope. Catastrophists aren't mentioned in the passage and so can be eliminated, but you can guess that they believed the opposite of the uniformitarians: that mountains and other large structures formed due to catastrophic events.
(B): Out of Scope. While Darwinists presumably believe this too, the author only mentions uniformitarians as specifically championing this view.
(C): Opposite. Creationists, unless they were in the vein of LeClerc, would likely argue that mountain ranges would have been created rather than developing over a long period of time. The author specifically states that the new geological evidence challenged "accounts from scripture."

PASSAGE V

Topic and Scope:
Bark's overly compassionate biography of Nicholas II and the importance of reality over perception.

Mapping the Passage:
¶1 suggests that America focuses too much on compassion.
¶2 summarizes Bark's main argument: Nicholas was a victim of the Russian Revolution, not responsible for it.
¶3 summarizes Bark's review of the "social, economic, and political" conditions during Nicholas' era.
¶4 quotes Bark, describing the quote as a "confused and confusing attempt to vindicate Nicholas."
¶5 asserts that the book is unsatisfying because Nicholas wasn't worthy of historical compassion, and provides an argument to support this contention.
¶6 summarizes Bark's discussion of Count Pobedonostsev, who informed Nicholas' unfortunate views.

Questions:
29. B Read the line in context. It's part of Bark's quote, which immediately knocks out (C) and (D). Bark is arguing that traditional approaches are best in difficult times: "turbulent times are perfect for redoubling the faith of ages." If Woodrow Wilson was "stalwart" and history smiled on him, that must mean that Wilson was also committed to traditional ideas. Why does Bark say that "the rest is detail"? Predict: Possibly to argue that the difference between what Nicholas did and what

Wilson did was minor. (B) paraphrases this in saying that they both followed a traditional approach.

Wrong Answers:
(A): Distortion. Though Bark does believe that commitment to core values during troubled times is important, there's nothing in the quote to indicate that Bark believes the values are subjective.
(C): Out of Scope. Since the quote is Bark, Bark is making the point rather than the author.
(D): Out of Scope. As above.

30. A Review the author's discussion of the Hohenzollerns in lines 62–65. The author argues that the Hohenzollerns fell before World War I just like Nicholas did, but dealt earlier with modernism and would have fallen even faster "had they behaved as Nicholas did." What is the conclusion? That the Hohenzollerns dealt better with their problems than Nicholas. What is the evidence? Only what the author gives in comparing the two. What must a critical assumption be? Predict: The problems that Nicholas and the Hohenzollerns dealt with were comparable; if they weren't, the author's comparison is pointless. (A) paraphrases the prediction.

Wrong Answers:
(B): Out of Scope. The author doesn't give any indication of what the Hohenzollerns thought about their mandate.
(C): Out of Scope. While the author may believe this, it's not an assumption critical to the comparison of the Hohenzollerns to Nicholas. Even if the author didn't believe this, the comparison could still hold up.
(D): Out of Scope. Though the author does believe that Nicholas should have modernized, there's no indication that he should have done so in the same way that the Hohenzollerns did. Tossing in other countries outside the scope of the comparison is a tip-off to the fact that this choice is out of scope.

31. D An unusual question: while most would ask what the support was, this asks you to evaluate the strength of the support. Go back to the lines mentioned. After the author makes the claim, examples are given of monarchies that at least delayed collapse by embracing modernism. The author's support is therefore fairly strong because it uses several contemporary examples to show how Nicholas *could* have behaved. (D) fits.

Wrong Answers:
(A): Out of Scope. It makes no sense that the author would support the claim that Nicholas could have delayed the collapse of the monarchy by giving an example of a ruler *other* than Nicholas who could have saved it for him.
(B): Opposite. The author's argument is strong precisely because it acknowledges that other monarchs did embrace modernity. Whether they did so reluctantly or not is outside the scope of the argument.

(C): Out of Scope. Though the author's support is strong, it has nothing to do with the quote, which is just part of the author's overall argument, and not evidence.

32. B An incorporation question. Summarize the situation: Workers strike, Nicholas' advisors want Nicholas to respond, and he doesn't because he follows traditional advice. The strikes eventually contribute to his downfall. Who would this situation support or contradict? Predict: it would support the author's view that Nicholas isn't worthy of historical compassion, and would weaken Bark's view that Nicholas couldn't have done anything to prevent the Revolution. (B) fits most closely with this idea.

Wrong Answers:

(A): Distortion. Bark acknowledges in ¶2 that "Nicholas was a poor leader," but that Nicholas couldn't have done anything about the Revolution. This choice is therefore half-right in that it *does* provide counter-evidence to Bark, but half-wrong in that it doesn't counter the contention that Nicholas was a good leader (no one argues that).

(C): Out of Scope. There's nothing in the new situation specifically discussing what happened after 1860. Striking workers would suggest *more* modernity, though, and so there's no way this would contradict Bark's argument in any case.

(D): Opposite. Since the situation suggests that there was a way Nicholas could have responded better to the crisis, it undermines Bark's idea that the czarism was doomed no matter what Nicholas did.

33. D What would challenge the author's contention in ¶1 that America's "compassion craze" is intruding into biography? Predict: Something that shows that America's obsession with compassion and biographies aren't as closely linked as the author says they are. (D) gives us just this: if Bark hadn't been exposed to American culture when writing the biography, it makes no sense to say that her book is an example of biography being swept up by the American compassion craze.

Wrong Answers:

(A): Out of Scope. The author argues that Bark is overly compassionate towards *Nicholas*; her treatment of the Count has no impact on this argument.

(B): Out of Scope. Even if this is true, it could still be that most biographers do this because they've been swept up in the compassion craze.

(C): Out of Scope. What Nicholas did is outside the scope: the author is concerned with whether or not the biography is overly compassionate towards Nicholas.

Strategy Point:
When asked to weaken a chain of cause and effect, keep an eye out for alternate explanations for the effect.

PASSAGE VI

Topic and Scope:
Critiques of the positivist approach to studying international relations and the positivist response

Mapping the Passage:
¶1 notes the conflict between historico-deductivists and positivists and describes the former's main critique of positivism: it tries to be completely objective in a field where complete objectivity is impossible.
¶2 provides an example: the causes of World War I can't be precisely pinned down.
¶3 presents one of the positivists' defenses: they don't pretend to be completely objective, but it's still best to be as objective as possible.
¶4 presents a second defense: positivism can lead to unexpected conclusions. The author also argues that the conflict between the two groups is good for research.
¶5 presents third defense of positivism: even if positivists are biased, historico-deductivists are too.

Questions:
34. A A tough question full of tough words. Since *a posteriori* is in italics, it's easy to spot. Go back to ¶2 to review what this is. Immediately after the phrase the passage says that in natural sciences, lab experiments can have "nomothetic status." What must this mean? Paraphrase: Probably that the findings are assumed to be definitely true. Read on: there's a "however" keyword that contrasts international relations with science, saying that "such lawlike generalizations about cause and effect are rarely if ever possible." Therefore, nomothetic status must involve "lawlike generalizations," and *a posteriori* overgeneralization must *challenge* positivists' attempts to do this because the historico-deductivists consider it a "case in point." RN I says the same, and so (B) and (D) can be eliminated. RN II is false because the example of World War II talks about *causes*, not effects. Though there's no need to evaluate RN III at this point, quickly confirm: there's no suggestion that historico-deductivism is exempt from the problem of *a posteriori* overdetermination, so that by itself doesn't suggest that the historico-positivist approach is inherently better. (A) must be correct.

Wrong Answers:

(B): Opposite. As described above.
(C): Opposite. As above.
(D): Opposite. As above.

Strategy Point:
You don't need to understand exactly what's going on to answer a question! Paying close attention to structure can help you to get through tough questions even when the details may be fuzzy to you.

35. B Read the word in context. The sentence in which the word appears immediately follows the positivists' "moderate rule" which says that "the propensity to error should make us cautious, but not so desperate that we fear to come as close as possible to apodictic findings." Paraphrase, keeping the main positivist idea of a scientific approach in mind: just because we can't eliminate error doesn't mean that we shouldn't try to work scientifically. What does the "torch" that the positivists want to grasp represent, then? Predict: The conclusions that they think they'll find. Three choices can be eliminated, leaving you with (B). You know that (B) must be true in any case from the mention of nomothetic propositions in ¶2: they're described as absolute scientific findings, exactly the sort of thing that the positivists want.

Wrong Answers:
(A): Faulty Use of Detail. The positivists acknowledge that error can't be eliminated, but that they can still grasp the "torch": the scientific certainty that they're after.
(C): Distortion. The positivists aren't trying to grasp political phenomena; they're trying to grasp an *understanding* of political phenomena.
(D): Distortion. As above, positivists don't want to get a handle on methodological commitments; they want to use methodology in order to get to the "torch" of understanding.

Strategy Point:
Pay close attention whenever a rule or definition is mentioned. The MCAT loves to test you on things which are clearly defined but in a difficult context.

36. D Go back to ¶2 to review. Historico-deductivists believe that *a posteriori* overdetermination presents some sort of problem for positivists trying to find nomothetic propositions. They also believe that nomothetic propositions, the "lawlike generalizations" used in science, aren't applicable to the study of international relations because one event can have many possible causes. What assumption is necessary to bridge these two beliefs? Predict: Nomothetic propositions can't explain events by relying on multiple causes. If they could, there presumably wouldn't be a problem with applying them to international relations. (D) paraphrases this.

Wrong Answers:
(A): Faulty Use of Detail. While historico-deductivists probably do believe this, it's not an assumption. Try denying it: even if they didn't believe this, or if they believed that positivists *could* provide a fully scientific account of World War I, their argument about overdetermination wouldn't necessarily fall apart.
(B): Distortion. The historico-deductivists probably believe that complex events aren't susceptible to the scientific analysis that the positivists are trying to use, but they must believe that they can be analyzed somehow; they'd be out of work otherwise!

(C): Out of Scope. The passage suggests no distinction between replicability and verifiability. Since both of these are part of the scientific method, it's an irrelevant distinction.

37. C Where is Dougherty mentioned? Go back to the end of ¶1. Immediately above the quote in the question is the argument that "the precision of an answer cannot exceed that of its question." The implication is that positivists want certainty where there isn't any. Tie it back into the metaphor: the "clocks and necessity" represent the certainty positivists want, while the "clouds and contingency" represent that uncertainty that actually exists. Only one of the answer choices deals with a positivist study, and it's a study of international relations, which the critics of positivists believe is full of uncertainty. (C) must be correct.

Wrong Answers:
(A): Out of Scope. A historico-deductivist study wouldn't be looking for "clocks and necessity" since the approach of the historico-deductivists is fuzzier than that of the positivists.
(B): Out of Scope. As above.
(D): Out of Scope. While the chemist *would* probably be looking for "clocks and necessity," there's reason to believe, especially from the discussion in ¶2, that historico-deductivists would acknowledge natural science as a field where this precision is justified.

38. C Review the "moderate rule" from the lines mentioned, using your work from Question 35 to help. Paraphrase the rule: the likelihood of error should make positivists cautious, but not so cautious that they give up trying to find scientific explanations as best as they can. Look for a situation that matches with this: (C) fits. Just because a worker can't earn a lot of money doesn't mean he shouldn't try to earn as much as he can.

Wrong Answers:
(A): Out of Scope. The principle behind this seems to be that the opinion of someone who creates a work is more important than that of anyone else judging the work, which is irrelevant to Williams' rule.
(B): Out of Scope. This principle behind this is most likely that different kinds of intelligence can be equal, which has nothing to do Williams' principle of trying to do the best one individually can.
(D): Opposite. If anything, this is the opposite of what Williams suggests. The principle behind this situation seems to suggest that one should hold back from acting because of possible dangers, while Williams says that one should do as much as one can.

39. B A quick scan of the answer choice shows a variety of professions. Who would be most likely to write a passage about a disagreement over how to study international relations? Predict: someone who studied international relations. (B) immediately recommends itself.

Wrong Answers:
(A): Distortion. Though history is mentioned frequently in the passage, it's always in the context of international relations. The author argues that the debate is "among international relations scholars," and so a history professor would be less likely to write about it than an international relations professor.
(C): Distortion. While diplomats are *involved* in international relations, they're not necessarily dedicated to the *study* of it. A professor of international relations would be more likely to be interested in the academic side of the topic.
(D): Out of Scope. There's no reason to think that a journalist would be concerned with an academic debate about the study of international relations.

Strategy Point:
Be willing to skip over hard questions! Easier questions are sometimes found at the end of a passage; make sure you have time to get to them by skipping the most difficult questions and coming back later.

PASSAGE VII

Topic and Scope:
The effects of quality control on Nixon-era welfare programs

Mapping the Passage:
¶1 describes problems in welfare during the Nixon era: high caseloads, high cost, and the inability to pass welfare reform legislatively.
¶2 describes performance monitoring, a way the Nixon administration tried to effect change without legislation.
¶s3 and 4 discuss the stated purpose of quality control and its actual effects.
¶4 continues the discussion of quality control's consequences: bias and harassment in the welfare application process increased.
¶5 describes the contradictory nature of quality control: it was intended to protect the right to welfare, but instead harmed it, and was supposed to instill accountability in government, but instead eroded accountability.

Questions:
40. A What sort of effort was quality control? Go back to ¶s1-3. In ¶2 quality control is described as "a mechanism of policy change." In the paragraph below, the author says that what Nixon did was "part of the administrative efforts to circumvent legislative obstacles." Therefore, quality control came from the ability to get around the inability to find a legislative solution. (A) paraphrases this tongue twister.

Wrong Answers:
(B): Faulty Use of Detail. While these factors may have *indirectly* led to quality control, ¶1 is clear that they first led to attempts to legislate, the failure of which directly led to the establishment of quality control.
(C): Out of Scope. The allegations in this answer choice are never mentioned or suggested in the passage.
(D): Distortion. The author argues that the administration's efforts *did* stem the increase of caseloads, though not in a good way. In any case, reduced caseloads was a *result*, not a cause, of quality control.

41. C A scattered detail question. Eliminate answer choices based on the passage or look for one that doesn't seem to fit. (C) does just this. While the author discusses decreases in the numbers of people who actually received welfare, there's no suggestion that the number of people *eligible* for welfare decreased. In fact, the author thinks that quality control was bad because people eligible for welfare weren't able to get it.

Wrong Answers:
(A): Opposite. This is mentioned in ¶4, among other places; the author notes "demands that welfare applicants routinely produce scores of documents of dubious relevance."
(B): Opposite. The author states in the middle of ¶2 that quality control penalized for overpayments and payments made in error, but not for underpayments, delays, and denials. These penalties were therefore both arbitrary and inconsistent.
(D): Opposite. This is a paraphrase of the author's point in the last paragraph that "government institutions and officials were thus insulated from the effects of their actions" and that "quality control ironically eroded the government accountability."

42. B An inference question without any clue in the question itself. The correct answer will therefore likely deal with main ideas in the passage as a whole. Predict the author's main point: the Nixon administration's policy of quality control made the welfare system worse off than it had been. Looking for an answer that ties into this turns up (B): if the author believes that national quality control hurt the welfare system, then the author must also believe that the welfare system would be better off with more state oversight.

Wrong Answers:
(A): Distortion. The author believes that quality control made welfare more restrictive, but doesn't believe that this made the system more *effective*. The author believes that quality control "appears to have initiated a process of effective disentitlement," which can't be considered an effective solution (note the negative tone)
(C): Out of Scope. The author never makes any suggestions for legislative reform, sticking only to the problems with performance measurement.

(D): Opposite. The author argues that quality control *has* caused disenfranchisement, so wouldn't argue that this claim was unjust.

43. D An evaluation question. Go back to ¶4 to review the phrase in context. The author argues that "quality control's effectiveness" depended on the bureaucrats in "hundreds of local welfare offices," and describes the poor results that came from that dependence. Why does the author mention the bureaucrats? Predict: to show why a national system of quality control turned out so poorly on the local level. (D) paraphrases this.

Wrong Answers:
(A): Faulty Use of Detail. The author does make this claim, but not until the last sentence of the paragraph, and the mention of bureaucrats isn't designed to support this. Rather, this claim supports the argument that local bureaucrats caused problems, which in turn supports the point made in (D) that performance monitoring was ineffective.
(B): Out of Scope. The author never tries to refute this theory, but only to show in the first half of the paragraph why the push for fiscal responsibility had negative effects.
(C): Faulty Use of Detail. While the author states that quality control "served a latent, political function," but supports it in the discussion of what errors were and were not punished. The reactions of bureaucrats to new demands doesn't support this particular statement.

44. B What common managerial tool is mentioned in the passage? Paraphrase: Quality control. What does the author think about quality control in the case of welfare reform? That it was too restrictive and kept people who were entitled to welfare from getting it. What would the author think about the use of "common managerial tools" to effect change in welfare? Predict: Probably the same thing; it's too restrictive. (B) rewards the careful reasoning with a nearly word-for-word paraphrase.

Wrong Answers:
(A): Opposite. If anything, the author argues that over-adherence to regulations was the cause of the problem in the first place.
(C): Opposite. The author uses to passage to cite quality control as an example of a case in which national welfare administration *wasn't* effective at doing this.
(D): Out of Scope. The only accountability that the author mentions is the accountability at the state and local level; federal accountability is never discussed.

45. B A question asking which of a list of activities quality control included. Predict by paraphrasing the general purpose of quality control: to "achieve fiscal accountability," as stated at the beginning of ¶2. Only (B) directly deals with fiscal accountability, and is supported by the author's point in ¶2 that quality control penalized states for overpayments.

Wrong Answers:
(A): Opposite. The author states explicitly in ¶2 that states were *not* held accountable for unreasonable delays.
(C): Opposite. Easing rules for reimbursement would *lessen* fiscal accountability, since more money would be distributed.
(D): Opposite. The author argues in the last paragraph that quality control "did not overtly breach the integrity of theoretical entitlement to welfare promised by statute and supported by legal precedent." In other words, quality control didn't change the statues. Even if it *did* change the statues, there's no clue in the answer whether the statues would have been made more or less restrictive; (B) is much more specific.

46. D How would the author improve the quality control system? Predict by identifying the main problem: the author says in ¶2 that quality control didn't work because it penalized bureaucrats for being too generous, but didn't punish them for not being generous enough, thus unjustly harming those eligible for welfare. Therefore, the author would probably be inclined to make the system less arbitrary and to punish for overpayment and underpayment alike, thus protecting those eligible for welfare. (D) paraphrases this.

Wrong Answers:
(A): Opposite. The author argues that quality control already unfairly limits the ability of people eligible for welfare to get paid; arbitrarily setting a limit of applications would just encourage this.
(B): Out of Scope. The author argues that the problem is with quality control, not with the caseworkers themselves, who are just trying to stick to the regulations. More careful screening therefore wouldn't seem to do much good.
(C): Out of Scope. There's no reason to believe the author wants to spend more money on welfare; the author deals only with the injustice of how the money being spent currently is distributed.

PASSAGE VIII

Topic and Scope:
The formation and location of hydrocarbon reserves

Mapping the Passage:
¶1 explains how hydrocarbons form in pockets underground.
¶2 gives some background for our global dependence on fossil fuels.
¶3 describes the two types of hydrocarbon traps: structural traps and stratigraphic traps.
¶4 notes that new sources of hydrocarbons will come from reserves that are difficult to locate, and describes generally how reserves are located and extracted.

¶5 notes that most new oil will be found in stratigraphic traps and outlines the method for finding oil when surface geology doesn't help: seismic exploration.

¶6 describes the limitations to seismic exploration of stratigraphic traps.

¶7 notes recent developments in refining seismic exploration, and raises hope that discovery of stratigraphic traps will be easier in the future.

Questions:

47. D A global question: predict with topic, scope, and purpose. The author discusses how hydrocarbon reserves are formed (especially in ¶s 1 and 3) and how they can be located (throughout the passage, but especially in the second half of the passage). (D) repeats this nearly word-for-word.

Wrong Answers:
(A): Faulty Use of Detail. While the passage does this, this choice says nothing about the location of reserves, which the passage spends significant time on.
(B): Faulty Use of Detail. The flip side of the above answer choice. The passage discusses seismic exploration, but it also discusses the formation of hydrocarbons before this.
(C): Faulty Use of Detail. The author argues in ¶5 that stratigraphic traps are harder to locate than structural traps, but this isn't itself the main idea of the passage; the author mentions this in order to explain the method for discovering stratigraphic traps.

48. B A detail question; "According to the passage..." tips you off. Where are difficulties mentioned? Go back to ¶6. The last sentence of ¶6 states what the question does, that it's difficult to distinguish reflections between the two materials. The beginning of the sentence gives the reason: "the density contrasts between oil-bearing sandstones and the shales that provide stratigraphic seals for the oil are often very small." (B) says the same.

Wrong Answers:
(A): Faulty Use of Detail. While the author mentions this in the same paragraph, it's used in the context of how resolution can be improved, not why it's difficult to distinguish between the sandstone and shale.
(C): Faulty Use of Detail. This is part of the "primary limitation with the seismic method" that the author discusses towards the beginning of the paragraph, not the direct cause of the particular problem in the question.
(D): Out of Scope. As above, thinness has to do with the primary limitation of the method, not the specific problem mentioned in the question.

49. C An evaluation question; review the lines in context. The author provides the example immediately after defining how stratigraphic traps are forming by stating "For example..." (note the keyword!). Predict

the use: the author is simply giving an example of how the traps are formed. (C) says the same.

Wrong Answers:
(A): Out of Scope. The author doesn't provide any contrast to structural traps in the example.
(B): Faulty Use of Detail. The author does explain this, but only in order to explain how stratigraphic traps are formed. This is another part of the example rather than the point of the example.
(D): Out of Scope. The author doesn't discuss difficulties in locating stratigraphic traps with seismic tools until ¶6.

50. C A scattered detail question. Either eliminate wrong answer choices or look for a choice that sticks out as correct. (C) should jump out immediately; since not all traps are stratigraphic, it wouldn't make sense for the author to have said that oil couldn't be extracted without a density contrast between reservoir rocks and a stratigraphic seal.

Wrong Answers:
(A): Opposite. The author states in ¶1 that "hydrocarbons...will eventually reach the surface and be lost unless they encounter impermeable rocks."
(B): Opposite. The author ties oil reserves to hydrocarbons in ¶s1 and 4, so it's reasonable to believe that it's not possible to get oil if an original source of hydrocarbons aren't present.
(D): Opposite. The author says in ¶1 that "if the rock within which they are trapped is highly permeable...the hydrocarbons can be extracted by drilling." In other words, drilling can't happen unless hydrocarbons are trapped within permeable rocks.

51. D Where are carbonate reservoirs mentioned? Review the beginning of ¶6: the passage says that "the most common stratigraphic traps (with the possible exception of carbonate reservoirs) are in sandstone layers that are much thinner than a seismic wavelet." What is the author implying? Predict: carbonate reservoirs are in layers that *aren't* much thinner than a seismic wavelet. (D) comes close to this.

Wrong Answers:
(A): Out of Scope. Density has nothing to do with the thickness of the layer, which is what we're concerned with in this part of the passage.
(B): Out of Scope. While carbonate layers might be *easier* to find than other stratigraphic traps because of their relative thickness, the author doesn't give any indication that they are in fact *easy* to find.
(C): Out of Scope. The author says nothing about the importance or lack thereof of carbonate traps.

52. A What is the author's opinion of seismology? The author discusses why seismology isn't a great way to find stratigraphic traps in ¶6, and raises the hope that seismology will become more effective in the future in ¶7. Paraphrase: Seismology has its problems, but will hopefully improve in the future. (A) says the same.

Wrong Answers:
(B): Distortion. Though seismology has limitations, there's no indication that it's intrinsically flawed. If it were, the author wouldn't argue for its improvement.
(C): Distortion. The author believes that seismology has promise, but spends a significant part of the passage explaining why seismology *isn't* extremely effective. Nothing at all is said about profitability, so this choice is out of scope also.
(D): Distortion. The author doesn't discuss the theory of seismology, instead focusing exclusively on the practical method and its limitations. Further, the author only suggests that seismology is ineffective for stratigraphic exploration, not completely ineffectual.

53. B What sort of development would improve seismic exploration the most? Predict: something that overcame the seismic method's primary limitation. The author states in ¶6 that the primary limitation is resolution, and that the wavelets are too large to be useful in discovering stratigraphic traps. Therefore, something that allowed for higher resolution would be a major development, and if it overcame the problem of attenuation that the author mentioned, it would sidestep the current problems with high frequencies. (B) fits.

Wrong Answers:
(A): Opposite. While it would be good for the frequency to increase, increasing the *attenuation* of the wavelength only exacerbates the problem with high frequencies that the author mentions.
(C): Distortion. While this would be an improvement, since the author mentions a problem associated with this in the paragraph, it wouldn't be as big an improvement as something that overcame the "principal limitation" of seismology.
(D): Distortion. As above, while further research might be helpful in other ways, it wouldn't be as helpful as a practical way to overcome the main problems with seismology.

PASSAGE IX

Topic and Scope:
The three social functions of popular music

Mapping the Passage:
¶1 Discusses the advent of pop music and the birth of Rock and Roll.
¶s2 and 3 discuss popular music's function of creating identity.
¶4 discusses its function in the management of feelings.

¶5 discusses its third function, organizing time, and notes that this is particularly important to the definition of youth.

Questions:
54. D What is the author's primary purpose in the passage? A gimme: the author wants to discuss the social functions of music. (D) fits the bill.

Wrong Answers:
(A): Faulty Use of Detail. The author does this as a side-note to describing popular music's function of organizing time, but it's only a detail.
(B): Out of Scope. There are no theories other than the author's own in the passage.
(C): Out of Scope. The author discusses other forms of popular culture, like sports, but only as a way of further describing the functions of music.

Strategy Point: Don't over think the easy questions! Take the quick points and move on.

55. C Where is classical music mentioned in the passage? It isn't! How could we figure out anything about classical music, then? Predict: by relating it to music in general. The author notes in ¶5 that "one of the effects of all music, not just pop, is to focus our attention on the feeling of time, and intensify our experience of the present." Therefore, both pop music and classical music must focus attention on time, since this is a general quality of music. (C) says the same.

Wrong Answers:
(A): Faulty Use of Detail. This is a social function of pop music, but the author doesn't suggest that it's a function of music in general.
(B): Faulty Use of Detail. The author uses this phrasing in describing "popular love songs" but again gives no indication that it's a function of music in general.
(D): Faulty Use of Detail. The author argues in ¶5 that pop music defines what youth is, but doesn't argue a similar function for music in general.

Strategy Point:
Don't panic when a question throws a curve ball in the form of an unfamiliar situation or terminology that's not in the passage. If it's in a question, it can be related back to the passage; you just need to figure out how.

56. C A question about the author's tone, scan the answer choices and note that only (C) is positive. Is the author's tone positive? Go back to ¶4 to review: the author says that the love songs "give shape and voice to emotions that otherwise cannot be expressed without embarrassment or incoherence." The author also notes that the songs express feeling "for us in interesting and involving ways." The author is positive, and therefore (C) is correct.

Wrong Answers:

(A): Opposite. The author argues that love songs are the antidote to banal language by expressing the same ideas in interesting ways.

(B): Opposite. The author argues that our own expressions of feeling can be emotionally incoherent and that love songs help to compensate for this.

(D): Opposite. The author clearly believes that popular love songs have an important social function: the management of feelings.

Note: Noting the author's tone (positive, negative, or neutral) helps narrow down answer choices with a quick vertical scan.

57. A Why does the author discuss sports in ¶2? Go back to review: the author says that "music, like sport, is clearly a setting in which people directly experience community..." Sport is used as an example of a case in which something similar happens, or, in other words, a parallel. (A) says the same.

Wrong Answers:

(B): Opposite. The author says that music is like sport: "like" indicates a parallel, not a contrast.

(C): Out of Scope. There's no assumption mentioned that could be challenged.

(D): Opposite. The mention of sport is used to elaborate on the *same* idea, not to introduce a new one.

58. B What does the author do in the last paragraph? Predict from your map: The author describes the third function of popular music, the organization of time, and its relevance to the definition of youth. (B) captures the author's focus on youth.

Wrong Answers:

(A): Distortion. The author briefly discusses the experience of youth, but only in the context of how youth relates to popular music, which this choice leaves out entirely.

(C): Out of Scope. This choice tries to capitalize on words familiar from the passage: "organization" and "youth." *Time* is organized, and youth is defined through popular music, but nothing at all is said about the organization of youth movements.

(D): Faulty Use of Detail. Though the author does discuss the relationship between music and time, it's done so particularly in the context of how it relates to youth, a topic that this choice completely omits.

Strategy Point:
Watch out for answer choices that take familiar wording and rearrange it into nonsensical, contradictory, or irrelevant answer choices. Familiar wording should be used to figure out what part of the passage to review, not to answer the question from the familiarity alone!

59. D Where is the creation of identity discussed? Go back to the ¶2. Review the author's main points: pop music helps us "directly experience community" and at the same time has an "individualizing" effect. The author uses these ideas to show how identity is created through pop music. (D) paraphrases the idea that pop music operates on the communal and individual levels.

Wrong Answers:

(A): Out of Scope. Though the author says in ¶5 that young people are most concerned with pop music, this doesn't mean that it's unpopular with the older set. In any case, it's irrelevant to the author's point about identity, which is restricted to ¶2.

(B): Faulty Use of Detail. The author makes this point in ¶4, but to support the idea that pop music helps to manage feelings, not to support pop music's role of creating identity.

(C): Opposite. The author says that pop songs are "open to appropriation for personal use in a way that other popular cultural forms...are not." Pop music is therefore *unique* in this way.

60. D Why does the author believe that popular music is important for social organization in youth? Go back to review the relevant text. The author makes the assertion in lines 45–46, and immediately above says that it's because good music has the ability to stop time, with "no memory or anxiety about what has come before us, what will come after." What would weaken this? Predict: something that said that good music *doesn't* stop time. (D) does just this.

Wrong Answers:

(A): Opposite. This would support the author's argument at the end of the passage that the moments associated with youth "have nostalgia coded into them" without necessarily weakening the author's point about forgetting the past.

(B): Opposite. This would support, and in fact paraphrases, the author's argument that "youth is experienced...through an impatience for time to pass and a regret that it is doing so."

(C): Opposite. This would also support the author's argument about youth, and in particular the author's claim that "we invest most in popular music when we are teenagers and young adults."

Materials used in this test section were adapted from the following source(s):

Edward Gibbon, *The History of the Decline and Fall of the Roman Empire*, Volume 6

Verbal Reasoning Test Eleven

Time—85 minutes
Question 1–60

DIRECTIONS: Each of the passages in this test is followed by a set of questions based on the passage's content. After reading each passage, decide on the one best response to each question and mark it on your answer sheet. If you are unsure of an answer, eliminate the choices you know are wrong and choose from the remaining choices. You may refer to the passages while answering the questions.

Passage I (Questions 1-6)

The best-known platonic depiction of tyranny appears in *Republic*, where the tyrant is beastly, subject to base and unnecessary appetites: power, vainglory, luxury, lust, and gluttony. To the extent that passions control him—a decidedly male figure—the tyrant is a sort of slave, who depends on both taxation to support him and his "drink-mates…and…mistresses," as well as bodyguards to protect him from assassins and other "worthless creatures" who proliferate under tyrannical rule.

An argument recently propounded by the historian of philosophy Matteo Giovannini threatens to unsettle this widely held view of the platonic tyrant as a brutish slave. According to Giovannini, the traditional view, while sound as far as it goes, is incomplete in that it ignores insights into the tyrannical character that are offered by Plato in the earlier and more obscure dialogue, *Lysis*.

If the ancient Greeks first inspired the ideological commitment to democracy that gripped Western thought especially during and after the Enlightenment, the Greek philosophers contributed to this development less by their embrace of the democratic principle than by their rejection of tyranny. In Aristotle's schema, tyranny is the most perverse of six types of government; Plato designated five types, with tyranny the least desirable, followed by democracy. Yet less clear than Plato's disregard for the tyrannical character is his sense of its basic constitution.

Giovannini's account purports to complicate the one-dimensional view of tyranny associated with *Republic*. But this account, while ingenious and provocative, is not beyond question. Most significantly, Giovannini appears not to have anticipated an obvious objection to his research design. While *Lysis* first appeared during Plato's formative period of aporetic dialogues in which the principal interlocutors frequently pose questions but rarely provide lasting answers, *Republic* dates from a later, more mature period in the development of Plato's thought, when conclusions are more frequent and less concealed. If Plato intended the conception of tyranny that appears in *Republic* to be somehow bound up in a paradox with the conception of tyranny in *Lysis*, he would presumably have hinted as much. Absent such indications, the danger is heightened that Giovannini may have invented, rather than discovered, subtle interconnections in Plato's thought.

According to Giovannini, *Lysis* forms a counterpoint to *Republic* by depicting a tyrant whose status derives, not from his slavish dependency, but from his utter self-sufficiency; he is complete, or (to use the language of the ancient philosophers) perfect. For such a figure, friendship—for many of the Greek philosophers, the foundation of healthy political community—is ultimately impossible, because "the one who is perfect does not depend on the many who are imperfect, but the many who are imperfect depend on the one who is perfect." In short, Giovannini argues, the tyranny found in *Lysis* is the wake of a doomed union between the needy masses and the singular, complete one. Viewed in the double light of *Republic* and *Lysis*, the platonic tyrant depicted by Giovannini is a paradoxical figure: here a slave; there the epitome of wholeness.

---

1. The author makes a few different points throughout the passage. In paragraph 4, the author is primarily concerned with:

    A. providing a richer alternative to the one-dimensional view of tyranny furnished in *Republic*.

    B. establishing a relationship between the content of platonic dialogues and the order in which they first appeared.

    C. dismissing Giovannini's findings on the grounds that they are more imagined than real.

    D. supplying an overall assessment of Giovannini's argument about the platonic conception of tyranny.

GO TO THE NEXT PAGE.

2. According to the information put forth by the author in the passage, what does Giovannini suggest about tyrannical regimes as depicted in *Lysis*?

A. They fulfill the brutish desires of the tyrant.

B. They are typically incompatible with the political community.

C. They result from a severe imbalance in the relationship between the ruler and the ruled.

D. They promote strength and self-reliance among the general populace.

3. The author most likely mentions Aristotle in order to:

A. illustrate Greek philosophers' rejection of tyranny as a desirable form of government.

B. link ancient Greek political thought with that of the Enlightenment.

C. exemplify the seminal nature of Plato's political thought.

D. provide a contrast to the position of tyranny in Plato's classification of regimes.

4. Which of the following is NOT presented as evidence for the best-known platonic characterization of the tyrannical figure?

A. Reliance on taxation to support his personal social pursuits

B. Slavish attachment to the friendship of the populace

C. Excessive indulgence of base desires

D. Dependence on physical protection from enemies

5. Suppose conclusive evidence emerged that, in order to shield his audience from confusion, Plato on occasion intentionally avoided revealing complex or seemingly contradictory conclusions in his dialogues. What relevance would this information have to the passage?

A. It would weaken Giovannini's claim that the platonic tyrant is a paradoxical figure.

B. It would verify the author's assertion that *Republic* provides a reasonable but only partial depiction of Plato's conception of the tyrannical character.

C. It would weaken the author's major criticism of Giovannini's research.

D. It would weaken the author's assessment of Giovannini's work as ingenious and provocative.

6. The author of this passage criticizes Giovannini. This criticism is primarily on the basis of his:

A. bias against the slavish dependency of the platonic tyrant.

B. over concern for the situation of the "needy masses."

C. failure to use original source materials in his research.

D. treating Plato's earliest works as deliberate contrasts to his mature works.

GO TO THE NEXT PAGE.

Passage II (Questions 7–12)

It is still an open question precisely how Hobbes conceptualized the state of nature; neither he nor his interpreters have been completely clear. Hobbes offers three scenarios. In *De Cive*, the state of nature is an empirical physical location in which war "is perpetuated in its own nature….They of America are examples hereof." In *Leviathan*, Hobbes appears to conceive of the state of nature as a facet of personality, accessible through introspection or intuition: "*Nosce teipsum*, read thyself…whosoever looketh into himself…shall thereby read and know what are the thoughts and passions of all other men."

In *De Corpore*, Hobbes suggests that principles of human nature can be derived by ratiocination from "the first part of philosophy, namely, geometry and physics." Among Hobbes scholars consensus lacks regarding how, and indeed whether, these scenarios reconcile. Conclusions seem to change sometimes within a single tract. Within the space of two lines in Konstantin's influential *Leviathan Logic*, the state of nature changes from a mere "act of imagination" into a far more ambitious "ideal conception." (What is more, Konstantin's assertion that the state of nature could never be empirically observed contradicts Hobbes's own reference to "they of America.") LaJoie calls the state of nature a creation of logic, not history, while for Saccente the state of nature is a "thought-experiment" designed not to chronicle the essential condition of humankind, but to illuminate it.

It has long been a commonplace idea that a state of nature is the conceptual starting point of Hobbesian political thought. A war in which "every man is Enemy to every man" chiefly characterizes this state in which, because of limited resources and the absence of any *summum bonum* to fortify a moral order, anarchy rules and life is never without want and fear. Even scholars who offer otherwise contrasting readings of Hobbes agree that its foundation is the state of nature. For LaJoie, Hobbes's state of nature "sets in motion the dominoes of deduction" from which ultimately issue the politics proper. Saccente cautions against framing Hobbes's thought within an "architectural analogue according to which the state of nature is the foundation of a structure and civil philosophy is its roof," yet she too maintains that for Hobbes "civil philosophy begins with knowledge of human nature." Hobbes presents no exception to the rule that at the outset, every social theorist, whatever else he or she argues, of necessity makes fundamental and seminal assumptions concerning human nature.

To the extent that it involves a politics—what Hobbes calls civil philosophy—built on a philosophy of human nature, Hobbes's thought constitutes a system in which the problems of political life in civil society are intertwined with the basic nature of the human condition. By this view, humankind exists in a universe the entire content of which is no more or less than matter and motion. A strict, raw, nominalist materialism circumscribes reality in this billiard-ball world of efficient causes, which manifest in personality as the passions that drive behavior.

What is usually termed 'will' is unreal, nothing more than the final derivative of appetite or aversion. To understand the operation of these passions in human behavior, we are invited by Hobbes to explore a setting in which nothing impedes people's acting on appetites and aversions. This setting is, of course, the state of nature. In addition to the absence in this state of any positive law, there is also no natural law in the scholastic sense of providentially-prescribed rational commands of right conduct for everyone. 'Good' is radically individual and utilitarian; it is always and only that to which appetite or aversion drives a person. Possessed of a natural liberty to compete for limited resources and to win what security they can by whatever means they choose, actors in the natural state vie, according to the famous phrase, for "Power after power, that ceaseth only on Death."

---

7. Of all of the following, which is NOT addressed by the author in the passage?

   A. The relationship between physics and human nature

   B. Hobbes's basic conception of the nature of universe

   C. The role of self-reflection in relation to the principles of human nature

   D. The requirements for emergence from the state of nature into civil society

GO TO THE NEXT PAGE.

8. As used in the end of the fourth passage in the sentence, "A strict, raw, nominalist materialism circumscribes reality in this billiard-ball world of efficient causes, which manifest in personality as the passions that drive behavior," the words "billiard-ball world of efficient causes" refer to:

A. the rejection of belief in transcendent or universal standards of right conduct.

B. the philosophical relationship between political and pre-political society.

C. the foundation of positive law in human nature.

D. the derivation of will from basic appetites and aversions.

9. Which of the following best characterizes the claim (lines 47–49) that "every social theorist, whatever else he or she argues, of necessity makes fundamental and seminal assumptions concerning human nature?"

A. It supports a viewpoint regarded by the author as widespread but groundless.

B. It is at odds with the subsequent claim that Hobbes's conception of the state of nature is an open question.

C. It broadens the scope of a claim with which the author agrees.

D. It demonstrates the systemic character of Hobbesian thought.

10. A key distinction between two types of social agreements—compacts of immediate performance and covenants of mutual trust—is that the latter, unlike the former, depend significantly on the presence of good faith and the expectation of long-term future cooperation among the parties to the covenant. Given this, which of the following does the passage suggest would be LEAST likely to occur?

A. A compact of immediate performance in the state of nature

B. A compact of immediate performance in civil society

C. A covenant of mutual trust in the state of nature

D. A covenant of mutual trust in civil society

11. According to the author, which of the following would be most analogous to conditions in the state of nature?

A. In a nuclear family, parents allow children to share in decision-making as the children develop a capacity to communicate increasingly thoughtful opinions.

B. In warfare, belligerents adhere to principles such as proportionality, non-combatant immunity, and other norms of the "just war" principle.

C. In international politics, sovereign states pursue their individual interests without reference to an overarching authority whose laws are backed by the threat of coercive force.

D. In a crime-ridden neighborhood, a paroled criminal burgles homes and businesses despite the emergence of a vigilante group of hostile neighborhood residents convinced that police are incapable of capturing the criminal.

12. The passage suggests that LaJoie's characterization of the state of nature is most consistent with that expressed in:

A. *Leviathan.*

B. *De Corpore.*

C. *De Cive.*

D. *Leviathan Logic.*

GO TO THE NEXT PAGE.

Passage III (Questions 13–18)

The apparent change from the rather mechanistic explanation of evolution put forth by the Greeks to the more creationist reasoning found later in Europe was a significant paradigm shift, yet it is clear that the idea of
5 evolution was not first pioneered by Darwin himself.

It is essential to confront the creationist issue and to look at it in a scientific manner. Creationism is not science and doesn't belong in the science classroom. However, a frank discussion of creationism with stu-
10 dents is also important. To avoid it may suggest that perhaps there is something valid there, lurking in the irrationality.

The late Carl Sagan, one of the staunchest advocates of rationality and reason in the increasingly irra-
15 tional and superstitious world in which we live, has defended the importance of good science teaching by saying: "In the demon-haunted world that we inhabit by virtue of being human, [science] may be all that stands between us and the enveloping darkness." In its most
20 simple form, the concept of evolution is that populations of organisms change over time. One can trace the origins of evolutionary thought at least as far back as the Greeks.

Anaximander, in 500 BC, held the belief that living
25 creatures were formed from water and that humans and other animals were descended from fishes. Empedocles, around 400 BC, proposed an evolutionary hypothesis in which he stated that heads, limbs, and various other parts of animals were continuously joined in random
30 combinations – e.g. human heads with cows' bodies – and that only some of these combinations were fit for survival.

Christian philosophers later elaborated on the ideas of Aristotle and Plato when they reasoned that because
35 existence is a good thing and because God is considered benevolent, God must have bestowed existence on all creatures. This twist of circular reasoning, to which the name "natural theology" was applied, dominated the period preceding Darwin, and this philosophy resisted
40 change long after Darwin published his theory of natural selection in 1859. Soon after Charles Darwin published his landmark work, universal school education began in Britain, and the teaching of evolution was a top priority in that new system.

45 Thomas Huxley, one of Darwin's most ardent supporters, was one of the founding members of the powerful London School Board, which helped to set curriculum guidelines for students and teachers. However, in the United States a strong biblical funda-
50 mentalism was taking hold, using the Bible as both a means of consolation as well as a guide for moral conduct. Many states passed laws banning the teaching of evolution in schools, and teachers who persisted either did so quietly or allowed themselves to be martyred, as
55 in the case of John Scopes, the Tennessee teacher convicted in 1925 of teaching evolution in his public school biology class. Despite his conviction, his trial scored enough of a public victory for the teaching of evolution that the rising tide of creationism slowed considerably
60 until many decades later. Most recently, those opposed to the teaching of evolution in schools have pressed the idea of "creation science," a tactic devised by creationists in the late 1960s to infiltrate America's science classrooms with religious ideas.

65 Creation science, despite the apparent oxymoron, is a phrase that has been widely used by creationists to add legitimacy to their claims by stating that creationism is a scientific theory just as much as evolution. By claiming that their ideas are scientific, creationists could then
70 demand equal time in the classroom devoted to both evolutionary theory and the "theory" of creationism. This extremely dangerous idea has been at the forefront of battles waged by so-called "creation-scientists" since the early 1970s in their attempts to overturn school cur-
75 ricula.

---

13. In the passage the author contrasts the presence of Thomas Huxley on the London School Board with the growing biblical fundamentalism in the United States in order to:

A. show how unimportant the Bible was in British education.

B. suggest that creationism was a movement specific to the United States.

C. suggest that Darwin's ideas needed a great deal of support in order to be allowed into England's classrooms.

D. demonstrate the continued presence of natural theology in United States curricula.

GO TO THE NEXT PAGE.

14. When Carl Sagan speaks of "the demon-haunted world that we inhabit by virtue of being human," what is he trying to say about us?

   A. Human claims that demons and other creatures exist on Earth should be believed.
   B. Humans are innately superstitious beings and irrationality is part of being human.
   C. We should put more emphasis into the teaching of science and reason so that we can understand better what makes us human.
   D. We tend to turn to fantastic and irrational explanations in order to explain phenomena in the world which we do not understand.

15. Alfred Russell Wallace is widely credited with having arrived at an almost identical theory of natural selection to Darwin's at about the same time that Darwin was ready to go public with his ideas. Yet, the one aspect of natural history that Wallace could not reconcile based on his theory was human intelligence, crediting something supernatural for the evolution of this trait. Thus, Wallace's ideas on evolution might be best characterized as:

   A. Thomas Huxley's views with some natural theology mixed in.
   B. those of a natural theologist.
   C. entirely creationist.
   D. a combination of biblical fundamentalism and natural theology.

16. When reviewing all of the arguments made in the passage it becomes apparent that the author's main idea in this passage is:

   A. to explain the differences between natural selection and creation science.
   B. to show how the continued spread of creationist views is a potentially dangerous affront to a rational, scientific understanding of evolution.
   C. to contrast the creationist viewpoints, such as fundamentalism and natural theology with more ancient views of evolution.
   D. to explain why the concepts of evolution are more scientifically correct than those of "creation science."

17. If presented in an open debate on the topic of teaching creationism and evolution in schools, the author would most likely agree with which of the following statements?

   A. All discussions of creationism and creation science should be eliminated from science classrooms.
   B. Teachers who teach evolution would agree to splitting time in their classrooms equally between evolutionary theory and creation science.
   C. There is no room for irrationality and superstition, since it hides scientific truth and derails reason.
   D. The Bible may be a valuable tool for guiding certain human behaviors, such as morals and ethics.

18. The author brings up Greek philosophers to point out which of the following:

   A. that the origins of evolutionary thought comprised some silly notions such as heads, limbs, and various other parts of animals were always being joined in random combinations.
   B. that the origins of evolutionary thought began long before Darwin.
   C. that both evolutionary thought and creationism have their origins among the Greeks.
   D. Anaximander first came up with the theory of evolution.

GO TO THE NEXT PAGE.

Passage IV (Questions 19–25)

The variety of fish reproduction techniques provides an example of the adaptive complexity that ecologists have found. Most spawning is synchronized with phases of the moon, and eggs are fertilized in the water
5 column. However, some species lay eggs on the sea bottom or in a protected area. Damselfishes will guard their nests quite aggressively, while jawfish and cardinalfish incubate eggs in the mouth. Seahorse and pipefish carry their eggs in a pouch. For some species sex is deter-
10 mined at an early stage of development, while others have the ability to alter sex depending on circumstance.

Most hermaphroditic species follow the protogynous pattern of the fairy basselet. If the male disappears, the dominant female in his harem will change sex within
15 days and take over his role within hours. However, a few species are protandrous, where the fish are male first and then become female. Much remains to be learned about fish reproduction, and evolutionary biologists find that the coral environment provides them with many oppor-
20 tunities to observe a variety of species and specialized behaviors.

The reef itself is alive with many billions of coral colonies plus other limestone-depositing organisms, growing among the skeletons of their predecessors.
25 Reefs grow on the continental shelf edge, on the shelf itself, along islands and atolls, and from the continental mainland. Reefs are found in two general locations: the Indo-Pacific, where Australia's Great Barrier Reef is located, and the Western Atlantic, which includes
30 Caribbean reefs. While strict requirements concerning the amount of available light, and the ocean's clarity, temperature, and movement have restricted the geographic locations of the Earth's reefs, these requirements have not limited the ecological complexity of reef
35 communities.

Species representing more phyla than those found in a tropical rainforest live on coral reefs. Scientists counted 1,441 worms on one coral head alone, and these worms belonged to over a hundred different families.
40 Six of the Earth's seven species of marine turtles inhabit the Great Barrier Reef. Four thousand species of fishes, more than a third of all marine fish species, make coral ecosystems their home. Cartilaginous sharks and rays, perciform fish families, and some lower teleost are
45 found. Perhaps more notably, representatives from all fish families and most genera are reef inhabitants. Although annelid, mollusk, and insect faunas eclipse

reef fish assemblages, fish diversity exemplifies the richness of coral environments.

50 Scientists study reef fishes not only because of the diverse sampling of species but also because of the range of behaviors and relationships between species and other animals that is available for analysis. Intense competition and predation have caused fishes to carve
55 out special niches. Mimicry and camouflage offer just two ways for species to blend in with their surroundings. Juvenile rockmover wrasses mimic dead leaves by floating along with currents, and peacock flounder blend in so well with the sea floor that only their sudden move-
60 ment will betray location. Symbiotic relationships between fish and other organisms also occur with frequency on coral reefs. Small cleaner wrasse and gobies enter the mouth of larger species and emerge unscathed because cleaner fishes eat dead skin and
65 external parasites from other fishes. Cleaner fishes are necessary to sustain the health of organisms on a reef. The anemonefish share their habitat with sea anemones in a symbiotic relationship that scientists have yet to unravel completely. The defensive nematocysts of the
70 anemone are used to stun prey, but the anemonefish are resistant to these stinging cells. Researchers believe that the fish secretes a mucous coating that mimics that of the anemone allowing for chemical signals to prohibit the firing of the cells. One theory holds that the fish obtain
75 these chemicals by rubbing against the sea anemone's tentacles. The benefits, if any, to the anemone for having these fish live with them is not clear.

---

19. Based on the information set down in the passage by the author, with which of the following statements would the author most likely agree?

   A. More effort should be made to protect Australia's Great Barrier Reef.
   B. The absence of diverse phyla in terrestrial ecosystems makes them irrelevant for Earth's biodiversity.
   C. The richness of coral reef diversity should be recognized and studied.
   D. Ecologists should focus research efforts on environments other than coral reefs.

GO TO THE NEXT PAGE.

20. By examining the points made by the author, it can be inferred from the passage that scientists studying hermaphroditic reef fishes would be most interested in research concerning:

    A. the complexity of reproductive behaviors of perciform families in light of fish evolution.

    B. the prevalence of shark attacks on reef divers.

    C. the development of coral spawning behavior in reef communities.

    D. the specific temperature requirements, broken down by latitude, for coral growth.

21. The author discusses the number of species found on a coral head in the fourth paragraph in order to:

    A. provide an example of an abnormal phenomenon.

    B. emphasize how much greater the diversity of worms on a reef than fish.

    C. highlight the importance of coral reef preservation.

    D. illustrate the diversity found in coral reefs.

22. It can be inferred from the passage that changes in an ocean's water clarity and temperature would concern researchers studying coral reefs because:

    A. water clarity and temperature directly limit ecological biodiversity.

    B. symbiotic relationships between organisms are complex and interesting.

    C. water clarity and temperature affect the growth of coral communities.

    D. scientists studying reefs also study climate change.

23. Which of the following theories is supported by the author through the example of the anemonefish in lines 67–71?

    A. Coral animals and fish often operate independently in the same realm.

    B. Complex symbiotic relationships operate on different levels.

    C. Symbiotic relationships only work when both species receive tangible benefits.

    D. Many smaller fish will hide in coral nooks and crannies to avoid predators.

24. Evidence of which of the following would most *weaken* the author's argument concerning fish diversity?

    A. More mollusk diversity can be found on a reef than fish diversity.

    B. Evidence of the diversity of fish behavior in other ecosystems surpasses that of the Great Barrier Reef.

    C. The discovery of new teleost species not found in marine environments.

    D. Coral bleaching causes fish species to die off.

25. The passage suggests that which of the following is implicit in discussions concerning biodiversity?

    A. The larger the number of marine turtle species, the greater the biodiversity.

    B. Higher population numbers mean greater biodiversity.

    C. The larger the number of phyla, the greater the biodiversity.

    D. Geographic location correlates with the amount of biodiversity.

GO TO THE NEXT PAGE.

Passage V (Questions 26–31

Tracking seems to contradict the oft-stated assumption that "all kids can learn." If certain students are better in certain subjects, they must be allowed to excel in those areas and not be relegated to an inferior class simply because they have been tracked in another subject in which they don't excel. The major obstacle to eliminate tracking seems to be scheduling, and tracking has become, in many ways, a means to alleviate difficulties faced by administrators in scheduling their student body for classes.

Tracking has the ability to create divergent experiences, even in identical courses that are meant to be taught at the same level and speed. Administrators who support tracking generally assume that it promotes student achievement, citing that most students seem to learn best and develop the most confidence when they are grouped amongst classmates with similar capabilities. Yet, at least for the lower level tracks, this method of class assignment can encourage "dumbing down," or teaching to the lowest common denominator of ability within a particular class, rather than accommodating differences and pushing all students equally hard.

Tracking places different students in groups that are usually based on academic ability as demonstrated by their grades and as described in teacher reports. These tracks mean that a student will proceed through every school day with essentially the same group of peers, assigned to classes at a particular level of difficulty. Researcher R. Slavin notes that "students at various track levels experience school differently," depending on their track assignments. There are differences, for example, in how fast a class progresses through material, how talkative and energetic the classroom is, even how stressed or relaxed the teacher appears.

One of the major problems with tracking is that the level in which students are initially placed often determines not only where they remain throughout high school, but also the kinds of courses they are allowed to take. For example, schools that offer Advanced Placement (AP) courses often require that students take the honors-level version of the introductory course before enrolling in the AP course a year or two later. A student who is tracked into the "regular" introductory course, rather than the honors level, may not be able to take the AP course even after doing an exemplary job in the introductory course, simply because the honors course is offered a year earlier than the regular one—allowing honors-track students to complete enough other graduation requirements to have time for the AP course later on. And, even if the "regular"-track student could make it into the AP course, he or she would be at a disadvantage, because the introductory course couldn't cover key concepts when the teacher was compelled to slow down the class for the less able students.

---

26. If it were found that students who were tracked did better overall on standardized tests than those who were not tracked, this would most likely *weaken* the author's argument that:

    A. tracking has the ability to create a diversity of student experience in the classroom.
    B. tracking encourages teaching to the lowest common denominator.
    C. tracking allows administrators to overcome scheduling difficulties.
    D. tracking allows students to learn best when grouped with similar-ability classmates.

27. According specifically to the points laid out by the author in the various paragraphs of the passage, the main idea of the passage is that:

    A. tracking should not be used by schools to try and promote student achievement.
    B. tracking may be detrimental to many students' success in school.
    C. teachers of tracked classes are often stressed and run their classes at a slow pace.
    D. scheduling is a major problem for school administrators.

28. The author's argument that tracking contradicts the assumption that "all kids can learn" would be *strengthened* by which of the following findings?

    I. Honors-track students almost always have AP classes on their transcripts, while regular-track students do not.
    II. Students in tracked classes do significantly better on standardized tests appropriate for their class level.
    III. Teachers of the lower math track in a particular school were unable to cover more than $\frac{3}{4}$ of the textbook over the past few years.

    A. I only
    B. III only
    C. II and III
    D. I and III

GO TO THE NEXT PAGE.

29. According to the arguments made in the passage, students may fall into a particular track because of all of the following conditions EXCEPT:

   A. high grades.
   B. learning difficulties.
   C. honors-course enrollment.
   D. how talkative and energetic they are.

30. If the author were to encounter a student in a class who was not doing the work because he or she claimed to be so bored by the material, the author would most likely conclude that:

   A. the student has been placed in a track that is too high.
   B. the student is unmotivated and should be disciplined.
   C. the student has been placed in a track that is too low.
   D. the student should be in AP level classes.

31. In spite of what points may be made in other parts of the passage, in paragraph 2, the author is primarily concerned with:

   A. contrasting administrative views of tracking with his own views.
   B. defining "dumbing down" and its effect on students.
   C. describing the diverse experiences students face when tracked.
   D. conveying the importance of pushing all students equally hard.

GO TO THE NEXT PAGE.

Passage VI (Questions 32–39)

This civil rights movement in the United States developed at the same time as the development of pluralist politics in the US. And very much of the latter, especially in the northern urban area, was infused with a heavy dose of ethnicity. As Blacks were coming out of slavery and going into courts, immigrant groups were coming out of Europe, passing through Ellis Island, and going into local political clubs and machines.

The politics of race has been mainly a struggle to restructure constitutional meaning and to establish certain legal claims. This emphasis was necessary precisely because the citizenship status of Blacks was defined for a long period as quite different from that of Whites. After the abolition of slavery, approximately one hundred years ensued—into the 1960s—that were devoted essentially to interpreting the new *constitutional* status of the emancipated Black citizens.

A "civil rights" movement developed that saw ninety-five years (1870-1965) devoted to establishing the privilege of Blacks to vote unencumbered by racial barriers. The main arena was the court system. Congress and the presidency were not principal participants, because the political constituencies supporting their elections did not favor such participation. Civil rights advocates went to federal courts to challenge "grandfather clauses," White primaries, evasive voter registration practices, as well as economic intimidation. These important, tedious battles created a cadre of constitutional lawyers who became in a real sense the focal points of the civil rights struggle. Such was the situation in the famous Montgomery, Alabama bus boycott from 1955 to 1957, which began when Rosa Parks refused to abide by a municipal law requiring her to sit in the rear of the city bus, and ended when the U.S. Supreme Court in *Gayle v. Browder* said she did not have to do so.

But while the politics of race was characterized by a struggle for rights, the politics of plural-ethnicity was characterized by a struggle for resources. The latter was a struggle to capture and control public office and the ability to dispense patronage and divisible and indivisible benefits. Instead of nurturing and training lawyers and plaintiffs, plural-ethnicity focused on precinct captains and patronage. While the Black racial political struggle utilized constitutional lawyers as sophisticated interpreters of new constitutional meaning, those focusing on ethnicity utilized lawyers to interpret immigration rules, obtain pushcart licenses, and negotiate the bureaucratic passage from alien to citizen. Both roles were fundamentally critical, but also fundamentally different. The point is the following: when the civil rights struggle evolved from rights to resources, as it certainly did beginning substantially in the 1960s, it took with it the orientation, language, and some of the tactics of the earlier struggle for constitutional rights.

---

32. The author of the passage mentions the *Gayle v. Browder* case in order to:

    A. provide an example of civil disobedience that led to a change in the law.
    B. show how civil rights activists distrusted the higher court system.
    C. examine how the struggle for resources utilized the lower court systems to achieve certain goals.
    D. refute the claim that the federal government was not involved in the civil rights movement.

33. According to the passage, how did the struggle for resources differ from the struggle for rights?

    A. It focused on grass-roots activism instead of electoral power
    B. It emphasized on control and political representation at a local level
    C. It was dedicated to effecting changes through election to national political positions
    D. It cooperated with newly-arrived immigrant populations

34. According evidence put forth by the author of the passage, why was the Executive Branch of the government not targeted for civil rights participation in the 1950s?

    A. Early activists had little political clout on a federal level at that time.
    B. Federal policies banned lobbying of Congress by civil rights advocates.
    C. Elected officials acted according to the expressed opinions of their voters.
    D. No members of Congress were interested in enforcing new voting laws.

GO TO THE NEXT PAGE.

35. Paying particular attention to the thematic organization of the passage, which of the following statements best describes the structure of the passage?

   A. Two historical developments are described and contrasted.

   B. A historical movement is praised using two closely connected examples.

   C. A general history of a struggle is presented, with a suggestion of how it will be resolved in the future.

   D. Two different approaches to a problem are analyzed and then combined.

36. According to the author, prior to 1965 the civil rights movement on behalf of Blacks was characterized by none of the following EXCEPT?

   A. An emphasis on removing restrictions on Black voting through court cases

   B. A struggle to overturn the decisions of constitutional lawyers

   C. The increasing ability of Black voters to mobilize and elect Black politicians to office

   D. Frequent conflict between the Congress and Supreme Court over controversial issues

37. In the passage, the author cites the Montgomery, Alabama bus boycott as an example of:

   A. a crucial incident which marked the turn of the civil rights movement toward the goal of controlling resources.

   B. an event important because it began the leadership career of Martin Luther King, Jr.

   C. one of the better-known battles to assert the civil rights of Blacks.

   D. an event whose primary importance was its impact on the enforcement of constitutional rights.

38. According to the author, the "politics of plural-ethnicity" discussed in the fourth paragraph differed from the Black civil rights movement before 1965 in all of the following ways EXCEPT that it:

   A. concentrated more on elections as a way to achieve important goals.

   B. initiated court cases for more sophisticated and theoretical reasons.

   C. was more concerned with the dispensation and control of patronage benefits.

   D. was more based on immigrant ethnicity in northern urban regions.

39. The author would most likely agree with which of the following statements regarding the relationship between pluralist politics and the civil rights movement?

   A. In the 1960s, the civil rights movement took on some of the less legalistic characteristics of pluralist politics.

   B. The civil rights movement remained fundamentally unaffected by pluralist politics.

   C. During the 1950s, the tactics of pluralist politics came to dominate the civil rights movement.

   D. The civil rights movement benefited from the constitutional rights achieved by pluralist politics.

GO TO THE NEXT PAGE.

Passage VII (Questions 40–47)

As Stanley Cavell wrote: "The most characteristic fact about actions is that they can—in various specific ways—go wrong, that they can be performed incorrectly. This is not, in any restricted sense, a moral assertion, though it points the moral of intelligent activity. And it is as true of describing as it is of calculating or of promising or plotting or warning or asserting or defining...These are actions which we perform, and our successful performance of them depends upon our adopting and following the ways in which the action in question is done, upon what is normative for it." Thus, in talking about virtue, we are talking about normative matters, matters taught and learned in terms of successful or unsuccessful human action. As such, we are speaking about the cultivation of human skills and practices, human ways of acting (or ways of acting humanly) in this world.

That virtue is taught (and learned) performatively has something to do with the ineluctably normative quality of human action or activity. Norms are ways of doing something, getting something done; these ways of acting are taught by doing and showing how to do. Being normative, however, human actions can go wrong. They can be done wrong, or be wrongly done.

Virtue is not so much a matter of learning specific rules or principles or maxims as it is one of developing the knack of exercising one's capacity for right action. Since "virtue" can mean both "moral goodness" and "successful or excellent action," my comments about the teaching of virtue are intended to apply to both senses or uses of the term, narrow and broad. Both are matters of human action or activity and, as such, are taught nondidactically, performatively.

Whether virtue is narrowly or broadly understood, the teaching is the teaching of a skill within a practice or form of life, the training of a capacity. Memorization may indeed play some part in teaching a skill within a practice, but it is not all, or even most, of what I understand this teaching to be. Virtue is embodied in action; accordingly, our knowledge of virtue is a kind of performative knowledge—both knowledge acquired through action and knowledge expressed or revealed in action, in performing a task.

Our knowledge of virtue is not, then, a matter of *propositional* knowledge, but rather a matter of performative knowledge. This helps account for our relative inability to define or say what virtue is with any confidence or assurance. Knowing what virtue is, is not the same as knowing what some kind of object is, because virtue is not an object. And since so much of Western thought uses our knowledge of objects as *the* paradigm of knowledge, any kind of knowledge that does not fit the model is apt to seem not quite or fully knowledge at all. In this respect, virtue is like language. Both are taught by example. Hence, an inability to articulate the meaning of virtue is not a sign of the lack of knowledge of virtue, contrary to Socrates (or Plato). Instead, it is a part of the grammar of virtue.

---

40. In the last paragraph of the passage, the most probable reason for the author's comparison between virtue and language is to:

- **A.** suggest that neither skill can be learned through indoctrination.
- **B.** prove that both skills are more easily acquired at a young age.
- **C.** show that both skills are based on certain human actions.
- **D.** make a case for the theoretical acquisition of language.

41. Which of the following is/are used in the passage to bolster the author's assertion in the second paragraph that "human actions can go wrong"?

- **I.** Reference to the inherent nature of virtue as propositional knowledge
- **II.** Expert testimony that supports the author's definition of virtue
- **III.** Additional explanation of the nature of human actions

- **A.** I only
- **B.** III only
- **C.** I, II, and III
- **D.** II and III

42. Based on the information given in the passage, we can infer that if presented with the following assertions, the author would most likely agree that:

- **A.** moral values must be learned through memorization of societal norms.
- **B.** abstract ideas can only be understood through extensive study of human nature.
- **C.** virtue can be explained through intensive philosophical discussion.
- **D.** some skills can only be demonstrated by the completion of a certain action.

GO TO THE NEXT PAGE.

43. As the term is used by the author in the first paragraph of the passage, "normative" human actions are based on:

- **A.** lessons learned from life experiences and observations.
- **B.** examples provided by historical precedents.
- **C.** cultivation and development of skills and practices.
- **D.** comprehension of what is right and what is wrong.

44. In the passage, the author mentions that virtue can be narrowly or broadly understood. Whether broadly narrowly defined, the teaching of virtue is NOT:

- **A.** a matter of propositional knowledge.
- **B.** the training of a capacity.
- **C.** the teaching of a skill.
- **D.** a matter of indoctrination of rules or guidelines.

45. The author would be most likely to agree with which of the following statements about norms?

- **A.** They are derived from specific maxims that define different aspects of virtue.
- **B.** Only by faithfully following behavioral norms can virtue be acquired.
- **C.** Many norms are simply the correct way of performing a certain action.
- **D.** They are the product of didactic teaching.

46. According to the passage, a person who is unable to define virtue:

- **A.** cannot successfully teach virtue to others.
- **B.** may impart knowledge of excellent action but not of moral goodness.
- **C.** can teach didactically but not performatively.
- **D.** may still have a knowledge of virtue.

47. Which of the following would the author consider an example of the "propositional knowledge" referred to in line 45?

- **A.** Experiments conducted on a trial and error basis
- **B.** Practicing virtue by imitating moral actions
- **C.** Learning a language in conversational classes
- **D.** Memorizing various philosophical definitions of virtue

GO TO THE NEXT PAGE.

Passage VIII (Questions 48–53)

The first great penal code in the Benthamite tradition, although never enacted, was prepared by an American, Edward Livingston, for the state of Louisiana in 1826. What led to the appearance of this draft code at this time in Louisiana? Many factors, doubtlessly, but conspicuously among them was the commitment of one man to the idea of codification. Livingston was a learned man, well read in Continental as well as English intellectual and social developments. He was captured by the ideas of Bentham and the ferment for legal reform and codification in revolutionary America and France. Earlier in his career as a United States Congressman he sought a revision of the United States penal law. That his code was drafted for Louisiana may be due simply to the accident that led him to leave New York and to transplant his legal and public career there.

The modern codification tradition to which the Model Penal Code (1962) belongs has its roots in the new rationalism of the eighteenth century Enlightenment, which saw reason as the instrument both for understanding and mastering the world. For law, reason provided a lodestar and an instrument for reform. The ideas of the Enlightenment took hold in England as well as the Continent and led to a powerful movement toward codification of law. But it was through the work of one man, Jeremy Bentham, that these ideas had their greatest influence on law reform. Bentham's thinking on codification of criminal law had a powerful influence on every codification effort in the English-speaking world in the nineteenth and twentieth centuries, not excluding the Model Penal Code.

Within Bentham's legacy are such concepts as: law defined in advance with clarity and certainty to maximize its potential for guiding behavior; judicial discretion to make or change the law eliminated as productive of uncertainty and arbitrariness; the doctrines of the criminal law and the principles of punishment justified only by their service to the purpose of the criminal law to prevent crime; penalties proportioned to the offense; and refusal to punish where it would be "groundless, inefficacious, unprofitable, or needless."

The Penal Code, breathtaking in conception and achievement, included a Code of Procedure, a Code of Evidence, a Code of Reform and Prison Discipline, and a Code of Crimes and Punishments. Livingston's unassisted completion of this task within three years was one of those prodigious, virtuoso performances that is scarcely imaginable today. His Benthamite philosophy was manifested in many of the Code's provisions, notably those relating to the judicial function. Livingston distrusted judges no less than Bentham; consequently, common-law crimes, use of common-law terms, and all means through which judges might infuse their own moral views into the definition of crimes were outlawed. The object of the Code, to leave as little as possible to judicial creativity, is apparent in its preference for exhaustive and detailed specifications of rules. Other notable characteristics of the Code include its rejection of capital punishment, its moderation of punishments, its forceful protection of freedom of speech and the rights of the accused, the prominent place it gave to reform of the offender and its provision of means to accomplish it.

---

48. If the author read the following statements in an article on the topic of the development of the Penal Code, he would most likely agree with which of the following statements?

   A. Edward Livingston's personal commitment to the codification of laws greatly influenced his colleagues, including Jeremy Bentham.
   B. English and Continental lawmakers agreed wholeheartedly on the need for standardization of laws during the eighteenth and nineteenth centuries.
   C. Developments in intellectual and philosophical thought during the Enlightenment were a major factor in leading to the establishment of the first penal codes.
   D. The Benthamite concept of penal codes has been highly influential in theory, but rarely successful when written into law.

49. The author spends some time disussing Bentham's work on legal reform. Which of the following is NOT attributed by the author to Bentham's work on legal reform?

   I. Making sure the punishment fits the crime
   II. Outlawing unjust and arbitrary penalties
   III. Legalization of capital punishment

   A. II only
   B. III only
   C. I and III
   D. I, II, and III

GO TO THE NEXT PAGE.

50. According to information put forth and argued by the author of the passage, which of the following was one of the primary reasons for the creation of Livingston's penal code?

 A. Influence from previous codification efforts had finally spread from other parts of the country into Louisiana.
 B. American legal figures were impressed by the legal systems in England and wished to emulate them.
 C. Livingston was inspired by intellectual and social changes and progress from abroad.
 D. Colleagues in the legal profession encouraged Livingston to develop a Penal Code based on the Benthamite tradition.

51. All of the following are strengths of Livingston's penal code EXCEPT:

 A. specific protection of defendants' civil rights.
 B. emphasis on reform rather than on punishment.
 C. constraints on judicial discretion to modify rules and legal procedures.
 D. successful implementation and expansion of his code.

52. Assuming that the author was correct and complete in his analysis of Livingston, one of the guiding motivations for Livingston's development of a penal code was:

 A. to afford broader rights and less severe punishments to convicted criminals.
 B. to decrease the possibility of judicial misinterpretation of laws.
 C. to define penalties and crimes based on common-law terms.
 D. to protect certain freedoms and civil rights of defendants.

53. Looking back on the form the passage takes as a whole, which of the following best describes the method used by the author to structure this passage?

 A. Presentation of a thesis, historical background of a topic, refutation of the thesis and suggestion of a different explanation
 B. Introduction of a controversial thesis, discussion of an example of the thesis, defense of a potential alternative thesis
 C. Objective presentation of a historical legal development, description of successive stages in this development, judgment of the outcome of this development
 D. Application of a theory, contextualization of the theory, description of the new application and comparison to the original

GO TO THE NEXT PAGE.

Passage IX (Questions 54–60)

Because we have so deeply interiorized writing, we find it difficult to consider writing to be an alien technology, as we commonly assume printing and the computer to be. Most people are surprised to learn that
5 essentially the same objections commonly urged today against computers were urged by Plato in the *Phaedrus*, against writing.

Writing, Plato has Socrates say, is inhuman, pretending to establish outside the mind what in reality can
10 be only in the mind. Secondly, Plato's Socrates urges, writing destroys memory. Those who use writing will become forgetful, relying on external resource for what they lack in internal resources. Thirdly, a written text is basically unresponsive, whereas real speech and thought
15 always exist essentially in a context of give-and-take between real persons.

Without writing, words as such have no visual presence, even when the objects they represent are visual. Thus, for most literates, to think of words as totally dis-
20 associated from writing is psychologically threatening, for literates' sense of control over language is closely tied to the visual transformations of language. Writing makes "words" appear similar to things because we think of words as the visible marks signaling words to
25 decoders, and we have an inability to represent to our minds a heritage of verbally organized materials except as some variant of writing. A literate person, asked to think of the word "nevertheless" will normally have some image of the spelled-out word and be quite unable
30 to think of the word without adverting to the lettering. Thus the thought processes of functionally literate human beings do not grow out of simply natural powers but out of these powers as structured by the technology of writing.

35 Without writing, human consciousness cannot achieve its fuller potentials, cannot produce other beautiful and powerful creations. Literacy is absolutely necessary for the development not only of science, but also of history, philosophy, explicative understanding of lit-
40 erature and of any art, and indeed for the explanation of language (including oral speech) itself. Literate users of a grapholect such as standard English have access to vocabularies hundreds of times larger than any oral language can manage. Thus, in many ways, writing
45 heightens consciousness. Technology, properly interiorized, does not degrade human life but enhances it.

In the total absence of any writing, there is nothing outside the writer, no text, to enable him or her to pro-
50 duce the same line of thought again or even verify whether he has done so or not. In primary oral culture, to solve effectively the problem of retaining and retrieving carefully articulated thought, you have to do your thinking in mnemonic patterns, shaped for ready oral recurrence. A judge in an oral culture is often called upon
55 to articulate sets of relevant proverbs out of which he can produce equitable decisions in the cases under formal litigation under him. The more sophisticated orally patterned thought is, the more it is likely to be marked by set expressions skillfully used. Among the ancient
60 Greeks, Hesiod, who was intermediate between oral Homeric Greece and fully developed Greek literacy, delivered quasiphilosophic material in the formulaic verse forms from which he had emerged.

---

54. In paragraph 5 of the passage, the author mentions Hesiod in order to:

   A. prove that oral poets were more creative than those who put their verses in written words.
   B. show that some sophisticated expressions can be found among the pre-literate ancient Greeks.
   C. demonstrate that a culture that is partially oral and partially literate forms the basis of an ideal society.
   D. thinking in mnemonic patterns is an unsuccessful memory device.

55. According to the passage, the thought patterns of most literates are based on various processes. to which of the following processes does the author point?

   A. Consistent reference to the written word as a visual coding device
   B. Acquired abilities to interpret oral communication in a textual context
   C. Learned abilities that are acquired by all humans during the early childhood years
   D. Conscious transformation of viewed objects into visual language

GO TO THE NEXT PAGE.

56. If given the chance to respond to the following assertions, the author of the passage would most likely agree that:

   A. computer advances in the recent decades will prove to be advantageous to human life.

   B. the development of writing has been detrimental to the progress of intellectual thought.

   C. communication in primary oral cultures was flawed and untrustworthy.

   D. beautiful and powerful creations cannot be produced through oral communication.

57. Suppose all of the following conclusions from tests or research are true and accurate. Which of the following would most *weaken* the author's conclusion about the benefits of writing?

   A. Data from a study of primary oral cultures prove that advances in philosophy in these cultures have been sophisticated and meaningful.

   B. Researchers have shown that children who are blind from birth and are never exposed to writing are just as likely to excel in all academic and artistic endeavors as sighted children.

   C. Historical evidence suggests that fewer developments in history and art were achieved in pre-literate ancient cultures.

   D. Tests on stroke patients whose language processing centers have been damaged have shown no proof of an increased reliance on oral communication

58. According to the author, an important difference between oral and literate cultures can be expressed in terms of:

   A. extensive versus limited reliance on memory.

   B. chaotic versus structured modes of thought.

   C. simple versus complex use of language.

   D. barbaric versus civilized forms of communication.

59. The author refers to Plato in the first and second paragraphs. He brings the philosopher up primarily in order to:

   A. provide an example of literate Greek philosophy.

   B. suggest the possible disadvantages of writing.

   C. illustrate common misconceptions about writing.

   D. define the differences between writing and computer technology.

60. According to points he brings up in various parts of the passage, the author views the technology of writing as:

   A. conflicting with the structure of human consciousness.

   B. enriching the possibilities of human achievement.

   C. damaging to essential human resources.

   D. essential for any artistic creation.

STOP. If you finish before time is called, check your work. You may go back to any question in this test booklet.

ANSWER KEY
VERBAL REASONING TEST 11

1.	D	16.	B	31.	A	46.	D
2.	C	17.	D	32.	A	47.	D
3.	A	18.	C	33.	B	48.	C
4.	B	19.	C	34.	C	49.	B
5.	C	20.	A	35.	A	50.	C
6.	D	21.	D	36.	A	51.	D
7.	D	22.	C	37.	D	52.	B
8.	A	23.	B	38.	B	53.	D
9.	C	24.	B	39.	A	54.	B
10.	C	25.	C	40.	C	55.	A
11.	C	26.	B	41.	B	56.	A
12.	B	27.	B	42.	D	57.	B
13.	B	28.	D	43.	A	58.	A
14.	D	29.	D	44.	D	59.	B
15.	A	30.	C	45.	C	60.	B

EXPLANATIONS

PASSAGE I

Topic and Scope:
Giovannini's interpretation of Plato's tyrant

Mapping the Passage:
¶1 discusses Plato's view in the *Republic* of what tyranny is (traditional view of tyranny).
¶2 introduces Giovannini's argument that this traditional view of what Plato thought is incomplete and ignores Plato's earlier depiction of tyranny in *Lysis*.
¶3 argues that the Greek philosophers rejected tyranny, and that Plato's conception of what tyranny constitutes is unclear.
¶4 critiques Giovannini's argument, suggesting that the *Republic* may represent a more mature view of tyranny than the earlier *Lysis*.
¶5 outlines Giovannini's argument that Plato describes tyrants as "perfect" in *Lysis* and that Plato's conception of tyranny between the two books is paradoxical.

Questions:
1. D An evaluation question: review your map of ¶4. Predict what the correct answer must look like: it has to note the author's critique of Giovannini's theory. Only (C) and (D) involve Giovannini, and (C) is much too harsh. (D) provides a balanced summary of what the author does, matching the prediction from your map closely. Note that the author's tone is neutral. He simply discusses the pros and cons of Giovannini's account.

Wrong Answers:
(A): Out of Scope. The author isn't concerned with critiquing Plato, only Giovannini.
(B): Faulty Use of Detail. The author discusses content and order in discussing Plato's more mature work in the *Republic* as compared to *Lysis*, but only as a way of critiquing Giovannini's overall interpretation of the two works.
(C): Distortion. The author says "the danger is heightened that Giovannini may have invented, rather than discovered, subtle interconnections in Plato's thought." While the author is therefore raising the *possibility* that Giovannini's findings are more imagined than real, he doesn't dismiss Giovannini outright.

2. C Review Giovannini's view of tyranny in *Lysis* (¶5), keeping in mind that the answer choices will try to confuse you with the views of others or from other books. The passage states: as "Giovannini argues, the tyranny found in *Lysis* is the wake of a doomed union between the needy masses and the singular, complete one." (C) paraphrases this contrast between the state of the masses and the state of the tyrant.

Wrong Answers:
(A): Faulty Use of Detail. This is the Plato's opinion of tyrannical regimes as described in the *Republic*, not *Lysis*.
(B): Distortion. Giovannini believes that Plato considers tyranny incompatible with a *healthy* political community, but this doesn't mean that it's incompatible with politics in general. The fact that ¶2 lists tyranny as one of the types of governments that Plato recognizes further suggests that tyranny is in fact compatible with the political community.
(D): Opposite. Giovannini describes the masses as "needy," suggesting that if anything, tyranny discourages self-reliance and strength.

3. A Review the mention of Aristotle in ¶2. What purpose does Aristotle have in this paragraph? The author says that Aristotle considered tyranny "the most perverse" form of government, and then follows this with Plato's similar view. Immediately before the mention of Aristotle, the author argues that the Greeks rejected tyranny. Predict the purpose: the author wants to show that Greeks in general rejected tyranny before focusing on Plato. (A) paraphrases this.

Wrong Answers:
(B): Out of Scope. The Enlightenment is only mentioned in passing, and the author connects it to ancient Greece by a commitment to democracy. The mention of Aristotle, however, is explicitly focused on the issue of tyranny.
(C): Out of Scope. Even if you don't know what "seminal" means (creative or original), you can still eliminate this answer choice. The mention of Aristotle doesn't shed light on Plato, except to say that Plato thought like at least one other Greek philosopher.
(D): Opposite. The only difference noted between Aristotle's and Plato's position is the number of governments they classified; they both put tyranny at the bottom of the heap.

4. B Start out by determining where exactly the best-known Platonic characterization of the tyrannical

KAPLAN

figure appears. What book would it be from? The beginning of ¶1 says that "the best-known platonic depiction of tyranny appears in *Republic*." All the wrong choices are mentioned in support of this depiction in ¶1 except for (B): the author does mention the tyrant's slavishness, but never slavish attachment to the friendship of the people he rules.

Wrong Answers:
(A): Opposite. The passage says that the tyrant "depends on…taxation to support him and his 'drinkmates…and…mistresses.'"
(C): Opposite. The passage says that the tyrant is "subject to base and unnecessary appetites."
(D): Opposite. The passage also states that the tyrant depends on "bodyguards to protect him from assassins."

5. C An incorporation question. Paraphrase the situation given in the question: Plato avoids confusing his audience by not revealing contradictory conclusions. How would this be relevant to the passage? Predict: Plato might have had a paradoxical conclusion about tyranny, just like Giovannini argues, between *Lysis* and the *Republic*, but avoided revealing the contradiction in the *Republic* to keep his audience from being confused. This would contradict the author's point in the fourth paragraph that "if Plato intended the conception of tyranny that appears in *Republic* to be somehow bound up in a paradox with the conception of tyranny in *Lysis*, he would presumably have hinted as much." Look for an answer choice that summarizes this: (C) fits the bill.

Wrong Answers:
(A): Opposite. The new information would strengthen Giovannini's claim since it increases the possibility that Plato did have a paradoxical view, but kept from revealing it for the sake of clarity.
(B): Distortion. The author doesn't argue this; Giovannini does. The author in fact argues that the *Republic* is the most complete reflection of Plato's views on tyranny since it was written when his views had matured.
(D): Distortion. While it *does* weaken the author's view, it can't weaken the argument given in this choice because the author never describes Giovannini's work as ingenious. In any case, the new information would support Giovannini, and so it couldn't weaken any praise given to him.

6. D Use your work from the previous questions and your map to help form a prediction. On what basis does the author criticize Giovannini in ¶4? The author argues that "Giovannini may have invented" connections in Plato's thought because if Plato had wanted to provide a paradoxical view of tyranny, he would have made it clear in the Republic. (D) paraphrases this: while Giovannini treats both *Lysis* and the *Republic* as works of equal

weight, the author believes that the *Republic* should trump any contradictions in the previous work.

Wrong Answers:
(A): Distortion. Though Giovannini suggests a possible view of Plato that isn't necessarily dependent on the tyrant's slavish dependency, Giovannini himself isn't necessarily biased against this view of tyranny.
(B): Distortion. While the description of the "needy masses" is part of Plato's view of tyranny in *Lysis* as described by Giovannini, Giovannini himself isn't overly concerned with the needy masses. Again, his focus is on Plato alone.
(C): Out of Scope. The author never makes this claim, and Giovannini is clearly going back to the source since his theory is based on Plato's original works.

Strategy Point: To answer the last questions, you can usually use research from previous questions, cutting down your time and earning quick points.

PASSAGE II

Topic and Scope:
Hobbes' conception of the state of nature

Mapping the Passage:
¶s1 and 2 discuss the uncertainties over what Hobbes thought the state of nature was.
¶3 describes the agreement among scholars that the basis of Hobbes' thought is the "state of nature."
¶s4 and 5 describe the state of nature.

Questions:
7. D A scattered detail question. While three of the answer choices summarize ideas or points made throughout the passage, (D) is never discussed in the passage. Though Hobbes may address this question somewhere in his writings (and many reading this passage will know that he *does*), it's not mentioned anywhere in the passage itself.

Wrong Answers:
(A): Opposite. Lines 12-14 discuss Hobbes' argument that the laws of human nature can be derived from laws of geometry and physics.
(B): Opposite. ¶4 describes Hobbes' view of the universe as one "the entire content of which is no more or less than matter and motion."
(C): Opposite. ¶1 discusses introspection, stating that "Hobbes appears to conceive of the state of nature as a facet of personality, accessible through introspection or intuition."

Strategy Point:
Remember not to bring outside knowledge into your reading of the passage! Everything you need to score perfectly on the passage is on the page.

8. A Read the lines in context. Immediately before, the author says that a "strict, raw, nominalist materialism circumscribes reality". A short jump afterwards, the author argues that Hobbes believes "what is usually termed 'will' is unreal, nothing more than the final derivative of appetite or aversion." Predict the general thrust of all these lines: Hobbes believes that the universe is materialist, without any sort of outside standards: the universe is deterministic, with effects coming from "efficient causes" just as a billiard ball moves because another one hit it. (A) most closely paraphrases this.

Wrong Answers:
(B): Out of Scope. While the passage mentions "the problems of political life in civil society," there's no mention of the two types of society mentioned in the question, nor would a phrase discussing "efficient causes" have anything to do with their relationship.
(C): Opposite. The author mentions positive law in ¶5, but only to suggest that it's lacking in Hobbes' universe. Therefore, Hobbes would argue that there is no foundation of this sort of law in human nature.
(D): Faulty Use of Detail. While the passage says that what people call "will" is actually just "the final derivative of appetite or aversion," this only explains part of the "world of efficient causes" that the phrase is referring to, leaving out the "universe the entire content of which is no more or less than matter and motion."

9. C An evaluation question in a somewhat unusual format. The answer choices are broad, so remember to read them back into the passage to make sure that any potential right choice actually matches with what's going on in the passage. Read the quote in context: the author says immediately before that Hobbes "presents no exception" to the rule quoted in the question. Paraphrase it all: The author believes that Hobbes makes assumptions about human nature. How does this belief fit in with everything else in the paragraph? It immediately follows claims by scholars that the foundation of Hobbes' thought is the state of nature. Evaluate: the author agrees with the scholars' claims and says that it's a trait of *every* social theorist. (C) accurately describes the author's agreement and broadening.

Wrong Answers:
(A): Opposite. The author doesn't believe that the view the scholars outline is groundless; rather, that it's true not just for Hobbes but for all social theorists.
(B): Out of Scope. The author makes a clear distinction between what everyone more or less agrees on, that Hobbes' foundation is in the state of nature, and what they don't: what exactly he thought that state of nature was.
(D): Faulty Use of Detail. While ¶4 discusses the fact that Hobbes' thought is systemic, this quote refers to the points made *above* it. The author also isn't trying to prove anything about Hobbes' thought here, but rather only to agree with what has been said before and to broaden it to social theorists in general.

10. C A lot of information to sort through here. Start by reminding yourself about the passage's topic and scope: most of the passage is concerned with the state of nature, and odds are that the correct answer will be also. What does the state of nature involve? Predict: As ¶5 says, it's a state in which everyone acts according to "appetite or aversion." What type of contract discussed in the question would be least likely to occur in a state of nature? Predict: a covenant of mutual trust, since there's no place for trust in Hobbes' conception of the state of nature. (C) rewards the careful thought.

Wrong Answers:
(A): Opposite. Since the state of nature is described as a cause-and-effect situation where everything happens for its own sake, it would make sense that the only workable agreement would be one that *doesn't* depend on mutual trust.
(B): Out of Scope. The passage doesn't give us enough information about civil society to hazard a guess on how likely this would be.
(D): Out of Scope. As above, we don't have enough information about civil society in the passage to say that this type of covenant would be the least likely.

11. C Another state of nature question. Predict by summarizing again what the state of nature is, using your work from previous questions to help. The state of nature is an every-man-for-himself sort of world where everyone acts according to their own immediate best interests. Armed with this prediction, (C) immediately recommends itself, just substituting countries for individuals.

Wrong Answers:
(A): Opposite. This choice involves cooperation and a sort of social order, both of which the passage suggests wouldn't exist in the state of nature.
(B): Opposite. Another example in which rules are followed, when in the state of nature there would be no rules.
(D): Distortion. Though the burglar might be acting according to the state of nature, the vigilante group that is trying to restore order suggests that there's an order to be restored, and therefore that the community isn't actually in the state of nature.

12. B Start out by paraphrasing LaJoie's characterization of the state of nature. In ¶3 LaJoie says that the state of nature "'sets in motion the dominoes of deduction' from which ultimately issue the politics proper." In other words, politics and society eventually evolve from the state of nature. LaJoie also describes the state of nature as "a creation of logic, not history" in ¶2. What do these two observations have in common? They both emphasize the importance of logic and deduction. The answer choices list four books: in which one is the importance of logic most clearly emphasized? *De Corpore*: the author says that in this books, Hobbes believes "the principles of human nature can be derived by ratiocination," in other words, that logic is important. (B) is therefore correct.

Wrong Answers:
(A): Opposite. The author suggests that *Leviathan* is more concerned with "intuition" than with logic.
(C): Opposite. In *De Cive* "the state of nature is an empirical physical location." In other words, it's not something constructed by logic, as LeJoie suggests, but an actual place.
(D): Opposite. As the only book not written by Hobbes, this choice is an oddball—consider it with suspicion (especially since "logic" is in the title—a bit too easy!). Konstantin describes the state of nature as an "ideal conception," which doesn't necessarily have anything to do with logic. A little above all this, the author says that "among Hobbes scholars consensus lacks," which further suggests that Konstantin's view will be different from LaJoie's.

PASSAGE III

Topic and Scope:
The history of theories of evolution and the appropriateness of teaching evolution, rather than "creation science" in the classroom

Mapping the Passage:
¶1 points out that Darwin was not the first person to argue for evolution.
¶2 argues that science classes should not teach creation science.
¶3 introduces a quote from Carl Sagan arguing the above statement and points to the simplest form of the concept of evolution.
¶4 introduces ancient analogues of evolutionary theory.
¶5 discusses the Christian philosophy of "natural theology" which dominated the period before Darwin.
¶6 outlines the beginning of evolution's acceptance in classrooms, as well as the resistance it met in America.
¶s6 and 7 discuss recent attempts to combat the teaching of evolution by introducing the "dangerous" "creation science."

Questions:
13. B An evaluation question: use your map to help you determine the author's purpose. What paragraph is Thomas Huxley mentioned in? ¶6, which has to do with the introduction of evolution into the classroom. What is the author's point? Paraphrase: Evolution was accepted fairly readily in England at least partly due to Huxley's influence, but in America it was resisted because "a strong biblical fundamentalism was taking hold." The author is therefore explaining why evolution found greater resistance in American classrooms. (B) most closely fits this prediction.

Wrong Answers:
(A): Distortion. Though the British clearly accepted evolution in education more readily than the Americans, this doesn't necessarily say anything about the Bible.
(C): Distortion. Though evolution was helped by having one of Darwin's "most ardent supporters" as a member of the school board, it didn't necessarily *need* this support.
(D): Out of Scope. Though the author suggests that American classrooms preferred creationism to evolution, the schools didn't necessarily teach natural theology, which the author discusses in ¶5 (a hint that it's probably out of scope) and which isn't strict creationism anyway.

14. D Go back to review the quote in context in ¶3. Immediately before the quote, Carl Sagan is referred to as an advocate "of rationality and reason in the increasingly irrational and superstitious world in which we live." How does the quote about a "demon-haunted world" play into this? Predict: It says the same thing the author did right before; humans tend to be irrational and superstitious. (D) paraphrases this very closely.

Wrong Answers:
(A): Distortion. Though Sagan refers to demons, he's clearly doing so as a way of arguing that we *shouldn't* believe in things for which we don't have hard evidence, rather than suggesting that demons do exist.
(B): Distortion. Though this choice comes close to Sagan's viewpoint, it goes to far in arguing that humans are innately superstitious, which Sagan doesn't argue. If we were innately superstitious, it would be pointless to argue for increased rationality, nor would the author discuss an "increasingly...superstitious" world: clearly, both Sagan and the author believe that superstition is something that can be overcome.
(C): Distortion. Though Sagan might agree with the first half of this choice, there's no indication that he believes that we should focus on science and reason specifically to learn about what makes us human.

15. A An application question. How would we characterize the views of someone who came up with a theory of evolution much like Darwin's, but who also believed that the supernatural created human intelligence? Predict: Wallace must be a combination of evolutionary and religious thought. Looking for a choice that matches might not turn up anything on a first pass, but remember that the passage describes Thomas Huxley as a firm believer in Darwin's theory. Therefore, (A) describes a combination of evolutionary beliefs and the Christian natural theology mentioned in ¶5, a perfect fit with the prediction.

Wrong Answers:
(B): Distortion. While this might explain the belief in a supernatural source for human intelligence, it does nothing to explain Wallace's evolutionary leanings.

(C): Opposite. Since Wallace's theory was almost identical to Darwin's, it can't be described as entirely creationist at all.

(D): Opposite. This choice also leaves out any hint of evolution, since neither biblical fundamentalism nor natural theology incorporate Darwin's ideas.

16. B A main idea question hidden in the middle of the question set. Predict using topic, scope, and purpose: The author wants to promote the teaching of evolution and to argue against the teaching of creation in the classroom. Only (B) and (D) suggest that the author is trying to argue for and against something, and of the two only (B) incorporates the idea of learning and understanding, which the author focuses on extensively in the discussion of classroom instruction.

Wrong Answers:
(A): Faulty Use of Detail. While the author discusses the differences briefly in ¶7, it's only to show that creation science isn't in fact science at all (despite what creationists say) and to argue that it shouldn't be taught in the classroom, a point that this choice leaves out.

(C): Out of Scope. The author describes all these things, but makes no attempt to contrast them. This choice also leaves out the author's attack on creation science, which takes up the latter half of the passage.

(D): Faulty Use of Detail. Though the author does this very briefly in arguing that creation science isn't science at all, it's only to make the larger point that creation science shouldn't be taught in the classroom.

17. D)
An inference question. Finding the correct answer here is a process of elimination. (A) and (C) are closely related so start there. (C) is not true because while Sagan would seem to argue this (¶3), and the author clearly dislikes influencing people through irrational ideas, the author does point out in ¶2 that "a frank discussion of creationism" is also important. To avoid it may give it credence. (A) is also not correct because of the same quote in the second paragraph. Without ever bringing up an alternate forum for this discussion, it can be assumed that this would have to take place in the same science classroom. (B) is wrong because in the last paragraph the author states that creationists, not teachers, have fought for equal time, and the passage never discusses what teachers believe. Also, it cannot be assumed that the teachers would agree en masse. This leaves (D). While the author never mentions specifically what he thinks the value of the Bible might be in other circles, there is no reason to assume that he would think it *might* not be a valuable tool.

Wrong Answers:
(A): Opposite. As described above.
(B): Out of Scope. As above.
(C): Opposite. As above.

18. C) While this question is straightforward, the answer choices are meant to trick the test taker who does not take time to read through all the possibilities. The author brings up Anaximander and Empedocles in ¶3 as evidence of his claim that "one can trace the origins of evolutionary thought at least as far back as the Greeks." But be careful—he also brings up Plato and Aristotle in ¶4, stating that Christian philosophers elaborated on their ideas when they came up with what became creationism. Therefore both evolution and creationism have their origins in Greece. (C) is correct.

Wrong Answers:
(A): Faulty Use of Detail. The later part of this answer is taken from ¶3 when the author details Empedocles' theory, but his point was never to show is was silly.
(B): Faulty Use of Detail. This is the point of ¶3, but it ignores the evidence in ¶4.
(D): Out of Scope. Anaximander is the earliest source mentioned as a precursor to evolutionary theory, but the author never claims that he is the original source.

PASSAGE IV

Topic and Scope:
Diversity and adaptation of organisms in coral reefs

Mapping the Passage:
¶s1 and 2 give examples of reproductive adaptations among reef animals (¶2, hermaphrodites).
¶3 describes the great diversity in types of reefs, and their geography.
¶4 describes the great diversity in reef ecosystems.
¶5 gives examples of unique adaptations among reef animals.

Strategy Point:
Get through examples-heavy passages quickly (in no more than two or three minutes at most, usually). Specific examples cited by a question can always be found in the passage, and most examples won't be mentioned at all in any given question set.

Questions:
19. C An inference question without any clues to help narrow it down, so chances are it will have to do with the author's main points. What does the author generally believe? Predict: The coral reefs harbor unusually rich ecosystems. (C) echoes this and adds the point at the end of the passage that "much remains to be learned."

Wrong Answers:
(A): Out of Scope. The author doesn't discuss conservation efforts in the passage, and so while the author *may* agree with this, it can't be inferred from the passage.
(B): Distortion. Saying that the biodiversity in coral reefs is exceptional doesn't equate with saying that the

biodiversity on land is irrelevant. Watch out for choices that suggest false contrasts!

(D): Out of Scope. The author doesn't discuss what should be done in terms of studying non-reef ecosystems.

20. A Find the example in ¶2 to which the question refers. What would scientists studying hermaphroditic fishes be most interested in? Predict: Reproductive behavior. Only (A) deals with fish reproductive behavior and adaptation, while the other choices are out of scope. Don't be put off by the mention of "perciform families," which are mentioned as one type of reef inhabitant in ¶4.

Wrong Answers:
(B): Out of Scope. Sharks, neat though they are, are never mentioned in the passage.
(C): Out of Scope. Coral spawning behavior wouldn't have anything to do with fish reproduction, and so would be outside the scope of hermaphroditic fish studies.
(D): Out of Scope. Temperature requirements also would seem to have little to do with fish reproductive behavior and adaptation.

21. D An evaluation question; predict an answer by looking at what comes before and after. Immediately before, the author notes that there are more phyla in coral reefs than tropical rainforests, and immediately afterwards the author notes that coral reefs have a large diversity of marine turtles. The purpose of the whole paragraph is to demonstrate the diversity of the coral reefs. Predict the purpose of this specific example: to give a further example of the diversity in coral reefs. (D) says the same.

Wrong Answers:
(A): Distortion. While the author suggests that coral reef diversity is unique, there's no indication that it's abnormal.
(B): Distortion. The author doesn't want to suggest that worms represent greater diversity, but rather simply give another example supporting the overall diversity of the coral reefs. This choice suggests a false contrast that the author doesn't make.
(C): Out of Scope. The author emphasizes diversity, but says nothing about preservation.

22. C Where does the author discuss water clarity and temperature? Go back to ¶3, where the author says that "the ocean's clarity, temperature, and movement have restricted the geographic locations of the Earth's reefs." What can be inferred about water clarity and temperature from this information? Predict: they're important to forming coral reefs. (C) repeats this.

Wrong Answers:
(A): Opposite. Though the two factors limit the location for coral reefs, this doesn't mean that they limit

diversity. In fact, the author argues immediately after discussing clarity and temperature, "these requirements have not limited the ecological complexity of reef communities."

(B): Out of Scope. While this may be true, it doesn't necessarily follow from a discussion of water clarity and temperature, which are completely irrelevant to whether or not a phenomenon is interesting.

(D): Distortion. Though climate change *might* be something that scientists studying reefs are interested in, this conclusion can't be drawn from the information in the passage.

23. B Review the example in context and paraphrase the main points: the symbiotic relationship between the anemonefish and the sea anemone is complex and scientists haven't determined completely how it works. (B) most closely approaches this summary with the idea that complex relationships have different levels of action, which would explain why scientists haven't been able to easily untangle the specifics of the relationship.

Wrong Answers:
(A): Opposite. A symbiotic relationship wouldn't support a theory arguing that species operate independently from one another.
(C): Opposite. Since the passage says that "the benefits, if any, to the anemone for having these fish live with them is not clear," the author clearly believes that symbiosis can work when the benefits for one species are not easily observable.
(D): Out of Scope. The example of the anemonefish has nothing to do with hiding from predators.

24. B What would weaken the author's argument that reef ecosystems have exceptional diversity? Predict: Either evidence that the reef ecosystems *aren't* diverse (which is unlikely since the author gives so much evidence that they are) or evidence that other ecosystems are relatively more diverse. (B) suggests evidence of the latter, immediately rewarding careful prediction with quick points.

Wrong Answers:
(A): Out of Scope. This is an irrelevant comparison; the different levels of diversity *within* the reef ecosystem have nothing to do with the overall level of diversity in the ecosystem.
(C): Out of Scope. Though the passage mentions teleost species in ¶4, simply finding a new species that didn't live in a marine environment would do nothing to challenge the ecosystem's overall diversity.
(D): Out of Scope. Even if this is true, it does nothing to challenge the fact that there are a diverse number of species to die off in the first place.

25. C Where is the main discussion of biodiversity? Focus your search on ¶s3 and 4. A quick scan of the choices turns up (C) as a likely answer. Verify it with text from the passage: the author says that "species representing more phyla than those found in a tropical rainforest live on coral reefs." Since the author mentions this in order to support the claim that reefs have exceptional biodiversity, it follows that the author considers the number of phyla to be a good measure of biodiversity.

Wrong Answers:
(A): Distortion. While the author mentions the number of species of marine turtle to emphasize the biodiversity of the coral reef, it doesn't make sense to think that the author considers this a good measure of biodiversity. If it were, rainforests, which obviously have *no* species of *marine* turtle, wouldn't be diverse at all!
(B): Out of Scope. The author never suggests that greater numbers within species indicate biodiversity, nor would this make sense anyway: the author would certainly believe that a coral reef with small numbers of many species would have more diversity than a homogeneous ecosystem with large numbers of only a few species.
(D): Distortion. Though geographic location is indirectly related to biodiversity in that the author says that coral reefs can only grow in certain places, there's no indication that there's an overall linkage between geography and biodiversity.

PASSAGE V

Topic and Scope:
The disadvantages of "tracking" in schools

Mapping the Passage:
¶1 argues that tracking contradicts the philosophy that all can learn, and presents an obstacle to eliminating tracking: it makes scheduling easier.
¶2 responds to the argument that tracking improves learning by stating that tracking can "dumb down" lower level tracks.
¶3 defines tracking and notes that it is common in the nation's schools.
¶4 notes a major problem with tracking: inability for some students in lower tracks to get into higher-level classes later.

Questions:
26. B An incorporation question. How would the author's argument be affected if tracked students did better than their non-tracked counterparts? The question tells you that the argument would be weakened, so you just need to find an answer choice summarizing an argument the author makes against tracking on the basis of performance. (B) is just such a choice: the author argues in ¶2 that tracking encourages "dumbing down"

Wrong Answers:
(A): Faulty Use of Detail. The author does argue this at the beginning of ¶2, but the statement isn't made in order to argue directly that tracking hurts academic performance. Therefore, it wouldn't be weakened by evidence that indicates higher performance.
(C): Faulty Use of Detail. The author makes this point in ¶1, but this is an advantage of tracking, and one of the reasons it sticks around. If evidence that tracking was also good for test scores came out, it would presumably *strengthen* this argument.
(D): Faulty Use of Detail. As above, the author notes this in ¶1 when discussing the advantages of tracking. It doesn't have anything to do with academic performance, however, and so the argument wouldn't be directly affected by the new evidence in the question stem.

27. B)
A main idea question. Predict using topic, scope, and purpose. The author argues that tracking in schools leads to disadvantages for the students. Clearly, he is not in favor of tracking. This knowledge allows us to focus in on the global choices (A) and (B). Of the two, (A) oversteps the scope of the passage. Only (B) accurately encompasses what the author is arguing.

Wrong Answers:
(A): Out of Scope. The author never actually argues that tracking should be eliminated, only that it has some negative consequences .
(C): Faulty Use of Detail. Stress level is mentioned at the end of ¶3, but this is not the author's main point of the passage.
(D): Faulty Use of Detail. Scheduling is mentioned at the end of ¶1, but this is not the author's main point of the passage.

28. D Review the argument referenced by the question; it's at the beginning of ¶1. Why does the author believe this is the case? Paraphrase the argument: If students are assigned to a lower track, the school is assuming that they're unable to perform at a higher level, and so they might be held back when the teacher has to slow down the class. Look for evidence that would support this, starting with RN III, which appears in three out of the four choices. RN III would strengthen the author's argument: lower-track classes that couldn't finish the work they were given would be an example of exactly what the author is discussing at the end of ¶4. Eliminate (A). RN I also supports the author's argument, echoing the argument at the end of ¶4 that lower-track students find it hard to take AP courses. Only (C) remains, and there's no need to check RN II. RN II, however, would *weaken* the author's argument, since it would suggest that tracking leads to a level of instruction appropriate to the student's abilities.

Wrong Answers:
(A): **Opposite.** As described above.
(B): **Opposite.** As above.
(C): **Opposite.** As above.

Strategy Point:
Some questions will very clearly reward you for attention to structure rather than detail. In this question, the relevant information was in the paragraph above *the lines quoted. Catching the keywords that tip this off will allow you to answer this question very quickly, since the correct Roman Numerals are simply details from that paragraph. Remember: Structure before Detail!*

29. D A scattered detail question. Either eliminate or look for a choice that seems foreign. While the first three are mentioned as criteria for tracking in the passage, (D) isn't mentioned as a criterion for tracking. While the author notes in ¶3 that "there are differences…in…how talkative and energetic the classroom is" depending on tracking, there's no suggestion that students are tracked *based* on how talkative or energetic they are individually.

Wrong Answers:
(A): **Opposite.** The author mentions grades as a criterion in the opening lines of ¶3.
(B): **Opposite.** The author cites "academic ability" as a criterion for tracking in ¶3.
(C): **Opposite.** The author discusses the way students get locked in to higher tracks (i.e. AP courses) with honors courses (¶4).

30. C An application question. The trick to many application questions is simply remembering that the author believes his own argument. How would the author respond to a situation in which a student underachieves because of boredom in a way that would strengthen the author's argument? Predict: He'd argue that the student was put in a track that isn't sufficiently challenging, a problem discussed at the end of ¶4. (C) rewards the careful prediction.

Wrong Answers:
(A): **Opposite.** The author doesn't address the possibility that students might be tracked too high; he's far more concerned with the "dumbing down" of classrooms.
(B): **Out of Scope.** There's nothing in the passage to suggest that the author considers lack of motivation in students a particular problem.
(D): **Distortion.** Though the author might agree that the student should be in a higher track, the higher track doesn't necessarily need to include AP classes, which represent a very specific situation mentioned in ¶4.

31. A Use your map to predict the purpose of ¶2: the author first describes why administrators like tracking (it promotes achievement) and then argues that it in fact does the opposite. (A) captures this structure of administrative views and authorial response.

Wrong Answers:
(B): **Faulty Use of Detail.** While this represents the author's view in the paragraph, it neglects the administrative views in the first half of the paragraph.
(C): **Faulty Use of Detail.** The author mentions "divergent experiences" that occur in tracking, but only as an introduction to discussing the arguments for and against the practice.
(D): **Faulty Use of Detail.** As in (B), while this is part of the author's argument against tracking, it neglects the views of the administrators.

PASSAGE VI

Topic and Scope:
The evolution of the civil rights movement and its relation to pluralist politics

Mapping the Passage:
¶1 points out that the civil rights movement came about at the same time new immigrants established political clout by banding together and joining organizations.
¶s2 and 3 describe the way that the civil rights movement fought for legal and constitutional legitimacy for blacks primarily through the court system.
¶4 contrasts the tactics of the civil rights movement with those of immigrants engaging in pluralist politics: the former worked for rights through the courts, while the latter worked for resources through politics.

Questions:
32. A Review the reference at the end of ¶3. Why does the author discuss Rosa Parks and the court case that repealed the law she violated? Paraphrase the situation: Rosa Parks violated the law, which led eventually to the law being changed. This supports the author's argument that the civil rights movement worked for change through the courts. Looking for an answer that paraphrases this leads quickly to (A).

Wrong Answers:
(B): **Opposite.** The author argues throughout the passage that the civil rights movement *relied* on the higher court system for its gains, and there's no evidence at all that it mistrusted the court system.
(C): **Distortion.** The author notes in ¶4 that the civil rights movement fought through the courts for rights, and only later for resources (after the Rosa Parks example).
(D): **Distortion.** The author in fact argues that "Congress and the presidency were not principal participants" in the civil rights movement, but that the courts were.

33. B A detail question that focuses on the main contrast in ¶4. Predict: the movement for rights worked through the courts, while the movement for resources worked through politics. Only (B) and (C) incorporate this idea of politics, and of these, only (B) focuses on the local politics that the author suggests when discussing "local clubs and machines" and "precinct captains and patronage."

Wrong Answers:
(A): Opposite. The author argues that the fight for resources *did* involve electoral power, and that any grass-roots activism was an attempt to gain this power.
(C): Distortion. While this choice does include a focus on politics, it specifically mentions national politics, when the author discusses "local political clubs and machines."
(D): Out of Scope. The author never mentions cooperation with new immigrant groups, and even if this did occur, the cooperation would presumably just be a means to the end of increasing political power.

34. C Review the author's discussion of the executive branch, which appears in ¶3. The author argues that the presidency and Congress didn't get involved "because the political constituencies supporting their elections did not favor such participation." Paraphrase: the President didn't help with the civil rights movement because it was politically unpopular. (C) paraphrases this.

Wrong Answers:
(A): Out of Scope. The national clout of activists isn't discussed, and the author is clear that the executive branch didn't act out of concern for voters rather than lack of concern for activists.
(B): Out of Scope. This discusses the legislative branch and is never mentioned in the passage anyhow.
(D): Out of Scope. Another answer choice dealing with the legislative branch rather than the executive branch.

35. A A rare question asking about the structure of the whole passage; use your map to help you build a prediction. ¶s2 and 3 describe attempts to gain rights through the courts, while ¶4 contrasts this effort with attempts to gain resources through politics. (A), though lacking in specifics, closely matches the structure of the prediction.

Wrong Answers:
(B): Out of Scope. The author doesn't praise the movements, and describes two completely different movements, not a single movement with two examples.
(C): Out of Scope. The author gives a general history of one struggle, but gives no indication of how it will play out in the future. This choice also leaves out the political struggle for resources discussed in ¶4.
(D): Distortion. The author discusses two different approaches, but they're two different approaches to

different problems, not the same problem suggested in this choice.

Strategy Point:
When evaluating the structure of a passage or paragraph, begin broadly, check the answers, and refine your prediction as needed. Most evaluation questions have straightforward answers; too much complexity in your prediction will waste time and make the right answer tougher to spot.

36. A A detail question: Start by finding where 1965 is mentioned in the passage. The author says in ¶3 that "a 'civil rights' movement developed that saw ninety-five years (1870-1965) devoted to establishing the privilege of Blacks to vote unencumbered by racial barriers." Paraphrase: Before 1965, the civil rights movement was primarily interested in the right to vote freely. (A) fits the bill.

Wrong Answers:
(B): Opposite. The author argues that the movement "created a cadre of constitutional lawyers who became in a real sense the focal points of the civil rights struggle." In other words, the author likely believes that constitutional lawyers were the ones struggling to overturn unjust decisions, not the other way around.
(C): Distortion. This characterizes the civil rights movement using the language the author reserves for the struggle for *resources* in ¶4.
(D): Out of Scope. The author never discusses any conflict and suggests that Congress kept a hands-off approach to the civil rights movement anyway.

37. D Review the lines describing the boycott: it started in response to the actions of Rosa Parks. Since you're dealing with an evaluation question, you can use a lot of your work from Question 32, which is also an evaluation question touching on the same events. The correct answer to 32 stated that the Supreme Court case vindicating Rosa Parks provided "an example of civil disobedience that led to a change in law," which seems to be a good description of the author's mention of the boycott also. Looking for choice that fits turns up (D), which simply focuses a little more on rights in general rather than the specific change in law.

Wrong Answers:
(A): Distortion. The author says at the end of ¶4 that the civil rights movement did eventually move from rights to resources, but says that it was an *evolution*, not something marked by a sudden turning point. In any case, the case of Rosa Parks clearly represents a struggle for rights rather than resources.
(B): Out of Scope. Martin Luther King, Jr. isn't mentioned in the passage; this choice tries to play on your outside knowledge. Remember to stick only to what is said and necessarily implied by the passage!

(C): Out of Scope. As above, though it may very well be one of the better-known battles, the author doesn't suggest anywhere in the passage that this is the case, and the example isn't making this point.

Strategy Point:
Many questions will test you on the same basic concepts; don't hesitate to use your work from previous questions if it's relevant!

38. B A scattered detail question. Since the question deals with the main contrast in the passage, review the basics: the civil rights movement fought for rights through the courts, while the movement of "plural ethnicity" fought for resources through politics. While three answer choices fit with the summary and with details from ¶s1 and 4, (B) suggests that the second movement used the courts to advance its ends, while the author says that this was a trait of the *civil rights* movement.

Wrong Answers:
(A): Opposite. This is the author's main characterization of the movement in ¶4: politics instead of courts.
(C): Opposite. This paraphrases the author's point that "plural-ethnicity focused on precinct captains and patronage."
(D): Opposite. The author, in ¶1, discusses immigrants "passing through Ellis Island, and going into local political clubs and machines," which suggests that most of the action was in northern cities.

Strategy Point:
In scattered detail questions, be on the lookout for a correct answer which contradicts the author's point of view or distorts a detail from another part of the passage.

39. A Predict an answer by paraphrasing what the author says when comparing the two movements in ¶4: though they took different approaches for different goals, the civil rights movement eventually "evolved from rights to resources." The author says at the end of ¶4 that the civil rights movement took "some of the tactics" of the earlier struggle for rights, suggesting that it still retained some of its reliance on the courts. What is the implication? Predict: It also took some of the tactics of plural ethnicity. (A) paraphrases this.

Wrong Answers:
(B): Opposite. The author discusses pluralist politics in order to shed light on the civil rights movement, as evidenced by the fact that he refers back to the civil rights movement throughout ¶4. It wouldn't make sense to introduce pluralist politics at all, then, if it had no effect on civil rights. As describe above, the author implies at the end of ¶4 that it in fact did.
(C): Opposite. The author argues that the civil rights movement didn't evolve into a fight for resources until the 1960s, and also argues that even when it did evolve,

it retained some of its earlier tactics. This choice is therefore wrong both in its substance and its time frame.
(D): Opposite. The author argues that pluralist politics focused on resources rather than rights, so there's no reason to believe that there were any rights won by pluralist politics.

PASSAGE VII

Topic and Scope:
The nature and teaching of virtue

Mapping the Passage:
¶s1 and 2 discuss how norms aid in learning virtue: they give instruction in how to act correctly.
¶3 argues that virtue involves learning certain actions rather than rules.
¶s4 and 5 argue that virtue can't be easily defined, but rather is understood as a certain way of acting.

Questions:
40. C Review the comparison between virtue and language. The author says in lines 54–55 that "virtue is like language. Both are taught by example." Paraphrase the similarity, keeping in mind the author's overall point: just as language has to be learned through speaking, virtue has to be learned by acting virtuously. (C) captures this focus on actions rather than rules.

Wrong Answers:
(A): Faulty Use of Detail. While the author does believe that virtue can't be taught through indoctrination and that language presumably can't be either, this point is made only to show that virtue has to be taught through action. The author is more concerned with how virtue and language *are* taught than how they *aren't.*
(B): Out of Scope. The author doesn't discuss age as a factor in learning either thing.
(D): Opposite. The author argues the opposite: that language has to be practiced to be learned, and can't remain theoretical, just as virtue must be practiced rather than indoctrinated.

41. B Review the author's argument that "human actions can go wrong." Immediately afterwards, he says that "they can be done wrong, or be wrongly done," Preceding this is a quote that discusses the nature of human actions. Armed with all this, hit the Roman Numerals. Start with RN III, which appears in three choices. The author does provide additional explanation, both when explaining how actions can go wrong and in the quote by Stanley Cavell, which focuses exclusively on the nature of actions. Eliminate (A). Look at RN I next: the author believes that virtue *isn't* propositional knowledge, which he argues in ¶5. Eliminate (C). Finally, check RN II: Though testimony is cited, there's no suggestion that it's expert, and it never refers to virtue, only to actions. Only RN III is correct, then, and (B) must be the correct answer.

Wrong Answers:
(A): Opposite. As described above.
(C): Opposite. As above.
(D): Opposite. As above.

42. D An inference question without any clues in the question stem, so keep the author's main idea in mind: virtue has to be taught by action rather than by rules. While three of the answer choices either distort or contradict this idea, (D) fits it well. The author would agree that some skills can only be shown through action, since virtue is just such a skill.

Wrong Answers:
(A): Opposite. The author argues right off the bat that "virtue is not so much a matter of learning specific rules," and argues throughout the passage that the learning of virtue requires action rather than simple memorization.
(B): Opposite. The author would probably agree, given the discussion in ¶s4 and 5, that virtue is an abstract idea, but would argue that it has to be understood through "performative knowledge," rather than through studying human action.
(C): Opposite. The author argues at the end of ¶5 that "an inability to articulate the meaning of virtue is not a sign of the lack of knowledge of virtue," but "shows what kind of thing virtue is," and suggests that this view runs counter to that of some philosophers. The author clearly believes, then, that virtue is better understood through methods *other* than philosophical discussion.

43. A Review what the author says about norms: "Norms are ways of doing something, getting something done; these ways of acting are taught by doing and showing how to do." Predict what norms are based on, as always keeping the author's main idea in mind: norms depend on actions, just like virtue! (A) paraphrases this: since norms are "taught by doing and showing how to do," it makes sense that they're learned by experiencing and observing.

Wrong Answers:
(B): Out of Scope. Historical precedents aren't mentioned, and so this choice can be safely eliminated.
(C): Faulty Use of Detail. The author uses this phrase at the end of ¶1, but in describing virtue specifically, rather than human actions in general.
(D): Opposite. The author believes that action is more important than theoretical knowledge, as he emphasizes in ¶5 when distinguishing between propositional knowledge and performative knowledge.

44. D
Look to the beginning of ¶4 for the answer to this detail question. The author states that "Whether virtue is narrowly or broadly understood, the teaching is the teaching of a skill [(C)] within a practice or form of life, the training of a capacity [(B)]." Here, the author explains what the teaching of virtue is. He continues by

describing what he knows it not to be, "Memorization may indeed play some part in teaching a skill within a practice, but it is not all, or even most, of what I understand this teaching to be." (D) fits this most closely.

Wrong Answers:
(A): Faulty use of Detail. The author says in the beginning of ¶5 that "knowledge of virtue" (not the teaching of virtue) is not a matter of propositional knowledge
(B): Opposite. In the beginning of ¶4 the author says that this is what the teaching of virtue is.
(C): Opposite. As in (B).

45. C What is the author's main point about norms in ¶s1 and 2? Predict: The author believes that norms are ways of acting correctly. (C) catches this belief that "Norms are ways of...getting something done."

Wrong Answers:
(A): Opposite. The author argues *against* maxims, and says that virtue can't be defined.
(B): Distortion. The author implies that norms are ways of teaching virtue through action, but doesn't argue that virtue can be learned *only* through norms.
(D): Opposite. The author says that norms "are taught by doing and showing how to do," which rules out the didactic teaching that the author argues against.

Strategy Point:
Be wary of extreme words like "only" whenever they appear in questions. Make them justify themselves!

46. D A detail question, as tipped off by the "According the passage" wording. What does the author say about defining virtue? Review the end of ¶5: The author says that "an inability to articulate the meaning of virtue is not a sign of the lack of knowledge of virtue." In other words, someone can still have virtue even if they can't say exactly what it is. (D) paraphrases this.

Wrong Answers:
(A): Out of Scope. The author seems to approve of people who can't define virtue, and so would probably argue that they're the ones best suited to teach it through action. However, there's not enough information given to know one way or the other.
(B): Opposite. This draws a distinction between the two definitions of virtue mentioned in ¶3, but the author makes a point of treating them as part of the same question, saying "my comments...are intended to apply to both sense or uses of the term" virtue.
(C): Opposite. The author argues that the only way to teach virtue is performatively, and in any case this question doesn't mention *what* the person is teaching, and is therefore also outside the scope.

47. D An application question. Review the mention of propositional knowledge. The author is contrasting it with performative knowledge, which he suggests is knowledge that comes from action. Predict what performative knowledge is: knowledge that *doesn't* come from action, i.e. learning by indoctrination. Look for an example that contradicts the author's idea of learning through action: (D) does this explicitly.

Wrong Answers:
(A): Opposite. This is an example of learning through action, which the author defines as performative knowledge.
(B): Opposite. Another example of performative knowledge.
(C): Opposite. Yet another example of performative knowledge which helpfully ties into the author's comparison between virtue and language later on in the paragraph.

PASSAGE VIII

Topic and Scope:
The precursors and traditions leading up to the Modern Penal Code

Mapping the Passage:
¶1 introduces Livingston's penal code, and his background.
¶2 describes the intellectual tradition leading to the Model Penal Code, and in particular the influence of Jeremy Bentham.
¶3 lists the concepts within Bentham's legacy.
¶4 describes the details of Livingston's Penal Code.

Questions:
48. C A broad inference question; review the author's main ideas: the author spends the passage discussing the traditions and people that led to the modern penal code. (C) paraphrases this closely, echoing the author's points at the beginning of ¶2.

Wrong Answers:
(A): Out of Scope. The author never suggests that Livingston influenced his colleagues, and reverses the order of influence between Livingston and Bentham, who preceded Livingston.
(B): Distortion. The author says that there was a "powerful movement toward codification of law" in both these places, but doesn't mention lawmakers specifically, nor is it suggested that they agreed wholeheartedly.
(D): Opposite. The author speaks very highly of the Benthamite codes, and so there's no reason to believe that he thinks that they aren't successful in practice. The answer is also off scope in that the author never discusses the practical application of the code.

49. B Where will things attributed to Bentham's work be found? Predict: Probably in the monster of a sentence that is ¶3, which starts out, "Within Bentham's legacy are such concepts as:" RNs I and II are mentioned in the list, but RN III is not and runs counter to Livingston's prohibition of capital punishment in his code, which was presumably borrowed from Bentham's ideas. (B) must therefore be correct.

Wrong Answers:
(A): Opposite. As described above.
(C): Opposite. As above.
(D): Opposite. As above.

50. C Where are the reasons for Livingston's creation of his penal code described? Review ¶1. The author says that "many factors" were responsible, and then describes Livingston's commitment to the idea. (C) paraphrases the author's point that Livingston "was captured by the ideas of Bentham and the ferment for legal reform and codification in revolutionary America and France."

Wrong Answers:
(A): Opposite. The author describes Livingston's code as "the first great penal code in the Benthamite tradition," which suggests that the idea hadn't spread to Louisiana from other parts of the country, but originated in the country with Livingston.
(B): Opposite. As above, since Livingston's code was the first of its kind, it can't have come about as an attempt to emulate the legal system of another country.
(D): Opposite. The author emphasizes that the code came about as "the commitment of one man to the idea of codification," and states in ¶4 that Livingston's creation of the code was "unassisted," which suggests that Livingston's colleagues had nothing to do with the effort.

51. D A scattered detail question, though not too scattered since you know that the strengths of Livingston's code are mentioned in the second half of ¶4. All are mentioned except (D), which is specifically contradicted in ¶1 by the author's note that Livingston's code was "never enacted."

Wrong Answers:
(A): Opposite. The author notes that protection of "the rights of the accused" is part of Livingston's code.
(B): Opposite. The author also mentions "the prominent place [Livingston's code] gave to reform."
(C): Opposite. The author notes that "Livingston distrusted judges no less than Bentham" and notes that that the point of the code was "to leave as little as possible to judicial creativity."

52. B Why did Livingston want to create the code? The author gives several reasons, so review the basics in ¶s 1 and 4 and look for an answer that fits. (B) echoes the author's point in ¶4 that the point of the code was "to leave as little as possible to judicial creativity," and notes that "all means through which judges might infuse their own moral views into the definition of crimes were outlawed." (Note that you can use your research from question 51 to help you here).

Wrong Answers:
(A): Faulty Use of Detail. While these were characteristics of the code, there's no indication that it was one of the guiding motivations, while the author states explicitly that reigning judges in was *the* object of the code.
(C): Opposite. The author notes that "use of common-law terms" was outlawed in Livingston's code.
(D): Faulty Use of Detail. Though these are also described as characteristics of the code, like (A), they're not explicitly mentioned as reasons for creating the code.

53. D An evaluation question dealing with the structure of the whole passage; use your map to help build a prediction. The author begins by describing the background for the Model Penal Code, gives an example of the first code in the tradition, and explains why the code was an improvement. Look for an answer that roughly matches each of these points in the correct order: (D) does just that. Livingston's code provides an application of a theory, the historical background contextualizes Bentham's theories, and the final paragraph compares Livingston's ideas both to Bentham's original ideas and to traditional legal systems.

Wrong Answers:
(A): Out of Scope. While the part about historical background fits, everything else veers away from the passage since the author presents no thesis to refute.
(B): Out of Scope. The author doesn't mention any controversial theses, and so this choice can be quickly knocked out.
(C): Out of Scope. This choice is in the wrong order and it suggests that the author describes multiple stages of development when he discusses only Livingston, and mentions judgment of an outcome when no such judgment is made.

Strategy Point:
When faced with abstract answer choices (which will appear often on evaluation questions), be sure to compare them to the specifics of the passage to make sure you understand what they're saying.

PASSAGE IX

Topic and Scope:
How writing has influenced human consciousness

Mapping the Passage:
¶s1 and 2 note that writing was once considered an "alien" technology by outlining Plato's objections to it.
¶3 introduces the author's thesis that writing has transformed human consciousness by explaining that thought processes for those who can read depend on writing.
¶4 argues that human consciousness depends on writing to achieve its full potential, and argues that technology in general can enhance human life.
¶5 describes how people in a completely oral culture function and gives an example of an intermediate between oral and written cultures.

Questions:
54. B An evaluation question. What is the purpose of mentioning Hesiod at the end of ¶5? The author describes Hesiod as "intermediate between oral Homeric Greece and fully developed Greek literacy," and immediately before says that "the more sophisticated orally patterned thought is, the more likely it is likely to be marked by set expressions skillfully used." Paraphrase all this: Hesiod is an example of an oral culture that produced sophisticated thought in sophisticated patterns. (B) paraphrases this.

Wrong Answers:
(A): Distortion. The author suggests that oral poets relied more on "set expressions skillfully used," but this doesn't mean that oral poets were more creative overall than those who wrote. In fact, the author would certainly argue that the ability to write could only enhance consciousness and vocabulary, and by extension, creativity.
(C): Opposite. Though Hesiod is described as the product of a culture midway between the oral and the written, the author never argues that this is the ideal society. The author believes that writing is important to full human consciousness, and so any ideal society would presumably have to include writing.
(D): Opposite. The author argues in ¶5 that mnemonics are *essential* to "retaining and retrieving carefully articulated thought," and therefore must be very successful memory devices.

55. A Where are thought patterns for those who write mentioned? Go back to ¶3 and paraphrase the author's argument about words and thought: people who write depend on the representation of words in order to think. (A) paraphrases this, and echoes the author's point that "we think of words as the visible marks signaling words to decoders."

Wrong Answers:
(B): Distortion. A potentially confusing answer choice. There's no need to spend too much time untangling what it means; since the author never describes literate thought as being based on the interpretation of oral communication, it can be eliminated quickly.

(C): Out of Scope. The author never discusses learning during childhood.

(D): Distortion. Though the transformation of objects into visual language seems to fit with what the author is saying, there's no indication that this is conscious behavior.

Strategy Point:
There's no need to fully understand what every wrong answer choice is saying. Remember that every right answer choice is categorically *right, and every wrong choice is* categorically *wrong. If you can find something wrong with an answer, it can be eliminated immediately, even if you don't know exactly what the rest means!*

56. A A broadly-worded inference question; review the author's main points before scanning the answers. In paragraph four, The author argues that technology in general, if properly assimilated, is good for human life, and at the beginning of the passage uses the computer as an example of technology that seems "alien" just as writing once did. The implication, then, is that if the computer is "properly interiorized" it will enhance human life. (A) says the same.

Wrong Answers:
(B): Opposite. The author argues that "without writing, human consciousness cannot achieve its fuller potentials, cannot produce other beautiful and powerful creations." The word "detrimental" should set off warning signs—the author is very positive about writing.
(C): Distortion. While the author argues that human thought has advanced because of writing, that doesn't imply that the method of communication before that time was flawed, let alone untrustworthy.
(D): Distortion. As above, though the author argues that *other* beautiful and powerful creations can't be made without writing, that doesn't mean that oral culture can't produce *any* such creations. Since the author cites "other" creations, the implication is that writing itself is a beautiful and powerful creation, which must have originated out of oral culture.

Strategy Point:
Watch out for choices in inference questions which suggest that because the author believes one thing is good, the author believes that the alternative is bad. While sometimes this is the case, one doesn't necessarily follow from the other. The MCAT will test you repeatedly on your ability to keep this distinction in mind as you read unfamiliar passages.

57. B An incorporation question. Paraphrase the author's main argument about the benefits of writing: it helps us to think on a higher level than we otherwise would be able to. What will the correct answer likely look like? Predict: It will provide an example or evidence suggesting that writing *doesn't* lead to a higher level of thought, or that the same level of thought can exist without writing. (B) fits this structure, providing an example suggesting that the same level of thought can be achieved without writing.

Wrong Answers:
(A): Out of Scope. The author would respond to this by saying that oral culture can produce sophisticated thought, but that literature culture can produce thought that's even *more* sophisticated.
(C): Opposite. This would support the author's argument that writing has enhanced human thought over time.
(D): Out of Scope. Whether or not stroke patients don't rely more on oral communication after having damaged their language centers has no bearing on whether written communication can enhance thought.

Strategy Point:
Get in the habit of predicting the general structure of answer choices whenever possible. Some structures, like those of correct answers to weaken questions, will be almost identical from question to question, with only the details changing. Focusing on how a choice looks rather than what's in it yields big dividends on test day.

58. A Review the differences between oral and written cultures, which are mentioned throughout the passage. (A) represents a major difference that author discusses in a few places. The author notes in ¶5 that oral culture depends on mnemonic patterns to remember, and in ¶2 the author quotes an ancient objection to writing: "writing destroys memory." Oral cultures, therefore, rely extensively on memory while written cultures much less so.

Wrong Answers:
(B): Out of Scope. The author doesn't discuss chaotic thought in the passage, noting that thought in oral culture is highly structured.
(C): Out of Scope. The author suggests that writing enables more complex *thought*, but suggests in ¶5 that some oral language can be highly sophisticated and complex.
(D): Out of Scope. The author only draws distinctions between level of advancement in thought; there's no suggestion that either type of communication is barbaric.

59. B What role does Plato serve in ¶s1 and 2? The author says that "essentially the same objections…were urged by Plato…against writing." The prediction is easy: Plato is used to introduce ancient objections to writing. (B) paraphrases this closely.

Wrong Answers:
(A): Out of Scope. The author doesn't discuss whether Plato's philosophy was literate or oral, and Plato is clearly used as more than an example of a type of philosophy: he's the source of objections to writing in general.

(C): **Out of Scope.** The author doesn't suggest that Plato's objections are misconceptions, and in fact seems to agree with the assertion that writing makes memory less important when discussing oral memorization in ¶5.

(D): **Out of Scope.** The author wants to show *similarities* between writing and computer technology; there's no mention of any differences.

60. B A broad question; predict a broad answer. What is the author's view of writing? Predict: It has the potential to expand human consciousness and creation. (B) paraphrases this.

Wrong Answers:
(A): **Opposite.** The author argues that writing has fit in very well with human consciousness, and has become a foundation of consciousness for literate people.

(C): **Opposite.** The author only has good things to say about writing and suggests that it can enhance human achievement, contradicting the idea that writing damages human resources.

(D): **Distortion.** Though literacy is described as "absolutely necessary for the development...of... explicative understanding of literature and of any art," literacy isn't necessarily needed for the development of art itself. Be careful! It's easy to misread the quote as suggesting that literacy is necessary for art, while the author is arguing that it's necessary for the *explanation* of art.

These conversion charts are based on the scores of past test takers and may not accurately reflect your actual MCAT score. (Data for Tests 1–3 are unavailable.)

Verbal Reasoning Test 4 Conversion Scale		
Scaled	Raw Scale Range	
1	0	12
2	13	18
3	19	22
4	23	27
5	28	30
6	31	35
7	36	38
8	39	42
9	43	45
10	46	47
11	48	50
12	51	53
13	54	56
14	57	58
15	59	60

Verbal Reasoning Test 6 Conversion Scale		
Scaled	Raw Scale Range	
1	0	12
2	13	18
3	19	22
4	23	26
5	27	28
6	29	30
7	31	33
8	34	37
9	38	40
10	41	45
11	46	48
12	49	50
13	51	53
14	54	56
15	57	60

Verbal Reasoning Test 5 Conversion Scale		
Scaled	Raw Scale Range	
1	0	12
2	13	18
3	19	22
4	23	26
5	27	28
6	29	32
7	33	36
8	36	38
9	39	41
10	42	44
11	45	47
12	48	50
13	51	53
14	54	56
15	57	60

Verbal Reasoning Test 7 Conversion Scale		
Scaled	Raw Scale Range	
1	0	12
2	13	18
3	19	22
4	23	26
5	27	29
6	30	32
7	33	36
8	37	38
9	39	41
10	42	43
11	44	46
12	47	50
13	51	54
14	55	56
15	57	60

Verbal Reasoning Test 8 Conversion Scale		
Scaled	Raw Scale Range	
1	0	14
2	15	20
3	21	27
4	28	31
5	32	34
6	35	38
7	39	40
8	41	42
9	43	44
10	45	46
11	47	48
12	49	50
13	51	53
14	54	56
15	57	60

Verbal Reasoning Test 10 Conversion Scale		
Scaled	Raw Scale Range	
1	0	9
2	10	13
3	14	18
4	19	25
5	26	27
6	28	31
7	32	34
8	35	36
9	37	40
10	41	44
11	45	49
12	50	51
13	52	53
14	54	56
15	57	60

Verbal Reasoning Test 9 Conversion Scale		
Scaled	Raw Scale Range	
1	0	9
2	10	13
3	14	16
4	17	21
5	22	24
6	25	29
7	30	31
8	32	34
9	35	37
10	38	40
11	41	45
12	46	51
13	52	53
14	54	56
15	57	60

Verbal Reasoning Test 11 Conversion Scale		
Scaled	Raw Scale Range	
1	0	9
2	10	13
3	14	18
4	19	26
5	27	31
6	32	34
7	35	27
8	39	40
9	41	43
10	44	46
11	47	48
12	49	50
13	51	53
14	54	56
15	57	60

KAPLAN

Writing Sample

CHAPTER ONE

INTRODUCTION

THE MCAT WRITING SAMPLE

The essay section of the MCAT that you take on Test Day will contain **two thirty-minute timed essays.** You will write your answers in a special booklet of lined paper. After working on the first question for thirty minutes, you will be told to stop and go on to the second essay question, for which you will again be allowed thirty minutes. It will be up to you to pace yourself during each thirty-minute period and not get bogged down.

You cannot choose to write on any other topic; you must write in English, not a foreign language; and you must try to accomplish everything the instructions require.

The Writing Sample's Purpose and Format

The writing sample tests your ability to:

1. develop a central idea,
2. synthesize ideas,
3. express ideas logically and cohesively, and
4. write clearly, using standard written English and proper punctuation.

In other words, it tests your ability to write a good brief essay. Of course, you are not expected to produce final-draft quality—the MCAT readers know you have only thirty minutes to write. But don't assume this means they have low standards. When you read the sample essays in the MCAT student manual, you will see that the test makers' expectation of a good essay really **is** a good essay.

The 10 Writing Sample Categories

Past writing sample statements have all fallen into one of these broad categories:

Advertising/Media
Business
Education/the Mind
Government
History
International Politics
Law
National Politics
Science/Technology
Sociology

Each essay question will have the same format: a statement followed by a set of instructions containing three distinct tasks. Each question will look something like this:

Consider this statement:

True leadership leads by example rather than by command.

Write a unified essay in which you perform the following tasks. Explain what you think the above statement means. Describe a specific situation in which true leaders lead by command rather than by example. Discuss what you think determines when a leader should lead by example or by command.

THE STATEMENT

On your test the statement may be an opinion, a widely shared belief, a philosophical dictum, or an assertion regarding general policy concerns in such areas as history, political science, business, or law.

You can be sure that the statement will **NOT** concern scientific or technical topics (e.g., biology, physics, or chemistry), your reasons for entering the medical profession, emotionally charged religious or social issues (e.g., abortion), or obscure social or political issues that might require specialized knowledge. In fact, you will not need any specialized knowledge to do well on this part of the MCAT.

THE INSTRUCTIONS:

Though worded slightly differently each time, the instructions that follow the statement will ask you to perform these **tasks** in a unified essay:

1. Provide your interpretation or explanation of the statement.
2. Offer a concrete example (hypothetical or actual) that illustrates a point of view directly **opposite** to the one expressed in the statement.
3. Explain how the conflict between the viewpoint expressed in the statement and the viewpoint you described for the second task might be resolved.

These tasks give you quite a lot to complete in a scant thirty minutes. It's a good idea, therefore, to approach this section prepared for what you'll find. That's where this booklet and the writing lessons will help: they'll familiarize you with the section and give you a firm sense of how to accomplish all necessary tasks. Actually, once you know what you're doing, the three tasks make your job somewhat easier since they "design" your essay for you (a good part of the battle!).

FREQUENTLY ASKED QUESTIONS ABOUT THE WRITING SAMPLE

Question: Is there a right or wrong answer to these essay questions?

Answer: No. Essays won't be judged on whether or not the readers agree with your position or think your points true. Furthermore, the essays' instructions will not ask you to take a position regarding the statements you discuss. If you feel that offering your position on the statement or a related issue will make a better essay, that's fine. But don't feel pressured to agree or disagree with the statement.

Question: Who grades my essays?

Answer: Two readers read each essay and score them independently—that means neither scorer knows how the other graded your essay. If the two scorers differ by more than a point (on a six-point scale), a third scorer is called in as a final judge.

Question: What kind of score will be reported?

Answer: Once the readers have graded your essays, the total scores for both essays will be added together. This combined score will then be converted into an alphabetic rating (ranging from J to T) and sent to you and to the medical schools that receive your other MCAT information. The medical schools will also get percentile information regarding how well you did compared to your peers. For more information on what constitutes a particular point score (say a score of four rather than six on any particular essay) consult your MCAT Student Manual, which contains detailed descriptions of what level of accomplishment each score represents.

Question: What's a good score?

Answer: Statistically speaking, there will be very few six-point essays. An essay of four or five would place you at the upper range of those taking this exam. But a good score is a personal estimation. After all, if you have very weak writing skills and pump up your skills using the Kaplan materials, you may feel very good about getting a score of three—and you'd be right to feel that way.

Question: How are my essays graded?

Answer: Your readers will use a holistic grading technique. That means that each reader supplies a single numeric score for the essay as a whole. (Organization, style, grammar, and so on are not graded separately.) Your readers will first of all determine how thoroughly and meaningfully you responded to the three writing tasks. They will note whether you offer appropriate illustrations or examples and how well you tie your thoughts together into a unified whole. In addition, they will pay attention to how well you organize your paragraphs individually and collectively. They will also look for varied sentence structure and word choice. This does not mean your readers want convoluted sentences or big "dictionary" words; they **do** want the kind of lively writing that comes with active **thinking.**

Question: I'm lousy at grammar and punctuation. Will those kinds of errors count for very much?

Answer: Your readers know you are writing under time pressure and expect you to make a certain number of mistakes in writing mechanics (grammar, spelling, etc.). A few scattered mistakes of this kind DO NOT carry much weight. However, a series of such mistakes can mar your work's overall impression. So while we suggest that you not be overly concerned with mistakes of this nature, don't ignore this area if it is a particularly weak one. If you're concerned to improve your grammar, punctuation, and sentence structure skills, spend some time with Part III of these Notes for a thorough review of writing mechanics.

Question: In writing my essays, do I have to follow a certain format?

Answer: Many students think they have to write a standard five-paragraph essay—an introductory paragraph, three body paragraphs, and a conclusion—the kind often taught in high schools. There is NO set format. As long as you address all three writing tasks, you can do so in whatever order and form you choose. However, since you will be scored partly on your essay's unity, giving the reader a sense of a definite beginning, middle, and end will be an advantage.

Question: My handwriting is terrible. Will this count against me?

Answer: Yes and no. Your readers are not grading your penmanship, but if they have to agonize over deciphering your scrawl, you can be sure their attitude toward your essay will be negatively affected. You must write legibly. If your printing is neater than your cursive writing, then by all means print your essays.

Question: Do I need to throw around a lot of big, impressive sounding words in order to do well?

Answer: Some test-prep companies tell their students to memorize impressive sounding words and work them into each essay. That's cynical and silly. People who have to memorize impressive words probably don't have much practice using them—so the words stick out and look awkward. Besides, the best essays make their points simply, concisely, and straightforwardly. If you have a large vocabulary this will help you make your points more convincingly since you'll be able to choose more precise words. If you're not comfortable using a large vocabulary, it's a poor idea to toss in fancy words for the sake of impressing a reader. What your readers want is **clarity.** You don't have to put on an act. Better to stick to the words you know than run the risk of a malapropism.

Question: What if I want to cross out a word or phrase . . . can I?

Answer: Your graders know that these are first-draft essays. You do not have time (and should **not** try to make time) to recopy your essay. Therefore, it is perfectly all right to cross out or make corrections. In fact, we suggest saving two minutes at the end of each half-hour to proofread your essay for small mistakes. However, remember that legibility and general neatness count.

THE KAPLAN APPROACH

To most writers, the process of essay writing is one filled with starts and stops. As writer working on drafting an essay thinks about the topic from several angles, coming up with ideas that eventually must be refined, rephrased, or thrown out. The writer might compose several introductory paragraphs before finding the right tack or be halfway through writing when a better idea comes to mind, requiring a major revision. This is the natural way for most people to compose.

But there is nothing natural about a timed essay test.

You simply don't have time to let your thoughts flow in their natural cyclic way. Yet it is essential to hash out and refine your ideas if you are going to produce an essay of any substance. Therefore, what you need is a method to speed up the writing process and make it more efficient.

We suggest you use a proven method that will help you take good advantage of each one of those thirty minutes. The purpose of the method is to provide you with a clearly defined track on which to move through the writing process, performing what needs to be done in as little time as possible. It consists of five steps:

THE FIVE STEPS
Step 1. Read and Annotate
Step 2. Prewrite Each Task
Step 3. Clarify Main Idea and Plan
Step 4. Write
Step 5. Proofread

Though they represent only about one-sixth of your total work time (or approximately five minutes), the most important steps in this method are 1–3. It is during this time, the **prewriting**, that you will do the hashing out, refining, and organizing of ideas that a writer usually does during the whole of the first-draft process.

In the rest of this booklet you'll have ample opportunity to practice the five-step approach. You'll become familiar with how each step relates to the whole. In time, you'll find yourself going through the steps in your own way—making them a natural part of your essay writing. As you do so, you'll find they take less and less time. Experienced Kaplan students can produce well-reasoned essays on the toughest topics within the thirty-minute time limit.

CHAPTER TWO

BUILDING YOUR ESSAY

PREWRITING—STEPS 1–3

Your ability to write is directly linked to your ability to think analytically and logically. You might have a wonderful command of the English language, but if you can't get your thoughts organized and your ideas clear in your mind, your essay will be a jumbled mess. So, since you don't have time to write a sloppy first draft and then revise it, you must do the basic part of refining your ideas *before* starting to write. In other words, you must *prewrite*.

The prewriting steps clarify what work you must get done before you are ready to write. Also, they help you get that work done efficiently. At first, you should practice these steps in sequence to familiarize yourself thoroughly with what prewriting involves. But as you get to know them, you'll probably find it more natural to jump around from one step to another rather than to work in a linear way.

For instance, you'll find that as you do Step 1 (read and annotate), ideas for any one of the other prewriting steps may well start popping into your mind right away. Task 2 (thinking of an opposing example) often helps to clarify your ideas about the statement's meaning (Task 1). Clarifying a main idea (Step 3) helps to focus all of your ideas for Steps 2 and 3. And so on. Once you learn the process, there is no need to feel that you must perfect each step before moving on to the next. Going back and refining your ideas as you move through the prewriting process will allow you to build a set of ideas that fit together into a coherent whole.

Taking Notes

It is essential to take notes during the prewriting process. Only a very extraordinary person can keep straight all of the ideas generated during prewriting. But note taking is a difficult thing to teach since each person must develop his or her own style. No one but you is going to read your notes; they don't need to be clear or comprehensible to anyone else. The trick is to develop a style that you can read and understand but that lets you abbreviate your ideas as much as possible. You don't want to waste time writing out whole sentences, but you must be able to make sense of your notes when you work on your essay. This takes practice.

STRATEGY: As you take your notes, categorize them according to the three tasks given in the essay instructions. Divide your note-taking page into three areas and number them, one for each task. Ideas that explain or illustrate the statement (the first task) get jotted down in area #1, ideas that explore the opposing view (the second task) go in area #2, et cetera. This method will automatically order your thoughts, even if you are not coming up with them in an orderly way.

All three steps in just five minutes?

As we discuss the prewriting process, it may seem as though it requires much too much time for a thirty-minute essay. Don't worry. At first, the steps take explaining and practice, but once you understand the process, you'll be able to work efficiently. You'll discover that the five minutes you spend prewriting will speed up the writing process.

MOST COMMON PREWRITING MISTAKES

* The student fails to pay close attention to the meaning of the statement and/or the instructions.
* The student rushes into writing, hoping to figure things out while composing the essay.
* The student is immediately struck by an idea that addresses the second or third task (the easier ones) and starts writing without prewriting the first task.

MOST COMMON SYMPTOMS OF POOR PREWRITING

* The essay does not thoroughly fulfill all of the tasks in the instructions.
* The essay has no clear main idea.
* The essay is poorly organized.
* The first paragraph or two are vague and pointless.
* All of the best ideas are jammed in at the end of the essay.
* The essay is incomplete: The student was "cut short" by the time limit and was unable to respond to all parts of the instructions.

Prewriting can be the single most important way of helping your final essay achieve clarity, order, and authority. Now let's look at the steps one by one.

STEP 1: READ AND ANNOTATE

PURPOSE: To clarify for yourself what the statement says and what the instructions require.

PROCESS: Read the statement and instructions carefully.

Annotate the statement: Mark any words or phrases that
* are easy to miss but are crucial to a good understanding of the statement
* are ambiguous or confusing
* refer to vague or abstract concepts (e.g., "freedom," "happiness," et cetera) that need clarification.

Annotate the instructions: Number the tasks and mark any words that will help you remember exactly what it is you're supposed to do.

Good communication requires more than just speaking or writing clearly—it first requires paying attention to what you are being asked to communicate *about*. And that means paying attention to what the given statement and instructions say. An essay that does not relate clearly and directly to the idea expressed in the statement or that does not fulfill the specific tasks put forth in the instructions is unlikely to receive more than a grade of three.

Why bother annotating?

Especially under pressure of a time limit, it is easy to waste the first few minutes with anxious worrying or nervous, unstructured thinking. Actually circling and underlining words puts your mind in gear. It helps you focus your attention on what needs to be done and forces you to concentrate on this important first step.

EXAMPLE OF STEP 1

Below is an example of one way this essay topic might be annotated. In the statement, this student has marked words that she felt required more careful thought. In the instructions, she numbered each task and marked those words that will help her zero in on exactly what she needs to do.

> *Consider this statement:*
>
> *True <u>leadership</u> leads by <u>example</u> rather than by command.*

Write a unified essay in which you perform the following tasks. ①*Explain what you think the above statement means.* ②*Describe a <u>specific situation</u> in which true leaders lead by* (command) *rather than by example.* ③*Discuss <u>what you think determines</u> when a leader should lead by example or by command.*

STEP 2: PREWRITE EACH TASK

TASK I

PURPOSE: To develop depth and clarity in your interpretation of the statement.
PROCESS:
- Think of one or more supporting examples.
- Clarify/define/interpret abstract, ambiguous, or pivotal words.
- Ask yourself questions to get beyond the superficial meaning of the statement.

The MCAT test makers say that the statement in the essay assignment will not be simply factual or self-evident. This means that, in order to explain the meaning of the statement, you must develop some ideas of your own about its meaning or about the meaning of certain words or concepts within it. But often it is difficult to see exactly where or why a statement *needs* explaining. It may *seem* perfectly self-evident to you. The trick is to imagine that you must explain this statement to your intelligent fifteen-year-old sibling and you want this fifteen-year-old to understand the statement on more than just a superficial level.

Take, for instance, the statement: The United States is a free country. This statement is often used in many different contexts. Yet, if you asked twenty different people what they thought about this statement, you'd get twenty different responses. So how do you explain to your fifteen-year-old why this is not just a simple statement of fact or opinion? You try to give an explanation of its *deeper* meaning. For one thing, there's a good deal of *history* behind the statement. The belief that the people of this country should be "free" to pursue their individual goals began with the first European settlers who came here in search of freedom from religious and economic oppression. But there is also the *philosophical* question: What *is* freedom? Much *controversy* revolves around this question. In fact, many people feel this country is "free" only for a privileged few. And so on. Thus, what might seem like a simple cliché is actually a very complex tangle of ideas and implications.

Obviously, you can't go into depth on all these subjects in a thirty-minute essay. (And your fifteen-year-old would fall asleep!) But to explain the statement with any clarity you must consider these issues, decide which ones you need to discuss, and put your ideas together to make the best interpretation you can. The MCAT essay readers are looking for a *thorough exploration* of the topic.

Here is a sampling of some of the many questions you can ask to get yourself started on an "exploration" of a statement:
- * What are some situations (hypothetical or real) that illustrate what this statement is saying?
- * Are there any specific words in the statement that need clarifying before you can discuss the meaning of the statement as a whole?
- * What is the historical background of the idea(s) in the statement? (Have the ideas been around for a long or a short time? Why? Where did they come from?)
- * What is the philosophical background of the statement? (Are there some basic beliefs or assumptions on which this statement depends?)
- * What people are concerned with this statement today and why are they concerned with it?
- * Does this statement mean different things to different people? If so, what are these different meanings? What meaning do *you* give it and why?

This is certainly a lot to think about!
With all these directions to go in, how do you keep your ideas from running all over the place? Here's one useful approach:

STRATEGY: Before trying to define the statement, think up one or two *illustrations* of it. This will give you something concrete to think about and will help you identify what areas you need to explore with this particular topic.

All MCAT Writing Sample topics will most likely strike you as at least partly true. Even if you disagree with the statement in a general way, you'll probably be able to think of *some* situation that illustrates a way in which the statement is true. This kind of illustration will help you figure out the *meaning* of the statement. (And if you want, you can use the example in your essay.)

Warning! Don't let a strong personal reaction to the statement ruin your essay.

A strong reaction to a statement can fool a student into rushing headlong into writing. But your powerful feelings or your eagerness to say a lot about a topic does not release you from having to follow the instructions.

REMEMBER: The first task asks you to explain what you think the statement means. You can talk about ideas that oppose the statement when you address the second task.

You don't have to take a stand.
You are not being tested on your opinions or your morals. The purpose of the essay assignment is to test your ability to think and to write. The instructions will not ask you to agree or disagree with the statement. You may take a stand if you feel that to do so will help you write a clearer essay, but you don't have to.

EXAMPLE
Below is the same essay topic shown in Step 1. Here, the student's prewriting notes for Task 1 have been added. These notes are just one student's response—each student will respond in his or her own way.

> *Consider this statement:*
> *True <u>leadership</u> leads by~~example~~ rather than by command.*

> *Write a unified essay in which you perform the following tasks.* ① <u>*Explain*</u> *what you think the above statement means.* ② *Describe a <u>specific situation</u> in which true leaders lead by command rather than by example.* ③ *Discuss <u>what you think determines when</u> a leader should lead by example or by command.*

> ① *By example–*
> *Alexander*
> *Gandhi*
> *Agassiz*
> *Clara B.*
> *– had a special gift* → *people compelled to follow*

You can see in the notes above that this student first got down to business by thinking up several examples of leaders who lead by example. With these in mind, she could generalize more clearly about the kind of leader who leads by example. The circled number 1 shows that these ideas all apply to the first task.

(The essay for which these notes were written can be found as Essay #1 in the discussion of Step 6.)

STEP 2: PREWRITE EACH TASK

TASK 2

PURPOSE: To further explore the meaning of the statement by examining a situation that represents an opposing point of view.

PROCESS: Think up one or more specific situations that demonstrate a way in which the statement is *not* true.

Of the three tasks, this one is the easiest for most students because it is so specific. Thinking up specific examples is a lot easier than defining abstract ideas. Furthermore, it's almost always easier to find a flaw in something than it is to explain what's true about it.

Once they learn to handle the prewriting process, many students find that it helps to work a bit on the second task before tackling the first. In any case, working on the second task is very likely to help you develop and clarify your ideas about a statement.

That the second task is helpful in clarifying ideas is no coincidence. The three tasks provided for you by the MCAT test makers follow a standard method of argument. The tasks, if you follow them, actually *help* you write a good essay. So follow them.

STRATEGY: Don't try to write or outline the essay in your head while you're prewriting the three tasks. Do the tasks first. They will help you develop a set of ideas on which you can build an essay. If you try to compose your essay before you're ready, you will only waste time.

Even if you agree completely with the statement you can come up with an opposing example.

The creators of the MCAT Writing Sample purposely pick statements that are sufficiently complex to have more than one side. If you are having trouble thinking of a good illustration, imagine a person who actively disagrees with the statement—what illustrations would he or she provide?

STRATEGY: Don't waste time struggling to think of an example from history or current events. If you can't think of a real-life example, make up a hypothetical one. You are not being tested on your knowledge of history, politics, or any other area.

If you disagree with the statement, the second task allows you to air your views.

It's difficult, if you have a strong reaction against a statement, not to launch right away into an explanation of that reaction. But your ideas will sound much more levelheaded if you take the time to clarify the meaning of the statement before talking about how that meaning is wrong. The second task (as well as the third) gives you a place to express an opposing opinion, so save your criticisms or revisions for your response to this task. The result will be a set of logical prewriting notes rather than a jumble of reactions.

It's OK to discuss more than one example, but don't spread yourself too thin.

Sometimes students find they can think of several different ways in which the statement is not true. Should this happen to you, focus on just one area. You may want to illustrate that the statement is untrue with a single example or with several examples—either way is fine. What's important is to make sure that all of the examples work together to illustrate the same general idea. You do not want to try to tackle more than one opposing idea. You don't have the time, and your essay is likely to lose focus.

EXAMPLE

Below is the same essay topic shown each. Here the student's notes for Task 2 have been added.

Consider this statement:

True <u>leadership</u> leads by <u>example</u> rather than by command.

Write a unified essay in which you perform the following tasks. ①*<u>Explain</u> what you think the above statement means.* ②*Describe a <u>specific situation</u> in which true leaders lead by* (command) *rather than by example.* ③*Discuss <u>what you think determines when</u> a leader should lead by example or by command.*

> ① By example—
>   Alexander
>   Gandhi
>   Agassiz
>   Clara B.
>   – had a special gift → people compelled to follow
>
> ② By command—
>   When people confused/defeated/need a common goal
>   leader takes charge
>   nations, businesses, etc.

From the notes responding to the second task (those next to the circled number 2) we can see that our student has developed the idea that leadership by command is appropriate in a certain kind of situation.

(The essay for which these notes were written can be found as Essay #1 in the discussion of Step 6.)

STEP 2: PREWRITE EACH TASK

TASK 3

PURPOSE: To find a way to resolve the conflict between the statement given in the essay topic and the opposing situation(s) you thought of for the second task.

PROCESS: Read the instructions for the third task carefully. Look back at the ideas you generated for the first and second tasks. Develop your response based on these ideas.

The third task follows naturally from the first and second tasks. If you think of an idea and then think of an opposition to that idea, it's only natural to try to reach some kind of resolution of the conflict. In fact, many students find that a resolution to the conflict just comes to them, before they even really think about the third task. That's fine. You often have your best ideas when your thoughts get rolling like that. Nonetheless, do take the time to carefully read the instructions regarding the third task.

STRATEGY: The instructions for the third task are likely to give you quite a specific approach to resolving the conflict. This approach will in turn make your job more specific and therefore easier. So, be sure to check back to the wording of the instructions for this task.

What if you can't think of a good way to resolve the conflict?

This task tests your ability to look at a *general* problem (the conflict) and, using your powers of judgment and evaluation, come up with a way of handling the problem. If your good judgment tells you that there is no easy or problem-free solution, then write what you think is the *best* solution. You are not expected to solve the problems of the world in this essay.

You don't have to resolve the conflict in support of, or in opposition to, the statement.

Remember, your readers don't care whether you agree or disagree with the statement. Use your own good judgment to resolve the conflict in any way that makes sense to you. Just be sure to explain your reasoning. Your reasoning is what counts, not your particular stance on the conflict.

EXAMPLE

Below is the same essay topic shown above. Here, the student's prewriting notes responding to the third task have been added.

Consider this statement:

True <u>leadership</u> leads by <u>example</u> rather than by command.

Write a unified essay in which you perform the following tasks. ①*<u>Explain</u> what you think the above statement means.* ②*Describe a <u>specific situation</u> in which true leaders lead by* (command) *rather than by example.* ③*Discuss <u>what you think determines</u> <u>when</u> a leader should lead by example or by command.*

① By example—
   Alexander
   Gandhi
   Agassiz
   Clara B.
   – had a special gift → people compelled to follow

② By command—
   When people confused/defeated/need a common goal
   leader takes charge
   nations, businesses, etc.

③ Followers shared a common vision
   If no shared vision → command is needed

The notes responding to the third task (next to the circled number 3) show that the student looked back over her notes and compared the kind of leadership she thought about in response to the first task with the kind of leadership she thought about in response to the second task. She apparently found a clear point of contrast between her two ideas of leadership. In one type of leadership, the followers share a common vision; in the other, they do not. As a result, she can clarify what determines when leadership should be by example or by command.

(The essay for which these notes were written can be found as Essay #1 in the discussion of Step 4.)

STEP 3: CLARIFY MAIN IDEA AND PLAN

PURPOSE: To do final organization and clarification of ideas. To take a mental "breath" before beginning to write.
PROCESS: Take a quick moment to look back over your notes in light of the ideas you have reached in prewriting the third task. Check to make sure your ideas are consistent with each other. Cross out those that no longer belong. Decide in what order your essay will address the three tasks.

Although it sounds like a lot to do, this step is actually the quickest of them all. If you have prewritten all three tasks, and have organized your notes so that you can clearly see which ideas pertain to which task, then most of your prewriting work is done. Having prewritten each of the tasks, you've now developed and refined your ideas in response to the essay topic.

You already have a main idea.
Many people find main ideas to be confusing things. But we don't need to bother with trying to define them. If you have prewritten the third task, then you have everything you need. You have reached a conclusion, an idea toward which all your other ideas lead. Treat this as your main idea.

Take a fast look over the rest of your notes to get rid of or clarify any ideas that don't relate to your main idea in a way that makes sense.

Then plan how you are going to order the ideas in your essay and you will be ready to write.

In fact, you already have a plan, too!
Although the MCAT people say that you can structure your essay any way you want, there is one very obvious and simple structure that helps make writing this essay quite a bit easier. The three tasks, in the order in which they are given, supply you with a straightforward structure that makes good sense.

STRATEGY: Use the Basic Essay Format Provided By the Three Tasks

First Part of Essay—Address the first task: This gives you the perfect opportunity to introduce the topic to be discussed and clarify its meaning. Establishing the basics in this way is essential for any argument to be clear.

Second Part of Essay—Provide an opposing idea to the one expressed in the statement: This lets you look at the statement from a different angle. Doing this lets you further develop your essay, delving more deeply into the nature of the statement and expanding on your ideas.

Third Part of Essay—Resolve the conflict between the statement and the opposing idea: This lets you synthesize your ideas into a focused conclusion—a natural ending to your discussion.

What do the prewriting notes for Step 3 look like?

Usually they are invisible, since most of Step 3 is done simply by looking over your notes and clarifying how your main idea will be the focus of the essay. You might cross out a phrase, add a word or two, draw an arrow between two ideas—whatever you need for that final mental preparation before actually writing.

FINAL PREWRITING REMINDER

Keep your notes in order by categorizing them according to the task they address: three tasks, three bunches of notes. You don't have to *think* of them in order, just record them in the fashion we suggest and you'll have an effective outline to help you through your essay.

STEP 4: WRITE

PURPOSE: Write a complete essay that addresses all three tasks in approximately twenty-three minutes.

PROCESS: Using your prewriting notes for guidance, compose a straightforward essay that thoroughly explains your response to each of the three tasks.

Writing an essay can truly be fun if you have sufficiently clarified your basic ideas beforehand. If you have a good general sense of what you want to say, you can let your mind roll along without fear of getting seriously off track or losing your focus. This is the time when you will get your best ideas—when you become creative.

But don't let the writing carry you away—stick to the tasks.

If the statement or some related idea inspires you to write an essay all your own, or only obliquely related to the topic, squelch that inspiration. You don't have time to fool around with experimental first drafts. If you want to produce a good essay *and* fulfill the three tasks, be conservative.

Does it seem boring, constraining or babyish to follow the tasks?

Follow them anyway. That's the requirement of the MCAT Writing Sample.

Does the length of the essay matter?

What matters is whether or not your essay is a good one, but good essays do tend to fill the three pages alloted. A well-written essay means a well-thought-out essay in which ideas are explained, illustrated, and developed until the implications are clear. Yet just filling up pages with blather, so it *looks* as if you are thinking, won't get you anywhere.

Following the tasks will help you produce a unified essay.

Unity in an essay means that all of the ideas focus on a common topic, and that they all lead to a central idea. If you fulfill each of the three tasks, you will probably achieve unity: The tasks should all relate to each other, and lead from first to second to third in a logical manner.

SOME COMMON TRANSITION WORDS AND PHRASES

Using transitions is an extremely important technique for achieving coherence and unity. Transitions provide the reader with signals about the structure of your essay's argument; the reader should be able to guess at your logical structure simply by looking at your transition words and phrases.

For contrast:
    although
    however, counterevidence
        suggests
    still
    on the other hand
    despite
    otherwise
    but
    yet
    though
	For comparison:
	    likewise
	    similarly
	    just as . . . so

For conclusion:
    in conclusion
    therefore
    if this is true, then
    hence
    finally
    in sum
    consequently
	For continuing argument:
	    also
	    moreover
	    further(more)
	    besides
	    in addition
	    not only... but also
	     this (argument)
	    that (attitude)
	    these (attempts)
	
	To introduce examples:
	    for instance
	    consider the case of
	    one reason for this is
	    another reason for this is
	    one example of this is
	    another example of this is

To introduce one idea and then suggest a better alternative:
    certainly . . . yet   granted . . . however
    undoubtedly . . . but   to be sure . . . nonetheless
    obviously . . . nevertheless admittedly . . . still	

EXAMPLE

Essay #1, below, and Essay #2, following, are both responses to the essay topic shown in the Examples of Steps 1 through 3. The prewriting notes shown in those earlier examples were written in preparation for Essay #1.

ESSAY #1

Even though we might all disagree about the precise definition of *leadership,* we could probably agree that, as one Supreme Court justice once wrote of pornography, we can recognize it when we see it. Through the lens of history, leadership can often seem mysteriously compelling, a kind of divine gift. In the story of Alexander the Great, legend and history combine to hand down the image of the brave, determined young man who fought more fiercely than his troops, proving by his own example that a band of Macedonians could indeed endure great hardship and overcome better-equipped adversaries in their conquest of the known world.

But we must not assume that leadership is only seen on the battlefield. By example, Clara Barton inspired the young women who helped make nursing a respected profession. It was by humble but powerful example that Gandhi taught his people that passive resistance could drive out their British oppressors . . . by example that great researcher/teachers like Louis Agassiz led a generation of budding scientists . . . and by example that writers like James Joyce can cause the development of literature to swerve in a new direction. Thus, no matter what the field of endeavor, it is usually the case that great leaders seem to lead by setting an example. Brave actions compel others to follow.

Yet these famous instances of successful leadership all benefit from a circumstance that does not always apply when strong leadership is needed. Those who followed Alexander, Gandhi, Barton, and Agassiz were already united in purpose. In each case, as well, the followers probably shared roughly similar backgrounds and social attitudes. By contrast, when a group is so diverse that common ground cannot be easily found or when there is no shared goal, leadership can only succeed when the leader commands, using his authority and inspiration to bring people together.

Consider the familiar cliché that a leader "forges" a nation, particularly when its people have suffered defeat. Is this not often the case in sports, business, and the arts, as well? A team, company, or theater group threatens to fall apart because the common vision has been lost. Its members are depressed, say, and they forget what brought them together in the first place. In such instances, a leader must take charge, order them to work together and ensure that a shared goal can be attained. Only after the work begins to take shape and the group regains its sense of purpose can the leader relax his command and lead by example. To my mind, it is always preferable to have leaders who can inspire us by example, for we as followers can therefore choose whether or not to follow. I do think we must recognize, however, that disorganized or confusing situations sometimes cry out for a leader who can assume command for the greater good of the group.

Evaluation and Discussion of Essay #1
Holistic Score: 6
Each of the three writing tasks is addressed separately in a response that is unified by a strong personal voice and a steady focus on the topic. All three tasks are addressed in a thorough way, demonstrating complexity of thought.

Paragraphs 1 and 2 address the first task in some depth. Paragraph 1 opens with an attention-getting, yet relevant, comparison to a famous comment about pornography. The author then goes on to provide a number of examples that work together to clarify the meaning of the statement. Notice that these paragraphs refrain from saying anything about what the statement does not mean; they are unified around ideas that refer to the first task only.

Paragraph 3 takes the tasks out of turn and addresses the third task. This method of organization is successful in this case for two reasons: 1) The author uses the third task as a transition to move from her description of leadership by example to her description of leadership by command; 2) The author returns to the ideas related to the third task in the final sentences of paragraph 4, and thus creates a unifying conclusion to the essay as a whole.

The first six sentences of paragraph 4 address the second task by describing a set of characteristics that make leading by command the best method. Although this discussion does not contain actual examples as in paragraphs 1 and 2, the characteristics described are specific and thorough enough to make the author's point clear.

The author's effective use of transitions (e.g., *yet, therefore, however*) creates a smooth progression of ideas. The transitional sentences beginning paragraphs 2 and 3 establish a clear relationship between the paragraphs.

STRATEGY: Variety in sentence structure and length keeps your writing from sounding monotonous or mechanical; it also adds sophistication.

The use of parallelism in paragraph 2 and the variety in sentence length, demonstrate a lively writing style. Variety of this sort shows energy—and it keeps the reader awake.

ESSAY #2

True leadership leads rather than commands. Where commands are given, followers do what they are told, but only what they are told, and only when they are told. When people are led by example they do as they are shown, not only when they are shown, but on their own as well. This is not to say that commanders do not get things done with their groups. Armies are run by commanders instead of leaders, because they want not soldiers who will work and think on their own, but who will do as they are told when they are told. But commanding is not the same as leadership.

True leaders lead by example rather than by command because leadership is different from command. In situations apart from the military, where it is preferable to have followers who think and act for themselves, leadership by example is a far more effective motivator and guiding force. Workers who are brow beaten into submission are far less motivated than workers encouraged to work steadily at their own pace, with their own ideas. Workers commanded to perform a duty a certain way are less productive than workers guided and trained to think cleverly and creatively about their tasks.

Commanding and leadership are two different things whose results are quite often similar, but also often not, depending on the situation. Leadership leads by example, not by command, because of its very nature. When leadership commands, it ceases to be leadership.

Evaluation and Discussion of Essay #2
Holistic Score: 3

This essay contains the beginnings of some interesting ideas and is written in language that is quite clear and straightforward. It does not focus, however, on providing a thorough explanation of the statement and its implications.

Nor does it fulfill all three tasks. In fact, only the first task is addressed, in a response that is poorly developed and organized. All three paragraphs work in some way to reinforce the statement that true leadership leads by example. Paragraphs 1 and 2 provide us with partial development of the idea by stating that people led by example can think for themselves and that workers who think for themselves perform better than those who do not. Although both of these ideas are interesting, they lack the necessary development. The author never clarifies why leading by example creates followers who can think for themselves. And he never pulls his ideas together into a coherent explanation of the meaning of the statement.

The author's main purpose in this essay seems to have been to establish that leadership and command are two different things. Yet he never makes clear what his purpose is in establishing this difference, nor does he use this difference to reach any conclusion. He simply restates the difference in each paragraph. The result is an excessive repetition of ideas.

It seems, therefore, that this author paid little attention to the tasks listed in the essay topic. Nonetheless, the paper receives a score of 3 rather than 2 for two reasons: 1) it succeeds in sustaining a focus on the topic provided without significant digression or distortion, and 2) the quality of language demonstrates adequate control of mechanics, sentence structure, and vocabulary.

In all likelihood, this author could have produced a significantly better essay had he paid closer attention to the precise requirements of the tasks. By prewriting, he would have had the chance to get himself on the right track before starting to write. By thinking about each task in turn, he would have had the opportunity to form a more fully developed sequence of ideas. By addressing each task in turn, he would have had the opportunity to produce paragraphs that had a single, logical purpose.

STRATEGY: To achieve unified paragraphs, address one task per paragraph. This will help ensure that the ideas in each paragraph all share a common focus.

STEP 5: PROOFREAD

This final step should be a quick one. You won't have much time at all to revise your essay substantially, so don't bother. What you should look for are blatant errors or significant omissions.

Here's a checklist of what to look for when proofing:

Problems in Meaning

1. Any missing words, transition phrases, or brief ideas?
2. Any sentence fragments or otherwise incomplete ideas?
3. Any incorrect or illegible words?
4. Any confusing punctuation?
5. Any incorrect grammatical forms?

Problems in Mechanics

1. Did you misspell a word?
2. Did you always capitalize when necessary?
3. Did you make unnecessary abbreviations?

STRATEGY: Learn the types of mistakes you tend to make and look for them.

Another important rule to follow in proofreading is to prioritize. For example, the problems in meaning are usually more important that those in mechanics. If your reader cannot follow your thinking, you stand to lose more ground than if he or she spots a misspelling.

STRATEGY: Write neatly! If you have bad penmanship, print. Carefully indent each paragraph, since clear paragraph breaks make your essay look well planned.

Once again, if you write up until the thirty-minute limit, you will miss being able to take Step 5. Plan to check your watch toward the end of the half hour and stick to the seven-step method. Even if you do not absolutely finish your thoughts, it is vital that you proofread. Be disciplined enough to leave yourself a minute or two to accomplish this step.

CHAPTER THREE

USAGE AND STYLE

You've learned how to analyze an essay topic, organize your thoughts, and outline an essay. Once you have an overall idea of what you want to say in your essay, you can start thinking about how to say it. The writing process is about producing clearly developed and well-organized essays. We'll now look at specific aspects of producing clear expository prose. **Remember:** The best strategy is to study this section and work the exercises in short, manageable blocks, interspersed with the study of other subjects in preparation for the MCAT.

Studies have shown that a writer's style improves dramatically when she knows what she is going to say. The message: Try not to generate too much anxiety over your writing style. Your goal here is not to become a Hemingway, but only to produce solid, thirty-minute, first-draft essays about general topics.

Most important—*keep it simple.* This applies to word choice, sentence structure, and argument. Obsession about how to spell a word correctly can throw off your flow of thought. The more complicated (and wordy) your sentences, the more likely they will be plagued by errors. The more convoluted your argument, the more likely you will get bogged down in convoluted sentence structure. Yet recall that *simple* does not mean *simplistic.* A clear, straightforward approach can be sophisticated.

Many students mistakenly believe that their essays will be "downgraded" for such mechanical errors as misplaced commas, poor choice of words, misspellings, faulty grammar, and so on. Occasional problems of this type won't dramatically affect your MCAT essay score. The test readers understand that you are writing first-draft essays. They will *not* be taking points off for such errors, provided the writer doesn't have a demonstrable pattern of such errors. If the essays are littered with misspellings and incorrect usage, then a more serious communication problem is indicated.

The moral is: Don't worry excessively about writing mechanics but do try to train yourself out of poor habits and do proofread your essays for obvious errors. Your objective in taking the MCAT is admission to medical school, and to achieve that objective you should probably give the medical schools what they want.

They do not expect eloquence in a thirty-minute assignment, but they do expect effectiveness. To help you achieve this effectiveness in your essay, we offer three broad objectives:

- be **CONCISE**
- be **FORCEFUL**
- be **CORRECT**

An effective essay is concise: it wastes no words. An effective essay is forceful: it makes its point. And an effective essay is correct: it conforms to the generally accepted rules of grammar and form.

The following pages break down the three broad objectives of **CONCISION, FORCEFULNESS,** and **CORRECTNESS** into twenty-three specific principles. **DON'T PANIC!** Many of them will already be familiar to you. And besides, you will have many chances to practice in the exercises and practice essays.

Use your time wisely. Don't do all the examples if you are confident that you know the point. Move on, spending extra time on those that give you trouble.

Principles 1 through 4 aim primarily at the first objective—concise writing; principles 5 through 11 aim primarily at the second objective—forceful writing; and principles 12 through 23 aim primarily at the third objective—grammatically correct writing. However, these three objectives are interrelated. For instance, a forceful sentence is usually not verbose, and correct sentences tend to be more forceful than incorrect ones.

The principles of concise and forceful writing are generally not as rigid as the principles of grammatically correct writing. Concision and forcefulness are matters of art and personal style as well as common sense and tradition. But if you are going to disregard a principle, we hope you will do so sparingly and out of educated choice. On the MCAT Writing Sample, sticking closely to the principles of standard English writing should produce a concise, forceful, and correct essay.

BE CONCISE

Principle 1. Avoid junk phrases.

Do not use several words when one word will do. Junk phrases are like junk food: they add only fat, no muscle. Many people make the mistake of writing *at the present time* or *at this point in time* instead of the simpler *now*, or *take into consideration* instead of simply *consider*, in an attempt to make their prose seem more scholarly or more formal. It does not work. Their prose ends up seeming inflated and pretentious. Writing junk phrases is a waste of words, a waste of limited time, and a distraction from the point of the essay.

JUNKY: I am of the opinion that the aforementioned managers should be advised that they will be evaluated with regard to the utilization of responsive organizational software for the purpose of devising a responsive network of customers.

CONCISE: We should tell the managers that we will evaluate their use of flexible computerized databases to develop a customer's network.

Exercise for Principle 1: Junk Phrases
Improve the following sentences by omitting or replacing junk phrases.

1. The agency is not prepared to undertake expansion at this point in time.

2. In view of the fact that John has prepared with much care for this presentation, it would be a good idea to award him with the project.

3. The airline has a problem with always having arrivals that come at least an hour late, despite the fact that the leaders of the airline promise that promptness is a goal that has a high priority for all the employees involved.

4. In spite of the fact that she only has a little bit of experience in photography right now, she will probably do well in the future because she has a great deal of motivation to succeed in her chosen profession.

5. The United States is not in a position to spend more money to alleviate the suffering of the people of other countries considering the problems of its own citizens.

6. Although not untactful, George is a man who says exactly what he believes.

7. Accuracy is a subject that has great importance to English teachers and company presidents alike.

8. The reason why humans kill each other is that they experience fear of those whom they do not understand.

9. Ms. Miller speaks with a high degree of intelligence with regard to many aspects of modern philosophy.

10. The best of all possible leaders is one who listens and inspires simultaneously.

Principle 2. Do not be redundant.

Redundancy means that the writer needlessly repeats an idea because he fails to realize the scope of a word or phrase that has already been used; for example, "a beginner lacking experience." (The word *beginner* implies lack of experience.) You can eliminate redundant words or phrases without changing the meaning of the sentence. Watch out for words that add nothing to the sense of the sentence.

Here are some common redundancies:

REDUNDANT	CONCISE
refer back	refer
few in number	few
small-sized	small
grouped together	grouped
in my own personal opinion	in my opinion
end result	result
serious crisis	crisis
new initiatives	initiatives

Redundancy often results from carelessness, but you can easily eliminate redundant elements in the proofreading stage.

Exercise for Principle 2: Redundancy

Repair the following sentences by marking out redundant elements.

1. All these problems have combined together to create a serious crisis.

2. A staff that large in size needs an effective supervisor who can get the job done.

3. He knows how to follow directions and he knows how to do what he is told.

4. The writer's technical skill and ability do not mask his poor plot line.

5. That monument continues to remain a significant tourist attraction.

6. The recent trend lately of spending on credit has created a more impoverished middle class.

7. Those who can follow directions are few in number.

8. She has deliberately chosen to change careers.

9. Such dialogue opens up many doors to compromise.

10. The ultimate conclusion is that environmental and economic concerns are intertwined.

Principle 3. Avoid needless qualification.

Since the object of your essay is to convince your reader, you will want to adopt a reasonable tone. There will likely be no single, clear-cut "answer" to the essay topic, so you should not overstate your case. Occasional use of such modifiers as *fairly, rather, somewhat, relatively* and of such expressions as *seems to be, a little,* and *a certain amount of* will let the reader know you are reasonable, but using such modifiers too often weakens your argument. Excessive qualification makes you sound hesitant; like junk phrases, they add bulk without adding substance.

WORDY: This rather serious breach of etiquette may possibly shake the very foundations of the corporate world.

CONCISE: This serious breach of etiquette may shake the foundations of the corporate world.

Just as bad is the overuse of the word *very*. Some writers use this intensifying adverb before almost every adjective in an attempt to be more forceful. If you need to add emphasis, look for a stronger adjective (or verb) instead.

WEAK: Novak is a very good pianist.

STRONG: Novak is a virtuoso pianist.

or

Novak plays beautifully.

And don't try to modify words that are already absolute.

WRONG	CORRECT
more unique	unique
the very worst	the worst
completely full	full

Exercise for Principle 3: Excessive qualification

Although reasonable qualification benefits an essay, excessive qualification debilitates your argument. Though the qualification in some of the sentences below might be appropriate in certain contexts, use these sentences, nevertheless, to practice achieving concision by eliminating qualification.

1.   She is a fairly excellent teacher.

2.   Ferrara seems to be sort of a slow worker.

3.   There are very many reasons technology has not permeated all countries equally.

4.   It is rather important to pay attention to all the details of a murder trial as well as to the "larger picture."

5.   You yourself are the very best person to decide what you should do for a living.

6.   It is possible that the author overstates his case somewhat.

7.   The president perhaps should use a certain amount of diplomacy before he resorts to force.

8.   In Italy I found about the best food I have ever eaten.

9.   Needless to say, children should be taught to cooperate at home and in school.

10.   The travel agent does not recommend the trip to Tripoli, since it is possible that one may be hurt.

Principle 4. Do not use water-treading sentences.

This principle suggests several things:

- Do not write a sentence that gets you nowhere.

- Do not ask a question only to answer it (unless you have hit upon a brilliant exception!).

- Do not merely copy the essay's directions.

- Do not write a whole sentence only to announce that you're changing the subject.

If you have something to say, say it without preamble. If you need to smooth over a change of subject, do so with a transitional word or phrase, rather than a meaningless sentence. If proofreading reveals unintentional wasted sentences, neatly cross them out.

WORDY: Which idea of the author's is more in line with what I believe? This is a very interesting . . .

CONCISE: The author's statement closely mirrors reality.

The author of the wordy example above is just treading water: wasting words and limited time and getting nowhere. Get to the point quickly and stay there. Remember, contrary to what you may have been taught, simplicity and clarity, not verbosity, win points.

ANSWERS TO EXERCISES

Answers to Exercise 1: Junk phrases

1.   The agency is not prepared to expand now.

2.   Since John has prepared for this presentation so carefully, we should award him the project.

3.   Flights are always at least an hour late on this airline, though its leaders promise that promptness is a high priority for all its employees.

4.   Although she is inexperienced in photography, she will probably succeed because she is motivated.

5.   The United States cannot spend more money to alleviate other countries' suffering when its own citizens suffer.

6.   Although tactful, George says exactly what he believes.

7.   Accuracy is important to English teachers and company presidents alike.

8.   Humans kill each other because they fear those whom they do not understand.

9.   Ms. Miller speaks intelligently about many aspects of modern philosophy.

10.   The best leader listens and inspires simultaneously.

Answers to Exercise 2: Redundancy

1.   All these problems have combined to create a crisis.

2.   A staff that large needs an effective supervisor.

3.   He knows how to follow directions.

4.   The writer's technical skill does not mask his poor plot line.

5.   That monument remains a significant tourist attraction.

6.   The recent trend of spending on credit has created a more impoverished middle class.

7. Few people can follow directions.

8. She has chosen to change careers.

9. Such dialogue opens many doors to compromise.

10. The conclusion is that environmental and economic concerns are intertwined.

Answers to Exercise 3: Excessive qualification

1. She is a good teacher.

2. Ferrara is a slow worker.

3. There are many reasons technology has not permeated all countries equally.

4. In a murder trial, it is important to pay attention to all the details as well as to the "larger picture."

5. You are the best person to decide what you should do for a living.

6. The author overstates his case.

7. The president should use diplomacy before he resorts to force.

8. In Italy I found the best food I have ever eaten.

9. Children should be taught to cooperate at home and in school. (If there's no need to say it, don't!)

10. The travel agent said not to go to Tripoli, since one may be hurt. (Saying it is *possible* that one *may* be hurt is an example of redundant qualification, since both *possible* and *may* indicate uncertainty.)

(No exercise for Principle 4)

BE FORCEFUL

Principle 5. Avoid needless self-reference.

You do not need to make repeated references to yourself in your essay. There is no need to keep reminding your reader that what you are writing is your opinion; your reader does not expect you to be expounding someone else's opinion. Avoid such unnecessary phrases as *I believe*, *I feel*, and *in my opinion*. Self-reference is generally superfluous and therefore detracts from your essay's concision. Self-reference also detracts from the forcefulness of your essay by constantly reminding your reader that you are expressing an opinion. Practice expressing self-confidence in your writing: your opinion is legitimate and deserves to be stated.

WEAK: I am of the opinion that air pollution is a more serious problem than the government has led us to believe.

FORCEFUL: Air pollution is a more serious problem than the government has led us to believe.

Self-reference is another form of qualifying what you say—a very obvious form. Sometimes, toning down your statement is appropriate, perhaps necessary. Using qualifiers like *probably* and *perhaps* can be effective if you do it sparingly. One or two self-references in an essay might even be appropriate. Being forceful and unreasonable is certainly not a winning combination. You must practice walking the middle ground between overstatement and wishy-washy qualification. Practicing different approaches to stating your opinion is the only sure way to improve your writing.

Exercise for Principle 5: Needless self-reference

1. I feel we ought to pay teachers more than we pay senators.

2. The author, in my personal opinion, is stuck in the past.

3. I do not think this argument can be generalized to most business owners.

4. My own experience shows me that food is the best social lubricant.

5. I doubt more people would vote even if they had more information about candidates.

6. Although I am no expert, I do not think privacy should be valued more than social concerns.

7. My guess is that most people want to do good work, but many are bored or frustrated with their jobs.

8. I must emphasize that I am not saying the author does not have a point.

9. If I were a college president, I would implement several specific reforms to combat apathy.

10. It is my belief that either alternative would prove disastrous.

Principle 6. Avoid the passive voice.

Using the passive voice is another way writers avoid accountability. Put verbs in the active voice whenever possible. In the active voice, the subject performs the action (we should do it . . .). In the passive voice, the subject is the receiver of the action and is often only implied (it should be done . . .).

You should avoid the passive voice **EXCEPT** in the following cases:

- when you do not know who performed the action (The letter was opened before I received it.)

- when you prefer not to refer directly to the person who performs the action (An error has been made in computing this data.)

PASSIVE: The estimate of this year's tax revenues was prepared by the General Accounting Office.

ACTIVE: The General Accounting Office prepared the estimate of this year's tax revenues.

In order to change from the passive to the active voice, ask yourself WHO or WHAT is performing the action. In the case above, the General Accounting Office is performing the action. Therefore, the GAO should be the subject of the sentence. Your prewriting, especially the game plan in which you begin to outline ideas for sentences, should give you an idea of your sentence's purpose. Weak sentences are usually the product of writing before thinking. Take a few seconds to find out what your sentence is going to do before you ask it to perform.

Exercise for Principle 6: Undesirable passives

1. The Spanish-American War was fought by brave but misguided men.

2. The bill was passed in time, but it was not signed by the president until the time for action had passed.

3. Advice is usually requested by those who need it least; it is not sought out by the truly lost and ignorant.

 397

4. That building should be relocated where it can be appreciated by the citizens.

5. Garbage collectors should be generously rewarded for their dirty, smelly labors.

6. The conditions of the contract agreement were ironed out minutes before the strike deadline.

7. The minutes of the City Council meeting should be taken by the city clerk.

8. With sugar, water, or salt, many ailments contracted in less-developed countries could be treated.

9. Test results were distributed with no concern for confidentiality.

10. The report was compiled by a number of field anthropologists and marriage experts.

Principle 7. Avoid weak openings.

Try not to begin a sentence with *There is, There are,* or *It is.* These are roundabout ways of getting to the main point of the sentence and usually indicate to your reader that you are trying to distance yourself from the position you are taking. Again, whatever the appearance, the problem usually results from writing before thinking about the sentence, hedging until you find out what you want to say.

Exercise for Principle 7: Weak Openings

1. It would be unwise for businesses to ignore the illiteracy problem.

2. It can be seen that in many fields experience is more important than training.

3. There are several reasons why this plane is obsolete.

4. It would be of no use to fight a drug war without waging a battle against demand for illicit substances.

5. There are many strong points in the candidate's favor; intelligence, unfortunately, is not among them.

6. It is difficult to justify building a more handsome prison.

7. It has been decided that we, as a society, can tolerate homelessness.

8. There seems to be little doubt that Americans like watching television better than conversing.

9. It is clear that cats make better pets than mice.

10. It is obvious that intelligence is a product of environment and heredity.

Principle 8. Avoid vague language.

Choose specific, descriptive words. Notice, the key is to choose your words, not let them flow uncontrolled from your pencil. Vague language weakens your writing because it forces the reader to guess what you mean instead of allowing the reader to concentrate fully on your ideas and style. You will find that the essay topic will supply you with an abundance of specifics; your argument will be more forceful if you replace vague phrases with the particular facts at hand.

WEAK: Brown is highly educated.

FORCEFUL: Brown has a master's degree in business administration.

WEAK: She is a great communicator.

FORCEFUL: She speaks persuasively.

Notice that sometimes, to be more specific and concrete, you will have to use more words than you might with vague language. This principle is not in conflict with the general objective of concision. Being concise means eliminating unnecessary words; avoiding vagueness will sometimes mean adding necessary words.

(No exercise for this principle)

Principle 9. Avoid clichés.

Clichés are expressions that may once have seemed colorful and powerful but now seem dull and lifeless because of overuse. When working under time pressure, you can easily let trite phrases slip into your writing. Clichés are often vague, even meaningless in the context of a sentence. A reliance on vague or meaningless clichés will suggest you are a lazy thinker; keep them out of your essay.

WEAK: Performance in a crisis is the acid test for a leader.

FORCEFUL: Performance in a crisis is the best indicator of a leader's abilities.

Putting a cliché in quotation marks in order to indicate your distance from the clichés does not strengthen the sentence; if anything, it merely calls attention to the weakness. If you are going to use a cliché, be aware that you are using one and ask yourself whether the reader will understand what you mean and whether the cliché says exactly what you mean.

Exercise for Principle 9: Clichés

Make the following sentences more forceful by replacing clichés.

1. Beyond the shadow of a doubt Jefferson was a great leader.

2. I have a sneaking suspicion that families spend less time together than they did fifteen years ago.

3. The pizza delivery man arrived in the sequestered jury's hour of need.

4. Trying to find the employee responsible for this embarrassing information leak is like trying to find a needle in a haystack.

5. Both strategies would be expensive and completely ineffective, so it's six of one and half a dozen of the other.

6. The military is putting all its eggs in one basket by relying so heavily on nuclear missiles for the nation's defense.

7. Older doctors should be required to update their techniques, but you can't teach an old dog new tricks.

8. You have to take this new fad with a grain of salt.

9. The politician reminds me of Abraham Lincoln: he's like a diamond in the rough.

10. A ballpark estimate of the number of fans in the stadium would be 120,000.

Principle 10. Avoid jargon.

Jargon includes two categories of words that you should avoid. First is the specialized vocabulary of a group, such as doctors, lawyers, or baseball coaches. Second is the overly inflated and complex language that burdens many students' essays. You will not impress anyone with big words that do not fit the tone or context of your essay, especially if you misuse them.

If you are not certain of a word's meaning or appropriateness, leave it out. An appropriate vocabulary, even if simple, will add impact to your argument. One proofreading technique is to ask yourself as you come across words you are unsure of, "Would a reader in a different field be able to understand exactly what I mean from the words I've chosen?" If you are not sure, change the word or phrase to a simpler and clearer version.

WEAK: The international banks are cognizant of the new law's significance.

FORCEFUL: The international banks are aware of the new law's significance.

WRONG: The new law would negatively impact each of the nations involved.

CORRECT: The new law would hurt each of the nations involved. (*Impact* is also used to mean *affect* or *benefit*.)

The following are commonly used jargon words:

prioritize

optimize

utilize (use)

finalize (end, complete)

conceptualize (imagine, think)

maximize

designate

originate (start, begin)

facilitate (help, speed up)

bottom line

time frame

alternatives (choices)

parameter (boundary, limit)

user-friendly (responsive, flexible, easy-to-understand)

input/output

mutually beneficial

assistance

target (v.)

blindside

downside

viable

dialogue

ongoing (continuing)

Exercise for Principle 10: Jargon

Replace the jargon in the following sentences with more appropriate language.

1. We anticipate utilizing hundreds of paper clips in the foreseeable future.

2. The research-oriented person should not be hired for a people-oriented position.

3. Educationwise, our schoolchildren have been neglected.

4. Foreign diplomats should always interface with local leaders.

5. Pursuant to your being claimed as a dependent on the returns of another taxpayer or resident wage earner, you may not consider yourself exempt if your current nonwage income exceeds five hundred dollars or if your non-wage income combined with current wage income amounts to or exceeds five hundred dollars.

6. There is considerable evidentiary support for the assertion that Vienna sausages are good for you.

7. With reference to the poem, I submit that the second and third stanzas connote a certain despair.

8. Allow me to elucidate my position: this horse is the epitome, the very quintessence of equine excellence.

9. In the case of the recent railway disaster, it is clear that governmental regulatory agencies obfuscated in the preparation of materials for release to the public through both the electronic and print media.

10. Having been blindsided by innumerable unforeseen crises, this office has not been able to prepare for the afore-mentioned exigencies.

Principle 11. Vary sentences in length and structure.

Even when writing is clear and correct it can be tedious if sentences are all similar in length and structure. Take the following passage:

> The author suggests that a conflict exists between devoting limited resources to many people who would be affected positively or to a needy few for whom the effects would be less impressive. This conflict underlies many political arguments in the United States today about education, welfare, health care, and other issues that are costly and complex. We should direct resources where they will have the broadest impact if taxpayers are willing to devote only a limited portion of their income to the "general welfare" of the American people.

Each sentence, taken singly, is adequate stylistically and grammatically, but the passage lacks force because the same construction is repeated in each sentence. Each sentence is more than twenty-five words long. All of the sentences begin with the subject (*the author, this conflict, we*).

Monotonous sentence construction makes the content seem monotonous and suggests that the writer may lack imagination. Your ideas will make more of an impact if you break up a series of long, complicated sentences by occasionally inserting a short and simple one. Usually you can do this by cutting one long, convoluted sentence into two shorter sentences. Changing the length of a sentence usually necessitates changing its structure as well, but if you concentrate on length, it will often be easier to restructure a sentence. You can also create dependent clauses for variation.

Now compare the passage above with the following revised version:

> According to the author, a conflict exists between devoting limited resources to many people who would be affected positively or to a needy few for whom the effects would be less impressive. This conflict underlies many political arguments in the United States today. People fight about how to distribute resources for education, welfare, health care, and other issues that are costly and complex. But taxpayers are willing to devote only a limited portion of their income to the "general welfare" of the American people. As long as this is true, we should direct those resources where they will have the broadest impact.

The two passages contain the same information, often use the same phrasing, and are roughly the same length, yet the second passage is more interesting and persuasive because it is varied. Sentence length ranges from eleven to thirty-two words, and structure is varied by the use of dependent clauses.

(No exercise for this principle)

ANSWERS TO EXERCISES

Answers to Exercise 5: Needless self-reference

1. We ought to pay teachers more than we pay senators.

2. The author is stuck in the past.

3. This argument cannot be generalized to most business owners.

4. Food is perhaps the best social lubricant.

5. More people would not vote even if they had more information about candidates.

6. Privacy should not be valued more than social concerns.

7. Most people want to do good work, but many are bored or frustrated with their jobs.

8. The author has a point.

9. College presidents should implement several specific reforms to combat apathy.

10. Either alternative would prove disastrous.

Answers to Exercise 6: Undesirable passives

1. Brave but misguided men fought the Spanish-American War.

2. Congress passed the bill in time, but the president did not sign it until the time for action had passed.

3. Those who need advice least usually request it; the truly lost and ignorant do not seek it at all.

4. We should relocate that building where citizens can appreciate it.

5. City government should generously reward garbage collectors for their dirty, smelly labors.

6. Negotiators ironed out the conditions of the contract agreement minutes before the strike deadline.

7. The city clerk should take the minutes of the City Council meeting.

8. With sugar, water, or salt, doctors can treat many of the ailments that citizens of less-developed countries contract.

9. The teacher distributed test results with no concern for confidentiality.

10. A number of field anthropologists and marriage experts compiled the report.

Answers to Exercise 7: Weak Openings

1. Businesses cannot ignore the illiteracy problem without suffering.

2. Experience is more important than training in many fields.

3. This plane is obsolete for several reasons.

4. The government cannot fight a drug war effectively without waging a battle against demand for illicit substances.

5. The candidate has many strong points; intelligence, unfortunately, is not among them.

6. The city cannot justify building a more handsome prison.

7. We, as a society, have decided to tolerate homelessness.

8. Americans must like watching television better than conversing.

9. Cats make better pets than mice.

10. Intelligence is a product of environment and heredity.

(No exercises for Principle 8)

Answers to Exercise 9: Clichés

1. Jefferson was certainly a great leader.

2. Families probably spend less time together than they did fifteen years ago.

3. The pizza delivery man arrived just when the sequestered jury most needed him.

4. Trying to find the employee responsible for this embarrassing information leak may be impossible.

5. Both strategies would be expensive and completely ineffective: they have an equal chance of failing.

6. The military should diversify its defense rather than rely so heavily on nuclear missiles.

7. Older doctors should be required to update their techniques, but many seem resistant to changes in technology.

8. You need not take this new fad very seriously; it will surely pass.

9. The politician reminds me of Abraham Lincoln with his rough appearance and warm heart.

10. I estimate that 120,000 fans were in the stadium. (Even when a cliché is used in its original context, it sounds old.)

Answers to Exercise 10: Jargon

1. We expect to use hundreds of paper clips in the next two months.

2. A person who likes research should not be hired for a position that requires someone to interact with customers all day.

3. Our schoolchildren's education has been neglected.

4. Foreign diplomats should always talk to local leaders.

5. If someone claims you as a dependent on a tax return, you may still have to pay taxes on your income in excess of five hundred dollars.

6. Two recent studies suggest that Vienna sausages are good for you.

7. When the poet wrote the second and third stanzas, he must have felt despair.

8. This is a fine horse.

9. Government regulatory agencies were not honest in their press releases about the recent railway accident.

10. Having spent our time responding to many unexpected problems this month, we have not been able to prepare for these longer-term needs.

(No exercises for Principle 11)

BE CORRECT

Correctness is perhaps the most difficult objective for writers to achieve. The complex rules of standard English usage can leave you feeling unsure of your writing and more than a bit confused. But remember, the **MOST IMPORTANT LESSON** you can take from this course is how to organize your thoughts into a strong, well-supported argument. Style and grammar are important but secondary concerns; your readers will *not* mark you down for occasional errors common to first-draft writing.

Do the exercises and then compare your answers to ours, making sure you understand what the error was in each sentence. Proofread your practice essays in PART II; later, return to your practice essays and edit them. Better yet, ask a friend to edit them, paying special attention to correctness. Remember, thirty minutes is not enough time to achieve perfection. Luckily, your readers will not expect perfection. So just think of this section as helping you to improve the details of good writing. If it begins to overwhelm you, stop and take a break. The brain needs time to absorb all this information.

As you work through this section on the form of the English language, you will come across a few technical words that describe particular functions that words have in a sentence. You will not be expected to know these terms, only to understand the essence of a word's function in the sentence so that you can recognize an error when you see one. You do *not* need to memorize these terms. A list of definitions is provided at the end of this chapter with examples of each of these parts of speech. You will also find basic explanations throughout the text. Our use of grammatical terms merely allows us to simplify what would otherwise be needlessly roundabout explanations.

PRINCIPLES OF CONSISTENCY

Many of the rules of English usage are designed to force the writer to stick with one structure or usage throughout a sentence or even an entire essay in order to give the reader as many clues as possible about meaning.

Principle 12. Do not shift narrative voice.

Principle 5 above advised you to avoid needless self-reference. Since you are asked to write an explanatory essay, however, an occasional self-reference may be appropriate. You may even call yourself "I" if you want, as long as you keep the number of first-person pronouns to a minimum. Less egocentric ways of referring to the narrator include "we" and "one." If these more formal ways of writing seem stilted, stay with "I."

I suggest that individuals best cherish principles of free speech when such principles are challenged.

We can see . . .

One must admit . . .

The method of self-reference you select is called the narrative voice of your essay. Any of the above narrative voices are acceptable. Nevertheless, whichever you choose, you must be careful not to shift narrative voice in your essay. If you use *I* in the first sentence, for example, do not use *we* in a later sentence.

INCORRECT: I suggest that individuals best cherish principles of free speech when such principles are challenged. We can see how a free society can get too complacent when free speech is taken for granted.

It is likewise wrong to shift from *you* to *one*:

INCORRECT: You can readily see how politicians have a vested interest in pleasing powerful interest groups, though one should not generalize about this tendency.

To correct each of the above sentences, you need to change one pronoun to agree with the other:

CORRECT: "*We* can readily see..." (to agree with "though we should not generalize...")

CORRECT: "*I* can readily see..." (to agree with "though I would not generalize...")

CORRECT: "*One* can readily see..."(to agree with "though one should not generalize...")

Exercise for Principle 12: Shifting narrative voice

Rewrite these sentences to give them consistent points of view.

1. I am disgusted with the waste we tolerate in this country. One cannot simply stand by without adding to such waste: living here makes you wasteful.

2. You must take care not to take these grammar rules too seriously, since one can often become bogged down in details and forget why he is writing at all.

3. We all must take a stand against waste in this country; how else will one be able to look oneself in the mirror?

Principle 13. Be sure that the verb agrees with the subject.

Singular subjects and plural subjects take different forms of the verb in the present tense. Usually the difference lies in the presence or absence of a final *-s* (he becomes and they become), but sometimes the difference is more radical (he is, they are). If you are a native speaker of English, you can usually trust your ear to give you the correct verb form, but certain situations cause difficulty: When the subject and verb are separated by a number of words, when the subject is an indefinite pronoun, and when the subject consists of more than one noun.

- **A verb must agree with its subject in number regardless of intervening phrases.**

Do not let the words that come between the subject and the verb confuse you as to the number (singular or plural) of the subject. Usually one word can be pinpointed as the grammatical subject of the sentence, and the verb, no matter how far removed, must agree with that subject in number.

INCORRECT: The joys of climbing mountains, especially if one is a novice climber without the proper equipment, escapes me.

CORRECT: The *joys* of climbing mountains, especially if one is a novice climber without the proper equipment, *escape* me.

INCORRECT: A group of jockeys who have already finished the first race and who wish to have their pictures taken are blocking my view of the horses.

CORRECT: A *group* of jockeys who have already finished the first race and who wish to have their pictures taken *is* blocking my view of the horses. (The long prepositional phrase beginning with the preposition *of* qualifies the noun *group.* The subject of the sentence is the noun *group,* which takes a singular verb *is*).

In both examples, the phrases and clauses between subject and verb do not affect the grammatical relationship between subject and verb. An intervening phrase that is plural does not change a singular subject into a plural one.

LOOK OUT FOR PREPOSITIONAL PHRASES INTERVENING
BETWEEN SUBJECT AND VERB!

What follows is a list of some of the most common prepositions:

in, out, up, down, over, under, between, off, on, behind, of, with, about, to, from, by, onto, before, after, through, despite, concerning, against

Also, watch out for collective nouns like *group*—such nouns are often plural in meaning but are nevertheless grammatically singular. The word *number* takes a singular verb when preceded by *the* and a plural verb when preceded by *a:*

CORRECT: A *number* of fans *hope* for a mere glimpse of his handsome face; unfortunately, they are rarely satisfied with a mere glimpse.

CORRECT: The *number* of fans who catch a glimpse of his handsome face *seems* to grow exponentially each time the tabloids write a story of his seclusion.

- **A subject that consists of two or more nouns connected by *and* takes the plural form of the verb.**

CORRECT: *Karl,* who is expert in cooking Hunan spicy duck, and *George,* who is expert in eating Hunan spicy duck, *have* combined their expertise to start a new restaurant.

- **When the subject consists of two or more nouns connected by *or* or *nor,* the verb agrees with the CLOSEST noun.**

CORRECT: Either the senators or the President *is* misinformed.

CORRECT: Either the President or the senators *are* misinformed.

There are some connecting phrases that look as though they should make a group of words into a plural but actually do not. The only connecting word that can made a series of singular nouns into a plural subject is *and.* In particular, the following connecting words and phrases do NOT result in a plural subject:

along with   besides   together with   as well as   in addition to

INCORRECT: The president, along with the secretary of state and the director of the CIA, are misinformed.

CORRECT: The president, along with the secretary of state and the director of the CIA, is misinformed.

If a sentence that is grammatically correct still sounds awkward, you should probably rephrase your thought.

LESS AWKWARD: Along with the secretary of state and the director of the CIA, the president is misinformed.

A note on the subjunctive: After verbs such as *recommend, require, suggest, ask, demand,* and *insist* and after expressions of requirement, suggestion, and demand (for example, *I demand that*), use the subjunctive form of the verb—that is, the form of the verb used after such expressions as *I want to* _____."

CORRECT: I recommend that the chocolate cake *be* reinstated on your menu.

CORRECT: It is essential that the reader *understand* what you are trying to say.

Exercise for Principle 13: Subject-verb agreement
Repair the incorrect verbs.

1. The logical structure of his complicated and rather tortuous arguments are always the same.

2. The majority of the organization's members is over sixty years old.

3. Both the young child and her grandfather was depressed for months after discovering that the oldest ice cream parlor in the city had closed its doors forever.

4. Hartz brought the blueprints and model that was still on the table instead of the ones that Mackenzie had returned to the cabinet.

5. A case of bananas have been sent to the local distributor in compensation for the fruit that was damaged in transit.

6. A total of fifty editors read each article, a process that takes at least a week, sometimes six months.

7. Neither the shipping clerk who packed the equipment nor the truckers who transported it admits responsibility for the dented circuit box.

8. Either Georgette or Robespierre are going to be asked to dinner by the madcap Calvin. I dread the results in either case.

9. I can never decide whether to eat an orange or a Belgian chocolate; each of them have their wondrous qualities.

10. Everyone in the United States, as well as the Canadians, expect the timber agreement to fall through.

Principle 14. Beware of faulty parallelism.
A common style problem, faulty parallelism, results from not seeing the structure of the sentence you are constructing. Matching constructions must be expressed in parallel form. It is often rhetorically effective to use a particular construction several times in succession, in order to provide emphasis. The technique is called parallel construction, and it is effective only when used sparingly. If your sentences are varied, a parallel construction will stand out. If your sentences are already repetitive, a parallel structure will further obscure your meaning. As an example of how parallel construction should be used, look at the following sentence:

As a leader, Lincoln inspired a nation to throw off the chains of slavery; *as a philosopher,* he proclaimed the greatness of the little man; *as a human being,* he served as a timeless example of humility.

The repetition of the *underlined* construction provides a strong sense of rhythm and organization to the sentence and alerts the reader to yet another aspect of Lincoln's character.

Writers often use a parallel structure for dissimilar items.

INCORRECT: They are sturdy, attractive, and cost only a dollar each. (The phrase, *they are,* makes sense preceding the adjectives *sturdy* and *attractive,* but cannot be understood before *cost only a dollar each.*)

CORRECT: They are sturdy and attractive, and they cost only a dollar each.

Parallel constructions must be expressed in parallel grammatical form. In other words, each segment of the parallel must be in similar form to the other segments: all nouns, all infinitives, all gerunds, all prepositional phrases, or all clauses.

INCORRECT: All business students should learn word processing, accounting, and how to program computers.

CORRECT: All business students should learn word processing, accounting, and computer programming.

This principle applies to any words that might begin each item in a series: prepositions (*in, on, by, with,* etc.), articles (*the, a, an*), helping verbs (*had, has, would,* etc.) and possessives (*his, her, our,* etc.). Either repeat the word before every element in a series or include it only in the first item. Anything else violates the rules of parallelism.

In effect, your treatment of the second element of the series determines the form of all subsequent elements:

INCORRECT: He invested his money in stocks, in real estate, and a home for retired performers.

CORRECT: He invested his money in stocks, in real estate, and in a home for retired performers.

CORRECT: He invested his money in stocks, real estate, and a home for retired performers.

When proofreading, check that each item in the series agrees with the word or phrase that begins the series. In the above example, *invested his money* is the common phrase that each item shares. You would read, "He invested his money in real estate, *invested his money in stocks, and invested his money . . . in a home for retired performers.*"

A number of constructions call for you to always express ideas in parallel form. These constructions include:

X is as _____ as Y.

X is more _____ than Y.

X is less _____ than Y.

Both X and Y . . .

Either X or Y . . .

Neither X nor Y . . .

Not only X but also Y . . .

X and Y can stand for as little as one word or as much as a whole clause, but in any case the grammatical structure of X and Y must be identical.

INCORRECT: The view from this apartment is not nearly as spectacular as from that mountain lodge.

CORRECT: *The view from this apartment* is not nearly as spectacular as *the one from that mountain lodge.*

Exercise for Principle 14: Parallelism
Correct the faulty parallelism in the following sentences.

1. This organization will not tolerate the consumption, trafficking, or promoting the use of drugs.

2. The dancer taught her understudy how to move, how to dress, and how to work with choreographers and deal with professional competition.

3. The student's knowledge of chemistry is as extensive as what the professor knows.

4. They should not allow that man either to supervise the project or assist another supervisor, since he has proven himself to be thoroughly incompetent.

5. Either the balloon business will have to expand or declare bankruptcy.

6. Before Gertrude begins to design the set, as well as hiring laborers to help her construct it, she should consult the director.

7. Merrill based his confidence on the futures market, the bond market, and on the strength of the president's popularity.

8. The grocery baggers were ready, able, and were quite determined to do a great job.

9. The requirements for a business degree are not as stringent as a law degree.
10. Not only did we sail, fish, and canoe that day, but also visited the quaint town on the island across the bay.

Principle 15. Be sure that pronouns refer clearly and properly to their antecedents.
A pronoun is a word that replaces a noun in a sentence. Every time you write a pronoun—*he, him, his, she, her, it, its, they, their, that,* and *which*—be sure there can be absolutely no doubt about which particular noun the pronoun refers to (the antecedent). Careless use of pronouns (a common mistake) can obscure your intended meaning.

AMBIGUOUS: The teacher told the student he was lazy. (Does *he* refer to *teacher* or *student*?)

AMBIGUOUS: Sara knows more about history than Irina because she learned it from her father. (Does *she* refer to *Sara* or *Irina*?)

You can usually rearrange a sentence to avoid ambiguous pronoun reference.

CLEAR: The student was lazy, and the teacher told him so.

CLEAR: The teacher considered himself lazy and told the student so.

CLEAR: Since Sara learned history from her father, she knows more than Irina does.

CLEAR: Because Irina learned history from her father, she knows less about it than Sara does.

If you are worried that a pronoun reference will be ambiguous, rewrite the sentence so that there is no doubt. Do not be afraid to repeat the antecedent (the noun that the pronoun refers to) if necessary:

AMBIGUOUS: I would rather settle in Phoenix than in Albuquerque, although it lacks wonderful restaurants.

CLEAR: I would rather settle in Phoenix than in Albuquerque, although Phoenix lacks wonderful restaurants.

A reader must be able to pinpoint the pronoun's antecedent. Even if you think the reader will know what you mean, do not use a pronoun without a clear and appropriate antecedent.

INCORRECT: When you are painting, be sure not to get it on the floor. (*It* could refer only to the noun *paint*; pronouns cannot refer to implied nouns.)

CORRECT: When you are painting, be sure not to get any paint on the floor.

Avoid using *this, that, it,* or *which* to refer to a whole phrase, sentence, or idea. Even when these pronouns are placed very close to their intended antecedent, the references may still be unclear.

UNCLEAR: United States consumers use larger amounts of nonrecyclable diapers every year. This will someday turn the earth into a giant trashcan.

CLEAR: United States consumers use larger amounts of nonrecyclable diapers every year. This ever-growing mass of waste products will someday turn the earth into a giant trashcan. (A good rule of thumb is to try not to begin a sentence with *that* or *this* unless accompanying a noun.)

UNCLEAR: The salesman spoke loudly, swayed back and forth, and tapped the table nervously, which made his customers extremely nervous.

CLEAR: The salesman spoke loudly, swayed back and forth, and tapped the table nervously, mannerisms which made his customers extremely nervous.

Also, unless you are talking about the weather, avoid beginning a sentence with *it*. (See Principle 7: Avoid weak openings.)

WEAK: It is difficult to distinguish between the rights of criminals and those of victims.

BETTER: Distinguishing between the rights of criminals and those of victims is difficult.

> Some nouns and pronouns are singular in one context and plural in another, depending on the number of the antecedent.

A few of the indefinite pronouns that can be either singular or plural are *some, all, most, any,* and *none*. When using one of these words as the subject, check to see whether the antecedent is singular or plural.

CORRECT: He was unable to finish his *work* last night. *Some remains* to be done today. *None of it is* easy. (Read: *Some* of his work *remains; none* of his work *is*)

CORRECT: His *superiors* have been following his progress. *Some are* more impressed than others. *None are* overwhelmed. (Read: *Some* of his superiors *are; none* of his superiors *are*)

Other indefinite pronouns are invariable in number:

SINGULAR:	anybody	everybody	somebody	either	one
	anyone	everyone	someone	neither	each
	anything	every one	some one	no one	

(NOTE: Just remember that -*body*, -*one*, and -*thing* pronouns are singular.)

PLURAL:	both	few	many	several

A related problem has arisen recently because of concern over using gender-specific words to describe individuals or groups that are not necessarily of one gender. The writer will often mistakenly substitute the traditional generic singular pronoun *he* with the plural form *they*. But other methods exist to avoid using *he* as a generic pronoun.

INCORRECT: The author makes a strong statement about the individual: each *person* must protect *their* individuality if *one* wants to remain individual.

CORRECT: The author makes a strong statement about individualism: *people* must protect *their* individuality if *they* want to remain individuals.

Beware using the wrong form of the pronoun in a sentence.

When writing a sentence containing a relative clause (one that begins with the relative pronoun *who, whom, that,* or *which*), authors often become confused about which pronoun to use.

CORRECT: Those people, whom I have been calling all day, never returned my call.

CORRECT: Those people, who have been calling all day, are harassing me.

A useful technique for choosing the correct pronoun is to turn the clause into a question. In the first sentence, you would mentally ask, "I have been calling *who* or *whom*?" Answer your question, substituting a pronoun: "I have been calling *them*." In the second sentence, you would ask, "*Who* or *whom* has been calling all day?" Answer your question, substituting a pronoun: "*They* have been calling all day." If you use *her, him, them,* or *us* to answer the question, the appropriate relative pronoun is *whom*. If you use *she, he, they,* or *we* to answer the question, the appropriate relative pronoun is *who*.

That and *which* are often used interchangeably, but as a rule, *that* is a defining, or restrictive, pronoun, while *which* is a nondefining, or nonrestrictive, pronoun. Usually, this can be translated into a simple rule of thumb: If the relative clause is set off with commas (i.e., the clause is not crucial to the meaning of the sentence), use *which*. If the relative clause is not set off by commas (i.e., the clause *is* crucial to the meaning of the sentence), use *that*. (See also Principle 19: Use commas correctly when you punctuate.)

EXAMPLE: The movie, which was released two years behind schedule, was one of the few that were real box office hits this spring.

Exercise for Principle 15: Faulty pronoun reference

1. Clausen's dog won first place at the show because he was well bred.

2. The critic's review made the novel a commercial success. He is now a rich man.

3. The military advisor was more conventional than his commander, but he was a superior strategist.

4. Bertha telephoned her friends in California before going home for the night, which she had not done in weeks.

5. Although John hoped and prayed for the job, it did no good. He called him the next morning; they had hired someone else.

6. You must pay attention when fishing—otherwise, you might lose it.

7. Zolsta Karmagi is the better musician, but he had more formal training.

8. The director wanted to give the lead part to her, but the star, his girlfriend, disagreed and insisted that she was better qualified for the job.

9. Zalmen showed us his credentials, but Koenig refused to answer our inquiries.

10. A retirement community offers more activities than a private dwelling does, but it is cheaper.

Principle 16. Be sure that modification is clear.

In English, the position of the word within a sentence often establishes the word's relationship to other words in the sentence. This is especially true with modifying phrases. Modifiers, like pronouns, are generally connected to the nearest word that agrees with the modifier in person and number. If a modifier is placed too far from the word it modifies, the meaning may be lost or obscured. Notice in the following sentences that ambiguity results when the modifying phrases are misplaced in the sentence.

AMBIGUOUS: Gary and Martha sat talking about the movie in the office.

AMBIGUOUS: They wondered how much the house was really worth when they bought it.

Avoid ambiguity by placing modifiers as close as possible to the words they are intended to modify.

CLEAR: Gary and Martha sat in the office talking about the movie.

CLEAR: When they bought the house, they wondered how much it was really worth.

Modifiers can refer to words that either precede or follow them. Ambiguity can also result when a modifier is squeezed between two possible referents and the reader has no way of throwing which is the intended referent:

AMBIGUOUS: The dentist instructed him regularly to brush his teeth.

AMBIGUOUS: Tom said in the car he had a map of New Jersey.

Be sure that the modifier is closest to the intended referent and that there is no other possible referent on the other side of the modifier. If when proofreading your essay you find a misplaced modifier, just enclose it in parentheses and draw an arrow to its proper place in the sentence.

CLEAR: The dentist instructed him to brush his teeth regularly.

CLEAR: Tom said he had a map of New Jersey in the car.

All the ambiguous sentences above are examples of misplaced modifiers: modifiers whose placement makes the intended reference unclear. In addition to misplaced modifiers, watch for dangling modifiers: modifiers whose intended referents are not even present.

INCORRECT: Coming out of context, Peter was startled by Julia's perceptiveness.

The modifying phrase *coming out of context* is probably not intended to refer to *Peter,* but if not, then to whom or what? *Julia? Perceptiveness?* None of these makes sense as the referent of *coming out of context.* What came out of context was more likely a *statement* or *remark.* The sentence is incorrect because there is no word or phrase that can be pinpointed as the referent of the opening modifying phrase. Rearrangement and rewording solved the problem.

CORRECT: Julia's remark, coming out of context, startled Peter with its perceptiveness.

Exercise for Principle 16: Faulty modification

1.   Bentley advised him quickly to make up his mind.

2.   I agree with the author's statements in principle.

3.   Coming out of the woodwork, he was surprised to see termites.

4.   The governor's conference met to discuss racial unrest in the auditorium.

5.   Hernandez said in her office she had all the necessary documents.

6.   All of his friends were not able to come, but he decided that he preferred small parties anyway.

7.   Margolis remembered she had to place a telephone call when she got home.

8.   George told Suzette he did not like to discuss politics as they walked through the museum.

9.   Having worked in publishing for ten years, Stokely's résumé shows that he is well qualified.

10.   Without experience in community service, holding political office would be a farce.

OTHER THINGS TO WATCH FOR

Principle 17. Avoid slang and colloquialisms.
Conversational speech is filled with slang and colloquial expressions. However, you should avoid using these informal expressions in the formal expository writing appropriate for the MCAT writing sample. Slang terms and colloquialisms can be confusing to the reader, since these expressions are not universally understood. Even worse, such informal writing may give readers the impression that you are poorly educated or arrogant.

INAPPROPRIATE: He is really into gardening.

CORRECT: He enjoys gardening.

INAPPROPRIATE: She plays a wicked game of tennis.

CORRECT: She excels in tennis.

INAPPROPRIATE: Myra has got to go to Memphis for a week.

CORRECT: Myra must go to Memphis for a week.

INAPPROPRIATE: Joan has been doing science for eight years now.

CORRECT: Joan has been a scientist for eight years now.

Many graders consider contractions to be too informal also. We recommend that you avoid contractions in your MCAT essay and spell out all words.

INAPPROPRIATE: The blackened salmon's been one of the restaurant's most popular entrees.

CORRECT: The blackened salmon has been one of the restaurant's most popular entrees.

INAPPROPRIATE: He hasn't missed a deadline in years.

CORRECT: He has not missed a deadline in years.

The English language has such a rich vocabulary that you should never have to resort to using a colloquialism to make a point. With a little thought you will find the right word. Using informal language is risky; play it safe by sticking to standard usage.

Exercise for Principle 17: Slang and colloquialisms

Avoid slang and colloquialisms. Replace the informal elements of the following sentences with more appropriate terms.

1.   Cynthia Larson sure knows her stuff.

2.   The crowd was really into watching the fire-eating juggler, but then the dancing horse grabbed their attention.

3.   As soon as the personnel department checks out his résumé, I am sure we will hear gales of laughter issuing from the office.

4.   Having something funny to say seems awfully important in our culture.

5.   The chef had a nice way with salmon: his sauce was simple but the effect was sublime.

6.   Normal human beings can't cope with repeated humiliation.

7.   The world hasn't got much time to stop polluting; soon, we all will have to wear face masks.

8.   If you want a good cheesecake, you must make a top-notch crust.

9.   International organizations should try and cooperate on global issues like hunger and party decorations.

10.   The environmentalists aren't in it for the prestige; they really care about protecting the yellow-throated hornswoggler.

Principle 18. Do not write sentence fragments and run-on sentences.

The time pressure of the MCAT Writing Sample could cause you to lose track as you are writing a sentence and end up with a sentence fragment or a run-on sentence. A sentence fragment has no independent clause; a run-on sentence has two or more independent clauses that are improperly connected. As you edit your practice essays, check your sentence constructions, noting any tendency toward fragments or run-on sentences.

Sentence Fragments

Every sentence in formal expository writing must have an independent clause: a clause that contains a subject and a predicate and does *not* begin with a subordinate conjunction such as:

after	if	so that	whenever
although	in order that	than	where
as	provided that	though	whether
because	since	unless	while
before		until	

When you proofread your essays, make sure that every sentence has at least one independent clause.

INCORRECT: Global warming. That is what the scientists and journalists are worried about this month.

CORRECT: Global warming *is* the cause of concern for scientists and journalists this month.

INCORRECT: Seattle is a wonderful place to live. Having mountains, ocean, and forests all within easy driving distance. If you can ignore the rain.

CORRECT: Seattle is a wonderful place to live, with mountains, ocean, and forests all within easy driving distance, but it certainly does rain often.

INCORRECT: Why do I think the author's position is preposterous? Because he makes generalizations that I know are rarely true.

CORRECT: I think the author's position is preposterous because he makes generalizations that I know are rarely true.

NOTE: **Beginning single-clause sentences with coordinate conjunctions—*and, but, or, nor,* and *for*—is acceptable in moderation, although some readers may object to beginning a sentence with** *and.*)

CORRECT: Most people would agree that indigent patients should receive wonderful health care. But every treatment has its price.

Run-on Sentences

Time pressure may also cause you to write two or more sentences as one. When you proofread your essays, watch out for independent clauses that are not joined with any punctuation at all or are only joined with a comma.

RUN-ON SENTENCE: Current insurance practices are unfair they discriminate against the people who need insurance most.

RUN-ON SENTENCE: Current insurance practices are unfair, they discriminate against the people who need insurance most.

You can repair run-on sentences in any one of three ways. First you could use a period to make separate sentences of the independent clauses.

CORRECT: Current insurance practices are unfair. They discriminate against the people who need insurance most.

Second, you could use a semicolon. A semicolon is a weak period: it separates independent clauses but signals to the reader that the ideas in the clauses are related.

CORRECT: Current insurance practices are unfair; they discriminate against the people who need insurance most.

The third method of repairing a run-on sentence is usually the most effective. Use a conjunction to turn an independent clause into a dependent one and to make explicit how the clauses are related.

CORRECT: Current insurance practices are unfair, in that they discriminate against the people who need insurance most.

One common way to end up with a run-on sentence is to try to use transitional adverbs like *however, nevertheless, furthermore, likewise,* and *therefore* as conjunctions.

RUN-ON SENTENCE: Current insurance practices are discriminatory, furthermore they make insurance too expensive for the poor.

CORRECT: Current insurance practices are discriminatory. Furthermore, they make insurance too expensive for the poor.

RUN-ON SENTENCE: Current insurance practices are discriminatory, however they make insurance too expensive for the poor.

CORRECT: Current insurance practices are discriminatory; however, they make insurance too expensive for the poor.

Exercise for Principle 18: Sentence fragments and run-on sentences
Repair the following by eliminating sentence fragments and run-on sentences.

1. The private academy has all the programs Angie will need. Except that the sports program has been phased out.

2. Leadership ability. This is the elusive quality that our current government employees have yet to capture.

3. Antonio just joined the athletic club staff this year but Barry has been with us since 1975, therefore we would expect Barry to be more skilled with the weight-lifting equipment. What a surprise to find Barry pinned beneath a barbell on the weight-lifting bench with Antonio struggling to lift the 300-pound weight from poor Barry's chest.

4. However much she tries to act like a Southern belle, she cannot hide her roots. The daughter of a Yankee fisherman, taciturn and always polite.
5. There is always time to invest in property ownership. After one has established oneself in the business world, however.

6. Sentence fragments are often used in casual conversation, however they should not be used in written English under normal circumstances.

7. A documentary film, which at least has an aura of reality and truth, and which in this case is very well produced, however there is less overall impact than a personal biography, particularly one of someone the public knows and likes.

8. After living for many years alone, the decision to move into a retirement community, despite the many restrictions entailed, was a difficult one—made all the more difficult by the seeming impossibility of finding one that met all Mrs. Casey's needs, which is why the decision took a long time.

PRINCIPLES OF PUNCTUATION

Principle 19. Use commas correctly when you punctuate.

When using the comma, follow these rules:

A. Use commas to separate items in a series. If more than two items are listed in a series, they should be separated by commas; the final comma, the one that precedes the word *and,* is optional.

CORRECT: My recipe for buttermilk biscuits contains flour, baking soda, salt, shortening, and buttermilk.

ALSO CORRECT: My recipe for chocolate cake contains flour, baking soda, sugar, eggs, milk, and chocolate.

B. Do not place commas before the first element of a series or after the last element.

WRONG: My investment advisor recommended that I construct a portfolio of, stocks, bonds, commodities futures, and precious metals.

WRONG: The elephants, tigers, and dancing bears, were the highlights of the circus parade.

C. Use commas to separate two or more adjectives before a noun; do not use a comma after the last adjective in the series.

CORRECT: I can't believe you sat through that long, dull, uninspired movie three times.

WRONG: The manatee is a round, blubbery, bewhiskered, creature whose continued presence in American waters is endangered by careless boaters.

D. Use commas to set off parenthetical clauses and phrases. (A parenthetical expression is one that is not necessary to the main idea of the sentence.)

CORRECT: Gordon, who is a writer by profession, bakes an excellent cheesecake.

The main idea is that Gordon bakes an excellent cheesecake. The intervening clause merely serves to identify Gordon; thus, it should be set off with commas.

CORRECT: The newspaper that has the most insipid editorials is the *Daily Times.*

CORRECT: The newspaper, which has the most insipid editorials of any I have read, won numerous awards last week.

In the first of these examples the clause beginning with that defines which paper the author is discussing. In the second example, the main point is that the newspaper won numerous awards, the intervening clause beginning with which identifies the paper.

E. Use commas after introductory participial or prepositional phrases.

CORRECT: Having watered his petunias every day during the drought, Harold was very disappointed when his garden was destroyed by insects.

CORRECT: After the banquet, Harold and Martha went dancing.

F.   Use commas to separate independent clauses (clauses that could stand alone as complete sentences) connected by a coordinate conjunction such as *and, but, not, yet,* etcetera.

CORRECT: Susan's old car has been belching blue smoke from the tailpipe for two weeks, but it has not broken down yet.

CORRECT: Zachariah's pet frog eats fifty flies a day, yet it has never gotten indigestion.

NOTE: **Make sure the comma separates two *independent* clauses, each containing its own subject and verb. It is incorrect to use a comma to separate the two parts of a compound verb.**

WRONG: Barbara went to the grocery store, and bought two quarts of milk.

WRONG: Zachariah's pet frog eats fifty flies a day, and never gets indigestion.

Exercise for Principle 19: Commas
Correct the punctuation errors in the following sentences.

1. Peter wants me to bring records games candy and soda to his party.

2. I need, lumber, nails, a hammer and a saw to build the shelf.

3. It takes a friendly energetic person to be a successful salesman.

4. I was shocked to discover that a large, modern, glass-sheathed, office building had replaced my old school.

5. The country club, a cluster of ivy-covered whitewashed buildings was the site of the president's first speech.

6. As we entered the park, a police officer clad in a crisp, well-starched uniform directed us to the theater.

7. Pushing through the panicked crowd the security guards frantically searched for the suspect.

8. Despite careful analysis of the advantages and disadvantages of each proposal Harry found it hard to reach a decision.

Principle 20. Use semicolons correctly when you punctuate.

A.   Use a semicolon instead of a coordinate conjunction such as *and, or,* or *but* to link two closely related independent clauses.

CORRECT: Whooping cranes are an endangered species; there are only fifty whooping cranes in New Jersey today.

CORRECT: Whooping cranes are an endangered species, and they are unlikely to survive if we continue to pollute.

WRONG: Whooping cranes are an endangered species; and they are unlikely to survive if we continue to pollute.

B.   Use a semicolon between independent clauses connected by words like *therefore, nevertheless,* and *moreover.*

CORRECT: The staff meeting has been postponed until next Thursday; therefore, I will be unable to get approval for my project until then.

CORRECT: Farm prices have been falling rapidly for two years; nevertheless, the traditional American farm is not in danger of disappearing.

Exercise for Principle 20: Semicolons

1. Morgan has five years' experience in karate; but Thompson has even more.

2. Very few students wanted to take the class in physics, only the professor's kindness kept it from being canceled.

3. You should always be prepared when you go on a camping trip, however you must avoid carrying unnecessary weight.

Principle 21. Use the colon correctly when you punctuate.

A. In formal writing the colon is used only as a means of signaling that what follows is a list, definition, explanation, or concise summary of what has gone before. The colon usually follows an independent clause, and it will frequently be accompanied by a reinforcing expression like *the following, as follows,* or *namely,* or by an explicit demonstrative like *this.*

CORRECT: Your instructions are as follows: read the passage carefully, answer the questions on the last page, and turn over your answer sheet.

CORRECT: This is what I found in the refrigerator: a moldy lime, half a bottle of stale soda, and a jar of peanut butter.

CORRECT: The biggest problem with America today is apathy: the corrosive element that will destroy our democracy.

B. Be careful not to separate a verb from its direct object with a colon.

WRONG: I want: a slice of pizza and a small green salad.

CORRECT: This is what I want: a slice of pizza and a small green salad. (The colon serves to announce that a list is forthcoming.)

CORRECT: I don't want much for lunch: just a slice of pizza and a small green salad. (Here, what follows the colon defines what "don't want much" means.)

C. Context will occasionally make clear that a second independent clause is closely linked to its predecessor, even without an explicit expression like those used above. Here, too, a colon is appropriate, although a period will always be correct too.

CORRECT: We were aghast: the "charming country inn" that had been advertised in such glowing terms proved to be a leaking cabin full of mosquitoes.

ALSO CORRECT: We were aghast. The "charming country inn" that had been advertised in such glowing terms proved to be a leaking cabin full of mosquitoes.

Exercise for Principle 21: Colons

1. I am sick and tired of: your whining, your complaining, your nagging, your teasing, and most of all, your barbed comments.

2. The chef has created a masterpiece, the pasta is delicate yet firm, the mustard greens are fresh, and the medallions of veal are melting in my mouth.

3. In order to write a good essay, you must: get plenty of sleep, eat a good breakfast, and practice until you drop.

Principle 22. Use hyphens and dashes correctly when you punctuate.

A. Use the hyphen to separate a word at the end of a line.

B. Use the hyphen with the compound numbers twenty-one through ninety-nine, and with fractions used as adjectives.

CORRECT: Sixty-five students constituted a majority.
CORRECT: A two-thirds vote was necessary to carry the measure.

C. Use the hyphen with the prefixes *ex, all,* and *self* and with the suffix *elect.*

CORRECT: The constitution protects against self-incrimination.
CORRECT: The President-elect was invited to chair the meeting.

D. Use the hyphen with a compound adjective when it comes BEFORE the word it modifies, but not when it comes after the word it modifies.

CORRECT: The no-holds-barred argument continued into the night.
CORRECT: The argument continued with no holds barred.

E. Use the hyphen with any prefix used before a proper noun or adjective.

CORRECT: His pro-African sentiments were heartily applauded.
CORRECT: They believed that his activities were un-American.

F. Use a hyphen to separate component parts of a word in order to avoid confusion with other words or to avoid the use of a double vowel.

CORRECT: The sculptor was able to re-form the clay after the dog knocked over the bust.

CORRECT: They had to be reintroduced, since it had been so long since they last met.

G. Use the dash to indicate an abrupt change of thought. In general, however, formal writing is best when you think out what you want to say in advance and avoid abrupt changes of thought.

CORRECT: The inheritance must cover the entire cost of the proposal—Gail has no other money to invest.

CORRECT: To get a high score—and who doesn't want to get a high score—you need to devote yourself to prolonged and concentrated study.

Exercise for Principle 22: Hyphens and dashes

1. The child was able to count from one to ninety nine.

2. The adults only movie was banned from commercial TV.

3. It was the first time she had seen a movie that was for adults-only.

4. John and his ex wife remained on friendly terms.

5. A two thirds majority would be needed to pass the budget reforms.

6. The house, and it was the most dilapidated house that I had ever seen was a bargain because the land was so valuable.

Principle 23. Use the apostrophe correctly when you punctuate.

A. Use the apostrophe with contracted forms of verbs to indicate that one or more letters have been eliminated in writing (just as sounds have been eliminated or shortened in speaking). Now that you know this, please do not use your knowledge on the MCAT essay. (For an explanation, see Principle 17: Avoid slang and colloquialisms.)

FULL FORMS:	you are	it is	you have	the boy is
	Harry has	we would	was not	
CONTRACTED:	you're	it's	you've	the boy's
	Harry's	we'd	wasn't	

One of the most common errors involving use of the apostrophe is using it in the contraction *you're* or *it's* to indicate the possessive form of *you* or *it*. When you write *you're*, ask yourself whether you mean *you are*. If not, the correct word is *your*. Similarly, are you sure you mean *it is*? If not, use the possessive form *its*.

INCORRECT: You're chest of drawers is ugly.

INCORRECT: The dog hurt it's paw.

CORRECT: Your chest of drawers is ugly.

CORRECT: The dog hurt its paw.

B.   Use the apostrophe to indicate the possessive form of a noun.

NOT POSSESSIVE:	the boy	Harry	the children	the boys
POSSESSIVE FORM:	the boy's	Harry's	the children's	the boys'

NOTE: The word *boy's* could have one of three meanings:

- The boy's an expert at chess. (The boy is . . .)

- The boy's left for the day. (The boy has . . .)

- The boy's face was covered with pie. (possessive: the face of the boy)

The word *boys'* can have only one meaning: a plural possessive (the . . . of the boys).

CORRECT: I caught a glimpse of the fox's red tail as the hunters sped by. (The *'s* ending indicates that one fox is the owner of the tail.)

CORRECT: Ms. Fox's office is on the first floor. (One person possesses the office.)

CORRECT: The Foxes' apartment has a wonderful view. (There are several people named Fox living in the same apartment. First you must form the plural, then add the apostrophe to indicate possession.)

C.   The apostrophe is used to indicate possession only with nouns; in the case of pronouns there are separate possessives for each person and number.

my, mine	our, ours
your, yours	your, yours
his, his	their, theirs
her, hers	
its, its	

The exception is the neutral *one*, which forms its possessive by adding an apostrophe and an *s*.

Exercises for Principle 23: Apostrophes

1.   The Presidents limousine had a flat tire.

2.   You're tickets for the show will be at the box office.

3.   The opportunity to change ones lifestyle does not come often.

4.   The desks' surface was immaculate, but it's drawers were messy.

5.   The cat on the bed is hers'.

ANSWERS TO EXERCISES

Answers to Exercise 12: Shifting narrative voice

1. I am disgusted with the waste we tolerate in this country. People cannot simply stand by without adding to such waste: living here makes all of us wasteful.

2. You must take care not to take these grammar rules too seriously, since you can often become bogged down in details and forget why you are writing at all. (Or use *one* consistently.)

3. We all must take a stand against waste in this country; else how will we be able to look ourselves in the mirror? (When using *we*, you must make sure to use the plural form of verbs and pronouns.)

Answers to Exercise 13: Subject-verb agreement

1. The logical *structure* of his complicated and rather tortuous arguments *is* always the same.

2. The *majority* of the organization's members *are* over sixty years old.

3. *Both* the young child and her grandfather *were* depressed for months after discovering that the oldest ice cream parlor in the city had closed its doors forever.

4. Hartz brought the *blueprints* and *model* that *were* still on the table instead of the ones that Mackenzie had returned to the cabinet. (The restrictive phrase beginning with *that* defines the noun phrase *blueprints and model*.)

5. A *case* of bananas *has* been sent to the local distributor in compensation for the fruit that was damaged in transit.

6. A *total* of fifty editors *reads* each article, a process that takes at least a week, sometimes six months.

7. Neither the shipping clerk who packed the equipment nor the *truckers* who transported it *admit* responsibility for the dented circuit box.

8. Either Georgette or *Robespierre is* going to be asked to dinner by the madcap Calvin. I dread the results in either case.

9. I can never decide whether to eat an orange or a Belgian chocolate; *each* of them *has* its wondrous qualities. (Note that you must also change the possessive pronoun to the singular form.)

10. *Everyone* in the United States, as well as in Canada, *expects* the timber agreement to fall through.

Answers to Exercise 14: Parallelism

1. This organization will not tolerate the consumption, trafficking, or promotion of drugs.

2. The dancer taught her understudy how to move, dress, work with choreographers, and deal with professional competition.

3. *The student's knowledge* of chemistry is as extensive as *the professor's knowledge*.

4. They should not allow that man *either to supervise* the project or to *assist* another supervisor, since he has proven himself to be thoroughly incompetent.

5. The balloon business will have to either expand or declare bankruptcy.

6. Before Gertrude begins to design the set, as well as to hire laborers to help her construct it, she should consult the director.

7. Merrill based his confidence on the futures market, the bond market, and the strength of the president's popularity.

8. The grocery baggers were ready, able, and quite determined to do a great job.

9. The *requirements for a business degree* are not as stringent as *those for a law degree.*

10. Not *only* did we sail, fish, and canoe that day, *but also* we visited the quaint town on the island across the bay.

Answers to Exercise 15: Faulty pronoun reference

1. The structure of the sentence might leave us wondering whether Clausen or his dog was well bred. Instead, use the impersonal *it.*
    Sample Rewrite: Clausen's dog won first place at the show because it was well bred.

2. *He* is probably meant to refer to the author of the book reviewed by the critic, but the context makes *he* appear to refer to *the critic,* who could be an author as well as a critic.
    Sample Rewrite: The critic's review made the novel a commercial success, and the novelist is now a rich man.

3. We cannot tell from the context whether the military advisor or his superior was the superior strategist.
    Sample Rewrite: The military advisor was more conventional than his commander, but the advisor was a superior strategist.

4. *Which* is the problem here: We do not know whether Bertha had not spent the night at home in weeks or whether she had not telephoned her friends in weeks.

    Sample Rewrite: Because she had not telephoned her California friends in weeks, Bertha called them before she went home for the night.

5. Referring to some ambiguous *they* without identifying who *they* are beforehand is incorrect.
    Sample Rewrite: John wanted the job badly, but when he called the employer the next morning he found that the company had hired someone else.

6. We don't know exactly what *it* is, but we can assume that *it* is a fish.
    Sample Rewrite: You must pay attention when fishing, or you might lose your catch.

7. We do not know whether *he* refers to Zolsta or to the unnamed lesser musician.
    Sample Rewrite: Zolsta Karmagi is the better musician, but Sven Wonderup had more formal training.

8. This sentence is extremely confusing because the reference of the two pronouns (*her, she*) is unclear. Who are *all* these women?
    Sample Rewrite: The director wanted to give the lead part to another woman, but the star, his girlfriend, disagreed and insisted that she, the star of so many fine productions, was better qualified for the job.

9. Whose credentials? Zalmen's or Koenig's?
    Sample Rewrite: Zalmen showed us his credentials, and was allowed into the press conference, but Koenig refused to answer our inquiries and was turned away.

10.   Which is cheaper, the private dwelling or the retirement community? The pronoun *it* has no clear antecedent.
Sample Rewrite: A retirement community offers more activities than a private dwelling does, but a private dwelling is cheaper.

Answers for Exercise 16: Faulty modification

1.   *Quickly* is sandwiched between two verbs, and it could refer to either one.
Sample Rewrite: Bentley advised him to make up his mind quickly.

2.   *In principle* probably modifies *agreed,* but its placement makes it appear to modify *statement.*
Sample Rewrite: I agree in principle with the author's statements.

3.   Termites are probably coming out of the woodwork, not the man, but an introductory modifying phrase always refers to the grammatical subject of the sentence.
Sample Rewrite: He was surprised to see termites coming out of the woodwork.

4.   Was the racial unrest in the auditorium, or was the conference merely held there?
Sample Rewrite: The governor's conference met in the auditorium to discuss racial unrest.

5.   Did she say it in her office? Were the documents in her office? Or both?
Sample Rewrite: Hernandez said that she had all the necessary documents in her office.

6.   If none of his friends came, it must have been a small party indeed.
Sample Rewrite: Not all of his friends were able to come, but he decided that he preferred small parties anyway.

7.   Did she remember when she got home? Or did she have to call when she got home?
Sample Rewrite: When she got home, Margolis remembered she had to place a telephone call.

8.   Either he didn't like discussing politics in the museum, or he didn't like discussing it at all.
Sample Rewrite: As they walked through the museum, George told Suzette he did not like to discuss politics.

9.   Was it Stokely's résumé that worked in publishing for ten years?
Sample Rewrite: Stokely, who has worked in publishing for ten years, appears from his résumé to be well qualified.

10.   It is the person holding the job, not the job itself, that requires experience in community service.
Sample Rewrite: A politician without experience in community service would fail to serve his constituents.

Answers to Exercise 17: Slang and colloquialisms

1.   Cynthia Larson is surely an expert. (It may go without saying that *knows her stuff* is a slang expression, but the substitution of *sure* for *surely* may be more difficult to identify as an error. *Sure* is an adjective, *surely* is an adverb, and an adverb is needed in this case, since the word is meant to modify *knows.*)

2.   The crowd was absorbed in watching the fire-eating juggler, but then the dancing horse caught their attention.

3.   As soon as the personnel department tries to verify his résumé, I am sure we will hear gales of laughter issuing from the office.

4.   Having something funny to say seems to be very important in our culture.

5.   The chef is skillful with salmon: his sauce was simple but the effect was sublime.

6.   Normal human beings cannot tolerate repeated humiliation.

7. The world does not have much time to stop polluting; soon, we all will have to wear face masks. (*Hasn't got* is both a contraction and an example of the colloquial substitution of *have got* for *have*.)

8. If you want a good cheesecake, you must make a superb crust.

9. International organizations should try to cooperate on global issues like hunger and party decorations.

10. The environmentalists are not involved in the project for prestige; they truly care about protecting the yellow-throated hornswoggler.

Answers to Exercise 18: Sentence fragments and run-on sentences

1. In this context, *except* is a conjunction, and as such makes the clause to which it is attached a dependent one.
   Sample Rewrite: The private academy has all the programs Angie will need, except that the sports program has been phased out.

2. *Leadership ability* is a sentence fragment, since it has no predicate.
   Sample Rewrite: Leadership ability: this is the elusive quality that our current government employees have yet to capture.

3. Here we have both a run-on sentence (two independent clauses linked by *therefore* and a comma) and a sentence fragment ("What a surprise to find . . ." contains no subject or predicate).
   Sample Rewrite: Antonio just joined the athletic club staff this year, but Barry has been with us since 1975; therefore, we would expect Barry to be more skilled with the weight-lifting equipment. It was quite a surprise to find Barry pinned beneath a barbell on the weight-lifting bench with Antonio struggling to lift the 300-pound weight from poor Barry's chest.

4. *The daughter of a Yankee fisherman* is a sentence fragment, since the group of words contains no verb.
   Sample Rewrite: However much she tries to act like a Southern belle, she cannot hide her roots. She will always be the daughter of a Yankee fisherman, taciturn and ever polite.

5. The conjunction *after* makes the second group of words a sentence fragment.
   Sample Rewrite: There is always time to invest in property ownership after one has established oneself in the business world, however.

6. Since transitional words like *however* do not subordinate a clause, this is a run-on sentence. You could either change the first comma to a semicolon or separate the clauses with a period.
   Sample Rewrite: Sentence fragments are often used in casual conversation. They should not, however, be used in written English under normal circumstances.

7. The trouble here is that the sentence is made up of dependent clauses with no independent clauses to serve as a base.
   Sample Rewrite: A truthful, well-produced documentary film has less impact than a biographical film about someone well-liked by the public.

8. This sentence must be broken down into two or more sentences.
   Sample Rewrite: After living alone for many years, Mrs. Casey had difficulty making the decision to move into a retirement community. Many restrictions were entailed, and none of the homes met all Mrs. Casey's needs. For all these reasons, the decision took a long time.

Answers for Exercise 19: Commas

1. Peter wants me to bring records, games, candy, and soda to his party.

2. I need lumber, nails, a hammer, and a saw to build the shelf.

3. It takes a friendly, energetic person to be a successful salesman.

4. I was shocked to discover that a large, modern, glass-sheathed office building had replaced my old school.

5. The country club, a cluster of ivy-covered whitewashed buildings, was the site of the president's first speech.

6. As we entered the park, a police officer, clad in a crisp, well-starched uniform, directed us to the theater.

7. Pushing through the panicked crowd, the security guards frantically searched for the suspect.

8. Despite careful analysis of the advantages and disadvantages of each proposal, Harry found it hard to reach a decision.

Answers for Exercise 20: Semicolons

1. Morgan has five years' experience in karate, but Thompson has even more.

2. Very few students wanted to take the class in physics; only the professor's kindness kept it from being canceled.

3. You should always be prepared when you go on a camping trip; however, you must avoid carrying unnecessary weight.

Exercise for Principle 21: Colons

1. I am sick and tired of your whining, your complaining, your nagging, your teasing, and most of all, your barbed comments.

2. The chef has created a masterpiece: the pasta is delicate yet firm, the mustard greens are fresh, and the medallions of veal are melting in my mouth.

3. In order to write a good essay, you must do the following: get plenty of sleep, eat a good breakfast, and practice until you drop.

Answers to Exercise 22: Hyphens and dashes

1. The child was able to count from one to ninety-nine.

2. The adults-only movie was banned from commercial TV.

3. It was the first time she had seen a movie that was for adults only.

4. John and his ex-wife remained on friendly terms.

5. A two-thirds majority would be needed to pass the budget reforms.

6. The house—and it was the most dilapidated house that I had ever seen—was a bargain because the land was so valuable.

Answers to Exercise 23: Apostrophes

1. The President's limousine had a flat tire.

2. Your tickets for the show will be at the box office.

3. The opportunity to change one's lifestyle does not come often.

4. The desk's surface was immaculate, but its drawers were messy.

5. The cat on the bed is hers.

LIST OF COMMONLY MISUSED WORDS

This list includes common diction errors and common idiomatic errors.

A diction error results from use of a word whose meaning does not fit in a particular context. Often the word that is needed and the word that is misused sound or look alike (e.g., *affect/effect*).

Idioms are established and accepted expressions. Idiomatic errors usually involve use of the wrong preposition (*different than* versus *different from*).

accept/except	To *accept* is to willingly receive; to *except* is to omit or exclude. **Example:** Peter was *accepted* by the college because, if you *except* his failing grades in two courses, his academic record is excellent. **NOTE:** *Except* is usually used as a preposition meaning "with the exception of." **Example:** I'll be home every day except Friday, when I have a dance class.
adapt/adopt	To *adapt* is to change something to make it suitable for a certain purpose; to *adopt* is to make something one's own. **Example:** *To Have and Have Not* was adapted for the screen by William Faulkner. **Example:** The Robinsons have *adopted* a baby.
affect/effect	To *affect* is to influence or change; to *effect* is to cause or to make (something) happen. **Examples:** The size of the harvest was *affected* by the lack of rainfall. The medicine Allen took *effected* a rapid recovery. **NOTE:** *Effect* is usually used as a noun meaning "influence." **Example:** The illegible signs on this road have a bad *effect* on safety.
allusion/delusion/ illusion	An *allusion* is an indirect reference; a *delusion* is something that is falsely believed; an *illusion* is a false, misleading, or deceptive appearance. **Examples:** Mr. Harmon fills his talk with *allusions* to literature and art to create the *illusion* that he is very learned. He has *delusions* that he is quite a scholar.
among/between	In most cases, you should use *between* for two items and *among* for more than two. There are exceptions, however; *among* tends to be used for less definite or exact relationships. **Examples:** The competition *between* Anne and Fred has grown more intense. He is always at his best *among* strangers. BUT: Plant the trees *between* the road, the wall, and the fence.
amount/number	*Amount* should be used to refer to a singular or noncountable word; *number* should be used to refer to a countable quantity. **Examples:** The *amount* of cloth on the bolt was enough for several suits. I was not sure of the *number* of yards of cloth on the bolt.

another/the other	*Another* refers to any other; *the other* is more specific; it refers to one particular other. **Examples:** Put *another* log on the fire (any one). Put *the other* log on the fire (the last one). The men were passing the pipe from one to the other (two men, back and forth). They passed the pipe from one to *another* (three or more).
as/like	*Like* is a preposition; it introduces a prepositional phrase. Remember, a phrase is a group of words that does not contain a subject and verb; *as,* when functioning as a conjunction, introduces a subordinate clause. Remember, a clause is a part of a sentence containing a subject and verb. **Examples:** She sings *like* an angel. She sings as an angel sings.
as . . . as . . .	The idiom is *as . . . . as . . . .* **Example:** That suit is as expensive as (NOT *than*) this one.
assure/ensure/ insure	To *ensure* is to make certain, safe, or secure; to *insure* is to provide for financial payment in case of loss; to *assure* is to inform positively. **Example:** Mr. Green *assured* his mother-in-law that he had *insured* his life for $30,000 to *ensure* that his wife would not suffer poverty if he died.
because	To say "the reason is *because . . .* " is considered ungrammatical in formal English. Use *that* instead. **Examples:** The reason I'm late is that my car refused to start. OR: I'm late *because* my car refused to start.
beside/besides	*Beside* means "next to" something; *besides* means "in addition to." **Examples:** She sat *beside* me at the basketball game. *Besides* the basketball team, there were only three other people in the gym.
between . . . and . . .	The idiom is *between . . . and . . .* **Example:** Call *between* five *and* (NOT *to*) six o'clock. He chose *between* meat *and* (NOT *or*) fish.
criteria/data	These are *plural* nouns that are often mistakenly used as singular nouns. **Examples:** One *criterion* (not *criteria*) for employment in this company is a willingness to work with surly people. The recently collected *data prove* (NOT *proves*) our original hypothesis was correct.
different from	*Different* is usually used with the preposition *from,* usually not with *than.* **Example:** Frank's attitude is *different* from Charlie's. **NOTE:** Remember that you say *differ* from, never *differ than. Differ* can also be used with *with.* **Example:** On that issue, I *differ* with you.
each other/ one another	In formal writing, *each other* is used to refer to two things, and *one another* is used for three or more. **Examples:** Len and Amy love each other. Those three theories contradict one another.
eminent/imminent/ immanent	*Eminent* means prominent or outstanding; *imminent* means likely to happen soon, impending; *immanent* means existing within, intrinsic. **Examples:** The whole school was excited about the *imminent* arrival of the *eminent* scientist. Scrooge was characterized by *immanent* selfishness.
fewer/less	Use *fewer* before a plural noun, *less* before a singular one. **Examples:** This amazing product contains *less* fat, *less* salt, and *fewer* calories.
if/whether	*If* is used in conditional clauses. Examples: *If* I have the money, I will go. I do not know *whether* to go. (Nothing is conditional in this sentence.)

imply/infer	To *imply* is to state or indicate indirectly; to *infer* is to deduce or conclude. Authors and speakers *imply;* readers and listeners *infer.* **Examples:** Pete sarcastically implied that he was angry. Joe inferred from Mary's dejected look that she had failed the exam.
ingenious/ ingenuous	*Ingenious* means intelligent, clever, or resourceful; *ingenuous* means innocent, naive, or simple. **Examples:** The thief entered the bank vault by means of an *ingenious* magnetic device. Alice is so *ingenuous* that she refuses to believe anyone would deliberately do harm.
irregardless	The correct word is *regardless,* regardless of the context.
its/it's	*It's* is a contraction of it is; *its* is a possessive pronoun meaning something belongs to it. **Examples:** *It's* obvious that something is wrong with that dog; *it's* whining and chewing its paw. (Hint: During proofreading, if you have written *it's,* ask yourself, "Does this mean it is in the sentence?" If so, write out *it is.* If not, remove the apostrophe.)
maybe	Don't use *maybe* to modify an adjective or other adverb. **Example:** That is a potentially (NOT *maybe* a) dangerous thing to do.
neither . . . nor	The correlative conjunction is neither . . . nor, not neither . . .or. **Example:** He is *neither* strong nor flexible. **NOTE:** Avoid the redundancy caused by *neither . . . nor* following a negative. **Example:** Unnoticed by Debby or Sue (not *neither* Debby *nor* Sue), Naomi left.
not only . . . but (also)	If you use *not only,* it must be followed by *but;* the word *also* is optional. The words following *not only* must be parallel to the words following *but also.* **Example:** The book is not only fascinating, but also instructive.
number	*The number* should be followed by a singular verb, a *number* by a plural. **Examples:** *The number* of errors in his statement is astounding. A *number* of us are going camping.
regard as	*Regard as* is the correct idiom; *regard to be* is wrong. **Example:** I regard you *as* (NOT *to be*) a close friend.
to be able	Do not use a form of *to be able* preceding the passive form of an infinitive. **Example:** My old television cannot (NOT is *not able to*) be repaired. NOTE: *Is not able to* is wrong because it implies the TV lacks ability; it's the TV repairer who lacks ability. **Example:** He is *not able to* repair the TV.
when/where	Do not use *when* or *where* in a definition, or where *that* would be more appropriate. **Examples:** A convention is a meeting of people with something in common. (NOT *a convention is where a number of people . . .*) A diagram is a sketch *that* illustrates (NOT *is when a sketch is made to illustrate . . .*) the parts of something. I read that (NOT *where*) you had to leave town. Also, do not use *where* when you mean *when,* and vice versa. **Example:** She moved to New York in 1970, *when* (NOT *where*) she left for college.
that/which	These two words are used interchangeably, though rules govern when to use each of them appropriately. (See Principle 15.)
their/they're/ there	*Their* is a possessive pronoun meaning something belonging to them; *they're* is a contraction of *they are; there* means *that place* (among other things) **Examples:** *They're* placing *their* bets over *there* at the race track, but there's no chance they will win *their* money back.

DEFINITIONS

subject	Who or what the sentence is about. **Example:** The author embraces an idealistic philosophy. (Who or what embraces? The *author* embraces.)
verb	The part of the sentence that expresses an action or state of being of the subject. **Example:** The author embraces an idealistic philosophy. (The author is what or does what? The author *embraces*.)
sentence	A group of words that expresses a complete thought; it must contain a SUBJECT and a VERB. **Example:** DOGS BARK. **Example:** The EXPLORERS SLEPT in a tent.
sentence fragment	A group of words that purports to be a sentence but lacks either a subject or a verb or some element necessary to make the sentence a complete thought. **Example:** Shrimp and cod on sale at the fish market. (This "sentence" lacks a verb.)
run-on sentence	Two or more complete sentences connected with just a comma or with no punctuation at all. **Example:** Sushi bores me, on the other hand teriyaki is one of my favorite dishes.
clause	A group of words that contains a subject and a verb.
phrase	A group of words that does not have a subject and a verb. **Example:** Considering the weather, I think I'll stay indoors.

| Phrase | Clause |

relative clause A clause beginning with a relative pronoun—*who, whom, that,* or *which*. The pronoun relates the information in the clause to the noun immediately preceding it.

Example:	This group, *which* has made a vocation of proving other people wrong, offers nothing positive to the world. **Example:** Those people, *whom* I have been calling all day, never returned my phone calls.
subordinate conjunction	A word or phrase that connects a dependent clause to a main, or independent, clause. **Example:** *Although* scientists argue that wearing a helmet reduces the risk of dying in a motorcycle accident, many riders choose to ride without a helmet.
participle	A word usually ending in *-ing* or *-ed*. They look like verbs but are used as adjectives. They are often found in modifying phrases. **Example:** The *pouring* rain depresses me. **Example:** *Looking* through the window, I watch the rain pouring into the gutters. (*Looking through the window* is a participial phrase modifying *I*.)
preposition	Word used to show the relationship of a *noun* or *pronoun* to another part of the sentence. **Example:** The author suggests that man cannot live *by* bread alone.

prepositional phrase	A phrase beginning with a preposition. Be careful with subject-verb agreement when a prepositional phrase intervenes. (In this sentence, *with subject-verb agreement* is a prepositional phrase.) **Example:** A group *of six German men* is taking the train to Belgium this afternoon.
modifier	A word or phrase that qualifies the meaning of another word by making it more definite. A modifier can be a word (an adjective or an adverb) or a phrase (participial, adverbial, adjectival, or prepositional). The modifier should be placed as near as possible to the thing being modified. A modifying phrase that begins a sentence refers to the noun or subjective case pronoun immediately following the phrase.
referent	The word or phrase to which the modifier refers.
misplaced modifier	A modifier that seems to modify the wrong part of a sentence.
Example:	Misplaced modifier: She served cookies to the ladies *arranged on her best china.* Correctly placed modifier: She served cookies *arranged on her best china* to the ladies. (It is the cookies that are on the china, not the ladies.)
noun	A word that names a person, place, thing, event, or idea. **Example:** *Tolerance* is a *virtue* that few *people,* not even *Diane,* discuss these *days.*
pronoun	A word that stands for or takes the place of one or more nouns.
antecedent	The noun to which a pronoun refers. **Example:** *Tolerance* is not discussed these days; *it* demands too much hard work to be a popular virtue.
adverb	A word that modifies a verb, an adjective, or another adverb. **Example:** She *lovingly* patted her dog on the head, before throwing him a very fine bone.
adjective or	A word or phrase that modifies or describes a noun or pronoun. (You
adjectival phrase	can ask, "What kind of _____ is it?") **Example:** One *excellent* example of bureaucratic ineptitude is the fact that I received my *office* fan in January. (What kind of example is it? It is an *excellent* example.) **Example:** The cheesecake, *which won the prize at the county fair for three consecutive years,* turned out to be an import from a New York bakery. (The underlined phrase describes the noun *cheesecake.*)

PUTTING IT ALL TOGETHER: PRACTICE ESSAY

Now that we've discussed the basics of good writing, use the Kaplan Five-Step Method to write a sample essay on the topic we discussed in Writing Sample Lesson 1. Do an entirely different prewrite. Try using your own favorite subjects as a source of examples – a hobby, for example.

Consider this statement:

To run a successful campaign, a political candidate must treat complex issues as if they were simple choices.

Write a unified essay in which you perform the following tasks. Explain what you think the above statement means. Descirbe a specific situation in which a political candidate could run a successful campaign by not treating complex issues as if they were simple choices. Discuss what you think determines when a political candidate should or should not simplify complex issues.

Observe the time limit and use the lined pages that follow. Use the blank space below each question for your prewriting notes.

Time Limit: Each essay should take no longer than thirty minutes.

CHAPTER FOUR

PRACTICE ESSAY

Using the Kaplan Five-Step Method and the principles of good writing discussed in the lessons and in preceding chapters, write a unified essay on the following topic. We will be discussing this topic in Writing Sample Lesson 2, comparing several sample responses.

Consider this statement:

Opportunity favors those who work hard.

Write a unified essay in which you perform the following tasks. Explain what you think the above statement means. Descirbe a specific situation in which a hard-working person might not be favored by opportunity. Discuss what you think determines when opportunity favors those who work hard.

Observe the time limit, use the lined pages that follow each question, and confine yourself to the space provided. Use the blank space below each question for your prewriting notes.

Time Limit: Each essay should take no longer than thirty minutes.

CHAPTER FIVE

PRACTICE QUESTIONS AND RESPONSES

Practice is vital for this as well as other sections of the MCAT. There is simply no substitute for sitting down and taking a test question under test conditions. In the first section of this chapter, you will have opportunities to practice writing essays of your own on four topics that closely resemble the kind you are likely to get on Test Day. Don't allow yourself any extra minutes to complete an essay; don't look at an essay topic in advance of taking a practice test. Being tough on yourself now will give you an edge on Test Day.

In the next section, you will see sample student essays responding to the same four topics. These sample essays have been evaluated using the MCAT-style holistic grading technique discussed in the Introduction to these Review Notes. As a special plus, we've included a "reactions" page after each essay. Here the student writer gives you his or her first reactions to the special problems encountered while taking this particular test.

Essay Questions Give You Important Practice
The first section, as stated, provides you with four practice essay questions. You should spend thirty minutes and only thirty minutes answering each essay question.

Since the actual MCAT will require you to write two essays back-to-back, you may want to take these practice topics in two one-hour sittings. In this way you can test yourself under conditions as close as possible to those you'll encounter on Test Day. Or you may want to give yourself four single-topic practice tests. This method will give you more sustained practice as well as the chance to critique each essay before trying the next. Or you may want to combine the methods: take the first two essay topics on separate occasions and then take the last two together in a full one-hour test. It's up to you.

Sample Student Essays Help You Develop Your Critical Skills
After writing on an essay topic, or on a pair of topics, turn to the sample essays that correspond to the topics you chose and see how other students responded.

Please do NOT look at a sample essay before writing on the topic yourself! Doing so would defeat the purpose of these practice test questions.

When you do look at a sample essay, try first to form your **own** opinion regarding the essay's merits. Pretend you are a professional MCAT reader and give the essay a grade based on the criteria the MCAT people care about. (These criteria are described in the Introduction to these Home Study Notes and more fully in the MCAT Student Manual.) <u>Then</u> look at how our readers evaluated the essay. Doing this will help you develop your own critical skills, a crucial step to becoming a good writer.

By the way, we hope you're interested in reading comments from the writers themselves on how they assessed their own performances. These brief and informal comments are personal glimpses into the problems they encountered in writing on these topics, and we feel they offer good insights into how your peers cope with this demanding assignment.

Ask Someone Else to Critique Your Essay

Another way to critique your own work is to ask someone else's opinion. If you know someone else taking the Kaplan course, it might be a good idea to swap essays. Or you can give your work to someone whose writing skills you respect: a friend, teacher, or family member. If you do so, tell them about the nature of the assignment and about the time limit. If your readers are not knowledgeable about the MCAT essay section, you may find it a good idea to show them the student essays and evaluations found in the latter part of this section. In that way, your readers will become better critics of your work.

If you do find someone to comment on your work, do your best to take their criticism with a cool head. To get the most out of these practice essays, you must put aside your emotional attachment to your writing and try to achieve a certain degree of objectivity. Remember that your evaluators are not trying to tear you down when they point out certain areas that need further practice.

Remember the Five Steps

When judging your own essays' merits, think about your performance in terms of the five steps. Could your initial approach to the topic be better? Did you skip or skimp on any of the prewriting? If so, you may want to review the appropriate sections in Chapter I of these Notes. Did you fail to finish your essay or to leave time to proofread? If so, you probably need to practice the prewriting a bit more in order to improve your ability to accomplish them in the five minutes we recommend. You can become comfortable with this efficient method only by practicing it. If you are not clear about any part of it, go back over Part I of these Notes to refresh your memory.

Take the Practice Tests Seriously

Give yourself thirty minutes; don't allow yourself "extra" minutes to finish that last paragraph. You won't get extras on Test Day.

Take each practice test under testlike conditions. You should have total peace and quiet in which to write. Do not use a computer or word processor. Use a pen, write on the lined paper provided, and take notes on a separate piece of paper, just as you will do on Test Day.

PRACTICE ESSAY QUESTIONS

Observe the time limit. Use the blank space below each question for your prewriting notes.

Time Limit: Each essay should take no longer than thirty minutes.

PART 1

Consider the following statement:

The best kind of education encourages students to question authority.

Write a unified essay in which you accomplish the following tasks. Explain what you think the above statement means. Describe a specific situation in which encouraging students to question authority is <u>not</u> the best kind of education. Discuss what you think determines when students should be encouraged to question authority.

PART 2

Consider this statement:

Violence is never a real solution to a political crisis.

Write a unified essay in which you accomplish the following tasks. Explain what you think the above statement means. Describe a specific situation in which violence could be considered a real solution to a political crisis. Discuss what you think determines when violence is justified in solving such a crisis.

PART 3

Consider this statement:

To be effective, government officials must have completely crime-free pasts.

Write a unified essay in which you accomplish the following tasks. Explain what you think the above statement means. Describe a specific situation in which a government official who once committed a crime might be able to perform effectively. Discuss what you believe determines when a criminal past would not interfere with a government official's effectiveness.

PART 4

Consider this statement:

The government should fund scientific research only when it has a direct application to societal problems.

Write a unified essay in which you accomplish the following tasks. Explain what you think the above statement means. Describe a specific situation in which the government should fund scientific research that does <u>not</u> have a direct application to societal problems. Discuss what you think determines whether or not the government should fund scientific research that has no direct application to societal problems.

STUDENT RESPONSES AND EVALUATIONS

The following pages contain student essays written in response to the questions provided in the previous section. Read each response only after you have first attempted to write on the question yourself.

Student's Essay in Response to Part 1

Education that consists of just memorizing details and facts is hardly education at all. True education demands active participation of both teacher and student. In true education, the roles of the student and the teacher are somewhat flexible: the teacher can learn from the student as well as the student learn from the teacher. By actively participating, instead of taking for granted the truth of everything the teacher says, the student thinks about the issues more thoroughly. Rather than just parroting the views of the teacher, the student by questioning authority develops views that are his own, and also learns a way to think critically about future issues. He learns how to think rather than what to think. This gives him intellectual freedom and a framework for thinking that he can use throughout his life.

But there are moments when the best kind of education does not encourage students to question authority. For instance, education in the hard sciences requires an acceptance of basic formulas and theorems if the student is to make any progress at all. A basic foundation must be laid before the challenges can begin. In other words, questioning authority must take place within the proper sequence. If the student is unable to accept the teacher's authority at least partially, then he will find himself unable to learn from the teacher at all. Questioning authority should develop out of a mutual trust and if such questioning comes about prior to the establishment of such a trust, a student will do his education a real injury. To begin by questioning the teacher's authority, without first having a solid foundation of knowledge, would be counterproductive and tend to impede learning.

In determining when education that encourages students to question authority is the best, we must consider two main factors. First, what type of education is in question? If we are dealing with the physical sciences, a basic groundwork must be agreed upon before questioning authority can begin. Second, to what degree is the authority being questioned? If the authority is seen as totally questionable, the validity of the authority as an authority will be destroyed.

It is important to remember that when a student is taught to question authority he must be also taught to question his <u>own</u> authority as well as that of a teacher or textbook. The purpose of questioning authority is not to teach the student to place himself in the role of the authority figure while totally disregarding the teacher. In such a situation the learning process will fail miserably. The purpose of questioning authority is to examine and analyze ideas before accepting them as true. When a student learns to do this with his own ideas as well as with others', he will truly have received the best education.

Student's Self-Evaluation

In general, I feel good about this essay. I managed my time well and stuck to my prewriting main idea and defense. I also benefited from keeping track of the time and pacing myself accordingly.

I felt a bit nervous about using the example of the hard sciences in paragraph 2. Perhaps that wasn't specific enough. Perhaps I'd have done better to use just one of the sciences—like physics—and thus avoid potential problems of over-generalization.

Reader's Evaluation of Student's Response to Part 1
Holistic Score: 6

This paper presents a thorough and thoughtful response to all three writing tasks, focusing clearly on the issue defined by the given statement. Paragraphs 1 and 2 address the first and second tasks, respectively; paragraphs 3 and 4 address the third task.

Paragraph 1 introduces the topic with a straightforward clarification of the statement's meaning (sentences 1 through 3), and then continues with some analysis of the statement's meaning as it relates to the benefits of an education that questions authority (Sentences 4 through 6). Paragraph 2's first sentence is a clear topic sentence, leading to the counterexample of education in the hard sciences. The bulk of paragraph 2 explores the implications of a student's premature questioning. The discussion is abstract, since it quickly leaves the specifics of the example behind, but precisely argued. It amply satisfies the requirement of the second task; it also paves the way for paragraph 3's examination of the two factors that should be taken into account in resolving the conflict between the ideas in the preceding two paragraphs. Paragraph 4 extends this discussion by introducing the related idea that students should question their own authority. These last two paragraphs amply discuss the third task: the author has explored the grounds for questioning authority, the problems associated with premature or unrestricted questioning, and the need for self-questioning.

The discussion in each of the paragraphs is organized around a unifying idea and is presented coherently and logically. Furthermore, the paragraphs relate well to each other. For example, the transitional phrase, "But there are moments" (paragraph 2, sentence 1), effectively guides the reader from the discussion in paragraph 1 to the new idea to be discussed in paragraph 2. The use of such transitional phrases occurs throughout the essay, creating a smooth and coherent argument. General statements are given an appropriate amount of specific explanation and/or illustration (Paragraph 4, for instance).

The language is clear and effective throughout. The essay also provides variety in sentence structure (e.g., the fourth, fifth, and sixth sentences of paragraph 1).

Student's Essay in Response to Part 2

In a political crisis, violence is often the first reaction in trying to reach a solution, much as a tantrum is the first reaction when a child fails to get his way. Yet if anything is to be resolved, violence in itself is not a solution. While violence may have an immediate effect on a crisis, it does not solve the crisis. It may control the situation temporarily, but the roots are still there and may flare up once the violence has passed.

Certainly there are situations where violence seems justified. Terrorists' acts of violence must sometimes be curtailed with violence when negotiations have failed. Similarly, defense from offensive military maneuvers. But violence in and of itself is not a full solution. The bombing of Hiroshima was seen by some as the only solution to a long and bloody war. Yet this act of violence in a violent political crisis has left terrible scars on all of humanity, and further development of nuclear weapons has led to deeper political crises, crises too dangerous to the entire planet to be resolved by violence.

Yet violence, like an occasional tantrum, does get attention and does often begin a series of events that lead to a solution. The storming of the Bastille did lead—after years of violence and terror in France—to freedom from the aristocracy. And storming the beaches at Normandy did save Europe from Nazi rule.

Violence in itself is not a real solution to a political crisis, but it can be an effective step in reaching a solution. On that ground alone, one can say that it is justifiable. Nonetheless, violence in itself can lead to a bigger crisis. But violence can play a vital part as an intermediate step toward a real resolution of hostilities.

Student's Self-Evaluation

I guess the main problem with this essay is that it got kind of repetitive. By the time I got around to really focussing on the third task, I felt I had said everything I had to say on the subject. As a result, I'm not happy with my final paragraph since it doesn't say much of substance. I wish I had focussed more directly on each task.

Reader's Evaluation of Student's Response to Part 2

Holistic Score: 4

This essay addresses the first and second tasks in paragraphs 1, 2, and 3. In paragraph 4, the third task is addressed as well.

The essay is confusingly organized and does not adequately respond to the third task; it is for these two reasons that it did not receive a score of 5. On the other hand, its use of relevant and interpreted examples raised it from a score of 3.

While paragraphs 1 and 4 are organized around central ideas, the remainder of the essay is confusingly put together. For example, paragraph 2's first sentence seems as if it is introducing a paragraph that will take up the second task, but the rest of the paragraph reverts to a discussion of task 1.

The essay addresses the third task in the final paragraph—introducing the notion that violence can be an "intermediate step" in solving a political crisis—however, the essay presents no clear analysis of what constitutes justified use of violence in such circumstances. Instead, the author repeats the idea that violence can make bad things worse.

The essay's allusions to the Hiroshima catastrophe, the storming of the Bastille, and the invasion at Normandy create a solid sense of specificity. If the essay were better organized, such examples would gain more force. Furthermore, the essay lacks clear transitions between paragraphs (between paragraphs 3 and 4, for example); the author could improve the overall flow of the argument by creating more substantive links between major groups of ideas.

Though generally clear, the language at times lacks vigor (the repeated use of the word "violence," for instance). Sentence structure does show some variety (paragraph 3, for example), though there are occasional problems in sentence construction (e.g., the third sentence in paragraph 2 is missing a verb and predicate, and therefore constitutes a sentence fragment).

Student's Essay in Response to Part 3

Of his own free will, no one would elect a known criminal to an important government post. In a free society, we like to have government leaders who honor and support the laws that we have made to protect the people and to keep the society smoothly running. When we find that a candidate or officeholder has not upheld the law in his earlier life, we doubt that he will do so in office. Hence, to be an effective politician, one must have a completely crime-free past.

Electing leaders with "clean records" must be kept in mind. We would not elect a known gangster or an individual with a long record of hideous or outrageous crimes or even a person accused of taking bribes because we fear that such individuals would continue such actions in office. Yet certainly one or two small spots on one's record in one's youth when for many years he has been "crime-free" cannot be considered reason enough not to elect an otherwise fine candidate. Certainly we would not want Al Capone or Charles Manson as our Senators, but even if John Kennedy had swiped an apple when he was ten years old or had a parking infraction at twenty, he would have still been one of our greatest leaders.

Having crime-free officials is a great idea, but there is a difference between <u>completely</u> crime-free and <u>generally</u> crime-free pasts. An effective official is more than merely one who has never committed a major crime. After all, Capone would probably be a more effective leader (in some ways) than many of the Presidents we have had in the U.S. simply because he knew how to run a big organization and get things done quickly. Of course, his style of power is not how we would like to have things done in a free society, but it was effective.

The question of crime-free or not crime-free hinges on what we mean by "effective." In a free democracy, we like our leaders to be nearly crime-free, but we can see that it is nearly impossible to have officials who are completely crime-free.

Student's Self-Evaluation

I could have spent more time planning this essay. I started writing almost immediately because I felt I knew exactly what I wanted to say. But half way in, I felt a bit lost. I also wondered whether my use of "we" to make general remarks about society was appropriate.

Reader's Evaluation of Student's Response to Part 3
Holistic Score: 4

This essay accomplished all three writing tasks: paragraph 1 discusses the first task, paragraph 2 discusses the second, and paragraphs 3 and 4 discuss the third. Despite this relatively clear organization, however, the discussion lacks the depth of a level 5 essay.

Paragraph 1 introduces the topic by examining the meaning of the statement. The paragraph's ideas are well organized, but the writer does not closely analyze certain key terms, such as "effective" or "completely." Doing so would have improved the essay's general clarity and sharpened its argument. Paragraph 1, in addition, ends somewhat too abruptly. Sentence 3 raises the issue of people doubting tainted candidates, but this is not linked to the next sentence's assertion that effectiveness requires a politician to have a completely crime-free past.

Paragraph 2 describes a counterexample—the case of people having a slightly tarnished record, such as a Kennedy—

but spends too much time arguing that career criminals would not be trusted. Hence the paragraph does not elucidate the meaning of the counterexample as much as it could have. In addition, the writer's failure to specify what "completely crime-free" means causes a lack of depth in this paragraph.

This last conceptual weakness carries over into paragraphs 3 and 4, which examine the grounds for effectiveness by discussing the difference between degrees of criminality. The example of Capone in paragraph 3 directly addresses the third task, but the discussion borders on the simplistic. The final paragraph's first sentence makes a good point, but the essay never clarifies what "effectiveness" entails. Hence, the conclusion lacks clarity.

This paper would be most improved by a clarification of the author's main ideas. The last paragraph is headed in a productive direction since its extension would logically take up the definition of "effective." Yet this attempt is not enough and it comes too late to add direction to the preceding discussion.

The writing shows a basic control of vocabulary and sentence structure. Transitions, however, could be more effectively used. The first sentence of paragraph 2, for example, does not effectively lead into paragraph 2's main topic, nor does it link this paragraph to the preceding one. Similarly, paragraph 3 could be better tied to paragraph 2's discussion; the phrase "having crime-free officials is a great idea" does not adequately make the necessary transition.

Student's Essay in Response to Part 4

The statement "The government should restrict its funding of scientific research to programs with a direct application to societal problems" is defined by me as follows: no monies shall be allocated to commercial, military or other programs not of benefit on some humanistic level.

In the case of space research, many would say that no funding should be given, in that this research is either pure adventurism or only of military or theoretical importance. But I believe that space research should be funded for two reasons: 1) it represents a solution other than population control for the problem of global overcrowding and 2) it advances many helpful technologies such as food preservation, fuel conservation and computer applications.

The criteria used to determine whether or not government funds should be used for any individual research project are difficult to put boundaries on. But I will outline some parameters here.

Programs should not concern military issues. The funding of such programs is the responsibility of the Defense Department and are a different issue altogether. For non-military research, researchers should be required to describe, in layman's terms, what their project is, what its history has been and what they think its future will be. There should be a board with as fair a cross-section of the people as possible to decide on funding. And there should be a set of regulations to add weight to research that does have a more direct application to immediate social problems.

Student's Self-Evaluation

I think that when tested I get too hung up on trying to use fancy language and then lose track of my own thoughts. I think my ideas would flow better if I could get them clearer before I jump into building a sentence, but the time pressure makes me too nervous.

Answering the third task seemed the hardest to me. I felt as if I had to start all over again and write a whole new essay.

Reader's Evaluation of Student's Response to Part 4
Holistic Score: 3

This paper addresses all three tasks, focuses consistently on the given topic, presents paragraphs that are unified around a central topic, and contains a clear organization of ideas. Furthermore, the ideas are all substantial enough to be appropriate for an assignment of this kind. None of the ideas are sufficiently developed, however, and as a result the paper is simplistic.

Paragraph 1 addresses the first task but merely rephrases the statement in different words. No attempt is made to expand our understanding of its meaning by explaining why or in what way it is valid.

Paragraph 2 addresses the second task by offering an example in which scientific research without direct application to societal problems deserves funding. The author provides a bit more explanation here than in paragraph 1, but it is still insufficient. Vague phrases such as "pure adventurism" and "theoretical importance" are left unexplained. More importantly, the author's defense for why space research should be supported is one-sided. Since paragraph 1 gives us no insight into why someone would *oppose* such research, the argument in paragraph 2 for *supporting* the research lacks a relevant context.

Paragraph 3 responds to the third task, but the ideas presented have little relation to the ideas in paragraph 2. Therefore, though the paper is unified in its focus on the statement provided, it lacks coherency—the ideas do not relate to each other.

The language of the essay is quite clear, on the whole, and the ideas are expressed without difficulty. In addition, variety in sentence length adds some energy to the style (see first two sentences of paragraph 4).

The most significant improvements to be made in this essay involve a more thorough exploration of ideas and a greater emphasis on the relationship between those ideas. The first place to work on improving these weaknesses is in the prewriting process. Asking questions will help expand the explanation of a topic (the first task). Looking back over the first and second tasks' prewriting notes (the third task) will help develop a central idea that will create a coherent relationship between all the ideas in the essay.